Comparative Democratization and Peaceful Change in Single-Party-Dominant Countries

Edited by
Marco Rimanelli

St. Martin's Press
New York

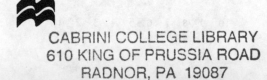

ISBN 0-312-16595-1

Library of Congress Cataloging-in-Publication Data
Comparative democratization and peaceful change in single-party
-dominant countries / Marco Rimanelli, editor.
    p.   cm.
  Includes bibliographical references.
  ISBN 0-312-16595-1
  1. Democratization.   2. One party systems.   3. Comparative
government.   4. World politics—1989-   I. Rimanelli, Marco, 1957-

JC421.C58   1999
320.3'09'049—dc21   99–23099
                                                                    CIP

Design by Letra Libre, Inc.

10 9 8 7 6 5 4 3 2 1

Table of Contents

Acknowledgments

Endless thanks to the National Italian American Foundation (NIAF) and its Executive Director Fred Rotondaro for awarding me two NIAF Summer Grants to complete this book; to the George Washington University-Elliott School for welcoming me as a Research Associate to complete the work's final revision; and to Senior Editor Michael Flamini of St. Martin's Press for always having faith in my work. Equal thanks go to all my dear colleagues in this book for having helped me on this difficult project with their papers, advice, and patience. Yet we all understand that our intellectual contribution to this work and field will hardly constitute the definitive or last word on single-party dominance or their transition to democratic pluralism.

Marco Rimanelli Ph.D.,
Director, Center on Inter-American & World Studies
Saint Leo University, Tampa, Florida, 1999

INTRODUCTION

Peaceful Democratization Trends in Single-Party-Dominant Countries

Marco Rimanelli

I. The Meaning of Democracy: The Traditional Approach

This work draws a comparative analysis of an international trend towards radical but peaceful political change and democratization in countries previously monopolized by single-party-dominant political systems (be they authoritarian or even democratic). This quiet change was easily overlooked in the wake of the momentous international changes unleashed since 1989 by the post–Cold War period. On one hand, the overwhelming uncertainty thrust in international relations by the fall of the Soviet Union and the redrawing of the world maps led to a rush to reassess at a regional level the old, waning, international security balance (nuclear arsenals, non-proliferations, arms control, insurgencies), especially once the positive impact of dismantling East-West arsenals and waning ideologies (capitalist democracy versus totalitarian Communism and Fascism) was replaced instead by the return of even older destabilizing demons (nationalism, secessionism, civil wars and "ethnic cleansing") in both Europe and the former Soviet Union, which the Cold War had long suppressed. On the other hand, international observers have been traditionally mesmerized by the more spectacular impact of violent change on political systems, which automatically self-reinforced the standard assumption that most radical domestic changes are either the result of, or lead to, some sort of violent, bloody revolution, which finally opens the way for a new political system to be established over the remnants of older ones.

The impact of revolution and/or peaceful change on authoritarian régimes is all the more important as until 1989 democracies were perceived to be in the minority compared to the proliferation of one-party states, which restricted politico-electoral competition to just a single, "legitimate" party with a fixed candidate list. Such states were Marxists ones with their local Communist party (USSR, China, Eastern Europe, etc.), right-wing authoritarian régimes, and many Third World states where a single party dominates the political system. Instead, democratic societies are mostly based on the periodic electoral alternance between two major parties, or more often broad, ruling coalitions. But democratization is not a recent international phenomenon, as the modern wave of transition from authoritarianism to democracy started with the 1974 "Carnations' Revolution" in southern Europe (Portugal, Greece, Spain), and culminated with the 1989–91 collapse of Communism in Eastern Europe and the ex-USSR. In hindsight, it was the sudden collapse of the Soviet Union and the end of the Cold War that had a fundamental catalyst role in allowing all types of pent-up domestic pressures for change to finally emerge in a less charged and "frozen" international environment. Yet, this should not be construed as an assertion that the lack of democratic development in many countries selected as case-studies for this book is the direct result of the East-West ideological-military polarization of the world during the Cold War. Nevertheless, the end of the Cold War and the demise of the Soviet/Communist stranglehold over the East did accelerate this trend and stimulated by example similar pressures for democratic change and political accountability of national leaders worldwide, be it in ex-Marxist states (Russia, Poland, Hungary, Czechoslovakia, Nicaragua), in unstable Third World countries (Mexico, South Africa, Nigeria, Taiwan, India, Brazil, and Argentina), or even among stable, but flawed, Western states (Italy, Japan, Spain, Greece, Portugal, and Israel).[1]

What is democracy? As there are many abstract forms of democracy, no rigid set of rules can be relied upon. Instead, each country's type of democracy derives from specific local socio-politico-economic conditions, state structures, and policy practices. The definition of democracy has changed throughout time, becoming more structured than in the past as a system of governance with publicly binding rules. Thus,

> Modern democracy is an institutionalized political system of governance where the rulers' policy decisions/actions are binding on the collectivity, but must be undertaken in the national interests and are held accountable by the country's citizens, acting indirectly through the competitive election of public officials and the judiciary's coercive enforcement of the law.[2]

Democratic rules of conduct and procedure/strategies for political access or exclusion, are institutionalized through a written *constitution,* although this by itself is not a vital element of democracy (neither Britain nor Israel have theirs on paper, while dictatorships do not respect constitutions, nor are they held accountable by them). Concerning governing strategies, a Liberal-type democracy advocates a narrow style of governance and public realm (the enforced collective norms that bind society) backing an independent individualistic private sector, while a Leftist-type democracy supports a proactive governance based on extensive public regulations, subsidies, redistribution of wealth, and partial nationalization of property for the collective good. Both are acceptable forms of democracy with variations in their implementation. Also acceptable are differences in democratic electoral systems (proportional popular vote versus uninominal single college; single ballot versus primaries or double-turn elections), or variations in political systems (presidential republic versus parliamentarian republic or constitutional monarchy).

In all democracies, *rulers* are elected officials, whose legitimate authority and independent decisions on behalf of the collective remain always accountable to the citizens (through free and fair elections), even when overriding considerations of national interest might justify controversial, unpopular policies. The *citizens'* civic rights and duties, and their equal, fair treatment *under the law,* allows them direct influence on the state, although the actual rate of voter participation differs among countries (80 percent to 90 percent in Europe and Japan versus 50 percent in the United States). All citizens cooperate, compete, and debate alternative policies either individually, or in parties and interest groups, without abusing laws and minority rights through a "tyranny of the majority." Minorities and local interests are also protected through constitutional provisions; federal and local governing autonomies; "consociationist" governments of national unity (like Italy's frozen bi-polar rivalry between the Christian-Democrats [DC] and the Communists [PCI]); or neo-corporatist social pacts (right-wing groups). However popular, "civic culture" values (tolerance, mutual respect, fair play, compromise, moderation, trust in public authority) do not provide any operative guideline for democracy, given the need for long-term absorption of such values in the society. Furthermore, federalism, republicanism, and independent checks and balances between the three branches of government are not elements of democracy *per se,* but pertain only to the U.S. brand, while the overwhelming majority of democracies are based on fusions of powers between executives and legislatives (parliamentarian democracies), centralized governments, and few severely limited kingdoms (constitutional monarchies). Thus, Robert Dahl stresses that there are only seven key procedural conditions for modern democracies, but four more are also usually tagged on, while Michael I. Sodaro and others also include the interaction between elites and disadvantaged segments of society:

1. Governmental decision-making is constitutionally vested in elected officials.
2. Elected officials are chosen in frequent, free, and fair popular elections (routinely "nominated" officials and "electoralism" devoid of other democratic conditions are equally unacceptable). Legislative and executive share decisional responsibility and accountability.
3. All adult citizens have voting and civic rights.
4. All adult citizens have the right to run for public office and be elected.
5. Full freedom of speech and expression for all without retribution.
6. Free and uncensored information and media sources, protected and available to citizens.
7. Citizens have the right of association and to form independent associations/political parties/interest groups with equal access.
8. Democratically-elected officials must exercise their constitutional duties without being opposed, overruled, or vetoed by unelected officials (like entrenched civil servants, authoritarian Military Councils/*Juntas* unencumbered by institutional civilian-military controls, paramilitary groups, or socio-religious forces).
9. Every state's national government must be a self-governing autonomous political institution with internal sovereignty (the right to defend and exercise exclusive legal authority within the country's borders), external sovereignty (the right to go to war, exchange diplomats, and trade), and freedom from any external control by other states (as "satellites," dominions, protectorates), or overarching political systems as colonies and territories).
10. Democratic representatives formally/informally agree not to use their temporary electoral/legislative/governmental superiority to disenfranchise the minority and oppositions from ever competing for power and higher office, while the losers will respect the majority's decisions.
11. Citizens must obey the law and governmental decisions despite uncertainties on the outcome of elections, as long as these acts of authority reflect the contingent collective preferences ("democratic bargain") as expressed through regular, free and fair elections.[3]

Whatever their form, all democracies practically incorporate all of these conditions. The same is true for single-party-dominant systems where one party perpetually wins all elections and rules either alone or through its tight control of coalitions. In fact, these few single-party-dominant systems always recognize the legal possibility for political change through independent elections should the voters alter their preferences in an indeterminate future (Japan, Sweden, Italy, Mexico), while the very lack of institutional channels for electoral change denies democracy and soon leaves in its stead just an authoritarian one-party system (Indonesia).

However, if democracies have more open societies and polities than authoritarian systems, they neither have automatically more open economies (free trade versus protectionism and regulations), nor are more efficient economically than non-democratic régimes, especially during the difficult and chaotic initial transition to democracy. Improvement in socio-economic conditions come in time, never immediately. Democracies are also not more administratively efficient in their political decision-making compared to non-democracies. Moreover the costs of administration may include substantial resources for patronage and "paying-off" clients and opponents. Democracies might not appear stable in the short-run when freedom of expression and political disagreements/protests over the new institutions and rules of conduct increase domestic tension and politico-ideological polarization. Thus, democracy per se will not automatically bring in its wake capitalist economic growth, social peace, political harmony, administrative efficiency, and tolerance. But it does foster the growth of political institutions peacefully competing to govern, modify, and influence public policy on behalf of the collective good's changing needs, channeling socio-economic contrasts through regular procedures and the rule of law.

II. The Meaning of Democracy:
Single-Party Dominance or the "Uncommon" Approach

Less attention and research has been traditionally devoted to more subtle shifts in political power and change, which although potentially significant in their long-term domestic repercussions were consistently overlooked as the affected political system did not appear poised on the edge of either bloody revolution or convulsive disintegration. Thus, according to common wisdom, peaceful domestic change and transition to a stable, classical, multi-party democratic system carries the most enduring hopes for future stability and prosperity. But such peaceful transition could also be the most misunderstood, not only when it took place in former dictatorships, but also surprisingly, in countries already fully democratic, or semi-democratic. In fact, in the latter cases the ruling élites had successfully perpetuated their monopoly of power through single-party-dominant systems, which assured domestic order under a democratic façade of peace and stability.[4]

Until 1989, the common opinion had been that long-term one-party states thrived only in rigidly controlled Communist, authoritarian, or semi-authoritarian régimes (Marxists; right-wing authoritarian régimes; Third

World states), due to social stagnation and politico-economic control by small oligarchies.[5] In the late 1980s T. J. Pempel overcame the dearth of scholarly research on single-party dominance to conclusively prove how in industrialized states also the democratic process could perversely deny alternance and allow instead, at times, the emergence of "one-party-dominant systems" (or "uncommon" democracies). Such single-party hegemony, or the dominance by one leading party on ruling democratic coalitions, is still a relatively uncommon occurrence, as the party in question must successfully hold on to power uninterruptedly over very long periods of time beyond a decade, and/or as the dominant member of over 12 successive governments (Pempel prefers a difficult 30-to-50 years high benchmark, attained only by Japan, Italy, Sweden, and Israel). Within the party-bureaucratic and state-society relations of industrialized states, the successful emergence of single-party-dominant systems is tied both to the hegemonic party's skill as an electoral machine and governmental coalition-builder through different socio-economic sectors, while effectively addressing, through public policies, the various needs of the community and of different social groups, which in turn strengthen the party's own electoral base and cyclical reelection. However, the four most successful single-party-dominant systems of all times (Italy, Japan, Israel, and Sweden) are balanced both by sudden losses of hegemony in similar cases (Israel, Sweden, Spain, Greece, Italy) and by many cases of "failed dominance," given that single-party dominance over time is never a sure outcome compared to outright bi-party alternance or coalition governments, even in the most favorable of circumstances (Great Britain, West Germany, France, Norway, or Australia).[6]

Thus, according to Pempel, four vital criteria assure a party's politico-electoral "dominance" over all other parties, while monopolizing the formation of governments and national policy agendas for successive decades: (1) electoral "dominance" (in relative numerical terms) compared to its opponents by securing a plurality of parliamentary seats; (2) even without an absolute parliamentary majority it controls all parties through its "dominant bargaining position" in forming all ruling coalitions with minor partners, while strategically denying the viability of any other governmental formula that would exclude it (yet this does not take into account the minor partners' ability at times to blackmail the dominant party for more power lest the junior partner splits and dooms the coalition); (3) "chronological dominance" with control of all successive governments over very long periods of 30-to-50 years; (4) and "governmental dominance" to fulfill through time the party's own historical-ideological vision by shaping national policy agendas through a series of interrelated public policies. However, these rules reflect mostly common records of success, not rigid criteria vital for success, as all countries do not behave similarly in their attempts to retain hegemony.[7]

In all democratic systems (pluralist, bi-party, or single-party-dominant), parties are the key element in influencing broad socio-economic coalitions, policy-making structures, and public policies, beyond traditional electoral campaigning, fund-raising, organizational support, competing ideological manifestos, and legislative policy support. But traditional Party System and Voting Behavior Theories for democracies are so ideologically and conceptually committed to the automatic equation "democracy = party alternance in power" that they fail to explain why the electorate in socially dynamic democracies keeps reconfirming in power single-party-dominant systems through continuous strings of electoral victories, without deserting it for other parties. The same applies for Organizational Theory's focus on the natural difficulty of all organizations to adapt to changing external circumstances, which they resist to the point of dangerous stagnation, so that the longer parties remain in power, the more atrophied their policies become compared to challengers previously defeated at the polls. Instead, the political reality of single-party dominance proves that at least for those few parties who survive in power over decades despite pressures for politico-electoral alternance or policy stagnation, long-term dominance is the result of interlocking, exceptional circumstances (the traumatic transition to democracy from authoritarianism or independence), external support (a foreign Power's politico-military and financial support, like that of the United States during the Cold War), continuous electoral victories and monopoly of governmental formation as the dominant party is reconfirmed an absolute or relative majority, a long-term but flexible socio-politico-ideological vision attracting the electorate's support, and a close interrelationship with most domestic social groups (even those initially hostile to dominance). In single-party dominant countries, the dominant party becomes the sole agent and glue of the political system, while serving many functions to mobilize vast socio-economic blocs and the electorate to implement its policies and reconfirm its hegemony and semi-permanent governance over the country's political system through a "virtuous cycle of dominance": ideological-electoral success and control of state resources create both a favorable situation of dominance and the conditions to perpetuate through mutually reinforcing flexible strategies aimed at strengthening the party's electoral base through wise governance, tactical bargaining, public policies, politico-ideological monopoly of the national agenda ("cycle of dominance"), flexible strategies to mobilize core voters, and new socio-economic groups through governmental control of state resources for "targeted" public-policies and "hidden" patronage, while being able to adapt its dominance to domestic changes affecting the socio-economic coalition supporting the single-party-dominant system.[8]

Yet as circumstances change, and society becomes more industrialized and secular, single-party dominance is threatened by its very success, so that its survival demands the skillful reliance on consolidating and expanding its own electorate through the dominant party's unlimited access to state resources for patronage. As waning ideological differences and election results influence governmental behavior less and less, national power distribution and political choice become dependent on practical élite "consociationism" (inter-party cooperation and bargaining) to prevent socio-political pluralistic fragmentation and to control national politics and electoral choices to continue the parties' traditional role as institutionalized socio-political assimilators of domestic issues. This is even more important if single-party-dominance must rely on an electoral relative majority, rather than outright dominance, forcing it into coalition governments with quarrelsome junior partners. Such coalition governments, however, still reflect predominantly the single party's bargaining dominance and public policy initiatives (as well as its historical agenda), while balancing the interests of coalition partners to keep their respective voting bases mobilized and political opponents isolated. In all cases, success requires a mutually reinforcing cycle of dominance over all adversaries by the mobilization of vast socio-economic blocs, strategy, inter-party bargaining, governmental formation, public policy shaping, and especially long-term semi-permanent governance through the skillful reliance on the state's resources to establish a patronage system to reward loyal voters.[9]

Therefore, does long-term single-party dominance challenge to the core the general assumption of democracy's identity as exclusively tied to a traditional system based on politico-economic alternance via the polls in changing societies? Can we consider democratic single-party dominance, based on the extensive reliance on state resources, to reward followers and reshape the country at large while preserving power? Traditional democratic literature implicitly or explicitly rejects the notion that uninterrupted rule by a single governmental party over several decades is a "democracy," the traditional assumption is that democracy calls for a close relationship between electoral change, pluralistic parties, and alternance in power to replace ruling parties. And yet, despite pent-up socio-economic imbalances and corrupt patronage, successful single-party dominance in democracies is still a practically acceptable, albeit less desirable, democratic outcome: Italy's DC, Japan's LDP, or Israel's Labor always remained proud of their twin role in holding on to power, while socializing their countries to democracy, although the glue to all these competing socio-politico-economic pressures for domestic control is the inevitable reliance on patronage to "capture votes." Both DC and LDP, each with a record of almost 50 years of uninterrupted rule, represented the most extensive and successful conservative parties in the industrialized West (just like Israel's Labor dominance represented "legitimacy" for the Left), enjoying tactical bargaining and monopolizing the ideological agenda and public policy, which further consolidated their local hegemony in government and helped them in turn to strengthen their electoral base by relying on state resources to finance public policies of patronage and stimulate economic growth. In Japan and Italy, the LDP and DC relied on the foreign backing of the United States during the Cold War to "delegitimize" the Left as "non-democratic," while their control of governments, legislatures, and public sectors allowed them to defuse threats and shore-up supporters through economic policies and massive public works to create jobs in local and rural communities (where they were strongest electorally, rather than in the politically more volatile urban areas).

However, fewer democratic parties succeed in the long-run as single-party-dominant systems (over several decades), because success is truly an art form, rather than a given when favorable conditions exist. While Pempel's implicit cut-off limit for single-party-dominant systems of 30 or more years of continuous government is met only by Sweden, Japan, Italy, and Israel, the reality of dominance shows that it is still only marginally more frequent if a decade is used as benchmark and repeated returns to power bring back the lost power-base. Thus, Germany's CDU/CSU electoral durability (1949–68, 1982–98) has proven how dominance can be rekindled in an "imperfect bi-party" system (where the two dominant parties are flanked by tiny coalition partners) even after a hiatus of more than a decade. The success of Japan, Italy, Sweden, and Israel as single-party-dominant systems is quite individualized for each case, given their different historical origins and unlikely socio-economic mixes supporting the dominant parties. Socio-political and even foreign constraints always exist in democracies, constraining the degree of political change through time, while loss of power can be either wholly devastating for some ex-dominant parties (since 1976, Labor in Israel has been politically weakened, despite occasional coalitions with *Likud;* in Italy the DC collapsed and was disbanded in the early 1990s after the entire political system was indicted by the judiciary for systemic corruption, illegal financing, and patronage), or mostly irrelevant and temporary by reconfirming in power the dominant party (Japan, Sweden). Nevertheless, if today Israel and Greece seem poised to follow Germany into a cyclical pattern of alternating dominance between rival parties/blocs (CDU/CDS versus SPD in Germany; *Likud* versus Labor in Israel; PASOK versus *Nea Demokratia* in Greece), the reality is that most other democratic countries where conditions for dominance existed in the past are now evolving instead into traditional coalition-based alternance systems (such unintended "failed dominance" in the long run is illustrated in this book's case-studies of Italy, Spain, and Portugal). In ex-Communist and Third World countries, as well as newly democratizing countries, where one-party authoritarian dominance existed, the peaceful evolution into traditional democratic alternance is still more common (Brazil,

Argentina, Poland, Hungary, Czech Republic, Russia, Nicaragua), despite their fragile new democratic roots, than the preservation of a democratic single-party dominance (Mexico, Taiwan, possibly India), or even its rare replacement by another democratic dominant party (the black ANC replacing the white Nationalists in south).[10]

Thus, both Pempel's and this work confirm that three interrelated commonalties exist in the origins, maintenance, and effects of long-term rule in all cases, although no single component is able to assure dominance and create a reinforcing "syndrome of conditions."

(1) Each dominant party benefited from variants of proportional electoral systems fostering a multi-party system, rather than uninominal elections and bi-party systems (such as in the United States and Britain, where victory requires almost 50 percent of the votes for a single candidate to win and consolidates the system into two main parties whose ideological differences are also tempered by the common political need to recruit the moderate voter), or dictatorial one-party states (USSR, China, Cuba, where elections are just propaganda show cases, devoid of any opportunity for change for the voters). Proportional electoral systems assure both a fragmented multi-party system and greater stability in actual popular-party representation than does a uninominal electoral system, which favors sudden electoral alternance by penalizing the losers at the polls. Moreover, the proportional system assures dominance to parties with less than 50 percent majority at the polls in a multi-party system, thus papering over internal factional rivalries (which could otherwise splinter the party into insignificance), while winning a plurality allows each party to keep undiluted its politico-ideological distinctiveness and core voters). The larger the number of parties in any given political system, the stronger the tactical bargaining power existing for any leading party capable of holding just 35 percent of the votes, and thus of dominating the system through coalition-building (Italy's DC, Israel's Labor), especially if the opposition is split into several competing parties unable to unite. But the electoral system alone cannot guarantee victory or dominance, as many "failed dominance" cases prove. Thus, only Japan's LDP came close to receiving 50 percent of the vote, but often fell below (Japan's electoral system allowed several LDP candidates to run for the same seat keeping the party in power whatever the result). Israel's *Mapai*/Labor and Italy's DC each secured usually 30-to-40 percent of the vote, although both were able to govern through politico-ideological polarization against the disunited opposition and coalition-building with smaller partners, to secure the necessary legislative majority to pass bills and retain dominance in a fragmented multi-party system, even if the majority of voters were left temporarily dissatisfied (Japan, Italy).

(2) Although prolonged dominance is difficult to predict, each single-party-dominant system benefited from a historical "cycle of dominance," transforming many initial victories into a few self-perpetuating, long-term success stories. The origins of a single-party-dominant system involve either a "mobilization crisis" (or key political reorientations of the country's main socio-economic groups, as during transitions to democratization in Israel, Italy, Japan, and West Germany, where the *Mapai*/Labor, DC, LDP, and CDU/CSU all emerged as dominant parties by identifying themselves at the beginning as both new political parties and the key democratization agents), or new mobilization opportunities for parties initially left behind but able to secure dominance at a later period (Sweden's SAP, Portugal's Communists, Spain's PSOE, Greece's PASOK). Indeed, in this second case the initial, apparently dominant, democratization party soon collapsed into a "false dominance" when it could no longer capitalize on its earlier electoral-identity advantage alone (Sweden's Conservatives, France's MRP Conservatives and Gaullists, Greece's *Nea Demokratia,* Spain's Union of Democratic Center). Moreover, dominance requires fixed patterns of electoral mobilization based on core socio-economic blocs polarized by distinct ideological differences, reinforced through time by vital reliance on extensive patronage, to hold on to a volatile electorate to recruit new socio-economic groups to replace its shrinking, aged, core cadres, so as to become almost a "catch-all party" (Italy's DC, Japan's LDP, Sweden's SAP, Israel's *Mapai*/Labor, Germany's CDU/CSU and SPD). Failure to cope with changing circumstances by renewing and/or expanding the party's support base, due to ideological rigidities or interrupted absorption of new groups, leads to stagnation and "false dominance" (France's MRP in the late 1940s and Gaullists in mid 1970s; Israel's Labor in 1977; Greece's *Nea Demokratia* in 1980s; Spain's UDC in 1981 and PSOE in 1995; Italy's DC in 1992–94), or temporary erosion of power (Japan's LDP in 1970s and 1990s; Italy's DC in 1980–85; Sweden's SAP in 1976–82; West Germany's CDU in 1968–82).[11]

(3) Long-term victory allowed a dominant party both the access to state resources to increase the opportunity (not the guarantee) for further electoral successes, and the authority to shape wisely over time the country's public policies, political discourse, patronage rewards for supporting socio-economic groups, and isolating opponents through ideological polarization. In Japan the LDP's initial support core consisted of business, financiers, shopkeepers, farmers, and anti-Communists, while workers, urban dwellers, and intellectuals tended to side with the Left (Socialists and Communists). The same was true for Italy's DC, which benefited additionally from organized Catholic/Vatican support, Catholic unions, and women. Instead, organized trade unions were the key element for victory in both Sweden's SAP and Israel's *Mapai*/Labor, while bourgeois, agrarian, and religious votes got

dispersed among several competing small Center-Right parties. In all countries, domestic polarization preserved as solid blocks the respective socioeconomic bases supporting each party, while governmental alternatives often aborted due to ideological-economic-religious incompatibility, or the numerical weakness of a divided opposition. Thus, the ideologically-loyal dominant party bases were rewarded through patronage and "pork-barrel" public policies (Italy, Israel, Japan). The dominant party also succeeded in shaping through time the national politico-ideological and economic agenda, while consolidating its power in a virtuous cycle of dominance by rewarding supporters and isolating opponents, if no major backlashes occurred. In specific circumstances of structural weakness by the dominant party, successful retention of power requires a highly flexible, non-ideological "soft hegemony" through extensive coalition-building and patronage-sharing to co-opt and split when possible its socio-ideological opponents (the Catholic DC versus its anti-clerical Lay partners and Communist-unionist opponents). Nevertheless, the DC's failure during the 1960s–80s period to socialize the old unions, immigrants, young voters, and new socio-economic groups led to its slow electoral erosion, which only increased patronage and tactical sleight of hand (the "Historical Compromise" with the PCI in the late 1970s; the Craxi-Andreotti-Forlani/C.A.F. secret policy-patronage sharing pact with the PSI in the 1980s). The DC could delay until the 1992 collapse of the entire political system after its widespread corrupt patronage was fully revealed and then dismantled by the judiciary and popular revulsion.

III. Beyond Single-Party Dominance: A Return to Pluralism?

Dominance can also lead to defeat, sooner or later. Due to the failure to continue to pursue those three vital conditions through time, there were many cases of "failed dominance." Should the dominant party lose control and an opponent reach dominance as well (rather than evolving into a multi-party system), it can seek to dismantle the old order and replace it with a new ideological vision through an identical implementation process (*Likud* versus Labor in Israel after 1977; PSOE versus UDC in Spain in 1981; PASOK versus *Nea Demokratia* in Greece in the 1980s–90s; Portugal's Socialists and moderates versus the Communists in the 1970s; Thatcher's Conservatives versus Labor in Britain in the 1980s–90s; the ex-*Contras* versus the *Sandinistas* in Nicaragua; the black ANC versus the white Nationalists in South Africa). Or instead, the path towards a traditional multi-party democracy is finally opened, as in the case of ex-authoritarian and Third World states (Poland, Hungary, Czech Republic, Brazil, India, tentatively Russia). Despite the collapse of dominance in Israel, Spain, Italy, Greece, and a host of Third World countries, single-party-dominant systems will continue regardless, albeit further reduced in numbers, whenever the right circumstances exist and are skillfully exploited by old or new dominant parties. For example: (1) despite doubts about its commitment to democracy and the anti-corruption gains of the small opposition parties, Mexico's PRI continues to rule uninterruptedly and weather all storms, much like Japan's LDP; (2) the demise of Sweden's SAP, Japan's LDP, Taiwan's Nationalists, and Argentina's Folics proved to be only brief, temporary parentheses, given the lack of suitable long-term alternatives in each country; (3) likewise, the second recent return to power of Germany's CDU/CSU symbolized its resurgent successful drive to regain dominance over the medium-term (1982–98), which could also be imitated in the future by Italy's new Leftist *Ulivo* Pole if it succeeds in consolidating its 1995 success and galvanizing in the long-run its support base along a new leadership and domestic strategy; (4) finally, the 1999 electoral victory of the ANC in South Africa confirms its role as the most recent new dominant party, replacing since 1994 the white-Boer Nationalist Party's monopoly (1948–94), due to changes in electoral suffrage and the race card. Instead, the mid 1990s electoral victories of Israel's *Likud*, Greece's PASOK and France's Gaullists, should not be construed as examples of resurgent dominance because their politico-electoral successes are still too volatile in such highly polarized domestic political scenes where incumbents and opponents command rigid ideological poles along a nearly 50/50 electoral fault line (in the same manner that Israel's 1999 elections brought a fragile Labor-led coalition back to power, and France's Socialist parliamentary success versus a Gaullist president reconfirms the deep split in the political scene and a systemic *Co-habitation*).[12]

On the basis of these assumptions, the case-studies selected follow specific criteria: (1) A focus on the success and evolution of peaceful political change (not bloody revolutionary uprisings) as the key element of a radical alteration of the countries' pre-existing political régimes based on single-party-dominant polities (where one-party rule, or hegemony by a single political force, can no longer be sustained after decades of success).

In such cases, domestic pressures for peaceful change and the repercussions of corruption scandals and/or pre-existing political polarization can lead these countries to evolve into truly pluralistic democratic societies. Moreover, given the unpredictability of politics under stress, especially when entrenched élites are confronted by forceful popular pressures for better accountability and democratic representation, this work does also make some allowances in a few of the case-studies for a degree of pre-existing violence, but still controllable as turmoil (terrorism, localized insurgency, but no civil war or bloody revolution), as a key factor in accelerating domestic change towards democratization and multi-party models. Thus, the impact of long-term, violent, civil disobedience (South Africa, Israel, Poland), or localized guerrilla warfare (Nicaragua, Mexico, Russia) are taken into account to assess their influence in promoting a final, negotiated, radical, but still relatively peaceful, political change in these specific countries. Most of the democratizing changes that ultimately lead to the emergence of a well-established pluri-party democracy are the product of post-crisis developments through many years or decades, and this is the real focus of the book's analysis of democratization patterns and trends towards pluri-partitism from pre-existing single-party-dominant countries.

(2) All countries selected in this book are single-party-dominant systems, irrespective of geographical location, ethnic make-up, and degrees of economic development. In the past, the common assumption was that democratic pluri-party systems could thrive only in countries with stable political systems, mostly Eurocentric in make-up and politico-cultural traditions, where a sufficiently high level of economic development supported a large, law-abiding middle class. These were also the necessary socio-political and economic infrastructures needed to sustain any national democratic system. Thus, one-party systems all had to be traditional authoritarian régimes from the ex-Communist bloc and Third World.

While not refuting this view as a recipe for long-term democratic stability and growth, this book instead focuses mostly on the domestic pitfalls affecting, with equal abandon, either democratic or ex-authoritarian and ex-Communist states throughout the world, during their "forced" peaceful transition from single-party-dominant régimes to truly pluralistic democratic systems. Single-party-dominant polities are characterized by the systemic monopolization of domestic political power, all national structures, and the decision-making process (governmental and local policies, plus bureaucracies), by an entrenched, single party over a long period of time (even several decades). This openly contrasts with normal electoral alternance or political give-and-take among different poles of domestic power in any pluralistic society.

Thus, in this work, single-party-dominant systems are roughly divided into five categories:

a. One-party quasi-democratic régimes (Mexico, post-1980s Taiwan, India);

b/c. One-party authoritarian régimes and dictatorships of either Marxist (Russia, Poland, Czechoslovakia, Hungary, and Nicaragua), or right-wing persuasion (pre-1975 Greece, Portugal and Spain; pre-1980s Brazil, Argentina, Taiwan, and South Africa; Nigeria);

d. Dominant majoritarian single-party democratic systems, where the party's long-term and overwhelming predominance over smaller coalition partners and rivals makes it virtually impossible for any weak opposition to attain any democratic alternance in power (Italy, Japan, post-1975 Spain);

e. Other democratic systems, where the long drawn-out tenure in office and ideological polarization among two opposing mass-parties (be it within the context of essentially bi-party systems, or among two majoritarian parties within a fragmented multi-party system where the other parties are uniformly small and weak), makes any pluralistic democratic alternance to power not a formality, but instead a veritable national trauma in a perceived historical struggle for the soul of that country (Greece, Israel, Italy in the late 1940s and 1970s).

(3) In all these case-studies, the book seeks to analyze:

a. the comparative development and long-term impact of single-party-dominant systems, or majoritarian parties' monopoly over long periods of time on national politics and economies;

b. the inevitable trend towards corruption and finance embezzlement by single-party governments, accustomed to decades-old monopoly on national politics to preserve power;

c. the chance and success of effective pluralistic democratic change in offsetting single-party dominance and systemic political corruption.

The national peaceful transition process from a single-party dominance to an untried, pluralist democracy, can be initiated either by the same single party in a desperate effort to stem, without losing power, the pressures to reform itself (Italy, Mexico, Japan, South Africa), or by the opposition if it is capable of rallying most of the dissatisfied domestic forces behind a national coalition movement for change once the ruling single party is on the verge of collapse (Poland, Czech Republic, Hungary, Argentina, Brazil, Portugal, Greece). In some cases the peaceful transition to democracy is short-lived and stalled by the lack of real change in either the structures of national and military power (Nigeria), or by the dearth of economic growth necessary to reintegrate ex-guerrilla fighters into a peaceful society (Nicaragua).

Conversely, it would be quite interesting to also compare this international trend with the changes simmering within the U.S. political system, one of the most traditional embodiments of democratic alternance to power, of federalist autonomy, and of checks and balances constraining governmental authority. Yet the United States' success has shrouded the down-side of its "pure bi-party" system: since last century the stable but exclusive alternance to power of the Democratic and Republican Parties has effectively shut out any independent third party competitor. On one hand, America's "institutionalized" democratic "bi-party" alternance to power (in the presidency and to a lesser extent in congress) has lead to a stable democratic system, whose structure prevents the dominant party entrenched in power from becoming corrupt or remaining in power unchallenged for decades. On the other hand, however, the "pure bi-party" system excludes all other, smaller and local, political/grass-roots forces independent from and not represented within the dominant Democratic and Republican Parties' dichotomy. Non-traditional independentist opposition movements in the United States are thus excluded from expanding and playing a critical, domestic political role, due to the negative impact of frequent uninominal/single-college electoral laws, media access, access to PAC and private finances, (compared to that of incumbents) politico-ideological messages, electoral response and general apathy, party-finance campaigns, and smear tactics. Thus, both the doomed 1980 Anderson and 1992 Ross Perot independent campaigns against Presidents Jimmy Carter (D) and George Bush (R) respectively, as well as the brief Colin Powell phenomena of 1995, were instrumental in injecting interesting issues into an essentially bi-party domestic debate, but in the end still failed to sway the electorate in sufficient numbers to affect the election's outcome except as a negative drain on the incumbent. Thus, Perot's radicals siphoned more votes from the dominant Republicans than the challenger Democrats; a Jesse Jackson independentist challenge always threatened to siphon mostly black voters from the Democrats, while the Powell meteor affected equally voters of both parties before the General declared himself to be pro-Republican and out of the race. However, the insularity and complexity of U.S. domestic politics militate against their inclusion in this work.

Each chapter in this book analyzes on one hand the historical reasons for the success in developing self-perpetuating, long-term, single-party-dominant structures, and, on the other hand, the current political evolution affecting these countries' transition towards a true pluri-party democratic system based on governmental alternance, irrespective of when the actual transition from single-party dominance to pluralistic democratic system took place. Thus, right-wing military régimes (Greece, Portugal, Spain, Brazil and Argentina) became pluralistic democracies in the 1970s and early 1980s, after the erosion of their domestic power-bases. Ex-Marxist states instead became democratic only in the tumultuous 1989–90s period, following the end of the Cold War and the ideological and politico-military collapse of the Soviet Union. Finally, democratic single-party-dominant countries, like Italy and Japan, entered into a painful reassessment of the validity and strictures of their democratic system in the early 1990s, following widespread corruption and scandals, which toppled traditionally dominant parties and paralyzed the country.

In the chapter "Political Immobilism, Clientelism, Collapse, and Democratic Renewal in Italy" by Dr. Marco Rimanelli of Saint Leo University

(Tampa, Florida), Italy appears as both a trendsetter among single-party-dominant countries and a peculiar case-study. The almost 50-year-old triumph of the Christian Democrats' (DC) brand of "soft hegemony" was due to the unique combination of Pempel's dominance prerequisites, the Italians' peculiar anarchical politico-cultural mind-set, and a widespread, corrupt patronage system ("to lock-in the vote"). Through these policies the DC monopolized the state apparatus at large to reward its political supporters with jobs and targeted social programs that would keep them loyal and consolidate its single-party hegemony through the decades, despite domestic socio-economic changes, or political challenges by other parties. But in the end, this clientelistic system became so entrenched, pervasive, and greedy that it consumed the entire politico-economic system from within, destroying by 1992–95 all parties and political leaders. In its wake, a new, untested, chaotic multi-party system has emerged, still caught between bi-party alternance and fragmentation, but now more accountable democratically through the current Left-Center government (the PDS-led *Ulivo* Pole).

Dr. Platon N. Rigos of the University of South Florida–Tampa analyzes, in "Greece: The Perils of Incorporation," the local Left-Right contraposition since World War II, and especially the long, controversial rule of Papandreou's PASOK in creating a single-party-dominant Leftist-populist front (deeply mired in corruption and patronage), rather than a traditional Socialist party. Following Papandreou's death in 1996 the Greek political system is still trying to come to terms with the long-term issues of democratic alternance and corruption management.

Dr. Alfred G. Cuzán of the University of West Florida–Pensacola argues in his chapter "Democratic Transitions: The Portuguese Case" that Portugal's change from dictatorship to democracy since the 1974 military coup, highlights the socio-economic prerequisites for democracy, the subordination of the military to the new democracy's civilian authorities and constitution, and the different advantages of implementing parliamentarism or presidentialism in new democracies.

Likewise, Dr. Anthony N. Celso of Valley Forge Military College (Wayne, Pennsylvania) analyzes, in "Neo-Liberal *Renovation,* Democratic Transition and Fragmentation: The Fall of Spain's Socialist Hegemony," both the decade-long triumph of the Socialist PSOE in establishing a functional single-party hegemony over post-Franco Spanish politics, and the failure to preserve such hegemony in the long term. Essential in both situations was the PSOE's adoption of a "renovation" strategy, which first gave it a strong mandate to govern Spain in the 1980s, while neo-Liberal economic programs alienated the party's core Leftist blocs and unions. In the end, the PSOE's imperial leadership, its neo-Liberal policies, and the effective isolation of government from party control, split the PSOE by 1996 in bitter factionalism leading to the loss of governmental hegemony after a 14-year reign.

Dr. Jack J. McTague of Saint Leo University (Tampa, Florida) analyzes in "Political Polarization and Electoral Change in Israel," the suffered political alternance in power between the Labor and *Likud* blocs, against the backdrop of corruption, terrorism and the Palestinian problem. But neither the 1996 and 1999 elections nor the Arab-Israeli peace process seem to have finally settled the issue of political pre-eminence between the governing Labor and the rival *Likud* in their relationship with the festering Palestinian problem.

From the experience accumulated in more than 40 years of U.S. governmental service in Japan and East Asia, Mr. Jack P. Horgan ("Politics, Culture, and Democratic Reform in Japan") stresses that Japan's success as the first major working democracy in Asia, rests on pre-democratic, socio-cultural elements in feudal Japan, which were deepened after the Meiji Restoration in 1868 when the previously secluded Japan was first opened to the modern industrial world. But this limited pre-war democratic process was derailed by a bureaucratic military polity, which led the nation first to war in Asia and then to the disaster of World War II. The Allied occupation instituted major reforms, which the Japanese have melded into their own unique vision of democracy and capitalism, with its current transition from a Confucian-type control "for the people," towards a new balance between bureaucratic and political control "in the people." Japan provides a pattern for Western and Asian nations, although the traditional Japanese cultural aspects are difficult to duplicate. A major problem for Japanese democracy both before the war and since has been political reform including what they call the "prevention of corruption." It has taken a pluralistic alternation of power, nearly ending the 37 years of the LDP's single-party-dominant rule, to produce a new electoral system, which politicians predict will provide the basis of a new polity, although only time will tell.

Among ex-Marxist states, Poland, Hungary, and the Czech Republic have all embarked on a process of political democratization since the revolutionary upheavals of 1989 and the collapse of Communist régimes in Eastern Europe. Dr. Beat Kernen of Southwest Missouri State University–Springfield, evaluates in "Out from the Cold: Peaceful Democratization in Hungary, Poland, and the Czech Republic," the variables of system stability, régime support, ethnic tolerance, and electoral competition in the development of a strong, stable, multi-party democratization after Communist one-party totalitarian rule in all three states.

Instead, systemic instability and corruption by the new ruling élites in Russia only aggravate the dangerous sense of drift and powerlessness gripping the country in "The Russian Case: Élite Self-Emancipation" by Dr. Robert V.

Barylski of the University of South Florida–New School in Sarasota. Thus all four countries, but especially Russia, remain "immature" democracies, which nevertheless have been largely successful in developing a high degree of systemic and socio-economic stability, and have consolidated their fragmented political parties and their overly competitive electoral systems. Russia's economic woes and political instability poses the most serious of threats to its domestic order, but the parallel weakness of President Yeltsin, the Duma, and the military, precludes any authoritarian return at the present.

In "Evolution and Demise of One-Party Rule in Nicaragua" Dr. Harry Vanden of the University of South Florida–Tampa argues that the process of stabilization and multi-party democracy in Nicaragua put in place by the Marxist *Sandinista* régime finally collapsed due to the failure of economic reconstruction and integration of the ex-militias (*Sandinistas, Contras*). Saddled by both the heritage of political oppression (Somoza's right-wing dictatorship; *Contras*) and left-wing revolution (*Sandinistas*), Nicaragua's current post-*Contra* democratic government seems frozen in a bi-polar confrontation with the *Sandinista* opposition, twice defeated at the polls, but still strong.

Drs. Waltraud Q. Morales of the University of Central Florida–Orlando and Corinne B. Young of the University of Tampa argue in "Mexico: Revolution in the Revolution?" whether Mexico's political and economic system, dominated for most of the twentieth century by the Party of the Institutionalized Revolution (PRI), is on the verge of a democratic transformation and free-market growth through NAFTA. Popular dissatisfaction, crime, drugs, and corruption may see the defeat of the PRI in the 2000 national presidential elections and the formation of a two-party coalition government with the leading opposition National Action Party (PAN). Democratic reforms are vital if Mexico is to function either like a democratic single-party-dominant system found in Europe, or as an alternating multi-party system, in its effort to maintain régime stability and economic growth. However, various threats to a democratic transition come from guerrilla insurgency (*Zapatistas*), drug mafias, and pervasive corruption.

Instead, in South America's *Cono Sul,* according to Dr. Franco Mazzella of Southwest Missouri State University–Springfield ("Peaceful Democratic Change in Brazil and Argentina: A Comparison") both countries moved into a cycle of democratization after decades of military authoritarianism and failed political economy of *statism* (active governmental intervention in the economy). Democracy in both countries has been strengthened by the emergence of civic organizations, new constitutional guarantees, and economic policies that blend free-market models, regional economic cooperation like MERCOSUR and social investments. Democracy in both countries is still hampered by the legacy of mistrust of civilian politicians and the lack of party structures as vehicles of political participation, public choice, and accountability. However, despite recent economic woes, the conditions for return to a one-party military rule, or the eventual growth of a civilian single-party-dominant régime remain slim in both countries.

Dr. Renu Khator of the University of South Florida–Tampa ("The Political Party System of India: From One-Party Dominance to No-Party Dominance") studies the evolution of the world's largest democracy, where despite poverty, unemployment, and widespread illiteracy, 90 percent of the population regularly votes. In a fragile multi-ethnic country, this electoral loyalty benefited for decades the Congress Party of India, whose leadership (Gandhi, Nehru, Indira Gandhi) and successful single-party hegemony deeply conditioned Indian politics and the local-regional relationship between patronage, political power, and corruption. But since the death of the Gandhis and the popular revolt against Congress's corruption, India has been marred by further political instability and weak ruling coalitions influenced by Hindu fundamentalism, and unsuccessful in developing a stable and effective bi-party alternance.

Dr. James Robinson of the University of West Florida–Pensacola ("Local and Provincial Elections in Taiwan: Appraising Steps in Democratization") examines Taiwan's evolution from a right-wing nationalist one-party state to a democratic single-party hegemony, where recent electoral trends at the national and local levels foster the inner democratization and generational change of the old Kuomintang. Additional pressures for democratization come from the country's relations with the West, although Communist China's scare tactics to oppose an independentist democratic Taiwan might ultimately reintegrate Taiwan to the Mainland and bring to an end the island's recent democratic experiment (similar to what has happened since 1998 in Hong-Kong).

In the chapter "South Africa" Drs. Charles W. Arnade of the University of South Florida–Tampa and Keith Tankard of Cape Town explore the country's recent transition from apartheid and single-party dominance by the whites (who disenfranchised the black majority at least since 1948) to the current multi-party and multi-ethnic democratic system under Nelson Mandela of the ANC. Local crime, unemployment, regional terrorism, and "white-flight" give pause to the initial post-apartheid elation. However, the recent transition in Presidency from Mandela to Tabo Mbecki, sanctioned by the ANC's repeated strong victory in the 1999 elections, prove that the ANC can still count on an immense reservoir of goodwill among the local population to continue domestic reforms.

Finally, the concluding chapter by Dr. Festus Ugboaja Ohaegbulam of the University of South Florida–Tampa ("The Dilemmas of Democracy in Nigeria") asserts that the entrenchment of democratic values in society, for which Nigerian and other African nationalists struggled against Western European imperial powers, has continued to elude Nigeria since its independence in 1960. Since then Nigeria has experienced two civilian administrations and seven military régimes, whose collective misconduct have stymied democracy and economic growth, despite Nigeria's attempts to strengthen the federal system and defuse ethno-nationalist rivalries through the country's subdivision into 36 states of relatively comparative population. The major dilemma of democracy in Nigeria is the failure of local leadership (both civilian politicians and military rulers) to implement democratic strategies, while overcoming regional, ethno-nationalist, and religious rivalries. To restore democracy in the near future, Nigerians need to alter the relationship between the Nigerian state, as the source of all wealth, and the multi-ethnic society, composed of competing ethno-religiously rival consumers. Nigeria is the only case-study where the transition from single-party dominance, or one-party authoritarianism, has been a glaring failure, while outrageous local governmental corruption, civil rights abuse, and ethno-nationalist tensions prove the difficulty of securing a stable, democratic alternance. However, recent changes since the 1998 death of strongman Abacha seem to have finally brought back that civilian democratic rule that Nigeria dearly misses.

Notes

1. T. J. Pempel, "Introduction," p. VII-VIII, in T. J. Pempel ed., *Uncommon Democracies. The One-Party Dominant Regimes* (Ithaca, NY: Cornell University Press, 1996).

2. Philippe C. Schmitter & Terry L. Karl, "What Democracy Is and Is Not," *Journal of Democracy* (summer 1991).

3. Robert Dahl, *Dilemmas of Pluralist Democracy* (New Haven, CT: Yale University Press, 1982), p. 11; Michael J. Sodaro ed., *Comparative Politics: A Global Introduction* (New York: McGraw-Hill, 2000), chapter 10.

4. Pempel, ed., *Uncommon Democracies*, p. 3–314.

5. Samuel P. Huntington, *Political Order in Changing Societies* (New Haven, CT: Yale University Press, 1968); Samuel P. Huntington & Clement Moore, eds., *Authoritarian Politics in Modern Societies: the Dynamics of Establishing One-Party Systems* (New York: Basic Books, 1970); David Apter, *The Politics of Modernization* (Chicago: Chicago University Press, 1965); Geoffrey Barraclough, *An Introduction to Contemporary History* (London: Penguin, 1964), p. 124–232.

6. Giovanni Sartori, *Parties and Party Systems, Vol. I* (London: Cambridge University Press, 1976), p. 193; Ronald H. McDonald, *Party Systems and Elections in Latin America* (Chicago: Markham, 1971), p. 220; Maurice Duverger, *Political Parties: Their Organization and Activities in the Modern State* (New York: Wiley, 1963); Jean Blondel, *Comparing Political Systems*

(New York: Praeger, 1972), p. 99–102; Asher Arian & Samuel Barnes, "The Dominant Party System: A Neglected Model of Democratic Stability," in *Journal of Politics,* vol. 36, no. 3 (1974): p. 592–614; Ariel Levite & Sidney Tarrow, "The Legitimation of Excluded Parties in Dominant Systems: A Comparison of Israel and Italy," in *Comparative Politics,* n.15 (1983): p. 295–327.

7. Pempel, "Introduction. Uncommon Democracies: the One-Party Dominant Regimes," p. 1–4.

8. Pempel, ed., *Uncommon Democracies,* p. 4–258; Angelo Panebianco, *Political Parties: Organization and Power* (Cambridge: Cambridge University Press, 1988).

9. Pempel, "Introduction," p. 4–33; P. A. Allum, *Italy, Republic without Government?* (New York: Norton, 1973); Giorgio Galli & Alfonso Prandi, *Patterns of Political Participation in Italy* (New Haven, CT: Yale University Press, 1970).

10. Pempel, "Conclusion: One-Party Dominance and the Creation of Regimes," p. 333–360, in Pempel, ed., *Uncommon Democracies.*

11. Pempel, ed., *Uncommon Democracies,* p. 167–187, 333–341, 340–360. See also Part I, "Single-Party-Dominant Systems and Western Plural Democracies" in the current volume.

12. Pempel, ed., *Uncommon Democracies,* p. 333–341, 340–360. See also Parts II and III of the current volume, regarding the democratization of ex-one-party countries in former Marxist and Third World states.

PART I

*Single-Party-Dominant Systems
and Western Pluralist Democracies*

ONE

Political Immobilism, Clientelism, Collapse, and Democratic Renewal in Italy

Marco Rimanelli

In his seminal work, T. J. Pempel lists four criteria for a party to forge a long-lasting single-party-dominant political system within any given country. First, it must dominate numerically the political scene, in terms of seats won in parliament and numbers of votes nationally. Second, it must hold the controlling political bargaining position, so that no government can ever be formed without its participation and leadership. Third, the dominant single-party must rule the government over an extended period of time (possibly over 30 years) through several successful and democratic elections. Fourth, it must dominate the governments that it forms, by monopolizing key positions such as the prime minister, foreign minister, defense minister, economic portfolios, and the state apparatus at large, to be able to reward its political supporters with jobs and targeted social programs that would keep them loyal to it and thus consolidate its single-party dominance despite domestic changes or challenges by other parties. In all instances, Italy emerges as both a trendsetter among single-party-dominant countries and a peculiar case-study. The almost 50-year-old triumph of the Christian Democrats' (DC) brand of "soft hegemony" was due to the unique combination of Pempel's dominance prerequisites, the Italians' peculiar anarchical politico-cultural mind-set, and a widespread patronage system ("to lock-in the vote") so pervasive and greedy that in the end it consumed the entire politico-economic system from within, destroying all parties and political figures, leaving in its wake an untested, chaotic, new multi-party system, still caught between bi-party alternance and party fragmentation, corruption, and accountable democratic renewal through the current new government of the Center-Left (the *Ulivo* Pole).[1]

I. The Weight of the Past:
Trasformismo and Imperialism, 1800s–1945

To talk about Italy is always difficult, given the almost surreal complexity of local politics and social issues. This is particularly trying for what concerns the unexpected political implosion of the early 1990s, which destroyed from within Italy's post-war political system (or "First Republic"). Since the fall of the Fascist dictatorship in 1943–45, domestic political crises have been nothing new in the fragile democratic country, which boasts the embarrassing record of 50 governments in 50 years, and where instances of political scandals over graft and corruption resurfaced repeatedly since the late 1950s. But amidst recurrent political and economic crises, or governmental reshuffling, the *Tangentopoli* corruption scandal of the early 1990s became the ultimate and most destructive "Italian Crisis": a modern cancer, long festering in a fragile country barely a century-old (National Unification took place in 1859–70), which developed from decades of rampant, institutionalized, secret, political clientelism and corruption, spilling from the highest national levels unto the society at large, until *Tangentopoli* uncovered it.

Italy is a country of complex paradoxes, a country of endless, often unnecessary trials and inefficiencies, but also a country of unexpected survivals, where political sins and national crises often go hand in hand, only to be routinely swept under the rug, in the hope that all problems will "miraculously" disappear, once the public opinion's attention has receded. Italians have long learned the difficult "art of surviving" against all odds—at times well, but more often just barely—while personal and family gain is all that really matters. Symbolically, the collapse of the Ancient Roman Empire 1,500 years ago, marked not only the passing of a long world hegemony, but even more that of a model of Roman bureaucratic efficiency, law, and maniacal sense of state duty. Thus, from the Middle Ages to Italy's National Unification in 1859–70, the Italian character was deeply singed by centuries of wars, foreign invasions, poverty, political fragmentation, intrigue, lawlessness, and inefficient government. Only the Renaissance marked a long period of governmental efficiency and accountability, commercial growth, wealth, and socio-cultural renewal, but at the price of worse political intrigues and widespread secret political assassinations. Today's Italy remains haunted by the incompetent mistakes of 20 years of Fascist dictatorship, and tarred by the equally widespread ruin left behind during the Cold War by a permanent, unaccountable ruling class, led by the Christian Democrats, which dominated the ultra-bureaucratized, democratic "First Republic" with the willing cooperation of most other parties.[2]

The lessons Italians drew from their checkered history was not a thirst for democratic renewal and national unity, but instead a deep distrust of all governments and laws, both seen as inevitable evils which people's ingenuity strove to bypass and minimize. Italians reacted to this environment through extreme selfish individualism, a constant quest for individual protection from the powerful, and the vital reliance on the solidarity of family, friends, or clan against a threatening world (yet outside such circles, Italians are equally apt at backstabbing fellow Italians, or foreigners when it suits them, although this is not uncommon in other cultures as well). Consequently, a systemic, semi-anarchical mind-set prevails with everybody cutting corners around state regulations and legal barriers, while in an otherwise inefficient and closed labor and housing market, success still depends on reliance upon the extended clan of family, friends and powerful associates as the traditional first help and last resort to solve all important or menial problems. This combination of national, semi-anarchical attitude, anti-governmental distrust, and a penchant for subverting all rules, has turned Italy into one of the most heavily regulated countries in the world in an effort to prevent widespread cheating. But as the common saying goes: *Fatta la legge, trovato l'inganno* (Once a law is enacted, fresh ways to by-pass it are readily discovered).

Two consequences emerge from this peculiar situation. On one hand, the country remains a fragile political system, almost irrelevant to the people's personal lives and beset by a slow, difficult, power-alternance among competing political parties. On the other hand, in the absence of clear-cut political-electoral majorities favoring competing political programs, Italy's prevailing rulers traditionally held on to power through patronage and graft to cement the very socio-political coalition-building vital to govern and legislate, while stalling any political alternance by radical oppositions. Whenever the opposition could not be secluded outright from power, it still could be emasculated (without resorting to anti-democratic repression) by "buying-off" key rival leaders, or co-opting to power the more readily controllable smaller political forces. These political maneuvers preserved the old ruling class in power, while perpetuating a polarized domestic political arena, where ideologically hostile oppositions rarely succeeded in replacing, or joining, ruling coalitions.[3]

Such political style of ruling first emerged during the process of National Unification (or *Risorgimento*, 1848–70): Piedmont's moderate-conservative, Savoy kingdom monopolized both the Italian crown and institutional control by channeling national patriotism behind its efficient army and the diplomatic cunning of Prime Minister Count Camillo Cavour to offset both foreign threats (Austria, France, Prussia, Russia, Britain), and domestic rivals (the disorganized, populist, republican revolutionary forces of Giuseppe Mazzini and General Giuseppe Garibaldi). Cavour relied on a mix of nationalism, constitutional liberalism, and economic reforms to secure the support of both the more moderate political factions and the traditional authoritarian forces in each of the sub-Italian regional states just annexed, whose local élites were kept in power in exchange for their loyalty to the new nation and its fiscally conservative Piedmontese ruling class ("Old Right") until 1876.

This dynamic coalition of different political forces tied by power-sharing was evident in the semi-colonial exploitation of the underdeveloped South (*Mezzogiorno*), and opposition to the secular socio-political interference of the Catholic Church. In the first instance, the overcrowded, impoverished *Mezzogiorno* remained dominated by feudal absentee landlords, whose political loyalty was "bought" in exchange for preserving their traditional local controls, administrative non-interference, and scuttling vital land reforms. In the second instance, Pope Pius IX's loss of political power following Italy's annexation of Papal Rome in 1870 led to the excommunication of the country's ruling élite, and the religious prohibition of all Catholics from voting and working in the government. But this policy, rather than destroying the fragile new state, turned into a "God-send" for the nationalist Liberal-Conservative rulers and Radical-Republican opposition who controlled half of the country. United behind their common anti-clericalism, the two groups could now mold the new Italy without compromising with a powerful, national Catholic party until 1913 (a paralyzing political force in France under Napoleon III in 1848–70, and a besieged rival in Bismarckian Germany in 1870–90s). The "Old Right" successfully absorbed less organized rival factions thanks to a restrictive electoral suffrage favoring the upper middle class. Politicians remained semi-independent and perpetually in power through loose personalistic coalitions in a socially homogeneous parliamentarian system lacking major ideological cleavages, mass-parties, or direct popular involvement in politics.[4]

The emergence since the late 1880s of a truly Italian, broad, political class (encompassing northern Moderate-Conservatives, northern and southern Liberal-Radicals, southern ex-Bourbonic Conservatives) did not foster the adoption of sorely needed radical socio-economic reforms and political changes as many feared at the time. Instead, once co-opted into power, the previously excluded "Old Left" (Liberal-Radicals) reconciled themselves to the monarchy and Moderate-Conservative order, without trying to widen the government's political basis through significant electoral, or land reforms. The "Old Left" had to cater to Moderate-Conservative forces and even single, influential members of parliament to pass legislation through a mix of a few cosmetic reforms and a complex patronage system, which would secure key votes and the politico-ideological switch of members (*Trasformismo*) on behalf of the government. As a policy of intra-party personalistic coalitions, *Trasformismo* transcended political loyalties and ideologies, while getting the job done without threatening the socio-economic status quo. Instead, the masses' political apathy and secular poverty were aggravated by chronic unemployment, overpopulation, landlessness, political exclusion, and crushing taxation of basic goods to redress national finances. As a partial safety-valve, the government tolerated unregulated internal migration from the country (urbanization), while actively supporting industrialization in the North (the Milan-Turin-Genova "Industrial Triangle") and mass emigration abroad (Mediterranean, France, South America, United States, East Africa) to defuse the internal pressures of unemployment and overpopulation, rather than solve directly their underlining socio-economic causes.

The fact that even a "progressist" Leftist government proved unwilling or unable to address the core issues of land reform and socio-economic justice or expand electoral suffrage led to popular disillusionment against all ruling parties, widespread despair and occasional peasant and labor revolts, which were firmly repressed by the state and army (the anti-taxation peasant revolts in the 1870s–80s; the 1880s "Sicilian Fasces" Revolt). Even when material change and progress did occur, it was mostly in localized areas of northern Italy, where both the nascent industry in the Industrial Triangle and the more efficient agricultural farms of the fertile Po Valley fostered both national economic growth and a widening chasm between the wealthy north and the backward, rural *Mezzogiorno*. Thus since the 1880s, Italy's ruling élites integrated northerners and southerners; common southern folks flocked to the civil service and legal and military jobs, quickly becoming the backbone of national bureaucracy, while northerners preferred instead commercial risk-taking ventures. But the key negative factor in the long run was Italy's traditional shallow nationalism and suspicion of centralized authority: most of the population remained estranged from Risorgimental and Savoyard traditions, which involved only smaller nationalist-Liberal élites and the middle class in control of domestic power. During the Liberal Era (1870s–1922) the bulk of the population felt psychologically "anti-Italian," deprived of meaningful political participation (universal male suffrage came only in 1913, and female suffrage in 1946), and coalesced along rival anti-state traditions of religion, ideology, and socio-economic class: the Catholics rallied around the Vatican's anti-Liberal command to reject political participation, while Leftist workers joined a neutralist revolutionary Socialist Party against the Liberal state.[5]

Abroad, Italy's economic-colonial rivalry with France and her politico-military fragility led her to join the Triple Alliance with Germany and

Austria-Hungary (1881–1914), while British friendship and hegemony over the Mediterranean assured Italy's maritime and trade security as well as the opportunity to slowly expand her colonies in Africa. But by 1896–1911, domestic opposition to these new colonial conquests (Eritrea, Somalia, Ethiopia, Libya) and the radicalization of the northern industrial working class in the radical Socialist Party exploded in widespread anti-governmental demonstrations, once strong-man Premier Francesco Crispi fell on the twin horns of the humiliating colonial disaster of Adua (which halted the conquest of Ethiopia) and the 1896 Banca Romana Scandal (which exposed nationwide patronage and political-industrial collusion). Tensions peaked when open royal support allowed a reactionary, military-based government to use artillery fire against demonstrators in the 1899 "Milan Riots," which in turn led to the revenge assassination of King Umberto I by an anarchist. By 1903–14 Liberal Premier Giovanni Giolitti's skillful, moderate statesmanship had successfully contained further political instabilities and widespread Socialist political strikes through a savvy mix of restrained law enforcement and meaningful labor and electoral reforms (including, by 1913, universal male suffrage), while playing-off all factions and winning the support of both moderate Socialists and the Catholic Populars.

However, Socialist domestic opposition flared again with anti-war demonstrations during the 1911–12 Italian-Turkish War to conquer Libya, and against Italian attempts to occupy chaotic Albania. Thus, the government engineered the controversial 1913 Gentiloni Pact with the Vatican to let the opposition Catholic forces rejoin the political arena by forming the moderate Popular Party and cooperating with the government against the atheist Socialists. But World War I, the emergence of an anti-German entente bloc (France, Russia, Britain, Serbia), and parallel Italian and Slav irredentist ethnic tensions against Austria-Hungary demoted Italy's national security and new-found fragile domestic consensus. The expedient turn towards neutrality in 1914–15 could not hide the deep split in the country, where the monarchy, Liberal-Conservatives, and Nationalists pressed to join the war on the Allies' side, while Giolitti's Liberals, plus Catholics and Socialists, remained vocal neutralists. Even the government's 1915 secret alliance with the Allies failed to sway the Socialists and most Catholics from their anti-war boycott, which left the two parties once again on the fringes of Italian political life, just when their sheer number seemed sufficient to propel them into power by 1914. After World War I, the devastating impact of war-time human losses and socio-economic dislocations on Italy's limited resources, coupled with national outrage against the Allies' slight of Italy's extreme nationalist claims at the 1919 Versailles Peace Treaty, plunged the country into political chaos, splitting her along class and ideological lines, equally inimical to the old Liberal state. Bloody street clashes, socio-economic turmoil, Leftist and Catholic land occupations, strikes, and factory occupations ("Red Biennial") ensued, while the government floundered hopelessly.[6]

In such a vacuum of domestic political power and virtual anarchy, Benito Mussolini's right-wing Fascist Party mobilized unemployed ultra-nationalist veterans, Nationalist-Conservatives, the middle class, and rural landlords against Leftist workers, landless peasants, and activist Catholic peasants. Backed by conservative industrialists and rural landlords, and with the tacit quiescence of governmental forces and the monarchy, Fascist paramilitary black-shirts ("Squadrists") engaged in bloody street fights and rural raids to quash their ideological rivals. By the fall of 1922, Mussolini capitalized on his regional success and the government's disarray: his brazen bid to seize power with a massive show of force by his armed "Squadrists" ("March on Rome") led the monarchy to appoint him premier. Mussolini's success was also due to the willing cooperation of the ruling élites, monarchy, and armed forces: as many times in the past, they sought to control the opposition by co-opting the unruly Fascists as an institutionalized, anti-Left bulwark, under the élites' political control. Instead, within two years Mussolini emasculated both the democratic oppositions (Liberals, Catholics, Socialists, Communists) and his own Conservative-Nationalist backers (which he forcibly absorbed). The Fascist dictatorship always banked on the ambiguous acquiescence of King Vittorio-Emanuele III and the Vatican (appeased by the 1926 Concordat's politico-religious concessions and Fascism's virulent anti-Communism). The Savoyard Monarchy and conservative forces retained power by supporting Mussolini's creeping Fascist dictatorship and forced assimilation of the political oppositions through superficial mass "nationalism" and patriotism. During the *"Ventennio,"* Fascist leadership and conservative interests merged in a common quest for graft, influence, and dictatorial rule, under the blustering façade of nationalist power-politics, militarism, occasional social reforms, and renewed expansionism abroad.

Fascism's politico-military strengthening of Italy as the "least" of the world's great powers was followed by its fateful ideological alliance with Hitler's Nazi Germany (1936 Axis; 1937–38 Anti-Komintern Pact; 1939 Pact of Steel; 1940 Tripartite Pact with Germany and Japan) against the Anglo-French Allies. Thereafter, Fascist Italy's belated entry into World War II in 1940 to exploit Germany's apparent victory (rather than stay neutral like Francoist Spain, or Turkey), led to military defeats against the Allies (strengthened in 1941 by the USSR and the United States) and the loss of all recent conquests (Mussolini's "Neo-Roman Empire" in the Mediterranean). By July-September 1943 both Fascism and Italy collapsed under a twin Allied versus German invasion threatening the country's existence as a Nation-state.[7]

During Fascism, Mussolini had reluctantly shared political power with the Savoyard Monarchy, and by 1943 such liaison tainted both the *Duce* and King Vittorio-Emanuele III in the eyes of public opinion and anti-Fascist opposition. While Italy's collapse in World War II left Mussolini's rump-Italian Republic of Salò (1943–45) on Hitler's losing side, the Savoyards in the south had already shifted allegiance to the winning Allies under the military-monarchist régime of General Umberto Badoglio (1943–44) and then the CLN anti-Fascist national front (1944–45). Yet King Vittorio-Emanuele III's refusal to step down until 1945 also tainted politically his son King Umberto II's brief tenure. The collapse of Fascism as a one-party dictatorship, and the ideological hatreds unleashed by the Partisan/Civil War of 1943–45, deprived the Italians of the old veneer of nationalist identity after 20 years of dictatorship (two generations had never been exposed to democracy), while Italy's reemergence as a fragile, pro-Western democracy was beset by new conflicting socio-ideological forces struggling for control over a broken, defeated country.

Under the Fascist dictatorship, true anti-Fascists were always a small minority (mostly Leftists), either imprisoned or in exile, while most Catholics and Liberals chose passive, silent acquiescence. Only Italy's World War II military débâcle and the Partisan/Civil War against the Nazi-Fascists expanded the anti-Fascists' ranks and democratic influence on a previously supine society with a sudden proliferation of different ideologies and political parties (Catholics, Moderates, Conservatives, Socialists, Communists). In the backward *Mezzogiorno,* where the Allied liberation came rapidly, the anti-Fascist resistance's influence was limited to introducing the population to these new democratic ideals and multi-party system, to which southerners remained indifferent compared to the overriding desire for economic growth and employment, while local bosses easily shifted allegiance from monarchy and Fascism, and now the new democratic system, to preserve their stranglehold. Instead, in Northern Italy the growth of radical CLN partisans (80,000 in summer 1944; 250,000 in spring 1945) behind Nazi-Fascist lines, and the lack of a unifying, conservative figurehead capable of reining in the partisans (like General Charles De Gaulle in France), worried the occupying Anglo-American Allies who feared a partisan Leftist take-over (like Yugoslavia, Albania, and Greece, where the rival East and West spheres of influence clashed). However, the CLN coalition strove to paper-over domestic politico-ideological rivalries between its components, both in wartime and in the immediate post-war refoundation of the state, while struggling for independence from the oppressive Allied politico-military controls.

Thus, the "First Republic's" democratic institutions symbolized a sharp break with the past: the 1946 Institutional Referendum was approved by 54 percent of Italians, while the monarchists' close loss (46 percent) reflected mostly loyalty and fears of an uncertain post-war future, rather than foreshadow a long, divisive institutional crisis, like the old Risorgimental versus Catholic one after Unification (1870–1913). Instead, the 1946 Republic versus monarchy clash became the symbol of the clash between olden ways and modernity, although the modernists' 1946 victory ushered only moderate, weak reforms to ease the transition from the old authoritarian monarchy to an anti-Fascist, modern, democratic republic focused on national reconstruction and reconciliation. Thereafter, except for a minority of diehards in the south, most monarchists accepted the "First Republic," once political stability and economic growth within the Allied Western bloc appeased earlier fears.[8]

II. Establishing Single-Party Dominance: DC, Cold War, and Clientelism, 1945–70

According to Giuseppe Di Palma and other scholars, any war-ravaged country where the demise of its previous dictatorial régime was followed by foreign military occupation should normally lean towards establishing a single-party-dominant system during the difficult post-war political birth of a new democratic system, rather than develop a more difficult, full-fledged, multi- party system with alternance in power. Moreover, according to Pempel, any such party securing political dominance should be able then to preserve a durable hegemony over domestic politics, economics, and society. Yet after World War II only Italy and Japan emerged as single-party-dominant countries, but within a reconstructed Western-style, democratic, multi-party system devoid of alternance (DC in Italy, 1945–92; LDP in Japan, 1955–98). However, in both countries political dominance seemed unrelated to the electoral system, as Italy shifted from her traditional uninominal system ("winner-takes-all") to a pure proportional one, while in Japan the LDP still relies on the uninominal system. Instead, other war-ravaged countries like West Germany, France, and Austria emerged as traditional multi-party democratic systems with party-alternance to power, despite decade-long periods of single-party dominance (Germany's CDU in 1949–66 and 1982–98; France's RpR/UDF bloc in 1958–82 once De Gaulle replaced the chaotic IV Republic with his Right-leaning V Republic). Instead, in Austria the rival Socialists and Catholics formed long-lasting national coalitions until the 1990s to avoid party dominance and polarization. More recently, Greece and Spain (both since the end of local Fascist dictatorships in 1973–75) experienced occasional single-party dominance during the 1980s under the Socialist PASOK and PSOE leadership respectively. Likewise, after the 1989 revolutions the ex-Communist Eastern European democracies faced similar situations, although multi-party alternance seems to have prevailed there as well.[9]

Italy and Japan are the only democracies to have developed single-party-dominant systems parallel to both countries' post-war economic reconstruction, along Pempel's theories of dominance. But even in Italy, where wartime defeat and economic-political reconstruction favored the DC's rise to single-party dominance, this was neither easy nor preordained. Instead, in the immediate post-war Italy's new competitive political system pitted all parties in a race for power, in which initially the Marxist Left bloc (PSI-PCI in 1944–48) seemed favored. Indeed, within any step-by-step transition to a new democracy, the emergence of a single-party-dominant system through both inter-party democratic cooperation and the delegitimization of the extreme oppositions is quite rare, yet in Italy exceptional circumstances propelled the Christian Democrats (DC) to power through skilled politics and long-term consensus-building strategies. But the Cold War's ideological polarization between rival U.S. and Soviet blocs, and Italy's own alignment with the U.S.-led West, consolidated the DC's domestic rival hegemony on power. However, Di Palma rightly demonstrated that any moderate party like the DC could retain dominance in domestic politics not exclusively on the basis of the party's own peculiar qualities of leadership, but mostly through a mix of political alliances and periodic reshuffling of party strategies to guarantee loyalty from disparate groups.

The DC retained power by constantly delegitimizing the undemocratic extreme oppositions and their entrenched constituencies: the MSI's neo-Fascist Right (that backed Mussolini's dictatorship), and the PSI-PCI Leftist front (which fought against Fascism, but in the Cold War remained loyal to the USSR more than to the new pro-Western democracy). This policy, however, requires a constant, skillful balance between delegitimization and inclusion to avoid otherwise inevitable risks of unacceptable domestic turmoil in a fragile new democracy, should such exclusionary policy be too rigid. Often, but not always, domestic extremist forces wither away naturally at the onset of democracy, and in this case it is not an impossible political task to engineer the transfer of their loyalty from a dictatorial system to a full-fledged democracy, as few anti-democratic opponents are ideological diehards compared to the majority interested mostly in personal opportunity. Thus, any dominant party pursuing inclusive, non-confrontational strategies of political participation can gradually absorb part of the extremes in the new democratic system, as long as clear-cut participation rules equally benefit all parties and allows any party to become a winner. Since the mid 1940s, the DC did attract some of the extreme parties' constituencies into the democratic transition process by appealing to inter-party cooperation across ideologies, and by relying on non-competitive alliance-building and power-sharing formulas on an equal (50/50 percent) or proportional basis during both the governments of national unity (1945–48) and DC-led broad political coalitions (1948–92).[10]

Initially, the emergence of democracy in an ex-authoritarian country is paralleled or followed closely by the rapid development of new political forces and ideological issues mobilizing the electorate and ruling élites committed to democracy-building. Thus, the earlier process of democracy-building is overshadowed by issues of national and ideological identity: at home power distribution, electioneering, labor-industrial relations, and socio-economic interests soon redistribute to other political actors the initial dominant position enjoyed by the first forces to seize control of the political system, while abroad national diplomacy is conditioned by the international politico-economic system and the hegemonic power influencing the country. Certainly, single-party dominance in the early stages of democratization is one of many potential political scenarios that can develop in such a chaotic transition process. But early in the second period, any initially dominant party in power must, in order to survive, then change strategy to better preserve or extend its dominance through a strategy of coalition-building and democratic consolidation. Only moderate parties through all-inclusive strategies (ideologically difficult for both the extreme Left and Right) are the most likely ones to secure domestic political hegemony and establish a successful single-party-dominant system.

A strategy of one-party dominance and delegitimization of the oppositions is often more appealing to Leftist parties after the transition from right-wing dictatorship, even when they were not involved in the initial overthrow and/or had to collaborate with moderate forces. But the extreme Left's type of single-party dominance in new democracies is soon undone as the result of their orthodox Marxist view of political hegemony and system-legitimization as morally and politically identical. By fusing ideology with their hold to power, Leftist single-party-dominant systems herald the "purity" of their cause against the morally and politically bankrupt socio-economic forces, that supported, or acquiesced to, the past dictatorship. Thus, the Marxists would combine legitimization of their initial hegemony through substantial policy reforms of the state, economy, and society, while underplaying institutional guarantees for democratic competitiveness and power-sharing alliances with moderate parties. But if the single-party-dominant extreme Left does not quickly promote at home a revolutionary Marxist régime by delegitimizing all other rival parties, it could soon lose its dominance under the joint pressure of the moderate parties, whose vital political consent for legislation is contingent on the government accepting new rules of competitive, democratic access to power (like in Italy in 1945–48, or in Portugal in 1973–76). In Italy and France, local Communist parties played a central role in the Partisan/Civil War against the Nazi-Fascist dictatorial forces during World War II and seemed poised to gain domestic hegemony during the initial phase of reconstruction until 1948. But neither one pursued an exclusionary ideological strategy of extreme Left dominance turning into an outright Marxist dictatorship (such as happened in Soviet-controlled Eastern Europe), although this was a hotly divisive and threatened possibility. Instead, both the pro-USSR PCI and PCF chose not to act for fear of domestic turmoil, governmental repression, and an international backlash during the Cold War, as the United States supported moderate democratic forces as well as right-wing dictatorial régimes against the Left.[11]

Instead, if the extreme Right is the initiator of the transition to democracy after the failure of domestic dictatorship, it too could sometimes maintain its single-party dominance within a new democratic context, by playing an ambiguous role initially. But the need to overcome the discredit of its past dictatorial affiliation, would force the Right to push beyond liberalization and internal reforms to embrace full democratization, regardless of the risk of losing control. In such case, to seize control of the democratic process, the reformed-Right must compromise with the other emerging democratic opponents, as did the UDC (Union of the Democratic Center) in post-Franco Spain after 1975. However, the natural tendency is for the single-party-dominant models of the reformed-Right to disappear in time under the twin pressure of its democratic opponents (whose political support requires power-sharing alliances), and the latent sabotage by hard-core dictatorial elements within the Right (whose negative influence could undermine any liberalization). Either situation would then factionalize the Right into several ideologically similar, but smaller parties (as happened with the sudden demise of the UDC in Spain in 1980), unable to hold on to dominance. Instead, outright collapse would be the result of holding onto its discredited power by mobilizing state resources and institutions against strong pressures for devolution by the emerging democratic opponents: thus in Italy the discredited Savoyard monarchy and Badoglio's military-monarchist government (July 1943–June 1944), were soon marginalized by the CLN anti-Fascist democratic coalition of national unity, and the monarchy abolished by 1946.

Although the reemergence of Moderate-Conservative parties is slower after a dictatorship compared to the Left's ability to preserve its structures underground, after World War II the occupying Anglo-American Allies openly favored the reemergence, legitimization, and political control of sympathetic democratic forces in Italy, France, Scandinavia, BE.NE.LUX, West Germany, Greece, Austria, and Japan. Thus, regardless of their commitment to democratic openness, moderate-conservative parties were better poised to consolidate governmental control and secure the support of the pro-democratic, occupying Allies to achieve dominance and defuse the challenge of radical oppositions. Likewise, in Eastern Europe it was the occupying Soviet forces' and Stalin's brutal satellization policies that imposed a thorough and uniform model of Marxist dictatorship on behalf of local Communist parties who had already secured a single-party-dominant status after World War II. However, the Moderates' initial advantage as the indispensable guarantors of an orderly and stable transition to democracy was not sufficient to assure continuing dominance once the occupying Allies left and/or the reconstruction period was completed. Only Italy's DC and Japan's LDP succeeded in preserving their politico-electoral single-party dominance over nearly 50 years, while the similar initial dominance by the CDU in West Germany (1949–66), the UDC in Spain (1976–80), and the *Nea Demokratia* in Greece (1975–80) soon whittled away. The fact that the DC and the CDU were Christian parties, and did mobilize the popular vote against their Marxist challengers on the basis of both religious and conservative anti-Communism, plays no role in explaining Japan's LDP's success as it is not a religious party. Moreover, no hegemonic Catholic party emerged in France, Spain, Portugal, or Austria out of this same sub-culture. In Italy the DC offered a more popular religious-nationalist alternative to Marxism, untainted by collaboration with the previous Fascist régime, and on this basis the DC constantly rallied to its side the religious constituency, through the capillary support of the Church, while expanding its vast sub-cultural appeal and social basis to the non-religious middle class and moderate public opinion.[12]

As the legitimate guarantor of the new democracy, the DC successfully consolidated its single-party dominance through non-ideological, political alliances and politico-electoral strategies, while withholding democratic credibility and government posts from rival parties (either moderates excluded from government coalitions, or extremist Left and Right oppositions). This difficult balancing act to establish single-party dominance in a fragile, multi-party democratic system depended on various concomitant factors, including the DC's early central role in the transition to democracy, its capillary socio-cultural reach, its international alignments, and its solicited support from the United States (Italy's main occupying power), while political in-fighting with other parties allowed the DC the delegitimizing of the extremist Right and Left. In the context of open, routine, democratic elections, neither the moderate parties nor the extreme oppositions could mutually exclude each other, although the extremes' vocal opposition to democracy played into the DC's hands by narrowing the field of credible, rival ruling parties. For the extreme parties, exclusive power and ideological "purity" would lead to repression of their democratic opponents and the return to dictatorship, but also cause severe international repercussions against either dictatorial Leftists or Rightist régimes within the West. Instead, democracy would assure—albeit narrowly—the survival of all extreme oppositions not openly engaged in subversion. Thus, in post-Francoist Spain both the reformed Right and Left quickly adopted democratic rules and in turn dominated the system, while in Italy and France both extreme Left and Right were long excluded from power and only occasionally brought into coalition governments.

In Italy after World War II, Catholics and Leftists (Socialists and Communists) who had been excluded from national power by both the Liberal and Fascist states, strove to build a new national democratic consciousness within a republican state to integrate their own alienated supporters. In 1945–48 the Italian Left (PSI-PCI) controlled 40 percent of the voters, mostly in Northern Italy, through a vast and efficient political network, affiliated organizations, trade unions, professional cadres, and strict ideological loyalty to the USSR. For the first time, in 1943–48 the Left made inroads among the conservative southern peasants through popular appeals for land occupations and redistribution of land, given the massive local overpopulation and backwardness. But post-war unemployment in the unionized northern urban-industrial areas forced the PCI to soften its revolutionary nationalization programs and adopt a conciliatory line towards Catholics, industrialists, and the Liberal Right to guarantee national unity and governmental influence for the Left. PCI leader Palmiro Togliatti sought to dispel the fears of both the occupying Anglo-Americans and the middle class of a Soviet-supported domestic Communist revolution, but many ex-partisan units hid their weapons for a future revolution. However, both Leftists and Liberals remained relative minoritarian political forces compared to the disenfranchised masses of loyal Catholics. While Don Luigi Sturzo's earlier non-clerical Popular Party was abandoned by the Vatican after it normalized relations with the Fascist state, since 1943 the DC was the fastest party to reorganize itself thanks to the Vatican's prestige and network of Catholic organizations. Long excluded from the political fabric by both the Liberal and Fascist states, the Church exploited Fascism's collapse to replace the state as the country's chief socio-moral guide, while using the DC for outright political influence. Likewise, devout DC Premier Alcide De Gasperi relied on Pope Pius XII's authoritative influence to turn the DC into the catch-all mass-party of Catholic unity, whose clerical, classless, Moderate-Conservative ideology against the materialism of both capitalists and the atheist Left attracted monarchists, republicans, conservatives, reformists, peasants, ex-Fascists and Leftist Christians.[13]

Soon the Vatican-backed DC monopolized the Catholic vote and national politics. Since the resistance, the DC kept alive the difficult political cooperation among the ideologically opposed democratic components of the wartime anti-Fascist coalition so as to jointly promote a post-war "institutional" democratic break with Italy's disreputable Fascist and Savoyard pasts. On one hand, Premier De Gasperi and the DC indirectly allowed the "First Republic" to prevail by abstaining from taking sides in the clash between monarchy ("old") and republic ("new"), given the widespread monarchist sentiment among DC rank-and-file. On the other hand, the DC and other democratic parties permanently occupied state power to strengthen Italy's traditionally weak national identity, while rallying masses of voters and cadres through their party machinery to loyally embrace the country's new democratic national consciousness. As official guarantors of the republic's democratic institutions (while keeping the executive weak to prevent any new "strong man" from prevailing), the "constitutional arc parties" became completely identified in the public mind with the "First Republic" and state institutions. This ambiguous party-nation relationship allowed the political system to reward its supporters, while constantly bypassing national institutions and social pressures. But the parties also quickly monopolized state resources to perpetuate their governmental coalitions and political partitioning ("Partitocracy") of the economy and country, while in time a thick web of secret inter-party trade-offs and negotiations (*"patteggiamenti"*) did politically emasculate the independence of parliament, governments, and premiers. This instrumental twin party-state and party-nation identification (political integration and loyalty towards the nation as a result of the parties' ability to channel state resources to their own rival constituencies) left most Italians dissatisfied with the performance of the "official" state institutions. Yet both Catholics and Marxists relied on such party-state identification to strengthen their own ideological brand of "democracy" and help their respective constituencies though permanent state intervention in the country's economic growth and employment (White "clientelism" versus Red nationalizations).

For moderate parties, the exclusive reliance on nationalism, international alignments, and anti-extremist rhetoric (anti-Communism, anti-Fascism) as factors in mobilizing mass loyalty and marginalization of the opposition are less effective over time in a competitive, open democracy, especially as the promise of capitalist growth and affluence falter (i.e.: Russia and Eastern European in the late 1990s). As Italy's dominant moderate party, the DC undertook a strategy of concerted inter-partisan cooperation between moderate parties and even the extreme oppositions, which consolidated as well her hegemonic leadership. This strategy of political inclusion required formal inter-party agreements to engineer politico-constitutional and socio-economic coexistence through rigid power-sharing formulas (*pactismo*), or strict proportional allocation of positions and resources based on each party's actual political strength ("proportionalism"). These anti-hegemonic solutions are easier to achieve between two opposite blocs of similar strength to prevent either one from becoming dominant (like in Austria, or Latin America). Instead, in Italy a moderate Center was always confronted by political extremism from both Right and Left. Thus, a complex strategy of inter-partisan cooperation, constitutional accommodation, and an open political system guaranteed maximal political access through parliamentary rules and proportional elections (*garantismo*). Also the extreme parties accepted the rules of *garantismo* and the interplay of an open democratic system, rather than seeking to attain exclusive power and then failing. Thus, the DC's moderate centerism emerged as a nuanced single-party-dominant force in domestic politics, although on this strength she could even at times abandon inter-partisan cooperation with impunity.[14]

The DC embraced *garantismo* since the anti-Fascist wartime national coalitions (1943–45) and throughout the early post-war governments of national unity (1945–48) with both Moderates and the Left (PCI and PSI). Also Italy's 1946 constitution enshrines *garantismo* to benefit both the DC and the Left. By 1948 the Cold War imposed a sharp realignment of the country and government with the U.S.-led West, while the DC's emphasis on identity, ideology, international alignments and economic reconstruction relegated the extremes into permanent opposition. The DC's ability to manipulate *garantismo* and its ability to act as a linchpin in lending legitimacy to inter-partisan policies of reconciliation helped it avoid an initial clash with an electorally stronger Left, which allowed De Gasperi to hold together the centrist coalition and appealed to Italy's electorate threatened by the extremes until the victorious show-down with the 1948 elections. However, the Left also benefited from *garantismo,* first by joining the governing coalition, and later by relying on its constitutional shield when the Cold War excluded it from power and propelled the DC into politico-electoral hegemony from 1948. The DC's dominance was always nuanced and strengthened through time by forcing potential opponents into governmental coalitions, both to reduce their disloyalty and expand the area of governmental consensus. In Italy, as in other countries, dominance was the result of both repeated electoral victories and the continued (perceived or real) inability of the oppositions to govern (due to their lack of political credibility and their ideological rejection of the country's core democratic values and pro-Western international alignment), rather than just an issue of sheer numerical strength. Likewise in West Germany and Japan, national identity and domestic and foreign politics, remained for a long time the monopoly of the conservative parties, whose unchallenged domination benefited also from international factors (the Cold War; U.S./NATO alliance, anti-Communism, Western trade), while their public opinions supported the exclusion of the domestic Left until it too adopted pro-Western democratic values. Instead, should the extreme oppositions be insignificant, and other moderate parties share basic values, then single-party dominance would be impossible and be replaced by inter-party alternance in government.

Since the second post-war period, the single-party dominance by conservatives in West Germany, Japan, and Italy benefited both from their early monopoly of the democratic transition process and from the Cold War's frozen geo-political structure, which in turn allowed the CDU, LDP, and DC to exclude the extremists and the democratic Socialist oppositions from domestic policies. Both West Germany's and Japan's geo-strategic international location on the border of the Soviet "Iron Curtain" during the Cold War taxed the West into balancing pro-democratic repressive policies (like "de-Nazification") and constitutional-economic reconstruction with the need to build a sturdy local democracy free of past imperialism, but still capable of providing a military bulwark against an expansionist USSR. Thus, the close collaboration between U.S. occupation authorities and local Japanese and West German conservative-business forces and bureaucracies made it easier for the German CDU and Japanese LDP governments to dispense with inter-party cooperation, and stress conservative continuity under the cover of a foreign-guided democratization, free-trade, and anti-Soviet alignment with the U.S.-led West. In Germany and Japan this successful "winner-take-all" strategy and popular economic growth policies rewarded the conservatives with political dominance, while marginalizing the oppositions (both extremists and moderates) through constant electoral victories, which undercut any need for inter-partisan accommodation. But should the ruling party suddenly lose popular support, any electoral reversal could immediately wipe out this long-suffered dominance (as happened in Germany to the CDU both in the late 1960s and 1990s, and in Greece and Spain to their conservative parties in the early 1980s).[15]

By 1947 the Cold War forced all Italian parties to take sides in the Super Powers' confrontation between the United States and USSR, while the DC was under strong conservative, Vatican and U.S. pressures to jettison the rival PCI-PSI bloc from the old anti-Fascist government of national unity. Conversely, the PSI split as the PSDI supported the government, while Pietro Nenni's PSI remained alongside their PCI ally in their common revolutionary class struggle. Likewise the Leftist-dominated Italian Trade Union (CGIL) and working class were infiltrated by Catholic and moderates supported by the United States and AFL, splitting the Union into three parallel structures (CGIL, CISL, UIL) and weakening their common labor and political agendas. The DC was mightily aided by the Church's massive anti-Communist crusade, demonstrations, and excommunication threats, while the United States openly threatened to terminate vital economic aid (Marshall Plan), while organizing a large write-in campaign by Italian-American immigrants to their relatives in Italy. Thus, the 1948 elections saw the majority of Italy's popular opinion among all classes swing its support behind the pro-Western DC-led government (69 percent of votes, with the DC at 48 percent compared to 35 percent in 1946) against the pro-Soviet Left (31 percent). right-wing forces even sought to disenfranchise the PCI as an anti-democratic party tied to a foreign enemy (the USSR), especially once Togliatti's failed assassination and coma brought the PCI rank-and-file spontaneously into bloody street clashes with the police, while several buried weapons caches were unearthed for the "imminent" revolution. But Togliatti's recovery allowed the PCI to stop its most militant "hot-heads," fearing that a military and political débâcle would ensue, while De Gasperi rejected the Right's calls to disband the PCI fearing a renewed civil war. Instead the Left remained frozen into a perpetual opposition, while all other democratic parties joined the new DC-led government spanning from the moderate Right (PLI) to the Center-Left (PRI, PSDI). This preserved also the DC's own inter-class factionalism (DC-Right, DC-Left and other "currents"), while the Left's political marginalization was consolidated by Italy's international alignment with the U.S.-led NATO military alliance from 1949. De Gasperi had justified Italy's Western alignment during the Cold War as inevitable, given Italy's geo-political location and his desire to join an integrated a Christian Europe at both the military (NATO, EDC, WEU) and economic levels (ECSC, European Union). This would protect Italy as the weakest European nation and preserve national security, despite her defeat as a Great Power in World War II. Also Lay and business forces supported a parallel vision of an integrated, peaceful, capitalist, European market, similar to that of the United States, while exports and domestic growth introduced the very Western materialist prosperity so much dreaded by the Church, as well as radical socio-economic changes.

Premier De Gasperi's strategy to turn the DC into the democratic anchor of all Centrist government coalitions by sharing the benefits of coalition power among a broad socio-politico-economic constituency, strengthened her political dominance and prevented divisive domestic polarizations between Left and Right, labor versus capitalism, atheism versus intolerant Catholicism. The DC's Centrist socio-political and capitalist economic strategies, together with its anti-Communism, were fully backed by the United States in its quest to sustain a liberal, pluralistic, Western democracy in Italy. Moreover, Italy's membership in the U.S./NATO military alliance was domestically countered by the strong rival presence of the pro-Soviet PCI/PSI and CGIL union during the Cold War, as bi-polar domestic political tensions between the DC-led Centrist governments and the Left mirrored the international clash between the super powers. Often the United States' rigid anti-Communist ideology left it baffled at the DC's ambiguous, "soft hegemonic" strategy of including the Left in domestic and national policies, even after both PCI and PSI had been jettisoned from the government, while at the same time marginalizing it from power (1945–48, 1958–61, 1976–79). But the DC's support for democracy deflected U.S. pressures to outlaw the Left, allowing the extreme oppositions to survive and slowly be reabsorbed into the democratic system. Thus, the DC's strategy of inclusive coalition governments and patronage helped democratize the ex-dictatorial country to the routine ballot-box squelching of the oppositions, without the violence of the past (exalted by Fascism during the *Ventennio* and later by right-wing extremists through para-military coup attempts or Black terrorism in the 1960s–70s, while also the post-partisan Left seemed ready to use it in the mid 1940s, as did the Red terrorists of the 1970s).[16]

Although much feared, incidents of direct and covert U.S. interference in Italian politics became infrequent after the 1950s. Nevertheless, the U.S. presence assured that any rival politico-ideological style of nation-building (from the Left or extreme Right) would have been impossible to attain (as attested by the virtual and "not so implicit" veto exercised on Italian politics by U.S. Ambassador Claire Luce on behalf of the Republican Eisenhower administration in the 1950s, or by U.S. National Security Advisors Henry Kissinger and Zbignew Brzezinski in the 1970s for the Nixon's Republican and Carter's Democratic administrations). The DC benefited immensely from U. S. military protection and economic aid: (1) with the internationalization of domestic contrasts, the rival Leftist unions were fragmented between their Marxist and Catholic-Liberal components, allowing a degree of control by the government; (2) the PSI lost its moderate wing, which as PSDI provided DC-led governments with a legitimate, albeit small, foothold within the Left; (3) U.S. politico-economic support allowed the DC virtual local autonomy from the Vatican's conservative stranglehold; (4) the U.S./Western free trade capitalism allowed Italian enterprises to finally flourish in international trade, while domestic economic growth ("Economic Miracle") transformed the country's socio-cultural make-up.

Italy's strategy of *garantismo* combined institutional protections of all parties with broad moderate coalition governments, while the DC's single-party dominance monopolized state's institutions for almost 50 years. At the same time, constitutional *garantismo* allowed the DC to defuse political tensions by letting the delegitimized extreme Left and Right (PCI and MSI) participate in selected areas of domestic politics, parliaments, local governments, and society, while the DC selectively co-opted the government into the more "malleable" opposition forces (PSDI in the 1940s and PSI in the 1960s) to strengthen the government's hold on power, and further isolate the extreme ones. Delegitimization, in fact, remains difficult to dispel for excluded parties accused of being undemocratic. Both Right and Left were persistently criticized over the slow cosmetic nature of their internal changes: the discredited

MSI, for its attachment to its Fascist past and ambiguous backing of right-wing violence; the allegedly pro-Soviet PCI, for its reluctant, ambiguous acceptance of Italy's key pro-Western foreign policy (NATO, the United States, and a united Europe) while retaining a non-democratic party structure. But despite 50 years of exclusion, the neo-Fascist MSI still kept its constituency (between 5 to 9 percent), and the PCI even increased its own to 30 percent by the 1970s. After the collapse of Italy's "First Republic" in 1992 and the fall of all its tainted traditional parties, the reformed ex-PCI split (losing its more Marxist extremists) and its democratic successor, the PDS, finally become the new dominant force in Italian governments after 1995. Likewise, the ex-MSI benefited from an electoral expansion among the former DC-Right, while its more "humane" façade gave it both brief governmental experience (1994) and a new democratic legitimacy as a Right/conservative party, only mildly tainted by its Fascist heritage.[17]

Although the establishment of single-party dominance by moderate parties is often the result of strategies focused on democratic identity (reaping the benefits of creating a new democratic system), or loyalty (excluding from power extreme oppositions, labeled as "disloyal" anti-democratic), still many other obstacles in the long term can deny political dominance, rather than consolidate such control. In any case, strategies of *garantismo*, or outright exclusion of the extreme parties, work best in the earlier phase of transition to democracy to achieve single-party dominance. Afterwards, new strategies and/or infusion of politically targeted new resources, are constantly needed to preserve dominance past the initial phase of democratic consolidation to "reinvigorate" the single-party-dominant system. Thus, the dominant party's control of the state's apparatus and national economy presents a tempting opportunity to turn it to partisan use and "reward" the civil service, the corporate-economic structure, and targeted constituencies for their permanent electoral and financial support of the ruling party. Finally, in time, a widening stifling net of patronage, corruption, and vote peddling permeates both the political system and society-at large with its many-faceted negative repercussions, just as in Italy under the DC's clientelist policies.

The DC-led governments consistently failed to implement key constitutional provisions (a constitutional court, decentralized regions, referendum), due to obsessive fears of uncontrollable social strife should the Left exploit Italy's Constitution to penetrate the country's institutions and regional governments. Both the Church and the DC exercised an overwhelming influence on the society to preserve social peace and order against the twin threats of Communism and capitalist materialism, while the Vatican's conservative hierarchy sought to preserve its recent heightened politico-moral influence and Italy's backward rural Catholic life as a bulwark for the Church's religious-societal influence (65–70 percent are loyal practicing Catholics). But despite the "Communist threat," the PCI never deviated from its strict respect of democracy, because this also protected the PCI from destruction (notwithstanding its politico-ideological ties to the USSR) even as it kept the Left politically marginalized. These contrasts also fostered a relentless, underground, cultural-religious-ideological clash between the Catholic societal sub-culture ("White") against both the rival Leftist ("Red") one, and the smaller Liberal-Democratic ("Lay") middle class. Although minoritarian in the Red-White struggle between dominant sub-cultures, the Lay parties dominated the country's intelligentsia and business, seeking to build a modern, capitalist, industrial, non-clerical, and progressist Western nation. Moreover, soon the old rural Italy started to wane, due to the country's politico-economic integration in the U.S.-led capitalist West, which favored strong industrial growth after 1952 (agriculture declined from 32.8 percent of GNP in 1948 to 22.8 percent in 1951, 19.2 percent in 1956, and by 1960 more people were employed in the industrial sector than in agriculture), massive urbanization, and the inflow of Western materialist culture through the mass media.[18]

At the same time, to please the activist DC-Left, De Gasperi promoted the political-economic penetration of the backward southern countryside by supporting the Leftist-leaning landless peasants' agrarian struggles through a limited land reform aimed at creating a loyal network of Catholic independent farmers, backed by the new (and soon debt-ridden) governmental fund for southern infrastructural development (*Cassa per il Mezzogiorno*). Local social peace was achieved not through increased and efficient production, but mostly through massive flight from the countryside to southern cities and new northern industrial poles, while the *Cassa per il Mezzogiorno* soon became a massive conduit for clientelistic support by targeting public works and financing for only those areas promptly bankrolled by the DC, while organized crime quickly secured the most lucrative contracts. The lack of state powers and southern cynicism contributed to the rapid rise in local corruption after 1943, while southern organized crime (Sicily's Mafia, Naples' Camorra, the Calabrese *'ndrangheta*) flourished in the power-vacuum left by a weak state unable to quickly offset southern poverty. Southern organized crime expanded its reach from traditional rural production rackets to contraband, gambling, and prostitution in the 1940s–70s, construction speculation in the 1950s–80s, and drugs in the 1970s–90s. The Mafia especially expanded its local political role by guaranteeing prompt "captive votes" to anti-Leftist politicians, while backing land-owners against Leftist peasants. Thus, most local politicians and the DC as well, had to build a power base in Sicily through some agreement with the Mafia (and the Camorra in Naples).

By the early 1950s the DC-Vatican alliance had turned too conservative for most Italian public opinion, leaving the DC with an eroding political base. On one hand, this rapid industrialization and urbanization of the peasantry siphoned votes from the Church-backed countryside and the conservative DC to the despised progressist influence of its Leftist and Liberal rivals, as over 4.2 million southerners migrated to the fast-growing industries of Northern Italy; of these over 500,000 moved abroad to Europe (86 percent to Germany, Switzerland and Belgium), but only 250,000 went overseas (United States, Canada, Australia, Latin America) in the 1951–74 period. On the other hand, southern ex-peasants were directed by their priests to local northern Catholic circles and the CISL Catholic Union whose renewed social activism (dissenting with the Vatican) together with the DC-Left sought to provide Christian aid to the immigrant workers and prevent their flight to the rival Leftist unions. Also the DC's Lay junior coalition partners became restive and hostile to excessive clerical interference in the society. Thus the DC sought to halt the erosion of conservative votes to the extreme Right, while expanding its politico-electoral power through the 1952 electoral reform law (dubbed "Fraud Law"), which removed the nation's pure proportional representation system with local preferences in favor of a large reward in extra seats to the majoritarian party, or coalition, capable of reaching 50.1 percent of popular votes. However, widespread opposition by the Left, extreme Right, and even the DC's smaller Lay partners to the 1952 electoral law crippled the Centrist coalition government, whose victory in 1953 was beset by the loss of so many electors that it failed to reach the 50.1 percent minimum (DC 40 percent; PRI + PLI + PSDI 9 percent). Thereafter, DC leader Amintore Fanfani replaced De Gasperi in 1953 and boldly sought to open the country to the reformist Left (PSI), while introducing "clientelism" as a hidden system to increase party strength by trading state funds and contracts for "captive" White votes.[19]

III. Retaining Single-Party Dominance through Alliance-Building and Patronage, 1955–80

Notwithstanding nearly 50 years of democracy, Italy still remains one of the most divided democratic countries. From the end of World War II, the DC based its dominant role at home on a combination of religious faith, anti-Communism, democracy, *garantismo,* and the skillful allocation of patronage to capture vaster strata of the electorate, although in the immediate post-war period the DC's single-party dominance was hard to establish. Yet the DC was never a particularly strong party, and after the 1955 death of De Gasperi could no longer rely on a charismatic leader. But for almost 50 years no realistic alternative existed to challenge the DC's dominance, given the existing frozen quasi-bi-party system according to Giorgio Galli. Instead, France's revered V Republic constitutional system under General Charles De

Gaulle's charismatic leadership failed to preserve single-party dominance for the Gaullist party (RpR), once De Gaulle's 1969 departure left the party mired in squabbles, despite the conservative RpR/UDF bloc still holding on to power until 1980 (and precariously in the 1990s). As the DC's hegemonic position in domestic politics was never really challenged (except briefly in the late 1970s by the PCI and 1980s by the PSI), it was the slow decline of her overall electoral strength since the early 1950s that forced her to rely upon varying Center-Right and Center-Left coalitions with minor moderate parties. In the 1940s–50s, coalition-building was electorally unnecessary for the DC, but helped widen the area of governance and isolate extremist forces. Thereafter, the DC soon replaced its earlier dependence on the Vatican and its network of parishes with a nationwide, loose, party organization, whose notorious factionalism became institutionalized in autonomous political "currents." Moreover, Italy's rapid socio-economic transformation into the fifth most industrialized country also undercut traditional Catholic values cherished by the DC and Vatican. By the late 1960s social tensions boiled out of control and protest within the Catholic base merged with a Leftist student-unionist front seeking to undermine the DC's successful governmental hold to her status of single-party dominance. Further intermittent criticism and challenges to the DC's political dominance came in the 1960s–80s from a slowly reforming but powerful PCI within the constitutional party-system, and by the parallel onslaught of Fascist and Red terrorists. But the DC succeeded in remaining in power for almost 50 years because no realistic alternative existed to challenge her weakened political dominance.

The DC's institutionalized single-party dominance (or "soft hegemony" according to Sydney Tarrow) was the product of several interlocking politico-economic factors: (1) an inter-class Catholic social base; (2) a non-dogmatic cultural-religious Catholic identity; (3) the Vatican's support for a single Catholic party; (4) anti-Communism; (5) moderate conservatism; (6) the coexistence of several semi-independent ideological-personalistic "currents" within an umbrella, catch-all party structure favoring unity rather than schism; (7) a flexible Centrist governing formula heavily based on distributive policies; (8) a vast system of clientelistic patronage and corruption, which was the most extreme expression of its distributive governance style (the "unofficial" proportional parceling of the state apparatus among the governing coalition, while trading public jobs/contracts for votes or favors); (9) the domestic political exclusion from power of extreme parties (PCI and MSI), tempered by parliamentarian and local governance cooperation with them, extending occasionally to the national level (Ferdinando Tambroni's brief 1959 government with the MSI; the late 1970s "Historical Compromise" with the PCI); (10) the international constraints of a bi-polar world during the Cold War with the vital need to secure U.S. approval for any major domestic political change towards the Left; (11) strong support of business, but also catering to marginal vocal groups (unions, peasants, immigrants, Arab world); (12) political leadership in institutionalizing the DC's national dominance (De Gasperi) and preserving it against changing socio-economic situations (Fanfani's *clientelismo,* Moro's "Opening to the Left" and "Historical Compromise," Andreotti's C.A.F. secret alliance).[20]

After Fascism's long dictatorial régime, Italy's post-war democratic system was embraced as the least divisive one on socio-political and economic grounds, but still carried little loyalty among the people and political forces, whose main interest remained personal gain and group aggrandizement masked through official slogans. Thus, Italy's "First Republic" privileged a constitutionally sanctioned, proportionally elected, parliamentarian system with a weak executive, while the creation of a constitutional court, regional decentralization, and referendum to repeal unpopular laws were long delayed. But the ensuing volatile, multi-party system proved too fragile and lacking firm decision-making, while revolving-door, fragile coalition governments and premiers dashed through the political system too quickly to leave any stable mark, or even see through national policies. Moreover, a weak parliamentarian system strengthened beyond all controls the key domestic influence of the parties (and especially the DC) as king-makers of legislative policies and governmental coalitions, while fragile coalition governments implemented inclusive patronage strategies. Italians in general resented such a weak, scandal-prone, political system, but could not get the parties that virtually dominated it to pass needed constitutional reforms until the early 1990s when the system collapsed on itself.

This resulting *partitocrazia* system self-perpetuated an immobile political status quo, dominated by jockeying for power among the parties, rival interests, and control of both public policy and national politics. As parties and parliamentary coalitions made and unmade prime ministers and ruling coalitions, all governmental crises and reshufflings (for influence and key ministerial posts) were mediated through complicated, long, intra-party negotiations outside parliament itself. In such a weak coalition system, the DC thrived and preserved her single-party dominance. In fact, no longer able to rule Italian politics through sheer electoral strength, or through its post-war democratic appeal, the DC's "soft hegemony" successfully relied on DC-led Centrist coalitions with the prestigious external backing of the United States ("tutelage") during the Cold War to isolate and undermine anti-governmental Left and Right oppositions. By fully exploiting and even expanding the government-based distributive/patronage network, the DC could support and reward both party loyalty and coalition partners, reduce socio-political polarization by redirecting national resources to satisfy all social interests and protest groups, while disarming the oppositions by either co-opting them (PSDI in 1946; PSI in the 1960s "Opening to the Left"), or excluding them from government and related benefits of a state-run patronage system. Consequently, during the post-war period a variety of socio-economic and political interests became tied to the DC, and remained wholly committed through over 45 years to the DC's survival in power as the best guarantee for their its continued gain and influence (including also the Mafia), especially during the transition phases of democratization (1943–48), economic reconstruction (1945–55), and "Economic Miracle" (1955–69).[21]

In time, the DC's decline forced it to share the state-based patronage system with all other governmental political partners as well, on the basis of their willingness to collaborate with it. Three traditional explanations sought to rationalize the DC's "soft hegemony" through different voting-behavior models, which although valid remain too narrowly focused to provide a comprehensive political strategy, while Di Palma's *Institutional Structuring Model,* redefined by Tarrow, truly provides a thorough understanding of the DC's successful strategy.

(1) The older *Religious/Subcultural Voting Model* focused on the political ties between the DC's Catholic identity and the electorate's deep faith, which kept in check the opposing undemocratic Marxist sub-culture. Tarrow rightly criticizes this: had this religious-political identity been the only factor explaining the DC's dominance, the party would have then lost her hold on power by the mid 1970s at the latest, mirroring the overall decline in religiosity in Italy and the West in the 1960s–70s following the country's industrialization and adoption of secular materialistic values (*Laicizzazione*). Indeed, a similar collapse from religious-based dominance happened in France, where Gaullist control of the religious vote did not prevent its later politico-electoral erosion in the 1970s. Yet in Italy the DC still preserved her dominance, while the PCI's hopes to numerically bypass the DC (*sorpasso*) never materialized.

(2) The *Tactical Voting Model* was frequently used in Italy in the 1960s–70s by scholars and journalists critical of the DC, who explained the DC's political dominance as the country's sole anti-Communist bulwark: the DC could constantly attract also large segments of normally anti-DC moderate swing voters, exclusively through her capacity to oppose any PCI's challenge to power. But as the Left was successfully marginalized and the initial contentious period of democratic transition and economic reconstruction drew to a close, the declining importance of the DC's old hegemony against the Left should lead voters to turn rationally to other parties. Although the popular criticism of the DC's inefficiency favored in the 1970s a widespread protest vote benefiting the PCI, the DC too stepped up her anti-Communist and religious crusades to retain the swing voters with alternate

success: temporary politico-electoral triumphs came in 1974–76 and 1979 against the threatened *sorpasso* by the PCI, but abject defeats came also on the politicized socio-religious referenda attempting to repeal the divorce and abortion laws in 1974 and 1982. Tarrow and Giacomo Sani criticized as improbable such type of implicit collective voting-behavior rationality. However, despite the decline of ideological polarization both abroad and domestically, the DC succeeded surprisingly in reigniting the electorate's old anti-Communism to defeat electorally contain the PCI's rise during the 1970s' East-West Détente, while Silvio Berlusconi as well could rely on these same anti-Communist fears to attain electoral victory over the ex-Communist PDS in 1994 during the post–Cold War.[22]

(3) The *Economic Performance Model* narrowly focused on voting patterns that reward the DC's dominance in times of business expansion, and punish the ruling coalition if the economy performs poorly. Although this model is often referred to in explaining electoral shifts and defeats in the United States and Germany, it is not applicable to Italy, where coalition governments spread the blame around all members rather than just the DC, while the country's stunning economic decline in the 1970s translated only in temporary declines, not political alternance.

(4) Di Palma's *Institutional Structuring Model,* instead, rightly stresses that during the earlier transition to democracy, the DC's dominance was crafted by exploiting the country's new republican, democratic institutions (parliamentarism, proportional representation, freedom of speech and assembly), and related *garantismo* whose institutional engineering did allow other parties and extreme oppositions (monarchists and MSI on the Right; the PCI on the Left) free and equal access to the political process. In time, such equal access allowed the extreme oppositions to become constitutionalized within a democratic structure that "institutionally" marginalized them, yet protected their survival through constitutional guarantees, which they too shared, once they realized they could never win numerically, or subvert the system. The politico-military cooperation among all parties and the PCI during the resistance (1944–45) and later governments of national unity (1944–48), plus their collective effort in crafting a new democratic constitution, created a unique inter-party and cross-ideological bond (the "constitutional arc parties" excluded the stalwart neo-Fascist MSI and the dying monarchists, absorbed by the MSI). The DC's non-exclusionary role perpetuated her dominance and politico-electoral image as the country's vital democratic pillar, and as the sole conduit of U.S./Western international support. In turn, this also assured that the larger, threatening Leftist opposition would end up supporting the DC's system of *garantismo* to insure its constitutional protection. However, as Italy's reconstruction was compete by the 1960s, the DC lost this inherent strategic advantage and had to rely on other

policies to reinvent its sources of hegemony past the transition period to preserve domestic hegemony. Created by DC Premier Fanfani since the mid
1950s, patronage for vote (or "political exchange") became the vital strategy
to preserve dominance, coupled with political "immobilism," secret bribes
for foreign contracts (Lockheed and ENI-Petronim scandals), and occasional
ideological-religious crusades (the 1974 anti-divorce and 1982 anti-abortion
referenda). But as some policies failed (divorce; abortion), or were limited in
gains ("immobilism," the 1970s ideological-political anti-Communist
clashes), the DC started a slow decline, exacerbated by constant popular criticism and dissatisfaction over the party's corrupt inefficiency, patronage,
"immobilism," and inability to solve Italy's economic morass.[23]

Since 1955 DC Premier Fanfani adopted a two-pronged strategy to revitalize the DC's declining politico-electoral power. The first strategy was
to continue De Gasperi's cautious political independence from Vatican interference, notwithstanding the Church's vital role in rallying voters. Fanfani sought to create a "captive" electorate tied to the DC through
clientelistic debts of gratitude and employment, by promoting activist
state intervention (*"dirigisme"*) in the national economy (supported by the
Left and unions). Private enterprises had limited resources and invested
following strictly selfish capitalist rules, but state enterprises could instead
draw upon the vast national treasury reserves to marry prosperity with social justice, guaranteeing large employment levels even during recessions,
as well as subsidized social services for the poor and marginalized rural
areas. While the economy grew during the "Economic Miracle," state intervention spread also to public housing, infrastructures, railways, high-
ways, roads, and aqueducts (yet all mostly in central and northern Italy) to
meet Italy's explosive urban, industrial, and trade expansion. Starting with
Cassa del Mezzogiorno Agency, Fanfani also placed DC loyalists as heads of
state enterprises to subtly tie public expenditures to the party's clientelistic
needs by redirecting the flow of state investments and permanent ("safe")
state jobs to support mostly local communities electorally loyal to the DC,
while attracting through "pork-barrel" public works (at times economically irrational) local votes, which the DC's Catholic ideology and propaganda had failed to rally earlier. Permanent "mass conversions" to DC local
rule always followed the impact of the *Cassa del Mezzogiorno*, and any disloyalty was likewise swiftly punished with the termination of state investments and jobs. As a closed, influential, conservative class, the private
sector was initially cold to any state intervention, abhorred social upheavals, and backed any political system (Giolitti's moderate Liberalism in
1900–10s, Mussolini's Fascists in 1920s–30s; De Gasperi's DC-led Republic since 1946) which shielded the industrialists' profit and influence
from politico-unionist pressures. U.S. pressures forced on them free trade,

while in the late 1950s they slowly converted to Fanfani's *"dirigisme,"* once the inherent advantages for the capitalist system of state-sponsored road-rail and popular housing constructions helped distribute goods nationwide and kept indirect production costs low. Through time, the DC's corrupt, clientelistic "milking" of public enterprises for party gain and votes spread to the entire political system, which became addicted to its clientelistic rewards. But by the 1970s new criticism from the private sector focused on the public sector's slide into permanent unproductive deficits, routinely bankrolled by higher taxes and the political impossibility for the government to either restructure public enterprises or cut a bloated, unqualified workforce.

Fanfani's second strategy was to enlarge the fragile ruling Centrist coalition to cope with Italy's rapid socio-economic transformation and hold on to a volatile electorate after the disastrous 1953 elections. As the Cold War temporarily abated in the mid 1950s, in Italy the domestic ideological divide also softened. Within the Left, the PSI abandoned the PCI by 1956 due to the PCI's political hegemony, which siphoned votes from its junior partner, especially following the Soviet repression of the 1956 Hungarian Revolution (although this policy change was strongly resisted by both Socialist and Communist cadres). The PSI understood that with the Cold War polarization, Italy would remain a Western capitalist country, with the USSR as the West's main international threat, thus leaving the Left permanently out of power domestically. Thereafter, the PSI openly supported NATO, European integration, and a reformist government to channel resources to the working class, the poor, and the South. But any political reorientation of the governing coalitions was impeded by its very weakness in 1953–61, which prevented it from either ruling effectively, or forging a stronger national realignment with the extreme parties (on the extreme Right the Monarchists and MSI Neo-Fascists; on the Left the PSI and PCI). Either a Center-Left or a Center-Right alliance would inevitably alienate important DC party "currents" and electors on the opposite ideological spectrum whose support was so important for the broader, inter-class DC party, or even fracture the DC into smaller, rival Catholic parties, each vying for Vatican support. Thus, "immobilism" dominated these fleeting Centrist governments, which routinely postponed addressing the country's many crises, while Fanfani and the DC-Left tried to improve relations with the PSI.[24]

Governmental immobilism and DC irresolution on socio-political reforms left fleeting DC-led governments dependent on monarchist and MSI votes to survive constant attacks by the Left and by "sharpshooters" within their midst (*franchi tiratori:* ruling party members who sabotage the government by secretly voting against their own party during vital votes of confidence on key laws, hoping to gain future posts once the government's defeat forced early elections or governmental reshuffling). Thus, as each fleeting Centrist government became hostage to the Right for survival, it was quickly jettisoned by the DC-Left and Lay parties, forcing in another ruling coalition just as weak, due to the DC's unwillingness to interrupt this vicious cycle with an open Center-Left alliance with the PSI. But in 1960 DC Premier Tambroni refused to step down and openly remained in power with the MSI's support (MSI Secretary-General Arturo Michelini hoped to "legitimize" this Center-Right government as an anti-Communist force and democratically join any Center-Right government as an equal partner). Soon anti-governmental and anti-Fascist protests exploded throughout Italy, until Tambroni fell and the dissatisfied MSI hard-liners split away from their party to promote subversion and, in time, terrorism too. Finally, a Center-Left coalition (a Centrist coalition with the PSI's external support) was engineered by new DC Secretary-General Aldo Moro against the DC-Right. The Right still felt that without Vatican and U.S. backing the DC was too weak to contain the Leftists/Communists while a Center-Left government with the PSI would symbolize the DC's political surrender to the Left, and in time to the PCI as well. Thus, the neo-Fascists' street violence and the PCI's anti-capitalist ideology, together with both the extremes' opposition of DC-led governments kept alive for decades a sense of political intolerance, poisoning Italy's fragile democracy, while right-wing forces (including governmental sectors infected by ex-Fascist members) started to secretly support terrorist violence and plans for military coups as a tool to retain power at all costs against the Center-Left and the unions.

Paradoxically, the PCI's strong socio-institutional presence, which had been condemned into perennial opposition by the DC-led governments (Giorgio Galli's "imperfect bi-party system"), also ended up helping to preserve the DC's "soft hegemony" by unwillingly participating in its system of distributive policy and competition at regional and institutional levels. The PCI had a strong rural base in the Center-North, and a strong but limited influence in the north's "Industrial Triangle" (where blue-collar and artisan labor were split between Communist, Socialist, Catholic, and Liberal unions), while its unsuccessful courting of the southern rural and middle-class votes helped soften its doctrinaire ideology ("Italian road to Socialism"). Certainly, a revolutionary PCI could never wrestle power from the DC, given its U.S. connection in the internationally polarized Cold War, while any clash would have pushed the DC further towards the Right and possibly even fomented an outright bloody right-wing military coup backed by the United States, such as Chile's in 1973 ("K factor"). All PCI leaders since Togliatti dreaded just such polarization and potential total ban of the PCI's limited, but solid, regional presence. Thus, Togliatti pursued a democratic-leaning strategy, rather than all-out revolutionary confrontation, given the PCI's isolation in the West beyond the Iron Curtain. Unable to compete with the DC in overwhelming Catholic and peasant rural areas and the South, Togliatti and his successors sought to expand party membership beyond the traditional blue-collar proletariat by also courting the same middle-class voters, which the DC successfully influenced. During the 1950s–70s, both DC and PCI were strengthened by their respective bloc of mass organizations, unions, and professional associations. With East-West Détente in full swing, both parties de-emphasized their earlier fierce ideological clash and redoubled efforts to "capture" moderate voters through inter-class electoral appeal, policy competition, and loose partisanship, to the chagrin of both sides' ideological cadres. Thus, an uneasy, subtle "consocialist" cooperation in parliament and local governments developed between the DC-led governments and PCI, while political clashes remained limited to inter-class strategies and policy competition, because neither party could rely on extreme national polarization to rule alone, without risking a backlash.[25]

The result of this complex politico-economic interrelationship was a softening of post-war domestic tensions and ideological divide, with a steady increase in practical inter-partisan cooperation at the base and in municipal/regional governments. This inter-class electoral strategy and inter-partisan cooperation over governmental-based patronage was the key to reducing polarization and consolidating Italy's political system in two, mostly antagonistic, immobile poles. But despite inter-partisan cooperation, political "immobilism" prevented any possible government-based political alliance with the Left until the 1960s co-opting of the PSI ("Opening to the Left") and the 1970s ambiguous, brief, external liaison with the PCI ("Historical Compromise"). Moreover, "immobilism" undermined the politico-ideological chances for a strong Centrist party to emerge as a more dynamic alternative to power between DC and PCI. Thus, a unified, moderate PSI always failed to attract significant voters from both Left and Center to expand beyond its 10 to 15 percent range and overcome the DC's dominance. Tarrow denies that either the DC or PCI really became "catch-all parties" thanks to their inter-classist political strategies, but in reality the DC always attracted, from the beginning, a larger share of the inter-classist moderate vote, beyond its small, clerical sub-culture. The PCI basically failed in such efforts (beyond siphoning votes from the PSI and moderate Left) until the rapid electoral expansion in the 1970s capitalized on a widespread, anti-DC and anti-governmental middle-class "protest vote." Inter-classist cooperation between the rival DC and PCI grew the strongest at the base of the political system (local and regional governments), with an unofficial "consociation" of distributed patronage through discreet parliamentary *leggine* (committee bills) since the early 1960s. But inter-classist cooperation also carried high costs: in both parties (and to a minor degree across the political spectrum) the clash between several competing interests and entrenched "constituencies" prevented or delayed vital legislation on issues splitting any party.

In the 1960s, facing the risk of losing its dominance to a relatively moderate Leftist bloc during the socio-economic crises, the DC revamped its strategy of co-opting new governmental allies around the DC's leadership by sharing patronage of state resources with old partners to keep them from drifting away (the small, conservative Liberal; moderate Social-Democratic; and Republican parties), while DC Premier Moro slowly co-opted the PSI (the third-largest party with 15 percent of votes) back into the government in 1963–64. The "Opening to the Left" consolidated the DC's "soft hegemony" and isolated the PCI into its opposition ghetto, although the PCI's electoral strength also rose in the 1960s–70s. But this strategy also produced continuous legislative delays, political crises, and socio-political outbursts from the country at large, while the cost of "sharing" the patronage machine with the larger and more demanding PSI became difficult at a time of economic decline in the 1970s. The Center-Left's political weakness, inter-partisan dissent, and factional alliances prevented the government from either performing its programmatic duties (legislation, economic shepherding, vital internal reforms), or keeping the PCI isolated in the unions and polls for long. Thus, appropriation bills (*"leggine"*) by powerful individual parliamentarians ("notables") skyrocketed beyond any governmental control, but the economy remained adrift due to the executive's weakness and the proliferation of factions ("currents") within the DC and other ruling parties. Each party's "notables" became virtually independent of governmental control, locally siphoning patronage and even secretly undercutting its majority to grasp coveted ministerial seats during subsequent governmental reshuffling, in a game of political "musical chairs." Paradoxically, during the crises of the 1960s–80s the DC gained from the proliferation of party "currents," which gave it the political flexibility to avoid the collapse befalling other dominant, but rigidly centralized and ideological parties, unable to adapt to change (France's Gaullists or Israel's Labor in the 1970s), while relying on "current" leaders from the Left (Fanfani), Right (Cossiga, De Mita), or mixed factions (Andreotti's move from Right to Left, or Moro's *"Dorotei"*) to swing the DC along the rapidly changing political winds.[26]

The Centrist government had co-opted the PSI in the 1960s to strengthen its domestic stability and authority, while the DC sought to use the PSI alliance to stay in touch with the evolving Italian society and labor force. However, persistent opposition to the Center-Left, both within the ruling coalition and the country at large, stifled domestic reforms, while the 1963 national elections failed to reward the government and weakened both DC (–4 percent) and PSI (no growth at all). It was clear now that Fanfani's and Moro's strategy of political co-opting of the moderate Left and middle class had failed. In fact, the DC had never been a truly bourgeois party, regardless of its interest in wavering middle-class voters: the DC's Catholicism and anti-materialism opposed both liberalism and capitalism, although the DC's role as essential post-war intermediary of U.S. politico-economic assistance had created temporary politico-economic alliances between business and Lay forces with DC-led governments. As Italy's economic boom required a mature industrial policy and middle-class values, the DC's fractured rival Left and Right political "currents" (kept together only by their common religious faith), were unable to support either Left versus Right domestic political bi-polarism, or governmental alternance without being ripped apart at the core. The DC therefore successfully kept her single-party dominance by sabotaging both the PSI's reformist programs and any moderate-conservative ("legitimate") Right rival, as either alternative would have undermined the DC's exclusion from power of both the PCI and the MSI (as "illegitimate" forces).

Instead, PSI leader Pietro Nenni had joined the government to create a democratic, Leftist alternative to the ideologically ostracized PCI, but the PSI's inability to push the DC and Center-Left to implement agreed-upon socio-economic reforms (limited nationalizations, national economic planning, the regions' politico-administrative decentralization) penalized the Socialists in both the 1963 and 1968 elections, while militants rewarded the PCI with large electoral gains, which nullified Nenni's alternative Leftist strategy. Worse, in 1964 the PSI's Leftist, anti-governmental wing split as PSIUP (Italian Socialist Party of Proletarian Unity) with a third of party cadres, while Nenni's crafty remerger with the ultra-moderate PSDI (whose 20 percent of militants had split from the PSI in 1947 to support Western DC-led governments) formed the new PSU (Unified Socialist Party), which however upset both its remaining ex-PSI Leftists and labor voters (who feared absorption by the Right), as well as the ex-PSDI moderates (who feared any shift to a radical Left). Yet the PSI had no alternative long-term strategy, as the PCI's growth spelled suicide for the tainted Socialists. Further erosion was halted by the PSU's split again in 1969 into its PSI and PSDI components, while the PSI recuperated some electors out of its activist involvement in the "Hot Autumn" strikes.[27]

The DC's single-party dominance was based on an inter-class coalition of patronage, religion, conservatism, and anti-Communism, attracting the declining electoral support of peasants and old middle class, but was shallowest among the working-class, the fast-growing immigrants, and new professional middle class. The DC always held on to its loyalist base and U.S. backers, while perpetuating her "soft dominance" at home, even when forced to share its patronage and power with other coalition parties, because only such political strategy defused ideological polarization and kept the DC in control of the system. These coalitions of patronage benefiting all ruling parties became in time the primary, albeit hidden, function of national politics, given the presence of a strong Left (not easily excluded from the country or from Parliament), while the DC's own Catholic Centrist-populist loyalists could not hope to shepherd their platform alone (due to the DC's electoral inability to secure absolute majority), or in any hard-to-balance coalitions with the anti-clerical Lay parties (PRI, PLI, PSDI, PSI). Only the DC could provide the necessary—albeit seemingly chaotic—balance among competing parties and long-term political support to sustain both the country's economic growth and the clientelistic demands of the population. Thus, given its relative electoral weakness, the DC's single-party dominance turned into a "soft hegemony" fueled by Centrist policies and patronage-driven ruling coalitions, rather than DC-only governments. Throughout the years, as the opposition and the media exposed scandals, corruption, clientelism and waste, the DC's popularity waned, but all efforts to reform remained cosmetic. Worse, until 1992 neither the politicians nor the people were willing to eradicate patronage, because it was the only tool to share power proportionately among competing coalition partners and still secure vital votes by diverting state finances into generous governmental contracts on behalf of this or that political fiefdom.

In the economy, the DC never backed an openly polarized business versus labor confrontation, as this would have alienated its supporters within both fields, while undercutting its ability to rival the Left for working-class votes. Moreover, Italy's industrial and business circles were too narrow and relatively weak to sustain a purely capitalist-driven economic growth at home and abroad. Until 1969 the DC's political "soft hegemony" was able to benefit both her business and populist constituencies, as Italy's remarkable "Economic Miracle" was based on market-oriented but politically-assisted growth, thanks to generous state interventions and migration of cheap labor from the overpopulated *Mezzogiorno* to the northern "Industrial Triangle." In 30 years (1946–76) over 4 million southerners relocated to North-Central Italy, altering local demographics (17 percent of residents by 1971), while many others settled also along southern coastal urban areas, which were unable to absorb the massive flux of unemployed (by 1971 Naples accounted for 20 percent of the entire southern population). But the growth of Italy's industrial base (25 percent of GNP in 1951; 29 percent in 1976) was still too slow to match the even faster demand for labor, while the income gap between north and south worsened as poverty, unemployment, and organized crime became endemic, especially in major southern centers. Moreover, Italy's small domestic market and reliance on exports was cyclically vulnerable to international recessions, inimical to economic growth. The DC could extend her control by relying on close business relations and generous infusions of state investments in the economy, but there was never a commonality of identity and interests between government and business, which never trusted DC-led governments as capable of engineering long-term planning and sustained economic growth in either an activist Keynesian (planned state interventions), or neo-Liberal direction (market capitalism). Unable to develop any centralized economic direction, Rome's economic policies were all too easily altered under organized pressure from the unions or interest groups (business groups, peasants, artisans, etc.). The massive flow of state resources was traditionally channeled to pork-barrel/private projects, rather than national ones, due to the inescapable patronage intervention of political parties and clientelistic contacts (the *Cassa del Mezzogiorno*'s failure after over 35 years to develop a self-sufficient southern economy beyond vital infrastructures is the worst example). Governmental economic intervention was mainly through interest-free export loans to industry, a rapidly expanding public sector stimulating both the economy and a reservoir of perennially employed public workers, especially in the South (yet youth unemployment has risen to 13 percent since the 1970s), while routinely relying on the Bank of Italy to implement restrictive monetary policies and to curtail inflation and labor wage-hikes (rather than public expenditures, given the vital need to appease public workers).[28]

The DC's catering to inter-class social forces and voters gave a disproportionate politico-economic influence to the peasants in rural areas (due to their electoral strength and Social-Catholic appeal), shopkeepers, artisans, small businesses in the provinces, the urban middle class and professionals. In all cases, the electoral importance of these voters made it difficult to cut public expenditures in times of inflation and reduce huge governmental deficits (1970s–90s). The DC's success in shepherding national economic growth during the 1950s–60s "Economic Miracle" and Italy's transformation in an industrial society also spurred the rapid growth of a newly educated, professional middle class (10 to 17 percent in 1951–71), which socially replaced the older middle-class and artisan base loyal to the DC, but remained marginal to the DC's social coalition and even threatened her traditional dominance. This new professional middle class pressed the DC for civic modernization, education reform, and urban planning, while their large "baby-boom" produced an uncontrollable anti-DC young electorate (mostly Leftist, but also many neo-Fascists), which became radicalized by the 1967–77 student-labor protest movement. Another new social force came from the millions of unskilled southern immigrants in northern urban-industrial areas in 1951–71, which had little ties to the unions. Yet the DC failed to benefit electorally from this massive influx of southern Catholics: transplanted to northern secular areas, immigrants met open discrimination, appalling lack of housing and services, and a weak DC party infrastructure. The parallel decline of anti-Communism and religiosity, together with the DC's failure to politically attract the new middle class and immigrants, left it unable to further consolidate its "soft hegemony" by extending patronage benefits to these new groups of voters and "capture" their loyalty (the way Israel's Labor Party used to successfully integrate new waves of immigrants until the 1970s). But as the South remained stagnant and underdeveloped, the 1969 Reggio-Calabria revolt provoked a growth in the local and national protest vote in 1970–72 on behalf of the neo-Fascist MSI, which captured 20 percent of the votes in southern provinces. The DC, PSI, and other governmental parties could react only by flooding the *Mezzogiorno* in the 1970s–80s with easy state investments (roads, dams, harbor facilities, steel plants, petrochemical industries) to stop electoral erosion and redress southern underdevelopment. Yet this fostered organized crime's siphoning of local contracts, while the artificial creation of new and redundant southern industrial centers (Naples, Taranto, Gela, Reggio-Calabria) failed also to develop economically the southern hinterland, nor could it foster the growth of a local middle class. By 1973 the international downsizing of steel and petrochemical industries burdened by high energy costs and overcapacity devastated Italy, and threw the West into recession.

During the 1960s, the Centrist government's co-opting of the PSI had brought on-board a host of socio-economic issues affecting the country's modernization (internal migration, limited nationalizations) and the PSI's tradition of social mobilization. But the Center-Left's paralysis left most of these issues unresolved, until their later radicalization left the government vulnerable to massive and often violent domestic, anti-government protests over its socioeconomic failings. Moreover, the DC's rival socio-political factions loosened party controls over Catholic labor, while the party's refusal to represent labor as a class left it unable to seriously rival the Left in influencing the workers or keeping the unions split on ideological grounds at a time of tight government economic policies: (1) The 1967 pension reform bill triggered massive workers' demonstrations beyond the unions' own expectations. (2) The "Economic Miracle" and massive internal migrations of cheap, non-unionized, southern labor, whose low wages and 'round-the-clock work-weeks boosted productivity and exports, also created hundreds of thousands of restive new blue-collar workers in heavy and light industries. Italy's unions were forced by 1969 to mobilize to rein in the impatience of younger, radical and non-unionized workers (CUB: *Comitati Unitari di Base,* or "Amalgamated Floor shops Committees," later known as *"Autonomi"*) demanding fast-rising wages. Already since 1968 militant Leftist and Catholic students strove to merge labor and student protests with their opposition to the old stifling order, while attracting also the PSI/PCI's youth federations (who criticized the PSI for joining the government, and the PCI opposition for being "too soft"). But the student-labor coalition soon lost control of their vast mobilized forces and street demonstrations during the unending 1969–72 strikes ("Hot Autumn"), while the unions reasserted their new-found political independence from the Center-Left ruling parties through the powerful joint CGIL-CISL-UIL Federation, which "recaptured" leadership of the 1969–72 strikes and secured major syndicalist victories also thanks to the Center-Left's acceptance of inflation-indexed higher salaries and institutionalized industrial-labor relations (1970 *"statuto dei lavoratori"* act). (3/4) Unknown to the unions and the government, these historical labor gains effectively stopped Italy's "Economic Miracle" by wiping out her traditional trade and labor competitiveness abroad, while the 1973 and 1979 "Oil Shocks," plus the 1970s international monetary crises, precipitated the West into stagflation and severely harmed Italy (which imports 80 percent of its energy needs and most raw materials for industrial transformation). But economic crises only spurred renewed labor unrest to "defend" and "index" wages against inflation, rather than reform labor-industrial relations.[29]

These waves of protest could not be curbed by traditional reliance on anti-Communist counter-mobilization and police repression (except occasionally as a deterrent/containment strategy during emergencies and against violent urban guerrillas), or recessionary economic policies to dull wage hikes. In fact, the PSI's dual, ambiguous presence in both the Center-Left governments and in the streets as a militant member of the protesting Leftist student-labor front, forced the DC to alternate between unending negotiations with all challenging socio-political groups, or outright capitulation to street riots. But the socio-economic cost of political weakness and compromise with any street challenge was high, as the DC kept subsidizing her patronage machine and her electorally vital, traditional, social coalition, while trying to defuse all new crises by "throwing money" at the protesters, keeping uneconomic industries operational, expanding public sector deficits, and fueling inflation through unrestrained currency printing.

With all governments paralyzed by competing socio-economic and socio-political demands from both supporters and opponents that had to be appeased, the DC felt the brunt of national dissent and criticism, just as extremist right-wing and left-wing terrorists plunged the country into years of bloodshed in the vain effort to topple democracy and a weak judiciary under the cover of street protest (*"anni di piombo"*). Already in summer 1964, General Giovanni De Lorenzo of the Italian Secret Service (SIFAR) had organized a failed para-military coup d'état ("Solo Plan") with the complicity and veiled support of certain DC sectors. The "Solo Plan" adapted 1950s secret Western para-military counter-measures to resist a potential Communist take-over, and was geared now at neutralizing all domestic oppositions. Although tense secret negotiations between Premier Moro, President Segni, and De Lorenzo finally pre-empted the coup from being carried out, it was kept hidden from the public and judiciary until 1967, while the DC strenuously derailed all judiciary inquests to keep the scandal from also unveiling embarrassing local pro-coup support within the DC. More threatening to Italy's socio-political order were the neo-Nazi terrorist bombing campaigns beginning in 1969 ("Strategy of Tension") geared at exploiting existing domestic socio-economic contrasts, the "Hot Autumn" general strikes, and Red-Black university strife to destabilize the political system. Initially, the Left's perceived revolutionary ideology was blamed for such turmoil, while failed Rightist coups were uncovered (the "Borghese Coup" and the *Rosa dei Venti* conspiracy in the early 1970s). Thereafter, both Black and Red terrorism exploded, while the MSI grew electorally as a pseudo-legitimized party of law and order by merging with the monarchists (MSI-DN) and supporting the DC and Vatican through their losing joint struggles over the divorce act and divorce referendum. Most of the extremist political strife plaguing Italy in the 1970s was essentially ultra-Leftist, through university-based, splinter, extremist groups who opposed the PCI and unions (seen as "sell-outs" to the government), and promoted constant demonstrations and clashes against neo-Fascist rivals, the government, and the police. These extremists were driven by a blind state of exulting "pre-revolutionary" belief that their "armed struggle" could attract the dissatisfied non-unionized working class to "overthrow the system" and prevent a mythical U.S.-backed Rightist military coup (as in Greece in 1967 and Chile in 1973). Leftist extra-parliamentarians and terrorists were anti-Western and supported militant domestic labor disputes and Third World revolutionary movements, while criticizing the PCI's post-1956 subtle co-existence with the capitalist West. But by the mid 1970s the electoral pendulum shifted towards the Constitutional Left (PCI/PSI), isolating Black and Red extremists, as well as the corrupt and socially backward DC.[30]

The DC's electoral decline in the mid 1970s was also the direct result of public disgust with the unearthing of several corruption scandals affecting many governmental partics, but especially top DC leaders and even the DC president of the Republic Giovanni Leone (impeached in 1978). The scandals involved: expanding public bureaucracy to provide easy, permanent jobs to loyal voters; illegally influencing state contracts; exacting bribes on all national economic transactions; running into the ground and making insolvent the great state corporations by focusing only on employment and not strict business accountability; giving bribes to Middle Eastern countries over vital oil import contracts (Italy imports 80 percent of her energy needs); accepting bribes on arms contracts from the U.S. company Lockheed; covering up the Sindona financial scandal. Nevertheless, national indignation was short-lived given the DC's public self-flagellation and promises of reforms, and especially the public's misappreciation of how severe was the actual degree of political corruption—most judicial inquests were routinely covered up. Moreover, domestic political reform was endlessly postponed, because few political forces were willing to openly denounce the national network of politico-economic corruption and "unprosecuted" illicit favors, which lined the pockets of too many politicians of all parties with illicit donations in exchange for political support. Although cut-off from the DC's patronage system, the PCI benefited from politico-financial ties to the USSR until the early 1980s, plus its large networks of committed cadres and volunteers. Thus, all parties opposed addressing domestic political corruption, and only when forced by the public outcry did they hastily pass a 1974 law against all private donations to political parties, limiting party fundings to public funds provided through a percentage ratio dependent on each party's electoral vote.

> . . . [N]one of the parties which milked the state funds with impudence had any clear perception of the illegality of their type of financing . . . , including the communist opposition. . . . The entire political class feels justified in such behavior in the firm belief that [without] parties . . . the democratic state would likely collapse. . . . [Thus, it is at the parties'] discretion to decide when and how much to "withdraw" from the bottomless public treasury. Unavoidable is also the percentage that disappears in the [politicians' own] private pockets, while especially devoid of any transparency or accountability is the mechanism behind the whole disbursement of public expenditures. . . .
>
> [N]o one realized that those same political parties which had been used to milk the system for years would never respect the fund-raising limits imposed by the new legislation. The state's political financing were insufficient to meet the ever growing needs of party machines, and only supplement the same financial flows of before. . . . Thus the parties become just a little bit richer, but remain as corrupt as ever, if not more. . . . [31]

Despite scandals, terrorism, corruption, inflation, oil/energy hikes, the collapse of the Lira, economic-financial turmoil, and restiveness among its coalition partners, the DC weathered all storms and kept its hegemony over both its "currents" and governmental coalitions, while its steady electoral losses remained relatively contained in size. Indeed, throughout the post-war years, the DC remained the party of "relative majority" whenever it ruled from positions of strength, or even from weakness, which forced on it brief experiments in power-sharing with smaller, but vocal, partners. The DC's strategy of "soft hegemony" remained unchanged and quite flexible given the fast-changing times, while relying on state resource-sharing in an ever-vaster patronage machine that defused contrasting ideological policies and satisfied grievances from different socio-political groups (although this became increasingly difficult in the 1970s–80s), especially with the huge increases in income taxation. However, without clear programmatic planning, the DC left Italy to fend for herself during the chaotic economic growth of the post-war period, postponing for years, if not whole decades, all controversial legislation that threatened key constituencies (tax reform, regional autonomy, divorce, abortion, labor-industrial relations). When in the 1970s the DC became too weak and despised nationally, it sought to hold onto its dominance by sharing power and co-opting the PCI in the mid 1970s to halt the Left's electoral challenge. In fact, the 1975–76 regional and parliamentary elections became the conduit for a tumultuous mass protest vote by the youth and middle class, which enhanced the PCI's new, moderate, pro-Western, "Euro-Communist" image, until finally the Left seemed poised to bypass the DC ("*sorpasso*"). After an extremely ugly political campaign dominated by the DC's virulent anti-Communist crusade, the DC still managed to prevail by siphoning most votes from its smaller partners to surge at 38.2 percent against a rising PCI at 35 percent. But after the elections the DC was unable to form a new government without the PSI, which left the coalition once the electorate had punished it for its 15-year alliance with the scandal-ridden DC (the PSI fell from 14 to 9 percent). Thus, the DC secretly sought the PCI's willing abstention from challenging a minority DC government.

The PCI had remained the only Western, Marxist mass party, with a tightly organized and hierarchical control of the party cadres, denying real democratic input from its cadres, while the party was dependent on Moscow for its ideological-political legitimacy. Since 1956 Togliatti and the PCI leadership co-opted into the leadership mid level, post-war cadres not tied to the USSR to avoid stifling party rigidity and decline, while modernizing the PCI in tune with the fast-changing Italian society. Following the 1968 Soviet invasion of Czechoslovakia and the 1963–69 Sino-Soviet clash, the PCI openly criticized the USSR's "*Nomenklatura*" and imperialist policies (and "almost completely broke" its relations after the Soviet invasion of Afghanistan in 1979–80 and the 1981 Soviet-sponsored Polish military coup against the union *Solidarność*). But change within the PCI was still deemed too slow by both moderates and radicals, while in the 1970s radicalized ex-student protesters joined Red terrorist groups (BR, GAP, etc.) and openly attacked the PCI as a "sell-out" to the West, following the moderate policies of reformist PCI Secretary-General Enrico Berlinguer. The Italian society's rejection of the old socio-politico-clerical shackles of Church and DC moral controls in favor of materialism, consumerism, and progressist civil rights strengthened the PCI's appeal as a "uncorrupted" party and the only one capable of finally overcoming 30 years of DC-led political "immobilism" and corruption. Berlinguer, moreover, sought to present the PCI as a reformed member of Europe's Social-Democratic parties by exploiting the

PSI/PSDI's electoral decline, and having support from Germany's SPD and Britain's Labor Party.

Thereafter, the sweeping 1975 anti-DC protest vote gave to a fractured Left (PCI and PSI) 45 percent of the national, as well as regional and city-wide control over Italy's Center-North industrial and agrarian heartland, major cities, and local administrative coalitions, leaving the DC and MSI in opposition. Any renewed Leftist front (first developed during the highly polarized divorce referendum) would attract some of the Lay parties and secure 50 percent of the electorate (both blue-collar and middle-class) for a government of Left-Center alternance. This would finally terminate the DC's 30-year-old single-party dominance as the country's power-broker and patronage provider to loyalists and allies alike. But the PSI always remained hostile to cooperation, while Berlinguer realized that to keep increasing its new middle-class votes the "Euro-communist" PCI had to become even more "democratic" and integrated in the capitalist society, while "legitimacy" abroad came by joining the weakened DC into loyally accepting Italy's Western politico-military orientation towards the United States, NATO, and European integration. Indeed, to overcome its ideological isolation the PCI had already engaged since the 1960s in secret political cooperation with both DC and PSI by supporting in parliament most governmental reforms and establishing a constructive government-opposition debate. Yet under criticism by the extra-parliamentarian Left, the PCI stopped that pro-democratic ideological shift internally hoping to reassure its confused, pro-Soviet rank-and-file (fearing that orthodox Communist stalwarts would split away and get Soviet-sponsorship to run a rival, Stalinist, Communist party).[32]

The costs of such political schizophrenia were heavy: since the early 1970s Berlinguer rejected challenging the DC's hold on power and pursuing the PSI's left-wing offer to form a fragile PSI-PCI Leftist governmental alternance. In face, despite the 1968 student protests and the 1969 "Hot Autumn" union strikes, Berlinguer saw Italy as still too fragile a country to withstand uncontrollable strong socio-political domestic turmoil and radical changes without collapsing into a right-wing dictatorship (like General Pinochet's Chile) with secret U.S. backing ("K factor"). Berlinguer proposed instead an "Historical Compromise" (a coalition government under DC leadership) as a way to prevent the DC from turning against a Leftist opposition government, or supporting a right-wing military coup. DC ex-Premier Moro, who in the 1960s had engineered the "Opening to the Left" and Center-Left governments with the PSI, also sought to strengthen the DC's own "dominance" by neutralizing the working class and PCI. Moro wanted all governmental cooperation with the opposition reduced to a minimum. But both PCI and DC were pushed towards closer governmental cooperation by the parallel Black and Red terrorist emergency of the mid 1970s, and the country's economic collapse in a sudden stagflationist crisis (inflation and recession, due to international exchange rate instabilities and rising oil prices savaging Italy's economy).

Moro's 1977–79 ambiguous "Historical Compromise" politically sponsored the PCI's membership in a DC-led government of national solidarity, after a period of external support to jointly revamp the economy with vital controversial legislation against stagflation, freezing union-backed wage hikes to curb labor demands, and destroying the Red and Black terrorist threats. The 1978 clamorous kidnapping and execution of Moro by the terrorist Red Brigades allowed the DC-Right and DC Premier Giulio Andreotti to secure the mantle of defenders of state institutions, while turning him into a slain "martyr" for democracy. Despite strenuous objections by the United States (Nixon, Ford, and Carter administrations) and anti-PCI forces in Italy, which feared a permanent PCI governmental influence, Premier Andreotti kept Moro's design alive, albeit skillfully postponing indefinitely the PCI's eventual entry into the government, while forcing it to accept unpopular anti-inflation economic policies (hurting the unions) and anti-terrorist legislation (which destroyed both Black and Red terrorism by 1981). Having so consolidated the DC's shaky hold on power, Andreotti succeeded in preserving both the DC's electoral base and its dominance over the government. Instead, the PCI had been so compromised by its governmental support and anti-labor policies to redress the economy that its electoral rise stopped abruptly as many young voters left to join the extra-parliamentary Left, while recently acquired middle-class voters returned to moderate parties. Then by 1979 Andreotti jettisoned the PCI back into opposition in favor of a new power-sharing Center-Left alliance with the rival PSI under Bettino Craxi's unscrupulous leadership.[33]

IV. *De Profundis:* Collapse and Renewal of Italy's Political System, 1980s–2000

Italy's self-image at home and abroad traditionally focused on negative visions (corruption, elephantine bureaucracy, Mafia, terrorism, social volubility, and economic backwardness), rather than her accomplishments. Likewise, domestic and foreign commentators dismissed both Italy as a serious political actor and the DC as a truly powerful hegemonic party, like France's Gaullists, by focusing superficially on her volatile 50-plus governments in half a century of democracy, rather than on the "immovable" political leadership and party élites, which routinely rotated in power with every new government. Instead, the enduring triumph of the DC's "soft hegemony" and pervasive patronage always succeeded in defusing, during the Cold War, all ideological-political and socio-economic threats to her dominance by co-opting, buying-off, or isolating her opponents, while preserving a slowly shrinking electoral base. The DC's own endurance was closely tied to its cautious policy of shrouding its hegemony within governmental power-sharing with smaller partners, while rejecting permanent, rigid politico-ideological stands, which would backfire in the long run by polarizing the country in an unstable Right-Left bi-polarism, and demoting the DC's "soft hegemony." Such politico-strategic malleability and massive patronage machine also made it difficult to pry power away from the DC's institutional grasp, despite its slowly declining socio-politico-electoral appeal. After surviving its worst crises in the 1970s, Moro's assassination deprived the DC of its most innovative strategist in co-opting opponents, and left an increasingly weakened DC under the self-focused, Machiavellian leadership of Andreotti and Arnaldo Forlani to fend-off the PCI's quest for power, while wrestling with Craxi's PSI rival challenge for premiership through ever more difficult policy intrigues and pluralistic patronage-sharing. Then in the 1980s the DC's persistent electoral weakness, national economic woes, and popular backlash against *immobilismo* prevented it from retaining exclusive control of the premiership: at first minor political partners symbolically shared the top post under the DC's reluctant tutelage, until Craxi's PSI openly blackmailed the DC for an "equal" 50/50 share in the political and patronage spoils as the price to save the DC's "soft hegemony," rather than replace it with a potentially competing PSI/PCI "Leftist alternance." This led to a secret, corrupt pact between Craxi, Andreotti, and Forlani to monopolize patronage and higher offices among themselves and their parties (the "C.A.F. triumvirate"), jointly alternating PSI and DC in power, while sucking dry state resources. The C.A.F. triumvirate was the ultimate fruit of this secret pact for corruption, and its greed paradoxically hastened the system's sudden collapse in 1992.

The DC's dominance and centrality in Italy's fragile, new, democratic system and economic growth assured both the widest possible coalition governments and power-sharing under its pluralistic patronage system, as well as guaranteeing the constitutional survival of the oppositions (PCI, PSI, MSI). Despite their isolation, the oppositions had an implicit vital stake in preserving the pluralistic system, rather than risking outright defeat and destruction should they radicalize and try to topple the U.S.-backed DC hegemony over the "First Republic." Moreover, unlike other democratic Western countries, Italy's DC-led governments never imposed, in times of crises, even selective censorship on the media (Israel, Britain), or on banned radical parties (West Germany, Israel), nor did they discriminate against individuals over their political beliefs (West Germany, Israel, Britain). As Italy's democracy survived, the DC preserved its "soft hegemony" by remaining malleable in its governmental strategies until the early 1990s: those who could not be co-opted into the system (PLI, PSDI, PRI, Nenni's PSI), or bought-off through patronage (Craxi's PSI, new interest groups, Süd Tyroler separatists), were destroyed eventually (secessionists, Red and Black terrorists), or marginalized within their respective spheres of influence (PCI, MSI, Mafia), while preserving a degree of secret political exchange with the government.[34]

The DC's chronic political weakness within the country at large was compounded by the emergence of militant Catholic groups (*Comunione e Liberazione*) adamantly opposed to modern materialism, Marxism, and capitalism alike. Together with the 1978 election of Karol Wojtyla as Pope John-Paul II, the Church tried to reassert its interventionist policies and spiritual values on an indifferent lay society. Caught in the middle between a religiously militant youth and Vatican pressures, the DC—now under Fanfani's brief leadership—rejoined the Church, hoping to rejuvenate itself through the anti-abortion crusade with which the Polish Pope had sought to spiritually cleanse the society. But the Italian society as a whole rejected clericalism in 1981 with 67.5 percent of votes preserving the abortion law. The DC's defeat led the DC's new secretary-general, Ciriaco De Mita, to immediately abandon the Vatican's neo-spiritualism, while seeking in the business/industrial community a new source of political and financial support. But Italy's business community was struggling against the international decline of traditional manufactures and the rise of electronics hastened by the twin "Oil Shocks" (1973–74, 1979) and the 1970s stagflation crisis, which left the country deeply in debt (public expenditures doubled from 31.2 percent of GNP in 1960 to 62.5 percent in 1983 with a L.140 billion national deficit), while inflation rose to 20 percent in 1981, the Lira was devalued 6 percent and recession slowly redressed. Only the small- and medium-sized enterprises kept continued to increase profits, while unemployment undermined the unions' old strategy of higher salaries cutting into the industry's profit-margins (1969 "Hot Autumn" strikes). Thus, as the Church's stifling embrace had twice alienated the DC from large sectors of Italian society (the 1974 divorce and 1981 abortion referenda), so the business community kept its distance, given the DC's unending record of scandals and corruption, which tarnished its national image: the 1972 Lockheed Scandal; the ENI-Petronim Scandal; the 1978 impeachment and resigning of DC President Giovanni Leone; the P2 rogue Massonic Lodge 1981 scandal with its business connection and right-wing extremism under Licio Gelli; maxi-bankers Roberto Calvi's mysterious "suicide" in London in 1982 and Michele Sindona's arrest and later poisoning in jail in 1986. The P2 Scandal in particular, unveiled a secret network of members among DC and PSI politicians, plus key figures from all government parties, together with higher officers in the armed forces, police, judiciary, bureaucracy, media and organized crime as well, supporting Gelli's anti-democratic right-wing intrigues. But whatever secret ties existed between P2, Black terrorists, and organized crime

(Mafia, Camorra) and elements of the DC party structure, these revealed mostly the corrupting malaise of holding on to power (national and local) at any cost, affecting a party that had for too long monopolized the country's government, rather than unveiling widespread anti-democratic tendencies within the DC. In fact, the exclusive, unchecked politico-electoral fiefdoms of local party leaders always required a thick web of "clientelistic" loyalties and complicities to secure massive local electoral and financial support to DC candidates in exchange for steady flows of state aid, jobs, and benefits (pensions, insurance, health, housing).

The DC's twin political débâcle in 1981 (the anti-abortion referendum and the P2 scandal) forced it for the first time to cede the government's leadership to the small PRI ally with Premier Giovanni Spadolini, rather than choosing PSI leader Craxi, given the Socialists' image, equally tarnished by the P2 scandal. The new government sought to both clean the political house and revitalize the economy, while cutting public expenditures, but with mixed results given the entrenched resistance to down-size the excessively generous and inefficient Italian welfare system, similar to the radical anti-welfare policies of U.S. President Ronald Reagan and British Prime Minister Margaret Thatcher. Independently from the covert need to expand their funding sources, all parties including the PCI (which was ideologically loath to undermine the state's popular programs) shared the vision of a *Stato assistenziale* where state resources, banking, and public enterprises should constantly expand to meet the population's needs and state-driven economic development, rather than strictly focusing on profit-making. Thus, no party—corrupt or otherwise—and government ever had the vision and will to alter such bankrupt development strategy to arrest the perverse growth of Italy's inefficient public sector. Instead, as political corruption reached the highest levels ever, deeply impacting the entire society, the parties in power conspired to prevent any meaningful, vital, economic reform and cuts of the bloated public sector, for fear that even minimal reductions in the traditional flow of public expenditures and clientelistic welfare services would shrink their own access to resources and local power, losing altogether their own main source of party loyalty and electoral votes.[35]

The widespread politico-industrial ties of corruption, and the lack of well-established work-ethics revealed instead Italy's still unsolved limitations as a mature, Western, capitalist society, leaving her closer to Eastern European countries, or even Third World ones. By the 1980s the Italian political system and its weak, cynical governmental parties were long fossilized into an unchangeable balance of power, chronically unable to either rule, or quickly pass vital legislation to address the needs and ills of an evolving society. Thus, despite an immobile political system wrecked by constant governmental crises, the very frequency of national and local elections paradoxically routinely reconfirmed all parties to power virtually unchanged thanks to their loyal electoral base and high turn-out (about 90 percent of the electorate compared to 50 percent in the United States), but only as long as they could buttress their waning politico-ideological appeal with ever-expanding clientelistic ties and favors. At the same time, the business sector (both public and private) was deeply harmed by its thorough clientelistic partitioning among all ruling parties, whose political control over the public sector, banking system, and state bureaucracy expanded well beyond any capacity for efficient and productive influence. However, by the mid 1980s Italy's economic stimulation measures started to work, thanks mostly to sudden international impact of the parallel drop of oil prices (long-term) and of the dollar (temporary) against the Italian Lira (both oil and raw materials imported in Italy are paid in dollars). The consequent growth in Italian industrial production and sales at home and worldwide benefited mostly the country's small and medium enterprises in North, North-East, and Central Italy. This "New Economic Miracle" propelled Italy into fifth place among the world's most-industrialized powers (after the United States, Japan, Germany, and France, but ahead of Great Britain), while most people reacted with a frenzy of consumeristic spending and greed.

Italy's "First Republic" had essentially run its course by the collapse of the "Historical Compromise" in 1979. Collectively enslaved to their own shadowy network of clientelistic dependency, multimedia appeals for votes, and the constant infusions of fundings to maintain a pervasive grip on voters, the DC-led new Center-Left coalition (*Pentapartito*) kept the PCI isolated, while becoming consumed by internecine rivalries and competition for hegemony between Craxi's raging PSI (seeking more power and votes) and the status-quo DC (seeking to stem further erosions of its electorate and single-party dominance). But despite previous scandals, the crisis of the Italian state really exploded only in 1992, for two reasons. On one hand, the PSI played a key role first in shoring up the political system in both the 1960s and 1980s, but only by 1992 did its unlimited greed for power and patronage finally destroy the clientelistic order supporting Italian politics. On the other hand, the Cold War's international polarization still indirectly influenced Italian domestic politics in 1979–91 by preserving its "imperfect bi-polarism" (the DC-led ruling coalition versus the isolated PCI opposition). In this context, as the third (but small) Italian party, the PSI could not challenge the "imperfect bi-party system" with the DC in constant control of all government coalitions and the PCI as its perennial opponent from the side-lines. Since the early 1960s when the PSI returned to government with the DC, it had hoped to expand its electoral base in competition with the PCI on the Left and by reabsorbing the more moderate PSDI. But the electorate never forgave either the PSI's immediate plunge into the DC-sponsored corrupt patronage system, or its failure to implement much heralded reforms. Thus, after a decade of Center-Left rule the PSI still polled only at 9.6 percent (1972 national elections) and could not capitalize even from the 1976 electoral surge on behalf of the Left in protest of the DC's corruption and clientelism. Thereafter, the young mid-level cadres seized control under Bettino Craxi's leadership in 1976. To revive the stagnant PSI, Craxi pursued a twin strategy of independent self-assertiveness from the DC and open confrontation with the PCI. Craxi's politico-ideological offensive sought to isolate the PCI from any governing alliance with either the DC (the 1970s "Historical Compromise," which squeezed the smaller PSI), or the PSI itself (the old 1940s–50s "Leftist alternance," which siphoned out PSI votes to the PCI), while savaging the PCI for its limited adoption of pro-Western democratic ways ("Euro-Communism") and its authoritarian, Leninist party structure. The PSI's left-wing still hoped to return to a united Left between PCI and PSI, but as long as PCI and DC collaborated in the "Historical Compromise" both strategies coexisted, although Craxi feared that the PCI's rivalry would destroy the PSI. Moro's 1978 kidnapping and slaying by the terrorist Red Brigades gave Craxi the chance to split DC and PCI by advocating concessions to the terrorists in contrast with the official DC-PCI line of no compromises. Once the PCI returned into opposition in 1979, Craxi's autonomist anti-PCI line was vindicated.[36]

East-West cooperation during Détente broke down the old religious-ideological barriers between Catholics and Communists, more Leftist Catholics joined the PCI in the 1980s, and the new middle class deserted the DC in turn, while the break-down of class and income cleavages turned workers into less militant, prosperous customers. The post-1980 loss of the youth and middle-class swing voters, which had almost pushed the PCI beyond the DC, left the PCI with a fast-aging Communist blue-collar electoral base (the working class grew from 41 percent in 1951 to 47.1 percent in 1971, but by 1983 it had shrunk to 42.7 percent), whose activism was spent, while agriculture too declined (43 percent in 1951; 18 percent in 1971; 13 percent in 1981). Although the *Mezzogiorno* remained hopelessly backward, overall the modern Italian society was now secular, Western, and capitalist, while rejecting old socio-economic loyalties to either the Church/DC, or the PCI and class, but openly displeased with the DC. Banking on the dual weakening of DC and PCI from the collapse of the "Historical Compromise," Craxi's anti-PCI strategy sought to perpetuate the PCI as an "illegitimate" political force in isolation, while the PSI returned to government in 1980 as an autonomous inter-class Leftist governmental party, challenging the DC's monopoly on power with tough bargaining (to secure a disproportionate number of ministerial seats) to become its principal political partner/rival, rather than a dependent. In any case, Craxi hoped to "capture" new voters from both the weakened DC and PCI. Craxi shaped the PSI with a mix of modern, slick "show-biz" and blustering personalistic, authoritarian leadership (reminiscent of Crispi and Mussolini). Yet Craxi's cult of personality within the PSI and his political strategy remained self-limiting by the focus on expanding the PSI at all costs (electorally and politically), even if this might damage the Left, or bring down non-accommodating governments.

Craxi's slick appeal to the growing middle class was based on a mix of libertarian social issues (supporting the abortion law) and unattainable institutional reforms of either the electoral system (which Craxi secretly opposed, fearing that adopting the uninominal system would eliminate the PSI) or a presidential republic (impossible but tempting). But the PSI's flashy initiatives and talk of modernization never amounted to much and by 1979 electoral returns were negligible, despite massive television ads and recruitment campaigns in the *Mezzogiorno,* based on clientelism and ties with organized crime. Thus, the longer the PSI shared power with the "immovable" DC, the more isolated its own reformist supporters became within the party, while Craxi's push for ever larger shares of the clientelist cake resulted in fresh embarrassing scandals and jail sentences for Socialist officers (ENI-Petronim scandal in 1979; P2 scandal in 1981; the 1981 imprisonment of maxi-banker Calvi who first revealed the PSI's lavish bribes and then escaped prosecution to mysteriously die as a "suicide" in London). Craxi responded to these scandals with a virulent, all-out politico-rhetorical campaign of indignant pressures and threats against the judiciary, until all investigations were discreetly dropped. Once again, these scandals harmed the PSI's electoral drive with only a 1.6 percent increase in the 1983 elections, just when the PCI was stagnating and the DC fell hard electorally because of its own corruption scandals and the economic repercussions of the 1979–80 second "Oil Shock" (which pushed inflation to 20 percent and left a $20 billion trade deficit). Despite the PSI's electoral failure to siphon votes from the DC and PCI, Craxi nevertheless secured a determinant national political influence as the DC's main coalition partner and guarantor of continuity and stability (*"governabilitá"*). As the DC-PSI political cooperation became vital to shore-up traditionally weak coalition governments (which usually lasted a couple of years, rather than the full five year legislature), Craxi's extracted full rights to "loot" the state alongside the DC:

> Despite the PSI's declining [electoral] strength at 9.8 percent, Craxi exploited to the max the coalition advantages and [virtual] veto power that the PSI had, which made it the de facto fulcrum of any possible governing [coalition]. The PSI was indispensable to a DC that wanted to free itself of the uncomfortable embrace of the Historical Compromise; . . . [but] the Center-Left became reality only when the DC was forced to grant all . . . PSI demands: . . . a 50 percent to 50 percent partition of power, despite their different electoral

strengths; half of the Ministries; half Under-Secretaries; half presidents of [state enterprises] . . . ; half directors and half of all officers within the state national and local administration; . . . so that from these positions [of power] the Socialists were sure now to attract those votes that society still denied them. . . . [37]

Then Craxi brilliantly succeeded in exploiting the DC's electoral fall to propel the PSI also into the premiership in 1983–87 (in alternance with DC Secretary-General De Mita, while Andreotti was foreign minister). Behind a façade of boldness, Craxi's premiership benefited from the fall of oil prices and the dollar, which enhanced Italy's economic recovery after 1983 (soon overtaking Britain's GNP) and halved inflation to 10 percent (but never really eliminated it). The price to pay was forcing delinquent shopkeepers and other "*evasori*" to pay most of their under-declared taxes, while abolishing the automatic wage-indexation for workers' salaries, notwithstanding the resolute opposition of the PCI and CGIL union. But Craxi failed utterly to stop the rise of the governmental debt fueled by the 1970s' run-away spending on social programs (like health care and pensions, vital for patronage and electoral purposes) and especially interest payments on the huge and fast-growing public debt (55 percent of GDP in 1981). Thus, Craxi's modernizing, prosperous, economic legacy was short-lived as the international recession hit in 1990–92, while the government's debt rose from 92 percent of GDP at the end of Craxi's term in 1987 to 108 percent by 1992. Nevertheless, Craxi's tough stand against the PCI and CGIL undermined the Communists' role as a solid opposition pushing the PCI's decline in the 1987 elections (26.6 percent). Internationally too, Craxi's prestige rose, following Italy's tough stance in favor of the 1985 Single European Act (breaking Britain's traditional opposition at the E.U. Summit in Milan) and by refusing to hand over to the United States those Palestinian terrorists who had hijacked the Italian *Achille Lauro* cruise-liner. Although in substance the PSI ruled much like the DC, Craxi's tough statesman style finally rewarded the PSI at the 1987 elections with 14.3 percent of the votes, consolidating Craxi's role as the power-broker of all future governmental coalitions. However, in the long run Craxi's political success and greedy prying of power and patronage from the DC (which outdid even the DC's record) unwittingly discredited Italy's institutions and undermined the whole politico-clientelistic structure once new corruption scandals in 1992 unveiled his secret power-sharing alliance (the C.A.F.) with the DC's most distrusted politicians (Andreotti and Forlani). In 1987 and 1989 the meddlesome, obstructionist PSI remained out of power after Craxi became unwilling to honor the earlier PSI/DC accord and relinquish the premiership to DC Secretary-General De Mita (the political rival of Andreotti and Forlani). Thus, Craxi attacked as incompetent Italy's President Francesco Cossiga, a DC leader and ex-premier, then precipitated two governmental crises against De Mita (1988–89), forcing him out of the premiership, which went then to Andreotti, while the DC secretary-generalship went to Forlani. The C.A.F. pact assured 50 percent of the DC's patronage network to the PSI, which thereafter bypassed the PCI as the second party in the *Mezzogiorno*, while Craxi was promised the premiership by 1992, to replace Andreotti who in turn would replace Cossiga as president (thus, when he became Premier, Andreotti refused to cut public spending, fearing a backlash against his future presidential bid), or if unsuccessful then both Craxi and Andreotti would support Forlani's own bid to the presidency.

As the 1980s–90s saw the slow demise of political ideologies, Marxism, religion, and old class divisions, Italy's cynical and volatile public opinion expressed in countless polls a 75 percent frustration rate with all of the parties' corrupt and inefficient monopoly over domestic politics (*"partitocrazia"*). But, unable any longer to either reform and efficiently lead the country, or to mobilize their electoral base along traditional, unifying socio-political themes, every party now had to rely exclusively on clientelism and corruption to keep their vital electoral ties from collapsing altogether. Thus, following the example of Craxi's PSI, in the 1980s all parties eagerly sought to widen their political appeal to an apathetic electorate by merging propaganda with multimedia show-biz and televised party congresses. The exponentially rising costs of administering such catch-all, politico-electoral, clientelistic machines demands ever-rising funds to pay for: televised propaganda and publicity spots; leadership and staff expenses for all parties (secretary-generals, deputies, senators, mayors, aldermen, etc.); salaries for party-cadres and fund-raising technical experts (two million people by 1985); hundreds of party offices and buildings nationwide; national congresses; and local party festivals. The generous flow of official state financing (in relation to each party's electoral percentage according to the 1974 Electoral Financing Act) was wholly insufficient to the task of administering party expenses and multimedia propaganda campaigns, so all parties redoubled their efforts to expand both traditional and unconventional flows of political financing. As a "trendsetter," Craxi's PSI benefited from free, preferential media access from magnate Berlusconi's network of private television stations and Fininvest financial holding. Once premier, Craxi rewarded Berlusconi with a deeply coveted, unprecedented full parity with the state RAI on TV programs and broadcast news, allowing him to expand his monopolistic media empire. Thus, the decline in the parties' capacity to control and condition the socio-political and economic system under the banner of collective interests led them to blindly " . . . drain all state resources to support their own electoral base in a country where political loyalty is reduced to a pervasive exchange-type of relationship, or clientelism," while in each party new individualized interests further siphoned state resources.[38]

Unrecognized, the end was near. As Italy's economy fell into recession again, popular distrust of the government and the unreformed DC rose to 49 percent by 1989, while the political system's malaise, together with the end of the Cold War, started to dismantle old ideological loyalties. On one hand, Italy's industrial modernization of the 1950s–70s had promoted prosperity, Western materialistic consumerism, and secular Lay values, which undercut the Catholic sub-culture and the DC's socio-economic base. On the other hand, economic specialization, decentralization, and pre-pensioning had demoted also the Red working class sub-culture, just when the young, moderate PCI leader Achille Occhetto, in 1989–91 hesitantly shepherd the PCI's painful transformation into a moderate PDS neo-Socialist party, *Partito della Sinistra* (Party of the Left). But this bold change was so slow and hesitant that the PCI/PDS split in two (with the smaller pro-Soviet Orthodox wing *Rifondazione Comunista* ("Communist Refoundation" or "Reconstructed Communists"), polling 6 percent of votes in 1992), while the PDS fell to 16.1 percent in the 1992 elections, rather than securing a much hoped for increase in both bourgeois and Leftist voters. Finally, the dramatic collapse in 1991–92 of the USSR and all old-style Soviet-led Communist régimes clamorously undermined the PDS' ex-Communist roots and threatened both its current identity and future. But cast adrift by the vagaries of world politics, the PDS was saved paradoxically by the parallel unexpected unraveling of Italy's entire political system with the disintegration of the PSI, DC, and most other parties. The secret C.A.F. pact and the tensions between DC and PSI soon broke the patronage system by fomenting internal rebellions against both parties' leaderships. Public dissatisfaction with the PSI rose, while within the DC, Mario Segni's constitutional reform and direct referendum campaign threatened the party's traditional political dominance. Likewise in Sicily, Leoluca Orlando distanced himself from the DC, becoming the Mayor of Palermo in 1993 after openly crusading against secret DC-Mafia ties, which clamorously exposed both Andreotti and his protégé, Palermo ex-Mayor Salvo Lima. But when a new anti-Mafia police campaign finally savaged Sicilian crime leaders previously protected by powerful groups within the DC, Lima was assassinated in 1992 by the dissatisfied Mafia to teach the DC and the government a lesson. This was followed by new "revenge" car bombs killing local Prosecutors Giovanni Falcone and Paolo Borsellino (like the 1980s Mafia car bomb assassination of anti-terrorist hero General Giovanni Della Chiesa), until new governmental crack-downs and a three-year-long military garrisoning of Palermo brought a semblance of control over the Mafia.

Then in early 1992 the DC-PSI C.A.F. was first trounced electorally by a strong protest vote, sending the DC reeling under 30 percent and the PSI to 13.6 percent. This defeat, in turn, freed Italy's dissatisfied magistrates from traditional governmental political control and retribution, allowing them to quickly turn into a veritable independent political force with virtual impunity. Almost immediately their wild spiraling "Clean Hands" judicial inquest (or the *Tangentopoli* corruption scandals) turned into an uncontrollable avalanche against both the PSI and DC patronage networks investigating corruption and illegal financing. After the indictment of Craxi's own PSI Milan headquarters in early 1992, *Tangentopoli* soon engulfed nationwide all governmental parties and public-private sector clientelism, destroying in turn the C.A.F.'s hold on power and devouring in a momentous political implosion most politicians and "old" parties: (1) Craxi was indicted on illicit financing and lost his bid for the premiership (which went in 1992–93 to PSI reformist advisor Giuliano Amato); (2) Craxi and his ex-protégé, Minister of Justice Claudio Martelli, soon tore the PSI in a fratricide clash for leadership, ending with the PSI's disintegration after Martelli too was indicted and forced out of both the Ministry of Justice and PSI, while Craxi lost his parliamentary immunity and fled into exile to Tunisia to avoid jail sentences; (3/4) clamorous revelations on DC-Mafia collusion and corruption indictments also doomed in spring 1992 DC ex-Premiers Andreotti and Forlani in their now bitter rival bids for president of the republic, while Forlani lost also the DC secretary-generalship. Of course, the Italian public had long been aware of the DC-based patronage system, but only the "Clean Hands" investigations and the flow of revelations from imprisoned, indicted "repentants" (granted immunity from prosecution) uncovered the stunning size and truly capillary nature of this greedy clientelistic system of corruption and plunder of the state and private sector by the DC and all governmental parties. Amidst nationwide shock and anger, from February 1992 to September 1993 alone, over 2600 people were indicted and seven committed suicide, while those arrested included five party secretaries, three ex-premiers, most party leaders, several sitting ministers and ex-ministers, 325 parliamentarians (one-third of total), top-ranking business executives, and scores of mid level party cadres, destroying both the administrative structure and political viability of every party (DC, PSI, PLI, PRI, PSDI) except for the Leftist PCI/PDS and the far-Right MSI oppositions who had been mostly excluded from patronage and power.[39]

At the same time, political militancy shifted in the early 1990s from the spent Marxist and Catholic ideologies and stagnant parties to new inter-partisan, anti-establishment groups: the Left-leaning ecologist *Verdi* (Greens); Orlando's Sicilian Catholic *Rete;* the revived MSI/AN (once the collective stigma of World War II faded and conservative votes migrated there from the defunct DC); and especially the populist Northern League (*Lega Nord*) regional protest movement. The Lombard *Lega Nord* began in 1984 as a small, regional-populist, protest movement under the colorful, venomous Umberto Bossi, who extolled northern virtues and condemned immigrants, "lazy" southerners, and the government's ("Roma") redistributive tax policies redirecting northern resources to the *Mezzogiorno*. Bossi quickly secured the backing of northern small business, the self-employed, and workers by opposing high interests rates on borrowing and heavy taxation. The *Lega Nord* got 3 percent of votes in Lombardy by 1987, then almost trebled to 8 percent in the 1989 European elections, and finally jumped to 19 percent in the 1990 regional elections by channeling the anti-tax protest vote of small and medium northern towns (rather than big cities), and in the wake of *Tangentopoli* it seized traditional DC, PSI, and PCI regional fiefdoms of Veneto, Lombardy, and Red Emilia.

As the economy soured and the political system collapsed into semi-anarchy, Premiers Amato (1992–93) and Ciampi (1992–94) set up efficient and "clean" governments of technicians who strove to craft an austerity-based recovery, while for the first time both governments were freed from the twin political conditioning of DC hegemony and PCI exclusion. Nevertheless, the prosperous northern socio-economic groups openly turned against the government, whose past patronage they never benefited from. Thus, the *Lega* secured 9.2 percent of national votes in 1992 (20 percent in Lombardy and 17 percent in the North), attracting over 65 percent of its voters from dissatisfied former DC, PSI and PCI supporters. Seizing upon *Tangentopoli's* devastation of the political system, in 1991 *"Senadur"* Bossi's successful populist movement absorbed other northern Italian regionalist forces on a common platform of anti-tax resentment, anti-southern racism, opposition to redistributing northern wealth to a backward corrupt *Mezzogiorno,* anger at governmental corruption, and trumpeting wild secessionist rhetoric to create the separate northern Italian "Padania" (or "Pontide") federal republic, above the Tuscan-Aemilian mountains, in a future loose confederation of three free-market Italian republics ("Etruria" in the center, and the "south") with economic-legislative decentralization and national powers limited to only diplomacy, defense, justice, and monetary policy. Nobody believed him, but tensions rose and insults frayed nerves as the country seemed on the verge of collapse. Bossi's vitriolic racism and intellectually flawed, anti-governmental, secessionist rhetoric alienated most Italians outside the north. Moreover, many "northerners" were integrated descendants of southern immigrants from that "Economic Miracle" that had fueled the north's industrial-economic growth and wealth, while *Tangentopoli's* finance and corruption scandals was as "home-grown" and widespread in the North as throughout Italy. In time, these internal contradictions led the *Lega* to split between the secessionist anti-establishment militants and the newer re-cruits' free-market views. Most of the latter (19 percent) switched by 1994–96 to Berlusconi's fast-growing new Center-Right party, *Forza Italia*, which gained acceptance with lightning speed during a pitched national campaign to stop the Left-Centrist PDS from winning the 1994 political elections. Bossi's sole recourse to halt the erosion of his party was to exacer-bate his secessionist rhetoric and symbolically proclaim in Venice the inde-pendent republic of Padania (15 September 1996), although only 10,000 supporters turned out, while the MSI/AN's nationalist counter-demonstra-tion in Milan rallied 100,000 people.[40]

Although the PCI/PDS was not tainted by *Tangentopoli* (except superfi-cially at the local level), the ex-Communists still failed to attract, in 1992–93, the bulk of the ex-PSI, ex-PSDI and ex-DC voters left adrift by the collapse of their old parties. By 1993 the PDS forged a successful, but fragile, regional coalition, the "Progressist Pole" (PDS, *Rifondazione Comu-nista*, Greens, Orlando's *Rete*, several smaller Center-Left parties, and Segni's Vatican-backed ex-DC dissidents) to exploit a new, mixed, uninominal-pro-portional electoral system promoted by Segni's referendum campaign and aimed at eliminating the political fragmentation of the old, entrenched pro-portionalism (whose popular vote favored a fragmented multi-party system). The new system assigned 75 percent of seats to uninominal "winner-takes-all" ballots, and 25 percent of seats to proportional lists with a 4 percent cut-off for eligibility, which would hopefully consolidate smaller parties and reward the winning coalition ("Pole") with extra seats. But Vatican hostility, plus the PDS's 1993 regional victories and controversial alliance with its un-repentant *Rifondazione Comunista* brethren, kept the PDS from preserving the strategic alliance with Segni's group (*Patto Segni*), which quit. This, in turn, fatally weakened both the PDS-led "Progressist Pole" and Segni's own independent Centrist ex-DC "Pole for Italy" (the reformist *Patto Segni* and the devout, pro-Vatican *Popular Party*-PPI), due to its inability to "capture" the Centrist void after the DC's collapse. The ex-DC rival splinters of PPI and *Patto Segni* together carried only 53 percent of the old DC's 1992 elec-torate (15.5 percent votes and 46 seats by 1994). No rival party (*Lega*, MSI, *Patto Segni*, PPI) seemed able to stop the PDS/"Progressist Pole" from an an-ticipated sweep of the 1994 political elections, or from forming the first gov-ernment by ex-Communists.

Overnight the political scene changed once private media magnate Berlusconi (dubbed *"Commendatore,"* a slick mix of Ted Turner, Robert Murdoch, and Ross Perot) entered into politics with a crafty, massive, U.S.-style media/advertising campaign with strident anti-Communist and neo-Liberal overtones, which hurled his brand-new *Forza Italia* party into absorbing in a few months the still dispersed, anti-Leftist, Center-Right forces, plus unaffiliated ex-DC and ex-PSI voters (all equally upset at the PDS/Progressists' imminent victory). Berlusconi easily won by preposterously turning the contest into an ideological crusade against the PDS's "Communist plot" for dominance (despite PDS abandonment of Communism, support for "Clean Hands" and state reforms, and anti-Mafia stand). Through relentless media blitzes on Berlusconi's unregulated private TV stations, *Forza Italia* forged a Center-Right coalition ("Pole of Liberties," or *Polo*) with the *Lega Nord* and the "post-Fascist" MSI/AN, which allowed them to win the elections with 47 percent of votes and 366 seats (104 to *Forza Italia,* 110 to MSI/AN, 118 to the *Lega Nord,* plus 34 to a smattering of Centrist mini-parties). Berlusconi's party attracted 40 percent of the youth vote, 6 percent of the industrial North-West and Milan, 26 percent of ex-DCs, 15 percent of ex-PSIs, and 19 percent of ex-*Leghisti,* Catholic Sicily, and Veneto, plus scores of blue-collar voters (to whom he promised a million new jobs). Berlusconi's unexpected electoral triumphs (the 1995 European elections gave a further 10 percent surge for *Forza Italia*), revealed also that the *Lega* had topped at only 8.4 percent of the vote: although the *Lega* declined, its 118 seats through Italy's new, mixed electoral system made it the largest "Pole" party, but Bossi remained strong only in the North, while losing the Veneto and some key municipalities. Likewise, the MSI/AN was localized in the Center and South, leaving the national vote, spotlight, and premiership to Berlusconi's *Forza Italia* (the third largest *Polo* party, yet the strongest nationwide), which soon rose to overcome its partners/rivals. Instead, the PDS-led "Progressist Pole" got 33 percent of the votes and 213 seats (PDS 110; Greens/Centrists 65; *Rifondazione* 38), with the PDS gaining only 4 percent of votes in the Red Belt and parts of the South, while Berlusconi's anti-Communist attacks and the dissent among the "Progressist Pole" smaller allies kept moderate northern voters away.[41]

In just two years the collapse of the "First Republic" was complete: *Tangentopoli*'s "Clean Hands" inquest had destroyed to the root the DC's single-party-dominant clientelistic system, while dooming all tainted traditional parties. The imperfect, new electoral system also freed Italy finally from the heavy politico-ideological and patronage constraints of the past. Although the "Second Republic" had already started with Premiers Amato (1992–93) and Ciampi (1993–94) transition governments of technicians, which were free from both the DC overbearing influence and the DC-PCI political contrast, their uphill fight to save the country and economy against the web of old interests never had a chance and was compromised by the lack of new elections to redress the capsized ship-of-state with a new "legitimate" majority. It was Berlusconi's government (1994) that seemed to have just such a "mandate" with a British-style premiership. But none of the largest new political forces held numerical supremacy, or even wished to recreate the DC's old dominant role. *Forza Italia's* artfully crafted party (born overnight without roots or experience) consolidated the new Center-Right *Polo* and filled the political void, while recreating a sort of "imperfect bi-polarism" with the rival PDS-Progressists once again denied alternance. Berlusconi had to rule with a skilled mix of savvy, tact, respectability, and leadership based on his businessman's financial empire and telegenic image as a "New Man," ostensibly "breaking" from the old régime. Yet Berlusconi was no "agent of political reform": his personal-financial ties with Craxi's PSI, questionable authoritarian leadership and attempts to revive clientelistic bonds, proved him to be just another creature of the "First Republic," rather than the vanguard of a reformed "Second Republic." In the end, Berlusconi's arrogant, authoritarian leadership and micro-managing clan rule stunted *Forza Italia's* growth as a party, and undermined his short-lived 1994 government (ten ministers were loyal Fininvest managers, while 51 percent of *Forza Italia's* parliamentary group comprised entrepreneurs and managers).

All too soon, anti-governmental criticism rose over the *Polo* government's inability to restart the economy and deliver Berlusconi's promise of "a million new jobs," while his financial and media empire sparked conflicts of interest charges (Berlusconi being both Premier and CEO of Fininvest Holding). Worse criticism came from the exposure of his embarrassing past clientelistic partnership with Craxi's PSI (Berlusconi's financial support and free "prime-time" commercial spots for the PSI during elections, which Craxi repaid by confirming Berlusconi's monopoly on private media and total freedom from state-run media oversight). Berlusconi's abrasive personal attacks and use of the Ministry of Justice to fight Milan's "Clean Hands Pool" made things worse and recalled Craxi's own doomed vitriolic campaign against the magistrature. By summer many became convinced that Berlusconi's political ambitions and virulent anti-Communist patriotism were just a front to use parliamentary immunity and the premiership to stymie new "Clean Hands" investigations of Fininvest. After July 1994 Berlusconi's charisma and political influence was severely weakened by a national anti-corruption uproar, which rebuffed (just like Premier Amato in 1993) his effort to save old friends and allies under indictment by seeking the immediate termination of the "Clean Hands" investigations. Moreover, *Forza Italia's* popular appeal was whittled away by Berlusconi's micro- managerial and authoritarian style: (1) the political equation, *Forza Italia* = Berlusconi, quashed the political autonomy of the party's grass-roots by tightly muzzling them through loyal Fininvest managers; (2) Italy's lack of national conservative traditions was aggravated by Berlusconi's arrogant managerial authoritarianism (which resembled U.S. presidential candidate Ross Perot's "proprietary" control over his grass-roots party in the 1992 and 1994 elections).[42]

Furthermore, Bossi's own spewing bitter rivalry against his allies was politically fateful, once *Forza Italia* led the "Pole of Liberties" government with a tight leash, forcing the reluctant *Lega* to switch from protest movement to governmental responsibility, while accepting a humiliating second place to avoid losing precious votes just won. Only Berlusconi could hold the fleeting Center-Right voters together and guarantee as democratic both the secessionist, anti-southerner and anti-Fascist *Lega* and the "post-Fascist" MSI/AN (strong in the *Mezzogiorno,* growing in the Center-North, but still embarrassingly shunned by foreign governments). Bossi's bitter drive to undermine Berlusconi's leadership started during the 1994 electoral campaign and continued thereafter against the new premier through vocal criticism that the *Polo* government under *Forza Italia* and MSI/AN was just a "corrupt" reincarnation of the despised old régime. Worse was the personal animosity and cultural divide between Bossi and Berlusconi, who saw themselves as entrusted with rival sacred missions. For the former, "to save Lombardy from Italy" was a personal crusade against any centralized governmental authority in Rome. For the latter, "to save Italy from Communism" (the purported sinister PDS-*Rifondazione Comunista-*"Progressist" coalition) was the key to national political pre- eminence by filling the political void left by the collapse of the DC and old Italian parties, while comparing himself to Christ gave Berlusconi a rhetorical image of a martyred "outsider," bludgeoned by his enemies. Bossi feared and vainly fought against the gradual, inevitable slide of his more moderate, recent supporters away from the *Lega's* anti-governmental protest platform towards Berlusconi's new, moderate, neo-Liberal government. Thus, Bossi kept distancing the *Lega* from the government, even at the cost of destabilizing it by constantly attacking Berlusconi as a member of Craxi's corrupt, old guard under a new guise, while the *Lega's* parliamentary group sought desperately to remain loyal to both Bossi and the government by pleasing its voters with moderate legislation. Finally, in December 1994 Bossi's quest for ideological "purity" led him to destroy the *Polo* government by ordering the *Lega's* withdrawal from the shaky government after Berlusconi's own indictment. Instead, the moderate *Leghisti* (in and out of parliament) revolted and joined Berlusconi's party, while corruption indictments savaged Milan's *Lega* and PPI local forces in 1995–96, allowing *Forza Italia* to sweep large areas of the *Lega's* northern fiefdom during in the 1996 elections.

The third *Polo* partner, Gianfranco Fini's MSI/AN, remained quietly grateful for the chance to govern and expand as a new ultra-conservative, democratic party, while rejecting only cosmetically old Fascist roots. Fini's twin strategy, built on tactical cooperation with Berlusconi (initially prized by the *Commendatore,* given Bossi's vicious backstabbing, but later dreaded as Fini in 1999 openly challenged a weakened Berlusconi for control), gave the post-Fascists political responsibility and a new national respectability. Fini also focused on penetrating the state's apparatus to inherit the DC's fallen clientelistic power-base, especially in the South, while masking this through nationalist rhetoric against the *Lega*'s secessionist ploys. Stung by international anti-Fascist criticism against the MSI/AN's inclusion in the government (and a 1 percent decline in the European elections), Fini was painfully aware that for all its better organizational basis, the MSI/AN needed Berlusconi's mantle of legitimacy to stay in power and prevent domestic electoral erosion. The MSI/AN put few political demands on Berlusconi's new government, and even backed his futile, imperious demands for immediate elections once the *Polo* government fell in December 1994. Yet, the MSI/AN's scramble to inherit the old DC's clientelistic power-base within the state apparatus and the South, also sought key posts in the influential state-run media, the farmers' organizations, and public enterprises. Inevitably, the MSI/AN sought more power by pursuing few openly divergent policies (social reform against governmental wishes; opposing the privatization program of *Forza Italia* and *Lega*), while initially keeping disagreements low-key with Berlusconi.[43]

The 1994 elections under the new mixed uninominal-proportional system had seen the triumph of the largest political coalitions (or Poles), although neither Berlusconi's shaky Center-Right "Pole of Liberties," nor the PDS-led Left-Center "Progressist Pole," secured an overwhelming success, while Segni's Centrist ex-DC "Pole for Italy" (*Patto Segni* and PPI) collapsed after failing to emerge as an alternative third-force electoral bloc, rather than support the "Progressists." The Catholic parties could survive further fragmentation only as an influential, national, swing voting bloc for either Berlusconi's Center-Right or the PDS. But the ex-DC (renamed PPI) under Rocco Buttiglione was split between the pro-Berlusconi faction (Roberto Formiglioni) and the pro-PDS one (Rosy Bindi). Buttiglione's contradictory, tortuous strategy favored a temporary, tactical PPI-PDS cooperation in the November 1994 local elections and backed the PDS and the pro-Bossi splintered *Lega* in the no-confidence vote (21 December 1994) that doomed Berlusconi's government. But Buttiglione's pro-Vatican ties both hampered and helped the PPI. The DC's collapse forced the Vatican to stop its historical support of Catholic unity in domestic politics and pursue a policy of cooperation and near-equidistance between six different splinter Catholic parties (the Centrists PPI and *Patto Segni,* the Rightists *Christian-Democratic Union*-UDC and *Christian-Democrat Center*-CCD, the Leftists *Christian-Socialists,* and Sicilian *Rete*).

Berlusconi's meteoric rise to power was equaled by his quick political enfeeblement due to: (1) the bitter internecine rivalry with Bossi's *Lega;* (2) his failure to pass a coherent budget to redress Italy's financial collapse under a crushing public debt at 110 percent of GNP; (3) his loss to the Left of the November 1994 regional administrative elections; (4) the loss of faith in him by the country's politico-economic élites; (5) a long struggle against the "Clean Hands" magistrates. Finally, Milan's "Clean Hands" prosecutors publicly humiliated Berlusconi by serving notice of his indictment on illicit campaign financing during his high-profile chairing of the U.N. Crimes Conference in Naples in December 1994 (the fourth premier humbled by the *Tangentopoli* corruption scandal, after Craxi, Andreotti, and Forlani). Berlusconi sought in vain to overturn both his indictment, and the governmental crisis, once Bossi abandoned the *Polo* government to join the PPI and PDS in a fateful no-confidence vote. Berlusconi then mobilized his followers in street demonstrations to denounce Bossi's betrayal, the "politically-motivated" indictments by the "Clean Hands" magistrates, and a "Communist-influenced illegitimate" parliament (thus embarrassing his own *Forza Italia* group and the lame-duck government of which he was still the premier). "Berlusconi, by appealing [directly] to the people, was now undermining the legitimacy of their [elected] representatives who, in turn, did not possess the resilience of the old DC. Berlusconi laid bare their fragility. . . ." But his imperious demands for immediate, early elections to regain a stronger mandate were opposed by most of the parliament (*Lega* included, as it and smaller parties feared their own electoral demise, while the PDS dreaded a repeat of the polarized 1994 electoral defeat): Berlusconi was backed by part of his own party and MSI/AN, plus the *Lega*'s splinter moderates who had joined him, while even *Forza Italia*'s parliamentary faction suggested that he cede power to his own finance minister and the ex-head of Italy's Central Bank, Lamberto Dini.[44]

Short of elections and with both the *Lega* and PPI split, neither Berlusconi's *Polo,* nor the strong PDS-led opposition, could numerically prevail and form a new government. Thus, Dini formed, in January 1995, a third caretaker technical government (like Amato and Ciampi), with the support of all parties and a limited mandate to introduce a "winner-take-all" regional electoral reform, and implicitly bring early elections by June. But Premier Dini immediately displayed his own independent political ambitions to actually govern on a fiscally conservative and pro-E.U. platform, thus politically weakening Berlusconi. From the Center-Right, Dini's reformist technical government repeatedly postponed elections a year and a half and secured the constant external parliamentary support of the PDS, *Lega,* and most of parliament to offset the steadfast opposition by *Forza Italia,* MSI/AN, and *Rifondazione.* The PDS used this precious time to reshape its democratic Left-Center image. The PDS-led "Progressist Pole" 1994 electoral defeat had been the result of the PDS's controversial alliance with their neo-Communist *Rifondazione* brethren, which kept the PDS from securing a strategic alliance with Segni's Centrist-Catholic "Pole for Italy," while on the other hand Berlusconi won by preposterously mounting an ideological crusade against the PDS's "Communist plot" for dominance. Now with *Rifondazione* in political isolation, the PDS replaced ardent reformist Occhetto as secretary-general with Massimo D'Alema, an ex-PCI cadre traditionalist who terminated constant internal party transformations while continuing the party's Social-Democratic reformist evolution and politico-electoral cooperation with Centrist forces, once the successful November 1994 local elections had reinvigorated the Left. But the PDS (or DS by the late 1990s) was hampered politically by its lack of a coherent vision of national socio-political reforms until, in 1995–96, D'Alema finally forged a stronger Center-Left bloc ("Olive Tree Pole," or *Ulivo*), which also included the PPI, and had as leader Romano Prodi, an ex-DC economist and ex-head of IRI (Italy's largest state industry conglomerate), while sponsoring a progressist, social image emulating U.S. President John F. Kennedy's 1960s "New Frontier" platform.

Soon after, Premier Dini also joined the PDS-led Center-Left *Ulivo* coalition in 1996, then called for spring elections, which were won handily by Prodi's and D'Alema's *Ulivo*. Dini became foreign minister under both Premiers Prodi (1996–98) and D'Alema (1998-current), while *Rifondazione* remained outside the new government as an ambiguous, temporary, external supporter. By 1998, Premier Prodi had received both domestic and international accolades for relentlessly driving Italy's annual inflation down to 1.7 percent, cutting governmental deficits from 7 percent to 3 percent, joining the E.U.'s monetary integration (despite German criticism), while imposing fiscal discipline in the face of parliamentary pressures for pork-barrel spending. However, Prodi's successful fiscal austerity policies took a toll on the *Ulivo* government's ability to pass domestic legislation: the government survived two no-confidence votes in Parliament on the narrowest of margins through the reluctant, external support of *Rifondazione Comunista,* but by late 1998 *Rifondazione* under Bertinotti split over withdrawing just such external support as a ploy to blackmail the *Ulivo* government into more Leftist policies. But *Rifondazione* badly misjudged its political bluff and influence: (1) Prodi's Center-Left coalition collapsed for want of just one vote; he was immediately replaced as premier by D'Alema in a virtually unchanged, *Ulivo* government with a slightly more progressist platform; (2) the neo-Communists fell into near-oblivion once the Cossutta faction split off (the only ideological difference between these two tiny neo-Communists parties is that Bertinotti's *Rifondazione* is pinned down into opposition, while Cossutta's Italian Communists Party backs the *Ulivo* government), and their combined political strength of 8.6 percent at the 1996 elections and 6.1 percent at the 1994 European ones tumbled to

4.3 percent for *Rifondazione* and 2 percent for the *Comunisti Italiani* at the 1999 E.U. elections.[45]

Premier D'Alema's *Ulivo* has ensured efficient governance, domestic stability and economic growth, but growing fissures emerged over controversial policy decisions (like the fight to cut back national pensions and welfare services, or the switch from a much-criticized ideological quest for diplomatic peace at all costs in the blood-soaked Yugoslavia to full support of NATO against Belgrade during the 1999 Kosovo War, lest D'Alema remind his Western Allies of his own Communist past). Italy's new-found stability and image was reflected by the reassuring role of economist leaders turned politicians: Dini remained as foreign minister; Prodi was internationally hailed as the new E.U. Commission's president in mid 1999 (to overcome a E.U. nepotism scandal); and Ciampi, the ex-head of Italy's Central Bank and ex-Premier became Italy's new president. But the more important task of completing Italy's domestic renewal rapidly waned away. Firstly, D'Alema's government backed a broad political referendum campaign to reform the disappointing 1995 uninominal-proportional electoral system by dropping its residual proportionalism (25 percent of the votes), and so overcome the stalled Constitutional Convention, while eliminating as well the volatile proliferation of mini-parties, which hid under the institutional electoral umbrella of the Poles. But, in 1999, the voters rejected the referendum and all hopes for a straight-uninominal electoral system with it, leaving the Italian political system deeply factionalized behind the two main parties (DS versus *Forza Italia*) and their broad ruling coalitions (*Ulivo* versus *Polo*).[46]

Secondly, Berlusconi's embarrassing triple convictions in December 1997 for fraud (a 16-month suspended sentence), and in July 1998 for both bribing tax inspectors and using an off-shore company to channel $12 million in bribes to his ex-friend, PSI ex-Premier Craxi (two years and nine months, plus two years and four months of jail-time, and a $5.6 million fine), failed to bring him down, as had happened to so many of his colleagues in the wake of *Tangentopoli*. The Italian court system routinely dismisses as time-served all jail sentences below three years; and Berlusconi retained his parliamentary immunity from prosecution as leader of *Forza Italia*. Craxi in turn, was condemned to four years jail-time and a $11.2 million fine; but, deprived of all immunities, he remains in voluntary "exile" in Tunisia behind a regiment of private corps, despite being sentenced *in absentia* five times for a total of 24 years. Both Berlusconi and Craxi violently protested their indictments, claiming to be victims of a long-standing vendetta by Milan's "Clean Hands" pool of judges, while Berlusconi, as usual, called for fresh street demonstrations by his party against the *Ulivo* government. Although these were trite political reactions, by 1999 the political climate had changed: *Forza Italia* fueled a now bitter political battle over whether Parliament should set up a special inquiry on the anti-corruption crusade of the "Clean Hands" judges, unjustly accused by many of overzealously prosecuting the *Tangentopoli* scandals to foster the collapse of Italy's political system in 1991–92. The "Clean Hands" judges had also virtually lost political clout and judicial autonomy by 1999 after failing to secure timely, serious convictions on corruption and illicit party-financing for all the thousands of imprisoned, corrupted politicians and staffers, given the exasperating, slow pace of Italy's judicial system.[47]

Finally, the bickering and divisiveness threatening the *Ulivo* coalition in 1998–99 was balanced by the near collapse of cohesion within the rival Center-Right *Polo:* the 1999 governmental reshuffle had only reconfirmed Italy's new political bi-polarism (*Ulivo* versus *Polo*), rather than allow the once triumphant Center-Right forces to stage a comeback. Nevertheless, the weakness of the *Polo's* opposition was aggravated by the *Lega's* near-demise (with most of its fiefdoms being absorbed by Berlusconi's *Forza Italia* in regional and local elections in 1996 and 1999), and by the parallel bitter struggle for leadership of the *Polo* staged by Fini's MSI/AN (or AN) in the wake of Berlusconi's judicial woes. However, Fini's separate list (with Segni's Catholics) in the June 1999 European and local elections performed badly nationally compared to *Forza Italia's* stunning rise to become Italy's first party compared to a distant second DS. At the 1999 E.U. elections the *Polo* gained 38.1 percent, of which *Forza Italia* had 25.2 percent (compared to 30.6 percent in the 1994 E.U. elections and 20.6 percent in the 1996 Italian political elections), outdistancing both its old partner-rivals of AN/Segni (10.3 percent, compared to 15.8 percent in the 1994 E.U. elections and 15.7 percent in the 1996 Italian political elections), and the *Lega* (4.5 percent, compared to 6.6 percent in the 1994 E.U. elections and 10 percent in the 1996 Italian political elections). *Forza Italia* kept 80 percent of its electoral strength, while "stealing" votes from its rival-partners of the *Polo:* 17 percent of AN's right-wing voters and 16 percent of the *Lega's* ones, plus 8 percent from the PPI Catholics. However, the forecasted governmental loss at the same elections, and especially the DS sharp fall, did not threaten D'Alema's rule through the *Ulivo,* as the winning coalition (E.U. elections: *Ulivo* 41.2 percent, of which DS 17.4 percent—compared to 19.1 percent in the 1994 E.U. elections and 21.1 percent in the 1996 Italian political elections). Moreover, European election results are traditionally seen more as a wild card than a precise indicator, while the sparsely attended Italian local elections (42 percent voter turnout, compared to 71 percent at the E.U. elections, or 80 percent to 90 percent in the political ones) are too scant as races and scattered nationwide to point anything but political trends. Thus, despite these reversals and an overall, cynical, political climate of uncertainty dogging the government's policies, it seems quite unlikely that D'Alema's weakened *Ulivo* coalition government will be unseated before the year 2000 national elections by an even weaker and divided *Polo* (whose only strength remains *Forza Italia*'s individual growth), if not at all.[48]

V. Conclusion: from Single-Party Dominance to Democratic Renewal

The DC's single-party dominance during Italy's "First Republic" provided the longest, most peaceful, and wealthiest period of national growth (1945–92). Nevertheless, as the party of "relative majority" the DC could never govern in complete isolation and keep a hold on power without the support of most parties (except the marginalized oppositions: PCI and MSI). When this proved insufficient to the task, the DC resorted to creative patronage and the gradual "looting" of state resources to permanently "capture" voter loyalty. Thus, Italy's "democratic state" soon evolved into an uncontrollably greedy "partitocratic state," devouring limited national resources to preserve its power and "captive" votes. But time and prosperity also eroded the original politico-ideological, religious, and socio-economic fragmentation of the Italian people in rival sub-groups and sub-cultures, while undermining the parties' claim for socio-political monopoly (partitocracy). All this ended up strengthening domestic calls for a more efficient, equitable investment of state resources.

Despite negative images of corruption, elephantine bureaucracy, Mafia, terrorism, economic backwardness, and 50 governments in half a century of democracy, the DC's "soft hegemony" and pervasive patronage always defused ideological-political and socio-economic threats to its dominance by co-opting, buying-off, or isolating her opponents, while preserving a slowly shrinking electoral base. The DC's endurance in power for almost 50 years (1945–92) was closely tied to its cautious policy of shrouding its single-party dominance under a façade of governmental power-sharing with smaller Lay partners, while rejecting permanent, rigid politico-ideological stands that would polarize the country in an unstable Right-Left bi-polarism inimical to the DC's "soft hegemony." Whenever fresh domestic crises or economic tensions weakened the DC's hold on power, the party soon revamped its "dominance" by co-opting new governmental allies around the DC's leadership and sharing patronage of state resources: thus the small Lay parties (PLI, PRI, PSDI) were turned into semi-permanent allies in Centrist coalitions after 1948, while in the early 1960s the DC slowly co-opted back into the government the PSI ("Opening to the Left"), in new Center-Left coalitions, to consolidate the DC's "soft hegemony" and isolate both the extreme Left (PCI) and Right (MSI) into permanent oppositions. When this was no longer sufficient, the ambiguous 1977 "Historical Compromise" gambit allowed the DC to endlessly promise future governmental membership to a now moderate PCI in exchange for its help in restoring the country's collapsing economy and defeating the Black and Red terrorist onslaught until unscrupulous Premier Andreotti jettisoned the PCI once the DC survived the ordeal intact. Such politico-strategic malleability and massive, systemic patronage also made it difficult to pry power away from the DC's institutional grasp, despite its slowly declining socio-politico-electoral appeal. But in the end it was the unrestricted "looting" of state resources by all parties, and especially the 1980s secret C.A.F. power-sharing pact between DC and PSI leaders (Andreotti and Craxi) to sustain their illegal patronage machines, that destroyed the "clientelistic" system, and with it the entire political system and its entrenched barons who fell as well by 1992–94. Thus, the contrast between the country's economic dynamism and its socio-political incoherence since the Cold War (which produced systemic patronage, corruption, and a widening gap between citizens and institutions) fostered the system's own demise when the clamorous 1992–94 prosecutions of entrenched, widespread political corruption and illicit campaign-finance scandals destroyed the governing "legitimacy" and politico-administrative structure of all old parties (DC, PSI, PSDI, PLI, PRI). Thus, Italy's single-party dominance survived the longest, together with Japan and few other countries, along Pempel's prerequisites (full democratic structures and liberties, 30–50 years in power, constant electoral success, modification of Italy's socio-political structure to preserve power and attract new voters), only to fall once the country's politico-economic system had been wholly consumed from within by an insatiable thirst for patronage and corruption.[49]

Other authoritative observers, like Giuseppe Prezzolini, Robert Putnam, Patrick McCarthy, and Simona Colarizi, also highlight the inextricable link between deep, established cultural traits and domestic politics in explaining both the success, uniqueness, and excesses of Italy's single-party-dominant system. Thus, the Italians' centennial-old anarchical aversion to state power and rules produced a deeply corrosive love-hate relationship between the new nation-state (1860–2000) and its citizens, whose provincial loyalties and personal interests rejected all forms of patriotic duty towards the country, while cynically pursuing a quest for individual/clan self-aggrandizement through favors and patronage (*"una mano lava l'altra"*). However, this does not extend automatically to the local level of governance as well. Throughout Italy regional governments work only when reflecting a thriving local "civic community," like the Center-North's Medieval democratic commune heritage, according to Putnam. In the Red Belt the PCI-PDS had relied on class solidarity and self-help associations like the Red co-operatives to foster just such a sense of "civic community," transferring its loyalty to the party. Likewise, the Catholic Church had successfully provided, for a time, an alternative socio-religious identity to the citizens through its network of parishes and devout associations in the north-east and south. But as the DC moved away from social reforms and Vatican control, it increasingly relied instead on the more direct source of clientelistic power by controlling the state apparatus to trade local job-creation and contracts for voting loyalty, especially in the impoverished south. In the process, the DC's single-party "soft" dominance provided socio-political peace and stability to a still immature and volatile society, even at the cost of patronage plundering. Certainly, *clientelism* existed one way or the other since the 1800s *Trasformismo*, but it became a systemic tool for order, power and votes only when DC Premier Fanfani used it in 1955 to free the party from conservative Vatican controls and replace fading anti-Communism with the channeling of state resources to reward loyal voters. But in the long-run patronage is fundamentally self-destructive of resources and engenders a desperate need to expand exponentially: systemic clientelism involved the plunder of all state resources by the DC and its allied governmental parties, then the parallel penetration and expansion of the public sector to secure even more resources since the late 1950s, and after 1964 the plunder of the private sector as well through hidden fees to use public services and state industries. Finally, bribes and illegal financing of political parties became the accepted norm to bypass state regulations and secure political favors until the state coffers were bankrupt and the citizen's patience exhausted.

But if today " . . . the designation of the old political class as scapegoat has absolved the mass of citizens from the task of self-scrutiny," the difficult task of changing the country's political culture has only just begun. Overall, Italy's national unification had failed to replace local loyalties and "civic communities" with a deeper sense of loyalty towards the nation-state, especially when the unresolved political clash between powerful interests and local poverty bred the transfer of citizens' loyalty to alternative networks of patronage and clientelism, be they quasi-legal, like Italy's "partitocracy" clientelistic power-sharing system, or outright illegal, like the parties' illicit financing and bribe system, the Mafia, and other local organized crime networks, to accomplish locally those same duties that an inefficient state had failed to provide legally and nationwide in the first place.[50]

> . . . Having achieved finally a sense of the Nation, Italians remain second-class citizens, lacking any strong sense of the state and are still uncertain on their rights and duties . . . once all those values promoted by the democratic institutions are daily denied and trashed by those who more than others should guarantee them

and model an adequate governmental intervention . . . until this perverse spiral
[of corruption] . . . turned on itself to strangle the very political system. . . . [51]

Today a "Second Republic" has come to life with the total—albeit
chaotic—remaking of the political system: over 50 tiny political groups
keep forming, splitting, and merging within the confines of the two intra-
party Poles: the PDS-led Center-Left *Ulivo* and the Center-Right "Pole of
Liberties." Although both *Tangentopoli* and the piece-meal altering of the
1948 constitution with important electoral reforms has been the driving
force behind the new fragmented "Second Republic's" parties, Italy's complete renewal still requires forging a new "social contract" between a non-
overbearing, or absentee, state and a politically responsible and honest
citizenry. Thus, effective decentralization of institutional powers would
tap the tradition of local "civic communities," while capitalist economic
growth and public-social goals must never again be sold to the highest bid-
ders, or partitioned in a renewed patronage system. Certainly election reforms per se are only a limited tool in achieving this task, although their
role was not indifferent in the final demise of the DC's long-lasting, single-
party "soft hegemony." Today the cumulative toll of scandals, inquests,
public disgust, and political chaos makes it highly unlikely that the DC-
style of single-party dominance and patronage machine could ever come
back to rule and haunt Italy's anarchical population. But if the socio-political and patronage premises for rebuilding a single-party-dominant system no longer exist, the country still lacks the necessary political maturity
to develop a stable Western-style democratic alternance to power and a viable bond/identity between state, nation, and citizens. Maybe the ruling
PDS-led *Ulivo* Pole can do the trick and provide sufficient stability, accountability, and responsibility to promote this necessary political and cultural evolution. Or maybe not, given the widespread underground
influence of cultural-political cynicism and greed. But should Italy's "Second Republic" flourish as a mature Western democracy, thanks to the leadership of the ex-Communist PDS/DS, it would be a fitful tribute to that
party's democratic evolution, and a sweet revenge for its reformist members who had for so long been marginalized from the body-politic as extreme Leftists and "Fifth-columnists" under foreign (Soviet) control. For
all the rest of the Italian population the main concern is different and as
old as the Italian nation-state: to have respect for and trust in a Western-
style democracy, whose efficient governments reflect a stable, reformed,
law-abiding, and de-ideologized political system, capable of assuring—no
matter the party in power—it would always cherish domestic stability and
tend to the country's needs without enriching its rulers or the coffers of patronage-driven party machines.[52]

Table 1.1 Italian Political Elections (House of Deputies), 1946–1996

	1946	1948	1953	1958	1963	1968	1972	1976	1979	1983	1987	1992	1994	1996
Percentage of voters	100.2	92.9	93.8	93.8	92.9	92.8	93.2	93.4	90.6	89	88.9	87.2	86.1	96.7
Blank ballots	n/a	2.2	4.6	2.9	3.2	3.6	3.2	2.7	4.1	5.8	4.9	5.2	n/a	n/a
DC[a]	35.2	48.5	40.1	42.3	38.3	39.1	38.7	38.7	38.3	32.9	34.3	29.7	—	—
PPI-Populars[a]	—	—	—	—	—	—	—	—	—	—	—	—	11.1	5 ca
Rete/Orlando[a]	—	—	—	—	—	—	—	—	—	—	—	1.9	1.9	n/a
Patto Segni[a]	—	—	—	—	—	—	—	—	—	—	—	—	4.6	n/a
CCD-CDU[a]	—	—	—	—	—	—	—	—	—	—	—	—	n/a	5.8
PlI-Liberals[i]	6.8	3.8	3	3.5	3.5	5.8	3.9	1.3	1.9	2.9	2.1	2.8	n/a	n/a
Partito d'Azone	1.5													
PRI[j]	4.4	2.5	1.6	1.4	1.4	2	2.9	3.1	3	5.1	3.7	4.4	—	n/a
PSIUP[d]						1.9	4.4							
PSDI[c]		7.1	4.5	4.6	6.1	14.5[c]	5.1	3.4	3.8	4.1	2.9	2.7	—	—
PSI-Socialists[c]	20.7	—	12.7	14.2	13.8	—	9.6	9.6	9.8	11.4	14.3	13.6	2.2	2 ca
PCI/PDS[b,e]	18.9	31[b]	22.6	22.7	25.3	26.9	27.1	34.4	30.4	29.9	26.6	16.1[e]	20.4	21.1
Rifondazione Comunista-RC[f]	—	—	—	—	—	—	—	—	—	—	—	5.6[f]	6.4	8.6
Ultra-Left[g]/DP[h]	—	—	—	—	—	4.5[g]	2.8[g]	1.5[h]	2.2/1.4	1.5[h]	1.7[h]	—	—	—
PR-Radicals	—	—	—	—	—	—	—	1.1	3.5	2.2	2.6	1.2	3.5	1.9
Verdi/Greens	—	—	—	—	—	—	—	—	—	—	2.6	2.8	2.7	2.5
Monarchists[l]	2.8	2.8	6.9	4.8	1.7	1.3	—	—	—	—	—	—	—	—
MSI/AN[l]	5.3	2	5.8	4.8	5.1	4.5	8.7	6.1	5.3	6.8	5.9	5.4	13.5	15.7

(continues)

Table 1.1 *(continued)*

	1946	1948	1953	1958	1963	1968	1972	1976	1979	1983	1987	1992	1994	1996
Lega Nord[k]	—	—	—	—	—	—	—	—	—	—	0.5	8.7	8.4	10.1
Forza Italia	—	—	—	—	—	—	—	—	—	—	—	—	21	20.6

Source: compiled by author from Italian governmental statistics (ISTAT).

[a]Christian-Democrats (DC-*Democrazia Cristiana*); after 1992 split in 6 parties (*La Rete; Patto Segni; PPI; UDC; CS; CCD*).

[b]Unitarian Leftist Front of Communists and Socialists (PCI + PSI), or *Fronte Popolare*.

[c]Unitarian Socialist Party (PSI + PSDI), or PSU-*Partito Socialista Unitario*, in 1943–1947 and 1966–1972.

[d]Leftist Socialists Splinter Party (PSIUP), or *Partito Socialista Italiano d'Unità Proletaria*.

[e]Ex-Communists/Democratic Party of the Left (PDS-*Partito Democratico della Sinistra-Quercia*, or lately DS-*Democratici di Sinistra*).

[f]Neo-Communists (*Rifondazione Communista*).

[g]Ultra-Left +

[h]*Democrazia Proletaria*; in 1992 merged with RC and PDS.

[i]Conservative-Liberals (PLI-*Partito Liberale*).

[j]Republicans/Moderate Liberals (PRI-*Partito Repubblicano*); absorbed by 1948 the Resistance Party/*Partito d'Azone*.

[k]Lombard/Northern League, or Secessionists (*Lega Nord*)

[l]Extreme-Right: "Common Man" (*L'Uomo Qualunque*); absorbed in 1948 by the Neo-Fascists (*Movimento Sociale Italiano*), then absorbed by the Monarchists in 1972 (MSI-DN); "Post-Fascists" since 1992 as MSI/AN. or *Alleanza Nazionale* (AN).

Table 1.2 Italian Governments, 1945–1999

Prime Ministers	Governments
1. Parri, Ferruccio (Pd'A)	DC + PCI + PSI + PLI + Pd'A + DL (6–11/1945)
2. De Gasperi, Alcide (DC)	DC + PCI + PSI + PLI + Pd'A + DL (12/1945–7/1946)
3. De Gasperi II (DC)	DC + PCI + PSI + PRI (7/1946–7/1947)
4. De Gasperi III (DC)	DC + PLI + PSI (2–5/1947)
5. De Gasperi IV (DC)	DC + PLI + PSDI + PRI (5/1947–5/1948)
6. De Gasperi V (DC)	DC + PLI + PSDI + PRI (5/1948–1/1950)
7. De Gasperi VI (DC)	DC + PSDI + PRI (1/1950–7/1951)
8. De Gasperi VII (DC)	DC + PRI (1/1951–6/1953)
9. De Gasperi VIII (DC)	DC (7–7/1953)
10. Pella, Giuseppe (DC)	DC (8/1953–1/1954)
11. Fanfani, Amintore (DC)	DC (1–1/1954)
12. Scelba, Mario (DC)	DC + PSDI + PLI (2/1954–6/1955)
13. Segni, Antonio (DC)	DC + PSDI + PLI (7/1955–5/1957)
14. Zoli, Adone (DC)	DC (5/1957–6/1958)
15. Fanfani II (DC)	DC + PSDI + PLI (7/1958–1/1959)
16. Segni II (DC)	DC (2/1959–2/1960)
17. Tambroni, Fernando (DC)	DC (3–7/1960)
18. Fanfani III (DC)	DC (7/1960–2/1962)
19. Fanfani IV (DC)	DC + PSDI + PRI (2/1962–5/1963)
20. Leone, Giovanni (DC)	DC (6–11/1963)
21. Moro, Aldo (DC)	DC + PSI + PSDI + PRI (12/1963–6/1964)
22. Moro II (DC)	DC + PSI + PSDI + PRI (7/1964–1/1966)
23. Moro III (DC)	DC + PSI + PSDI + PRI (2/1966–6/1968)
24. Leone II (DC)	DC (6–11/1968)
25. Rumor, Mariano (DC)	DC + PSU + PRI (12/1968–7/1969)
26. Rumor II (DC)	DC (8/1969–2/1970)
27. Rumor III (DC)	DC + PSI + PSDI + PRI (3–7/1970)
28. Colombo, Emilio (DC)	DC + PSI + PSDI + PRI (8/1970–1/1972)
29. Andreotti, Giulio (DC)	DC (2–2/1972)
30. Andreotti II (DC)	DC (6/1972–6/1973)
31. Rumor IV (DC)	DC + PSI + PSDI + PRI (7/1973–3/1974)
32. Rumor V (DC)	DC + PSI + PSDI (3–10/1974)
33. Moro IV (DC)	DC + PRI (1/1974–1/1975)
34. Moro V (DC)	DC (2–4/1976)
35. Andreotti III (DC)	DC (External Support: PCI + PSI + PRI) (7/1976–1/1978)
36. Andreotti IV (DC)	DC (External Support: PCI + PSI + PRI) (3/1978–1/1979)
37. Andreotti V (DC)	DC + PSDI + PRI (3–3/1979)
38. Cossiga, Francesco (DC)	DC + PSDI + PLI (8/1979–3/1980)
39. Cossiga II (DC)	DC + PSI + PRI (3–9/1980)
40. Forlani, Arnaldo (DC)	DC + PSI + PSDI + PRI (10/1980–5/1981)
41. Spadolini, Giovanni (PRI)	DC + PSI + PSDI + PRI + PLI (6/1981–8/1982)
42. Spadolini II (PRI)	DC + PSI + PSDI + PRI + PLI (8–11/1982)
43. Fanfani IV (DC)	DC + PSI + PSDI + PLI (12/1982–4/1983)
44. Craxi, Bettino (PSI)	DC + PSI + PSDI + PRI + PLI (8/1983–6/1986)

(continues)

Table 1.2   *(continued)*

Prime Ministers	Governments
45. Craxi II (PSI)	DC + PSI + PSDI + PRI + PLI (8/1986–3/1987)
46. Fanfani VI (DC)	DC (4–4/1987)
47. Goria, Giovanni (DC)	DC + PSI + PSDI + PRI + PLI (7/1987–3/1988)
48. De Mita, Ciriaco (DC)	DC + PSI + PSDI + PRI + PLI (4/1988–5/1989)
49. Andreotti VI (DC)	DC + PSI + PSDI + PRI + PLI (7/1989–3/1991)
50. Andreotti VII (DC)	DC + PSI + PSDI + PLI (4/1991–4/1992)
51. Amato, Giuliano (PSI/Independent)	Technical Government (C + PSI + PSDI + PLI) (6/1992–4/1993)
52. Ciampi, Carlo-Azeglio (Independent)	Technical Government (DC + PSI + PSDI + PLI) (4/1993–1/1994)
53. Berlusconi, Silvio (Forza Italia)	Pole of Liberties (Forza Italia + MSI/AN + Lega + CD + UDC) (5–12/1994)
54. Dino, Lamberto (Independent)	Technical Government (External Support: PDS + PPI + Center-Left + Lega) (1/1995–5/1996)
55. Prodi, Romano (Ulivo)	Ulivo Pole (PDS + PPI + Greens + Center-Left) (5/1996–10/1998)
56. D'Alema, Massimo (PDS/Ulivo)	Ulivo Pole (PDS + PPI + Greens + Center-Left) (10/1998–Current)

Source: compiled by author from Italian governmental statistics (ISTAT)

Notes

1. T. J. Pempel ed., *Uncommon Democracies: The One-Party Dominant Regimes* (Ithaca, NY: Cornell University Press, 1989); Michael Braun, *L'Italia da Andreotti a Berlusconi* (Milano: Feltrinelli, 1995).

2. Mario B. Mignone, *Italy Today: A Country in Transition* (New York: Peter Lang Publishing, 1995).

3. Patrick McCarthy, *The Crisis of the Italian state* (New York: St. Martin's Press, 1995). Quote, traditional saying.

4. René Albrecht-Carrié, *Italy from Napoleon to Mussolini* (New York: Columbia University Press, 1950); Denis Mack Smith, *Italy* (Ann Arbor: University of Michigan Press, 1969); Martin Clark, *Modern Italy, 1871–1982* (New York: Longmans, 1984).

5. Simona Colarizi, *Biografia della Prima Repubblica* (Roma-Bari: Laterza, 1996), p. 3–6; Giampiero Carocci, *L'Italia dall'Unità ad Oggi* (Milano: Feltrinelli, 1975); Claudio Fava, *Sud* (Milano: Mondadori, 1995).

6. Marco Rimanelli, *Italy between Europe and the Mediterranean: Diplomacy and Naval Strategy from Unification to NATO* (New York: Peter Lang Publishing, 1997), p. 3–423; Antonio Del Boca, *Gli Italiani in Africa Orientale dall'Unità alla Marcia su Roma* (Bari: Laterza, 1976); Claudio Morandi, *La Politica Estera Italiana da Porta Pia all'Età Giolittiana* (Firenze: Le Monnier, 1972); Migone, *Italy Today*, p. 2–95.

7. Adrian Lyttelton, *The Seizure of Power: Fascism in Italy, 1919–1929* (London: Weidenfeld & Nicholson, 1973); Renzo de Felice, *Interpretazioni del Fascismo* (Bari: Laterza, 1969); Ernst Nolte, *The Three Faces of Fascism* (New York: Mentor Books, 1969); Rimanelli, *Italy between Europe and the Mediterranean*, p. 425–622.

8. Giorgio Bocca, *Storia della Guerra fascista*, 2 vols. (Bari: Laterza, 1972); Giorgio Bocca, *Storia dell'Italia Partigiana* (Bari: Laterza, 1966); Colarizi, *Biografia della Prima Repubblica*, p. VII–XI, 6–11, 20; Rimanelli, *Italy between Europe and the Mediterranean*, p. 425–622, 671–922, 965–1002.

9. Giuseppe Di Palma, "Establishing Party Dominance: It Ain't Easy," p. 162–188, and Pempel, "Introduction," p. VII–VIII, 1–32, both in Pempel, ed., *Uncommon Democracies*.

10. Giuseppe Di Palma, "Government Performance: An Issue and Three Cases in Search of Theory," in *West European Politics*, no. 7 (April 1984): p. 172–187; Di Palma, "Establishing Party Dominance," p. 162–166, 169.

11. Di Palma, "Establishing Party Dominance," p. 166–169; Guillermo O'Donnell, Philippe Schmitter & Laurence Whitehead, eds., *Transitions from Authoritarian Rule in Latin America and southern Europe* (Baltimore: Johns Hopkins University Press, 1987); Claudio Pavone, *Alle origini della Repubblica* (Torino: Boringhieri, 1995).

12. Di Palma, "Establishing Party Dominance," p. 170–174; Pavone, *Origini della Repubblica*, p. 5–135.

13. Di Palma, "Establishing Party Dominance," p. 59–61, 174–176; Pavone, *Origini della Repubblica*, p. 95–235.

14. Colarizi, *Biografia della Repubblica*, p. VIII–XII, 5–17, 59–61; Pavone, *Origini della Repubblica*, p. 95–235.

15. Di Palma, "Establishing Party Dominance," p. 176–186; Pavone, *Origini della Repubblica*, p. 105–302.

16. Colarizi, *Biografia della Prima Repubblica*, p. 21–34, 78–81; Sidney Tarrow, "Maintaining Hegemony in Italy: The Softer They Rise, the Slower They Fall!" in Pempel, ed., *Uncommon Democracies*, p. 316–318; Rimanelli, *Italy between Europe and the Mediterranean*, p. 425–622, 671–922, 965- 1002; Leo J. Wollemborg, *L'Italia al Rallentatore* (Bologna: Mulino, 1966).

17. Tarrow, "Maintaining Hegemony in Italy," p. 314–316; Ariel Levite & Sidney Tarrow, "The Legitimation of Excluded Parties in Dominant Party Systems: A Comparison of Israel and Italy," in *Comparative Politics*, no. 15 (April 1983): p. 295–328; Leo J. Wollemborg, *Stelle, Strisce e Tricolore* (Milano: Mondadori, 1983).

18. Di Palma, "Establishing Party Dominance," p. 186–188; S. Colarizi, *Biografia della Prima Repubblica*, p. 33–44; Ennio Di Nolfo, *La Repubblica delle speranze e degli inganni* (Firenze: Ponte alle Grazie, 1996).

19. Colarizi, *Biografia della Prima Repubblica*, p. 28–33, 40–41, 45–51, 80–81; Fava, *Sud*, p. 3–234.

20. Tarrow, "Maintaining Hegemony in Italy," p. 306–332; Gianfranco Pasquino, "Italian Christian Democracy: A Party for All Seasons," in Peter Lange & Sidney Tarrow, eds., *Italy in Transition* (London: Cass, 1980).

21. Tarrow, "Maintaining Hegemony in Italy," p. 316–320; Silvio Lanaro, *Storia dell'Italia Repubblicana* (Venezia: Marsilio, 1992); Giorgio Galli, *Il Bipartitismo Imperfetto* (Bologna: Mulino, 1966).

22. Tarrow, "Maintaining Hegemony in Italy," p. 309–311, 318; Giacomo Sani, "The Italian Electorate in the Mid 1970s: Beyond Transition," in Howard Penniman, ed., *Italy at the Polls, 1976* (Washington DC: American Enterprise Institute, 1981), p. 118; Giorgio Galli & Alfonso Prandi, *Patterns of Political Participation in Italy* (New Haven, CT: Yale University Press, 1968); Joseph LaPalombara, *Democracy, Italian Style* (New Haven, CT: Yale University Press, 1987); Giacomo Sani, "Le elezioni degli anni settanta, terremoto o evoluzione?" in *Rivista Italiana di Scienza Politica*, no. 7 (1976): p. 261–288; Galli, *Il Bipartitismo Imperfetto*, p. 5–198.

23. Tarrow, "Maintaining Hegemony," p. 310–313; Michele Salvati, "May 1968 and 1969 Hot Autumn: Responses of Two Ruling Classes," in Suzanne Berger, ed., *Organizing Interests in Western Europe* (New York: Cambridge University Press, 1981); Joseph La Palombara, *Comportamento Politico in Italia* (Milano: Comunità, 1963).

24. Colarizi, *Biografia della Prima Repubblica*, p. 48–59, 61–67, 83; Raffaele Romanelli, ed., *Storia dello Stato Italiano* (Roma: Donzelli, 1995); Galli, *Bipartitismo Imperfetto*, p. 5–198.

25. Donald L.M. Blackmer & Sidney Tarrow, eds., *Communism in Italy and France* (Princeton: Princeton University Press, 1975); Peter Lange & Sidnet Tarrow, eds., *Italy: Crisis and Consensus* (London: F. Cass, 1980); Tarrow, "Maintaining Hegemony in Italy," p. 314–317; Colarizi, *Biografia della Prima Repubblica*, p. 67–77.

26. Giuseppe Di Palma, *Surviving without Governing: Italian Parties in Parliament* (Berkeley: University of California Press, 1977); Paolo Sylos-Labini, *Saggio sulle classi sociali* (Roma-Bari: Laterza, 1975); Tarrow, "Maintaining Hegemony in Italy," p. 316–326; Giorgio Galli, *Italia Sotterranea: Storia, Politica e Scandali* (Bologna: Mulino, 1980); Samuel H. Barnes, *Representation in Italy* (Chicago: University of Chicago Press, 1977); Paolo Farneti, *The Italian Party System, 1945–1980* (London: Pinter Publ., 1985);

27. Colarizi, *Biografia della Repubblica*, p. 96–102, 104; Enzo Santarelli, *Storia Critica della Repubblica* (Milano: Feltrinelli, 1996); Arrigo Levi, *Un'Idea dell'Italia* (Milano: Mondadori, 1979).

28. Martin Shefter, "Party and Patronage: Germany, England and Italy," in *Politics and Society*, no. 7 (1977): p. 403–451; Tarrow, "Maintaining Hegemony in Italy," p. 317–322; Giovanni Maria Bellu & Sandra Bonsanti, *Il crollo. Andreotti, Craxi e il loro regime* (Roma-Bari: Laterza, 1993); Michele Salvati, *Il sistema economico Italiano: analisi d'una crisi* (Bologna: Mulino, 1975); Colarizi, *Biografia della Prima Repubblica*, p. 108–110.

29. Colarizi, *Biografia della Prima Repubblica*, p. 83–96, 110–112; Tarrow, "Maintaining Hegemony in Italy," p. 322-326; Le Monde, *L'Économie Italienne sans Miracle* (Paris: Economica, 1982).

30. Tarrow, "Maintaining Hegemony," p. 326–329; Colarizi, *Biografia della Repubblica*, p. 100–120; Giorgio Galli, *Difficile Governo* (Bologna: Mulino,

1972); Marco Tarchi, *Cinquant anni di nostalgia. La Destra Italiana dopo il Fascismo* (Milano: Rizzoli, 1995); Marco Rimanelli, "Italian Terrorism and Society, 1940s–1980s: Roots, Ideologies, Evolution and International Ties," in *Terrorism: International Journal,* vol. 12, n.4 (December 1989).

31. Quotes: Colarizi, *Biografia della Prima Repubblica,* p. 130 & 131; see also p. 126–131.

32. Tarrow, "Maintaining Hegemony," p. 326–329; S. Colarizi, *Biografia della Repubblica,* p. 93–94, 120–126, 128- 134, 145–146; Marco Cesarini-Sforza & Enrico Nassi, *L'Eurocomunismo* (Milano: Rizzoli, 1977); Donald L.M. Blackmer & Sidney Tarrow, eds., *Communism in Italy and France* (Princeton: Princeton University Press, 1977), p. 3–20, 143–304, 373–419, 456–503, 541–640; Peter Lange & Maurizio Vannicelli, eds., *The Communist Parties of Italy, France and Spain* (London: Allen & Unwin, 1981), p. 1–53, 103–108, 157–162, 195–202, 279–286; P.A. Allum, *Italy, Republic without Government?* (New York: Norton, 1973); Giorgio Galli & Alfonso Prandi, *Patterns of Political Participation in Italy* (New Haven: Yale University Press, 1970).

33. Tarrow, "Maintaining Hegemony in Italy," p. 320, 326–329; S. Colarizi, *Biografia della Prima Repubblica,* p. 134–144, 149–150; Luigi Graziano & Sidney Tarrow, eds., *La Crisi Italiana,* 2 vols. (Torino: Einaudi, 1979).

34. Tarrow, "Maintaining Hegemony in Italy," p. 320, 326–332; Galli, *Bipartitismo Imperfetto,* p. 95–198.

35. Colarizi, *Biografia della Repubblica,* p. 142–161, 163, 170–172; Le Monde, *L'Économie Italienne,* p. 5–265.

36. Patrick McCarthy, *Crisis of the Italian state* (New York: St. Martin's Press, 1995), p. 2, 4–5, 123–128; Colarizi, *Biografia della Prima Repubblica,* p. 151–155, 163–169, 171–173; Galli, *Bipartitismo Imperfetto,* p. 95–258.

37. Quote: Colarizi, *Biografia della Repubblica,* p. 152, plus 151–155; McCarthy, *Crisis of Italian state,* p. 123–128; Frederic Spots & Theodor Wieser, *Italy: A Difficult Democracy* (London: Cambridge University Press, 1986)

38. Quote: Colarizi, *Biografia della Prima Repubblica,* p. 172, plus 169–179; McCarthy, *Crisis of Italian State,* p. 1–7, 74–80, 128–130, 134–137, 139–152; Giovanni-Maria Bellu & Sandra Bonsanti, *Il crollo. Andreotti, Craxi e il loro Regime* (Roma: Laterza, 1993); Jens Petersen, *Quo vadis Italia?* (Roma-Bari: Laterza, 1996).

39. Donald Sassoon, *Contemporary Italy* (New York: Longman, 1986); McCarthy, *Crisis of the Italian State,* p. 1–7, 74–80, 128–130, 134–137, 139–146, 150–152; Fabrizio Rizzi, *I Giudici di Milano* (Quarto: Musumeci, 1993); Adrian Lyttelton, "The Crusade Against Cosa Nostra," in *New York Times Review* (8 September 1995): p. 51–56; Alexander Stille, *Excellent Cadavers: The Mafia and the Death of the First Italian Republic* (New York: Pantheon, 1995); Alexander Stille, "The Fall of Caesar," in *The New Yorker* (11 September 1995): p. 68–83; Daniele Protti, "La DC corre il rischio di finire come il Libano," in *Europeo* (Milano: 25 October 1991): p. 6–7; Pialuisa Bianco, "Con la DC di Mario Segni tornerei a collaborare," in *Europeo* (Milano: 25 October 1991): p. 12–15.

40. McCarthy, *Crisis of Italian state*, p. 130–134, 144–167; Ilvo Diamanti, *La Lega* (Roma: Donzelli, 1993); Umberto Bossi & Daniele Vimercati, *Vento dal Nord* (Milano: Sperling & Kupfer Eds., 1992); "Northern Italian Politician Proclaims Independence," in *Tampa Tribune* (16 September 1996): p. 3; Pialuisa Bianco, "La Lega sono me. Castellazzi e C.? Traditori e venduti," *Europeo* (Milano: 25 October 1991): p. 18–19; Pino Belleri, "Bossi, chi ti dà i soldi?" *Europeo* (Milano: 25 October 1991): p. 20–23; Mack Smith, "Italy's Dirty Linen," p. 10–15.

41. Matt Frei, *Getting the Boot. Italy's Unfinished Revolution* (New York: Times Books, 1995); Marc Lazar, "Incertitudes Italiennes," *Revue Politique et Parlementaire*, vol. 98, no. 983 (May-June 1996): p. 31–36; Marc Lazar, "L'Italie au-delá du Rubicon?" *Politique Internationale*, no. 72 (summer 1996): p. 337–351; McCarthy, *Crisis of Italian state*, p. 186–191; Migone, *Italy Today*, p. 23–195; Mack Smith, "Italy's Dirty Linen," p. 10–15.

42. McCarthy, *Crisis of Italy's State*, p. 168–183; Stefano Bartolini & Roberto D'Alimonte, eds., *Maggioritario ma non troppo* (Bologna: Mulino, 1995); Braun, *L'Italia da Andreotti a Berlusconi*, p. 12–158.

43. McCarthy, *Crisis of Italy*, p. 184–191; Giovanni Ruggeri, *Berlusconi. Gli affari del Presidente* (Milano: Kaos Ed., 1994); Bettino Craxi, *Il Caso C.* (Milano: Giornalisti Ed., 1995); Mack Smith, "Italy's Dirty Linen," p. 10–15.

44. Quote from McCarthy, *Crisis of the Italian state*, p. 189, see also 183–186, 188–190; Giulio Savelli, *Che cosa vuole la Lega?* (Milano: Longanesi, 1992); Braun, *L'Italia da Andreotti a Berlusconi*, p. 150–268. See also: Robert H. Evans, "Italy . . . Quo Vadis?" p. 4–12, "Edmondo Berselli, "Solution on the Right: The Evolving Political Scenario," p. 13–21, and Massimo L. Salvadori, "From Regime to Regime: The Principle of the Missed Alternative," p. 22–26, all three essays in *Italian Journal*, vol. VIII, no. 1 & 2.

45. Gruppo Editoriale Oggi, "The June Referendum and the Next Elections: The Dini Government's Travails," in *Italian Journal*, vol. IX, no. 2: p. 3–7; McCarthy, *Crisis of Italian state*, p. 182–191; Pietro Scoppola, *La repubblica dei partiti* (Bologna: Mulino, 1996), p. 520–525; Mack Smith, "Italy's Dirty Linen," p. 10–15; author's interviews with Italian political observers, Rome, summer 1998.

46. Giovanni Fasanella & Daniele Martini, *D'Alema* (Milano: Longanesi, 1995); Massimo Franco, "Vita quotidiana d'un premier in guerra," p. 58–59, and Gianni Baget Bozzo, "La sinistra divisa alla prova del fuoco," p. 55; both in *Panorama* (Milano: 15 April 1999); Dennis Redmont, "NATO Commander Warns Threats," *AOL News/Associated Press* (12 July 1999); William Drozdiak, "Conflict of Interest Clouded Kosovo," in *International Herald Tribune* (21 July 1999); Stefano Brusadelli, "É l'ora del Referendum," in *Panorama* (Milano: 15 April 1999): p. 72–76; author's interviews with Italian political observers, Rome, summer 1999.

47. Tribunali di Milano e Napoli, *Le mazzette della Fininvest* (Milano: Kaos Ed., 1996); Alan Friedman, "Berlusconi gets Second Conviction in Week," *International Herald Tribune* (Paris: 14 July 1998): p. 1, 6; Anthony Lewis, "In

Came an Outsider to Make Italy a Top Player," in *International Herald Tribune* (Paris: 14 July 1998): p. 8.

48. "Recupero a sinistra per i DS. Bonino pesca da tutti i partiti," in *Repubblica* (Milano: 14 June 1999); "D'Alema: 'Nessun problema alla stabilità di governo'," in *Repubblica* (Milano: 14 June 1999); Victor L. Simpson, "Italy Elections could Fuel Shakeup," *AOL News/Associated Press* (28 June 1999).

49. Colarizi, *Biografia Prima Repubblica,* p. 10–17; Tarrow, "Maintaining Hegemony," p. 317–320; José Francisco Ruiz Massieu, "Italy and Mexico: a Political Analogy," *Voices of Mexico* (Mexico: October-December 1992): p. 93–95; Mack Smith, "Italy's Dirty Linen," p. 10–15.

50. Quote: McCarthy, *Crisis of Italian state,* p. 191. See: Giuseppe Prezzolini, *L'Italiano inutile* (Milano: Longanesi, 1958); Robert D. Putman, Robert Leonardi & Raffaella Y. Nanetti, *Making Democracy Work: Civic Traditions in Modern Italy* (Princeton: Princeton University Press, 1993); Scoppola, *Repubblica dei partiti,* p. 524–527; Luigi Barzini, *The Italians* (New York, 1970); La Palombara, *Comportamento Politico in Italia,* p. 5–201.

51. Quotes: Colarizi, *Biografia della Repubblica,* p. 168, also 189–191.

52. Pempel, "Introduction," p. VII-VIII, 1–32; Stephen Hellman, "Italy," p. 335–464, in Mark Kesselmann, Joel Krieger et alia, *European Politics in Transition* (Boston: Houghton Mifflin, 1997).

TWO

Greece: The Perils of Incorporation

Platon N. Rigos

I. Introduction

In the march towards democratization, political systems like the United States, France, Sweden, Spain, India, Mexico, and Argentina have gone through one or more periods of severe clashes, civil wars, or revolutions, which result in the political empowerment or incorporation[1] of religious and ethnic minorities. Political incorporation, when complete,[2] is more than a party representing the oppressed groups achieving power temporarily, or completing its historical agenda as T. J. Pempel indicates.[3] It means that large segments of the public are certain that they now have a stake in the system, that they can be part of the governing coalition. The concept of "political incorporation" is often used in American urban literature to denote the coming to power of African-American, Hispanic, or some white non-élites, but students of transitional societies also used it.[4]

Some countries have seen the process begin early, as in England with Oliver Cromwell, and be repeated more gently with the Labour Party dominance of the post-war years. Other countries started the process in the late eighteenth century (France) and continued it throughout the last two centuries in incomplete and repolarizing clashes and changes in party dominance. It is possible to generalize that democratizing political systems will not be stable until all previously oppressed groups feel they belong to it.

Unfortunately, political empowerment periods are rife not only with civil wars, political violence, and oppression, but also with rhetorical excesses, increased polarization and economic problems like inflation. If political incorporation results in rancor and anger among the middle or upper classes, instability will continue. If it heals rifts and cleavages through high indebtedness, a huge bureaucracy, and a stagnant economy, costly and perilous adjustments may be expected. This paper seeks to remind those who compare the performance of economic and political system of the importance of the nature and pace of the political incorporation process. In comparing one party-dominant or multi-party democracies, the perils and costs of political incorporation must be factored in. A political system such as Sweden's cannot be easily compared to one where the effects of political incorporation are very recent. There are also other factors that play a crucial role (e.g., the proximity of a security threat), and are often forgotten, but the costs and perils of political incorporation outweigh them all.

For the last 25 years, modern Greek politics have been characterized as hopelessly stuck into cycles of extremes such as the colonels' dictatorship in the early 1970s and the Papandreou policy swing to the Left in the 1980s. Serious analysts, including Greek scholars, found the cause of this instability to be rooted in a patron-client transitional system,[5] which harmed the creation of modern party systems and a merit civil service. Even Left-of-Center commentators criticized Papandreou policies as not truly socialist, but populist.

In the 1990s, foreign critics sought to emphasize Greece's location in the Balkans, and to use the Ottoman Turkish past as a means of explaining its position on Macedonia.[6] Some even questioned whether present-day Greeks and ancient Greeks had anything in common. Greece was said to belong to a non-Western civilization,[7] because the Orthodox Church was viewed as too dominant. The Greek economy was often described as a basket-case, particularly in the 1980s,[8] and still suffering from excessive indebtedness. Portugal was given as an example of a country putting its house in order in comparison to Greece. The influential magazine *The Economist* called the country "The Sick Man of Europe."[9]

In 1995, the consensus among friendly and unfriendly observers was that Papandreou's party, the PASOK (Panhellenic Socialist Movement), would fall prey to infighting after his death. New Democracy, the party representing the Right would climb back to power and continue a series of unstable swings from Left-of-Center to Thatcherite policies.

Yet the transition took place smoothly in June of 1996. A new prime minister emerged to rule and to be confirmed by national vote in September. The party that had dominated Greece's politics since 1981, the PASOK, began to resemble Social-Democratic parties elsewhere, and dropped some of its populist divisive rhetoric. It pushed its rival Right-of-Center party, the New Democracy (or *Nea Demokratia*), to the sidelines. If it could solve the fiscal problems it helped create, and remedy the perennial overcentralization of the Greek state, Greece would remain a one-party-dominant democratic system, like Sweden, well into the twenty-first century.

How is it that this quiet and swift transition has not affected the judgment of Greek and foreign analysts?[10] Greece is depicted as not sufficiently Western to belong to the European Union.[11] The reason for this misinterpretation of recent Greek political life is that few have noticed that the major project of *political incorporation of the marginalized social strata* was complete as early as the late 1980s.[12] When the Communist and New Democracy party made common cause for one whole year in 1989, to stop the abuses of a charismatic Peron-like leader bent on monopolizing power, this should have given students of Greek affairs cause to revisit old theories. The behavior of a free and noisy press at that crucial juncture should have been cause for reassessments.

This chapter shows how political incorporation in Greece has entailed a civil war, right-wing oppression, one-party Leftist dominance, populist demagoguery, high inflation, corruption, high deficits, and debt. Because previous studies of Greece have relied on "national character, cultural explanations,"[13] I will start with an inquiry into the meaning of political incorporation and its various facets. Next comes an overview of a few Greek social and economic features that help explain how political incorporation took place in this country. The purpose of this second part will be to isolate the few characteristics of Greek culture and economics that are incontrovertible parameters within which the past is to be understood and the present policy options can be defined.

A short history of modern Greek politics will focus on how some major themes, political incorporation efforts, and foreign power machinations have impacted on Greece's march to democratic stability to this very day. As elsewhere, the major variables (e.g., a bloody civil war) have repercussions on other factors (e.g., the role of big nations), which in turn can slow down the political incorporation process. The causal path is complicated and its direction is not always clear. Here is an attempt to analyze the major directions.

II. The Process of Political Incorporation: A Theory

Democratic development in most Western societies has often been described as requiring the separation of Church and state, urbanization, expansion of the franchise and general economic development. But at some point, countries like Germany and Italy in the 1920s and 1930s have taken an authoritarian, if not totalitarian, road. The nature and type of political incorporation has often made more difference than some factors like Church-state separation.

The accession to power of a Left-type party for a long period,[14] and the acceptance by most voters and élites that this change is legitimate and normal, is a very convincing sign that political incorporation has been successful. The Socialist-Communist coalition of the 1930s in France was not accepted as legitimate. A similar accession to power in the 1980s was at first feared, but led to a general consensus under François Mitterrand. Labor's accession to power in the post-war years demonstrated that even for Britain incorporation was not complete. The polarized class system was reflected in politics under Thatcher.

Yet, as mentioned earlier, political incorporations can be perilous. This is not the place to analyze when political incorporation is less perilous, or what conditions indicate that it is complete, but this study of Greece will show that some generalizations and future hypotheses are possible.

III. Greek Social and Economic Facts of Life

Greece is a small country (10.6 million in population) that does not easily fit into conventional categories. It does not fit into the class of wealthy small nations, like Belgium and Holland, because its manufacturing sector is weak. Yet it certainly does not belong in the group called underdeveloped nations. Even at the height of the poverty of the early post-war years, Athens' theater activity was comparable to that of Rome or Paris.[15]

Greece is also unique because its citizens have a very strong sense of national identity. This strong identity was not just the product of a strong centralizing state as some may have us believe.[16] It has been shaped by a long and rich history, a language that is as old as most civilizations, and a religion (Greek Orthodox) that sheltered this language through 400 years of Ottoman Turk rule. In many ways, the Church acted like the guarantor of the culture and of the Greek identity at a time when there was no state. This also makes Greece unique among Western societies because anti-clericalism never became a strong political movement as it did in France or Mexico. Greek intellectuals like Kazantzakis[17] show, in their work, a deep religiosity and an equally deep questioning of the role of religion in secular modern life. Greeks may poke fun at and even despise some clergy, but when the time comes to marry, to educate a child, to die, they all remain faithful to a religion, which is such an integral part of their identity.

This uniquely strong identity also makes for an equally unique homogeneity in an increasingly diverse world. Minorities of Slavs, Turks, and other ethnic groups have either been absorbed or ignored by the mainstream culture. While stories of subtle and not so subtle persecutions may have emerged during the last few years as part of the Macedonia issue, the fact remains that minority revolts or movements have been small and very few in comparison to other nations.[18]

Greeks have only had class structure to divide them, but that has been sufficient to create very damaging clashes, as their recent history demonstrates. The class struggle has been difficult to resolve until now. The remnants of a patron-client system was inherited from the foreign tutelage, but enhanced by Greeks into a well-practiced art. It has weakened parties, interest groups, and civil society. The role of strong personalities and powerful families has often created confusion on national issues of class cleavage.

The economy is Greece's weak spot for many reasons. Agriculture is still one of the largest productive sectors and one with great potential, but does not export enough of the excellent fruits and vegetables that are sold locally. Manufacturing has been weak since the 1960s, and has declined from its earlier 3 percent GDP level. Greek wages are not low enough to make local investment attractive. By the late 1970s wages had almost caught up with most of Western Europe and the entitlements given by government made investment even more risky.

A more fundamental reason for the shape of the economy, is that Greeks lack trust in each other.[19] Extreme individualism means that businesses are family-owned and collapse after the father dies. Fukuyama[20] has described a similar phenomenon among the Chinese.[21] This is why there are few large shareholder-owned corporations in Greece.

IV. Modern Greek Politics:
From the Civil War to the Colonels' *Junta*, 1940–74

In an extremely individualistic country, a strong state is the only point of cohesion and modern Greek history is marked by the primacy of the state over society. The state became a dominant force also because in part it modeled itself on France, although this primacy of the state has unfortunately weakened any measure of local self-governance until recently.[22] The state has had to be dominant also because national aspirations impelled it to recapture from Turkey lands populated by Greeks (Balkan Wars, 1912–13) and because of incessant threats to its territorial integrity. In 1940 Italy sought to annex Greece, Germany conquered it (1940–44), Britain liberated it just to keep the advancing Soviet Army out of the Mediterranean, while Turkey still claims parts of the Aegean.

Greek post-war political history can be viewed from a number of perspectives. From a political incorporation perspective, the post-war period is bounded by four major patterns: the Civil War, the *Junta*, Papandreou's political phenomenon, and Papandreou's later death drama. After the end of the Civil War (1944–50), a long period of dominance by parties of the Right lasted until 1962 and then the Center parties controlled the system until the Colonels' Coup. After the *Junta* régime in 1967–74, a short six-year stint by a weak "New Right" government led to an eight-year rule by PASOK. Although PASOK lost its grip for a while (1988–93), it came back for three years under Papandreou and won again under Simitis.[23]

Civil wars are among the cruelest forms of warfare. Greece had the bad fate of experiencing such a war, right after World War II, a very bloody and costly war in its own right. Even more than France and Italy, Greece found itself with a very dominant and popular Left and a strong Communist Party (KKE) in the middle of the resistance to the German occupation. The Communist-Socialist Alliance, or EAM (Greek Liberation Front) and its army, ELAS, did not even wait for the end of the war to exert its muscle. Left circles in Greece believe it could have easily established a government and ruled all of Greece by 1944 had it not been for the Stalin-Churchill "percentage Deal" to keep Greece in the Western sphere of influence (Stalin received from Churchill a promise of control in Bulgaria, Romania, and Hungary in exchange for no Soviet control of Greece). Thereafter, Stalin ordered Greek Leftist elements to cooperate. Since then, many Greeks have believed that Stalin's intervention robbed them of an opportunity to establish an independent Socialist Greece until the 1980s. An "alternative" government was created in March of 1944, headed by a non-Communist academic, Alexander Sovolos. In the EAM-controlled areas, friends of the Left thought a Socialist Greek government with a minority of Communists was not only feasible, but desirable. Peasants and even the intelligentsia were impressed with the competent and corruption-free officials that EAM put in the areas it controlled.[24]

This part of history is important to remember in interpreting the sheer hatred of the Right in some segments of Greek society, and how the accession to power of PASOK in 1980 was viewed as a revenge for past injustice. EAM lost the battle for Athens. As the Churchill-Stalin agreement became a dead letter (Stalin called for the withdrawal of British forces in early 1946), the final and bloodiest phase of the Civil War began. The British called on the Americans for help in 1947 and Truman responded immediately with the anti-Communist Truman Doctrine. The KKE leader Zakhariadis, a doctrinaire Stalinist, fought a conventional war that was a disaster both for Greece and his forces. A new government of northern Greece was proclaimed in northern Epirus, at the border of Greece and Albania. The partisans were trying to create a fully Communist base bordering on Soviet client states. EAM put more Greek villages to the torch than the Germans had during their 1941 invasion of Greece, and in the end Zakhariadis's strategy alienated any popular support EAM may have had. In retrospect it is difficult to see how Greece's fate could have differed from Bulgaria's or Romania's had the KKE won the civil war instead. The KKE leadership had no Tito among them. They proved to be hard Stalinists every step of the way.[25]

Right-wing circles, on the other hand, remember that as the Communist fortunes ebbed, the movement proceeded to take some 30,000 children and some families to various parts of the Soviet Empire, while the Greek Communist Party was declared illegal. Since 1975 these ex-partisans have been permitted to return to Greece under a clemency program that allowed even well-known war criminals to go unpunished. It is not surprising that a political system that emerged (partly because of American aid) out of a savage war against Communism (supported by Communist neighbors like Bulgaria, Albania, and Yugoslavia), would be virulently anti-Communist.

General Papagos, who had fought the resistance and won the Greek Civil War, was asked to organize the first government under King Paul I. Papagos created a "Grand Right Coalition" with his party, the Greek Rally, as the center. Papagos soon died (1953) and King Paul, with some influence from his wife Fredericki, passed over the governing coalition's next in command to select the younger Constantin Karamanlis in 1955. The latter went on to preside over a decade of improvements in national living standards and economic growth. But the polarization of Greek society was still there, reflected in anomalies in elections and occasional suppression of dissent. He was to return as president of the post-*Junta* republic.[26]

Greece after World War II and the Civil War was a devastated country, where children ran barefoot in the street, and inflation destroyed all savings. The Greek royal family, "imported" to the country from German and Danish royal lineage by Britain and other European great powers in the nineteenth century, held a dubious legitimacy throughout its short history and had a tendency for meddling in national politics. The Queen's meddling is said to have caused Karamanlis to quit his post and go into exile in 1963. During the 1950s, the armed forces were fiercely pro-monarchy and anti-Communist. The secret police and para-military elements fought and jailed a number of Leftist leaders. The CIA is believed to have had its hand in almost all parts of Greek political life. These assumptions may sometimes be exaggerated and reflect a widespread populist belief in foreign intervention and conspiracy theories, but even serious observers find some accusations well warranted. Assumptions of foreign intrigue and foreign linkages of the governing coalition is a common and constant theme in small democracies that were dominated by a major power. This foreign dimension cannot always be dismissed as a feeling of persecution and a refusal to take responsibility, since it occasionally emerges from the darkness of rumor to a stark and well-documented reality. It poisoned political speech with accusation of treason, while such rhetoric can be quite corrosive to democratic debate and political incorporation.[27]

In the middle of this climate of conspiracy and fears of repression, Greece nonetheless thrived economically, rebuilt its infrastructure and parts of its welfare state (social security, unemployment compensation, a minimal public health-care system). Under a Conservative like Karamanlis, the state established a prominent role in the economy, owning banks, phone companies, and some major industries. The abrupt departure of Karamanlis created an opportunity for Centrist political leaders like George Papandreou and Constantine Mitzotakis. They formed an alliance which lasted until the Colonels' Coup. Andreas Papandreou, who had served in the U.S. Navy and reached scholarly excellence as an economist at Harvard and Berkeley, had returned to his native Greece in 1957. By the mid 1960s he was known as a firebrand Socialist. Still, his father entrusted him with the important Ministry of Defense. A schism in the Centrist coalition emerged, when the *Aspida* affair was discovered in early 1966: George Papandreou fired his son; then, in a quarrel with the monarchy, he gave his resignation, expecting that no other government would be possible without his support. A transitional coalition was however crafted and future Prime Minister Constantin Mitzotakis, among others, joined this Center-Right government. A few months later the Colonels intervened with a right-wing military coup.[28]

This incident was to play an important role in the saga of Greek politics. It became an article of faith among the Populist and Communist Left that by joining with others to create a transition government, Mitzotakis had betrayed the forces of democracy and made the *Junta*'s accession possible. Andreas Papandreou and PASOK were to use this over and over to mobilize parts of the middle class against Mitzotakis. The camps for political prisoners (which included even Right-of-Center leaders) and the sheer lack of freedom of the press and expression were critiqued by the international press and Greeks of all political permutations abroad. But the most costly and lasting mistake the Colonels made was to give Turkey an excuse to intervene in Cyprus. The *Junta* in Athens encouraged some military elements to stage a coup against Archbishop Makarios who was seen as leaning too much to the Left and as not sufficiently enthusiastic about "*enosis,*" the union of Greece and Cyprus.[29]

The nature of the régime was oppressive, but not overly intrusive. Among the positive legacies of the régime is the elimination of the monarchy. Another positive legacy, was an awareness even among right-wing political leaders, that some of their followers were a threat to democratic rule. The legacy has an impact to this very day. It puts Right-of-Center leaders on the defensive and makes it difficult for them to present free-market policy alternatives. The *Junta* lost much of its effectiveness after four years, and in 1973 was operating in a power vacuum. It is in this vacuum that some elements made the colossal mistake of engineering a right-wing coup in Cyprus, which gave Turkey the opportunity to invade the island. The United States, alerted about the Turkish fleet's movements did nothing to prevent the invasion and enduring occupation of the northern part of the island. This enraged the Greek public. Anti-Americanism was widespread and helped to create the setting for the successes of PASOK in the 1980s and beyond (PASOK leader Papandreou campaigned on the promise of closing U.S. military bases in Greece).[30]

V. The Papandreou Era and Afterwards: The PASOK Legacy

The first government in power was headed by Karamanlis who expanded the welfare state and nationalized even more banks, shipyards, and airlines. The moderate Right, called the New Democracy Party, sought to occupy the Center and heal the wounds of the past. This was a battle New Democracy could not win as PASOK remained even more radical and fueled extreme nationalism. The old practice of coddling economic enterprises, even if unprofitable, continued. A tendency for wealthy individuals to play it safe and invest in real estate and land also reappeared. As in some developing democracies, the wealthy classes routinely transferred capital to foreign locations and were ready to leave at a moment's notice.

During the 1974–81 period, PASOK managed to establish itself as an entirely new party with a new political identity and novel ideas. It did this by exploiting, and at the same time transcending, the old divisions of Greek politics, namely, those between Conservatives and Liberals, Communists and anti-Communists. The party emerged as the champion of anti-right-wing forces and represented society as being split by the fundamental division between an all-embracing "non privileged" majority; which it claimed to stand for, and a tiny "privileged" oligarchy of foreign interests and domestic monopolies, identified as the enemy. The party's claim was that its main goal was nothing less than the Socialist transformation of society through a "third road to Socialism."[31]

PASOK soon became no more than the extension of its charismatic leader. The party managed to develop a well-organized and highly active mass-base and to introduce new political personnel into it ranks. Yet it is characteristic that during its first 16 years, PASOK held only two national congresses, the first in 1984 and the second in September 1990. The third one took place in June of 1996 after Papandreou's death.

The Greek middle class, then as now, included the salaried strata in both the public and the private sector, liberal professionals, shopkeepers, and the self employed in small and medium-size family businesses. These different groups are characterized by frequently contradictory interests and it is very difficult to lump them together under the same banner. It seems that these middle strata, dissatisfied with the performance of the right-wing governments of the 1960s–70s, were ready to switch their political allegiance to a new political force seeking change.[32]

In October 1981 an eight-year reign by Andreas Papandreou began. PASOK gained 48.1 percent of the vote (highest ever by a party in the postwar era) and a majority in parliament. It won again in 1985. PASOK thrived by weakening most parties on the Left. Greece's third road to Socialism experiment displayed some marks of a hard Socialist ideology. Squeezing the private sector did not involve nationalizations, since already most banks were owned by the government. The attack on the private sector took the form of a series of far more subtle, but effective, measures: (1) A 25 percent hike in all salaries. Indexing of salaries and pensions to the rate of inflation. (2) A law forbidding private firms to fire more than 20 percent of their employees. (3) Difficult loan conditions created by an inflation rate of 16 percent, high interest rates (25 percent), and the policies of the national banks. These banks loaned to agricultural cooperatives controlled by PASOK, and to state-managed firms, but rarely to businesses without links to the party. (4) A concerted effort to marginalize private agricultural producers (difficult loans) and favor agricultural cooperatives. (5) So-called "problematic industries" (those previously weak or made weak by the new laws) were brought under governmental protection. (6) Government spending: public spending increased during the 1982–88 period by 40 percent (compared to 28 percent 1975–81 under the New Democracy government). Public debt increased during the same period by 433 percent (compared to 106 percent in 1975–81), or from 12.5 percent of Gross Domestic Product (GDP) in 1983 to more than 20 percent of GDP in 1989. (7) Generous pension plans were granted to elements of the middle class that were friendly to the party. Civil War veterans, even ex-Communists returning from Soviet-controlled lands, were given such pensions. The implementation was so sloppy that it was possible for a healthy 35-year-old person to get a half pension and still hold another job.

State-controlled agencies and agricultural cooperatives for the promotion and export of agricultural products became very powerful. Many of these agencies were involved in serious economic scandals, among which was the notorious "corn scandal," which resulted in the prosecution and imprisonment of a PASOK minister. Large loans and subsidies were given even to inefficient cooperatives that accumulated large debts. The cooperative boards and executive structures were quickly filled with PASOK-appointed administrators. Farmers were made to understand that the only way they could get loans would be through joining the cooperative or the party. In a few years, even independent farmers joined the party, which could distribute large European Union subsidies.[33]

New boards and administrative positions were created and all were part of the burgeoning party nomenclature. "Problematic industries" (some 40 large firms) were allowed to fall even further into debt and became a place where the party could find jobs for its faithful. Overstaffing was a common occurrence. The Department of Problematic Industries became a giant make-work bureaucracy. On the positive side, women's rights were expanded in all areas. Aid was to be given to poor women who needed a dowry to get married. Women were given the right to receive a pension if divorced. Women's employee rights were also reinforced. Finally the welfare system was expanded. Health-care became more systematic throughout Greece, with the building of clinics in remote areas. The government's social reforms in the areas of health, education, and social security, though extremely popular with the middle and lower strata, were based on borrowed money and were used as a means for the creation of new state/party-controlled agencies.

Though most of these measures were taken during PASOK's first year in office and the government was later obliged to revert to an austerity program, they created the image of a responsive government. These measures did not help the economy: new productive investments and industrial growth declined, while unemployment and inflation increased. To cope with the deteriorating economic situation, PASOK had to turn to foreign loans. Yet even these loans were not channeled into productive investments. Instead, they financed PASOK's social policies and, above all, the expansion of an already overinflated public sector. PASOK's political reign was extended by Greece's entry into the European Community (E.C.), a membership Karamanlis had fought for and Papandreou opposed. But E.C. agricultural subsidies were ideally suited to attract the sympathies of farmers and peasants who in the past had tended towards conservative views. PASOK's operatives in every village and small town made it known that E.C. funds and state subsidies would go strictly to the party faithful. This was a major boost for PASOK's electoral base.[34]

This strategy paid off in electoral terms, as PASOK maintained an electoral base of about 38 percent, even in the middle of the huge corruption trials in 1990–91. From 1985 to this day, there were some signs of dissatisfaction and change within PASOK's electoral base. The unions rebelled against anti-strike measures. The Left-of-Center "upper-middle" and some intellectuals in "upper" social groups, gradually shifted their political allegiance to New Democracy. PASOK's diminishing appeal to these social strata reached a new low during the 1988–89 period. This dissatisfaction was manifested in PASOK's remarkable electoral losses in the big urban centers like Athens and Salonika. The scandals and PASOK's mistreatment of unions seeking to strike brought about a strange coalition between the Communist Party and New Democracy, which took office with the express purpose of allowing an impartial inquiry into the scandals and the corruption. Some of the accusations reached all the way to the top to Papandreou, who was indicted. This strange alliance lasted just a year to allow for a tribunal to be selected and new elections the following year.

Mitzotakis led his New Democracy party to victory with 46 percent of the vote in 1991. Although this plurality would have given room for effective governance, the strict proportional electoral system adopted by PASOK gave Mitzotakis a majority of one. Mitzotakis proceeded to change the system to favor the larger and smaller parties, but demurred from calling elections right away, as he could have. His slim majority nonetheless pushed through the privatization of the phone company (still incomplete to this day) and tax reform. Both measures alienated elements of the Right that had learned to live with a system of government contracts. They did not like privatization because "foreign firms" could benefit. They might lose some contracts. The new Right began to show the split between old Right politicians and those dedicated to true free-market capitalism, a split which bedevils New Democracy to this very day.[35]

The Macedonia issue also proved divisive within the ruling party. Even though the government adopted a firm rejection of the use of the name Macedonia, the young and charismatic Foreign Minister Antonios Samaras began using more inflammatory rhetoric. Mitzotakis was aware that Greece was being depicted by the foreign press as warlike and ill-intentioned towards a little country of one million. He had no other choice but to fire Samaras, although this did not appease the critics of Greek foreign policy. Despite his pro-American stance, Mitzotakis pursued an even-handed policy towards Serbia and warned European nations of the bloody consequences of the recognition of Bosnia. After the Bosnian War started, he maintained close contacts with the Serbs who had been Greece's traditional allies since 1912. This stance irritated U.S. policy-makers, who at the time were gearing up to bomb Bosnian Serb positions, similar to the bombings that eventually took place in the summer of 1995. It is interesting that Mr. Samaras, a member of the Council of Foreign Relations, decided to found a new party called "Political Spring" in October of 1993, precipitating the fall of the government, new elections, and a smashing victory by PASOK. The percentage of the vote for PASOK was not higher than 43 percent, but the electoral system devised by Mitzotakis gave PASOK a comfortable majority of 180 seats (30 more than needed for a majority).[36]

The second arrival of PASOK to power served only to reinforce the trends described above. The corruption continued through the awarding of contracts for public works. The newspapers, which had already been implicated in the Koskotas Affair, continued to reflect a style full of invective and bias. E.C. officials learned to be more careful that contracts for infrastructure did not go to unqualified PASOK supporters. They put in place procedures that made it difficult for PASOK to reward its minions. The government's reaction was to delay the awarding of contracts and to shift some of the funds to Portugal. Finally, after much wrangling among party members about the succession of Papandreou as prime minister, former Economy Minister (in 1986) Constantine Simitis, was elected. Papandreou remained as head of the party, even though many in the party asked him to relinquish that post.

As if the problem of managing the economy was not daunting enough, Simitis found himself in a foreign affairs crisis when Turkish journalists landed on the uninhabited Greek island of Imia, off the coast of Turkey, where they hoisted a Turkish flag. Furthermore, the Turkish government announced that it did not recognize the legality of the 1946 Italo-Greek Treaty, which ceded Italy's former possession of Rhodes and the Dodecanese Archipelago to Greece. The U.S. government intervened and persuaded both sides to go back to the *status quo ante:* both sides left the island, which returned to uninhabited status with no flag on it.[37]

Polls before Papandreou's hospitalization showed PASOK losing ground with only 38 percent of the electorate. But in December of 1995, as he lay close to death, Papandreou still refused to delegate power, while the consensus among many commentators was that PASOK would fall prey to infighting after his death, and break up. They were wrong. PASOK executed a smooth transition of power, knowing all too well that the break-up of the party would create the need for new elections. The incentive was at first to keep the system of patronage going. Fortunately for Simitis, Papandreou died a few days before the party was to hold an important convention. This allowed Simitis to face and defeat four of his challengers and emerge as undisputed leader of the party and the government.

Simitis has restored some confidence in the Greek economy by pledging to prepare Greece for entering into the European monetary union in 1999. Austerity measures have included a salary freeze and some efforts at privatization. Inflation has abated (down to 5 percent from 22 percent) and the economy is showing signs of revival. The Turkish provocations continued throughout summer 1996 and tested the new Greek government. Soon after that, the polls showed Simitis comfortably ahead of New Democracy leader Miltiadis Evert. Simitis called for early elections on 22 September 1996. New Democracy ran a simplistic tax-cut campaign with exaggerated nationalistic tones. The race tightened, but PASOK and Simitis still won by a 3 percent margin (41 percent to 38 percent). The same electoral system that exaggerates the margin in parliament, gave PASOK a majority of 160 deputies over 102 for New Democracy. On the other hand, the small parties of the Left increased their strength, while Samaras and his "Political Spring" party were shut out and received only 2.9 percent of the vote. Simitis has a new mandate to proceed to reform the economy, cut back the public sector, and reduce the colossal debt accumulated by his party over the years. Evert has been reelected as leader of New Democracy, but still hears rumblings of dissatisfaction. Greece had lurched slightly Left again, but to a more responsible Left, partly because the opposition had little to offer.[38]

VI. Analysis

Greek politics under Papandreou came very close to approximating the populist ideal seen in Argentina under Peron. The political incorporation of large numbers of Greek voters who thought they would never have influence was PASOK's greatest achievement. On the other hand, PASOK's failure to institutionalize democratic processes within its own organization until recently, was not healthy. Its reneging on promises of decentralization and civil service reforms was also unhealthy. Unions, newspapers, and farmer cooperatives were made subordinate.

The media's fate deserves particular attention. An invective tabloid style emerged in the 1980s, created by one of PASOK's newspapers known as *Avriani.* Eventually many of the middle-of-the-road media outlets imitated the style and became supporters of the party. Some Right-of-Center papers were bought and turned into milder versions of *Avriani.* The remaining right-wing papers such as *Apoyievmatini* copied the tabloid style of *Avriani.* Some of the methods employed to subvert the media included the use of secret funds in governmental agencies or state banks to subsidize the friendly press, the granting of preferential treatment (advertising) to these papers, and to those being asked to be neutral towards scandals emerging in the government. Selective leaks to friendly papers were another tool. Some newspaper owners ventured into the construction field to benefit from contracts from the government and public works subsidized by the European Union. Nonetheless a few serious papers remain. Despite all we have described, it was the same media outlets that opposed Papandreou's effort to silence all opposition.[39]

The damage done by PASOK's policies is similar to that created by other Left-of-Center parties elsewhere: the creation of a large class of people and businesses who depend on the government as if it was a common cash register. The difference is that in Greece all kinds of demands for private gain are transformed into legitimate rights of the "people." At that stage "anything is fair game"[40] and cynicism spreads. Papandreou's contribution was the creation of a party that seems to have survived him in good shape. Rid of the pervasive influence of the charismatic leader, the party may revert to its Socialist origins.

Clientelistic practices remain because both major political parties find them useful to their survival and expansion. This is where the need for a true meritocratic civil service fits in. Yet hardly anyone in Greece believes it is likely in the near future. Both elements in each party will need to develop the ethic of professionalism described by Christofilopoulou at the local level. It might come sooner if the E.U. demands professional standards, free competition in contracts, and privatization. There are signs that this could happen. In the United States, the spread of civil service was the result of federal social security regulations in the 1930s. Sheer economic rationality will eventually force the dismantling of the huge governmental machinery. Although the farmers shut down the country in a massive protest against the reduction in their subsidies, the Simitis government did not give in as Chirac did in France. Various unions are grumbling, but the government and opposition are both committed to the Maastricht Treaty and to eventually joining the monetary union.

The goal of full Europeanization is tied to national security considerations and no group is likely to derail it. The argument has been made that full entry into the European system is the best way to protect the country's borders. Even though the European Union has not ventured to say that an attack on any member country is tantamount to an attack on the whole union, the implication is that once Greece is thoroughly integrated into Europe, it will be even more difficult for Turkey to attack or challenge Greece's borders.[41]

VII. Conclusions

What are the prospects for Greek democracy? The army has been in its barracks since 1974, and will stay there unless war breaks out. The Communist threat has been virtually powerless in a country that fought a very bloody civil war over Communism. The elements of the Right that produced ugly episodes in the 1950s and the Colonels' dictatorship in 1968–74 have been in jail, dead or impotent. While strong on family values, Greece does not have to cope with the demands of a Christian fundamentalist or anti-immigrant movement. Despite almost two decades of perilous behavior by the major agent of political incorporation, some glaring facts remain. Opposing parties (Communist, other Leftists and New Democracy) made common cause when PASOK went too far into corruption and coercion. Even at the height of PASOK control, some of the larger municipalities (Athens, Salonika) were in the hands of the opposition party.

The Greek electorate may have been made cynical, but this occurs after incorporation diminishes the volume and sharpness of political discourse. Policy compromises within major parties is critiqued by the purists. Yet in

Greece the entry of small parties in the new parliament helps defuse some cynicism. Greece's proportional electoral system, which favors the largest party, enhances diversity without bringing chaos. The New Democracy party is in the process of transforming itself. The young nephew and namesake of Karamanlis has opted to move towards a free-market model of conservatism. Still, remnants of the Monarchist and clientelistic factions remain.[42]

Opposition newspapers have been functioning and constantly increasing in number. Two television channels, ANTENA and MEGA, have developed a neutral professional style that was a rare commodity in the 1980s. PASOK's major achievement is the feeling that all classes have now had access to power. Despite a tax system that allows too many tax evaders, Greece has an adequate safety net. New funds (from tax reform) and a lessening of tensions with Turkey could enhance higher education and state-sponsored high-technology efforts. The Greek character feature that makes it difficult to create large enterprises is not likely to change, but countries like Taiwan have shown it is possible to thrive with small businesses in high-technology sectors. Two major stumbling blocks remain: the size of defense spending, and the civil service's size and inefficient nature.[43]

In Greek foreign policy, what is off-limits is to negotiate with Turkey over the territorial integrity of Greece or Cyprus. But this pressure was not as strong as that which came from within PASOK itself. Simitis seemed close to compromise when elements within his party gave him an ultimatum. He emerged ever more popular after the summer of 1997 when Madeleine Albright seemed to have Bosnia negotiations on her mind. A so-called Madrid Conference Protocol at first promised a Greek-Turkish *détente*. All the efforts yielded little because of one event Turkey could not stomach. The E.U. announced it would begin the process of admitting Cyprus without waiting for the island to be unified and before considering Turkish accession. Turkey retorted that it would begin integrating northern Cyprus into Turkey as threatened earlier.[44]

In September of 1997, Athens was awarded the 2004 Olympics and Greeks reveled in the streets. Some may see in it the beginning of the end of this period of marginalization. They may be right. Greece has made enormous political progress and its last elections were so normal that a writer claimed that the system was "as close to perfect a democracy as one can expect today."[45]

Political incorporation gives those who study democratic development a new conceptual angle, which can explain variations in the process. It has shown that while Church-State separation was very important for some nations at certain periods of history, and seems to be an obstacle today for countries with large fundamentalist movements, it is mostly when religious and political cleavages coincide that Church-State issues become dangerous to the democratic system.[46]

Notes

1. R. De Leon, *Left-Coast City: Progressive Politics in San Francisco, 1975–1991* (Lawrence, KS: University Press of Kansas, 1996); R. Browning, D. R. Marshall & D. Tabb, *Protest Is Not Enough: The Struggle of Blacks and Hispanics for Equality in Urban Politics* (Berkeley: University of California Press, 1984).

2. There are many incorporations that start a process of inclusion, which may be continued by non-violent gradual processes later.

3. T. J. Pempel, ed., *Uncommon Democracies: The One-Party Dominant Regimes* (Ithaca, NY: Cornell University Press, 1990).

4. C. Lyrintzis, "PASOK in Power: Change to Disenchantment," in Richard Clogg, ed., *Greece, 1981–1989: The Populist Decade* (New York, St. Martin's Press, 1993) p. 120–130.

5. P. N. Diamandouros, "Politics and Culture in Greece, 1974–91: an Interpretation," in Clogg, ed., *Greece, 1981–1989*, p. 27. See also L. Tsoukalis, "Beyond the Greek Paradox," in G. T. Allison & K. Nicolaidis, eds., *The Greek Paradox* (Cambridge, MA: MIT Press, 1997), p. 163–174.

6. Greece's Macedonia stance was described as extreme nationalism. Sober newspapers like *Le Monde* brought up the Balkan analogy to denote an irrational tribalism assumed to exist in Yugoslavia.

7. Samuel P. Huntington, *The Clash of Civilizations and the Remaking of World Order* (New York: Simon & Schuster, 1996), p. 162, 20–27.

8. S. B. Thomadakis, "The Greek Economy: Performance, Expectations and Paradoxes," in Allison & Nicolaidis, eds., *The Greek Paradox*, p. 39–60.

9. "The Sick Man of Europe," in *The Economist* (22 June 1992).

10. Throughout 1996, articles in the *Economist* treated this change as a welcome improvement, but not as a sign of new trends. See Keith Legg & John M. Roberts, *Modern Greece: A Civilization on the Periphery* (Boulder, CO: Westview, 1997), p. 153, which expresses an otherwise pessimistic assessment of Greek politics, hoping that "future politics . . . may become more civil."

11. Legg & Roberts, *Modern Greece*, chp. 11.

12. Lyrintzis, "PASOK in Power," p. 120–130.

13. Cultural explanations are back in vogue ever since Putnam's work on Italy. See: Robert Putnam, *Making Democracy Work: Civic Traditions in Modern Italy* (Princeton, NJ: Princeton University Press, 1993). Those who use them (Huntington, *The Clash of Civilizations*) ought to be careful not to let such studies deteriorate into national character simplifications and caricature. The cultural approach should be relegated to explanations of last resort. Structural, historical explanations are less likely to lead to value-laden declarations and racist statements. See also Samuel P. Huntington, *The Third Wave: Democratization in the Late Twentieth Century* (Norman, OK: Oklahoma University Press, 1991).

14. This applies more to modern Western industrial nations. Today Iran is undergoing political incorporation of the lower classes through an extreme theocratic regime. England's Cromwellian Revolution was also a similar type of religion-based incorporation. See also: J. Markoff, *Waves of Democracy: Social Movements and Political Change* (Thousand Oaks: Pine Forge Press, 1996).

15. The most recent theatrical productions were quickly translated and presented in Athens; indigenous productions were also of high quality.

16. Legg & Roberts, in *Modern Greece,* p.10–19, argue that Greek identity was a mixture of Byzantine and Western orientations, shaped artificially by a strong state which imposed homogeneity through a single religion and language.

17. See among a huge assortment of works his *Report to Greco* (New York: Simon & Schuster, 1965).

18. At the time of this writing, France, another highly homogeneous nation, is fighting a poorly reported uprising in Corsica.

19. This is a cultural trait unlikely to change. Even Greeks in the United States work on the basis of extended families.

20. Francis Fukuyama, *Trust* (New York: Free Press, 1994).

21. This has not stopped the economy of Taiwan from thriving, or its politics from becoming democratic.

22. P. Christofilopoulou, *Decentralization in Post Dictatorial Greece* (Ph.D. Dissertation: London School of Economics and Political Science, 1989).

23. R. C. Macridis, *Greek Politics at a Crossroads: What Kind of Socialism* (Stanford, CA: Hoover Institution Press, 1984); R. S. Shinn, ed., *Government and Politics, Greece: A Country Study* (Washington D.C.: American University, 1985).

24. D. Close, *The Origins of the Greek Civil War* (New York: Longman, 1995).

25. C. M. Woodhouse, *The Struggle for Greece 1941–1949* (London, 1976).

26. Ibid.

27. One of the great personalities in Greek political history, Prime Minister Venizelos, and his Liberal Party had opposed the monarchy in the 1920s.

28. Andreas had created a subversive group of left-wing officers under the name of *Aspida* (the Shield).

29. J. A. Katris, *Eyewitness in Greece: The Colonels Come to Power* (St. Louis, MO: New Critics Press, 1971).

30. R. Clogg & G. Yannopoulos, eds., *Greece under Military Rule* (New York: Basic Books, 1972).

31. M. Spourdalakis, *The Rise of the Greek Socialist Party* (London: Routledge, 1988).

32. Lyrintzis, "PASOK in Power," p. 120–130.

33. Diamandouros, "Politics and Culture in Greece, 1974–91," p. 27–30.

34. C. Danopoulos, "Greek Bureaucracy and Public Administration: A Persistent Failure of Reform," in Ali Farazmand, ed., *Handbook of Comparative and Development Public Administration* (New York: Dekker, 1991).

35. P. N. Diamandouros, "Greek Politics and Society in the 1990s," in Allison & Nicolaidis, eds., *The Greek Paradox,* p. 89–121.

36. Ibid.

37. Ibid.
38. N. Kyprianos, "Viewpoint: What to expect from Simitis," in *Athens News* (24 September 1996)
39. S. Pezmazoglou, "The 1980s in the Looking Glass: PASOK and the Media," in Clogg, ed., *Greece, 1981–1989,* p. 125–135.
40. Quote: C. Lyrintzis, "PASOK in Power," p. 130.
41. P. Christofilopulou, "Professionalism and Public Policy-Making in Greece: The Influence of Engineers in the Local Government Reforms," in *Public Administration,* vol. 70 (spring 1992); C. Danopoulos, "Greek Bureaucracy and Public Administration," S. B. Thomadakis, "The Greek Economy: Performance, Expectations, and Paradoxes," p. 39–60.
42. "A Country on the Edge," in *The Economist,* vol. 335, n.7889 (22 May 1993), Special Insert, p. 1–19.
43. "Country Profiles, 1995," in *The Economist Newsletter* (January 1996).
44. S. Stearns, "Greek Security Issues," in Allison & Nicolaidis, eds., *The Greek Paradox,* p. 61–72.
45. Quote: Kyprianos, "Viewpoint: What to expect from Simitis."
46. Tsoukalis, "Beyond the Greek Paradox," p. 163–174.

THREE

Democratic Transitions: The Portuguese Case

Alfred G. Cuzán

The Portuguese régime change from dictatorship to democracy, set in motion by the April 1974 military coup and finalized with the 1982 and 1989 constitutional amendments, offers clues for answering contested questions about transitions to democracy. Among those questions are the following: Are there socio-economic prerequisites for democracy? What conditions facilitate subordination of the military to the new democracy's civilian authorities? Who are the parties to the agreement a democratic constitution represents? What is the relationship between market economy and democracy? What works best in new democracies: parliamentarism or presidentialism?

This chapter first examines the highlights of Portuguese political history with those questions in mind. The next section reviews the twentieth century's salient political features: the First Republic, 1910–26, when Portugal tried democracy for the first time; the Salazar-Caetano dictatorship, 1932–74, known as the Second Republic; and the transition and consolidation of democracy in the Third Republic, which, initially against heavy odds, has taken place in Portugal during the last quarter of a century. This is followed by an analytical section in which the failures of the First and the successes of the Third Republic are scrutinized to extract clues for answering the questions of the previous paragraph.

I. Highlights of Portuguese Political History

Portugal is probably Europe's oldest nation-state, having broken away from Spanish Castile in 1385. The Portuguese came again under Spanish domination for roughly a century beginning in the 1570s. In 1640 Duke João of Braganza declared independence from Spain, becoming King João IV, the first monarch of a dynasty that would reign for almost three centuries. But it took several decisive battles fought over some two decades before independence was finally secured, in 1665.[1]

For some three decades after the Napoleonic invasion, which the royal family sat out in Brazil, the country went through military coups and civil wars, the upshot of which was the adoption of a royal charter. Under the charter, the king still wielded extensive powers, more than any other monarch in Western Europe, including the power to dissolve parliament and rule by decrees under certain conditions. As the nineteenth century came to a close, the monarchy lost much of its legitimacy on account of its seeming inability to put the government on a sound financial footing or promote development at home or in the African colonies. Republicanism spread among the middle class, including much of the intelligentsia, bureaucracy, and, ominously for the monarchy, the armed forces. In 1908 King Carlos and his oldest son were assassinated on the streets of Lisbon. Less than two years after the regicide a rebellion of armed republican civilians, aided by non-commissioned officers and a few junior officers, broke out in the capital. The bulk of the military stayed on the sidelines, failing to come out in defense of the monarchy. After a few skirmishes, King Manuel II, aged 20, along with his mother, went into exile. Portugal's First Republic was declared with great fanfare. At the time, Portugal was Western Europe's poorest and least educated country, with 80 percent of the population illiterate.[2]

One of the first acts of the provisional government was to launch a frontal assault on the Roman Catholic Church. Much of its patrimony was confiscated, churches became state property, religious orders, including the Jesuits, were expelled, religious instruction, even in private schools, was banned, religious holidays were abolished, priests and nuns were forbidden to wear their habits in public, and even the times of religious worship came under state regulation. Many years later, when asked why the First Republic had fallen, Marcello Caetano, Portugal's second and last premier of the dictatorship (overthrown in 1974), cited the religious policy initially adopted as one of two reasons (the other reason he gave was a party system plagued by factionalism).

A Constitutional Assembly was elected under restricted suffrage, which included only literate males. Universal suffrage was rejected for fear that women and illiterates were susceptible to manipulation by the clergy and other forces of reaction (such as the monarchists). The principal issue dividing the Assembly was whether to constitute a parliamentary or a presidential system. After much wrangling, a parliamentary system, with a weak president elected by the assembly, was adopted. The president would in turn appoint the prime minister, the effective head of the government.

The parliamentary system proved to be very unstable, indeed the most unstable in Western Europe. Until the overthrow of the republic in 1926, there were 45 governments headed by 30 different prime ministers appointed by seven different presidents. The average life of a government was four months. Two governments were brought down by military coup and a constitutional change establishing a strong presidency elected by universal suffrage was imposed by a provisional *junta*, with opposition parties boycotting the election of President Sidonio Pais. Pais was assassinated one year later. Other political figures, including a prime minister, also met violent death, and one president and another prime minister independently chose voluntary exile. Between 3,000 and 5,000 people died during several outbreaks of street fighting during the life of the First Republic.

The immediate cause of the instability was the concentration of power in the national assembly, combined with one party's consistent winning of elections—the Democrats, which won six out of eight elections—its near monopoly over patronage, with which it rewarded not only its cadre and voters but also vigilante groups (known as the "White Ants"), which terrorized real or suspected monarchists and supporters of opposition parties. The asymmetry in power among the parties corrupted both the Democrats and their opposition, the former becoming arrogant and oppressive and the latter irresponsible to the point of egging on the military to bring down the government in the hope of capturing it for themselves. Another cause of instability was the cost of Portuguese involvement in World War I on the side of the British and French. The war was unpopular at home, where it contributed to skyrocketing inflation, and exposed Portugal's ill-equipped and badly trained military to humiliating defeats in the field of battle.

In 1926 a revolution by junior officers, known as the "Young Lieutenants," seized the government and dissolved the national assembly. By this time, the republic, like the monarchy it replaced, had few defenders left. As with the overthrow of the crown, the change was accomplished with little loss of blood. However, in a foreshadowing of what would happen in the 1970s, it proved easier for the military to overthrow a régime than to establish a new one on a stable footing. The same tendency to split into conflicting factions that plagued the First Republic afflicted the military, as well. In 1930, they turned the government over to Antonio Salazar, a former professor of law and economics from Coimbra University, who as the military government's minister of finance, had balanced the government budget for the first time in many years.

Salazar established a régime that would last for nearly half a century.[3] Sometimes mischaracterized as Fascist, the Salazar régime was a civilian dictatorship staffed by professors and lawyers, which exercised corporativist controls over labor and business. Unlike Fascist régimes, Salazar's "aim . . .

was depoliticization rather than mass mobilization within a single party seeking completely to identify with or to transcend the state."[4] Under Salazar, the military was at least nominally brought under civilian control by customarily electing as president a general or admiral hand-picked by Salazar who would in turn perform the constitutional duty of appointing the prime minister, a post always going to Salazar himself. However, the military enjoyed a great deal of institutional autonomy, and Salazar was careful to cultivate its support. Under Salazar, the privileges and properties of the Roman Catholic Church were partially restored (although the separation of Church and State enacted by the Republic was maintained). Also catered to by Salazar were small businesses and small farmers, who were granted certain protections from domestic and international competition. The press was censored, while the régime broadcast messages of patriotism, prudence and religion.

However, the régime was by no means totalitarian: opposition magazines and newspapers survived the dictatorship, and opposition organizations were allowed to contest elections for the National Assembly and, until 1958 (when a renegade military officer mounted a strong challenge to the official candidate), the presidency. The military was never rendered totally docile, however, there having taken place several coup attempts during the life of the régime. Still, a political police insured that recalcitrant opponents unwilling to live with the régime's political restrictions were jailed, exiled, or sometimes assassinated (the First Republic had abolished the death penalty, which was never restored). Ironically, the régime's suppression of opposition forces played into the hands of the one group with the ideology, internal organization, and external support capable of surviving, if not thriving under clandestine conditions: the Communist Party of Portugal (PCP).[5]

Salazar kept Portugal politically stable but also socially backward and economically poor. One of its main "exports" was human beings, who emigrated by the tens of thousands to greener pastures in Europe, Brazil, North America, and the African colonies. By 1974, approximately one in eight Portuguese resided abroad. Only during the last decade of the régime did Portugal experience exceptional economic growth, fueled by industrialization financed by foreign investment attracted by low wages and a construction boom stimulated by an inflow of tourists and émigré remittances. By the late 1960s Portugal was beginning to close the gap in per capita income with Spain, a trend that was reversed after the overthrow of the old régime.

In 1968, Salazar suffered an accident followed by a stroke, leaving him in a coma for over a year before he died in 1970. His successor, Marcello Caetano, also a professor, had the personality of "a follower, not a leader."[6] He promoted economic growth by easing some of the restrictions meant to protect small businesses from competition, a policy that dismayed a loyal constituency of the régime. He briefly flirted with political liberalization, satisfying neither the liberals, who thought the reforms did not go far enough, nor the *ultras,* or die-hard Salazarists.

But his biggest mistake was alienating the military. Since 1961, Portugal, having refused to follow the British and French into decolonization, had been fighting to retain its African empire, which included what is now Guinea Bissau, Angola and Mozambique. The war proved costly in terms of men and treasure. In the 1960s, 30 to 40 percent of the annual government budget was spent on the African war effort. By 1973, Portugal had 30 military personnel for every 1,000 inhabitants, one of the highest ratios in the world. A shortage of officers ensued. The government attempted to remedy the situation by making it easier to obtain battlefield commissions and promotions, something that outraged regular officers educated in the military academy who had waited years to rise slowly in the ranks. The controversy over the government's plan prompted some 200 professional officers, mostly in the middle ranks (captains and majors), to organize an Armed Forces Movement (MFA), ostensibly to address these personnel issues, but with larger political ends too.

The seemingly endless colonial wars had taken a toll on the military. A number of officers, including some high-ranking ones, came to the conclusion that the government's colonial policy was untenable and that the civilian leadership was indifferent to the sacrifices of the men in uniform. One of them, General Spinola, Governor of Guinea, had urged the government to grant greater autonomy to the colonies. Rebuffed in private, he published a book, *Portugal and the Future,* that was critical of the government's colonial policy. The book "shook the regime to its core."[7] Furthermore, a number of junior and middle-ranking officers became radicalized during their Africa tours. Sent to suppress guerrilla movements inspired by Marx, Lenin, Mao, "Che" Guevara, Castro, and other Third-World liberationists, they came to agree with their adversaries. These officers concluded that Portugal should not only grant its colonies independence, but go through a process of radical Third World–style "liberation" itself in which the army would take the leading role.

The MFA absorbed these various currents of military opinion and organized what turned into a bloodless overthrow of the dictatorship in April 1974. Caetano resigned in favor of General Spinola, whom the MFA, by now dominated by radical factions, was willing to accept as a temporary figurehead. Its program was summed up three "D's": decolonization, democracy, and development. The colonies were promised independence, elections for a constituent assembly were scheduled for no later than one year after the coup, and large properties in industry, agriculture, services, and banking, were slated for nationalization. The policies under the "D" of development were Socialist in nature, but proved counter-productive both economically and politically.

As with the First Republic, the initial euphoria soon evaporated. Portugal again plunged into chaotic, fierce factional infighting within the government and in the streets.[8] As the structures of the old régime were dismantled, a revolutionary situation ensued in which contingents of workers and peasants, some acting spontaneously, others in league with radical parties, took over factories, farms, buildings, and houses. MFA radicals working hand in glove with the Portuguese Communist Party, a Stalinist party that had endorsed the Soviet invasion of Czechoslovakia and rejected Euro-Communism, seized the initiative. In September they forced out General Spinola in favor of a more pliant figurehead. The PCP was granted unprecedented power over labor unions, the bureaucracy, agrarian policy and even foreign policy, where it facilitated the Soviet and Cuban intervention in Angola. Trade with Cuba increased several fold. After the revolutionary period, trade with the island declined to its previous level, which suggests that political, not economic, considerations had been behind the increase.

Not all MFA radicals were in league with the PCP, however. A military faction included officers who had come to view itself as a "national liberation movement" like those which, only a year or so earlier, had been combating in Africa. Some of them, as well as others, were "in day-to-day contact" with "small, but militant Marxist-Leninist and Maoist parties" to the Left of the PCP.[9] The spectrum of military opinion included non-radical shades, as well. One faction was sympathetic to the Socialists, led by Mario Soares. The Socialists are a Social-Democratic party member of the Socialist International, with good relations with English, German and Swedish parties, which came to their aid. Still another, smaller faction, was loyal to a reconstituted Right composed of two main parties, the Social Democratic Party (PSD; initially the Popular Democratic Party), which was founded by the liberal wing of the Caetano administration, and the Center Social Democrats (CDS). These democratic factions from the Center, Center-Left and Center-Right received aid from ideological counterparts outside of Portugal, including the Socialist International, the British Labor government and trade unions, and the CIA.[10] Finally, there was a rump of marginalized officers less concerned with partisan politics or economic ideology than with the interests of the military as a professional institution that should be autonomous in its domain.

Following Spinola's failure to stage a comeback in a botched coup in March 1975, the MFA radicals seized the opportunity to carry out another wave of expropriations and purge schools, universities, and other public institutions of "reactionary forces." More significantly, the MFA forced the parties poised to contest elections for the national assembly to sign a pact committing themselves to putting Portugal on a path to socialism and sharing power with two organs of the MFA: a General Assembly, which would act as a sort of second house of parliament, and a Council of the Revolution. This was a way of insuring "that the MFA political programme would be implemented regardless of any electoral results."[11] The parties were given 48 hours to read and sign the pact. Fearing that the elections would be cancelled unless they signed, the parties complied.

However, the April 1975 Constituent Assembly elections dealt the Communists and the MFA radicals a fatal blow. The Socialists came first, with 38 percent; the PSP second, with 25 percent; and the Communists only third, with less than 15 percent.[12]

Nevertheless, the outcome was in doubt through the summer, as the MFA radicals and their PCP allies attempted to circumvent the national assembly, carrying out additional expropriations and encouraging the taking over of the last independent newspaper, *La Republica,* as well as the Catholic radio station, by radical factions of employees. As during the First Republic, vigilante types (reminiscent of the "White Ants" of the First Republic) terrorized regime opponents. In fact, in an interview with an Italian journalist, Alvaro Cunhal, PCP general-secretary, confidently predicted that Portugal would never trade the revolutionary power of the streets for the electoral power of a parliamentary system.

What turned the tide was an anti-Communist backlash in the countryside, primarily in the north. Portugal is divided into two roughly equal parts by the Tagus River, at the estuary of which sits Lisbon. The north is a region of small proprietors and strong Catholic sentiment with a tradition for rebellion. It was here that Napoleon's occupation army encountered the fiercest resistance. Fearful that their land, too, would be confiscated by the State, and outraged at radical attacks on the Church, which warned of the threat of Communism, mobs sacked and burned PCP headquarters in at least 50 towns and villages, practically driving the party out of the region.[13]

The anti-Communist agitation in the north suggests that in the summer of 1975 the MFA was presented with a choice between backing down or sending an occupying army to subdue the region, a chancy prospect in any case, as it undoubtedly would have sparked a guerrilla war aided and abetted by exiles in Galicia, the neighboring northwestern Spanish province, linguistically close to Portugal. It would have been ironic indeed if the same military that had been motivated to overthrow Caetano, partly to end the war against African revolutionary guerrillas, had found itself waging a war against home-grown, counter-revolutionary guerrillas in Portugal itself. Had the military been of one Leftist mind, it might have taken the gamble. But it was not. If anything, the army was in danger of disintegrating, as units began to declare competing political allegiances and others mutinied. In September 1975 a Leftist faction of the military revolted but was suppressed under the command of General Antonio Eanes (elected president of Portugal less than a year later).

Following the suppression of the Leftist rebellion and the ousting of other radical officers from the government, a slow-motion counter-revolution got underway. A new pact between the parliamentary parties and the MFA reduced, but did not eliminate, the latter's role. It did away with the MFA General Assembly and provided for an elected president of the republic. However, it retained the prohibition against even amending the constitution so as to allow the reversing of the nationalizations of property carried out by the MFA in the previous two years. Also retained was the "Council of the Revolution," composed of 20 self-appointed officers who would advise the president on issues of national interest, legislate on all military matters, and pass on the constitutionality of parliamentary legislation to ensure that it would not reverse the "conquests of the revolution."

The constitution adopted in 1976 established a mixed system, with an elected president and an elected parliament. The president is elected for a five-year term and may stand for reelection once. Initially, the president was made chairman of the Council of the Revolution and chairman of the General Staff of the Armed Forces. The constitution included a commitment to socialism and a classless society, and similar Marxist-style phrases. Most significantly, Article 83 stipulated that the nationalizations carried out in the previous two years were irreversible conquests of the revolution and could not be undone.[14]

The 1976 elections, the first under the new constitution, again yielded a plurality for the Socialists, and Mario Soares was elected premier, or head of government. The presidential election was won handily by General Eanes, supported by the Socialists and the parties of the Right, the PSD and CSD. During his first term (he was reelected in 1981), General Eanes restored hierarchy and discipline to the military. Under his leadership, too, the military was reduced in size and its mission reoriented towards NATO.

For the next decade politics was reduced to a series of parallel struggles between parliament and president, between parliament and the military, and between the PSD and the Socialists. The first two struggles were won by parliament. In 1980 the PSD government obtained a legislative majority in favor of a bill providing for the privatization of nationalized banks. However, this was vetoed by the Council of the Revolution. Two years later, in the teeth of vehement opposition from President Eanes, the military, and the PCP, which organized two general strikes, the PSD, CSD, and Socialists joined forces in Parliament to amend the constitutional text by the required two-thirds majority so as to do away with the Council of the Revolution, establishing a Council of State advisory to the president and a thirteen-member Constitutional Court charged with vetting bills and reviewing laws for constitutionality. The amendment also curbed presidential powers, including the power to dismiss the government at will. The three parties again joined forces to override President Eanes' veto of a National Security Law, putting the military under effective control of the parliamentary government. A subsequent compromise provided for a sharing of appointments and removals of members of the general staff and top command posts between president and government. In 1989, another agreement between the Socialists and the PSD resulted in a second set of constitutional amendments allowing for the privatization of the nationalized properties and excising from the constitutional text all Marxist-style phraseology about socialism and the classless society. Article 83, which had prohibited future parliaments from amending the constitution so as to reverse the so-called conquests of the revolution, was unceremoniously dropped.[15]

As to the struggles between the parties, having won the 1979 election, the leader of the PSD argued in favor of a two-step process for constitutional revision that would require a parliamentary majority and popular ratification of all amendments. To this the Socialist Party would not consent. In 1982 the PSD wanted to revise the constitution both in its political and economic aspects, but the Socialists only went along with the political amendments that eliminated the Council of the Revolution. It was not until 1989 that the Socialists signed off on the economic amendments.

The two parties have been the main contenders in parliamentary and presidential elections. The Socialists have been more successful in presidential contests, having won three consecutive elections since 1986, while the PSD, which has yet to win a presidential election, has done better in parliament, having controlled the government either solely or in alliance with the CDS for all but two years between 1980 and 1995. In 1996, for the first time since the establishment of the Third Republic in 1976, president and premier are both from the same party, the Socialists.

II. What the Portuguese Case Suggests about Democratic Transitions

Transitology, or the study of transitions towards democracy, has wrestled with a number of important questions of both scholarly and practical interest, such as whether there are pre-conditions for democracy and what factors contribute to democratic consolidation and stability. The following sections scrutinize the Portuguese case in search of clues for answering such questions.

A. Pre-requisites for Democracy

Among the prerequisites for democracy that have been considered or suggested by, among others, Huntington, Lipset, Murphy and Neubauer[16] are those having to do with the level of literacy in the population and, relatedly, the density of the country's system of communications; ethnic, cultural, and religious homogeneity; minimal economic development; a culture that supports the values of constitutional democracy; a military and internal security apparatus not adamantly opposed to democracy; the contesting of elections by at least two mass-based political parties; and economic performance under the fledgling democratic government.

The Portuguese case suggests that the threshold of socio-economic development a country must cross before democracy can be established or sustained is rather modest. Portugal has had two experiences with democracy in 1910–26 and from 1976 to the present. In both the first and the start of the second period, Portugal was Western Europe's poorest and least literate country. Some might hold that fact at least partly responsible for the collapse of the First Republic. But it is not clear how illiteracy contributed to that, since illiterates were excluded from voting in most elections, precisely for fear that they would vote in favor of clerical and monarchist parties. Perhaps, had the suffrage been expanded to include them, elections during the First Republic would have yielded more conservative governments less willing to carry out those social and economic reforms that Di Palma advises would-be crafters of new democracies to avoid.[17]

Regarding the current period, at the time of the revolution Portugal was the poorest country in Western Europe. In 1975 life expectancy was 65 for males, the second lowest in all of Europe after Albania. In 1981, illiteracy was 21 percent of the total population (25 percent for females), the highest in all of Europe, bar none. As for the country's communication system, around 1974 there were only 11 telephones per 100 inhabitants; in 1980 there were fewer than 200 television sets per 1,000 inhabitants; and daily circulation of newspapers was 47 per 1,000 inhabitants. All these ratios are less than 20 percent the U.S. rate. In short, as Manuel puts it, "Even on 23 July 1976, when Portugal instituted a democratic system, the country did not 'measure' up on any of the modernization 'democratic' indicators in education, literacy, attitudes and industrialization."[18]

Thus, it seems that, while it may be true that some socio-economic threshold needs crossing before democratic crafting can succeed, the Portuguese case suggests that threshold may be fairly low. Indeed, Huntington sets it at a GNP per capita of $1,000 (in 1988 dollars). But even this constraint may not be rigid. Reflecting on the Portuguese case, Bruneau concludes that "[c]ontinuing underdevelopment may not be a good basis for liberal democracy, but it does not preclude it. There is much more involved that relates to political institutions."[19] The case of Costa Rica, Latin America's premier democracy, suggests likewise.

Regarding ethnic homogeneity, the Portuguese are one of the most homogeneous ethnic and linguistic peoples in the world. Roman Catholicism is by far the dominant religion. Yet, the country has experienced many civil wars, large and small, fought over ideological divisions. One of these, the rift between clericals and anti-clericals, contributed to the instability and final breakdown of the First Republic. It probably also led to greater support from Catholics for the Salazar régime than would otherwise have been forthcoming. By the 1980s, after the country had lived through a 50-year old dictatorship of the Right, and survived a revolutionary period in which the threat from a Communist and military Left loomed large, democracy appears to have gained wider acceptance among élites and the public alike. This suggests ideological cleavages trump ethnic and linguistic homogeneity. It is not social homogeneity but ideological consensus, i.e., widespread agreement about the political system and the scope of public policy, that is necessary for democracy. If this is lacking, as it was during the First Republic, ethnic and linguistic homogeneity count very little.

As for a culture that supports constitutional democracy, Portugal did have about a century of parliamentarism, first under the constitutional monarchy, then under the First Republic. But under the monarchy it was more of a parliamentary oligarchy and during the First Republic the suffrage was limited to 20 percent or so of the adult population, so the democracy had a narrow social base. Moreover, during the First Republic the behavior of parliamentarians in and out of the chamber was extremely uncivil. And for some half a century before the 1974 military coup, Portugal was under dictatorial rule. Nevertheless, the absence of a democratic culture did not prevent the establishment and apparent consolidation of democracy there in the last two decades. This suggests that democratic institutions may themselves produce a democratic culture where there is none.

B. Taming the Military

Concerning the military, Portugal has a tradition of *pronunciamientos,* or military uprisings in the name of a political program, dating at least as far back as the beginning of the nineteenth century. But its interventions have not been ideologically consistent, sometimes being in favor of liberalism, reform, or even radicalism, and other times in favor of authoritarianism or reaction. Once in power, the military has tended to fracture into contending factions. Both Salazar and the current democratic system were successful at subordinating the military to civilian control. In 1976, the democratic parties borrowed a page from Salazar's book, backing for president a senior military officer who would reinstate military discipline. Subsequently, the three principal democratic parties were able to present a united front in parliament vis-à-vis the very president whom they had helped elect. Two other measures helped in subordinating the military to parliament: a drastic reduction in the size of the military (under 70,000 in 1993, it was less than one-fourth the 1974 peak) and its integration into NATO. While reducing the size of the military is a measure which any democracy can adopt, the option to join NATO remains unavailable to new democracies outside Europe.[20]

The democrats' success in subordinating the military to civilian authority may be due, above all, to a stable political party system, which includes four main parties, each with an apparently secure political base.[21] Each succeeding election has essentially boiled down to a contest between two mass-based parties, the Left-of-Center Socialists and the Right-of-Center Social-Democrats, each of which has attained, if for a limited period, an absolute majority in parliament. During a brief period, the two parties formed a grand alliance. It may be that, when the two dominant political parties, their other policy differences notwithstanding, join in a common front to subordinate the soldiers to civilian authority, the military is brought to heel.

C. Democracy and Economic Efficacy

According to Lipset, disappointing economic performance saps the legitimacy of democracy.[22] If this is the case, then a fledgling democracy would be particularly vulnerable to economic downturns. However, this did not happen to Portugal. During the last decade of the old régime, Portugal was closing the gap with its Iberian neighbor: the ratio of Portuguese to Spanish per capita GNP peaked in 1973 at 69 percent. After the coup the trend reversed, with the ratio dropping below 50 percent under the impact of expropriations, nationalizations and the fear of Communism. In the 1990s the ratio has begun to recover, although as recently as 1993 it was lower than it had been in 1970. Thus, for nearly two decades the economy continued to underperform. This was one of the unwelcome legacies of the "Carnations' Revolution." It was not until the mid 1990s that the country resumed robust economic growth. Presently, it is once again gaining on its Spanish neighbor.

If Lipset is right, then Portugal's success in transitioning to and consolidating democracy during two decades of economic disappointment makes it an exceptional case. Either prosperity is less important for democratic consolidation than Lipset believes, or the relationship is mediated by contextual factors, such as who is to blame for the hardships. After all, it was not an elected government but a self-appointed military vanguard, working hand-in-glove with the Communist Party, that adopted the policies that drove the economy into the ground. It took years of political bargaining to build the parliamentary consensus necessary to overcome the military's opposition to reversing the bitter-tasting "conquests of the revolution." Thus, it is not unreasonable to assume that Portuguese voters, even as they held presidents and prime ministers accountable for economic conditions during their terms in office, did not blame democracy itself for their troubles. If so, they are now reaping the fruits of their perseverance.

D. Relationship between Democracy and the Market

Walter Murphy asks, "Does constitutional democracy need to be joined with a market economy?" Lipset answers yes.[23] The Portuguese case suggests that the democratic parties, from Center-Left to Center-Right, agree. Putting aside partisan differences, they enacted constitutional amendments that reversed the MFA-imposed constitutional provisions that committed the country to Socialism and a classless society and prohibited future parliaments from privatizing the nationalized properties. During the last several years, Portugal has begun to privatize those state enterprises, raising revenues for the government in the process.

Portugal's simultaneous pursuit of democracy and a market economy flies in the face of Elster's "impossibility" theorem.[24] He argues that to carry out reforms on both fronts involves several interdependencies that cannot be obtained simultaneously. To cite only two, privatization aggravates inequalities, which goes against the democratic grain, and the elimination of price controls sparks mass protests organized by labor unions and other constituencies, which intimidate vote-conscious political parties into backing down. The Portuguese case shows that, indeed, privatizations are opposed by certain groups, such as the PCP, capable of mobilizing tens of thousands of protesters to take to the streets. But, contra Elster, it is possible for the political parties bent on privatization to weather the storm and stay the course of privatization, as Portuguese governments have done.

E. The Constitution as a Pact

Who are "the parties to the agreement a constitution represents. Is the 'constitution' of a constitutional democracy a covenant *among* a people? *Between* a people and their rulers? Both?"[25] While these classical conceptions of constitutional democracy may help us understand earlier instances of democracy, the Portuguese case suggests still another possibility: that in contemporary times a constitution is, among other things, *a compact among political parties.* Election to the 1975 Portuguese constituent assembly was by party lists, so all members of the assembly were party members. Similarly, all constitutional amendments have been enacted by a two-thirds vote of the national assembly, a ratio obtained only by agreement among two or more parties in parliament. Interestingly, in 1979, having won the election but lacking a two-thirds majority, the PSD wanted to enact constitutional amendments in a two-step process consisting of a majority vote in parliament followed by popular ratification in a referendum. However, the Socialists, presumably the most "democratic" and "progressive" of the parties, balked (as did then-President Eanes), seemingly desirous of preserving the inter-party nature of the compact.

F. Parliamentary vs. Presidential Democracy

The hypothesis that parliamentary systems are more conducive to democratic stability than presidential systems has received a good deal of scholarly support recently, although Lipset demurs.[26] It is said that the winner-take-all presidential system is inferior to the parliamentary system at incorporating and balancing a wide range of interests, particularly those of small but passionate minorities, which, shut out from the winner-take-all presidential system, are less loyal to the democratic regime. Presidential systems are alleged to be polarizing, divisive, and rigid, less able to strike delicate balances among conflicting interests. Indeed, comparative and historical evidence suggests that parliamentary systems are longer-lived[27] and suffer less from political violence[28] than presidential systems. Drawing on the Spanish experience, Linz offers a counter-factual hypothesis in favor of parliamentarism: "There can be no doubt that in the Spain of 1977, a presidential election would have been far more divisive than the parliamentary elections that actually occurred. . . . Spanish politics since Franco has clearly felt the moderating influence of parliamentarism; without it, the transition to popular government and the consolidation of democratic rule would probably have taken a far different—and much rougher—course."[29]

Still, such apparent exceptions as the increase in political stability in France from the Fourth to the Fifth Republic, which incorporated a strong presidency in a hybrid system, not to mention the United States, stand out. Portugal may turn out to be another exception. The First Republic began as a parliamentary system with a nominal president. The ensuing chaos, however, led to a *de facto* constitutional change, shifting greater authority to a president. It was as if, during the First Republic, a balance between presidentialism and parliamentarism was being sought. The lesson was not lost by the crafters of the present constitution, which provided for a mixed system of president and parliament.[30] This resulted in a struggle for power between the two branches, a contest that, by the mid 1990s, had apparently been won by the legislature. However, this may turn out to have been but one swing of the pendulum, driven in that direction by special circumstances associated with the Third Republic's first two presidents. The first president, General Eanes, was a military man without a party base. The two major parties, seated in parliament, coalesced against him. And the second president, Mario Soares, had to contend with a parliament in which his party, the Socialists, were in the minority. Whether a shift in the opposite direction, towards greater presidential power, will follow, now that since 1996 both branches are under the Socialists' control, remains to be seen.

What is clear, however, is that the present hybrid system has apparently succeeded where the First Republic definitely did not. To be sure, a host of other variables have also taken different values in the interim. Nevertheless, it cannot be ruled out that the institution of the presidency has been a stabilizing force in Portugal. Between 1976 and 1996, General Eanes and Mario Soares each served two consecutive five-year terms, having been re-elected to a second term by a wide margin. That Portugal has had only one president per decade, it may be argued, has lent ballast to a ship of state that was being buffeted by strong gusts of discontent and frustrated ambitions left in the wake of the revolutionary upheavals of the 1970s. Presidential continuity has also acted as a corrective to relatively short-lived governments, the average tenure until recently being seven to eight months.[31] The office even seems to have had a moderating effect on the persona of the incumbent: Mario Soares, who as prime minister displayed a partisan, combative style, as president "gradually assumed the mantle of a constitutional monarch and a symbol of unity. Rather than using his office to crusade in favor of Socialism, as some had suspected, he settled for the role of a nonpartisan, establishment figure and became known affectionately as *Rei Mario* (King Mario)."[32] The performance of the presidency vis-à-vis parliament has been such as to lead one scholar to conclude that Portugal's constitution ought to be amended in the direction of presidentialism.[33] Thus, Portugal offers a sober counter-example, which enthusiasts of the parliamentary system need to take into account.

III. Conclusions

Portugal's transition demonstrates that a relatively poor country, with no prior experience with mass democracy, can emerge from 50 years of dictatorship, go through a chaotic period of revolution and counter-revolution, and still succeed in consolidating democracy. It also suggests that democracy and the market go together and, furthermore, that Socialism and democracy are incompatible. It seems that the wholesale nationalization of property can only be carried out and sustained by force of arms. From the point of view of a committed Socialist, elections are "reactionary," i.e., they produce parliamentary majorities favoring a return to the market. Finally, Portugal casts doubt on the notion that parliamentarism is always superior to presidentialism. As a statistical generalization, it may be true that parliamentary systems have a longer life and are less subject to political violence than presidential systems. But it is a long way from a statistical generalization to a policy prescription. When it comes to the actual crafting of institutions, contextual and historical contingencies become paramount. Portugal's hybrid régime, like France's, suggests that the presidency can be a stabilizing check to permutable parliamentary governments.

Notes

1. David Birmingham, *A Concise History of Portugal* (Cambridge: Cambridge University Press, 1993).

2. On the First Republic see Douglas L. Wheeler, *Republican Portugal: A Political History, 1910–1926* (Madison, WI: The University of Wisconsin Press, 1978); R. A. H. Robinson, *Contemporary Portugal. A History* (London: George Allen & Unwin, 1979).

3. Lawrence S. Graham, *The Portuguese Military and the State: Rethinking Transitions in Europe and Latin America* (Boulder, CO: Westview Press, 1993); Paul Christopher Manuel, *Uncertain Outcome. The Politics of the Portuguese Transition to Democracy* (Lanham, MD: University Press of America, 1995); Kenneth Maxwell, *The Making of Portuguese Democracy* (Cambridge: Cambridge University Press, 1995); Walter C. Opello Jr., *Portugal: From Monarchy to Pluralist Democracy* (Boulder, CO: Westview Press, 1991); Robinson, *Contemporary Portugal;* Paul Christopher Manuel, "Portuguese Civil Society under Dictatorship and Democracy, 1910–1996," in *Perspectives on Political Science,* vol. 27, no. 3 (1998): p. 142 ff.

4. Robinson, *Contemporary Portugal,* p. 52.

5. Carlos Cunha, *The Portuguese Communist Party's Strategy for Power, 1921–1986* (New York & London: Garland Publishing, 1992).

6. Maxwell, *Making of Portuguese Democracy,* p. 41.

7. Ibid., p. 32.

8. On the revolutionary period and subsequent reaction, see Nancy Bermeo, *The Revolution within the Revolution. Workers' Control in Rural Portugal* (Princeton: Princeton University Press, 1986); Martin Kayman, *Revolution and Counter-Revolution in Portugal* (London & Wolfeboro, NH: Merlin Press, 1987); Phil Mailer, *Portugal: The Impossible Revolution?* (Montréal: Black Rose Books, 1977); Audrey Wise, *Eyewitness in Revolutionary Portugal* (Nottingham: Spokesman Books, 1975); Cunha, *Portuguese Communist Party;* Manuel, *Uncertain Outcomes;* Maxwell, *Making of Portuguese Democracy;* Opello, *Portugal;* Robinson, *Contemporary Portugal.*

9. Maxwell, *Making of Portuguese Democracy,* p. 119.

10. On foreign support for one or the other of the main Portuguese protagonists, see the memoirs of the British Foreign Secretary: James Callahan, *Time and Chance* (London: Collins, 1987). See also: Rainer Eisfeld, "Influencias Externas sobre a Revolução Portuguesa: O Papel da Europa Ocidental," in Eduardo

de Sousa Ferreira & Walter C. Opello Jr., eds., *Conflitos e Mudanças em Portugal, 1974–1984* (Lisbon: Editorial Teorema, 1985), p. 79–99.

11. Hugo Gil Ferreira & Michael W. Marshall, *Portugal's Revolution: Ten Years On* (Cambridge: Cambridge University Press, 1986), p. 46.

12. Cesar Oliveira, "Transiçao e Consolidaçao da Democracia em Portugal," in *Pensamiento Iberoamericano*, no. 14 (1988): p. 300; Maxwell, *Making of Portuguese Democracy*, p. 112–113. Be it noted that the PCP's popularity has not increased in the intervening two decades. In the most recent parliamentary elections, held in 1995, the communists, in alliance with the Portuguese Greens, pulled less than 10 percent of the popular vote. See Agora's Elections Around the World website, http://www.agora.stm.it/elections/election/country/pt.htm.

13. Kayman, *Revolution and Counter-Revolution;* Mailer, *Portugal: The Impossible Revolution?;* Maxwell, *Making of Portuguese Democracy;* Wise, *Eyewitness in Revolutionary Portugal.*

14. On the politics of Portuguese constitution-making, see the collection of essays in Kenneth R. Maxwell & Scott C. Monje, eds., *Portugal: The Constitution and the Consolidation of Democracy, 1976–1989* (New York: Columbia University, Camoes Center Special Report No. 2, 1990).

15. On the political struggles between the two branches, see David Corkill, "The Political System and the Consolidation of Democracy in Portugal," in *Parliamentary Affairs,* vol. 46, no. 4 (1993): p. 517–533; David Corkill, "The Portuguese Presidential Election of 13 January 1991," in *West European Politics,* vol. 14, no. 4 (1991): p. 185–192; Francisco Pinto Balsemao, "The Constitution and Politics: Options for the Future," in Kenneth Maxwell, ed., *Portugal in the 1980s: Dilemmas of Democratic Consolidation* (Westport, CT: Greenwood Press, 1986), p. 197–232; Carlos Gaspar, "O Proceso Constitucional e a Estabilidade do Regime," *Analise Social,* vol. XXV, no. 1–2 (1990): p. 9–29. Graham, *Portuguese Military;* Maxwell & Monje, *Portugal: the Constitution;* Oliveira, *Tranciçao.*

16. Samuel p. Huntington, "Democracy's Third Wave," in *Journal of Democracy,* vol. 2, no. 2 (1991): p. 12–34; Seymour Martin Lipset, "The Social Requisites of Democracy Revisited," in *American Sociological Review,* vol. 59, no. 1 (1994): p. 1–22; Deane E. Neubauer, "Some Conditions of Democracy," in *American Political Science Review,* vol. 61 (1967): p. 1002–1009; Walter F. Murphy, "Constitutional Democracy," photocopy, 1996. The Murphy photocopy is the syllabus for a National Endowment for the Humanities Summer Seminar for College Teachers, which he directed at Princeton University.

17. Giuseppe Di Palma, *To Craft Democracies* (Berkeley: University of California Press, 1990).

18. Manuel, *Uncertain Outcome,* p. 3; Giulio Sapelli, *Southern Europe since 1945. Tradition and Modernity in Portugal, Spain, Italy, Greece and Turkey* (London: Longman, 1995).

19. Thomas C. Brueneau, "Portugal's Unexpected Transition," in Kenneth Maxwell & Michael H. Haltzel, eds., *Portugal: Ancient Country, Young Democracy*

(Washington: Wilson Center Press), p. 14. The case of Costa Rica, Latin America's premier democracy, suggests likewise: in 1974, 25 years after the establishing of democracy there infant mortality was higher and the number of telephones per 100 inhabitants less than half of Portugal's.

20. Portugal's experience, however, suggests a justification for NATO's eastward expansion that has nothing to do with defense against Russia, namely, to promote the subordination of the military to parliamentary control in the formerly Communist-ruled countries of Eastern Europe.

21. Joaquim Aguiar, "The Hidden Fluidity in an Ultra-Stable Party System," in Ferreira & Opello, *Conflitos e Mudanças*, p. 101–127. See also Daniel Nataf, *Democratization and Social Settlements. The Politics of Change in Contemporary Portugal* (Albany: State University of New York Press, 1995).

22. Lipset, *Social Requisites*, p. 17. On the relationship between economic conditions and government popularity in Portugal from the mid-1980's to the mid-1990's, see Linda Rosa Fonseca Gonçalves Veiga, "Popularity Functions for the Portuguese Prime Minister, Government, Parliament, and President," in *European Journal of Political Research*, no. 33 (1988): p. 347–361.

23. Murphy, *Constitutional Democracy*, p. 3; Lipset, *Social Requisites*, p. 3.

24. Jon Elster, "The Necessity and Impossibility of Simultaneous Economic and Political Reform," in Douglas Greenberg, Stanley N. Katz et alia, eds., *Constitutionalism and Democracy. Transitions in the Contemporary World* (New York & Oxford: Oxford University Press, 1993), p. 267–274.

25. Murphy, *Constitutional Democracy*, p. 41.

26. For forceful arguments against presidentialism see: Juan Linz, "The Perils of Presidentialism," in *Journal of Democracy*, vol. 1, no. 1 (1990): p. 51–69; Arturo Valenzuela, "The Crisis of Presidentialism," in *Journal of Democracy*, vol. 4, no. 4 (1993): p. 3–16. Lipset, *Social Requisites*, doubts that the case for presidentialism is all that strong.

27. Adam Przeworski et alia, "What Makes Democracy Endure?" in *Journal of Democracy*, vol. 7, no. 1 (1996): p. 39–55.

28. Arend Lijphart, *Democracy in Plural Societies: A Comparative Exploration* (New Haven, CT: Yale University Press, 1977).

29. Linz, *Perils of Presidentialism*, p. 59–60.

30. Tom Gallagher, "Democracy in Portugal since the 1974 Revolution," in Ferreira & Opello, *Conflitos e Mudanças*, p. 61–78.

31. Aguiar, *Hidden Fluidity*, p. 103.

32. Corkill, *Portuguese Presidential Elections*, p. 186.

33. Pinto Balsemao, *Constitution and Politics*.

FOUR

Neo-Liberal *Renovación,* Democratic Transition, and Fragmentation: The Fall of Spain's Socialist Hegemony

Anthony N. Celso

"They are no longer in the same family as the Left."[1]

The March 1996 electoral defeat of the Spanish Socialists may have some profound ramifications for the political Left outside of Spain. The Spanish Socialist Workers Party (PSOE) was viewed in the popular press and by leading academic observers as a model that other Social Democratic parties should emulate. The Socialists' pragmatic, centrist policies and their courting of the middle class and the business community seemed to secure four straight electoral victories. The PSOE, in effect, would dominate Spain's electoral landscape throughout its recent democratic period. The Socialist government's neo-Liberal, free-market policies, however, would contribute to severe internal divisions within the PSOE in the 1990s, compromising its hegemonic political status and contributing mightily to its 1996 defeat. What is surprising about the Spanish case is the rapidity and scale of the Socialist Party's organizational and ideological collapse in the mid 1990s after so much startling success.

The PSOE's stunning victory in the 1982 general election, and the Socialist's subsequent electoral triumphs in the 1986, 1989, and 1993 elections coincided with the general weakness and disarray of its competitors. The Spanish Communist Party, once considered to be the dominant force on the Spanish Left and a prime candidate to govern Spanish society in the post-Franco era disintegrated because of severe ideological and organizational problems. On the Right, the Popular Party had been notably unsuccessful in convincing the electorate that it had severed its Francoist legacy. The political disarray and ideological extremism of the Socialist's main adversaries contrasted strikingly with the PSOE's moderate, pragmatic image and tight centralized direction. Under the leadership of Felipe González and Alfonso Guerra, the PSOE embarked on a strategy of philosophical and organizational renovation that would broaden the Socialist's electoral appeal beyond its traditional working class base, isolate its left-wing, and ensconce the PSOE firmly in the electoral center of the Spanish body politic.

The Socialists' organizational structure in the 1970s and 1980s also played a role in securing its dominant position. The embryonic nature of the PSOE's organizational apparatus and its relatively low ratio of party members to voters, presented ample opportunities for upward mobility and central direction within the party. The leadership's allocation of patronage during the PSOE's formative growth years of the late 1970s, and the subsequent creation of a dependent party cadre, would set the stage for centralism within the PSOE during the González-Guerra period. Under the PSOE's organizational rules, which Paul Heywood has characterized as introducing a form of democratic centralism, member disobedience to the leadership can be punished with expulsion.[2]

The Socialists' reputation for efficient management was enhanced by its policy behavior and the technocratic, neo-Liberal image of successive González governments throughout the 1980s. Several cabinet ministers (Narcis Serra, Miguel Boyer and, above all, Carlos Solchaga) gained reputations as "modernizers" who were more concerned with growth than redistribution. The Socialist's courting of the international business community and their commitment to the European Community's open-market arrangement underscored the PSOE's ideological mutability and pragmatic sense. Accordingly, the González period would emphasize policies of monetarist austerity and industrial and financial policies that would strengthen, not weaken, the economic power of domestic and foreign capitalists.

The central direction of the PSOE's organizational structure and its neo-Liberal policies have been hailed as core elements in the party's political success in the 1980s and early 1990s.[3] The Socialist's organizational centralism and neo-Liberal ideology reflected a strategic calculation by the leadership in the late 1970s that the general weakening of Leftist ideologies, the constellation of power in the Spanish party system, and the need to broaden the party's electoral base to include large segments of the middle class, did necessitate a broad "renovation" of party practice and philosophy.

Usually discussed in terms of the Left's search for a new political-economic model, "renovation" implies that the old Social-Democratic model is no longer viable in an international post-Fordist society.[4] The renovation debate turns on the utility of expanding the welfare state and on the propriety of the a party-working class mobilization model: the former is viewed as excessively inflationary, while the latter is mitigated by the decline of the industrial workforce and the rise of the service sector.

Since its traditional constituency and policies are viewed as antiquated by many, the democratic Left should search for alternative operating principles and solutions. Within a general framework, renovation may imply a shift to the right, embracing the market, utilizing incentives for private sector growth, and reorienting party organization to include the salaried middle class, or it may portend a tilt to the Left, with concomitant emphasis on ecological issues and the incorporation of new social movements (feminists, pacifists, environmentalists) into the Socialist fold.

The PSOE began its renovation debate long before most Social-Democratic parties and its process of *renovación* has proceeded quite rapidly. During the late 1980s and 1990s the renovation process stalled and backfired on the PSOE. The days of robust economic growth and foreign investment during the mid 1980s have given way to recession, high unemployment and increased labor militancy. Consequently, fragmentation surfaced in the party's organizational structure over the social and equity implications of the González government's pursuit of a neoliberal agenda in the early 1990s. Factions within the party would call for more intra-party democracy and debate within the PSOE over the political trajectory of the Socialist's neo-Liberal model.

The Socialists' electoral fortunes and political standing underwent a profound transformation in the 1990s. The first signs of the party's erosion came with its slim electoral victories in the 1989 and 1993 elections, with the latter denying the PSOE an outright parliamentary majority. Exacerbating the Socialists' political standing would be the confluence of strong internal dissension within the PSOE's ranks, the rise of a non-Socialist Leftist coalition, and a series of corruption scandals that would force prominent government ministers and PSOE officials to resign. The refusal of the Catalán nationalists to honor their parliamentary pact with the PSOE government at the end of 1995, a reaction to the spectacular corruption allegations against the government, forced González to call an early election. The results of the March 1996 election, marking a first-time victory of the Rightist Popular Party, confirmed the end of Socialist political ascendancy in Spain.

This chapter is concerned with the PSOE's *renovación* campaign and its contribution to the Socialists' 1996 electoral defeat. In particular, the study is driven by several lines of inquiry. Firstly, what was the impetus and motivation for the renovation of the PSOE? Secondly, why did party élites choose a renovation model based on party democratic centralism and neoliberal ideology? Thirdly, what were the political costs associated with a Rightist renovation model and to what extent did it contribute to the Socialist fall from grace in March 1996? And, finally, what can theories on democratization and Social-Democratic parties tell us about the decline and potential rebirth of the Spanish Socialists.

I. The Gonzalez-Guerra Party Machine and the de-Marxianization of Spain's Socialism

". . . the party has an obligation to be a source of tranquility for society." [5]

The end of Franco's 36-year-old dictatorship in 1975 and the subsequent rapidity of the Center-Right's democratization in Spain would effect the bargaining power and position of the anti-Francoist forces. Donald Share has labeled the transfer of power in Spain as involving a process of "transactive democratization" where remnants of the Francoist régime determined the pace, scope, and institutional character of Spain's democratic opening.[6] Under this process, the Left could refuse to negotiate with the right (i.e., seek a clean break with the old order) or it could work under the rules, processes, and institutions specified by Franco's successors. The speed of the democratization process and the embryonic nature of Leftist political organization (both the Communists and the Socialists were outlawed during the Franco period) worked in favor of cooperation. The Left, having been locked out of power for practically a generation, looked at the prospect of attaining power, even under terms dictated by the Right, as too promising of an opportunity.

Prime Minister Suarez's dismemberment of Franco's political infrastructure and his democratization efforts in the mid 1970s would trigger a power struggle between three different socialist factions. During the Franco dictatorship, the Socialists experienced severe divisions characterized by the simultaneous development of three competing factions: the 1930s Popular Front veterans, still exiled in Paris, and the emergence of two clandestine factions in Spain. In the 1960s and 1970s the historic PSOE, because of its remoteness and its geriatric leadership, began to wither, while the indigenous Socialist movements grew in strength. The most populous of these factions, anchored in the Sevillian student protest movement, represented important elements in the Spanish new Left. The group's leadership, Felipe González and Alfonso Guerra, were young, charismatic, and determined not to temper their revolutionary zeal by accepting the Right's proposed electoral institutions. Their main rivals, a Madrid-based group of Christian-Democratic lawyers and intellectuals, rejected the anti-clericalism of the Left and were eager to accept the democratization initiatives of the Center-Right government.[6]

The Right's democratization proposals were apprehensively received by the Spanish Left: the Communists and the Sevillian Socialists initially rejected a political dialogue with Franco's successors and demanded general elections and the restoration of democracy. Their refusal to cooperate, however, became impractical over time as the proliferation of new parties on the Left, who were eager to accept power-sharing arrangements, threatened the Communists and Socialists with political extinction.

González and Guerra responded to Prime Minister Suarez's democratization efforts with a two-pronged strategy. On an internal level, ideological recruitment and mobilization of the party's rank and file would be furthered by deepening the PSOE's commitment to Marxist ideology. This intensification of the Socialists' Leftist identity would act as a locus of support for recruitment of new members. The embryonic nature of the PSOE's party organization, which promised rapid upward mobility and access to jobs for the party faithful, and a strict majoritarian voting scheme within the party's federal and regional committees, helped insure that the leadership would maintain tight control. Externally, González and Guerra reversed their initial position and, in 1975, entered into a political dialogue with Suarez. Within the party, a division of leadership roles occurred with Secretary-General González acting as the party's chief spokesman and symbol of moderation, while Vice Secretary-General Guerra governed organizational matters with a firm hand and enforced ideological norms on the rank and file. The González-Guerra strategy of internal radicalization and external moderation paid substantial political dividends: ideological intensification attracted a mass following and pragmatism enhanced the PSOE's leverage in constructing arrangements that would govern the country.

The pace of internal developments and the mobilization of party activists in the party would accelerate the PSOE's Leftist direction. During the mid 1970s the party's leadership openly avowed neo-Marxist themes, which departed sharply from the Social-Democratic ethos of previous PSOE leaders. Leftist ideology was most visibly demonstrated in the PSOE's 1976 conference in which the Socialists pledged a decisive break with the market economy by promising to nationalize key industrial and banking sectors.[7] Similar radical measures were expressed in the area of foreign policy (i.e., solidarity with the Third World, critiques of foreign multinational corporations and, above all, pulling Spain out of NATO) and in the area of labor relations with the Socialists actively endorsing worker self-management and an expansion in the welfare state.

Spain's first democratic election in the post-Franco era witnessed the emergence of the PSOE as the dominant opposition party in Spain and the secondary position of the Communists.[8] Given its strong showing (28 percent of the popular vote) the Socialists would play a formidable role in shaping Spain's constitution and emerging democratic institutions. With its strong electoral performance and pioneering efforts in building Spain's nascent democratic infrastructure, the PSOE had established its dominant position on the Left. From this vantage point, González had hoped to position the PSOE as the governing party in the 1 March 1979 elections.

The results of the election proved a bitter disappointment for the Socialists. The PSOE's poor performance (increasing their share of the vote by a little more than one percent) produced much soul-searching among the party's inner circle.[9] The Socialists' lackluster showing spurred a debate within the party over its future programmatic and ideological course. González and Guerra viewed the election result as evidence that a more centrist image was needed. The contradictions between the Socialists' conciliatory gestures towards the Center (i.e., cooperation with Suarez) and its Leftist ideological orientation were, in their view, quite clear to the electorate. During the 1979 campaign, Prime Minister Suarez's Rightist government reinforced this assessment by adroitly pointing out the inconsistencies between the Socialists' moderate campaign image and its programmatic radicalism.

The Socialists' extremist ideological discourse, so successful in mobilizing the party's rank and file, had become a serious campaign liability. Sensing the need for an abrupt U-turn, González recommended that all references to Marxism be deleted from the PSOE's 1979 party platform. The leadership's position on Socialist ideological recharacterization encountered severe opposition at the party's XXVIII Congress in May 1979. González's Leftist opponents (the so-called *críticos*) insisted on a Marxist identity for the PSOE, pressed for proportional representation in the González regional and national party organizations, and demanded an electoral pact with the Communists. The Congress gave González key victories on the alliance and intra-party democracy issues, but strongly rebuked his ideological agenda. Given the *críticos* victory on the ideology issue, González resigned as the party's general-secretary. González's sudden departure as party leader opened up a political void that the Left could not fill. The Left's inability to secure passage of an alternative party leadership at the XXVIII Congress resulted in an emergency party meeting in September 1977, convened under strict majority delegate-selection rules, which enhanced the position of the González-Guerra voting bloc.

The political isolation of the *críticos* increased as the party's membership clamored for González's return as the PSOE's leader. González dominated the September meeting and used his influence under the delegate-selection rules approved by the XXVIII Congress to give his forces a majority in the PSOE's regional and federal executive committees. Within the party's apparatus, internal discipline was intensified with disloyal members facing the penalty of expulsion. The Extraordinary Congress of September 1979 was a personal triumph for the González-Guerra faction and a validation of their arguments for more ideological moderation and central control over the party. Accordingly, all references to class struggle, mass nationalization, worker self-management, and the PSOE's Marxian roots were eliminated from the party's 1978 platform.[10]

The consolidation of central control over the party and the redirection of its ideological message encountered little serious opposition in the early 1980s. Most party members, dependent upon the leadership for resources and jobs, found that their ascension through the party's ranks could be facilitated by complete fidelity. James Petras, for example, has noted that a majority of party activists joined the PSOE for career advancement. As a result, this disproportionately young, professional, salaried middle class exhibited a high degree of ideological mutability.[11] Thus, access to money, prestige, positions, and, above all, electoral success, became the *sine qua non* of Socialist Party politics. Not all members freely agreed to the de-ideologization of the PSOE. In 1981 the party's radical wing formed the *Izquierda Socialista* (Left Socialists) as a protest and study group to contest the leadership's pursuit of moderate, Centrist policies. Modeled along the lines of the French Socialist CERES faction, *Izquierda Socialista* sought to push the PSOE into a more socially conscious programmatic agenda.[12] Despite this faction's energetic appeals, the PSOE's political trajectory of centrist politics and electoral opportunism proceeded unhampered for over a decade.

The party's de-Marxianization was used by the González faction to expand its potential electorate and to cultivate a more pragmatic image. Indeed, the Extraordinary Congress set the stage for more moderation at subsequent party conferences. The XXIX Congress, convened in October 1981, ensconced the PSOE as a Social-Democratic party whose platform called for limited social investments, the creation of 800,000 jobs over four years, better provision of social services, and labor reform.[13] Though light years from the party's earlier pledge of *"la ruptura,"* rupturing Spain from its capitalist base, the Socialists decisively rejected austerity and sought state intervention to cure social ills.

The Socialists' Centrist policy drift was furthered by the squabbling and eventual disintegration of Suarez's governing Centrist coalition. The fragmentation between UCD's Social-Democratic and Christian-Democratic partners contrasted strikingly with Socialist unity. The Socialists capitalized on UCD discord by reassuring voters that a PSOE victory would not threaten the Church, the military, or private enterprise, and that the party needed to carry out a bourgeois revolution before enacting redistributive measures. Throughout the 1982 election campaign, González minimized Leftist ideals, and emphasized the PSOE's commitment to stability and growth.[14] The political fragmentation of the Center parties and the inability of the Communists to establish a solid electoral presence allowed the PSOE to move to the Right and transcend the limitations of its working-class constituency. The fragile nature of Spain's democratic transition and the precarious status of the economy strengthened the Rightist tendencies within the PSOE, and once the Socialists were able to secure their electoral victory in 1982, ideological conservatism would proceed rapidly in the party.

II. The Refoundation of Socialist Economic Policy: Neo-Liberal Industrial Reconstruction

"In order to form tortillas, you have to break a few eggs."[15]

With 48 percent of the popular vote and a commanding legislative majority in the Cortes, the PSOE were well positioned to implement their program. The Socialists' 1981 party conference had sought to use the public sector to create 800,000 jobs over a four-year period. In the 1982 campaign González consistently rejected the austerity policies of the Right and pledged to stimulate the economy to produce growth and social equity. The constellation of political forces, it would seem, would facilitate implementation of the party's 1981 platform.

The Socialists' employment-creation policy had been supported by its sister organization in the labor movement, the General Workers Union (UGT).[16] In the late 1970s the PSOE and the UGT developed a symbiotic relationship in which trade union campaign mobilization on behalf of the PSOE would be rewarded by the Socialists' implementation of a pro-labor Social-Democratic agenda. The political alliance between the union and the party was furthered by an organizational connection involving joint executive committees and compulsory UGT membership for top PSOE members. With the Socialists' 1982 electoral victory, the UGT sought to establish a party-union axis for corporatist mediation of economic policy.

Economic forces, however, would work against the implementation of the Socialists' campaign promises. The policy freedom allowed by the PSOE's margin of victory and its close ties to the UGT would be constrained by the magnitude of Spain's economic problems. Upon taking office, the Socialists inherited a high unemployment rate and a huge trade deficit. The failure of Spanish industry to compete in the world market and the resulting expansion of production subsidies and unemployment assistance had ruined the central government's financial situation. By 1982 the magnitude of the public sector budget deficit severely limited the new government's policy options.

With the predominance of economic factors, including Spain's planned entrance into the European Community by 1986, power and prestige flowed to the free-market technocrats in González's government. For some observers, the González period represented the flowering of technocratic government in Spain. [17] Many of the top positions during the PSOE reign were filled by highly educated professionals with ties to Spain's banking and business communities. This technocratic element viewed the redistributive and employment creation emphasis of the Socialists' campaign pledges as potentially harmful to the economy and greatly hindering economic "modernization": Industry Minister Carlos Solchaga, for example, took the lead in urging Gonzalez to abandon his 1981 pledge to create 800,00 jobs, while Economy Minister Miguel Boyer established the taming of inflation as the government's number one priority. For the neo-Liberals in González's inner circle, growth and privatization, marketing, and technological rebirth should become standard terms in the PSOE's ideological lexicon. [18]

Solchaga and Boyer defined Spain's economic problems from an explicitly free market, monetarist perspective. From this vantage point, excessive wage costs, "inflexible" labor markets, and antiquated, often state-owned, companies stood in the way of Spain's modernization. The neo-Liberals, having deemed social democratic ideology and policy counterproductive, declared themselves in favor of a new political-economic trajectory (called *renovación* or *refoundación*) for the PSOE could set the stage for the Socialists' appeals to the salaried middle class. [19]

The neo-Liberals' dominance over economic policy was exacerbated by the hierarchical nature of the leadership's control over the PSOE's regional and national party organs. In the early years of the González administration, the cabinet was shielded from party controls. Once the neo-Liberal policy began, fidelity to the government's agenda (irrespective of ideological congruence) was expected. If opposition did erupt, the leadership could use its substantial patronage powers and, if necessary, expel recalcitrant party members. Thus, party centralism acted to support the governments neo-Liberal emphasis. The move away from the Socialists' 1981 electoral platform would be marked by the González administration's November 1983 white paper on reindustrialization. [20] Under this policy, the government committed itself to an industrial regeneration path involving substantial wage cuts and employment reductions in strategic industries. The workforce reductions and wage cuts planned for heavy industry would be offset by the creation of reindustrialization zones in depressed areas, which would offer tax incentives, loans, and subsidies to private capital interested in locating in these areas. Both the "zones for urgent reindustrialization" and phased workforce reduction programs sought to shift resources away from wages to research and investment, for the neo-Liberals envisioned such a shift as auguring Spain's competitive potential in the European market. Such a transformation, however, would entail substantial difficulties for the Socialists' trade union allies and impose substantial hardship on workers.

The government's July 1984 Law on Industrial Reconversion established a consultive framework for negotiation over the implementation of plant closings and employment reductions. The major unions sought to ease this painful economic transition by cooperating with the government and employers. After some initial friendly consultation, the government's relationship with the socialist UGT and the Communist Workers Commissions (CCOO) union began to deteriorate as the process of industrial reconversion unfolded. Within two years of the law's implementation, 83,000 jobs would be phased out. The government's emphasis on fiscal-monetary austerity and inflation fighting, a direct bid to encourage foreign investment, pushed unemployment well past the 20 percent mark in the mid 1980s. The government's much heralded zones for reindustrialization program resulted in too few permanent jobs and accelerated the expansion of fixed contract, temporary work. Faced with mounting unemployment and the government's rigid wage policy, the unions began to balk.[21]

Conflict between the unions and the government surfaced in a bitter public feud between UGT leader Rodondo (until 1986 a PSOE legislative deputy) and minister Solchaga. The UGT leader, who began to question the government's strategy as early as 1985, sharply criticized Solchaga's dominant status with the PSOE's inner circle. From Rodondo's perspective, Solchaga's defense of monetarist orthodoxy, and his exhortations that labor capitulate on wage and employment issues, personified the government's hostile attitude towards the unions. Despite threats of expulsion from the PSOE, the UGT leader sought to rally support within the party to limit the power of the neo-Liberal technocrats. Erosion in the PSOE's relationship with the unions (particularly the Socialist UGT) would increase after Rodondo's resignation as a Socialist legislative deputy in 1986. The polarizing effects of the government's neo-Liberal policies, and a number of corruption scandals within the PSOE, would weakened the position of González and his team of pro-market technocrats. By 1988 the government's failure to address key labor issues created an absurdist spectacle of Leftist unions striking against a Socialist government whose polices, in a Fellini-style turn, would be supported by major employer federations.[22]

Though the 1988 general strike failed to force the government to reconsider its free-market course, it did succeed in stimulating PSOE intra-party debate. The general strike's political consequences (it received massive support from the Spanish public) played a role in accelerating the party debate over the government's neo-Liberal political and economic trajectory: for the PSOE Right the conflict underscored the need to move away from the party's union constituency and embrace more market reforms to attract the middle class; for the party's Social-Democratic Left the strike symbolized the alienating effects of the government's regressive policies and above all, the insular and imperial nature of the PSOE's leadership. The PSOE's slim margin of victory in the 1989 general election added more fuel to dissension within the PSOE's ranks.

The party split, stimulated by the government's conflict with the unions, would widen appreciably in the 1990s. The political position of the neo-Liberals, once thought preeminent, began to be contested. Richard Gillespie argues that the Socialists' 1990 efforts to draft an ideological manifesto (*Programa 2000*) was designed to challenge neo-Liberal hegemony in the party.[23] The backers of this effort, most particularly PSOE Vice Secretary-General Guerra, sought to tie government policy to established social democratic norms and anchor the party to its trade union constituency. *Programa 2000*, if fully implemented, would repudiate the entire thrust of the party's neo-Liberal 1980s renovation and limit the González government's autonomy.

III. Fragmentation and the Guerrista Challenge: Whither Neo-Liberal Hegemony?

"I think he [PSOE Vice President Narcis Serra] has the habit of playing the piano, and does not understand what is occurring in the streets."[24]

Alfonso Guerra's search for a viable Social-Democratic model for the PSOE would exacerbate divisions within the party through much of the 1990s.[25] Widely viewed as the Socialists' second most powerful figure in the post-Franco Era, Guerra's position within the party has, in many ways, been more important than González's. Guerra's dual role as vice secretary-general and vice president of the government gave him an important party-state link to control PSOE's patronage policies. Having established financial leverage and control among the Socialists ranks, he has many friends and supporters within the party.

In the early 1990s Guerra assuaged regional PSOE party leaders angered over the abrasive tone and neo-Liberal political discourse of González's key advisors. During this period Guerra's role as peacemaker allowed him to articulate rank and files grievances against the government and urge that González pursue less draconian marketing polices. Guerra's tactics would be viewed with great suspicion by the PSOE Right, who would urge his removal from the government.

Guerra's position in the government would come to an end in 1991 as a consequence of a corruption scandal involving his brother, a minor regional PSOE functionary. The neo-Liberals in the party used the event to discredit and isolate Guerra, forcing his resignation as vice president and furthering the bad blood between the Rightist and Social-Democratic factions within the PSOE. With his departure, central control over the party's apparatus unraveled, setting the stage for battles between the neo-Liberal *renovadores* and the Social-Democratic *Guerristas* in the early 1990s. The PSOE's national and regional organs and executive committees would be beset by ideological factionalism and contending loyalties. Having retained his post as vice secretary-general of the PSOE, Guerra would establish political alliances with regional party barons to counter the González factions' domination of the PSOE's federal executive committee.[26]

The government's relationship with the unions would continue to worsen in the early and mid 1990s, accelerating even more factionalism in the party. González's efforts to control wages, cut public sector deficits, and restructure unemployment insurance encountered stiff labor resistance. In 1992 the major unions launched a second general strike against the Socialist government, which would provoke a militant neo-Liberal line in González's inner circle of advisors. The government's policy of convergence with Europe, moreover, came under increasing scrutiny and criticism within the PSOE.

The PSOE's balkanization into competing camps and the quarreling between the *renovadores* and the *Guerristas* was temporarily suspended by the need to close party ranks in the June 1993 election. The façade of unity presented by the PSOE's coalescence of forces succeeded in securing the party's fourth straight electoral victory, yet failed to stem the PSOE's steady electoral slide. The June 1992 election resulted in the government's worst electoral showing (38 percent of the vote) and the party failed to achieve a parliamentary majority in the Cortes.[27] The lack of a decisive showing in the election and the tenuous nature of the Socialists' legislative pact with the Catalán and Basque nationalists furthered dissension within the PSOE's ranks.

IV. The PSOE's XXXIII Congress: Dissent, Fragmentation, and the 1996 Electoral Defeat

"The party has to break its tendency toward tribalism."[28]

In January 1994 delegates to the Socialists' XXXIII Congress were selected by the PSOE's regional assemblies. The delegate selection process balkanized the party into warring ideological factions. The neo-Liberals were able to muster 60 percent of the delegates with the remainder controlled by forces loyal to the *Guerrista* camp. The Congress was viewed by many PSOE leaders as the most significant in the Socialists' post-Franco history and a possible watershed in the PSOE's ability to refound the party's organizational and ideological trajectory.

Given the excitement surrounding the Congress, the results were somewhat anti-climatic. Most of the Congress would be dominated by organizational and procedural matters. The composition of the PSOE's federal executive committee captured most of the delegates attention. In this regard, the *Guerristas* were successful in retaining their leader as the PSOE's vice secretary-general and the continuation of José Maria Benegas as the PSOE's organizational secretary, though the representation of the Left within the executive committee would be reduced.

González and his allies in the party were less accommodating on other more substantive issues. Faced with demands by the Left that the PSOE should renounce its legislative pact with the Cataláns and establish an alliance with the ex-Communist United Left (IU) party, the *renovadores* resisted any change in the government's policy. The Rightist forces, bolstered by 60 percent of the delegates, upheld the administrations neo-Liberal economic policy, making only minor concessions to pro-labor and Leftist currents in the party. The failure to bring the party's recalcitrant left-wing back into the fold resulted in defections from the party and contributed to the United Left's (IU) rise in the public opinion polls and its enhanced electoral standing.

The neo-Liberals' "victory" at the Congress proved ephemeral, and would set the stage for the PSOE's defeat in the 1996 election. The position of the Rightist faction in the party would be harmed by a series of corruption and other scandals that would force three prominent neo-Liberal cabinet ministers to step down in the mid 1990s. In late 1995 criticism continued to be leveled at González's neo-Liberal trajectory for the PSOE, and by the disclosure of government-assisted death squads directed at the Basque terrorist network, ETA, in the mid 1980s. Under such conditions, the Catalán (CiU) refused to honor its parliamentary pact with the Socialists, forcing the PSOE to call the March 1996 election.

The Socialists entered the March election badly divided, burdened by controversy and corruption, and facing strong challenges from the Left and Right. The confluence of these forces would end the PSOE's 14-year reign. The election results, however, were far from decisive: the Rightist Popular Party received only 38 percent of the vote compared with the PSOE's 37 percent.[29] Having failed to secure a legislative majority, the PP would be forced into an unstable alliance with the Cataláns. This situation would seem to auger a new round of unstable, perhaps even Italianesque, politics in Spain. What does this new electoral landscape mean for the opposition Socialists, and can the PSOE reposition its organizational and ideological model in ways to take advantage of this new environment? By drawing on a number of theories of party change and transformation, let us examine some explanations for the loss of Socialist hegemony and the capacity for the PSOE organizational and ideological rebirth.

V. The Endless Quest for Socialist Refoundation: Opportunities, Constraints, and Dilemmas

"No social democratic party can ignore the challenges of market efficiency or of libertarian community." [30]

The inevitable decline of the Social-Democratic, working-class party mobilization model has become almost an axiom among theorists studying the Left in the latter stages of the Twentieth Century. The post-Fordist economy and the emergence and political dominance of the salaried middle class has altered the terrain of electoral competition in most Western democracies. Social democratic parties must, accordingly, embrace the market, transcend the narrow limitations of their blue-collar support, and attract a more heterogeneous coalition. Such moves seem to suggest a less ideological, pragmatic political course.

Herbert Kitschelt, for example, argues that the old Right/Left distributional divisions have lost their saliency and have been increasingly replaced by a new "politics" centered around communitarian and libertarian concerns.[31] Such issues as workplace democracy, personal autonomy, ecological survival, feminism, ethnic rights, and the imperative of market efficiency have gained greater prominence in the new service economy, forcing Leftist parties to rethink established political coalitions and Social-Democratic norms.

Social-Democratic success in adapting to this new environment is dependent upon party organizational structure, the nature of intra-party competition, and the party's own ideological legacy. Some party structures may be too rigid to engineer this transition or the presence of a strong Leftist, libertarian, third party may impair the selection of this ideological model. A similar effect might come from the interplay of the party's traditionally strong organizational and ideological ties to its trade union constituency.

While Kitschelt is hesitant to recommend a Socialist renovation model, his preferences are fairly clear: to enhance their electoral position Socialist parties should, under the right circumstances, adopt an organizational-ideological model involving the confluence of party centralism and a market-libertarian ideology. Such circumstances (i.e., a weak Rightist party, the absence of a strong Left competitor, and an embryonic party organization) should allow Social-Democratic parties to transcend their established constituencies and past ideology. Kitschelt's theory of Social-Democratic transformation is especially useful in explaining the success and operating features of the Spanish Socialists' renovation process in the 1980s.

In the Spanish case, the collapse of the Center-Right in the early 1980s and the lack of an entrenched party structure allowed Gonzalez and Guerra to engineer a Rightist renovation path for both the party and successive PSOE governments in the 1980s. Yet the very nature of Socialist renovation in the 1980s created counter movements in the 1990s (a resurgent PSOE left-wing, the rise of the ex-Communist IU, and the erosion of union support) that would contribute to the Socialists' electoral demise. Kitschelt's theory of party change is less able to explain the loss of Socialist hegemony because, despite his protestations to the contrary, it is based on a fixed structural model (a post-Fordist service economy, a dominant salaried middle class and market efficiency imperatives) that makes the decline of the Social-Democratic/working-class model inevitable. In reality the structural foundations of advanced market economies may vary significantly from Kitschelt's formulation, with some retaining an increasingly larger pool of permanently unemployed, underemployed, and poor that would suggest the continued saliency of distributional politics.

The failure of the Spanish Socialists to maintain their dominant status in the 1990s occurred because the PSOE was too fixated on the "imperatives of market efficiency" and decoupled too rapidly and too severely from its working-class constituency. Thus, alternative frameworks will be needed to explain the Socialists' fall from grace. T. J. Pempel's work on one-party-dominant states may have some value in explaining the Socialists failure in Spain. Pempel argues that successful one-arty democratic states involve "a virtuous cycle of dominance."[32] The first stage of this process involves a party's electoral mobilization of "historic blocs" (i.e., dominant social groups) and its articulation of their needs and aspirations. Having organized this bloc of supporting groups, the party must establish ideological distance from its main opponents to establish its programmatic turf, so to speak.

The development of a fixed, distinctive, ideological position and the mobilization of important social blocs can be the springboard for electoral success. Once in office, the state should pursue policies that consolidate the social position of its historic blocs, while searching for new blocs to cement its hegemonic status. With each successive electoral victory, the party strengthens its core supporters, weakens its opponents, and sheer longevity of uninterrupted rule legitimates the dominant party, guaranteeing it future electoral victories.

Pempel's analysis, when applied to the Spanish Socialists from 1977 to 1996, explains a fair amount. From 1977 to 1982 the Socialists organized their historic bloc of trade union supporters, ensconced themselves as Social-Democratic standard bearers and defenders of Spain's democratic transition, and achieved an electoral landslide in 1982. Once in office, however, the PSOE progressively severed its organizational ties to the unions, moved to the neo-Liberal Right, and implemented polices that weakened its core constituency. Such measures, accepted only when necessary to facilitate Spain's democratic process, became increasingly suspect over time. The very nature of the party's Centralist tendencies would further alienate the PSOE's regional barons and rank and file. Within this context, the PSOE's neoliberal renovation model backfired for the Socialists, undermining its support among the unions, splitting the party into warring camps, and revitalizing the non-Socialist Left. The party's ideological transition to neo-Liberalism would fail to provide sufficient ideological distance from its right-wing competitor, and would make hollow its status as a Leftist party. Over time, these forces would weaken the electoral viability of the PSOE and contribute to its erosion in the late 1980s and 1990s.

While Pempel's model of one-party dominance captures a great deal, it may overestimate the capability and autonomy of regimes to use policy to consolidate and reward historic blocs. Written over five years ago, international markets now more strongly constrain the authority of even strong regimes and, as such, policies may not be so easily crafted or executed. Within this context, the difficult economic situation inherited by the Spanish Socialists and the government's commitment to European integration limited, to some degree, the types of policies the PSOE could pursue.

With the constraints and opportunities identified by Kitschelt and Pempel, what future philosophical and organizational courses might the PSOE entertain in the late 1990s. First, the Socialists might keep their neo-Liberal political trajectory and hope to exploit the PP's inexperience and its dependence on the Cataláns. Within this context, attacking the youth and inexperience of the Aznar government could be a holding action until the PP loses its Catalán parliamentary support, thus forcing new elections. Should this scenario play out, González could portray the PSOE as Spain's natural governing party and exploit Aznar's lack of decisive leadership. Given the still dominant position of Gonzalez and the *renovador* faction within the PSOE's political infrastructure and the tenuous nature of Aznar's PP coalition (a fragile mix of nationalists, Christian-Democrats, and economic Liberals) this option has some merit.

Such a course, however, is unlikely. The erosion of Left support for the PSOE, and the party's balkanization into competing ideological camps, threaten the party with organizational annihilation if the leadership continues its neo-Liberal model. Recent analysis of the 1996 election, moreover, shows a substantial defection of PSOE voters to the United Left Party and that the ex-Communists challenge to the PSOE's left flank would only intensify under a continued neo-Liberal model.[33] Indeed, the retention of the party's Leftist voters would have secured a PSOE victory in the 1996 election.

The Popular Party's successful renovation from a neo-Francoist party into a Centrist modernizing political force and the erosion of Leftist support for the PSOE suggest a rational Socialist policy would move to the Left. The intensification of Leftist ideology, an electoral alliance with the United Left, and greater intra-party democracy could turn the party's political fortunes around. Substantial sentiment exists for the option among the *Guerrista* and Leftist faction, and it would constitute a sharp rebuke of the party's neo-Liberal legacy of party centralism, corruption, and élitist politics.

The still dominant position of González and the PSOE Right would militate against this refoundation strategy and the Left could be forced to bolt the party. Should this happen, the PSOE in the late 1990s could be on the periphery of Spanish party politics and, with the defection of the party's Left to the ex-Communists, a reconstituted IU could be Spain's leading Leftist party. Past loyalties to González and the uncertain nature of Aznar's fragile hold on power will probably prevent the PSOE from pursuing a significant shift to the Left. How then will the PSOE resolve its organizational and ideological conundrums expressed in its XXXIII Congress? The most likely response would be a continued compromise between the *renovadores* and the *Guerristas* that allows some alteration in policy (i.e., neo-Liberalism with a human face) and intra-party reforms that assure dissidents greater outlets and opportunities to influence party practice.

Such a compromise, however, is likely to be transitory. In 14 years of PSOE rule the party has become battered and politically exhausted, and encased in intense factional conflicts. The work of formulating a new ideological message and organizational model (a second phase in the refoundation process) is likely to wait until the current crop of PSOE leaders either resign or are forced out. Without the strain of past conflicts, egos, and animosities, parties often find regenerative capabilities, and perhaps the Socialists will find a renovation model that does not have the Centralist and unequal tendencies of its neo-Liberal predecessor. Therefore, by 1999 the PSOE remains in disarray as an opposition party, still mired in the search for a common ideological and organizational model to reenergize the party. However, as no change in the Center-Right ruling coalition and balance between political forces has occurred since Aznar's 1996 victory, the Socialists will likely have to wait for the outcome of Spain's general elections in 2000 before they can succeed in completing their transformation.

Notes

1. Quote from Julio Anguita (leader of the United Left Party). Quoted in *El País* (Madrid, 6 June 1994).

2. Paul Heywood, "Mirror Images: The PCE and PSOE in the Transition to Democracy in Spain," in *West European Politics,* vol. 10, no. 2 (April 1987): p. 193–210.

3. Donald Share, *The Dilemmas of Social Democracy: The PSOE in the 1980s* (Westport, CT, Greenwood Press, 1989).

4. Richard Gillespie, "Programa 2000: The Appearance and Reality of Socialist Renewal in Spain," in *West European Politics,* vol. 16, no. 1 (January 1993): p. 78–96.

5. Felipe González interviewed by Fernando Claudídin, in *Zona Abierta,* vol. 20 (May-August 1979): p. 8.

6. Donald Share, "Dilemmas of Social Democracy in the 1980s: The PSOE in Comparative Perspective," in *Comparative Political Studies,* vol. 21, no. 3 (October 1988): p. 408–435.

7. Share, *Dilemmas of Social Democracy.*

8. Paul Heywood, "Mirror Images: The PCE and the PSOE in the Transition to Democracy," in *West European Politics,* vol. 10, no. 1 (January 1987): p. 193–210.

9. Robert Robinson, "From Change to Continuity: The 1986 Spanish Election," in *West European Politics,* vol. 10, no. 1 (January 1987): p. 120–124.

10. Share, *Dilemmas of Social Democracy.*

11. James Petras, "Spanish Socialism: The Politics of Neoliberalism," p. 95–127, in James Kurth & James Petras, eds., *Mediterranean Paradoxes: The Politics and Social Structure of Southern Europe* (Indianapolis, IN, Berg Publishers, 1993).

12. Richard Gillespie, *The Spanish Socialist Party: A History of Factionalism* (New York: Oxford Press, 1989).

13. Share, *Dilemmas of Social Democracy.*

14. Heywood, "Mirror Images," p. 193–210.

15. PSOE parliamentary leader Carlos Solchaga interviewed by Juan Ibáñez in *El País* (Madrid, 19 September 1993): p. 16.

16. Richard Gillespie, "The Break-up of the Socialist Family: Party-Union Relations in Spain, 1982–1989," in *West European Politics,* vol. 13, no. 1 (January 1990): p. 48–62

17. Anthony Ferner, *Governments, Managers and Industrial Relations: Public Enterprises and their Environments* (New York & London: Basil Blackwell, 1988).

18. Gillespie, "Programa 2000," p. 78–96.

19. PSOE parliamentary leader Carlos Solchaga talks on the *renovación* campaign in *El País* (Madrid, 19 September 1993).

20. Organization for Economic Cooperation & Development, *Economic Survey: Spain* (Paris: OECD, May 1984).

21. Organization for Economic Cooperation & Development, *Economic Survey: Spain* (Paris: OECD, 1988).

22. Gillespie, "Breakup of the Socialist Family," p. 48–62.

23. Miguel Martinez Lucio, "Employer Identity and the Politics of the Labor Market in Spain," in *West European Politics,* vol. 14, no. 1 (January 1991): p. 41–57.

24. Gillespie, "Programa 2000," p. 178–196.
25. UGT leader Nicholas Rodondo quoted in *El País* (Madrid, 18 April 1993).
26. For a good account of the PSOE's divisions and ideological camps see "La Fractura," in *ABC* (8 August 1993).
27. Ibid.
28. *El País* (Madrid, 6 June 1993).
29. For an account of the March 1996 election see *ABC* (5 March 1996).
30. Quote from Herbert Kitschelt, *The Transformation of European Social Democracy* (London: Cambridge University Press, 1994), p. 300.
31. Ibid.
32. T. J. Pempel, "Conclusion: One-Party Dominance and the Creation of Regimes," in T. J. Pempel ed., *Uncommon Democracies: The One-Party Dominant Regimes* (Ithaca, NY: Cornell University Press, 1990), p. 333–360.
33. Recent analyses done by the Centro de Investigaciones Sociologicas state that the PSOE experienced sizeable defections of PSOE voters (10 percent of members) to the United Left (IU) party in the 1996 election, which ended by costing the PSOE the election. The center's study is reported in *El Pais* (Madrid, 5 January 1997): p. 11.

FIVE

Political Polarization and Electoral Change in Israel

John J. McTague

In his recent book on one-party-dominant governments, T. J. Pempel lists four criteria for a party to be regarded as dominant within a given country. First, it must dominate numerically, in terms of seats in parliament and numbers of votes. Second, it must have the controlling bargaining position, i.e., no government can be formed without it. Third, the party must rule the government over a lengthy period of time. Fourth, it must dominate the governments that it forms by monopolizing the key positions such as prime minister, foreign minister, and defense minister.[1]

This chapter will attempt to demonstrate that from 1948 to 1977 Israel had such a dominant party, *Mapai*/Labor, which fulfilled all four criteria. It will explain the reasons for this dominance and why Labor lost its controlling position in the 1977 elections. Then, we will survey the Israeli electoral landscape since that election, a period in which the country has seen politics evolve into a competitive two-party and two-bloc system.

The Israeli government is based on a parliamentary system, with a figurehead president as head of state. Power is vested in the Knesset which, until 1996 (when direct election was introduced) had the power to select the prime minister. The Knesset has 120 seats, which are chosen by a pure proportional electoral system. Voters choose parties, not individuals, on election day and seats are awarded in strict proportion to the percentage of votes received by each party. Prior to the election, each party must submit a ranked list of candidates; members are then seated according to their position on that list. Until 1992, parties needed to secure only 1 percent of the total vote to qualify for a seat; for that election, the threshold was raised to 1.5 percent.

This system tends to encourage a multiplicity of parties. The minuscule threshold is so easily obtained that there is a constant temptation for larger parties to split up and new parties to arise, since the smaller units can still win seats and sometimes have even more power if they are needed to form a coalition. Consequently, in the 13 national elections that have been held since independence, there have never been fewer than ten parties represented in the Knesset.[2]

Nevertheless, in Israel's first eight elections, from 1949 to 1973, one party—*Mapai*—which in 1968 merged with other Socialist parties to form Labor, dominated the political landscape. This dominance extended back to the 1920s when *Mapai* became the strongest force in the *Yishuv* (the Jewish community in Palestine), due to its strength in the *Histradrut,* the national labor union, and the *kibbutz* movement. By the mid 1920s about 70 percent of Jewish workers belonged to the *Histradrut,* which made it easier for *Mapai* to recruit them. Moreover, "jobs, housing and other social benefits were distributed to [new] immigrants through the party machinery."[3] Most of Israel's "founding fathers"—David Ben-Gurion, Moshe Sharett, Golda Meir—came from *Mapai,* and that party and other socialist groups has strong support from the *Ashkenazim,* the East European Jews who comprised the majority of the state's population until the 1970s.

An analysis of Israeli elections shows that *Mapai*/Labor never received a serious challenge until 1973. In each of the first seven elections (1949 to 1969), *Mapai* and its Socialist partners, *Mapam* and *Achdut Ha'avodah,* never won fewer than 56 seats out of 120. In 1949, 1959, and 1965, they won an outright majority of seats, while in 1953, 1955, 1961, and 1969, they needed to add smaller parties such as the National Religious Party (NRP) to their coalition. As should be obvious in a pure proportional system, the Socialist parties also dominated the popular vote. In those first seven elections, they never won less than 46 percent of that vote and three times exceeded the 50 percent mark.

Why was *Mapai*/Labor able to dominate the electoral scene so completely? There were a variety of reasons. In its ideology and its policies, it had the support of a majority of Israelis for the first 30 years of the nation's existence. The party's goals—attracting and absorbing immigrants, promoting economic growth and developing national solidarity—were widely accepted by the body politic. Its leadership in Israel's first three wars (1948, 1956, and 1967), made heroes of the nation's generals and inspired admiration around the globe (at least in the West). And pragmatically, *Mapai*'s control of the military, bureaucracy, *Histradrut,* and the Jewish Agency (which supervised immigration) gave it enormous advantages over its opposition.[4] As Myron Aronoff put it succinctly:

Labor maintained its dominant position for as long as it did because it was relatively successful in meeting the major challenges which Israel faced in its first three decades: defense against hostile neighbors, the absorption of masses of immigrants, and the need for economic growth.[5]

Equally important to one-party dominance was the fact that *Mapai*/Labor faced no serious opposition until 1973. Prior to that year, the best performance of any opposition group in the seven elections had been that of *Gahal*, which in both 1965 and 1969 won 21 percent of the vote and 26 seats. *Gahal*, the forerunner of the *Likud*, was a combined slate of Menahem Begin's *Herut* Party and the Liberals, neither of whom had fared very well on their own up to that point. Even with their joint slate, they tallied less than half the votes and seats of *Mapai* (which had become the major component of the Labor party in 1968).

Why was the opposition so ineffectual? First, it was badly divided between secular and religious parties. Orthodox voters constituted a minority of the populace and could only take power in a coalition with parties of the Left or Right. And since only *Mapai*/Labor could form a government up to 1977, it was with them that the religious parties (particularly the NRP) chose to cast their lot. Among the secular parties, *Herut* and its leader, Begin, were the best known but their origins in the pre-state terrorist group, the *Irgun*, made them highly controversial, an issue which *Mapai*/Labor exploited to the fullest extent. The party was portrayed as extremist and injurious to Israel's image while Begin was turned into a pariah by Ben-Gurion, who refused to even utter the *Irgun* leader's name in the Knesset or consider bringing him or his party into the government coalition. The Liberals, on the other hand, were offered cabinet positions and other benefits such as government grants for business projects.[6]

The 1977 election is known in Israel as the "earthquake" but in retrospect it was the previous election of 1973 which began the trend from domination of a single party to a competitive system. By that time, *Gahal* had allied with several smaller parties to become the *Likud*, and had recruited one of the few heroes of the 1973 Yom Kippur War, Ariel Sharon, to its ranks. That war, fought just two months before the election, was regarded by many Israelis as their first military setback and was the first major blemish on Labor's record in power. The two people most responsible for conducting that war, Prime Minister Meir and Defense Minister Moshe Dayan, saw their popularity fall dramatically because the army was caught unaware by Egypt's surprise attack.

Moreover, as Labor's image was declining, the *Herut-Gahal-Likud* world view was becoming more respectable. From its inception in 1948, *Herut* had espoused control of all of *"Eretz Israel"* ("Greater Israel": from the Sinai to the West Bank and Golan Heights), a concept which had appeared to be an impossible dream until 1967. But during the 1967 Six-Day War that dream had become a reality, bringing the party closer to the mainstream of Israeli politics. And Begin himself, the former terrorist leader (*Irgun*) who had been treated as an outcast during the Ben-Gurion years (1948–63), had gained respectability by serving as minister without portfolio in the wall-to-wall coalition that had been created just before the Six-Day War began.[7]

Beyond changes in the political landscape, the economic situation was evolving to the detriment of Labor by the 1970s. The growth of the private sector, which had been stimulated by government policy in the 1950s and 1960s, was decreasing voter dependency on state largesse in some segments of the population, while corruption in the *Histradrut* weakened that vital agent of *Mapai* dominance.[8] Thus, voters were becoming less inclined for both political and economic reasons by the early 1970s to vote Labor, and the gradual rehabilitation of Begin and his party's image made them more palatable to the public as an alternative.

Consequently, the 1973 election was the most competitive in the state's history to that point. The Socialist parties (Labor Alignment) saw their vote fall below 40 percent for the first time (39.6 percent). Labor still had the most seats but its margin of victory (51–39) was the smallest ever, and the party found it difficult to put together a coalition (the NRP eventually joined but proved to be a difficult partner). American political scientist Don Peretz, who has analyzed Israeli elections for the *Middle-East Journal* for the past 25 years, wrote at the time that this election might be the beginning of a competitive two-party system in the Jewish state.[9]

The election of 1977 proved his prophecy correct. The movement away from Labor, which had begun in 1973, was greatly exacerbated by a number of events. In spring 1974, Golda Meir retired as prime minister, handing the job to the former chief of staff and ambassador to Washington, Yitzhak Rabin. She was the last representative of the "founding fathers" to run the country, and Rabin seemed to exemplify a new generation, untried and less trustworthy. Moreover, Rabin lacked the charisma of his predecessor and did not make a strong impression in his public appearances.

Demographic changes were also working against Labor. Immigration since the founding of the state had largely come from Asian and African countries, to the point where these *Sephardim* comprised about 45 percent of the population by the mid 1970s. Several studies have demonstrated that these *Sephardic* voters tended to feel that Labor had neglected their needs over the years and was primarily an *Ashkenazi* party. Moreover, they generally took more "hawkish" positions regarding the Occupied Territories and negotiations with the Arabs, which inclined them more towards the *Likud*.[10]

Other data showed that the *Likud* was more popular with younger voters, with Labor's strength resting with those over the age of 40. Older voters could remember that *Mapai*/Labor had created the state in 1948, while younger ones recalled that Labor had been caught unprepared in October 1973 when Anwar Sadat launched his attack. Since the *Sephardic* population tended to be younger than the *Ashkenazi* one, these two tendencies blended together in the *Likud*'s favor.[11]

Still, as the year 1977 began, few were predicting the "earthquake" that took place in May. New elections became mandatory when Rabin's coalition fell apart in December 1976, due to the NRP's abstention on a no-confidence vote over an official ceremony that partly overlapped the *Sabbath*. Most prognosticators predicted that Labor would be returned as usual, but a series of disastrous events helped to foil these predictions. First, Rabin was challenged for the party leadership by Defense Minister Shimon Peres, who at the time was regarded as more of a hawk than the prime minister. Rabin fought off the challenge but the battle left major scars which helped create the rivalry between the two men that persists to the present day.

Then a rash of scandals unfolded in spring 1977, which rocked the party to its foundations. First, Asher Yadlin, who had been the party's candidate to head the Bank of Israel, was tried and found guilty of bribery. Housing Minister Avraham Ofer committed suicide while under investigation for misappropriation of funds. Finally, in April, press accounts revealed that Rabin's wife, Leah, had broken the law by keeping an illegal bank account in the United States, dating back to their days in Washington. Rabin was forced to withdraw as head of the Labor list and Peres was chosen to replace him. This event happened less than two months before the election.

Compounding Labor's difficulties was the existence of a new party, the Democratic Movement for Change. Headed by the former chief of staff and noted archeologist, Yigael Yadin, the DMC appealed primarily to the same middle class *Ashkenazi* constituency as Labor. Its platform was similar to Labor's in many areas, but had one major difference, a commitment to change in the political system, specifically electoral reform. Attracting a smattering of politicians from all across the spectrum, it seemed to represent a fresh force in the nation's politics.[12]

Moreover, *Likud* ran a sophisticated campaign, orchestrated by Ezer Weizman (today Israel's president and identified with Labor). Begin, who had been slowed by a heart attack, was portrayed as a grandfatherly figure, in an attempt to further soften his image which had gradually become less demonized since 1967. With Labor also taking a hard line on the Occupied Territories, *Likud*'s position no longer appeared extremist, while its calls for more free enterprise also seemed sensible. Still, polls taken in early may by *Ma'ariv* and *Yediot Asharonot* showed Labor leading by between 4 and 9 percent, although over a fifth of all voters were undecided.[13]

Consequently, when the election results were announced, they caused shock waves not only in Israel but around the world. Labor had suffered major losses, dropping 19 seats (51 to 32) and 15 percent of its vote (39 percent to 24 percent). But the *Likud* made only modest gains, picking up four seats (39 to 43) and just 3 percent more of the popular vote than it had in 1973. The biggest surprise was the showing of the DMC, which in its first attempt won 11.6 percent of the vote and 15 seats. And the various religious parties, who generally hover between 10 and 20 seats, picked up two from 1973 for a total of 17.

How does one account for this earthquake? A gradual decline in Labor's support and increase in the *Likud's* had been evident in 1973, so some further move in that direction was not unexpected. The *Likud's* gain of four seats probably reflected that trend. But the collapse of Labor was so dramatic as to require greater explanation. It would appear that the combination of the headline-making scandals of early 1977 and the presence of the DMC can to some extent account for it. The scandals caused many long-time Labor voters to withhold their support this time around, yet most were unwilling to vote for the *Likud,* a party they had regarded as anathema since *Herut's* inception. But it was much easier for them to vote for the DMC, which almost seemed to represent Labor without the scandals. It appears likely that the new party's 11 percent of the vote and 15 seats came primarily from former Labor voters. By voting DMC they could send a message to their old party without crossing the political divide.[14] Summing up the Labor débâcle, Aronoff concluded that the party had failed to do a number of things:

> ... to socialize a new generation of supporters and leaders, to maintain responsive party institutions, truly to integrate the Eastern Jews, to maintain its historic coalition partnership with the NRP, to prevent the main nationalist opposition from gaining legitimacy, and to prevent or resolve the crisis of identity which emerged between the late 1960s and mid 1970s [over the Occupied Territories].[15]

Still, before the earthquake could be considered complete, Begin and *Likud* had to put together a coalition government. He had 43 seats to start with, then added two more when Sharon, who had run on a separate list and captured two seats, rejoined the party. Then the NRP and *Agudat Israel* (another religious party), which had grown increasingly uncomfortable with Labor, threw their 17 seats Begin's way. Two more were added by a one-man party, Flatto-Sharon, and the co-opting of Labor's Dayan as foreign minister, bringing the total to 64, a small but sufficient majority. Later in the autumn, the DMC joined the coalition, adding 15 more seats, but that decision ended up tearing the party apart, causing its dissolution before the 1981 election (the small *Shinui* Party, now part of *Meretz*, is all that remains of it).[16]

The year 1977 thus brought an end to 29 years of single-party and one-bloc domination in Israel, but what would take its place? Superficially, one might look at the fact that *Likud* held or shared power in 1977–92 and conclude that those 15 years were a period of one-party dominance also. But that was not really the case. It would be more accurate to describe the period since 1977 as one of competitive two-party or two-bloc politics, characterized by extremely close elections between Labor and parties of the Left versus *Likud*, parties of the Right, and religious parties.

Election results from five national contests (1977, 1981, 1984, 1988, and 1992) bear out this fact. In those five races, Labor has actually performed marginally better, averaging 41.2 seats compared to *Likud*'s 40.8 percent and 32.1 percent of the vote to 31.7 percent respectively. In 1984, Labor actually out-polled the *Likud* by three seats, and in 1981 and 1988 fell only one seat short of its rival. Partly due to these close results, the two parties governed together from 1984 to 1990 in a National Unity Coalition.

But the main reason that the *Likud* held a slight advantage over that 15-year period was that its bloc was generally larger than Labor's. The 1977 election inaugurated the era of two competing blocs, each revolving around one of the major parties. And the key for the *Likud* has been the fact that the "third force" in Israeli politics, the religious parties, joined its bloc in 1977 and has remained there ever since, with one exception. The religious parties, for the most part, are committed to the concept of *"Eretz Israel,"* which has been *Herut-Likud*'s raison d'être from the beginning. On the other hand, Labor, led by Peres from 1977 to 1992, stood for compromise under the slogan "land for peace," and the parties of the Left are also more secular in orientation than the *Likud* and its allies, making coalition even more difficult. The problem was clearly demonstrated in the first year of Rabin's 1992–95 government, via the frequent clashes between former Education Minister Shulamit Aloni (of the secular Citizens' Rights Movement) and the *Shas* Party (the one exception noted above to the rule of religious parties joining *Likud* Coalitions).[17]

Comparing the size of the two blocs in the last five elections, *Likud* had an average advantage of 63–54.[18] During that time the religious parties have never won fewer than 13 seats and these always went to the *Likud* bloc prior to 1992, tipping the scales in their favor. Without those religious Knesset members, *Likud* would not have been able to form a government after any election, except for the two *Likud*-Labor grand coalitions that governed in 1984–90. Only in 1992, when parties of the Left won 61 seats, thereby making a *Likud* government impossible, did *Shas*, which was the most dovish of the religious parties, choose to cross the aisle and join a Labor coalition. But the relationship was stormy; they quit the government in summer 1993 and did not rejoin.

Why does it appear that Israel has a competitive two-party and two-bloc system? Because each party and bloc has a solid base of support with a large number of voters who are loyal to it and its ideology. Labor and Leftist party loyalists tend to be *Ashkenazim,* middle class, less religious, and in favor of the "land for peace" concept. *Likud* and parties of the Right draw support mostly from the religiously observant, the lower classes, and those who want to hold onto the Occupied Territories. Labor and the Left's worst performance came in 1977 when they captured only 33 percent of the vote and 41 seats, but this was clearly an aberration, as it was at least 10 percent less than the Left has ever polled either before or since. The Labor bloc's best showing came in 1992 when it polled 49.4 percent of the vote.

Conversely, the bloc of Rightist and religious parties hit its nadir in 1992. But with 48.1 percent of the vote they barely fell short of the Left. Their highest total had come just four years earlier with 52.7 percent, demonstrating a remarkably consistent bloc of Rightist and religious voters. While *Likud* lost 6.2 percent and eight seats in 1992, parties allied to it partially compensated by picking up two of those seats. Labor's "blocking majority" was a razor-thin 61 seats and these included five places won by Arab anti-Zionist parties who could not be included in the government, due to an unwritten rule of Israeli politics. Only the addition of *Shas* to the coalition gave the government a "Jewish majority."[19] A shift of just two seats to the Right would have allowed the *Likud* to stay in power in 1992.

Still, thin as its margin was, Labor formed its first government since 1977 and *Likud* found itself out of power for the first time since then. A number of factors explained this result. First, the Russian immigrants who had poured into the country since 1990 were angry about their high unemployment rates and poor housing prospects; thus, they voted heavily against the *Likud.*[20] Second, many *Sephardim* in the party were upset because their hero, David Levy, had complained about the shabby treatment he had received from Yitzhak Shamir and other *Ashkenazi Likud* leaders; *Sephardic* support for the party consequently declined. Third, *Likud* was hurt by corruption scandals, particularly in Ariel Sharon's Housing Ministry.[21] Also, U.S. President George Bush's refusal to guarantee loans for new housing unless Shamir agreed to halt construction in the West Bank and Gaza indicated that normal relations with the United States were in jeopardy under *Likud.*[22] And finally, Labor helped its own cause by replacing the dovish four-time loser, Peres, at the top of the list with the hawkish and more popular Rabin.[23] Perhaps the biggest surprise of the election was the fact that, given all these handicaps, the *Likud* and its allies still came so close to retaining their hold on power.

Thus, if we return to the four factors necessary for dominance cited at the beginning of this chapter, we can conclude that *Mapai*/Labor possessed them in 1948–77, but the *Likud* did not in 1977–92. The first requirement, dominance in numbers, was clearly held by *Mapai* until 1973, when the *Likud* made its first strong showing. But conversely, the *Likud* itself only scored one dominant victory at the polls, in 1977, while its subsequent wins were much too narrow to be considered signs of domination. As for the second prerequisite, dominant bargaining position, *Mapai*/Labor clearly had such a status until 1977, for it would have been impossible to form a government without it, a claim no other party could make during those years. Such a bargaining position was also held by *Likud* after the 1977 and 1981 elections but not after the 1984 contest, when it was forced to share power with Labor, even to the point of rotating the prime minister's office between the two parties. In 1988, the *Likud*'s bargaining power marginally improved: it still had to form a grand coalition with Labor but was not required to share the top job.

With regard to chronological dominance, *Mapai*/Labor clearly controlled Israeli politics for a period of 29 years, but the *Likud*'s tenure is more difficult to judge. The party was continuously in office for 15 years but for six of those years (1984–90) it shared the government with Labor. And finally, in the category of dominance in government, the 1984–90 period also weakens *Likud*'s case. For those entire six years, Rabin served as defense minister, while Peres was successively prime minister (1984–86), foreign minister (1986–88) and finance minister (1988–90). Thus, the *Likud* only truly dominated the Israeli political system from 1977 to 1984, much too brief a time to establish an era.

The elections of May 1996 reinforced the pattern of a highly competitive two party and two-bloc system, but the four years leading up to them were among the most dramatic (and traumatic) in Israeli history. Rabin took office having pledged to complete an autonomy agreement with the Palestinians within nine months, but after negotiations in Washington appeared to stalemate, he turned to Foreign Minister Peres. His old rival had opened a channel to the PLO in Oslo, Norway, and this new opening quickly bore fruit. In September 1993, in a ceremony on the White House lawn, Rabin and Yasir Arafat shook hands and signed a declaration of principles to begin a three-stage process of constructing an agreement. This event took the whole world by surprise and became the major news story of the year.[24]

As a part of the agreement, Israel and the PLO officially recognized each other for the first time.[25] Stage one was to entail autonomy for Gaza and Jericho, a small town in the West Bank, but details were not finalized until May 1994. That month the Palestinian Authority was created and Palestinians were able to exercise some measure of self-rule for the first time in their history. But autonomy proved to be a double-edged sword. The economy of Gaza, already pathetically weak, grew worse under Arafat, due to the failure of the international community to provide sufficient financial help, the inexperience of the Palestinian Authority, and periodic closure of the Israeli border due to terrorist incidents.

Meanwhile, negotiations began over the second stage: autonomy for the major Palestinian cities in the West Bank, and elections to determine a president and a legislature for the Palestinian Authority. These negotiations proved difficult but were concluded in September 1995, climaxed by another White House lawn celebration.[26] Little did anyone at that ceremony know that the signing would commence a nine-month emotional roller coaster ride for both Israelis and Palestinians that would end in a *Likud* victory at the polls the following May.

Hope turned into despair just two months later when Rabin was assassinated by a right-wing Jewish Israeli after a peace rally in Tel-Aviv. This unprecedented act shocked the nation and brought discredit on parties of the Right, which had engaged in inflammatory rhetoric against Rabin and the peace process. Peres, who was sworn in as prime minister to replace his old comrade and rival, managed a smooth transition and continued the peace process unabated.[27]

Optimism seemed to return on both sides in January 1996 when the Palestinians held their first elections, which were generally regarded as successful. But that optimism was rudely shattered a month later when a series of bus bombings in Jerusalem and Tel-Aviv, carried out by the Islamic terrorist group *Hamas*, killed 60 Israelis and caused many others to question whether peace with the Palestinians was possible. Peres' double-digit lead over his challenger, the *Likud*'s Benjamin Netanyahu, vanished overnight with the election less than three months away.[28]

The final trauma was the attack on south Lebanon in April, undertaken in response to the firing of *Katyusha* rockets into northern Israel by *Hezbollah* guerrillas. The tragic shelling of a U.N. compound in Qana, which resulted in 100 deaths, gave Israel an international "black eye" and forced Peres to abandon the operation without ensuring security across the northern border. The election was held just one month later.[29]

In 1996 for the first time, Israelis cast two votes at the ballot box, the usual one for a party of their choice in the Knesset, a second to directly elect a prime minister. This change, which had been approved by the parliament in 1992, but delayed for four years, was intended to strengthen the power of the prime minister at the expense of the smaller parties in the coalition bargaining that always follows an election. One of its effects was to create a campaign resembling a U.S. presidential race, with a focus on the personalities and positions of the candidates.[30]

The provisions of this new electoral law called for a runoff between the top two candidates if no one received a majority on the first ballot. Rabin would have been the only candidate of the Left had he lived, and Peres, his replacement, was not challenged, as *Meretz* (a party to the left of Labor) and the Arab parties chose not to contest the prime minister's race. However, the Right seemed to be in major disarray. Following Labor's lead,[31] the *Likud* had instituted a primary in 1993 to replace Shamir, who had resigned following his defeat. Despite never having held any position higher than deputy minister, Netanyahu emerged as the victor, out-polling Levy (among others) who once again claimed discrimination. Levy subsequently quit the *Likud* and formed his own party, *Gesher*, announcing that he would run for prime minister. Similarly, Rafael Eitan, leader of the *Tsomet* Party, threw his hat into the ring, threatening to split the Right's vote three ways.

But in spring 1996 Sharon arranged a series of meetings between Netanyahu and his two rivals, which culminated in an agreement to merge both *Gesher* and *Tsomet* into the *Likud*. Both Levy and Eitan agreed to withdraw from the race, making this first direct election a straight fight between Peres and the *Likud* leader (and eliminating any need for a runoff).[32] Thus, the race took on even more of the aura of a U.S. two-party presidential campaign.

In fact, the news media, both in Israel and the U.S., focused almost exclusively on the prime ministerial contest while giving short shrift to the Knesset campaign. After the Rabin assassination, the combination of a sympathy vote and a backlash against the Right gave Peres an initial double digit lead, which he held steadily until the bus bombings of February-March 1996. Those terrorist atrocities wiped away most of that lead and the polls consistently forecast an extremely close race from then right up to election eve. The dominant issue of the campaign, by a large margin, was that of the "peace process" and its relation to national and personal security. Peres, backed by the Clinton administration, defended the pace of negotiations with the Palestinians and Syria, while Netanyahu argued that the peace process had instead worsened Israel's security position.[33]

Election results showed a country virtually split down the middle on this issue. After trailing in the early returns and having exit polls declare him the loser, Netanyahu emerged as the victor by a razor-thin margin: 50.4 percent to 49.5 percent, a difference of less than 30,000 votes. The Knesset race was equally close with Labor winning 34 seats to *Likud*'s 32. The bloc of Rightist and religious parties picked up a total of 57 seats, a loss of two from the last election, while the Labor-*Meretz*-Arab bloc, which had controlled the previous Knesset with 61 seats, fell to 52. Two new Centrist parties, the Russian Immigrants Party (*Yisrael Ba'aliya*) and the Third Way, won seven and four seats respectively.[25] Therefore, neither bloc could control the Knesset without at least one of these new parties, but each had previously indicated that they would support, under certain conditions, whichever man was chosen as prime minister.[35] Thus, Netanyahu was able to put together a coalition that could rely on a comfortable 68-seat majority (compared to Rabin's mere 61 votes).[36]

How does one account for these results, which would have to be termed an upset? Certainly, the absence of Rabin was a major factor. Known as "Mr. Security," he inspired widespread confidence from the Israeli public much more than Peres, who was considered too naive and trusting of Arafat and Syria's leader, Hafez Assad. Considering how narrow the margin turned out to be, it is likely that Rabin would have emerged victorious, even in the same circumstances.

One of those circumstances, which also played a huge role, was the series of bombings carried out by *Hamas* in late February and early March 1996. They caused many Israelis to have second thoughts about the pace of the peace process, and served to reinforce Peres' image as a "naive" leader. Without these tragic events, he almost certainly would have won.

Other factors were Netanyahu's gradual softening of the *Likud* hard line as the election drew closer, his "American-style" media campaign, and his performance in the one televised debate. Moreover, Labor antagonized both religious and Russian voters during its four years in power, the former by treating them as pariahs and the latter by neglecting their needs much as the *Likud* had done previously.

The direct election of the prime minister in some ways has had an effect opposite from what was intended: it may turn out to increase the powers of Netanyahu's office, but it certainly did not strengthen the two major parties. Labor lost 10 seats from its 1992 total and *Likud* (plus *Tsomet*) declined by eight seats. Their combined total of 66 seats was the smallest since these two parties were created in the late 1960s and early 1970s.

On the other hand, the smaller parties did much better than expected, capturing 54 seats, which was an all-time high. The most successful were the three religious parties: *Shas*–10, National Religious Party–9, and United Torah Judaism–4. The split vote apparently allowed their supporters, who generally back the Right, to help *Likud* by voting for Netanyahu and then help themselves by voting for their own party. And the Russian immigrants, who felt neglected by the *Likud* in 1992, were equally angry with Labor this time around. So they formed their own party, led by ex-dissident Natan (Anatoly) Sharansky, and won seven seats (three or four of those had gone to Labor in the previous election).[37]

Overall, the 1996 election results demonstrate the continued validity of the competitive two-party and two-bloc model in Israel. Both the prime minister's race and the Knesset contest were extremely close. Had a mere

15,000 voters shifted to Peres, he would have retained his office. And he could have formed a coalition with his 34 Labor seats, nine from *Meretz,* nine from the two Arab parties, and 11 from the two Centrist parties who were ready to support whichever candidate came out the winner. Once again, this election demonstrated that the overwhelming majority of voters were solidly attached to one of the two blocs and that the number of floating voters was quite small.[38]

After the break up of the Netanyahu government coalition, the May 1999 elections appeared to call that premise into question, as the *Likud* Bloc under Netanyahu's leadership suffered a disastrous defeat. After a tumultuous three-year-term during which he alienated many of his own cabinet ministers—Dan Meridor, David Levy, Yitzhak Mordechai and Benny Begin—Netanyahu was buried by an apparent political landslide (44 percent to 56 percent) by the One Israel Bloc (Labor plus two small parties) under its new leader, former Chief of Staff, General Ehud Barak. The prime minister's personal characteristics, rather than his policies, appear to have played the largest role in his crushing defeat. But his downfall was equally shared by the parties on the Right. *Likud* itself declined to 19 seats, its fewest since the 1960s, and along with its allies garnered only 37 mandates, clearly its poorest electoral showing in 30 years.

Another new trend in this election was the replacement of the "lands versus peace" issue as the salient one in the campaign. With *Likud* having continued to implement, however unwillingly, the Oslo Accords, that issue seemed to fade in comparison to the conflict between secular and religious Israeli. The biggest winners in the Knesset were *Meretz-Shinui,* which gained seven seats between 1996 and 1999 to reach a total of 16 through a fierce anti-*haredi* campaign, and *Shas,* the *Sephardim* religious party led by its recently convicted leader, Aryeh Deri, which also added seven new mandates to reach a total of 17 now. Other religious parties (NRP and UTJ) gained ten seats between them.

On the other hand, the May 1999 election saw the continuation of one pattern that has been evident since 1984: the gradual decline of the two biggest parties, Labor and *Likud.* After combining for 95 seats in 1981, the two saw their totals fall to 85 (1984), 79 (1988), 76 (1992) and 66 (1996). But the precipitous drop in this most recent election to a mere 45 seats meant that even if they joined forces again in a new coalition government, they would fall far short of a workable parliamentary majority. This development, which has alarmed members of both parties, has led a number of them to call for the repeal of the Direct Election Law, but the smaller parties, who obviously benefit from it, now hold the majority in the Knesset and are unlikely to back such a move.[39] The 1999 elections' twin trends may turn out to be aberrations, although it will require several more national elections to determine if that is the case. Whether the trends are aberrations or not, future changes in the electoral law seem quite remote.

But, if the most recent Israeli elections bode well for the future of a competitive political system, the inaugural Palestinian elections held in January 1996 did not. While these elections had many positive aspects, it would appear that they are a step, though not an irreversible one, towards one-party dominance in whatever political configuration the Palestinian Authority eventually evolves into. Of course, this development is hardly surprising. No democratic system exists anywhere in the Arab world and Palestinian politics has been dominated by the PLO and Yasir Arafat for the past 30 years. Moreover, throughout the non-Western world, new states freeing themselves from foreign rule have usually been dominated by the organizations and individuals who led the struggle for independence. Thus, Arafat and his *Fatah* faction are following a familiar pattern.

Palestinian elections were called for in the Interim Agreement (Oslo II) signed by Rabin and Arafat in September 1995.[40] They were to be held soon after the Israeli army completed its withdrawal from the major cities in the West Bank, which was accomplished by the end of December. The elections were held just three weeks after the withdrawal. As they approached, serious questions were raised that would never be asked about elections in Israel. Would they be free and fair? Would there be a high turnout? Would the Palestinian people accept the results? That is one of the differences between elections in an established democracy and those in a nation just beginning a democratic process.

Voters on 20 January 1996 choose a president and an 88-member legislature for the Palestinian Authority. From the beginning, it was obvious that Arafat and *Fatah* would triumph easily, due primarily to lack of serious opposition.[41] *Hamas,* the only other major political force in the West Bank and Gaza, chose not to contest the elections, although some of its members ran as independents.[42] Chairman Arafat himself faced only a token opponent, a woman named Samiha Khalil, in his campaign for the Presidency. Therefore, the results were predictable. Arafat was elected president with 88 percent of the vote to 9 percent for his opponent, while *Fatah* and other pro-Arafat candidates captured approximately three-quarters of the 88 seats (the estimates vary between 66 and 71).[43] But two prominent Palestinians who have broken with the Chairman, Hanan Ashrawi and Haidar Abdel Shafi, were elected in their respective districts (Jerusalem and Gaza). Consequently, there will be opposition in the council but how effective it will be remains to be seen.

Were these elections free and fair? The official statement of the heads of the international observer delegations drew both positive and negative conclusions. Negatively, they noted "certain measures which have inhibited the rights and freedoms normally associated with election campaigning," "a full understanding of the opportunities offered by democracy has still to develop in the body politic," and "a tendency to intimidate the media, which has been noted during the election process." On the other hand, the delegations applauded: "the very low level of election-related violence," the fact that "the electorate was presented with some variety of political views and a choice in most constituencies between official party-backed candidates and independents," and that "all candidates were offered the opportunity to make election broadcasts on Palestinian Radio." Overall, the observers concluded that "when judged against internationally acceptable standards, and after weighting in the balance some deficiencies which have been noted . . . [the elections] can reasonably be regarded as an accurate expression of the will of the voters on polling day."[44]

Voter turnout was also encouraging. Overall turnout was estimated at an impressive 79 percent, with close to 90 percent participating in Gaza and over 70 percent in the West Bank. Only in Jerusalem was the turnout disappointing (40 percent) and that was due to intimidation by Israeli soldiers, and the requirement that many people had to leave the city to cast their ballots.[45] For an inaugural election preceded by a brief two-week campaign, the results were impressive.

Has the Palestinian public accepted the results? The answer, so far, is a tentative yes, but the victory of the *Likud* has made it more difficult for Arafat to maintain his credibility, since he has found it more difficult to win concessions from Netanyahu than he did from Rabin and Peres. Thus, Arafat is not likely to be defeated at the ballot box, but could become the victim of an assassination or a revolution if his popularity wanes. Making judgments on Palestinian politics based on one single election is unwise. The likelihood of Palestine becoming a Western-style democracy may not be high, but this election was more democratic than those held in Egypt, Jordan, or any other Arab state. And that is an accomplishment in which Palestinians throughout the world can take justifiable pride.

Table 5.1 LABOR vs. *LIKUD* (seats won in election)

	1977	1981	1984	1988	1992	1996
Labor Party	32	47	44	39	44	34
Likud Party	43	48	41	40	32	32
Labor Bloc	41	54	59	55	61	52
Likud Bloc	64*	66	61	65	59	57*

*In both 1977 and 1996 Isreali parties not aligned with either bloc won seats in the Knesset. In 1977 the Democratic Movement for Change won 15 seats, and in 1996 the Russian Immigrants Party won seven and the Third Way four. In both ears, Isreali non-aligned parties wound up joining the *Likud* coalition.

Notes

1. T. J. Pempel, "Uncommon Democracies: the One-Party-Dominant Regimes," in T. J. Pempel ed., *Uncommon Democracies: The One-Party-Dominant Regimes* (Ithaca, NY: Cornell University Press, 1990), p. 3–4.
2. Gregory Mahler, *Israel: Government and Politics in a Maturing State* (New York: Harcourt, Brace, Jovanovich, 1990), Ch. 6.
3. Pempel, ed., *Uncommon Democracies,* p. 20.
4. Michael Shalev, "The Political Economy of Labor-Party Dominance and Decline in Israel," in Pempel, ed., *Uncommon Democracies,* p. 84–85.
5. Myron J. Aronoff, "Israel under Labor and the Likud: the Role of Dominance Considered," in Pempel ed., *Uncommon Democracies,* p. 266.
6. Shalev, "The Political Economy," p. 112–113.
7. Benjamin Akzin, "The Likud," in Howard R. Penniman, *Israel at the Polls: the Knesset Elections of 1977* (Washington: Books Demand, 1979), p. 91–114; Ilan Peleg, "The Legacy of Begin and Beginism for the Israeli Political System," in Gregory Mahler ed., *Israel after Begin* (Albany, NY: state University of New York Press, 1990), p. 19–49.
8. Shalev, "The Political Economy," p. 115–116; Aronoff, "Israel under Labor and Likud," p. 267.
9. Don Peretz, "The War Election and Israel's Eighth Knesset," in *Middle-East Journal,* vol. 28, no. 2 (1974): p. 111–125. The most complete analysis of this election is found in Asher Arian, ed., *The Elections in Israel—1973* (Jerusalem: Transaction Publishing, 1975).
10. Ofira Seliktar, "Ethnic Stratification and Foreign Policy in Israel: the Attitudes of Oriental Jews toward Arabs and the Arab-Israeli Conflict," in *Middle-East Journal,* vol. 38, no. 1 (1984): p. 34–50.
11. Asher Arian, *Politics in Israel, the Second Generation* (Chatham NJ: Chatham House, 1989), p. 147–170; Abraham Diskin, *Elections and Voters in Israel* (New York, 1992), p. 163–186.
12. Penniman, *Israel at The Polls, Jerusalem Post International Edition* (January–May 1977).
13. Don Peretz, "The Earthquake: Israel's Ninth Knesset Elections," in *Middle-East Journal,* vol. 31, no. 3 (1977): p. 251.
14. Peretz, "Earthquake," p. 252–255; Efraim Torgovnik, "A Movement for Change in a Stable System," in Penniman, *Israel at The Polls,* p. 147–172; C. Paul Bradley, *Parliamentary Elections in Israel: Three Case Studies* (Grantham, NH: Tompson & Rutter, 1985), p. 48–84.
15. Aronoff, "Israel Under Labor and the Likud," p. 271.
16. Peretz, "Earthquake," Penniman, *Israel at The Polls, 1977;* Bradley, *Three Case Studies.*
17. *Jerusalem Post International Edition* (July 1992-July 1993).
18. If we omit Labor's disastrous showing in 1977, the margin in the next four elections is much narrower, 63–57 in favor of the *Likud.* Arian, *The Second Generation,* and Diskin, *Elections and Voters,* provide excellent analysis of electoral behavior prior to 1992, as do Gershon Kieval & Bernard Reich eds., *Israeli Politics in the 1990s* (New York, 1992).

19. Sammy Smooha & Don Peretz, "Israel's 1992 Knesset Elections: Are They Critical?" in *Middle-East Journal*, vol. 47, no. 3 (1993): p. 444–463; Daniel Elazar & Shmuel Sandler, "The 1992 Knesset Elections: Mahapach or a Transfer of Power," in D. Elazar & S. Sandler, eds., *Israel at the Polls 1992* (Lanham, MD, 1995), p. 1–26.

20. Bernard Reich, Meyrav Wurmser & Noah Dropkin, "Playing Politics in Moscow and Jerusalem: Soviet Jewish Immigrants and the 1992 Knesset Elections," in Elazar & Sandler, *Israel at the Polls 1992*, p. 127–154.

21. Mordechai Nisan, "The Likud: the Delusion of Power," in Elazar & Sandler, *Israel at the Polls 1992*, p. 45–66.

22. Gerald M. Steinberg, "A Nation That Dwells Alone? Foreign Policy in the 1992 Elections," in Elazar & Sandler, *Israel at the Polls 1992*, p. 175–200.

23. Efraim Inbar, "Labor's Return to Power," in Elazar & Sandler, *Israel at the Polls 1992*, p. 27–44.

24. Text of Declaration of Principles in *Journal of Palestine Studies*, vol. XXIII, no. 1 (1994): p. 115–124.

25. Letters of Recognition between Rabin and Arafat, 9 September, 1993 in Ian J. Bickerton & Carla L. Klausner, *A Concise History of the Arab-Israeli Conflict* (Englewood Cliffs, NJ, 1995), p. 278–280.

26. Text of Interim Agreement in *Journal of Palestine Studies*, vol. XXV, no. 2 (1996): p. 123–140.

27. *New York Times* (5 November 1995): p. 1.

28. *Jerusalem Post International Edition* (2 March 1996): p. 1; and (9 March 1996): p. 1.

29. *Jerusalem Post International Edition* (20 April 1996): p. 1; and (27 April 1996): p. 1.

30. Liat Collins, "Yes, Mr. Prime Ministe," in *Jerusalem Post International Edition* (25 May 1996): p. 13.

31. The Labor Party held a primary for the first time in its history in February 1992, choosing Rabin over Peres as its candidate for prime minister. Inbar, "Labor's Return to Power," p. 29.

32. *Jerusalem Post International Edition* (7 February 1996): p. 1; and (9 March 1996): p. 1.

33. *New York Times* (30 May 1996): p. 1.

34. *New York Times* (1 June 1996): p. 1; *Jerusalem Post International Edition* (8 June 1996): p. 1–3.

35. Herb Keinon, "The Principal Thing," in *Jerusalem Post International Edition* (25 May 1996): p. 3.

36. *New York Times* (19 June 1996): p. 1.

37. Reich, Wurmser & Dropkin, "Soviet Jewish Immigrants," p. 127–128.

38. Don Peretz & Gideon Doron, "Israel's 1996 Elections: a Second Political Earthquake?" in *Middle-East Journal*, vol. 50, no. 4 (1996): p. 529–546.

39. *Jerusalem Post International Edition* (28 May 1999): p. 1–4; *New York Times* (18 May 1999): p. 1, 10; *New York Times* (19 May 1999): p. 1, 12.

40. Text of Interim Agreement, p. 123–140.

41. *New York Times* (21 January 1996); Lamis Andoni, "The Palestinian Elections: Moving toward Democracy or One-Party Rule," in *Journal of Palestine Studies,* vol. XXV, no. 3 (1996): p. 5–16. Although more than 670 candidates ran for the 88 seats, over 500 of them were independents. Salma Shawa, "The Palestinian Elections: a Strong Start into an Uncertain Future," in *Washington Report on Middle-East Affairs* (April 1996): p. 23.

43. Andoni, "Palestinian Elections," p. 7.

43. *New York Times* (23 January 1996): p. 4; Andoni, "Palestinian Elections," p. 14; Shawa, "Palestinian Elections," p. 98.

44. "Joint statement by Heads of International Observer Delegations to the Palestinian Elections, January 1996," in *Journal of Palestinian Studies,* vol. XXV, no. 3 (1996): p. 140–141.

45. *New York Times* (23 January 1996): p. 4; Andoni, "Palestinian Elections," p. 6; Shawa, p. 23; *Jerusalem Post International Edition* (27 January 1996): p. 2; Khalil Shikaki, "Palestinian Elections: an Assessment," in *Journal of Palestine Studies,* vol. XXV, no. 3 (1996): p. 17–22.

SIX

Politics, Culture, and
Democratic Reform in Japan

John P. Horgan

Certain indices serve as benchmarks for democracy. All but a tiny fringe of the Japanese people embrace the ideal of democracy and feel that they have a working democracy. Under universal suffrage of those over 20, elections are held by secret ballot to choose and change governments. Participation has been high until recently. Balloting is fair, however much the electoral system itself has needed revision. Governments reflect the nation's priorities.[1] They have brought freedom, peace, prosperity and prestige to the people. The Japanese have created a high level of resource distribution, which has fostered an open society where "If we work hard, our lives will improve accordingly."[2] The Constitution protects civil rights including free speech and assembly, enforced by a legal system, that has its singular accents. For instance, there are no political prisoners, however legal maneuvering allows for "unconvicted detention," which keeps extremists out of society long enough to dilute their effectiveness.[3] There is no official censorship. Mass media includes television critique, public debate, and one of the world's most prolific publication industries.[4] The nation has a highly trained, professional, and apolitical civil service, obedient to the nation's economic and political welfare, although it embodies the contradiction of a free economy managed by Mandarin bureaucrats. Interest groups have wide interaction in the policy process including public-private deliberation councils called *shingikai*. Furthermore, Japan boasts a healthy local government system based on a tradition of localism (*jimoto shugi*).[5] The education system creates a meritocracy—the foundation of Japan's social mobility—which has combined universal access with world-class standards.[6] No careful observer of Japan believes that the military are lurking in their barracks waiting to turn the clock back, or that fanatics of the Right or Left are poised to make a comeback.[7]

Nevertheless, dissatisfaction abounds and continued political and social improvement occupies the nation.[8] Change in the abstract means letting a "Japanized" democracy take root. In the concrete, it means change from a past of social order and a distrust of popular democracy to a future of increasing personal liberty and individualism within the framework of tradition. Democracy in Japan has meant consultation, compromise and harmony within a collective framework, not the Western concept of individual rights. While Japan has broken the bonds of political tyranny, some say the social system—the traditional hierarchical layering—remains tyrannous.[9] Specifically, the focus of this essay will be on the ongoing struggle for broad political reform through the means of revision of the electoral system—campaign finance, reapportionment, and the "political corruption prevention system."[10]

As always the past plays a strong role. Culture—the living remnants of tradition—functions like an operating system in a mental computer. On the order of 3500 BC, celestial observers in the Mesopotamian city-states found the heavens move at rates that can be defined predictably, leading to the great intellectual achievement of the idea of an all-embracing order embedded in the universe. Confucius read this universal "order" (*chitsujo*) as a grand hierarchy normative for society in a rational way—there is an order imbedded in the universe and there is an order embedded in society. "The collectivity, be it the family, corporation, or nation-state, takes priority over its individual members."[11] This idea is antithetical to the flowering of democracy.

Confucianism did not create the Japanese mind; however, its teachings over the centuries codified the Japanese temperament and proved useful for governing. Although undergoing steady change, society today is still loosely organized into overlapping Confucian-style "cones." One is a member of various groups requiring reciprocal obligations; one is either the leader or a follower (*oyabun-kobun*) and up or down (*sempai-kohai*) within them. One's cone is either up or down in relation to the other cones, and one has little chance to prosper outside one's cones. Life in the cones can be individually fulfilling or socially tyrannous depending on one's point of view. Outside groups are adversarial. Group differences are to be settled through consensus and harmony, a concept stated in the first article of Shotoku Taishi's 17-article constitution in AD 604 and the *Analects* of Confucius I, 12. Confucius values loyalty toward parents and elders. Even the organization of capitalism bears a distinctive Confucian stamp.[12] The Japanization of these principles added Buddhist benevolence and made the obligation reciprocal—the higher must care for the lower—a "pre-democratic" element. Again, Buddhism did not create the Japanese psyche, but provided a cosmology compatible with native insight.

These traditional ways of organizing society are now under heavy pressure from democratic ideals of individual freedom. Nevertheless, the Japanese language itself is structured to support such a traditional, hierarchical, and group-oriented society. *Keigo,* an integral grammatical component, announces the speaker's up/down relationship to the person addressed and the person being spoken about, as well as the speaker's view of his own rank. It is not optional, and Japanese social intercourse requires *keigo,* although the trend in society today is to lessen the impact of *keigo.*

As Japan's feudal political system had grown sclerotic, modern democracy developed after the arrival of U.S. Commodore Matthew Perry's "Black Ships" off the coast of Uraga in 1853. The Tokugawa feudal government had proved indecisive in the face of the guns of European colonialism and imperialism. Although an egalitarian middle class of artisans and small shopkeepers—a "pre-democratic" aspect—had grown up in the cities, they proved a drain on the countryside and the economy was nearing collapse.[13] Peasant uprisings grew common. The power and sway of the central government weakened as local warlords increasingly took matters into their own hands. In 1868 a pro-imperial alliance led by Satsuma and Choshu forces seized the imperial palace in Kyoto and proclaimed the imperial restoration. Then, in a series of battles in 1868 and 1869 called the "Boshin War," the alliance overthrew of the feudal government and "restored" the emperor, beginning the Meiji Era (1868–1912).

The first major political act of the new leaders was to issue the Charter Oath in the name of the new emperor. It promised: "(1) Deliberative assemblies shall be widely established and all matters decided by public discussion. (2) All classes, high and low, shall unite in vigorously carrying out the administration of affairs of state. (3) The common people, no less than the civil and military officials, shall each be allowed to pursue his own calling so that there may be no discontent. (4) Evil customs of the past shall be broken off and everything shall be based upon the laws of nature. (5) Knowledge shall be sought throughout the world so as to strengthen the foundations of imperial rule." This remarkable document can be considered another "pre-democratic" element in Japan, foreshadowing the ideals of the future, and certainly in stark contrast to the politics of the other nations of Asia.[14]

The middle class did not promote a revolt of the bourgeoisie. Rather, oligarchies, later called *genro* ("elders"), seized control. In order to serve the nation, the benevolent leaders of the new government, former *samurai* and court noblemen, created an industrial policy under the banner of *oitsuite oikosoo* (catch-up and overtake) and they directed investment to create wealth and power. They established capitalism by government fiat, or what has come to be known as a "capitalist development state,"[15] with its central bank and the *zaibatsu* cartels—Mitsui, Mitsubishi, Sumitomo and Yasuda. The state was a protectionist one with traditions like *kanson minpi* (respect officials, look down on the people). A sense of national purpose emerged. Furthermore, more seeds of Japan's later democracy were planted during the Meiji Era, as were the problems of later years. For instance, the new oligarchs jettisoned the feudal system of rigid caste differences—warriors, farmers, artisans, and tradesmen. Their doing so shows that tradition is like an oral tale agreed upon. On the negative side, party politics never rose to the task of replacing the *genro*.

Meiji Japan was the first non-Western state to adopt a constitutional form of government, when in 1889, Ito Hirobumi drafted a Prussian-style constitution.[16] It had a Confucian rather than a liberal democratic accent, and it summed up Japan's cautious attitude towards popular democracy.[17] The emperor was "inviolable," his rule "eternal," and his person "sacred." Within this context, the Constitution was the "immutable fundamental law" granted to the people by virtue of "the supreme prerogative inherited from our Imperial ancestors." The parliamentary-cabinet government imperfectly followed the prototypical British pattern. Ministers of state were responsible to the emperor and not to the parliament, while the military forces remained under direct imperial command, not under the cabinet whose members were not necessarily drawn from the Diet. The Diet's function was to serve the emperor and contribute its share to the harmonious workings of the family state. The bureaucracy, a meritocracy whose entrance was based on examinations, took the Prussian model and gradually took over the role of the *genro*.

Yoshino Sakuzo (1878–1933)[18] translated the word "democracy" as *minpon shugi*, which means that the aim of national sovereignty is rule *for the benefit of the people*. It is this same inflection that allows the "Democratic People's Republics" to borrow the "democratic" appellation. This definition sits well with Confucius, with an emperor system, and with a triumvirate of politicians, industrialists, and bureaucrats deciding national policy. Democracy in the sense of mass participation based on individual liberty was held in the darkest suspicion. How could one trust the self-centered masses to act magically in their overall interest, especially through "chaotic" devices like elections, embodying confrontation between interest groups, and settled by a majority instead of consensus? Incremental democratization through a carefully orchestrated process of the harmonious reconciliation of the various interests seemed in order; "full democracy" might have led the state to spin out of control, or so they thought then. Such thinking has not departed the political scene.

Nevertheless, other "pre-democratic" traits took root.[19] In the early 1900s Liberal ideas—the general trend in Europe and America—made steady progress among party politicians, businessmen, and élites such as journalists, educators, and diplomats. Those doctrines had appeal in themselves, but they were also the thinking of the most powerful nations on earth, lending them instant coin then as now. Two political parties emerged, backed by industrialists: the *Minseito* by Mitsubishi and the *Seiyukai* by Mitsui. The first party cabinet appeared in 1898 and immediately collapsed.

During the Taisho Era (1912–25), democracy vied to play a decisive role in governing at a time when no other government in Asia could be called democratic. By the 1920s, the pre-war liberal movement or "Taisho Democracy" reached its height in an embryonic pluralism. Its key tenets were: (1) that the government be conducted by party cabinets responsible to the lower house in the Diet; (2) that the lower house be elected by universal manhood suffrage; (3) that the people be guaranteed the exercise of their civil liberties; (4) that Japan abandon a policy of force in China and do no more than maintain the status in Manchuria; (5) that Japan follow a policy of international cooperation.[20]

"Taisho Democracy" stands as a great achievement in the development of democracy in Japan. The nation experienced a surge of hope for change, however, corrupt politicians and the world-wide Great Depression of 1930–35, called the *Showa* Depression in Japan, led to public disillusionment and, finally, terrorist assassinations by Rightist fundamentalists. The army struck in the infamous 26 February 1936 Incident. The coup failed, but party politics stood terrorized and discredited. Had democracy not ultimately failed, war might have been avoided.

Thereafter, the military assumed more and more power using its veto—the power to appoint military members of the cabinet. Unlike Hitler, Tojo did not lead a mass-movement to power. Still, the rise of Fascism and Nazism lent credibility to Japan's newfound theories of socio-economic controls based on Nazi and Fascist corporate ideas. The native religion, Shinto, was combined with neo-Confucianism to create a national mythology. The combination led to increasingly expansionist, militarist, and imperial policy. The neo-Confucian "mind-set" felt more comfortable with the totalitarian frame of mind, although Japan's native instinct is seclusion (*sakoku*), as shown by the ending of official embassies to China during the flowering of the Heian civilization (894 AD) and the virtual exclusion edicts of the Tokugawa Era (circa 1639). It is important to note that then, as now, foreign precedent is crucial, whether Confucian, Prussian, British, Nazi, or American.

After its defeat, Japan found itself in effect back in the year 1868 economically and militarily and with no international standing, particularly with its neighbors in Asia. However, the nation had patterns for development, and a trained workforce. But first came the Allied occupation. General Douglas MacArthur's first task was to feed and shelter the populace, but at the same time he set the policy framework: "Build the structure of representative government; modernize the constitution; hold free elections; enfranchise women; release political prisoners; liberate farmers; establish a free labor movement; encourage a free economy; liberalize education and decentralize political power."[21] The new constitution provided for a cabinet system, an independent judiciary, a supreme court, and a military under the control of the Diet, along with universal suffrage for women. It was approved in the first post-war elections on 10 April 1946 and went into effect in May 1947. The occupation proved a great historical watershed, but neither started nor finished the democratic process.

"Democracy" can also be translated as *minshu shugi*—the principle that sovereignty lies *in the people*. This had not been the system until the constitution of 1947. *Minshu shugi* is still not entirely digested. Hierarchical attitudes based on Confucian teachings linger in a complex way. Private or *shiteki* still connotes selfishness. Individualism is still a difficult concept to reconcile with social responsibility. The idea that all men are created equal is abstract when one's language relies on who others are and how they are ranked in relation to one. "Many Japanese find the concepts behind personal liberty, democracy, and free market economics to be foreign (*batakusai*). They do not share any universal religious beliefs or political ideals with other peoples in the world."[22] A university president said, "The new Constitution puts too much emphasis on the individual and his abstract (*chuushooteki*) relationships to the world. It does not take into sufficient account the needs of the Japanese family, community, and national life. It must be revised and brought into better balance."[23] Nevertheless, revision of the constitution is not a high priority, although a commission was set up in the Diet in 1999 to make a "preliminary" examination of the question. The question of revision is symbolic of the underlying drift and malaise in Japan today.

Within this post-war democratic framework, the protectionist patterns of Meiji resumed, abetted by the system of wartime controls which the occupation at first only imperfectly addressed and later strengthened.[24] The so-called "Yoshida Doctrine" established the priority of rebuilding industries, regaining foreign trade, and reconstituting reserves of cash and currencies. Based on Meiji precedents, the mechanism was a capitalism which did not use capital to maximize profit, but to maximize industrial potential—the concentration of public investment in infrastructure to the advantage of business while relying on domestic and international markets for price signals.[25] The ultimate beneficiaries were the abstract people, but it was not a consumer based economy. The policy was not spelled out, but has been given a mandate in elections ever since and remains, by default, the policy today. It has been legitimized by effectiveness, but it has now achieved its original goals and needs revision.

The occupation felt it had to rely on the bureaucracy to carry out its many reforms and unwittingly strengthened it. The Ministry of Finance continued to hold its power to shape and control the economy through its right to intervene in all transactions.[26] It can control which corporations receive bank credit, interest rates, and the prices of stocks, real estate and other investments. It need not explain its actions to either the Diet or the prime minister.[27] The Ministry of International Trade and Industry (MITI) was reborn with the avowed purpose of making the Japanese pre-eminent in world trade and even finance.[28] From this time forward it is difficult to dissect whether the politicians or the bureaucrats are in charge. This essay speaks of the "LDP's" achievements, but it could say "the LDP/bureaucracy." A U.S. president appoints well over 1,000 bureaucrats, whose ranks include camp followers, hangers-on, and many attorneys. With the concurrence of the factions, a prime minister appoints a total of 20 members of his cabinet, and his ministers may not be as powerful as their counterparts. Are we dealing with a feudal remnant, which impedes democracy, or a highly motivated élite who are free to make national policy without political interference from special interests? Party politics and the bureaucracy have been at odds since Meiji. Currently, the bureaucrats seem to be losing some ground, but party politics still seems unable to fill the vacuum.

The first major post-war Prime Minister, Yoshida Shigeru, faced two other fundamental problems—foreign affairs and security. The United States provided a protective umbrella throughout the period of the Cold War, allowing Japan to turn to economic development. The revision of the Security Treaty in 1960 yielded the diplomatic basis for Japan's return to the international community, but not without major turmoil, which threatened to bring democracy to the precipice.[29] On the social front, the LDP engaged the opposition in a struggle for control of the "hearts and minds," centering on educational policy. A sense of hard work, order, and hierarchy reemerged, with the people providing the disciplined, unselfish, and uncomplaining base for national regrowth. A sense of national purpose reemerged from the post-war malaise. Moral education—traditional rules for behavior—became a potent weapon in breaking the Leftist Japan Teacher's Union, a public employee union, and a key component of *Sohyo*, the Leftist labor federation. Decisive in this struggle was the public's fear of labor violence. In the process, the LDP took over the patriotic label as the "Japan Party" and was able to pursue its historical agenda.[30] Meanwhile the opposition grew increasingly divided and illegitimate, a process that soon created its own momentum and fed off itself in a vicious cycle.[31]

Left-wing intellectuals harkened back to their courageous record of opposition to pre-war Fascism. Vindicated by history, they took control of intellectual life. Although they received sympathy and support from the occupation, they did not see the United States as representative of democracy. It is ironic that the forces on the Left opposed the continued stationing of U.S. troops on Japanese soil when the U.S. umbrella was the best guarantee that democracy would further develop and the nation would not revert to totalitarianism, either Left or Right. Nor did the Left open a "great university" where all voices contended equally. They developed a system of political correctness—censorious, undemocratic, and heavily ideological. Intentionally or unintentionally, their major themes were supportive of Soviet foreign policy, as if an insurance policy against Scientific Socialism emerging victorious in the world struggle. Their key concept, subsuming all others, was the nuclear issue.[32]

A succession known as the "Yoshida School" (*Yoshida Gakko*) followed as prime minister. Sato, Kishi, and Ikeda were not formed in the crucible of party politics. They began as government bureaucrats. This succession of bureaucrats was broken by the rise of a party politician, Tanaka Kakuei, a businessman from the construction industry (*doken*) with no university education. Construction is still one of the largest industries and employed six million workers in Tanaka's era.[33] *Doken* is often synonymous with corruption and *"dango,"* an industry-wide system of bid rigging which provides the backbone of illegal political funding. The enigmatic Tanaka on the one hand fought for increased political control over the bureaucracy, while on the other he exploited the system without limit.[34] He brought both the strengths and weaknesses of democracy into high relief when he was arrested on 27 July 1976 and convicted in 1983 of accepting a $4.5 million bribe from the Lockheed Corporation. He dominated politics in and out of office, and created the largest and richest faction which forced "money makes right" (*kinken seiji*) on all politicians. He took pork to unimagined heights and nearly wrecked the financial system by funding construction projects. His alumni have played a pivotal role ever since, as have his legacies of power struggle with the bureaucrats, crony fiscal irresponsibility, massive corruption, and finally public reaction.

The Liberal Democratic Party grew in true Japanese fashion, a virtual umbrella of warlords under the leadership of a series of *daimyo,* with the electoral system feeding the machinery. A ground-breaking study by Nathaniel B. Thayer found that: (1) although the LDP had representatives in every part of the country, they seemed unable to become a mass party, and (2) the "factions" were central to the political process in spite of their being denounced on all sides.[35] The two problems are opposite sides of the coin. Each politician needs a support structure, usually with full panoply of women's and youth organizations. Each builds his own, called *koenkai*. Local politics then gravitates towards the *koenkai*, and not towards the national party, or even the local district. Even when the party itself raises funds, it still needs a way to decide allocation at the local level and makes such decisions through the factions. When he takes over power, each faction leader promises dissolution of the factions, political reform, and a mass national party. But it never happens. They boot-up their operating system and get a cultural "General Protection Fault." In defense of factions it should be noted that they brought a certain check on monolithic power within the LDP, a partial pluralism, and by default a substitute for alternation of parties.

The LDP has overcome many challenges since its inception in 1955, however corruption has proven insoluble. Politicians need large amounts of money to run elections and to take care of their supporters. They are expected to do far more than their counterparts in other democracies. They must care for their *koenkai* with gifts throughout the year as well as on special occasions like weddings. In 1990, reported political contributions amounted to $1.3 billion. Actual amounts were estimated to be much higher, and indirect contributions through stock manipulation, purchase of event tickets, and other subterfuges send the total even higher. Even at $1.3 billion, however, the figure dwarfs U.S. political contributions.[36] Such "structural" corruption, based on the then existing electoral system, has been seen as the root of all other evils.[37]

The old electoral system, a "single non-transferable vote (SNTV) in medium-sized constituencies," began in 1925 and was not modified by the occupation. Rare elsewhere, it may even be called the "Japanese System." Formerly, in a five-man district, for example, one could expect reelection with 20 percent to 25 percent (and sometimes as low as 12 to 15 percent) of the vote, giving the incumbent party a massive advantage, but also assuring the opposition of some representation. Apportionment has been increasingly skewered as the population has migrated to the cities. Furthermore, a prime minister is not directly elected, but chosen from among the LDP cadre, Diet members, and LDP local officials. The old system, what can be called a "controlled democracy," does not reflect even massive public indignation in a rapid way. It offered the citizens virtually no choices.

If money politics stems from the electoral process, the laxity of penalties and a lack of transparency in the campaign finance laws add to the problem.[38] Also custom shows ambivalence towards minor corruption and may wink at it.[39] Many citizens employ creative tax strategies (income taxes are a higher proportion of total taxes than in Europe). There is a dangerous mood of cynicism among people who have a low expectation of the Diet and even expect corruption to be a rule ("all politicians are dishonest").[40] Legal spending limits have been low. Other laws are vague and some offer ridiculous over-regulation (with an effect similar to the old 55-mile per-hour speed limit in the United States). Other cultural factors include a quest for consensus and eschewing confrontation.

While the Japanese can be proud of their economic achievements, and they may overlook small-scale corruption, large-scale corruption achieves "critical mass" and leads to massive indignation. The central moral message of the national religion is the idea of purification and cleanliness. "The basic moral idea is that the processes of nature cannot be evil. And to this there is the corollary that the pure heart follows the processes of nature."[41] Because Shintoism was hijacked in the service of totalitarianism by the right-wing nationalists of the pre-war period in collusion with neo-Confucianists, Shinto now languishes in a national and even international closet. This will not change soon, nor will the mandate of Shinto (stripped of political content) change in the innermost spirit of the Japanese people. A redefinition of the spirit of Shinto, devoid of its previous temporal political inflections, is vital for the psychic health of the nation.

From its beginnings in 1955 based on farmers and small shopkeepers, the LDP could never rest on its oars. It has become the "catch-almost-all" party.[42] Asanuma Inejiro, an early Socialist secretary-general, after the defeat in the 1958 elections bitterly complained that the conservatives stole many votes by promising old-age pensions, tax cuts, and other welfare measures.[43] Post-war Japan had no Willy Brandt, although Eda Saburo tried to reorient the Socialists after their defeat in 1960, only to be forced to resign as secretary-general.[44] The LDP and the bureaucracy together became a very pragmatic and not ideological but de facto Socialist Party. They have coordinated on behalf of less favored sectors, notably in rural areas and small business, and have repaired the broken parts of capitalist society. For instance, a mass migration of farmers to the cities changed the basis of political power,[45] leading to an agricultural policy that creates a rural "welfare" system, keeping overall income and wealth distribution among the most equitable in the industrialized world. Cynics ask if such adjustments represent democratic distribution of benefits or payoffs to core supporters.[46] Moreover, economic success created its own problems in a dialectic way—industrialization created massive pollution and revealed a pre-industrial welfare system. In the 1960s–70s the latter problems fed the rise of the opposition parties. After losing a series of local elections, the LDP and the bureaucrats saw their vulnerability and moved to provide social and economic security[47] by institutionalizing the policy-making role of various interest groups through "corporatism" or a system of "consultation on allotments" to avoid populism.[48]

While the LDP has pursued democratic development, political reform has proven more elusive. On the corruption issue, the LDP knew its vulnerability but was not able to face that reality until driven from office.

Cleaning up the system would mean smashing the "rice bowls" of the very people who would be expected to clean it up, on both sides of the fence. Furthermore, public indignation has been nuanced by the realization that LDP rule has been beneficial, and there seemed no viable alternative.

The high drama of political reform got underway when environmental and welfare policies led to budget deficits. In late 1988, the mandarins of the Finance Ministry (who were thinking of the overall benefit of all the people) had the LDP run a widely unpopular "3 percent national consumption sales tax" bill through the Diet, and the law went into force in April 1989. A second major negative element was injected into the scene when a massive scandal erupted the following month, and Prime Minister Takeshita Noboru was forced to resign in the wake of the Recruit Cosmos Affair. A brash young entrepreneur who built a small publishing business into a real estate and information conglomerate with $3.4 billion in annual sales aimed to use the company as leverage to propel himself into the élite circle of "rainmakers" who usually exclude such self-promoters. He offered cut-rate stock in companies soon to go public, and he donated in legal and illegal ways to political campaigns. He even loaned the money to buy the stocks.[49]

Uno Sosuke followed Takeshita in June of 1989, and was quickly caught in a scandal for payments of $21,000 to a *geisha* because he provided too little payoff in an era of big payoffs, and he looked *yabu,* or boorish. Thus the public had both a political and a pocketbook reason to protest in the upper house elections in July, and the LDP suffered its first electoral defeat in 34 years. While corruption was an important issue, the sales tax also played a key role in bringing out a labor, consumer, and women's vote that sealed the defeat. Also playing a role was the decision to open domestic markets to food imports as a concession to foreign pressure, creating a backlash among farmers, the LDP's central pillar.

The House of Councilors does not hold the power of the budget and is not as powerful as the House of Representatives. Loss of the Upper House election is largely symbolic. Nevertheless, this stunning defeat unleashed the forces of change both inside and outside the LDP. After only two months, Uno took responsibility and resigned in July 1989. There was for a time a heady and almost palpable feeling that change was at long last underway. Also, the younger LDP warlords grew restive. It would be wrong, however, to think that the old guard took the idea of political reform to heart. They were not ready to reverse years of stewardship for a "mood," and in the subsequent internal election for party president, chose image over substance by selecting Kaifu Toshiki. A former education minister with a clean, youthful, and vigorous demeanor, Kaifu took over in August 1989 with a much ballyhooed plan to overhaul the political system—a ceiling on donations to political parties, subsidies for elections, a change to single-seat constituencies, and reapportionment of the current system (long held unconstitutional by the supreme court).[50] He also vowed to repeal the sales tax of 1988.

Under Kaifu, the LDP stemmed its reverses in the national elections for the Lower House in February 1990. The voters played it safe. In an election characterized by Doi Takako, the chairwoman of the Socialist Party, as a "once in a lifetime chance" to end the LDP's old corrupt ways, the LDP won 275 out of 515 seats, with 240 going to the collected opposition. As a result, Ms. Doi resigned, and the LDP old guard quietly put electoral reform in a drawer while they faced looming trade problems with the United States.[51] The Socialist and Communist opposition also played a role in their own collapse. Japan is not a class-conflict nation. Most unions are enterprise unions. If it is the role of a political party to reform itself to take advantage of changing political realities and to move to where the votes are, then the opposition parties proved monumental failures. They clung to their Marxist ideology and waited for the voters to come to them.[52] Thus the Cold War had a negative influence on the development of pluralism—a less ideological party might have emerged much earlier as a viable opposition to single-party domination.

Kaifu was widely seen as an interim figure, the pawn of power brokers. One old guard leader even called him "little, stupid, sentimental on issues, and 'harping' on the past."[53] Nevertheless, he stubbornly refused to accept defeat and continued to espouse reform. That advocacy led to his downfall. He lost in the elections for party president of October 1991. By then he had his own scandals, which exposed the truth that the stock market was rigged to reinforce the relationship between the political and business worlds.[54]

The patrician Miyazawa Kiichi, a former bureaucrat with a clean reputation, replaced Kaifu. Miyazawa did not have a strong political base of his own, but ruled in accord with the tradition of *gaiseki,* a pattern enshrined since the Middle Ages when the *Shogun* and *Bakufu* ran the country in the name of the emperor. Kanemaru Shin, a true follower of the Tanaka legacy, moved into the position of wirepuller through undemocratic back-room deal making. Miyazawa had cordially despised him for many years, but was forced by real politic to elevate him to the post of party vice president in January of 1992. The deal was sealed at a "smoke-filled geisha party" on tatami floors with the *sake* flowing. This move confirmed Kanemaru's role as chief party log-roller and it revealed an ultimate weakness of Miyazawa and Japanese democracy.

The next month the police raided the offices of Tokyo Sagawa Kyubin, a start-up parcel delivery service that needed (highly regulated) routes in order to grow, providing the classic situation for corruption. Evidence of $80 million payoffs to more than 130 Diet members surfaced along with evidence the LDP had ties to the Japanese mob. As a follow-up, Kanemaru's home was raided by prosecutors on March 6, and $31 million in bonds, $960,000 in gold bars, and $391,000 in cash were found, all secreted from the tax office. Miyazawa was gravely wounded. The restive *daimyo* stirred—Ozawa Ichiro seized the issue and announced, "A leader is born of the needs of the times. My interest now is to achieve reform."[55] Unlike grass-roots protesters, these men were sophisticated politicians who knew the system from the inside and who embodied forces at work just beneath the surface. If the Kanemaru scandal were not enough, still another time-bomb began ticking with Upper House elections in the offing for 26 July 1992. Hosokawa Morihiro, a grandson of a *samurai* who had overthrown the government in the 1860s, announced a new party saying, "Everyone knows that we have a structural conspiracy among bureaucrats and businessmen."[56]

The House of Councilor's election was held during Japan's then worst post-war economic down-turn, which had the effect of challenging bureaucratic omniscience. But again the voters associated the LDP with Japan's rise. They won 68 seats (versus 39 in 1989), while the Socialists fell to 22 seats. Hosokawa's New Japan Party won five seats. The prophecy of the old guard, that the people would forget the 3 percent sales tax once it was in place, seemed borne out. A cynical 47 percent turnout proved the lowest in postwar history. Right after this victory the ever-widening waves from the trucking scandal consumed Kanemaru who resigned from parliament in October and "critical mass" had arrived for reform. By December the warlords were on the march: the Takeshita faction split; Hata Tsutomu, the finance minister, and Ozawa Ichiro took 43 members along to form another reform party in late June; and Kanemaru was arrested for evading $8.8 million in taxes.

Miyazawa pushed reform and was rebuked like Kaifu before him. If proof were needed of the fallibility of single-party dominance, the old guard announced the political reform bill would be put off, "until we win the upper house election two years from now."[57] This move sealed Miyazawa's fate. When rebels from the LDP joined the dissidents of Hosokawa, the government fell. Miyazawa called for elections of the House of Representatives in July 1993, triggering "the big one." The LDP suffered a massive era-ending defeat, turning it out of power after 37 years. They fell to 228 seats in the Diet, 28 less than a majority, and faced further defections.[58] Seven dissident groups formed a coalition under Hosokawa who became prime minister with a mandate for "reform at all costs." In January of 1994, he produced the unimaginable—laws for election and campaign reform—the prize sought since Tanaka. Corruption was the driving force, and it took an electoral defeat and an alternation of power to bring it about.

Still, Hosokawa's coalition was not a classic opposition party, rather more a factional shift within the LDP. Not only were all the players from the LDP, many were from the old Tanaka faction. Finding fresh blood in

Tokyo is like trying to find a politician in the ex-Soviet states who was not once a member of the Communist Party. Nevertheless, pluralism proved effective for change. On the heels of his stunning victory, Hosokawa was entwined in a corruption crisis of his own, stemming from the earlier parcel delivery scandal, and resigned on 8 April 1994. His ruling coalition nominated Hata Tsutomu who survived for two months until June when the Socialists introduced a non-confidence vote, which passed 261–214. Hata resigned on June 25. Meanwhile, Godzilla fled, and the economy continued its breakdown.[59]

In spite of defections, the LDP remained the strongest single party and held a strong desire do what had to be done to regain power, "Tearing out the most rotted pillars and rebuilding the temple with the Buddha inside."[60] In July 1994, the LDP and the Socialists shocked the world by agreeing on a coalition government. These are the two parties whose often-violent opposition—a reflection of the global Cold War—had defined Japanese politics for five decades. Nevertheless, in a death embrace, they elevated the Socialist Murayama Tomiichi to the position of prime minister. From the outside, this move appeared the equivalent of the Hatfields and the McCoys getting together for one last party on the *Titanic*.

From the inside, however, the situation looks a little different, as it always does. The LDP was the dominant partner and had learned some lessons from the past. In spite of the LDP's theoretical domination for 37 years, in fact they had expanded democratic practices. From the early days, they strove to incorporate all elements of society in consensus, harmony, and accord to the point of a fault. In the 1970s they experienced the *"hakuchuu"* or parity period when they learned to share control of key Diet committees. They had a conservative coalition partner in 1983.[61] For many years, some opposition parties took on the aspect of "clients." The only real confrontation with the opposition was over foreign ideology—tradition in the classrooms or Marxist dogma?[62] Is such a Right-Left coalition government unique to Japanese democracy? Probably it is. Professor Seizaburo Sato says the Japanese "are very lenient about philosophical differences."[63] Others note there is a deep cultural trait embedded in such behavior: "Ideology never meant that much in Japanese politics. From feudal days, power alliances meant more than ideas."[64] The secretary-general of the Japan Teacher's Union said: "When the Socialist Party was in opposition, its policies were just slogans, not policies it expected to be implemented."[66]

Great earthquakes have their after-shocks, and on 2 August 1994, Murayama announced the Socialist Party would henceforth consider the armed forces as legal entities under the constitution, there would be no shut-down of Japan's nuclear plants, and the flag and the national anthem would remain. Had he "erased" the Socialist Party or finally given it a chance to win?

Without a *raison d'être*, in all probability the former will be the case, although a Communist Party will continue to exist on the far Left like some medieval religious relic as long as China remains under Communism.

After the Great Hanshin earthquake in Kobe in January 1995, which Murayama heard about on TV, the government proved poorly prepared, indecisive, and inflexible. Murayama said, "It is natural to make mistakes."[67] In summer 1995 he resigned after inadvertently revealing he had made a secret deal with the LDP to become prime minister. He was replaced by his Finance Minister, Hashimoto Ryutaro, the sixth Prime Minister in six years, a further measure of the paralysis of party politics, and an indicator of the relative power of bureaucrats, either a tribute to democratic politics or its condemnation.

The heart and soul of the new electoral law is the change from the multi-seat constituency to a single-seat system from which all other reforms, including the "prevention of corruption," are to flow.[68] It reduces the number of electoral districts from 512 to 500, drawn on a reapportioned basis, with a single candidate elected per district. Two hundred seats are to be elected at large on a proportional basis, a system which has apparently led to less corruption in upper house elections.[69] Votes for the proportional seats will be counted by dividing the country into 11 blocs. A party must win 2 percent to qualify. Donations to individual politicians are prohibited. Political campaigns will have government financing.[70] Quantitative limits on annual political contributions to political parties by individuals, corporations, and labor unions have been set, however there is no limit to the number of support groups a politician can have, leaving a large loop-hole. Will the new system squeeze out smaller political organizations and eliminate dissenting views, that seemed protected under the old system? Could it lead to autocratic and monolithic government? "It is far from clear that Japan's political system will be less dependent on the influence of wealth in the future, or that corruption and bribery will be greatly diminished."[71]

The first election was held under the new system on 20 October 1996, and the results showed little change on the surface, the usual result for the first time around in Japanese politics. An apathetic 59.6 percent of eligible voters turned out, well below the previous low of 67 percent in 1993 for the lower house.[72] Again, the LDP failed to gain a majority and formed a coalition government with its partners in the previous government plus independents to obtain 262 votes, 12 over a majority. Hashimoto was reinstalled on 7 November 1996 with a promise to pursue administrative reform despite his coalition base. It will take several elections before the new system reveals its influence on the path of democracy.[73] Meanwhile, voices within the LDP have already called for the revival of the old system, but action is not likely.

On the economic side, the rising yen after the 1985 Plaza Accord, low interest rates, and an abundance of savings contributed to excess liquidity and an extraordinary speculative bubble in the country's stock and real estate market. In remarks before the Diet on 11 August 1998, former Finance Minister and Prime Minister Kiichi Miyazawa claimed the crucial mistake was made after the "Black Monday" stock market crash in New York in October 1987. He said the government did not clamp down on bank loans for real-estate development until April 1990, when it was too late.[74]

Governor Mieno Yasushi of the Bank of Japan (which functions like the Federal Reserve) faced down the Finance Ministry in order to protect the welfare of ordinary citizens and set interest rates to burst the so-called "bubble economy." The stock market collapsed in 1990. Real estate value has declined up to 80 percent. Equities are down an estimated 60 percent. A Western-style "slow growth" took hold in 1991, which actually slipped into reverse in 1992 and has yet to recover. Land and stock prices plummeted over 60 percent in a two-year period, leaving banks with non-performing loans and the worst banking crisis since the 1920s.[75] The bust of the bubble economy led to $6.8 billion in primary losses in the *jusen* bail-out, akin to the S&L bail-out in the United States, but much larger. Secondary losses were at $6 billion more, or a total of $12 billion, which represents only 3.2 percent of the outstanding bad loans according to the Ministry of Finance in 1995.[76] Calculated according to standards set by the U.S. Exchange Commission, in 1998 the government disclosed 35.2 trillion yen in non-performing loans by late March.[77] Most observers see these estimates as low. The banking crisis has yet to play out, and Japan still has not found its role in Asia. Nevertheless, with a current account surplus of $127 billion in 1994, the economy remains the world's second strongest.[78]

Ironically, the fiscal and political malaise led to a further incremental democratic development in summer 1998. The LDP lost the elections on 12 July for the Upper House. Keizo Obuchi replaced Hashimoto in turn. Obuchi's LDP was forced to deal with the opposition to pass desperately needed remedial financial legislation in the Diet. According to the leader of the opposition, Kan Naoto, "It was epoch-making, not only because the bills were based on those drawn up by the opposition camp, but also because lawmakers actually drew up the bills without depending on the bureaucrats. It showed that the Diet actually functions as a policymaking body."[79] The crisis may lead to further free-market thinking in the economic area along the line of Friedrich Hayek who believed that government control and intervention in a free market only forestalls recovery from economic ailments such as inflation, unemployment, recession, or depression. Time will tell.

Problems abound. In an increasingly interdependent world, Japan's international economic and political role in Asia and the world must be redefined.[80] There is no longer a defensive rationale for unlimited growth. "The question remains as to whether the bureaucratic businessman partnership will continue to be effective once industry has saturated the market at home and once overseas markets become inhospitable."[81] Trade surpluses with the United States can not forever be put aside as mere bilateral friction. Japan shows no inclination to allow truly reciprocal access to its market to the United States, much less to the Asians.[82] Japan relies as much on the world free-trade system as any country, and cannot continue to run surpluses with all its trading partners, especially as other Asian nations are becoming skillful players of the catch-up game and show no predilection to remain subordinate. Since the late 1980s Japan's companies have been the foremost competitors of Japan's companies. More and more manufacturing is moving overseas, and MITI has been losing its grip on foreign trade.[83] It is ironic that the Japanese, who are masters of long-range planning, seemed during the 1990s to be waiting head in-sand for the major crisis that is now upon them.

Government-sponsored development has had failures—the fifth generation of artificial intelligence,[84] the superspeed project in parallel processing, jet engines, and high definition TV. All these events have cast further doubts on bureaucratic omniscience and also the efficacy of party politics. The monastic Ministry of Finance has suffered its own corruption scandals and is under fire, while reform plans are being drawn up for it. MITI is reviewing its future direction after realizing that government intervention in private sector management is no longer an effective way to promote economic growth. An administrative vice-minister of the Defense Agency has been sacked for allowing overcharges of the Agency and covering up the crime.

Meanwhile, looking outward, there is a vexing problem on the Korean peninsula, while on the mainland the sleeping giant of China is now awakening. There is increased self-doubt and a national sense of rudderless malaise, reminiscent of the decade after the arrival of the "Black Ships." The national purpose of Meiji, wartime, and the post-war reconstruction is lacking. The ship of state has no one on the bridge making course corrections from the "Yoshida Doctrine." Instead, over the crisis in the financial system and insolvent banks there is debate about a "soft" landing, or doing nothing, or a "hard" landing (unlikely). No one seems to have ways to deal with the problems. Anyone with a vision, like the impatient Ozawa Ichiro, is isolated on the principle that "stakes that stand higher than others get hit."[85] After starting with one of the lowest popular ratings in history, however, Prime Minister Obuchi Keizo has taken on the problems in a dogged, tactical way, and his ratings are improving.

Sakakibara Eisuke, a University of Michigan Ph.D., established the foundations of a counter-reformation in his 1990 book *Beyond Capitalism*. He argues Japan's economic system should never be modeled on that of the United States.[86] For him, adopting a U.S.-style open economy will lead inevitably to crime, social breakdown, and declining prosperity. Many élite see The United States as a debtor nation of low competitiveness, running fiscal deficits, with drug ridden cities, violent crime, and a poor public education system, not to mention political scandal. Whither Japan and Japanese democracy?

If the past is prelude, Japanese democracy in the sense of individual freedom will continue to expand incrementally, but remain a unique indigenous creation, and not take on some "formula."[87] Democracy in the sense of economic freedom will, of necessity, follow more free-market thinking. It should also be noted that "Japan's non-Western, non-individualist sociolegal culture provides a useful counterpoint for nations like the United States which are in need of a more transcultural understanding of constitutional democracy for the next century. Perhaps it is time for people everywhere to look less at their own democracies and other forms of government through the glasses of Western political theory and constitutional experience, and to begin afresh to induce new democratic legal theory with eyes focused on some of the rich evidence coming from non-Western areas such as Japan."[88] In the future, Japanese will not easily give up their desire for education, welfare, wages, medical services, urban infrastructure, housing, and family and community life along with their new-found democratic freedoms, nor will they pose a threat to peace. It would take a rupture of the world's economy and the emergence of an international model to provide militarists and extremists any leverage.

> Many of their qualities, much of their thought and behavior, not only as revealed in their early legends but even as observed today, marks them off very distinctly from the Chinese, despite their great intellectual and even spiritual debt to successive dynasties of Han, T'ang, Sung and Ming. No student of Japanese history can fail to be impressed by this feature. The power and prestige of a foreign culture seem as if they would overwhelm and transform Japan, but always there is a hard, non-absorbent core of individual character, which resists and in turn works upon the invading influence.[89]

It is the genius of Shinto to adopt all the deities of Buddhism and the universal order of Confucianism as aspects of the "Way of the Spirits," a process called *honji suijyaku,* which can be translated, "the original substance manifests itself as traces." Although the concept of *Honji suijyaku* originated in Chinese thinking, its development by the Japanese has been called the most original Japanese contribution to philosophical thought." Put another way, the ideals of Western individualism and democracy have not been digested as "traces of the original substance." Individualism has not been mythologized as it has been in Western Europe and America.

The patterns of thought and action of a culture are by no means mystical agencies in history. "The concrete elements of history, the acts of politicians, the aspirations of people, the ideas, values, preferences and prejudices of an age, are the outward manifestations of its religion in the widest sense."[90] Tradition continues to play a powerful role in the national psyche, policy formation and the development of institutions, "the continued willingness of individuals to act in predictable ways."[91]

We should bear in mind the words of Ninomiya Sontoku:

Furu michi ni	"Brush aside
Tsumuro ko no ha o	the leaves
Kakiwakete	covering the old road
Amaterasu kami no	and see the footprints
Asiato o miru.	of the Sun Goddess."[92]

Notes

1. T. J. Pempel, *Policy and Politics in Japan: Creative Conservatism* (Philadelphia: Temple University Press, 1982), p. 255–271; T. J. Pempel ed., *Uncommon Democracies: The One-Party-Dominant Regimes* (Ithaca, NY: Cornell University Press, 1990), p. 3–4.

2. Takeshi Inagami, "The Japanese Will to Work," in *The Wheel Extended,* vol. 10, n.3 (January-March 1981): p. 21–29.

3. Patricia G. Steinhoff, "Protest and Democracy," in Ishida & Krauss, eds., *Democracy in Japan,* p. 188–190.

4. For a dissenting voice see Harold R. Kerbo & John A. McKinstry, *Who Rules Japan?* (Westport, CT: Praeger, 1995), p. 88–89, 104, 159–160.

5. Terry E. MacDougall, "Democracy and Local Government in Postwar Japan," in Ishida & Krauss, eds., *Democracy in Japan,* p. 139–170.

6. Edward Beauchamp, "Education," in Ishida & Krauss, eds., in *Democracy in Japan,* p. 225–251. Also see Thomas P. Rohlen, "Education in Japanese Society," in Daniel I. Okimoto & Thomas P. Rohlen, eds., *Inside the Japanese System: Readings on Contemporary Society and Political Economy* (Stanford University Press, 1988). For a dissenting voice see Kerbo & McKinstry *Who Rules Japan?* p. 161–162.

7. Kenneth Pyle, "The Future of Japanese Nationality: Essay in Contemporary History," in *Journal of Japanese Studies,* vol. 8, n. 2 (summer 1982): p. 242–263; Kerbo & McKinstry, *Who Rules Japan?,* p. 174–176.

8. Ichiro Ozawa, *Blueprint for a New Japan: The Rethinking of a Nation,* (Tokyo: Kodansha, 1994), p. 203–204; Miyamoto Masao, *The Straightjacket Society* (Tokyo: Kodansha International, 1994).

9. Yoichi Higuchi, a law professor at Sophia University, addressing United Nations University symposium in Kobe. Quoted in *Japan Times* (29 September 1998).

10. Those who find further undemocratic aspects are known as "revisionists," and include Chalmers Johnson, James Fallows, Clyde Prestowitz, and Karel van Wolferen. See James Fallows, *More Like Us* (New York: Houghton Mifflin, 1989).

11. Daniel I.Okimoto, "*Japan, the Societal state,*" Okimoto & Rohlen, eds., *Inside the Japanese System*, p. 211–214

12. Chie Nakane, *Japanese Society* (Berkeley: University of California Press, 1970), p. 2–99; Takeo Doi, *The Anatomy of Dependence* (Tokyo: Kodansha International, 1973); Michio Morishima, "The Power of Confucian Capitalism," in *The Observer* (London, June 1978).

13. McNeil, *Democracy in Japan*, p. 89.

14. Martin Collcutt, Marius Jansen & Isao Kumakura, Cultural Atlas of the World: Japan (Richmond, VA: Stonehenge & Time-Life Books, 1991), p. 169.

15. Chalmers Johnson, *MITI and the Japanese Miracle: The Growth of Industrial Policy, 1925–1975* (Stanford: Stanford University Press, 1982); Christopher Howe, *The Origins of Japanese Trade Supremacy: Development and Technology in Asia from 1540 to the Pacific War* (Chicago: University of Chicago Press, 1996).

16. William Theodore de Bary, ed., *Sources of the Japanese Tradition* (New York: Columbia University Press, 1958), p. 662.

17. Ito said: "The trends in our country today erroneously lead to a belief in works of the extreme liberals and radicals of England, America and France and to considering their theories the supreme norm. In having found principles and means of reversing these trends, I believe I have rendered an important service to my country, and I feel I can die a happy man." Quoted by Jon Halliday, *A Political History of Japanese Capitalism* (New York: Monthly Review Press, 1975), p. 38–39.

18. De Bary, ed., *Sources of the Japanese Tradition*, p. 728.

19. For a discussion of earlier pre-democratic traits in the Tokugawa Era, see Nakane, *Japanese Society;* Junichi Kyogoku, *The Political Dynamics of Japan* (Tokyo: University of Tokyo Press, 1987); Kazuo Kawai, *Japan's American Interlude* (Chicago: University of Chicago Press, 1960).

20. De Bary, ed., *Sources of the Japanese Tradition*, p. 718.

21. *Japan Now* (September 1995); Japan Information and Culture Center, 1155 21st Street NW, Washington DC, 20036.

22. Kazuo Ogura, Chief, Cultural Exchange Department, Ministry of Foreign Affairs, "The Crevice between the Empire of Ideas and the Lost People," in *Gaiko Forum* (June 1991): p. 4–11.

23. Lawrence Olson, *Dimensions of Japan* (New York: American University Field Staff, 1963), p 130.

24. James Sterngold, *New York Times* (25 July 1993): p. 8; Peter Calvocoressi, *World Politics Since 1945* (London: Longman, 1991), p. 71–82; Eisuke Sakakibara & Yukio Noguchi, "Dissecting the Finance Ministry–Bank of Japan Dynasty," in *Japan Echo*, vol. 4, no. 4 (1977): p. 88–124.

25. Peter F. Drucker, *"Economic Realities and Enterprise Strategies,"* in Ezra Vogel, ed., *Modern Japanese Organizations and Decision Making* (Berkeley: University of California Press, 1975), p. 228–244.

26. Akio Mikuni, "Behind Japan's Economic Crisis," in *New York Times* (1 February 1993); Karel van Wolferen, *The Enigma of Japanese Power, People and Politics in a stateless Nation* (New York: Random House, Vintage Books, 1990), p. 375–395.

27. John Creighton Campbell, *"Democracy and Bureaucracy in Japan,"* in Ishida & Krauss, eds., *Democracy in Japan,* p. 113–137.

28. Johnson, *MITI and the Japanese Miracle,* p. 18–31.

29. "But these nervous predictions were never borne out. Some observers have concluded that ideological conflict was a face-saving front to maintain organizational cohesion and to conceal backroom compromises not known to the public." Quote: Hans H. Baerwald, *Japan's Parliament: An Introduction* (London: Cambridge University Press, 1974), p. 103–120. Also Hideo Otake, "Defense Controversies and One-Party Dominance: The Opposition in Japan and West Germany," in Pempel, ed., *Uncommon Democracies,* p. 128–161; George R. Packard III, *Protest in Tokyo* (Princeton: Princeton University Press, 1966); Robert A. Scalapino & Junnosuke Masumi, *Parties and Politics in Contemporary Japan* (Berkeley: University of California Press, 1962), Ch. 5.

30. Van Wolferen, *The Enigma of Japanese Power,* p. 373. For reorganization of the labor movement see p. 71–72. For attitude of the Japan Teacher's Union see p. 75–80.

31. Pempel, ed., *Uncommon Democracies,* p. 6–7, 16–17.

32. In the February 1958 issue of *Sekai,* Arate Osada, President of the Japan Education Association, an organization of university professors wrote, "The morality of peace is perhaps the most important of moralities today. Once the nature of hydrogen warfare is made clear, the love of Christ, the compassion of Buddha, the humanity of Confucius, the greatest good of the greatest number of Spencer, Bentham and Mill all become impossible unless war is rejected and peace is safeguarded." Quoted in Olson, *Dimensions of Japan,* p. 132. Also Pempel, ed., *Uncommon Democracies,* p. 26–27.

33. Gavan McCormack, *The Emptiness of Japanese Affluence* (Armonk, NY: Sharpe, 1996), p. 25–77.

34. Ishizaka Taizo, Chief of Keidanren, declared, "We cannot give the position to a man who is an ignorant laborer," quoted in Van Wolferen, *The Enigma of Japanese Power,* p. 111, 127–139. Also Chalmers Johnson, *Japan: Who Governs: The Rise of the Developmental state* (New York: Norton, 1995), p. 77–79.

35. Nathaniel B. Thayer, *How the Conservatives Rule Japan* (Princeton: Princeton University Press, 1969); Gerald L. Curtis, *Election Campaigning, Japanese Style* (New York: Columbia University Press, 1971).

36. Steven R. Weisman, "Moves by Kaifu's Foes Leave Political Reform in Tatters," in *New York Times* (2 October, 1991); Johnson, *Japan: Who Governs?* p. 15.

37. Ozawa, "The Advantages of Creating Small Electoral Districts," in *Blueprint for a New Japan,* p. 62–75.
38. Japan Economic Institute, "Political Reform in Japan: How Near? How Far?" Report No. 5A (Washington, DC: 12 February 1993).
39. Van Wolferen, *The Enigma of Japanese Power,* p. 240–244.
40. McNeil, *Democracy in Japan,* p. 182.
41. Joseph Campbell, *The Masks of God: Oriental Mythology* (New York: Penguin Books, 1976), p. 477.
42. Ellis S. Krauss, "Politics and Policy-making Process" in Ishida & Krauss, eds., *Democracy in Japan,* p. 56.
43. Olson, *Dimensions of Japan,* p. 181.
44. Hideo Otake, "Defense Controversies" in Pempel, ed., *Uncommon Democracies,* p. 148–161.
45. Yasusuke Murakami, "The Age of New Middle Mass Politics: The Case of Japan," in *Journal of Japanese Studies,* vol. 8, no. 1 (winter 1982): p. 59–72.
46. Krauss, "Politics and the Policymaking Process," in Ishida &. Krauss, eds., *Democracy in Japan, p.* 56; J. A. Stockwin, "Political Parties and Political Opposition," in Pempel, ed., *Uncommon Democracies,* p. 98.
47. Takashi Inoguchi, "Conservative Resurgence Under Recession," and Ellis Krauss & Jon Pierre, "The Decline of Dominant Parties: Parliamentary Politics in Sweden and Japan in the 1970s," in Pempel, ed., *Uncommon Democracies,* p. 189–259. Also Ozawa, *Blueprint for a New Japan,* p. 62.
48. Pempel, ed., *Uncommon Democracies, p.* 10.
49. "Japan: A Scandal That Will Not Die," in *Time* (24 April 1989): p. 37; "Japan: Sand in a Well Oiled Machine," in *Time* (8 May 1989): p. 44.
50. James Sterngold, "Japanese Election: Unconstitutional but Valid," in *New York Times* (26 July 1993).
51. Barbara Rudolph, "Pop! Goes the Bubble," in *Time Magazine* (2 April 1990): p. 50.
52. Pempel, ed., *Uncommon Democracies;* J. A. A. Stockwin, "Political Parties and Political Opposition," in. Ishida & Krauss eds., *Democracy in Japan,* p. 107–109.
53. Quote: Michio Watanabe, Steven R. Weisman, *New York Times,* (29 December 1990): p. 3.
54. James Sterngold, "Beneath the Rocks on Japan Inc.'s Playing Field," *in New York Times* (28 July 1991).
55. George J. Church, "Japan: Good-bye to the Godzilla Myth," in *Time* (19 April 1993), p. 42; Japan Economic Institute, Report No. 5A.
56. Quote: Steven R. Weisman, "Blunt Strongman deals behind Scenes in Japan," in *New York Times* (29 March 1992).
57. Quote: Seiroku Kajiyama in David E.Sanger, "In Tokyo Hotel Room, Political Swords Were Drawn," in *New York Times* (25 June 1993).
58. Barbara Wanner, "Political Reform Passage Sets Stage for Shifting Alliances," in Japan Economic Institute, *Report No. 8A* (Washington DC: 25 February 1994).

59. Steven Butler, "Eclipse of the Rising Sun," in *U.S. News and World Report* (11 December 1995); Suzan Dentzer, "Downsizing: Will East Meet West?" in *U.S. News and World Report* (11 December 1995).

60. Quote: David E. Sanger, "Issue for Japan Voters Today: How Much Change?" in *New York Times* (18 July 1993): p. 4.

61. Michio Muramatsu & Ellis S. Krauss, "The Dominant Party and Social Coalitions in Japan," in Pempel, ed., *Uncommon Democracies, p.* 283–305.

62. E. S. Krauss, "Politics and the Policymaking Process," in Ishida & Krauss, eds., *Democracy in Japan, p.* 56; J.A.A. Stockwin, "Political Parties and Political Opposition," in Pempel, ed., *Uncommon Democracies,* p. 98.

63. Quote: David E. Sanger, "Surprise Alliance Picks a Socialist as Japan's Leader," *New York Times* (30 June 1994): p. 1.

64. Quote: David E. Sanger, "A Japanese Machiavelli Creates a Boom in Political Prescriptions," in *New York Times* (3 July 1994).

65. Quote: James Sterngold, "Japan Chief Speaks Out Ending Leftist Doctrine," in *New York Times* (3 August 1994): p. 2.

66. Quote: Sato Seizaburo & Sheryl WuDunn, "Japan Leaders Criticized on Response to Quake," in *New York Times* (24 January 1995): p. A-6.

67. For arguments for the change, I. Ozawa, *Blueprint for a New Japan,* p. 63–66.

68. Frank McNeil, *Japanese Politics: Decay or Reform?* (Washington, DC: Carnegie Endowment for International Peace, 1993), p. 71; J. A. A. Stockton, "Political Parties and Political Opposition," in Ishida & Krauss, eds., *Democracy in Japan,* p. 102–103.

69. Local Autonomy College, *Election System in Japan* (Tokyo: Ministry of Home Affairs, 1995).

70. Quote: David E. Sanger, "Japanese Premier Agrees With Foes on Voting Reform," in *New York Times* (29 January 1994): p. 1.

71. Nicholas D. Kristof, "Ex-Ruling Party Scores Comeback in Japanese Vote," in *New York Times* (21 October 1996): p. 1.

72. H. R. Kerbo, *Who Rules Japan?* p. 98.

73. *Japan Times* (11 April 1998).

74. Bill Emmott, *The Sun also Sets: The Limits of Japan's Economic Power* (New York: Simon & Schuster, 1991), p. VIII.

75. Douglas Ostrom, "Taxpayer Tab Rises for *Jusen* Bailout," in Japan Economic Institute, Report No. 4B (2 February 1996); "6.8 Billion Public Fund for *Jusen* Bailout is only a Drop in the Bucket of Total Bubble Economy," in *Real Japan Today* (Orlando, FL: Forum for Urban Development, February 1996).

76. *Japan Times* (11 August 1998).

77. Eamon Fingleton, *Blindside* (New York: Houghton Mifflin, 1995), p. 5–6, 204–256.

78. Quoted in *Japan Times* (2 October 1998), p. 1.

79. James C. Abegglen, "Narrow Self-Interest: Japan's Ultimate Vulnerability?" in Diane Tasca, ed., *United States-Japanese Economic Relations: Cooperation, Competition, and Confrontation* (New York: Pergamon Press, 1980), p. 21–31.

80. Van Wolferen, *The Enigma of Japanese Power,* p. 7.

81. Michael H. Armacost, *Friends or Rivals? The Insider's Account of U.S.-Japan Relations* (New York: Columbia University Press, 1996); Merrit Janow, "Trading with an Ally: Progress and Discontent in U.S.-Japan Trade Relations," in Gerald Curtis, ed., *The United States Japan and Asia* (New York: Norton, 1994), p. 53–95.

82. David E. Sanger, "Mighty MITI Loses Its Grip," in *New York Times* (9 July 1989): p. 1, Section 3. Also "In a certain sense MITI is a classic example of a bureaucracy that has pursued suicidally successful policies. The ministry is like a poverty agency that has succeeded in eliminating poverty." Quote from C. Johnson, "MITI and Japanese International Economic Policy" in R. A. Scalapino, ed., *The Foreign Policy of Modern Japan* (Berkeley: University of California Press, 1977), p. 23–45.

83. Edward A. Feigenbaum & Pamela McCorduck, *Fifth Generation: Artificial Intelligence and Japan's Computer Challenge to the World* (Reading, MA: Addison-Wesley, 1983); Scott Callon, *Divided Sun: MITI and the Breakdown of Japanese High-Tech Industrial Policy, 1975–1993* (Stanford: Stanford University Press, 1995).

84. For example, Steven R. Weisman in the 11 September 1994 issue of *The New York Times Book Review*, raises the ludicrous specter that Ozawa is "a closet rightist with a secret militarist agenda."

85. Quote: James Sterngold, "In Japan, the Clamor for Change Runs Headlong Into Old Groove," in *New York Times* (3 January 1995); Edmund L. Andrews, "A Blunt Economist in Japan Emerges as Mr. Yen," in *New York Times* (16 September 1995). Also "Too much deregulation would create great confusion, you could destroy things that are thousands of years old." "It's naked market forces against cultures. It would be the end of Japanese-style capitalism if we pushed this kind of change too far. Japan would be split, as America is split." "If [advocates of Americanism] believe in the universal value of Americanism, the 'reform' they are attempting is nothing but an act of barbarism against our own national cultural values."

86. For limits of pluralism, Pempel, ed., *Uncommon Democracies*, p. 13–15.

87. Lawrence W. Beer, "Law and Liberty," in Ishida & Krauss, eds., *Democracy in Japan*, p. 85.

88. George B. Sansom, *Japan: A Short Cultural History* (New York: Appleton-Century-Crofts, 1943), p. 14–15.

89. De Bary, ed., *Sources of the Japanese Tradition*, p. 268–271.

90. J. L. Talmon, *The Origins of Totalitarian Democracy* (New York: Prager, 1960).

91. Patricia G. Steinhoff, "Protest and Democracy," in Ishida & Krauss, eds., *Democracy in Japan*, p. 171–198.

92. W. T. de Bary, ed., *Sources of the Japanese Tradition*, p. 580; Van Wolferen, *The Enigma of Japanese Power*, p. 293; plus footnote on Thomas R. H. Havens, *Farm and Nation in Modern Japan* (Princeton: Princeton University Press, 1974), p. 25–26, 42–45.

PART II

Pluralist Democratization in Ex-Marxist Régimes

SEVEN

The Russian Case: Élite Self-Emancipation

Robert V. Barylski

W hen talking about democratization in Russia, I consider myself as one of the early skeptical realists. I support democratic ideals and free enterprise, but insist on realistic observation of what is actually taking place in the former Soviet Union (USSR). For years I had been observing civil-military relations and armed conflict. I had frank discussions with Soviet colleagues, civilian, and military professionals just before, during, and after the dismantling of the Soviet state. I felt that Western writers tended to lean too far in one of two directions. Some were excessively optimistic about the extent to which Russia had changed. Others were overly pessimistic and predicting an imminent Fascist dictatorship and a resurgence in Russian imperialism.

Personal encounters convinced me that most Soviet Communists were primarily managers and administrators who had no interest in radical Marxist-Leninist ideology. Party statistics confirm that they were para-professionals and professionals working in state bureaucracies which stifled initiative and systematically deprived them of the higher levels of personal security, material well-being, and personal liberty enjoyed by their élite counterparts in the advanced Western industrial states. It was such Communists who dismantled the authoritarian Socialist system in Russia. Such Communists were not overthrown, they emancipated themselves. They defended their interests by destroying the unitary Soviet state and the unitary Communist party system.

The chapter's first two sections set the historic context and explain the élite self-emancipation and self-defense thesis. The third section argues that there were two main élite emancipation strategies: *authoritarian* and *democratic reconstruction.* Some élites reconstructed themselves as one-party dominant, nationalist authoritarian, and semi-authoritarian régimes. This happened in Turkmenistan, and Uzbekistan. Others implemented more progressive, competitive political, and economic competition—what is popularly called "democracy." This happened first in Lithuania, but Ukraine and Russia also fit that model. Russia's managerial and administrative élite fragmented and created dozens of political parties instead of consolidating behind an effective, cohesive reform movement led by a popular charismatic leader. The new Russian élite pursued its self-interest by using political fragmentation to defend its new powers rooted in privatized wealth and special access to political leaders.

The chapter's fourth section examines Russia's fragmented body politic. It faults Boris Yeltsin for neglecting party-building tasks. It describes the general crisis of political effectiveness and legitimacy and warns that the same élites that used political fragmentation and democracy to advance their interests might turn to political reconsolidation and authoritarianism to protect themselves from radical populism. Marxist-Leninist and Western political science agree that threatened élites turn to dictatorship to protect their interests and to resolve major systemic crises. In the final analysis, no major political change can be successful until the new régime has established effective control over the armed forces. Military dimensions of Russian political change are discussed as well.

I. Gorbachëv's Reform Strategy and Yeltsin's Victory

Soviet Communists leaders such as Mikhail Gorbachëv knew their system's problems well. Gorbachëv understood that the Communist Party's corrupting monopoly on power was impeding societal adaptation. It was his duty as head of the Soviet Union to increase velocity of change. But how could that be done without precipitating a major systemic crisis? By summer 1988 he decided upon a general strategy. He would begin with competitive elections at the lower and middle levels of power. Next, a combination of indirect and direct elections would create a Communist-dominated, all-Union legislature that included a substantial, vocal minority—a mixture of reform Communists and independents, which could be counted upon to keep pressing for progressive reform. Expanded civil liberties and freer mass media would guarantee a lively national debate about policy and keep the political balance tilted towards change. During 1988 the official Party daily, *Pravda,* released a barrage of major reports designed to put more truth in history and the Communist youth organization's daily, *Komsomolskaya Pravda,* converted itself into a lively, fresh voice in Soviet society. Communists were behind these changes and enjoying these new liberties. But not all Communists agreed with the wholesale attack on established Soviet dogma and symbols.

In fall-winter 1988, Gorbachëv used his dictatorial powers to get the Soviet legislature to amend the Soviet constitution and to jump-start the competitive political process. At each critical juncture, he obtained formal legal approval from the appropriate political body. He saw himself as an enlightened dictator: "Perestroika—the process of change in our country—started from above. It could not have been otherwise in a totalitarian state."[1]

Under the Communist system there had been regular elections but in keeping with its élitist point of view, the party vetted all candidates. The country ran on a combination of governmental regulations, fiats, and basic laws. Party officials were at the center of all the important political decisions about who got what, when, where, and how. People knew that political contacts and political connections were far more important than formal law and due process. Smart politics meant cultivating excellent relationships with the entrenched party bosses at every level. They made things happen. Gorbachëv wanted to make those political leadership positions more competitive and to hold political leaders accountable to the people on a regular basis. But he wanted to preserve the Communist Party as the only institution capable of implementing reforms consistently across the vast expanse of the Soviet Union. He believed that a one-party system could be competitive and accountable to the people.

This bold undertaking threatened entrenched interests, élites that had never opened themselves to public criticism let alone run a competitive campaign. In the beginning, Gorbachëv and the reformers supporting him feared being overthrown by a conservative political *putsch*. They wanted to push basic change to the point where it would be irreversible. The Communist Party started to divide over his reform program. One part of the Communist élite demanded slow, cautious change. Another part began to press for more radical reform. Most Communists just went along for the ride. But all Communists had to consider how best to defend their personal and professional interests. Was it better to leave the Communist Party and to side with the new popular fronts springing up in the republics and demanding independence from Gorbachëv's Union? Or would it be wiser to join a coup against Gorbachëv and to restore the Soviet Union's political effectiveness by authoritarian means? Or was there a third option, a way to privatize Socialist property and to cripple the state's ability to destroy personal liberty and property?

A. The Russian Challenge to Soviet State and Party Unity

Russia—the largest of the 15 republics that formed the Union of Soviet Socialist Republics—was the key to the Soviet Union's future and to Gorbachëv's political fate. All the Communist Party's general-secretaries from Stalin to Gorbachëv had kept the Russian republic under extra firm control. They divided Russia into some 90 city and regional party machines, which they managed directly. The other 14 republics had their own Communist parties headed by their own Central Committees led by their own first secretaries but Russia did not. The Russian republic, with some 150 million people—just over half the population of the entire USSR—was prohibited from forming its own, free-standing Communist Party and from having its own first secretary. Why? Because the Soviet dictators—from Stalin through Gorbachëv—did not want to have to compete with a big, influential head of the largest Communist Party of the 15, namely Russia's.

Although the outside world focused attention on the challenges to the Soviet Union state and Gorbachëv's authority coming from small republics such as Estonia, Latvia, and Lithuania, the most serious threats to Soviet state viability and integral, one-party rule were brewing in Russia and Ukraine. The greater Moscow region's population is larger than the combined populations of the three Baltic republics. As Muscovites in particular and Russians in general began to imagine themselves as citizens of a free Russia rather than the capital of an authoritarian Soviet empire, the Soviet state was at risk. The second most important threat to Soviet state viability came from Ukraine since Ukrainians were the second largest ethnic group in the USSR and their republic had some 50 million people.

On 12 June 1990, the Russia parliament passed a declaration of Russian sovereignty. That same month, the Russian members of the Communist Party of the Soviet Union (CPSU) formed their own, free-standing Communist Party of the Russian Federation (CPRF), elected officers and soundly criticized Gorbachëv's handling of all-Union Communist Party reform. Both moves confirmed that Gorbachëv's effectiveness and legitimacy were in decline along with the presidency of the USSR and the General-Secretariat of the CPSU, which he headed. In July 1990, Yeltsin resigned from the Communist Party of the Soviet Union but did not join the Russian Communist Party. But as a well-connected, former Communist he knew the important leaders and members of Russia's political élite. He was confident that he could win elections and operate without building a new, big political party. He neither wanted to be co-opted nor defeated by a free-standing, well-organized Communist Party of Russia, especially one dedicated to Leninist principles.

Some pro-Yeltsin, CPRF members tried to get the 2768 delegates who attended its founding congress to adopt their *Democratic Platform* and to convert the CPRF into a democratic socialist party. But they found themselves in the minority.[2] What did it mean to be a Communist in 1990? Delegate V. A. Tyulkin pointedly asked the CPRF to define its political base. Was it the working people of Russia or the new entrepreneurial class? He warned the CPRF that it needed to answer such fundamental questions if it intended to become an effective political force.[3] The convention never answered that question. Neither did it really respond to conservatives such as Colonel General Albert Makashov, whose speeches sounded more like calls for emergency dictatorship than for reform. Party leaders tried to please all the main factions and adopted moderate positions. But the CPRF did call for Russian sovereignty in political and economic affairs within a reformed Soviet Union. It also adopted a decree on political power that prohibited CPRF full-time party functionaries from holding full-time political or administrative office in the formal institutions of government.[4] Thus, even the CPRF had been affected by *perestroika*. The new party elected Ivan K. Poloz'kov to serve as its first secretary and mandated that he work to defend the "Socialist choice" and to bring the reform process under control. The CPRF warned that old political and economic structures were breaking but the process of creating new ones was not keeping pace with their *demontage*.[5]

Boris Yeltsin forged ahead without the CPRF, or the CPSU machines to back him. He became the battering ram that destroyed Gorbachëv and the Soviet Union state. He worked without a political party of his own. He understood that the citizens of Russia—including nominal Communists—would support reform strategies that liberated them from Soviet authoritarian imperialism. After watching Russian soldiers in the Soviet Armed Forces being used to kill Georgian and Azeri civilians in April 1989 and January 1990 respectively, the Russian parliament, even with a Communist majority, passed legislation that forbade Soviet Union President Gorbachëv from sending Russian draftees to serve in hot spots outside Russia without the specific approval of the government of Russia. Russians did not want their sons to kill or to be killed by fellow Soviet citizens in political wars waged by the Soviet state.

Most other republics passed similar legislation. Soviet military officers also deeply resented these punitive expeditions and Gorbachëv's tendency to abandon the military to absorb the public wrath instead of admitting that he had sent them against fellow citizens for political reasons. Yeltsin invoked Russia's laws against Soviet Union President Gorbachëv and Union Defense Minister Dmitry Yazov in January 1991 when a botched a conspiracy to suppress Baltic nationalists caused more bloodshed. The Russian republic's refusal to back Gorbachëv's punitive expeditions forced him to renegotiate the division of powers between the USSR and the republics.

B. Yeltsin Defeats Gorbachëv

Moscow had become a city with two, competing political capitals. Boris Yeltsin and the Russian sovereignty movement were rising. They wanted to make Moscow primarily the capital of Russia. At one press conference in June 1990, a participant mockingly suggested that Gorbachëv make the city of Sverdlovsk—Yeltsin's old political base, the capital of the Russian republic and leave Moscow as the capital of the Soviet Union.[6] Yeltsin's natural allies against Gorbachëv and the Union state were the sovereignty movements in the other 14 republics. Together, they could destroy Gorbachëv and the Soviet Union state. Membership in this political coalition was not limited to liberals and democrats. Anti-Gorbachëv authoritarians in Central Asia were as welcome as democratic, nationalist-secessionists in the Baltic Republics and the Caucasus. Yeltsin needed the other 14 republics more than a Russian political party to drive Gorbachëv from the Kremlin, to take down the Soviet flag, and to replace it with the Russian tricolor.

In March 1991, Gorbachëv tried to form an alliance of convenience with his own conservative Communist critics in a vain attempt to remove Yeltsin and decapitate the Russian sovereignty movement. The purge was supposed to happen legally at the Russian Congress which had the power to remove Russia's government and to revise its constitution. But instead of rallying to Gorbachëv, the Communists broke ranks and enough sided with Yeltsin to secure his position and to implement direct, democratic presidential elections in Russia. Communists for Democracy, led by Air Force Colonel Aleksandr Rutskoi, delivered the Yeltsin victory. Yeltsin made Colonel Rutskoi his vice presidential running mate in the June 1991 presidential elections. The two won 60 percent of the popular vote on a pro-Russia, pro-reform, and pro-democracy ticket.[7] Elections took place less than three-months after the March 1991 showdown. There was not enough time to build a real national political machine to work every constituency. Yeltsin's victory seems all the more valid for that reason. He defeated five other teams including candidates endorsed by moderates and conservatives in the declining CPRF and the CPSU.

C. Yeltsin Emancipates the Élite

Newly elected, President Boris Yeltsin and the Russian parliament occupied a relatively new office complex known as the White House in downtown Moscow, not the Kremlin's power suites. This White House kept challenging Gorbachëv, whose ability to govern Russia and the other 14 republics kept falling. The June 1991 electoral victory increased Yeltsin's self-confidence. He was sworn in as Russia's first democratically elected president on 10 July 1991 and blessed in the name of all the faiths by Patriarch Aleksy II of Moscow and all Russia. On 20 July 1991 Yeltsin issued an official *ukaz* (edict) that banned the CPSU and the CPRF from using Russian state institutions and properties for Communist, partisan political work. This gutted the party's network of offices and meeting rooms which were located mainly where Party members worked. Yeltsin further ordered that security officers, managers and all Russian state employees immediately stop taking orders from CPSU and CPRF political bosses. Henceforth they were to observe only the legal, constitutional chains of command. *He thereby liberated Russia's professional élite from Communist Party dictatorship.* He imposed stiff fines on anyone violating these new decrees. He had thrown down the gauntlet. The old guard had to act or surrender. In August 1991 Gorbachëv's own cabinet turned against him and tried to impose a semi-authoritarian régime to prevent the Soviet Union's collapse and to save their jobs. But Yeltsin moved quickly and brilliantly and emerged as the dominant political leader. Yeltsin defeated the August Coup and prevented Gorbachëv from recovering the powers he had lost.

During the last ten days of August 1991, Yeltsin banned the Communist Party and seized its assets in the name of Russian democracy. Then he converted the CPSU's Central Committee buildings into his own presidential administrative complex. During the August Coup, Yeltsin nationalized all Soviet state property within the borders of the Russian Federation. The leaders of the other 14 republics, who had not already done so, immediately did the same. Thereafter, he and his supporters tried to orchestrate the privatization of Russia's public wealth. This gave him enormous patronage powers although some regional bosses also imitated him and insisted upon the right to privatize without interference from Moscow. Yeltsin also gained veto power over all key, post-coup appointments in the Soviet military and security forces, powers that made him the real commander-in-chief, not Gorbachëv.[8] Gorbachëv held on for four more months until Yeltsin and the heads of the other Soviet republics declared an end to the Soviet Union and the liquidation of Gorbachëv's presidency in December 1991.

Why did not the presumed conservative majority within the declining Communist Party and Soviet union state bureaucracy rally behind the coup? Why was it so easy for Yeltsin to defeat its State of Emergency Committee, Gorbachëv's Union state administration, and the Gorbachëv loyalists still holding full-time Communist Party positions? The answer is rooted in élite self-interest: Yeltsin served the rising élite's interests better than either Gorbachëv, who had already become ineffective, or the populist Reds who were already accusing them of stealing the revolution's gains and privatizing wealth and power at the expense of the average Russian citizen.

Yeltsin emancipated fellow members of the élite from the Soviet, one-party, one grand bureaucratic state. It was interested in consolidating these new personal liberties and economic opportunities. It therefore did not rally to the August authoritarians. This is a key insight into post-Soviet politics. To understand it well, it is necessary to restore élite theory analysis to our discussions of the one-party system's collapse. The same insight applies to military professionals who were tired of the one-party dictatorship and had no faith in Gorbachëv's ability to lead. Yeltsin pledged to liberate professional officers from political commissars. He publicly endorsed that position during the August coup and forced Gorbachëv to implement it immediately after the coup.

In the final analysis, the Union state fell because it could not defend itself. The armed forces resented Gorbachëv and the manner in which he treated soldiers and policemen who obeyed orders, used lethal power against nationalists in the republics, and were denounced for it. Gorbachëv soiled the military's reputation and self-esteem and deeply wounded military morale. Yeltsin supported and encouraged this military mood by condemning Gorbachëv for allowing, if not directly ordering, the political killings that took place when Soviet forces repressed Lithuanian nationalist in Vilnius in January 1991. At that time Yeltsin further chastised Gorbachëv for hiding behind others instead of accepting responsibility. Yeltsin even threatened to take Defense Minister Yazov to court for violating the Russian republic's laws by ordering Russian draftees to engage in illegal activities in other Soviet republics. If you want to topple a leader peacefully, you have to neutralize the armed forces and/or divide them from that leader. Yeltsin did both but Gorbachëv made it easy for him.

The top military leadership joined the plot to depose Gorbachëv and/or to impose a state of emergency. This was a predictable and logical response from a military establishment, which believed that Gorbachëv's continued presence in the Kremlin and indecisive leadership represented a clear and present danger to Soviet national security. The military moved with the state of emergency until Yeltsin swiftly organized opposition to it, offered himself as an alternative to Gorbachëv, and gave the military an honorable way out of the crisis. Only the several top civilian and military leaders were arrested. The senior military who supported the coup most enthusiastically were retired quietly on enhanced pensions. Those who actively supported Yeltsin took their still warm seats in the top leadership positions. The coup began on Sunday, 18 August 1991. By the morning of Thursday, 22 August 1991, when it was over, the Soviet military was taking its lead from Boris Yeltsin, the president of Russia, not Mikhail Gorbachëv, the president of the Soviet Union and their legal commander-in-chief.

II. Élite Self-Emancipation, not Popular Revolution

Élite self-interest is the critical factor in successful transitions from Marxist-Leninist authoritarian Socialist régimes to more openly competitive political economies. Peaceful transitions from authoritarian to more competitive systems have two main requirements. First, the dominant élites must have concluded that peaceful change best serves their self-interests. Second, when and if the competition for wealth and power approaches the point of confrontation, the rising group must permit the entrenched opposition to retreat gracefully. The defeated factions need an honorable way out and a tolerable place in the new order otherwise they will be more likely to organize armed resistance. In the Eastern European and Soviet transitions, the vast majority of the former élites needed to know that they faced no trial by anti-Communist tribunals, or other serious punishments. Quite the contrary, political change offered new opportunities to members of the former élite.

A. An Élitist Approach to Peaceful Change

What brought Russia to the point where the Communist élite wanted to transform itself into a property-owning bourgeoisie? There is nothing new about that basic trend. Vladimir Lenin, Joseph Stalin, and Nikita Khrushchëv had to struggle against the Party's tendency to transform itself into a secure élite capable of defending itself against central political leadership. However, from 1964 to 1982, under Leonid Brezhnev, the Communist élite achieved unprecedented levels of personal political security. China's experience confirms the same general tendencies in the evolution of Marxist-Leninist régimes. In the People's Republic of China, Mao Zedong fought a losing battle against such tendencies by launching his Great Leap Forward and his Great Proletarian Cultural Revolution. After Chairman Mao's death in 1976, the party abandoned left-wing radicalism and became a more normal managerial élite. In December 1978, under Comrade Deng Xiaoping, the party leadership legitimized elitist, pragmatic development strategies that encouraged and rewarded initiative and professionalism with enhanced wealth and power. By the mid 1980s both the Soviet Union and China were governed by authoritarian, socialist meritocracies.

Communist-led modernization plants the seeds of its own destruction. Western modernization theorists explained the process during the Cold War, but hesitated to follow their own theory through to the logical conclusion that the Communist Party of the Soviet Union would embrace political and economic markets. The modern industrial system's internal logic supports meritocracy and professional autonomy. Further, domestic and international economic competition place a high premium on innovation and access to new ideas and information. Such economic necessities support political liberalization and greater investments in public education. In this model, liberty is justified by the requirements of economic competition. This is what Gorbachëv came to believe after trying unsuccessfully to foster competition within the one-party dictatorship and state-owned, planned economy.

The Gorbachëv reformers engaged theoretically and politically with the fact that reformed capitalism produced more prosperity and liberty than so-called developed Socialism. *Perestroika* was an attempt to apply international modernization theory to Soviet conditions. That theory plus empirical observation of world trends since 1945 boiled down to the following observation: Competitive political systems produce better government than one-party dictatorships; and, competitive economic systems produce richer, more complex and dynamic economies than planned state Socialism.

In the mid 1980s when Gorbachëv surveyed the international scene, the most advanced Western European industrial states and Japan had standards of living about ten times higher than the Soviet Union's (around $20,000 per capita GDP versus the Soviet Union's $2000). Further, the competitive political economies had greater economic and technological dynamism than the Soviet bureaucratic command economy which Gorbachëv described as "stagnation." This had enormous implications for Soviet national defense and Moscow's ability to maintain defense parity with its Cold War and potential future rivals.

B. The USSR: An Authoritarian Socialist Meritocracy

The Soviet Union was an authoritarian Socialist meritocracy. The Communist Party defined itself as a meritocratic élite that governed in the name of the whole people as its vanguard. The party tried to recruit talented youth into the *Komsomol* and to move the most promising team-players into candidate and full membership status as they advanced in their careers. Mikhail Gorbachëv and Boris Yeltsin are prime examples of that process. During the last decades of Soviet rule, the party boasted that it had become a well-educated professional élite. The idea of giving the common people the power to determine the outcome of major national policy debates was incompatible with the Communist Party's élitist authoritarian, Socialist, meritocratic philosophy.

Modern professionalism has definite élitist elements. Modernization theory argues that experts should determine the outcome of policy debates, profession by profession, according to standards set by the respective professions. It also supports free debate within the professions in order to encourage perpetual innovation and progress. It does not invite non-experts to make key scientific and technological decisions by majority popular vote. For example, Soviet military professionals hoped that the end to Soviet dictatorship would enhance the military professional's ability to shape defense policy and reduce boorish, disruptive, civilian governance of national defense affairs. They knew that the military had suffered under Stalin and had been bullied by Khrushchëv. When they supported Gorbachëv's early reforms, they did not realize that they would face new forms of interference in professional military affairs by civilian politicians.

In March 1985, when Gorbachëv became general-secretary, the Communist Party numbered some 18 million working adults out of a total Soviet population of about 290 million. Managers, directors, and other leaders—the élite at all levels of Soviet society—were supposed to be party members. Appointment to high positions in society required special political clearance in Moscow at the CPSU Central Committee. This rule applied to military and civilian élites alike. The term *nomenklatura* was used to describe the élite within the élite: those appointments that required central approval. The Central Committee judged candidates on professional merit and political reliability, their ability to work constructively within the one-party, authoritarian meritocracy. For example, before Lieutenant-General Aleksandr Lebed could be given command of the important Tula paratrooper/special forces division, he was vetted by the Central Committee's personnel department through personal interviews and background checks, a process he deeply resented but nonetheless submitted to since that was the normal way people advanced in their careers.[9] He had to be a good soldier and in good standing as a party member. All higher ranking officers were party members.

In the 1980s, the party recruited about 600,000 to 620,000 new members annually.[10] A similar number left the party lists each year. This amounted to some 12,000 new members entering and a similar number leaving the party every week. In the Central Committee's main offices on *Staraya ploshchad* in Moscow, the party's personnel managers divided the 18 million full-time members into developmental categories and selected promising rising talent for special education. By the mid 1980s this advanced training had a strong managerial-science component. The party built and equipped a modern, national study center which it named the Academy of Social Sciences under the CPSU Central Committee. In June 1991 when I visited that institution and participated (as a foreign guest) in a Soviet seminar on ethnic conflict and political instability, the Academy was tense with gossip about the impending coup against Gorbachëv. It was an open secret. The Academy was also in the process of converting itself into the élite national school of business and public administration, which it subsequently became. The meaning of the term *Communist* had been changing for some time. The party was becoming the national association of professional managers, public administrators, and politicians. For example, in July 1991 there were approximately 1 million Communist Party members in the Soviet Armed Forces. Only 10 percent were engaged in full-time personnel and political education work; the rest were normal, professional military officers.[11]

As people rose through the Communist table of ranks, the expense budgets, living space, access to vacation homes, use of élite hospitals, automobiles, and chauffeur-driven limousines, in-town hotel space, better restaurants, and access to scarce consumer goods—these and other nonsalary benefits improved. Here is a bit of anecdotal evidence. A highly connected Soviet acquaintance—one of the pioneers organizing new money-making enterprises in the late 1980s—treated me to a fine meal in elegant surroundings at a lavish, clubby restaurant and hotel in Moscow, called the *Oktyabrskaya,* just before the August Coup in 1991. The restaurant was reserved only for the high *nomenklatura* and access was strictly controlled. Armed security guards were posted at the gates. Neither the general public, nor general party members could enter the grounds, let alone reside or dine there. Yet, even this was modest compared to the royal treatment that the top leadership enjoyed. It compared favorably with Western élite standards. One could live comfortably and well under the Communist system. However, the Soviet élite was prevented by its own system from having the higher levels of personal and financial security enjoyed by its Western counterparts.

Upwardly mobile élites were also expected to obtain advanced degrees and certificates through the party's continuing education programs. By 1985, the party boasted that some 99.9 percent of its top leadership had earned a higher degree. In 1939, the educational level for that cohort of district, city and area party committee secretaries was much lower—only 4.9 percent had higher education.[12] The Communist élite was used to living well and had carved out a special niche in society. The only hitch was that it did not own these rights and assets outright. They were attached to one's *nomenklatura* position and had to be surrendered along with the position. There were special rights for high-level retirees, but on the whole people suffered a loss in material support and access to special services upon retirement. For this reason, for example, Soviet military generals tried to hang on to their positions as long as possible, and by the end of the Soviet régime the Communist army had twice as many generals on its active-duty lists as it should have, given the overall number of troops to command. There were 3000 generals on the active-duty payroll lists even though Defense Minister Yazov told Gorbachëv that there were about 2000 generals in summer 1991. Further, more than 700 were beyond retirement age.[13] Additionally, the most prestigious officers earned post-retirement benefits by being placed in the General Inspectorate, an honorary advisory body.[14]

Although people owed their careers to the party, they were not willing to go down with the ship especially when there appeared to be better alternatives to one-party authoritarian living. The Soviet élite began to abandon the sinking ship. Between summer 1989 and summer 1991, about 4.2 million members resigned from the CPSU, about 25 percent of its total membership.[15] The élite of Soviet society was starting to reposition itself politically. Gorbachëv and Yeltsin knew those numbers and what they meant. The Communist Party was liquidating itself. Thus, in July 1991 when Yeltsin shut down party operations in Russian state enterprises and seized party assets in August 1991, he was only damaging the immediate interests of that 10 percent or so of party members who made their living as full-time party employees. The vast majority of (former) Communists had regular full-time jobs, and these were concentrated in élite societal positions.

III. Democratic and Authoritarian Élitism

Prior to 1988–89, personal wealth and power depended upon one's status in the Communist Party. By 1989–90 new ideas and practices for achieving wealth, power, and status were growing within and outside the Communist one-party system. Two strategies emerged for coping with change. The first strategy made political liberalization and the privatization of Socialist property, the dual foundation for the post-Soviet élite's wealth and personal security. This approach is normally called democratic political reconstruction because it made political leaders accountable to the electorate through regular competitive elections. The second strategy saved and rebuilt dictatorship but it also embraced the privatization of public property. Public property was privatized in the new authoritarian states and in the new democratic states. In both types of states, privatization strategies included a mixture of elitist and egalitarian distributions. There were also mixed forms of public/private ownership. However, the most salient feature was the emergence of a new property-owning élite in the democratic and the authoritarian states.

A. Democratic Élitist Self-Emancipation

Although democratic reformers are accused of having imposed radical changes too rapidly, they insist that they were only able to implement a series of half-measures. They argue, and I have reached the same conclusion, that beneath the surface of democratic market reforms, powerful segments of the former Communist Party élite were privatizing wealth and power. These groups were less interested in constitutional rule and a law-governed state than in creating political conditions favorable to their immediate enrichment and successful transformation into the post-Soviet élite.[16]

Because the Party was so large and included rising, as well as mature, members of Soviet society's natural élite, we should not be surprised to learn that most of the post-Soviet élite had been part of the Soviet élite. President Boris Yeltsin is a primary example of that phenomenon. Olga Kryshtanovskaya and

Stephen White found that on average some 70 percent of the political and business élite at the federal and regional levels in Russia circa 1994 had been part of the former Communist élite.[17] David Lane further determined that the general public perceived the reform movement as a top-down, élitist process.[18] He also found that Russian élites believed that the radical reform was a top-down process driven by the Yeltsin entourage rather than a bottom-up policy change demanded by the average Russian voter.[19] Leading reformers such as Yegor Gaidar have made similar points.[20]

Since the early 1980s Leonid Khotin has studied the Soviet managerial élite: the professionals who directed Russia's large industrial enterprises. He began with in-depth interviews with Soviet émigrés living in the United States and then moved into on-site research in the Soviet Union. His 1990 study surveyed 1200 directors in 14 major cities. Khotin's research discovered that Red directors were professional managers who understood basic Western managerial issues and their own system. He found that Soviet managers favored economic reform: when directors argued against rapid disruptive changes, pioneering reformers like Gennady Burbulis and Yegor Gaidar treated their warnings as efforts to prevent basic reform instead of accepting them as constructive criticism.[21]

After 1992 it became fashionable to attack Burbulis and Gaidar for imposing "shock therapy" on Russia. The thesis is that the pro-Western duo brashly precipitated Russia's economic decline. But Gaidar argues that entrenched interests prevented the Yeltsin administration from implementing deep reform. The Kremlin had to settle for half-measures and compromises because parts of the managerial élite mounted sufficient resistance to distort their grand reform plans. The moderates forced Yeltsin to remove Gaidar in December 1992. Viktor Chernomyrdin, a major Soviet energy executive, succeeded him. But like Gaidar before him, Chernomyrdin faced resistance from managers and entrepreneurs who wanted the liberty to take ownership of state enterprises and assets but did not want to subject themselves to fair, open-market competition. As a result, Russia got what *they* wanted: a hybrid economic system riddled with special deals, exemptions, quasi-monopolies, and corruption.

Ex-Communist directors and political bosses used insider positions, political connections, and access to capital flows to buy up the majority of shares in the enterprises they managed. They privatized socialist assets and converted them into private and corporate property which they now owned. According to Michael McFaul, by summer 1993 "insiders had acquired majority shares in two-thirds of Russia's privatized and privatizing firms." Although they were the primary beneficiaries of privatization, they used state subsidies and special exemptions from taxation to stay afloat.[22] Thus, they were adept at eating at the Socialist trough and sleeping in the capitalist bed.

According to McFaul, " . . . during the Soviet era enterprise directors had de facto already seized many of the rights associated with ownership of property."[23] During the transition from Soviet to post-Soviet property relationships they successfully defended their own interests and prevented wide-open, competitive privatization. The directors acted in a perfectly understandable manner. This was normal and predictable. Had they not mixed their lives and labor with the enterprises? Who had a higher "right" to ownership in the post-Soviet era?

The fragmentation of economic and political power took place simultaneously. The transformation of wealth from monopoly state ownership into private, corporate, and mixed forms of ownership is the economic foundation for political pluralism and the division of power between the federal government and the regions. Economic policy became the central issue in Russian political life as soon as the negative economic consequences of the break-up of the Soviet common market and planned economy became apparent (see Section IV below).

B. Defensive Emancipation: the New Post-Soviet Authoritarians

The second main form of élite self-defense and emancipation is authoritarian. It originated in élite self-defense against Gorbachëv's reforms. Traditional Communist élites had to emancipate themselves from Gorbachëv and Moscow in order to defend themselves against reforming liberals and local anti-Communists. They blamed Gorbachëv for their predicament. He ordered them to relax their grips on power. But when liberalization produced anti-Soviet secessionist movements and inter-ethnic conflict, Gorbachëv chastised Communists for failing to implement reforms properly. To make matters worse—from the traditional Communist élite's point of view—he refused to permit them to use force and intimidation in the old Soviet manner to restore order. Further, he demanded that local Communists obey him even when it had already become clear that the people, the future voters who would determine who would rule, wanted national independence and an end to the Communist élite's monopoly on power.

Gorbachëv's *democratizing* one-party system strategy was flawed, and it failed. One-party systems survived in some former Soviet republics but only as *authoritarian,* one-party régimes. This happened in Turkmenistan and Uzbekistan, where the traditional Communist élite blocked and then reversed Gorbachëv's liberalization program. Post-Soviet authoritarianism also took hold in Azerbaijan and Tajikistan after an initial period of political liberalization had ended in political crises. In those two countries, dictatorship followed unsuccessful efforts at political liberalization.

In the summers of 1991 and 1993, I had extensive discussions about this general problem with people at various levels of power in Azerbaijan. The Communist Party of Azerbaijan lost confidence in itself and in its ability to retain power, while having no faith in Gorbachëv's ability to make wise, timely decisions. From 1988 to 1990, he weakened dictatorship and this changed the balance of political forces in the Caucasus. Ethno-national conflict developed between Armenians and Azeris. But instead of clamping down firmly, Gorbachëv prevented the respective Communist parties from using coercive methods that might have prevented major armed conflict. In 1988 when ethnic riots turned lethal, he sacked the leaders of both Communist parties and ordered their successors to be patient and to promote inter-ethnic reconciliation. But more conflict followed and Azeri and Armenian Communists soon understood that they could not rely upon Gorbachëv. Unless they themselves embraced Azeri and Armenian nationalist platforms, they were politically doomed.

By December 1989 Gorbachëv's policies had so immobilized the Communist Party of Azerbaijan that the nationalist, Popular Front was positioned to assume power on a wave of truly massive public demonstrations of disgust with the faltering Communist élite. After weeks of negotiations, Gorbachëv decided to intervene directly and he used the Soviet armed forces to achieve his primary political objective. He thereby made domestic war an instrument of Kremlin policy. In January 1990, he sent the Soviet Armed Forces to occupy Baku, the capital of Azerbaijan, and other key cities the way Nikita Khrushchëv had sent troops to save and reform Communist rule in Hungary in 1956, and Leonid Brezhnev had sent Soviet and Warsaw Pact troops and special forces to save one-party rule in Czechoslovakia in 1968. Gorbachëv claimed that he was primarily motivated by humanitarian reasons since some ugly ethnic rioting had broken out. However, fighting between the Soviet military and the defenders of Baku took a greater toll in lives than the ethnic disorders they had been sent to prevent. And, oddly enough, the immediate ethnic problem had been resolved in Baku before the Communist army expanded its operations into full-scale military occupation. The Soviet military and the Popular Front had actually been systematically removing Armenian and ethnic Russians from Baku and other key cities in advance of the main military action. The 200 or so people killed in Azerbaijan destroyed the Communist Party's legitimacy and drove a wedge between Azeri nationalism and the Soviet state. It also made the Soviet Armed Forces think about the moral price it would have to pay if Gorbachëv or some other leader decided to use it against fellow Soviet citizens again.

Soviet guns kept a nominal Communist, pro-Soviet régime in power in Azerbaijan for another two years. But that régime lacked internal integrity, legitimacy, and confidence in itself. Meanwhile, in neighboring Armenia during 1990, the nationalists armed themselves and used peaceful elections to overthrow the Communist Party. In this environment, party labels began to lose meaning as both countries suffered from general political breakdown. The new Armenian régime waged its political and military war for control over Nagorno-Karabakh more successfully than the nationalist Communist régime, which Gorbachëv installed in Azerbaijan. As a result, Ayaz Mutalibov's pro-Moscow Communists lost legitimacy and were driven from power by the Popular Front in late spring 1992. Weeks later Mutalibov mounted a successful, short-lived counter-coup, but it failed in a day when the Popular Front sent hundreds of thousands of its supporters to besiege the government center and demand his immediate departure in May 1992. Special security troops were in position and could have caused a massacre, but Azeri and Russian officers decided not to. Mutalibov fled to Moscow where he was given political asylum. The Popular Front—a political coalition, rather than a well-organized political party—took power for a second time and held modestly competitive presidential elections which placed Abulfaz Elchibey in power. But after more defeats on the Armenian front, he was overthrown by a second series of armed rebellions and negotiated pacts in summer 1993. Heydar Aliyev, the experienced Soviet-era Communist leader of Azerbaijan whom Gorbachëv had forced into retirement, returned to power and tried to rebuild Azerbaijan's political infrastructure.

Aliyev used authoritarian and semi-authoritarian methods which, he argued, were required by the true state of emergency. But he also used the mass media skillfully and televised important speeches and parliamentary debates, explaining what he was doing to avert national political failure. He faced enormously complex intrigues fueled by the influx of major Western investments in Azerbaijan's Caspian oil fields, Russian efforts to get Azerbaijan to accept Russian military bases and border forces on its Iranian frontier, and Russo-Turkish competition over future oil pipeline routes and revenues.

The situation directly across the Caspian in Turkmenistan was quite different. Turkmenistan's Communist Party retained its viability in spite of Gorbachëv's reforms and the collapse of the Soviet Union. Turkmenistan also refused to join the Russian-sponsored Collective Security Treaty, but President Separmurad Niyazov negotiated security arrangements directly with Russia which helped to defend his country of 3.8 million people and long borders with Iran and Afghanistan. Niyazov converted the Communist Party into a Turkmen national élite and replaced Soviet with Turkmen symbols. He created a paternalistic, one-party régime that prevented opposition political movements from organizing and negotiated major natural gas production and sales contracts that gave his country a strong income flow.

Uzbekistan, the most populous state in former Soviet Central Asia, followed a similar path under Islam Karimov. That new nation of some

22 million is governed by an authoritarian régime dedicated to maintaining stability while promoting economic development. Karimov has argued that only one-party rule can guarantee the political stability required to create the climate in which Uzbekistan can attract major investments and reconstruct its economy successfully. His country borders on two states where civil war followed political fragmentation—Tajikistan and Afghanistan. Like Turkmenbashi Niyazov in Turkmenistan, Islam Karimov has revived national traditions and built a new Uzbek nationalism to replace Soviet proletarian internationalism. This process is best illustrated by his decision to take down the huge statue of Lenin in Tashkent and to replace it with one of Emir Timur whom Westerners call "Tamerlane the Conqueror."[24]

The cases of Turkmenistan and Uzbekistan illustrate the Soviet one-party system's durability, the Communist élite's ability to defend itself against political liberalization and the Soviet Union's collapse. After independence, the nativist élite benefited by preserving and enhancing its power at the expense of the Slavic *namestniki,* or Communists of European ethnic heritage who lorded over them under the Soviet system. By nationalizing the one-party system, the Turkmen and Uzbek Communist élite enhanced and improved its situation. Turkmen and Uzbek professionals steadily took the leading positions in key institutions after 1991, including the armed forces. For example, in 1992 Uzbekistan's officer corps was 94 percent Slavic (primarily of Russian and Ukrainian ethnicity), but by the end of 1996, it was 80 percent Uzbek.[25] The case of Azerbaijan illustrates how efforts to democratize the one-party system produced general political-system failure and led to authoritarian restorations. A similar set of circumstances developed in Tajikistan, which fragmented along political, regional, ethnic, and clan lines in 1992. It is particularly interesting because part of the opposition fled to Afghanistan where it continues to train and to send fighters into the protracted struggle for power in Tajikistan.[26]

IV. Political Fragmentation and Reconsolidation

Russian élitist emancipation produced political fragmentation and a general societal crisis in which the classical pre-conditions for defensive political reconsolidation began to manifest themselves. Russia's regional political bosses, managers, and entrepreneurs liberated themselves from Communist Party control by overthrowing the Soviet state. Political and economic entrepreneurs amassed new wealth and power but the new Russian state faced major systemic problems, which could not be resolved without repairing Russian state viability. Yeltsin tried to rule without a strong national political machine or political party in the traditional Soviet sense of the term. This strategy did not work.

A. Presidential Rule without Presidential Parties

Boris Yeltsin became the political leader of Russia without first having built a strong, national party to support his reform program in the federal legislature and at all levels of government. He had less than three months to organize his first campaign and that was not enough time to build a national party. After his victory, he neglected party development and tried to govern by making political deals and working with various parts of the fragmented political élite.

Boris Yeltsin believed that his election in June 1991 gave him a popular mandate to promote political democratization and market economy reforms. Yet, he faced a Russian national legislature with a more conservative majority and ambitious leaders who argued for a slower approach to reform and insisted that it also have a definite mandate from the people. He also faced demands for regional autonomy and negotiated settlements between the federal government and the 89 political units making up Russia. These tugs of war were mainly about economic issues related to federal taxes and privatization of state enterprises and state-owned natural resources. Only the Chechen drive for autonomy developed into a war for national independence. The Tatars' parallel one was settled in treaties and agreements that split wealth and power between Tatarstan and the federal government.

In liberal political theory, local and personal interests eventually form the national interest though political bargaining and a series of democratic elections that bring national leaders towards the political center. Yeltsin hoped to build such a national consensus. But the reform process became bogged down in post-Soviet politics: the politics of fragmentation in which the Russian state and national interests were chasing a run-away train pulled by personal and regional interests. Instead of serving as the engine-pulling reform, the Kremlin was expending energy putting out political fires and doing political maintenance work.

Yeltsin argued that Russia needed a powerful presidency. He insisted that parliament revise the Russian constitution and give him the powers required to impose political order and implement reforms efficiently. Parliament refused for two reasons. First, it disagreed with his reform strategy and insisted that the Russian public favored a more conservative approach. Second, it claimed that Russian democracy would suffer if too much power were placed in the executive branch. President Yeltisn and Speaker Ruslan Khasbulatov fired political warnings at each other for some 18 months.

In 1993 parliament turned itself into an armed camp and hired former Soviet Deputy Minister of Defense Vladislav Achalov as its chief of special security. It welcomed defectors from the Kremlin including Yeltsin's vice president, Colonel General Aleksandr Rutskoi, into its anti-Yeltsin coalition.

Yeltsin decided to resolve the festering crisis even if it meant violating the constitution. In September 1993 he ordered parliament to disband, refused to accept a compromise in which he and the parliament would both immediately stand for election, and permitted lapses in Moscow city security that allowed "Red" (Communist) and "Brown" (nationalist) hotheads in parliament (White House) to launch an armed *putsch*. On the morning of 3–4 October 1993, President Boris Yeltsin sent tanks against parliament's office and assembly complex, the very White House he had defended in August 1991. By sunset he had defeated the "Red-Brown" rebellion and captured Achalov, Khasbulatov, Rutskoi, and other opposition leaders. He kept them in jail without trial until after the December 1993 elections. He amnestied them in early 1994.

He put a new constitution before the people for a vote in December 1993. According to official results, it passed. The new constitution gives him direct control over all federal military, police, and security forces. The president has the right to appoint and dismiss all armed forces officers without the advice and consent of the federal legislature. He used his direct power over security and military affairs to launch covert operations against the Chechen secessionists in 1994 and to send the troops to overthrow the rebel régime in December 1994. By waging a civil war from December 1994 to July 1996, without legislative approval, he demonstrated that he had created a semi-authoritarian presidency.

B. The Duma Elections: Public Protests and Élite Indifference

Yeltsin neglected political party-building and tried to govern through executive powers and patronage. But political fragmentation damaged his political effectiveness. The political élites that had just liberated themselves from the old Communist Party did not seem interested in accepting any new presidential party discipline over their activities. Neither did they seem particularly worried about public protests against their new wealth and power. The three federal legislatures—the Supreme Soviet, which he overthrew in October 1993; the first Duma, elected in 1993; and the second Duma, elected in 1995—had mildly anti-Yeltsin majorities and very substantial anti-Yeltsin program minorities. Disaffected voters were protesting against the new élite by voting for politicians who echoed their complaints. However, no powerful, effective, charismatic leader emerged to galvanize popular discontent effectively.

Some 130 parties and associations registered for the 1993 Duma elections. This field narrowed itself down to 13 parties registered and approved for the party-list half of the Duma competition. Yegor Gaidar carried the flag for the pro-Yeltsin party, Russia's Choice. But Boris Yeltsin refused to campaign actively and astutely avoided linking his political prestige to Russia's Choice. Yeltsin had access to public opinion data and knew that Russia's

Choice would do poorly. The public was inclined to use the Duma vote to protest against the Yeltsin administration and it did. In the party-list voting, Vladimir Zhirinovsky's Liberal Democrats received 23 percent, Russia's Choice won 15.5 percent, and the Communist Party of the Russian Federation (CPRF) received 12.4 percent.[27]

The 1995 Duma elections produced similar results except that the CPRF came out on top and the Liberal Democrats slipped to second place. The openly pro-Yeltsin party, now called "Our Home Is Russia," came in third with 10 percent. Grigory Yavlinsky's *Yabloko* Party got 7 percent.[28] Dozens of parties ran, but only four received the 5 percent or more required to earn party-list seats. These four parties received about 50 percent of the party-list vote and the remaining 50 percent was divided among some 39 other political parties and movements. This patchwork reflected Russia's natural political fragmentation and the political élite's reluctance to build strong federal parties. Only the remnants of the Communist Party demonstrated a reasonable degree of organizational viability.

C. The 1996 Presidential Elections: Winning without a Party

At the beginning of 1996, Yeltsin's popularity ratings were in the 8 to 10 percent range. The Russian economy was still in deep decline, the war in Chechnya was grinding on, and the country suffered from widespread corruption and rising crime. Russia's new financial élite wanted to prevent the Communist populists from taking the Kremlin and they rallied to the pro-Yeltsin, anti-Communist campaign. It required a campaign, but did not rely upon a major pro-Yeltsin political party: "Our Home Is Russia" existed, but its poor performance in the Duma elections did not inspire confidence. Nevertheless, Yeltsin won the elections without a strong political party. It appears that modern presidential campaign techniques, which use the mass media skillfully and have solid financial backing, can deliver victories without strong grass-roots organizations. Yeltsin's team used presidential power and patronage to keep the media friendly, and the new financial élites kept his campaign treasury full.

The Yeltsin team's successful three-part strategy was logical and relatively simple. First, it had to present the "new" Communists as a Trojan horse for irresponsible authoritarians who dreamed of restoring the status quo ante. This was relatively easy since there were extremists in the CPRF who made radical statements, and the party had not really developed a coherent platform. Second, it had to convince voters that Boris Yeltsin was listening to the Russian people and taking action to address their complaints. As the president toured the country, he dispensed favors and made promises. Third, the Yeltsin campaign had to split the protest vote and to draw part of it into his coalition. Lieutenant-General (Ret.) Aleksandr Lebed's candidacy served that purpose. After the first round, the Yeltsin team co-opted Lebed and kept him in the Kremlin until his own maverick behavior forced Yeltsin to remove him.

D. *Élite Nervousness and Talk of Suspending Elections*[29]

On 5 May 1996, General Aleksandr Korzhakov, chief of Yeltsin's Kremlin leadership security services revealed that some Kremlin insiders were nervous about the presidential elections. He demonstrated élitist concerns about the public's ability to make the right choices. Korzhakov argued that the presidential elections should be postponed because voters needed more time to reach "mature conclusions" about candidates and issues. He told reporters, "Many influential people in Russia consider it desirable to postpone the election, myself among them, since we need stability." He said Russia's security services had information that the postponement option had widespread support in the country, and stressed that it was in the national interest.[30]

But Yeltsin rejected postponement and forged ahead. He told reporters that he had ordered the general not to poke his nose into politics. Yeltsin insisted that the elections be held on time and said that he had "faith in the wisdom of Russia's voters."[31] The Communists denounced Korzhakov, demanding that the elections be held as scheduled: they needed democracy and the constitution to protect their political rights.

Russia's new wealthy class realized that radical populism threatened its power and position in Russian society. It was vulnerable to a Russian counter-reformation with strong Socialist overtones. A week before Korzhakov's call for postponement, a group of 13 prominent business leaders, headed by Boris Berezovsky, published an appeal that attacked the competitive electoral process because it was encouraging each faction to take extreme positions instead of combining forces for the good of the country. Instead of letting the elections decide who will govern, they proposed that all major political leaders meet to negotiate power-sharing pacts, a series of binding compromises. Their appeal insisted, "Russian politicians must be induced to make very substantial mutual concessions and to conclude strategic political accords and to codify them in legal form. There is simply no other way out."[32] They wanted a business merger instead of an election. They considered the democratic process a threat to Russian reconstruction along Western lines.

E. *The Election*

Presidential voting takes place in two rounds. The top two vote-getters go on to the second round unless one candidate wins more than 50 percent in the first round. The first round had these results:

35 percent BORIS YELTSIN
32 percent GENNADY ZYUGANOV
15 percent ALEKSANDR LEBED
0.7 percent GRIGORY YAVLINSKY
0.6 percent VLADIMIR ZHIRINOVSKY
0.5 percent MIKHAIL GORBACHËV
0.4 percent MARTIN SHAKKUM
0.2 percent YURY VLASOV
0.2 percent VLADIMIR BRINTSALOV
0.1 percent SVYATOSLAV FYODOROV[33]

The two-stage election process encourages political groups to consolidate behind the two candidates that have a chance of winning. It is also supposed to motivate politicians to study public opinion and to aim their pitch at the majority of voters. Over time this type of behavior should encourage a two-party system to develop in Russia. If so, one party would be more socialist and statist in orientation than the other. This was starting to happen during the 1996 presidential campaign. Zyuganov's Communists tried to moderate their image and to distance themselves from the Stalinist legacy. The Communists were moving towards the political center.

Yeltsin moved in the same direction by pledging to clean house and to complete the reform process properly. To gain credibility he formed a political alliance of convenience with Lieutenant-General (Ret.) Aleksandr Lebed after the first round of voting. By linking up with Lebed, Yeltsin hoped to co-opt enough protest voters to win the second round handily. General Lebed pledged to fight corruption and to infuse honesty and justice into Russian politics. He also pledged to end the war between the federal government and the Chechen separatists. Yeltsin seemed to be grooming Lebed to be his successor. He put Lebed at the head of Russia's Security Council and announced that Lebed would review and advise him on top governmental military and civilian appointments. This gave the impression that Yeltsin was responding to the public's demand for action. Yeltsin claimed to be offering the Russian voters a clear choice between the Communist past and a new future based on liberty and prosperity. Nevertheless, 40 percent of the electorate still voted for Zyuganov, while 5 percent selected "neither." Yeltsin received about 55 percent of the popular vote.

F. The Economic Crisis, State Revenue and Democratic State Viability

The unanticipated consequences of political-economic change was a 50 percent drop in economic out-put, as measured by GDP, in the Russian Federation from 1991 to 1996.[34] The post-Soviet economic depression severely damaged the Russian state's ability to raise revenues and to fund the continuation of basic security, defense, and social-welfare functions. The Kremlin had to draw heavily upon revenue flows from foreign and domestic oil and gas sales—some 70 percent of 1996 revenues. This left those important industries starved for investment capital and vulnerable to foreign cash-rich élites who were eager to purchase major stakes in Russian natural resource industries. The Russian state took the easiest way out and essentially continued to bleed the energy sector just as Gorbachёv and Brezhnev had done. Russian oil executives complained, but had to toe the line. Minister of Energy and Fuel Pyotr Rodionov reported that some 70 percent of taxes collected for the Kremlin treasury came from the energy sector.[35] On the one hand, the Russian state's financial viability is directly dependent upon the energy sector; on the other hand, the energy sector's leading executive became Russia's prime minister in December 1992.

For several years, inflation raged as the Kremlin printed money to replenish the treasury and to make up for tax collection shortfalls. In 1995–96 the Yeltsin administration broke that pattern by resorting to belt-tightening measures, including not paying the state's bills owed to defense contractors, slowing down transfer payments, and delaying salary payments. During the 1996 election campaign, Yeltsin pledged to pay back wages and pensions without rekindling high rates of inflation. His administration made some progress by squeezing more taxes out of export industries, engaging in internal and foreign borrowing, and shifting rubles within accounts. Prime Minister Chernomyrdin discussed economic reform problems soberly and gave no hope of any rapid recovery. He told the public that the economy was bottoming out, that he would not permit major deficit spending, and that it would be several years before the general population felt the results of new growth. He pledged to continue keeping workers on the job at essentially bankrupt defense industries, but only at very low wages.[36]

By December 1996, the overall back pay and back pension-bill problem had returned with a vengeance. Yeltsin was informed that the Russian state, owed federal employees and pensioners a grand total of about 17 trillion rubles and that he could obtain a like sum by properly taxing the bootleg alcohol business. He fired Alla Vdovenko, the state's chief alcohol inspector. He ordered his staff to inspect the top 15 industrial enterprises, which collectively owed the state some 51 trillion less than state revenue estimates had predicted they would pay.[37] Meanwhile, it was widely believed that Russian entrepreneurs were exporting capital at an annual rate of some $50-to-$60 billion in 1995–96.[38] The Yeltsin administration did not take any decisive action to reverse these capital out-flows, which symbolically represent a major domestic entrepreneurial vote of no-confidence in the state of the Russian political economy and leadership.

G. *The Strong Hand Response*

As 1996 drew to a close, the Russian public listed economic problems—the wage and pension crisis—as the country's most important issue, and 62 percent, the first majority in the post-Communist period, responded positively to the question: "Do you agree with the proposition that imposing order in Russia today requires a change-over to a régime with a 'strong hand'?"[39] In his March 1997 "state of the Russian Federation Message" to the Russian legislature, Yeltsin pledged to resume the battle to complete the reform process he started in August 1991, when he led democratic Russia's successful political battle to defeat the state of emergency. But he incorporated emergency language into his message and put his administration on notice that national interest required an immediate, effective response to the problems of economic decline and corruption. The military had been demanding more effective government for years. During Yeltsin's first administration, the military was led by army General Pavel Grachev, a Yeltsin loyalist who normally avoided making alarming statements about the cumulative impact of five years of inept and inadequate national leadership in defense affairs. At Lebed's insistence, Grachev was retired before the presidential elections. Yeltsin then appointed army General Igor Rodionov to lead the military reform process. Rodionov tried to work constructively with Yeltsin and the presidential administration. But he refused to conceal military discontent with the Russian state's inability to impose economic discipline on the country and to increase federal revenue collections enough to maintain national defenses at a reasonable level.

Yeltsin insisted that Rodionov resign his military command and become post-Soviet Russia's first civilian minister of defense. He hailed this step as one more proof that Russia was adopting Western political standards for civilian-control over the armed forces. This step took Rodionov out of the legal military chain of command and prevented him from issuing binding military orders to generals. Rodionov reaffirmed his support for military reform and for a smaller but better trained and equipped military system capable of responding to external threats. The military knew that Russia's ability to support defense was shrinking and that no real progress could be made in military reform unless the Russian state began to rebuild its economy. In February 1997, Rodionov called for immediate changes in federal policy to save the Russian defense system from irreversible collapse. He even refused to endorse the Yeltsin administration's public line that assured foreign and domestic audiences that Russia's strategic rocket forces were being properly maintained.[40] His speech to Soviet and Russian military veterans on Armed Forces Day was the most scathing on-the-record assessment of defense policy mismanagement made since the collapse of the Soviet Union. He asked his audience of military heroes to use their political connections and authority among the people to press for effective reforms. The talk certainly made Yeltsin uneasy but it could not be ignored since Rodionov was a respected commander, strategic thinker, and statesman. It was another signal that military patriots were prepared to swing their support to any team of leaders capable of resolving the national political and economic crisis. In his "State of the Federation Message," Yeltsin again asked Russians to rally behind him and once against promised to complete the reform process properly.

H. Military Élite Dependency on Yeltsin

Although Boris Yeltsin did not build a powerful political party to back his reform programs, he kept an eye on the armed forces and placed them under direct, presidential control. But he refused to share civilian control over the military with the legislature. In effect, he made the armed forces his to command in the manner of civilian and military dictators. He flatly refused to give the Dumas elected in December 1993 and 1995 any power over military appointments. The constitution that his staff wrote, which the Russian public approved through a national referendum in December 1993, legitimized absolute presidential control over military appointments.

Direct presidential control over the armed forces makes it easier for democratically elected presidents to protect themselves against military coups or military involvement in civilian-led political intrigues. However, it also makes it too easy for presidents to convert the military high command into extensions of their personal political machines and to impose bad policies upon the country. The institutional structures legitimized by the Yeltsin constitution are better suited to dictatorship than to democracy. If the Russian legislature had a greater role in the supervision of national military affairs, Yeltsin would not have been able to launch the war against the Chechen separatists in November-December 1994. And, quite obviously, he could not have sent tanks under Defense Minister Grachev to fire upon his own parliament on 3–4 October 1993. Institutional arrangements influence political behavior. When a president is the dictator over the officer corps it is easier for the president to use military force to achieve domestic political objectives than when the president shares power with an elected legislative branch of government.

V. Conclusion: Élite Self-Emancipation Models

The Russian revolution of 1990–1991 was an élite-led political transformation not a *people's revolution*. No rival political movement overthrew the Communist Party in Russia. Instead, the political élite emancipated itself from authoritarian restraints. Its more progressive, adaptable, and agile members successfully managed the political and economic changes and set themselves up as Russia's new, post-Communist élite. Mikhail Gorbachëv suffered defeat in victory. He had wanted to preserve the Communist Party and to use it to coordinate economic and political reform throughout the 15 republics. But, élite self-interest—a heterogeneous mixture of progressive and authoritarian motives and instincts for self-preservation—moved against him.

We cannot understand what happened in the former Soviet Union unless we adjust the analytical paradigm—the main concepts used to study one-party-dominant systems in capitalist societies—to fit the realities of authoritarian, Socialist meritocracies. The Communist Party's national development strategy created a Soviet managerial and administrative élite, but it denied Soviet élites the type of personal autonomy and security that comes from owning and controlling assets and from living under a system of limited government. Élite emancipation required that the élite privatize economic assets and break the Communist Party's ability to deprive it of those gains. Many Soviet professionals were angry that their country's institutional structures and practices—*their system*—encouraged and perpetuated counterproductive behavior. Thus, they understood and supported the idea of systemic reconstruction, which is precisely what the Russian term *perestroika* means. Gorbachëv gave hope that such a future could be attained and he broke through the main barriers that had been blocking progressive reformation. However, Gorbachëv was stymied by his deep personal commitment to preserving the Soviet Union and reforming its one-party system, instead of jettisoning it altogether.

Yeltsin defeated Gorbachëv, pledged to complete the reform process swiftly, and dismantled the Soviet state without the benefit of a large, disciplined, national political party. He was associated with three short-lived political parties: Democratic Russia, Democratic Choice, and "Our Home Is Russia." The latter two turned in a poor showing in the Duma elections. But instead of creating a new, one-party-dominant system as a tool for preserving their democratic gains, Yeltsin and Russia's post-Communist élite limped along with a fragmented, weak party system. Why? The answer seems to be rooted in the new élite's enjoyment of post-Communist independence from tight party discipline. The economic foundations for this resistance to a strong, presidential party are clear. Regional bosses and entrepreneurs do not want to lose their new economic freedoms. The élite governing Russia could change its strategy and opt for a one-party system—a corporate model in which central political *generalissimos* manage politics by meeting demands, sector by sector, and by preventing open political competition. In some of the former Soviet republics the political élite defended its wealth and power by rebuilding one-party régimes with unabashedly nationalist, authoritarian ideologies.

Three different types of political régimes emerged on the territory of the former Soviet Union. Some of the newly independent states pursued democratization. But within this group some created ethno-national democracies that actively discriminated against unpopular minorities. Others quickly reconstructed and revitalized their own one-party dictatorships but replaced Marxist-Leninist symbols with ethno-national ones. And there was a third set, which fell somewhere between the two extremes. Indeed, the majority of former Soviet republics are under hybrid régimes.

The Communist Party established the habit of one-party dominance and a corporate approach to national politics. The élite, which originally emancipated itself from the one-party system, may decide to revise and revive that device in order to protect its new assets and interests. Rather than permit itself to be overthrown by radical populists seeking a more equitable redistribution of wealth, it is likely to make political alliances and to strike bargains to preserve as much of its new wealth and power as possible. Now that it owns and controls major economic assets, it has an interest in using a strong hand to promote economic recovery and prosperity.

When Gorbachëv reflected upon his political defeat and his inability to implement reforms in a controlled manner, he said he had become a general who issues orders but whom no one obeys. Gorbachëv described himself as "a commander surrounded by a staff, marshals and generals, but not having army units at his disposal."[41] The same was happening to Yeltsin for the same reasons it had happened to Gorbachëv. The political élite in the regions had broken away from General-Secretary Gorbachëv. It seized upon democratization and privatization to liberate itself from central control. Yeltsin promoted and took advantage of those sentiments and genuinely shared them. He closed down the unitary Communist Party and gave scant attention to building a new, national, presidential party in its place. Yet, the national political and economic crisis had become serious enough to warrant some political reconsolidation. It would be in the new Russian élite self-interest to lead political reconsolidation, rather than to risk having itself overthrown.

VI. Postscript

Western political theory argues that well-structured political and economic competition will produce better government, more liberty, and higher standards of living than its authoritarian rivals. But for this to happen the new structures and rules need to be designed to make ordinary venal human beings behave better than they would otherwise behave. It would be naive to expect rather corrupt one-party systems to reconstruct themselves quickly into dramatically more honest multi-party democracies. However, over the coming decades, if the international system keeps the pressure on and basic democratic institutions continue to function, Russia's new financial and business élites will slowly raise the national standards.

Although Russia formally became a political democracy and a mixed market economy in 1991–92, Yeltsin was unable to complete building the federal agencies required to implement market reforms properly. He gave only furtive attention to fighting corruption and to building an effective federal civil service system. Yeltsin's personal limitations are partly to blame for these deficiencies, but the main cause was resistance from Russia's political and economic élites. The corrupt business elite and the Communist opposition, each in its own way and for its own reasons, kept the federal government weak. Weak government created a favorable environment for corrupt, oligarchic business operations. And, as long as international lenders and native oligarchies found ways to rescue the federal budget, Yeltsin did not have to reform customs and taxation. For a time, weak government also enhanced the Communist-led opposition's popularity. Therefore, Communist and other opposition parties were reluctant to give Yeltsin the new laws he needed.

Yeltsin's financial plans began falling apart in winter 1997–98. The insider-dominated privatization schemes and the foreign borrowing that kept his government supplied with barely enough money to operate from 1992 to 1998 broke down. Yeltsin's plan for financing the 1998 budget required strong markets for shares in Russia's natural energy and communications industries and strong demand for Russian exports. But the Asian financial crisis that erupted in October 1997 ruined his plans.

World commodity prices fell because producers had brought too much oil, steel, and other goods on line in anticipation of *continued* rising Asian demand. Oil prices fell from $20 to around $10 a barrel in March 1998. Foreign investors balked at paying billions for non-controlling interests in Russian oil companies which could not remain profitable at those prices. The oil company share auctions failed. Further, the world oil price collapse cost the Russian state some three to four billion dollars in foreign currency earnings on oil sales. The same pattern held true for steel, timber, gold, diamond, and other export revenues. The financial crisis precipitated a political crisis. Yeltsin was desperate for money to pay the federal system's operating costs and desperate to rescue his declining political reputation. These pressures made his erratic political behavior all the worse. Russia entered a two-year period of leadership instability.

On 23 March 1998, Yeltsin fired his two most loyal and prominent administrators, Prime Minister Viktor Chernomyrdin and Vice Prime Minister Anatoly Chubais because they had not revived the Russian economy. He also fired Russia's top policeman, Internal Affairs Minister Anatoly Kulikov because he had done too little to fight corruption and criminality.

Yeltsin replaced Chernomyrdin with Sergei Kiriyenko, an intelligent, 35-five year old administrator with less than six months experience at the national level. Yeltsin described Kiriyenko as the energetic, young leader Russia needed to make the breakthrough into the healthy, honest market economy the country desired. Kiriyenko described himself as a manager and a technocrat, not a politician. Kiriyenko marched headlong into the battle for the economy. He demanded that the financial oligarchies pay their back taxes. He ordered that taxes be collected aggressively. He warned the oligarchies that their assets would be seized if they failed to cooperate. They balked. Rem Vyakhirev, the chief operating officer of Gazprom, Russia's mammoth natural gas corporation and biggest single contributor to the federal treasury, warned Kiriyenko against pressing too hard and destroying Russia's last viable corporations. The tax shakedown made little headway. And the campaign to force oligarchies to repatriate some $60 billion they had allegedly tucked away in secret off-shore bank accounts also failed.

In July 1998, Kiriyenko told the Duma that financial crisis was inevitable unless the Duma immediately passed a 26 point financial reform plan. The Duma did not cooperate. Kiriyenko and Yeltsin proclaimed a new war on alcohol bootleggers which made some progress but could not close the huge gap between tax collections and federal expenditures. Further, the major international lenders, the International Monetary Fund (IMF) and the World Bank, refused to pump new billion dollar infusions into the Russian financial system. They demanded fundamental reform first. They also demanded that the Russian federal government cut spending while increasing tax collections, a political impossibility.

The Kremlin had to choose between foreign lenders and the Russian people. Yeltsin and Kiriyenko opted for the people. If the Kremlin paid the interest due on its domestic and some $150 billion in foreign loans, it could not pay teachers, soldiers, policemen, pensioners, and other federal workers. Strikes and small marches on Moscow had already become common. Miners blocked major railroad lines until the federal government promised to pay some back salaries and benefits. They also demanded federal prosecution of corrupt élites who made fortunes while the mines went bankrupt. The Kremlin pledged to fight corruption but did not go beyond a few symbolic acts.

Many Russians abandoned the ruble for hard currency. The *Moscow Times Index (MTS)* fell from 1200 rubles in October 1997 to 400 rubles in July 1998, a loss of some two thirds. Russian bonds fell as well. On 17 August 1998, the Russian treasury and state banking system stopped paying interest on domestic and foreign debt. The MTS Index bottomed at around

200 rubles. The Russian equivalent to the *Dow Jones Industrial Average* lost more than 80 percent of its value in just ten months! There was a national banking crisis as well. On 21 June 1999, *Vremya* reported that the average Russian monthly salary, expressed in U.S. dollars, fell from $170 in May 1998 to just $60 in May 1999 because the ruble lost over half its value. Even the business oligarchy felt the pinch. In 1998 *Forbes* magazine named four Russian tycoons—Alekperov, Berezovsky, Potanin, and Vyakhirev to its list of the wealthiest men in the world. By 1999 there were no Russians on that list.

On Sunday 23 August 1998, Yeltsin fired Kiriyenko and tried to restore Chernomyrdin to his old post. Yeltsin explained that the country needed proven heavy weights like Chernomyrdin to fix the crisis. But the Communist-led opposition and liberal reformers in the Duma rejected Chernomyrdin, the business oligarchy's patriarch. The Duma threatened to impeach Yeltsin. With the ruble collapsing, banking in crisis, and the markets in a general mess, Yeltsin quickly found a compromise candidate, Foreign Minister Yevgeny Primakov. Primakov met with Duma opposition leaders and negotiated a compromise between old and new oligarchies. The idea was to save the economy by putting the new privatizers and some of the most-respected, old, Five-Year planners to work for the common good of Russia. This strategy made good political sense and worked.

By early 1999 the crisis passed and the economy stabilized even without major infusions of new cash from the IMF and the World Bank. The Primakov government made solid progress paying back salaries, beginning with the military. But Russia did not pay the interest on its $150 billion in foreign debt. However, Yeltsin began to worry about the next round of Duma elections in December 1999 and the presidential elections in the summer 2000. He wanted a dramatic breakthrough towards economic growth, not mere stabilization. Further, Yeltsin became jealous of Primakov's growing popularity. On 12 May 1999, he unceremoniously fired Primakov because economic stabilization was not enough. The Duma demanded that Yeltsin resign and allow Russia to elect a healthy, able president. Yeltsin refused, ploughed ahead, and nominated Minister of Internal Affairs Sergei Stepashin to be Primakov's successor. Yelstin described him as an honest, young, energetic leader, the type of person needed to restore discipline to the federal agencies, to fight corruption, and to get the economy moving (Defense Minister Sergeyev retained his position and provided defense leadership continuity through this political crisis).

Stepashin, like Kiriyenko before him, was a technocrat, a man who pledged to work hard, fight corruption honestly, and bring Russia closer to the ideal market economy and law-governed society. Why did Yeltsin make the country's top policeman and security chief its *fifth* prime minister? Was he preparing for a new political coup against the Duma whose neo-Communist majority was refusing to pass some of the basic laws the market economy needed and the IMF and the World Bank were demanding? At the end of his confirmation speech on 19 May 1999, Stepashin pledged to protect the constitution and he added: "I am *not* General Pinochet, my family name is Stepashin."

Stepashin started out as a political officer and professor in the MVD's elite academy in Leningrad. In 1989 he won a seat in Gorbachëv's first competitively elected Soviet parliament and quickly emerged as a defense system reformer. He supported smaller, better-trained, modern armed forces instead of the bloated defense establishment which the country could no longer afford. In 1991 Stepashin hitched his political wagon to Yeltsin and helped Yeltsin to reform the Russian security system. He served Yeltsin loyally throughout the Chechen War and took personal responsibility for some of its failures. Yeltsin put Stepashin in charge of the MVD in March 1998 and relied upon him to handle some very sensitive cases. Thus, in June 1999, when he became prime minister, Stepashin knew Russia's security and justice system, but had little experience in national economic management. How well could he fight the oligarchs and the opposition? How much progress could he make given Yeltsin's erratic style and the fact that Yeltsin had become a lame-duck president?

Stepashin assembled the country's business and financial élites and the political bosses of Russia's richest regions and appealed to their business interests and to the national interest. They faced a choice between intelligent reform and national disaster. On 16 June 1999 *Vremya* reported that some 50 top natural resource and energy corporation leaders pledged to hold the line on domestic price increases and to remit taxes more regularly. The World Bank and the IMF also began to show renewed interest in working with the Russian government. The national and international business and financial élites had their eyes on the coming Duma and presidential elections. They wanted to cooperate for the sake of stimulating Russian economic revival and preventing a proto-Communist electoral victory in December 1999. Changes in the international economy also gave Russia a financial boost. World commodity prices recovered moderately from their 1998 lows. And, on 23 June, the Duma passed most of the basic economic reform bills that the IMF and the World Bank demanded. The MTS Index rose from its September 1998 crash lows of 200 to just over 1000 at the end of June 1999. Russia had weathered yet another political and financial storm. Even sharp international tensions in spring 1999 between Russia and the West over the Kosovo War (pitting NATO and Yugoslavia) did not obscure the common interest in preventing Russia's financial and political collapse.

Yeltsin, the vain, capricious, old patriarch, had become Russia's biggest political problem, but time was quickly running out on his second term. It is conceivable that a younger, more intelligent, vigorous leader could have made more headway against the corrupt economic and political elite. Leaders are important but so are the national political and economic élites as a whole. The corrupt Communism of the Brezhnev-Gorbachëv era created managerial élites that were used to informal cozy arrangements not Western contract law. They knew how the West operated but saw their immediate self-interest more narrowly. Such energetic and ambitious Communists privatized the common wealth in 1990–91 and emancipated themselves from the one-party state. Their reluctance to resurrect a new strong state is understandable; but until they do, Russia will not realize its full economic potential and neither will they. Yeltsin served their needs during a rather primitive stage of economic reconstruction. A different type of leader is needed to build the more sophisticated law-governed system of economic and political competition that gave the West prosperity and political stability (in 1999 Yeltsin replaced Stepashin as Premier with Vladimir Putin, whose popularity rose with the second Chechen War, securing for him Yeltsin's and the military's support for his 2000 Presidential bid).[42]

Notes

1. Mikhail Gorbachëv, *Memoirs* (New York: Doubleday, 1996), p. 175.
2. See V. N. Lysenko's speech advocating progressive reform under a new type of Communist Party in *Pravda* (20 June 1990).
3. See V. A. Tyulkin's speech, in *Pravda* (20 June 1990), p. 1.
4. See the CPRF resolutions, in *Pravda* (22 June 1990), p. 1.
5. *Pravda* (24 June 1990).
6. See Gorbachëv's press conference in *Pravda* (26 June 1990).
7. The best work to date on Russia's elections is Stephen White, Richard Rose & Ian McAllister, *How Russia Votes* (Chatham, NJ: Chatham House, 1997), especially Chapter II.
8. Robert V. Barylski, *The Soldier in Russian Politics: 1985–1996* (Rutgers, NJ: Transaction, 1997).
9. Lt. General (Ret.) Aleksandr Lebed, *Za derzhavu obidno* (Moscow: Moskoversuskaya Pravda, 1995), p. 215–217.
10. "The Communist Party of the Soviet Union in Figures," in *The CPSU: Stages of History* (Moscow: Novosti, 1985), p. 90–118.
11. Robert V. Barylski, "The Soviet Military before and after the August Coup: Departization and Decentralization," in *The Armed Forces and Society*, vol. 19, no. 1 (1992): p. 27–45.
12. See *The CPSU: Stages of History*, p. 90–118.
13. Shaposhnikov, *Vybor*, p. 84.
14. Ibid., p. 87–89.

15. Reported by military Communist party organization leaders in *Krasnaya zvezda* (25 July 1991).

16. Yegor Gaidar, *Gosudarstvo i evolyutsiya* (Moscow: Evrazia, 1995); Dmitry Furman's "Nasha strannaya revolyutsiya" ("Our strange revolution") in *Svobodnaya mysl'* (Free Thought) no. 1 (1993): p. 8–19. *Svobodnaya mysl'* is published by the Gorbachëv Foundation. It is the successor to *Kommunist*, the theoretical journal of the Central Committee of the CPSU.

17. See the very interesting study of this phenomenon by Olga Kryshtanovskaya & Stephen White, "From Soviet *Nomenklatura* to Russian Élite," in *Europe-Asia Studies*, vol. 48, no. 5 (1996): p. 711–733.

18. Yegor Gaidar, *Gosudarstvo i evolutsiya* (state and evolution) (Moscow: Evrazia, 1995).

19. David Lane, "The Transformation of Russia: The Role of the Political Élite," in *Europe-Asia Studies*, vol. 48, no. 4 (1996): p. 535–549.

20. Lane, "The Transformation of Russia," p. 535–549.

21. Leonid Khotin, "Old and New Entrepreneurs in Today's Russia;" in *Problems of Post-Communism* (January-February 1996): p. 49–57.

22. Michael McFaul, "state Power, Institutional Change and the Politics of Privatization in Russia," in *World Politics*, vol. 47 (January 1956): p. 210–243.

23. Ibid., p. 211.

24. Ken Petersen, "Celebrating Amir Timur;" in *Central Asia Monitor (CAM)* no. 5 (1996): p. 14–15. For bibliography on Central Asian politics see: Edward Allworth's annotated bibliographies in *CAM*, no. 5 (1995), no. 2, 3, 5 (1996).

25. Col. Vladimir Kaloshin, Chief Department of Military Service & Educational Work, Editorial Board of the Uzbek defense journal, *Vatanparvar*, "Pyat' let na strazhe nezavisimosti," *Krasnaya zvezda* (14 January 1997).

26. Robert V. Barylski, "The Russian Federation and Eurasia's Islamic Crescent," in *Europe Asia Studies*, vol. 46, no. 3 (1994): p. 389–416.

27. White, Rose & McAllister, *How Russia Votes*, p. 122–224.

28. Ibid., p. 224.

29. This section draws upon my discussion of this topic in *The Soldier in Russian Politics: 1985–96*, Chapter 15.

30. Tatyana Malikin, "Personal: Aleksandr Korzhakov Believes the Presidential Election Should be Postponed," in *Sevodnya* (6 May 1996); *CDSP*, vol. XLVII, no. 18 (1996): p. 1.

31. Reported by Stephen Kiselyov, "Instant Analysis: A Warning Shot to the Head," in *Izvestiya* (7 May 1996); *CDSP*, vol. XLVIII, no. 18 (1996): p. 1–3.

32. B. A. Berezoversusky et al., "Get Out Of The Impasse!" in *Kommersant-Daily* (27 April 1996); *CDSP*, vol. XLVIII, no. 17 (1996): p. 1.

33. Results from the Central Electoral Commission as reported by Aleksandr Pel'ts, "Podvedenie itogov pervogo tura prezidentskikh vyborov prodolzhaetsya," in *Krasnaya zvezda* (19 June 1996). I rounded the figures.

34. Stefan Hedlung & Niclas Sundstrom, "The Russian Economy after Systemic Change," in *Europe-Asia Studies*, vol. 48, no. 6 (1996): p. 87–93.

35. Pyotr Rodionov as cited by Patrick Crow, "Oil: Russian Energy Sector's Weaker Sister?" in *Oil and Gas Journal* (13 January 1997): p. 32.
36. See Prime Minister Viktor Chernomyrdin's talks with defense industry workers as reported by Vladimir Gundarov, "Skvoz' prizmu reform," in *Krasnaya zvezda* (26 November 1996).
37. Aleksandr Pel'ts, "Prezident Rossii provel zasedanie VchK," in *Krasnaya zvezda* (27 December 1996).
38. Hedlung & Sundstrom, "The Russian Economy after Systemic Change," p. 87–93.
39. For the list of top events and concerns, see: Yury Levada (All Russian Center for the Study of Public Opinion), "Sociology: Year of Unpaid Debts," in *Moskoversuskiye novosti,* no. 1 (1997): p. 6; *Current Digest of the Soviet Press,* vol. XLIX, no. 1 (1997): p. 4–5. For the public opinion survey on the *strong hand,* see: *CDSP,* vol. XLIX, no. 1 (1997): p. 4; Georgy Bovt, "Four Countries in One," in *Kommersant-Daily* (20 December 1996).
40. Oleg Vladykin, "Ministr oborony RF Igor' Rodionov: 'Sokhranit' tot fundament, na kotorom postroim dostoinuyu Rossii armiyu," in *Krasnaya zvezda* (25 February 1997).
41. Gorbachëv, *Memoirs,* p. 323.
42. Michael Satchell, "Kremlin Gilt—Or Is It Guilt?" in *U.S. News & World Report* (20 September 1999): p. 36–37; Anne Nivat, "Dodging Death in the War Zone," in *U.S. News & World Report* (15 November 1999): p. 38–39.

EIGHT

Out from the Cold: Peaceful Democratization in Hungary, Poland, and the Czech Republic

Beat Kernen

D emocratization is a process that may endure for a long time and that cannot be followed according to a well-tested recipe or theory. It includes, therefore, many caveats, vagaries, and a strong element of unpredictability for any political system that finds itself in the transition from a non-democratic past to some form of democratic future.

Welkin and other commentators, however, have suggested a crude model of the democratization process that can be directly applied to Eastern Europe. The "democratic impulse" is triggered by a system's failure to fulfill people's needs, the "demonstration effect" from the international community, and indigenous leaders and élites who support change. Upon toppling the old order, the system assumes the characteristics of an "immature democracy," or one that lacks "generational age" or "institutionalized trust,"[1] but is "committed to democratic ideals and forms" and strives to translate these into practice. The third stage is the "mature democracy," which is a system that enjoys a "substantial reservoir of élite and popular 'institutional trust'."[2]

The former Eastern European "People's Democracies" definitely fall into the category of immature or unconsolidated democracies, given their general lack of a democratic experience and their decade-long tutelage under the former Soviet Union, which tainted them as "quasi-totalitarian" or "ideocratic" states.[3] The common denominator of Eastern European "ideocracies" was that their political system emulated that of the Soviet Union in that the régime derived its legitimacy from Marxist-Leninist doctrine, and the ruling Communist Party and its affiliates were the only organizations officially admitted into the political process. Furthermore, these "ideocratic" and "monolithic" characteristics resulted in controlled (mass) political participation, rigged elections biased towards official institutions and candidates, and the lack of de facto civil liberties and rights.

Democratization in Eastern Europe entails, therefore, replacing a political system that was based upon a single ideology, a dominant institution, a ruling élite recruited from the *nomenklatura,* and an enforced ideological consensus with one which tolerates competition, pluralism, and the general rules of the "democratic game."

An acute dearth of studies on the democratization process still exists, but the factors considered crucial for that process in this chapter do reflect the relevant literature. In order to allow comparison across Eastern Europe and eventually the former Soviet Union,[4] this chapter directly addresses the issues of system stability, régime support, and ethnic harmony,[5] and focuses on representation, pluralism, and competitiveness in, and resulting from, elections.[6]

This chapter evaluates the degree to which these elements of democracy prevail in Hungary, Poland, and the Czech Republic since the fall of Communist régimes in 1989. The selection of these countries is based on the notion that the three systems have shared similar features and experiences: they were at the forefront of the revolutionary upheaval in the late 1980s; their citizens enjoy a high standard of living relative to the rest of Eastern Europe; and they continue to be the region's leaders in implementing democratic, pluralistic, and market-oriented principles. The major assertion of this chapter is that the characteristics of the transition period in these three countries bode well for their domestic situation and international aspirations (membership in NATO and the European Union).

I. Hungary

Even under the régime of Janos Kádár, Hungary occupied a leading role by forging ahead with economic reforms (epitomized by "goulash Communism"), as well as by the underground opposition leading the country towards democracy. Crushed in 1956, intellectuals, students, and artists, united in opposition to the Kádár régime and relying on the *Samizdat* press, succeeded in putting pressure on the authorities and keeping alive the discussion of reforms throughout the 1970s and 1980s. By 1985, seats to the National Assembly were allocated on the basis of competitive, multi-candidate elections, which moved the legislature towards a more formidable competitor to the government. By the late 1980s, the Communist Party (Hungarian Socialist Workers Party) tolerated independent political organizations that eventually became the backbone of an emerging multi-party system. Prominent among these groupings were the Hungarian Democratic Forum (founded in September 1987), the Federation of Young Democrats (created in March 1988 as an alternative to the Communist Youth League), and the Network of Free Initiatives (established in March 1988), which renamed itself the Alliance of Free Democrats by the end of the year.

The Communist Party itself climbed onto the bandwagon of political reform when Kádár was forced to resign as general-secretary in May 1988 and replaced by Karoly Grosz and other reformers newly elected into the Politburo. In February 1989, the Communist Party proposed talks with the opposition on a new constitution and parliamentary multi-party elections. These talks culminated in an agreement on competitive elections to the National Assembly in 1990 and a referendum, held in November 1989, which approved a parliamentary system in electing a president. The spring 1990 elections to the legislature sealed (at least temporarily) the fate of the Communist Party. A two-round election brought the Hungarian Democratic Forum, together with two small coalition partners—the Independent Smallholders Party and the Christian Democratic People's Party—into power. The Democratic Forum's leader, Jozsef Antall, assumed the position of prime minister, and the new parliament elected Arpad Goncz (leader of the Alliance of Free Democrats), as Hungary's president.

A. System Stability, Regime Support, and Ethnic Tolerance

The peaceful transfer of power, epitomized by the March 1990 elections to the National Assembly, seemed to bode well for political stability in Hungary. The country adopted a European-style parliamentary system of government in which the legislature elects both the president (head of state) and the prime minister (governmental leader). On the other hand, the 1990 elections, based upon a complicated electoral law passed in the fall of 1989, also contained the seeds for political instability. The winning Hungarian Democratic Forum did not gain an absolute majority, and the ruling coalition did not enjoy the two-thirds majority necessary to pass laws or amend the constitution.[7] As a result, the government of Jozsef Antall failed to address important political and economic issues, and a growing social and economic crisis erupted within a year of the election.[8] By 1992, public dissatisfaction with both the political and economic situation had assumed more threatening proportions, when surveys indicated that almost two-thirds of Hungarians were dissatisfied with the general political situation, and primarily blamed the government of Jozsef Antall.[9] Over four-fifths of Hungarians expressed negative attitudes towards the economic situation, with more than half expecting a further decline in living standards. Again, most people blamed the government itself, although a greater percentage (but still less than a fifth) than in the case of political dissatisfaction thought the former Communist régime was responsible for the current economic shortcomings. Most ominously for Hungary's fledgling democracy, a bare majority indicated a strong determination to vote in future parliamentary elections, and half of those who would definitely stay away from polls gave disappointments with politics and the multi-party system as the principal reason.[10]

These discouraging political and economic trends, however, did not produce any large-scale social unrest that could threaten the stability of the system. The reason for this lethargic or complacent behavior may be sought in the fact that "economic issues were outside party rivalry and trade unions (which might mobilize working class citizens in a Western democracy) had a legitimacy deficit." In other words, Hungary (and other Eastern European post-Communist societies) was still distinguished by the lack of a traditional, or Western-type Social-Democratic Left whose absence explained the "weakness of class-based politics."[11]

Furthermore, compared to other Eastern European countries, Hungarian society is relatively homogeneous in its ethnic composition and lacks, therefore, the destabilizing conflicts that could undermine the political system itself. The country is home, however, to some one million people (about ten per cent of the population) of non-Hungarian ethnicity, of whom the *Roma,* or Gypsies, constitute by far the largest group, with several hundred thousand members. In summer 1993, the National Assembly passed a law on national and ethnic minorities that guaranteed these groups the right of self-government and other collective rights. It seems clear that the Assembly's motivation for the new law partially derived from Hungary's desire to induce other countries in the region with Hungarian minorities to emulate Hungary's example, an endeavor that appears to have failed so far.[12] Despite these legal guarantees, however, reports have surfaced indicating that *Roma,* especially, are victims of both official and private (skinhead) attacks.[13] Hungary also contains one of Europe's largest Jewish communities whose members have come under attack from nationalist forces. Most ominously and controversially, Istvan Csurka, vice president of the ruling Hungarian Democratic Forum, publicly promoted a nationalistic, anti-Semitic policy. Although he was subsequently expelled from the party, the democratic credentials of Antall's government were questioned by a number of political opponents and Western human rights organizations.[14] Whereas these disturbing incidences are not unique to Hungary, evidence that official circles are involved in, or at least tolerate, ill-treatment of *Roma,* Jews, foreigners, and other "non-Hungarians," casts a shadow of a doubt on Hungary's full commitment to democratic principles.

B. Representative Institutions, Political Parties, and Elections

Hungary's politics has been described as "politics by tribe," implying that personalities, trustworthiness, and other personal attributes of political candidates in post-1989 Hungary were at least as important as positions taken by political parties and their representatives.[15] One might, therefore, expect a highly fragmented and "hyperpluralistic" landscape characterizing both representative institutions and the political party system in Hungary. The degree of institutional and organizational fragmentation in Hungarian politics, however, has been moderate. As a result of the 1990 elections, six parties shared more than 97 percent of the seats in the new parliament, three of which (Hungarian Democratic Forum, Smallholders Party, and Christian Democratic People's Party) formed a coalition government, and the remaining three the opposition (Alliance of Free Democrats, Hungarian Socialist Party, and Federation of Young Democrats).[16] Furthermore, notwithstanding a subsequent split within the Smallholders Party's parliamentary faction, the parliament remained stable after 1990 in terms of both its political composition and party discipline.[17]

The stability in the parliament's composition and representatives' voting behavior has also translated into a stable Hungarian party system. The electorate's desire and support for political stability has expressed itself in the acceptance of existing parties to provide a sufficient choice to voters, despite a significant degree of apathy among the latter. A survey conducted in late 1992 revealed that a majority of Hungarians perceived no need for new parties, even though a quarter of the respondents welcomed the three most recently formed ones (Party of the Republic, National Democratic People's Party, and the Social Democratic People's Party).[18]

Thus, from 1990 until 1994, Hungary enjoyed the reputation of "an island of stability in Eastern Europe" and the coalition government led by the Hungarian Democratic Forum had become the region's longest lasting government.[19] The government's stability began to unravel in 1994, however. Facing growing unpopularity, largely due to the fact that over 80 percent of Hungarians felt that they were worse off than before,[20] the Hungarian Democratic Forum was soundly defeated, not only during the first round of elections in early May, but especially in the second round at the end of the month. The Hungarian Socialist Party (the former reform-oriented Communists) garnered a third of the vote during the first round, but increased its share to well over 50 percent in the final tally. The reasons for the Forum's defeat and the Socialists' victory are generally seen in voters' disillusionment with economic reforms, their longing for the security and the certainty that the Kádár régime provided (during the period of "goulash Communism"), the division between the political forces elected in 1990, and the Socialists' effective campaign strategy and convincing promise to voters to focus on their economic well-being without turning back the clock or abandoning democracy and market reforms.[21]

The election outcome, however, does not seem to have endangered prospects for continued stability and democratization. First of all, the new parliament contains the same six parties whose representatives were elected in 1990. They occupied over 97 percent of the seats in the 1990–94 National Assembly, and control virtually 100 percent in the recently elected legislature. These results do suggest, therefore, that the Hungarian party system remains stable and the electorate is unwilling to experiment with radical parties on either the far Left, or the far Right of the political spectrum. In addition, voters seem to have regained some of their interest in politics, as indicated by the higher voting turnout rates in 1994 compared to 1990 (almost 70 percent during the first round and over 55 percent in the second round). Secondly, the winning Hungarian Socialist Party entered into a coalition with the second largest parliamentary group—the Alliance of Free Democrats—through which the governing parties together enjoy the two-thirds majority necessary to advance their program.[22]

The return of the former Communists may be disconcerting to some and signal a growing danger to democratic gains made in Hungary and elsewhere in Eastern Europe.[23] A greater risk, however, seems to stem from potential instability within the government and growing social tensions because of the worsening economic situation. The two possibilities are, of course, intricately linked with one another: in Hungary, the failure of the government to improve the lives of average Hungarians may lead to socio-economic conflicts, which in turn could divide the governing coalition and the Socialist Party itself. The resulting governmental instability could threaten both the economic reform program and the democratization process.

II. Poland

In contrast to Hungary, Poland did not benefit from a regime willing to experiment with some economic reforms prior to the mid 1980s. It did, on the other hand, also not suffer from the legacy of a traumatic event such as Hungarians experienced in 1956 or Czechoslovaks in 1968. Moreover, Poland's Communist government gradually dismantled the repressive measures of the martial law period of the early 1980s and began to implement provisions for the protection of human rights and the granting of civil liberties, including freedom of the press. These steps, in turn, fostered the gradual, although not always peaceful, growth of a rival power center in the form of the *Solidarność* Union (Solidarity) that officially represented the working class, but became a symbol of opposition to the régime. After an initial attempt to crush the rebellious force by declaring martial law in the early 1980s, the Jaruzelski government felt compelled to negotiate with the competing movement (resulting in the famous Gdansk Agreement) and eventually recognized Solidarity as a result of the "round-table" talks held in 1989. These talks led to the creation of a second legislative chamber (the Senate, which was to coexist with the unicameral Sejm) and the position of president to be elected by the legislature. Competitive elections to all Senate seats and to 35 percent of the seats in the Sejm were held in summer 1989. The ensuing victory of Solidarity representatives and the defeat of Communist candidates were decisive: Solidarity won 99 out of 100 Senate seats, and the Communist Party even lost uncontested seats because voters crossed out the names of official (Communist) candidates.

A. System Stability, Regime Support, and Ethnic Tolerance

The political system created as a result of the "round-table" talks remained fragile, largely because of the dichotomy between officials from the Communist hierarchy who continued to occupy executive positions, and Solidarity members who had won legislative seats and enjoyed widespread popular support. Following the June 1989 legislative elections, the parliament elected General Jaruzelski as president and General Kiszczak as prime minister. Growing disillusionment with the Communists' lackadaisical pursuit of political reforms led to the resignation of Kiszczak less than three weeks after his election, and his replacement by Tadeusz Mazowiecki, a Catholic intellectual. In September 1990, Jaruzelski himself resigned, paving the way for competitive presidential elections in fall 1990. The surprising showing of Tyminski (a millionaire and former Polish exile) and a meager 40 percent support for Lech Walesa necessitated a runoff election between the two at the end of the year, which Walesa easily won.

Subsequent parliamentary elections (see below) witnessed a highly fragmented political landscape and, as a consequence, Poles were faced with weak, volatile, and short-lived governments. Nonetheless, the post-1989 political system has remained relatively stable due to two major factors. First, irrespective of governments and prime ministers, all leaders were supportive of and remained dedicated to economic reforms.[24] This provided, therefore, a degree of policy continuity that was relatively unaffected by leadership changes. Second, Lech Walesa, while less popular as president than as Solidarity leader in the 1980s, remained in office almost from the beginning of Poland's post-Communist experience until his recent electoral defeat. As president and symbol of the new Poland he was able to infuse stability into the system, especially in the face of economic hardships. In addition, although unable to adopt a new and comprehensive legal framework, the Polish parliament did accept a "Little Constitution" in October 1992, which helped to regulate the separation of power between the three branches of government and prevent debilitating turf wars.[25]

The fact that public dissatisfaction with governmental policies and the economic situation has not translated into widespread popular unrest is also contributing to stability. Protests against the government and its course of action have been expressed at the ballot box and, perhaps reflecting Poland's recent labor history, by a series of strikes. In addition, low voting turnout rates may be considered a form of non-destabilizing protest against the government. Thus, Polish citizens generally have not resorted to the streets as they did during the Communist period, and those who did have largely engaged in peaceful behavior. Finally, it is equally revealing that the most conspicuous expression of anti-government public opinion was not provoked by some economic issue, but the threat from the legislature and the Catholic Church to undo or restrict the right to abortion. Symptomatically, Poles' dissatisfaction with the government's position on this issue translated into support for "pro-choice" parties and candidates, not into protest marches.[26]

Even more than Hungary, Poland enjoys ethnically a highly homogeneous population, with non-Poles constituting a mere 4 percent. Ethnic conflict is, therefore, unlikely to destabilize the system or discredit the democratic credentials of the government. There have nonetheless been incidences of violence against *Romas* and reports of insufficient governmental response to them.[27] As part of the democratic process, post-Communist governments had to admit that Poland was ethnically not quite as homogeneous as some had traditionally proclaimed and, therefore, felt compelled to undertake steps to protect and promote the cultural identity of ethnic minorities.[28] In general, however, the relative homogeneity of Polish society,[29] and overall tolerant ethnic minority policies pursued by post-1989 governments, have greatly reduced the ethnic tensions in Poland. On the other hand, recent socio-political developments have created new minorities that are not ethnically defined and may be subject to official or unofficial reprisals. Examples of such groups are non-believers or members of non-Catholic nominations, and former Communist Party members accused of having committed human rights violations under the Communist régime. The question of "lustration" (how to treat such alleged perpetrators), however, is not unique to Poland and may be less pronounced here than in other Eastern European countries where repression was more severe and the desire for revenge is thus more pronounced.[30]

B. Representative Institutions, Political Parties, and Elections

Following local elections (the first free ones in Eastern Europe since the end of World War II) in May 1990, and presidential elections in December 1990, free and extremely competitive parliamentary elections took place in the fall of 1991 and 1993. If Hungary's politics can be described as "politics by tribe," that of Poland emerging after the 1991 elections may be labeled "politics of hyperpluralism." During the 1991 campaign, an astounding 69 parties participated, including such frivolous, but symptomatic, groups, as the "Polish Beer Lovers Party." Twenty-nine of these parties gained seats in the new parliament, but none collected more than 14 percent of the popular vote.[31] Consequently, the coalition government forged from this fragmented legislature was a "hotchpotch" of groups whose members were unified only in being "rabid anti-Communists [or] Roman Catholic nationalists."[32] Not surprisingly, the newly elected parliament might have been highly representative of Polish society (except for the former Communists), but it proved to be extremely fragile. It gave rise to five prime ministers and four different coalition governments between 1991 and 1993. Most importantly, these governments were too weak to tackle the most pressing economic problems such as the question of privatization. The privatization issue was not solved in Poland until 1994, despite the fact that Poland had developed a privatization plan (adopted in various Eastern European countries as well as Russia) as early as 1988.[33]

By 1993, the political situation had become untenable and, combined with the economic hardships many Poles experienced as a result of the continued "shock therapy," triggered a rude awakening for other Eastern Europeans and particularly Western observers. In September of that year, Polish voters returned to power the very parties that had been associated with the Communist régime and were virtually ousted by the 1991 elections: The Democratic Left Alliance (the former Communist Party) gained the largest share of votes with 20.4 percent, and was followed by the Polish Peasant Party with 15.4 percent.[34]

Before looking at the reasons for this "bolt out of the blue for the outside world,"[35] an examination of the evolving Polish party system is in order. In contrast to 1991, party "hyperpluralism" had moved towards "pluralism" by 1993 in that "only" 35 parties participated in the elections and a mere five individual parties and one coalition of parties reached the 5 percent and 8 percent threshold, respectively, needed to gain seats in the new parliament. Thus, the fear expressed in 1991 about excessive fragmentation that could potentially lead to anarchy, or the undoing of the democratization process, was unwarranted. The 1993 elections witnessed a transfer of power to the "moderate opposition," and most voters did not support extremist or "outsider" parties—"radical populists, extremists, cranks, and even beer lovers"—which received less than 6 percent of the total support, included Party X (2.7 percent) of Stanislaw Tyminski who had created an uproar in the 1990 presidential elections.[36] Thus, we may safely argue that Poland's party system had consolidated and "normalized" itself by 1993, with most voters backing reform-minded but moderate parties.

The return of former Communists in 1993 also supports this assertion. Whereas the Democratic Left Alliance and the Polish Peasant party benefited from the protest vote against economic hardships and the ensuing "angst" of uncertainty, other factors must be taken into account as well. First, the Catholic Church and its hardline stance on abortion and other religious issues (religious education, for example), turned away voters from the governing parties that were perceived to be too closely beholden to official Church dogma. Second, women, apart from the abortion issue, felt particularly hurt by the economic "shock therapy" pursued by the government, since they had often been the first to join the unemployment line or to suffer the consequences of inadequate fixed pensions and losses in social security benefits. Third, rural voters supported the Polish Peasant Party because of its promise to increase governmental farm subsidies and to introduce protectionist measures against agricultural imports from Western Europe. Fourth, pledges by incumbent members of parliament to "settle" with former Communists proved to be less appealing than proposals on how to deal with the economy and other everyday concerns of voters. Finally, both the Democratic Left Alliance and the Peasant Party ran well-organized and unified campaigns and offered a program that addressed issues of direct relevance to Polish citizens. By contrast, the losing side was fragmented, too ideological, and mired in personal rather than substantive differences.[37]

The power position of the winning parties, and thus increasing political stability, was further strengthened by the fact that one-third of the votes cast did not translate into any seats for those parties which did not reach the required voting percentage threshold and were subsequently allocated to the victorious parties. The end result, therefore, was a parliament in which the Democratic Left Alliance (171 seats) and the Peasant Party (132 seats) enjoy a two-thirds governing majority, and the Democratic Union and the Union of Labor form the opposition and constitute two of four power blocs. The inevitable regrouping predicted by one observer in early 1994 has not (yet) materialized, although there have been signs of tension between members of the Peasant Party and their coalition partners from the Left Alliance.[38]

On the eve of new parliamentary elections in 1997, the Polish political party landscape continues to be stable and has solidified into "Left," "Right" and "Centrist" blocs. Polish voters perceive the "Left" as the Democratic Left Alliance and the Polish Peasant Party, whereas Solidarity, the Movement for the Reconstruction of Poland, and the Freedom Union constitute the "Right." Somewhere in between these two blocs voters place the Union of Labor, although its leaders advocate a Socialist program.[39] If these preliminary surveys prove correct, Solidarity may again emerge as the winner and form a coalition government with other "Rightist" parties, whereas the Democratic Left Alliance and the Polish Peasant Party could be pushed into the opposition.

Potential changes in government or leaders do not, however, seem to threaten Polish political stability within the parliament or the Polish party system, but may simply be a reflection of voter apathy, or incumbent "burnout." Presidential elections held in December 1995 also did not motivate voters since Lech Walesa and his fierce anti-Communist rhetoric had lost much of their earlier appeal to Poles.[40] Walesa's electoral defeat is even more surprising if the notion is valid that these elections constituted the second political variable (besides the 1993 victory by the former Communists) to determine the future of Poland's transition to a market economy.[41] Although a second round between the incumbent President Walesa and the ex-Communist Kwasniewski was widely expected in these presidential elections, most experts bet on Walesa arguing that "a large majority" of Polish voters "simply [did] not want an ex-Communist in the presidency," especially since Kwasniewski's Democratic Left Alliance was already leading the governmental coalition.[42] When Polish voters proved these predictions incorrect and elected Kwasniewski over Walesa by a margin of 51.7 to 48.3 percent, they solidified a shift towards former Communists begun in Poland in 1993, emulated similar developments in Hungary, Lithuania, and Bulgaria, and foreshadowed events in Russia's 1995 parliamentary elections. In Poland and elsewhere, however, the electoral victory of ex-Communists has not signaled a return to the past, but more the de-mystification of the free market and (Western-style) democracy as *panaceae*.[43] The new president of Poland is generally regarded as a pragmatic and Western-oriented politician who will likely continue much of Walesa's agenda, with the exception of his strong stance on the separation of Church and state.[44] He and his government under Prime Minister Wlodzimierz Cimoszewicz (who replaced Josef Oleksy because of the latter's involvement in a spy scandal) are, therefore, unlikely to threaten socio-political stability in Poland.

III. The Czech Republic

In 1989 Czechoslovakia and the rest of the world witnessed one of the most remarkable events in post–World War II history: the "Velvet Revolution," a peaceful and short yet dramatic transfer of power from the Communist Party to intellectuals and former dissidents who were riding a wave of non-violent popular demonstrations. After two decades of harsh, neo-Stalinist rule under the post-1968 leadership, the Czech and Slovak populations got rid of their former rulers and embarked on a remarkably smooth journey of reforming the political, economic, and social features of the country. These reforms led Czechoslovakia, then Czecho-Slovakia, and finally the Czech Republic, to become one of the most stable and slowly prospering nation-states in Central Europe.

However, régime intransigence, i.e., the lack of response to social and political pressures for reform, distinguished Czechoslovakia before 1989 from Poland and Hungary. The reformist wings of the former-Communist Party in both Hungary and Poland were able to play a role in the political arena and eventually even to reassume power. By contrast, in Czechoslovakia the Communists were simply swept from power and have, in today's Czech Republic, not been able to exert any significant political influence.

Czechoslovakia also has the dubious distinction (besides Yugoslavia and East Germany) of having ceased to exist in its pre-1989 form. Initially, the Czech and Slovak parts of the federation seemed destined to remain united: the 1990 elections in Slovakia brought the pro-union coalition of the Public Against Violence and the Christian Democrats to power, and the Civic Forum led a pro-federation government in the Czech part. Furthermore, unity seemed strengthened after the election of the popular and globally respected Vaclav Havel as president of Czechoslovakia on 29 December 1989. By the 1992 elections, however, the Movement for a Democratic Slovakia under Vladimir Meciar and Vaclav Klaus' Civic Democratic Party in Prague made separation inevitable, which took place on 1 January 1993.[45] Ever since then, the Czech Republic has economically and politically surpassed Slovakia and today constitutes, along with Poland and Hungary, the core and vanguard of the East European transition movement towards democracy.

A. System Stability, Regime Support, and Ethnic Tolerance

The Czech Republic deservedly enjoys the reputation as the most stable country in Eastern Europe. Both its "Velvet Revolution" of 1989 and the "Velvet Divorce" of 1992–93 were conspicuously peaceful and consensual. Shortly before the break-up of Czecho-Slovakia into its two constituent parts, the Czech legislature adopted a new constitution that went into effect on 1 January, 1993, and consolidated the political and legal framework of the country.[46] System stability is further enhanced by the office of the Czech (formerly the Czechoslovak) Presidency occupied by Vaclav Havel. Although limited in his political and constitutional powers, and unable to prevent the break-up of the federation, Havel brought to the office the power of moral persuasion as an "apolitical" intellectual and writer, due to his worldwide prestige as a former political prisoner under the Communist régime. In addition, his longevity as the president of both Czechoslovakia and the Czech Republic has provided a sense of continuity and purpose to his fellow citizens.

Political stability in the Czech Republic cannot be divorced, however, from the economic policies implemented by the Klaus government. Vaclav Klaus, a self-professed economist and politician of Thatcherite persuasion, formed his own Civic Democratic Party in 1991, which he subsequently led successfully through the 1992 elections and into the position of senior partner in the four-party coalition government of the Czech Republic after 1 January 1993. Contrary to rhetoric and popular opinion both within and outside the Czech lands, he and his cabinet members are "far more paternalistic and interventionist than they would have the world believe," in order, according to Klaus, to "maintain the social peace and basic political consensus in this country."[47] Whereas the post-1989 Czech governments were aided by Czechoslovakia's history of democratization and industrialization and by the economic policies of the former Communist government (which, to its credit, bestowed neither huge debts nor macroeconomic imbalances to its successor), Klaus pursued a three-tier reform program designed to stabilize the system during the transition phase. First, in early 1991 the government implemented price liberalization, cuts in subsidies, currency convertibility (for trade), and exchange stability, in addition to governmental spending reductions during consecutive years, which allowed for a tight monetary policy that led to low inflation rates. Second, in 1993–94 the government launched a huge privatization program through the selling of vouchers to individual Czech citizens, through which 80 percent of the citizens acquired personal assets in the private sector and a stake in the well-being of the economic system. Thirdly, a social contract of sorts was established between the government and the working population. The contract provides for low wages for the workers (thereby making Czech exports cheaper and luring foreign investments because of cheap labor costs) who, in turn, benefit from high employment (with the government keeping afloat inefficient industrial enterprises) and low costs of living (through rent and utility price-controls).[48]

Despite some intra-coalition and inter-party quarrels,[49] the Civic Democratic Party has remained the strongest and most popular party in the Czech Republic. The alliance between the Civic Democratic Party, the Christian Democrats, and the Civic Democratic Alliance did experience, however, at least a partial setback in 1996. Parliamentary elections in the summer of that year denied the governing coalition a majority in the legislature, although voters returned the Civic Democratic Party as the largest political bloc, and the alliance still occupies 99 out of 200 parliamentary seats. The Left-of-Center Social Democratic Party registered, however, major gains, and Prime

Minister Klaus will have to come to terms with members of that party to assure a functioning government. Two major reasons explain this shift in voter support: First, as elsewhere in Eastern Europe, a growing number of Czech citizens have become disillusioned with the economic reform program and the lack of discernible effects on their daily lives. And second, the Civic Democratic Party under Klaus rested mostly on its laurels of low unemployment and inflation levels, increased wages, and disciplined monetary policies, but it ignored the fact that not every Czech had benefited from that record.[50] Given the Czech tradition of consensus-building, political stability does not seem to be at risk by these trends.

Ethnic intolerance will also hardly undermine the socio-political system of the Czech Republic, although it is the least homogeneous country compared to Poland and Hungary. Only 80 percent of the Czech population today is ethnically Czech, but the "populism factor," which could translate into support for extremist or hate groups, has little appeal among them.[51] The *Roma,* on the other hand, have raised concerns about their treatment in the Czech Republic. Like Hungary and other Eastern European countries, the Czech Republic has had its share of hate crimes against, and official neglect of, the *Roma* living on Czech territory. Whereas the government has undertaken some steps to address wrongs committed in the past, official steps have not gone far enough to prevent discrimination and violence against this ethnic minority. Indeed, Vaclav Havel has called the "Gypsy Problem" the litmus test for the Czech civil society.[52]

Most disturbing has been a law on Czech citizenship which went into effect on 1 January 1993, and is based, ironically, on a citizenship law adopted by the Communist authorities in 1969. Devoid of any meaning during the Communist period, the 1969 law provided for either Czech or Slovak citizenship in addition to citizenship of Socialist Czechoslovakia. In 1993, Slovakia expanded eligibility to Slovak citizenship to include all citizens of the former Czechoslovakia, whereas the Czech Republic restricted citizenship to those who were officially designated as "Czech" citizens under the 1969 law. The official justification for the restricted interpretation of Czech citizenship rights was the prevention of economic immigrants into the Czech Republic from poorer neighbors, namely, Slovakia.[53] Two provisions of the new law—"permanent" residency in the Czech Republic for a minimum of two years, and no criminal record for at least five years—had the specific effects, however, of expatriating those citizens who had lived in the country as "non-Czechs" or who were undesirable citizens, i.e., *Roma.* The organization Human Rights Watch estimated that the law affected about 100,000 "non-Czechs" or "Slovaks," most of whom were *Roma.*[54] None of these trends or policies threaten to undermine the Czech social or political system. They are disturbing signs, however, that the democratic credentials of that young nation-state are not as untainted as is commonly believed.

B. Representative Institutions, Political Parties, and Elections

The political institutions in the Czech Republic since 1 January 1993, were largely transferred from the former post-1989 Czechoslovakia: a presidency whose occupant is popularly elected and enjoys the constitutional prerogative to dissolve the lower chamber of parliament, and a legislature which follows standard parliamentary procedures and elects the government and controls its policies.

The relative institutional continuity stands in sharp contrast to the political party landscape in the Czech Republic, which has undergone dramatic changes since the days of the "Velvet Revolution." During the upheavals of 1989, two ill-defined and loosely organized movements—the Civic Forum, mostly active in the Czech part, and the Public Against Violence in Slovakia—were at the forefront of the struggle against the Communist régime. When the need for more formally organized and ideologically more coherent groups became apparent, generally dictated by the emergence of differing views on the economic and political reform programs proposed by the government, the two movements collapsed and split. By February 1991, the Civic Forum ceased to exist and gave birth to the Civic Democratic Party (Right-Centrist) led by Vaclav Klaus, the Civic Movement (Left-Centrist) headed by Foreign Minister Jiri Dienstbier, the Civic Democratic Alliance (Conservative), and the Social Democratic Party.[55] Similarly, other movements that had emerged during the heyday of the "Velvet Revolution" also splintered: the Association for Moravia and Silesia (promoting regional autonomy) split into a radical and moderate wing, and the Christian and Democratic Union had disintegrated into several Christian-Democratic parties by 1991. Finally, the Czechoslovak Communist Party itself broke into a predominantly Czech and a largely Slovak faction even before the dissolution of the federal system.[56] The consolidation, division, and renaming of political parties continued in 1992, but their proliferation never reached the proportions of post-1989 Poland. The number of major political parties in the Czech Republic remained relatively constant with about half a dozen being represented in both the 1990 and 1992 federal parliaments. Vaclav Klaus' Civic Democratic Party had become the largest political faction in the Czechoslovak Federal Assembly as early as the second half of 1991, controlling 43 out of 300 total seats, when the Civiv Forum split in 1991.[57] By the June 1992 elections, the composition of the Czech National Council (the future Czech parliament) consisted of the following groups and their respective seat distribution: the Civic Democratic Party (38 percent; allied with it was the small Christian Democratic Party), the Left Bloc (17.5 percent; consisting of the Communist Party of Bohemia and Moravia and the Democratic Left), the (Czechoslovak) Social Democracy (8 percent; now the Czech Social Democratic Party), the Liberal Social Union (8 percent; combining the Agricultural Party, the Czech Socialist Party, and the Party of the Greens), the Christian Democratic Union (7.5 percent; a mostly Catholic-oriented group without religion, however, being its primary concerns), the Association for the Republic (7 percent; considered an extreme right-wing party which, however, often joins forces with Leftist parties against the government), the Civic Democratic Alliance (7 percent), and the Association for Moravia and Silesia (7 percent; renamed the Movement for the Self-Governing Democracy of Moravia and Silesia after the 1992 elections).[58] The first post-"divorce" parliamentary elections took place in 1996 and witnessed the weakening of the governing alliance in favor of the Social Democrats, as well as the total disappearance from parliament of the Left Bloc and the gains made by the Communists and the right-wing Republicans.[59]

These shifts in political allegiance do not indicate a radical turnabout among Czech voters who continue to swim against currents in other parts of Eastern Europe: they have refused to bring back to power the former Communists. Although the Social Democrats now constitute the second largest faction in the Czech parliament and came in a close second in voter support, they are moderate Social-Democrats of a Western European mold. Two reasons explain why the Czechs have not followed the Hungarians and Poles. First, the government of Vaclav Klaus has adopted a unique program which combines economic market reforms and governmental support for industry designed to prevent large-scale unemployment. The social contract may, in turn, provide a partial answer for the government's and labor's shared commitment to market reforms and their mutual dislike of Communists. Second, unlike the Polish and Hungarian Communist Parties, the Communist Party in Czechoslovakia never shed its image of a hardline, neo-Stalinist party. In addition, the "Velvet Revolution" was too short to give the Communists sufficient time to regroup and emerge as an alternative to the reformers before other parties had established themselves.[60]

IV. Conclusion

The process of democratization is well under way in Poland, Hungary, and the Czech Republic. All three political systems have well-established representative and legal institutions. In the absence of any unforeseeable internal or external crises, the social, political, and economic foundations of these post-1989 systems are likely to remain stable, allowing the respective governments to pursue their reform programs and foreign policy aspirations.

For the sake of socio-economic stability, however, the process of implementing market reforms may decelerate, especially in Hungary and Poland. The Czech Republic under the Klaus government could, in this regard, serve as a model for Hungary and Poland to emulate, but the return to power of Polish and Hungarian reform-Communists may guarantee such an outcome in any case. On the other hand, the new governments of these two countries have proven to be committed to reforms and have thus allayed fears of a return to an authoritarian government that might destabilize the system by provoking intense opposition to its attempt to turn back the clock. Perhaps the most convincing argument against such fears may be found in the notion that the former Communists, as educated, experienced, and nowadays pragmatic politicians, have themselves benefited profoundly from the liberalization of economic and political activities. Whereas this does not guarantee against the reestablishment of patronage and clientele networks, it will ascertain stability which, in the long run, may be more beneficial than "lustration" campaigns that could erupt into witch-hunts.

The governments of all three countries must avoid complacency, especially if their economic reform programs are successfully implemented, as remains the case in the Czech Republic. The growing gap between the sections of society which benefit from the move to a market economy, and those who feel left behind and yearn for the days of welfare guaranteed by the state, must be addressed. Politically, the feeling of disillusionment with economic reforms seems to reflect itself in voter apathy and disinterest, particularly evident in Poland and Hungary, which could encourage further unresponsiveness or strengthen authoritarian tendencies.

The political-party landscape has consolidated itself as well. Led by the Czech Republic, all three countries appear to move towards a typical Western European pattern of governments and parliaments dominated alternately by Left-of-Center (the reform-Communists in Hungary and Poland), or Right-of-Center parties (Czech Civic Democrats). Despite the fact that they all share one precondition for the establishment of "one-party dominant regimes . . . an electoral system that fosters a multiparty system," it is too early to predict whether any of the three countries will create such a system, but the post-1989 history does not point in that direction.[61]

The treatment of ethnic minorities in all three countries gives some reason for concern, especially of the *Roma* living in Hungary and the Czech Republic. The latter has furthermore acquired the dubious reputation of having adopted one of the most restrictive citizenship laws. There is no evidence, however, to suggest that ethnic unrest in Poland, Hungary, or the Czech Republic could undermine the democratization process and systemic stability.

In sum, all three countries are stable and prospects for both continued stability and further democratization are promising. They are still transitional systems or "immature democracies," but their domestic history since 1989 and closeness to integration into NATO and the European Union warrants an overall optimistic assessment of the prospects of democracy.[62]

Notes

1. Samuel P. Huntington, *Political Order in Changing Societies* (New Haven: Yale University Press, 1968); Ralph M. Goldman, "The Nominating Process: Factionalism as a Force for Democratization," in Gary D. Wekkin et al., *Building Democracy in One-Party Systems: Theoretical Problems and Cross-Nation Experiences* (Westport, CT: Praeger, 1993), p. 47–69.

2. For a description of the model, see Wekkin et al., *Building Democracy in One-Party Systems,* p. 5–10.

3. Jaroslaw Piekalkiewicz & Alfred W. Payne, *Politics of Ideocracy* (New York: SUNY Press, 1995).

4. Judith Pataki, "Hungarians Dissatisfied with Political Changes," in *Radio Free Europe/Radio Liberty (RFE/RL) Research Report* (6 November 1992): p. 66–67.

5. Listed as "situational preconditions" in Sabrina P. Ramet, "Balkan Pluralism and Its Enemies," in *Orbis* (fall 1992): p. 547–564. For other sources of Ramet's criteria of democracy, see: Aristotle's *Politics;* Alvin Rabushka & Kenneth Shepsle, *Politics in Plural Societies: A Theory of Democratic Instability* (Columbia, Ohio: Merrill, 1992); Guglielmo Ferrero, *The Principles of Power* (New York: G.P. Putnam's Sons, 1942); Huntington, *Political Order in Changing Societies;* Crane Brinton, *Anatomy of a Revolution* (New York: Vintage Books, 1964); Valerie Bunce, "Rising Above the Past: The Struggle for Liberal Democracy in Eastern Europe," in Sabrina P. Ramet, ed., *Adaptation and Transformation in Communist and Post-Communist Systems* (Boulder, CO: Westview Press, 1993).

6. Free elections are one of several "institutional preconditions" according to Ramet, "Balkan Pluralism and Its Enemies." For other definitions of democracy see: Wekkin et al., *Building Democracy in One-Party Systems,* p. 9–10; Georg Sorensen, *Democracy and Democratization* (Boulder, CO: Westview Press, 1993), p. 13.

7. For data on the election outcome, see: Barnabas Racz, "Political Pluralization in Hungary: The 1990 Elections," in *Soviet Studies,* vol. XLIII, no. 1 (1991): p. 107–136. On the 1989 electoral law, see: Istvan Kukorelli, "The Birth, Testing, and Results of the 1989 Hungarian Election Law," p. 137–156.

8. Barnabas Racz, "The Hungarian Parliament's Rise and Challenges," in *RFE/RL Research Report* (14 February 1992): p. 23.

9. Judith Pataki, "Hungarians Dissatisfied with Political Changes," in *RFE/RL Research Report* (6 November 1992): p. 66–67.

10. Pataki, "Hungarians Dissatisfied with Political Changes," p. 67–68. Voter turnout rates were, however, also relatively low in the first post-Communist

Hungarian elections, a phenomenon that one observer explained as the consequence of a lack of mass mobilization in Hungary during the transition phase. See: Andras Korosenyi, "Stable or Fragile Democracy? Political Cleavages and Party System in Hungary," in *Government and Opposition*, vol. 28, no. 1 (winter 1993): p. 102.

11. Korosenyi, "Stable or Fragile Democracy?" p. 91, 99.

12. Commission on Security and Cooperation in Europe, "Human Rights and Democratization in Hungary" (Washington, DC: Commission on Security and Cooperation in Europe, December 1993), p. 17.

13. "Gypsies Suffering in Hungary's Shift," in *New York Times* (7 November 1993); "Boross: Ethnic Conflict Not Behind Gypsy Deaths," *Nepszabadsag* (15 September 1992), as translated in *Foreign Broadcast Information Service (FBIS)* (29 September 1992); U.S. State Department, *Human Rights Report 1992* (Washington, D.C.: state Department, 1993).

14. Commission on Security & Cooperation in Europe, "Human Rights & Democratization in Hungary," p. 18–21.

15. Quote attributed to Gaspar M. Tamas, leader of the Free Democratic Party in: Commission on Security and Cooperation in Europe, "Human Rights and Democratization in Hungary," p. 4.

16. Andras Korosenyi, "Hungary," in *Electoral Studies,* Special Issue, vol. 9, no. 4 (December 1990).

17. Korosenyi, "Stable or Fragile Democracy?" p. 89–90.

18. Judith Pataki, "Possible Newcomers to Hungary's Parliament," *RFE/RL Research Report* (9 April 1993): p. 20.

19. "Bring Back the Goulash," in *The Economist* (7 May 1994).

20. Ibid.

21. Ibid. For results and analyses of the 1994 elections, see: Edith Oltay, "Former Communists Win First Round of Hungarian Elections," in *RFE/RL Research Report* (27 May 1994); Edith Oltay, "The Former Communists' Election Victory in Hungary," in *RFE/RL Research Report* (24 June 1994).

22. "Horn's Dilemma," in *The Economist* (28 January 1995).

23. See: Anne Applebaum, "The Fall and Rise of the Communists," in *Foreign Affairs,* vol. 73, no. 6 (November- December 1994): p. 7–13.

24. Commission on Security and Cooperation in Europe, "Human Rights and Democratization in Poland" (Washington, D.C.: Commission on Security and Cooperation in Europe, January 1994), p. 7.

25. Commission on Security and Cooperation in Europe, "Human Rights and Democratization in Poland," p. 7; "Walesa Backs 'Small Constitution'," in *Facts on File World News Digest,* vol. 52, no. 2718 (31 December 1992): p. 994; "Poland: Government," in *The Europa World Yearbook* (London: Europa Publications, 1995).

26. Louisa Vinton, "'Outsider' Parties and the Political Process in Poland," in *RFE/RL Research Report,* vol. 3, no. 3 (21 January 1994): p. 14.

27. Commission on Security and Cooperation in Europe, "Human Rights and Democratization in Poland," p. 13.

28. Ibid., p. 8; Janusz L. Mucha, "Democratization and Cultural Minorities: The Polish Case of the 1980s–1990s," in *East European Quarterly,* vol. XXV, no. 4 (January 1992): p. 472.

29. Ethnic homogeneity in Poland was enhanced by momentous trends such as the reduction of the Jewish population because of Nazi Germany's occupation and the forced emigration of Germans after World War II.

30. Mucha, "Democratization and Cultural Minorities," p. 473–474; Commission on Security and Cooperation in Europe, "Human Rights and Democratization in Poland," p. 10.

31. Millard, Frances, "The Polish Parliamentary Elections of October 1991," in *Soviet Studies,* vol. 44, no. 5 (September 1992): p. 837–855.

32. Barry Newman, "As Election Day Nears, Governing Politicians in Poland Wonder Where They Went Wrong," in *Wall Street Journal* (16 September 1993).

33. Steven Silber, "Polish Premier Finally Opts for Privatization," in *Christian Science Monitor* (spring 1994).

34. Commission on Security and Cooperation in Europe, "Human Rights and Democratization in Poland," p. 8; Vinton, "'Outsider' Parties and the Political Process in Poland," p. 13–22.

35. Aleksandr Kuranov, "Eastern Europe's Pink Tide," in *Nezavisimaya Gazeta* (July 1994), translated in *World Press Review* (August 1994).

36. Vinton, "'Outsider' Parties and the Political Process in Poland," p. 14.

37. Commission on Security and Cooperation in Europe, "Human Rights and Democratization in Poland," p. 9–10; Kuranov, "Eastern Europe's Pink Tide," p. 3; John Pomfret, "Poland's Ex-Communists Say West Aided Win," in *Washington Post* (26 September 1993).

38. Vinton, "'Outsider' Parties and the Political Process in Poland," p. 22; "Canny Peasants," *The Economist* (12 February 1994); "Polish Parties Sign Agreement," in *Open Media Research Institute (OMRI) Daily Digest,* no. 34, Part II (16 February 1995).

39. Marius Janicki, "Two Sides of the Mirror; Parties, Party Leaders, Voters," *Polityka* (12 October 1996), as translated in *FBIS Daily Report* (8 November 1996): p. 2–4. If these preliminary surveys prove correct, Solidarity may once again emerge as the winner and form a coalition government with other "Rightist" parties, whereas the Left Democratic Alliance and the Polish Peasant Party could be pushed into the opposition.

40 "Rebel as Anti-Hero," in *The Economist* (22 October 1994).

41. Ben Slay, as paraphrased in Paula B. Smith, "The Polish Transition: Economic Success, Political Failure?" in *East European Studies* (Woodrow Wilson Center) (September-October 1995): p. 2.

42. Ruth Walker, "Poland's Anticommunists Aim to Rise Again in Presidential Bid," in *Christian Science Monitor* (3 November 1995); Ruth Walker, "Wary of Ex-Communists, Poles Boost Walesa in Vote," in *Christian Science Monitor* (7 November 1995); "Walesa by a Neck?" in *The Economist* (11 November 1995).

43. Marshall Ingwerson and Peter Ford, "Ex-Communists Retake the Helm," in *Christian Science Monitor* (21 November 1995).

44. Gregory Pitt, "Fresh Face, Same Agenda," in *Christian Science Monitor* (21 November 1995); George Moffett, "A Cold-War Reality Check: Didn't Communism Die?" in *Christian Science Monitor* (6 December 1995).

45. For a more detailed analysis of the split see: Commission on Security and Cooperation in Europe, "Human Rights and Democratization in the Czech Republic" (Washington, D.C.: Commission on Human Rights and Cooperation in Europe, September 1994), p. 9–10.

46. Ibid., p. 1.

47. "Vaclav Thatcher," in *The Economist* (6 August 1994).

48. Ibid.; "The New Bohemians,"in *The Economist* (22 October 1994).

49. For Vaclav Havel's vision of Czechoslovakia, see his "From the Czech Republic with Love and Dreams," in *Utne Reader* (May-June 1993): p. 90–92; "Vaclav Thatcher"; Jiri Pehe, "Civic Forum Splits," in *Report on Eastern Europe*, no. 10 (8 March 1991).

50. "Going West," in *The Economist* (25 May 1996); "Surprise," in *The Economist* (8 June 1996).

51. A term used by Leszek Balcerowicz, a Polish ex-finance minister, quoted in "The New Bohemians."

52. An example was the government's support for the Lety Archives and protection of the Lety camp, a site from which thousands of *Roma* were deported to Auschwitz during World War II; H. Kamm, "Havel Calls the Gypsies 'Litmus Test'," in *New York Times* (10 December 1993). Concerning the *Roma* in the Czech Republic see: Commission on Security and Cooperation in Europe, "Human Rights and Democratization in the Czech Republic," p. 18–21.

53. "Klaus Views Partnership, Migration," in *Lidove Noviny* (15 January 1994), translated in *FBIS Daily Report* (19 January 1994).

54. For details, see Commission on Security and Cooperation in Europe, "Human Rights and Democratization in the Czech Republic," p. 21–27; "HRW Criticizes Human Rights Observance by Czechs, Slovaks," in *CTK National News Wire* (9 December 1994).

55. Pehe, "Civic Forum Splits."

56. Ibid.; "Czechoslovakia's Changing Political Spectrum," in *RFL/RE Research Report* (31 January 1992): p. 2.

57. "Czechoslovakia's Changing Political Spectrum," p. 3; "Bulletin—Electoral Statistics and Public Opinion Research Data," in *East European Politics and Societies*, vol. 7, no. 3 (fall 1993): p. 555–564.

58. "Bulletin—Electoral Statistics," p. 558.

59. "Surprise."

60. For similar arguments, see: David B. Ottoway, "Czechs Defy Trend in Rebuffing Old Left," in *International Herald Tribune* (28–29 May 1994).

61. T. J. Pempel, ed. *Uncommon Democracies: The One-Party Dominant Regimes* (Ithaca, NY: Cornell University Press, 1990).

62. For the optimistic evaluation and the pessimistic view derived from the possibility of ethnic conflicts in East European countries see: Sorensen, *Democracy and Democratization*, p. 121–124.

NINE

Evolution and Demise of One-Party Rule in Nicaragua

Harry E. Vanden

Nicaragua is a small Central American state of three and a half million people. Like much of Central America, its economic development has been based on the export of bananas, coffee, and other primary products. It political history is replete with dictators, foreign intervention, factionalism, failed attempts at democracy, and one-party domination. As with similar cases from the south, Nicaraguan political history and political development are somewhat different from that of more industrialized countries. Nonetheless, as we endeavor to study political phenomena cross-culturally, we try to see if it is possible to discern some generalized similarities in a variety of different states. In works like *Uncommon Democracies: The One-Party-Dominant Regimes,* T. J. Pempel and his co-authors examine one-party domination in countries as diverse as Sweden, Italy, Israel, and Japan. Using some of their concepts it might be possible to better understand the evolution and development of the Nicaraguan political system and those of similar polities. By proceeding in this way, it might even be possible to see if such categorizations might be generally more applicable.

To qualify as a one-party-dominant régime, Pempel suggests that: "the dominant party must dominate the electorate, other political parties, the formation of government and the public policy agenda."[1] If we were to apply this criteria to Nicaragua, one would note at least two extended periods of one-party rule in this century. The first period of one-party rule in Nicaragua began in the mid 1930s when Anastacio Somoza García turned the Liberal Party into a political vehicle to consolidate his rule. He was formally elected president in 1936 and ruled for the next two decades. The second period was marked by *Sandinista* domination and extended from July 1979 until early 1990.

Examining the first period we note that even though the original Somoza dictator was assassinated in 1956, his sons' extended family and control of the Liberal Party allowed them to continue to rule the country well into the late 1970s. The Liberal Party became personalized by the Somoza family, but remained in power only until the Nicaraguan people finally overthrew the Somoza family régime in July 1979. By that time, the Liberal Party had become the dominant party in Nicaragua—albeit a party whose power and influence was always filtered through Somoza rule. Indeed, the entwined party and dictatorship monopolized power at all levels. Political opposition was factionalized and debilitated by four decades of being excluded from the halls of government. Only the Conservative Party showed any semblance of party unity and that too was shattered with the January 1978 assassination of its champion and arch-Somoza critic, Pedro Juaquín Chamorro. The one-party-dominant system that evolved could be even more precisely characterized as a personalized family dictatorship that vested power in the Somoza-controlled Liberal Party. Party and government were used both as instruments of subordination and domination.

Up to 1979 Nicaragua was one of the most conservative and authoritarian societies in Latin America. It could boast the longest family dictatorship in the hemisphere (1936–79). Indeed, it could be argued that Nicaragua was among the least democratic of the Latin American countries for the longest time and consequently had little experience with democracy or honest elections. Even the ultra-traditional régime in Paraguay could only date its existence to the early 1950s. One author even suggested that it not only had an authoritarian political culture, but that the factional nature of party interaction suggested a political system that was characterized by its underdevelopment.[2]

One person and one-party domination were significant factors in the skewed evolution of the political system in Nicaragua. The arbitrary and often capricious exercise of power led many to brand the small Central American state with the pejorative label of "banana republic." As suggested by the above and even the most cursory reading of Nicaraguan political history, one could easily conclude that power monopoly by a small group and one-party domination had been well institutionalized for some time before the *Sandinistas* came to power in 1979.

Originally, the first Somoza was able to exploit his close ties to Washington and his position as head of the National Guard. By the mid 1930s Anastacio Somoza García had emerged as the most powerful political figure in the country. He realized that the popular nationalist guerrilla leader Augusto César Sandino and his Army to Defend National Sovereignty favored popular rule and thus represented the greatest threat to the reestablishment of rule by a U.S.-backed élite. No doubt he also sensed that Sandino was a symbol of popular struggle and a possible key to the rediscovery of popular history and popular participation by the Nicaraguan people. The dictator was not content to have ordered the execution of the popular leader in 1933. He attempted to distort the popular memory of Sandino and his followers by having a slanderous anti-Sandino book published under his name. Somoza's efforts achieved some success, in that it was soon very difficult for the masses of Nicaraguans to obtain any favorable written accounts of the *Sandinista* struggle within the country.

After Somoza took direct control of the government in 1936, he instituted an increasingly repressive family dictatorship that—mostly because of its close ties to the United States—would endure until militarily defeated by the *Sandinista* National Liberation Front (FSLN) in 1979. However, despite bloody repression and the intense vilification of Sandino and his followers, sporadic popular struggle continued through the 1930s, 1940s, and 1950s, though clearly at a relatively low level.

By the 1940s, the full force of the Somoza dictatorship was being felt. Somoza had proven to be one of the United States' best "good neighbors," and had been lavishly received by President Franklin D. Roosevelt who is reputed to have opined that though Somoza was an "s.o.b." he was "our s.o.b." By the 1950s Nicaragua was a fully dependent producer of primary goods (mostly coffee and cotton), and an integral part of the U.S. system of political and economic control in the Western Hemisphere. Sandino's anti-imperialist popular struggle (1926–32) seemed to have been for naught. The guerrilla hero and the popular revolutionary's struggle seemed to be slowly disappearing from the popular mind and the people seemed to have less and less access to power. There were occasional armed actions or putsch attempts by old *Sandinistas* and other Nicaraguans who could no longer countenance the heavy-handed political and economic manipulation that characterized the Somozas and their friends. Students and workers (as in 1944) occasionally demonstrated against the régime, but lacked any clear ideological perspective in which to place their struggle. There was neither ideology nor organization for popular mobilization. Opposition to the dictatorship came to be symbolized by the sincere, but élitist, Conservative Party. Even the Nicaraguan Socialist Party (founded as a pro-Moscow Communist Party in 1944) often collaborated with traditional bourgeois politicians and Somoza-controlled unions, at the workers' expense. Somoza had taken over the Liberal Party and even went so far as to make pacts (1948 and 1950) with the Conservative Party in an attempt to co-opt the only major focal point of opposition to his régime. Without even the militant Liberalism that had initiated Sandino in his struggle, it was difficult for the diffuse opposition forces to gain the political perspective necessary to again mobilize the masses against the forces of dictatorship and imperialism.

In 1956 a young poet, Rigoberto López Pérez, assassinated Somoza. In so doing he not only avenged Sandino, but spurred a much-needed reexamination of national conscience that would increasingly challenge the status quo and free the Nicaraguan people from their lethargy. Rigoberto López Pérez's action and the different armed attacks and popular uprisings that the Nicaraguan people unleashed from 1956 to 1960 in great part reflect the gradual loss of Conservative political control over the popular masses. Party competition had proven increasingly ineffective.

Little by little the spirit of Sandino's struggle was once again being felt across the land. A new wave of guerrilla activities broke out in the countryside; one of the more famous of these was even led by Ramón Raudales, a veteran of Sandino's army. The university students also began to show a new militancy and, for the first time, a small group began to study Marxist theory.[3]

Founded in 1961, the *Sandinista* National Liberation Front (FSLN)—and not the traditional opposition—began to challenge the régime. But armed conflict did not ensure success either. In 1967 some of the FSLN's best cadres were isolated and surrounded at Pancasán in northern Nicaragua. However, while this was occurring in the countryside, things were even worse in the cities. The traditional opposition forces continued to demonstrate their ineptitude. One of the most notorious examples of this happened in Managua in January of 1967. Here, the Conservative leader Fernando Aguero took advantage of a large, peaceful demonstration against the dictatorship to try to carry out an ill-planned and unorganized putsch against Somoza. This resulted in the massacre of over 100 unarmed demonstrators and a further loss in prestige for the political opposition and the Conservative Party. In contrast, the tenacity of the resistance waged by the FSLN focused national attention on their struggle, and helped to turn a military defeat into a political victory. Beginning with the peasants and university students, the process of merging the vanguard and the mobilized masses into a unified fighting force was slowly getting underway.[4]

Unlike many other guerrilla movements in Latin America, the *Sandinistas* were able to learn from the mistakes they made. They demonstrated a great capacity for self-criticism and were thus able to transcend their initial error of isolating themselves from the masses.[5] Through painful trial and error and through an increasingly astute study of Sandino's thought and tactics, and those of other revolutionary movements throughout the world, they were able to fashion a strategy that would eventually unleash the full power of the Nicaraguan people against the dictatorship.

In the period after Pancasán and the 1967 elections, the FSLN's increased prestige brought many new recruits, especially from among students and youth in the cities. At this time the organization focused mainly on developing a base among the *campesinos* in the north-central part of the country, in the mountains around Zinica. It was there that the urban recruits were sent. The work bore fruit and became the axis of the "prolonged people's war" concept that dominated the *Sandinistas'* thinking at that time. While the Zinica front was the focus of the FSLN's armed activity following Pancasán, increased attention was being paid to urban work that was necessarily clandestine. The FSLN began to establish what it called "intermediate organizations": student organizations, worker organization, Christian movements, artistic groups, and others.

If the opposition parties were finding recruitment difficult, the *Sandinistas* were having considerable success winning *campesinos* to their cause in the mountains. This alarmed Somoza. Large-scale, brutal counterinsurgency operations were launched. Peasants suspected of collaborating with the FSLN "disappeared," were tortured, hurled out of helicopters, or otherwise murdered. What amounted to concentration camps were set up in Waslala and Rio Blanco at the northern and southern extremities of the area where the *Frente* was operating. The counterrevolutionary terror became so intense that the guerrillas were pushed back deep into the mountains, and progressively separated from the inhabited areas where they had been gaining political support. The "prolonged people's war" strategy, which demanded a secure rural base area, was reaching an impasse.

While the *Sandinistas* evolved their theory of mass struggle, progressive sectors within the Catholic Church became more and more concerned with the conditions of the masses. Motivated by this concern and the growing "Liberation Theology" movement, they began to intervene actively in the process of social change. Numerous Christian popular organizations emerged in the 1970s as the struggle against Somoza deepened. Eventually, an important unity was struck between the FSLN and these forces when prominent Church figures like Ernesto and Fernando Cardenal, and Miguel D'Escoto became part of the FSLN. In marked contrast to the decreasing legitimacy of the opposition parties, the *Sandinistas* began to be seen as the alternative to Somoza by the late 1970s.

The popular empowerment of the masses and the mobilization of grassroots participants through Christian Base Communities and the growing popular Church also interjected strong democratizing tendencies and helped to introduce ideas of direct democracy and less centralist views of governance into the *Sandinista* movement. Between Pancasán and late 1974, the FSLN carried on what it termed "accumulation of forces in silence." The calm was broken in a spectacular way with the 27 December 1974 seizure of the home of a wealthy and prominent Somoza cohort during a gala party for the U.S. Ambassador. A FSLN commando unit held more than a dozen foreign diplomats and top *Somocistas* for several days, finally forcing Somoza to release *Sandinista* political prisoners, pay a large sum of money, and broadcast and publish FSLN communiqués.

The FSLN's consciousness of the need to mobilize the masses was already apparent in Carlos Fonseca Amador's landmark article of 1968, "Nicaragua Hora Cero." Drawing a balance sheet on the Pancasán period, Fonseca wrote that: "Organized mass work (student, peasant, worker) was paralyzed. On the one hand, the quantity of cadres necessary for this work was lacking, and on the other, the importance this activity could have in the course of the development of the armed struggle was underrated."

Different tendencies in the FSLN finally converged around the fresh tactical and strategic questions brought to the fore by the upsurge of mass struggle that opened in late 1977. As the urban masses moved into action after Pedro Joaquín Chamorro's murder in early 1978, the trend was for all three tendencies to learn both from the masses and from each other. Disagreements over the question of alliances had led the Insurrectionalist tendency of the FSLN to participate in the Broad Opposition Front (FAO) through their supporters in the "Group of Twelve" while the FSLN's Prolonged People's War (GPP) faction and the *Proletarios* faction were concentrating on building the future United People's Movement (MPU). The political capitulation of the opposition party elements in the FAO to the U.S.-sponsored "mediation" in October 1978 quickly led the Insurrectionalists to adjust their policy and withdraw from the FAO. All tendencies then collaborated to establish the National Patriotic Front (FPN), which had the MPU as its axis. The FPN took on the character of an anti-imperialist united front, drawing in the trade unions, two of the three factions of the old PSN, student groups and petty bourgeois formations such as the Popular Social Christian and Independent Liberal Parties. Thus, many opposition parties ended under FSLN hegemony.

Finally, the experience of the September 1978 attempt at insurrection—which the Insurrectionalist tendency spearheaded most enthusiastically—taught the need for better organization and preparation. The cumulative effect of these lessons and the massive organized mobilization that resulted, paid off in June 1979 as the FSLN coordinated a massive popular insurrection.

I. The FSLN in Power

As the *Sandinistas* consolidated their political control after July 1979, more moderate elements of the victorious coalition left the government. After the initial euphoria of the revolutionary victory died down, the Nicaraguan political leadership engaged in actions that began to suggest that the participation and grass-roots democracy that had been initially envisioned as part of the *Sandinista* program might be sidetracked. Power became concentrated in the upper echelons of government and in the FSLN's National Directorate. Later, as the United States and its allies pressured the Nicaraguan leadership to bring the régime more in line with Western-style systems, steps were taken towards a system of representative democracy that the dominant group in the *Sandinista* leadership hoped would satisfy many of its detractors and thus increase the legitimacy of the Nicaraguan government in the eyes of the West.

When the FSLN took power on 19 July, 1979, the stage was set for a series of changes that included radical experimentation with forms of participatory and direct democracy, two of the most honest elections in Nicaraguan, if not Latin American, history (1984 and 1990), a very open constitution-making process, and the eventual return to representative democratic forms dominated by political élites. But these and subsequent events were, in turn, conditioned by a political culture that had been extremely traditional and authoritarian, and a political system that had been slow to develop. Opposition parties were tolerated and sometimes encouraged, but the *Sandinista* National Liberation Front soon became the dominant party in a newly configured régime. Traditional influences were difficult to lay to rest. In his essay on values in Nicaraguan Political Culture, the well-respected Nicaraguan political analyst Emilio Alvarez Montalván lists authoritarianism, élitism, and personalism as among the most prominent characteristics.[6] Even after years of *Sandinista* rule, many traditional values continued to permeate Nicaraguan political culture.

New values were, however, eventually interjected into the Nicaraguan context. Like many successful revolutions in the Third World, the 1979 *Sandinista* revolution promised democracy for the Nicaraguan people. Even before the triumph, the "Historic Program of the FSLN" had committed the revolutionaries to political structure(s) "that will permit the full participation of all of the people at the national as well as the local level. Further, as an ever wider coalition of forces joined the revolutionary movement in 1978 and 1979, the prospects for Nicaraguan democracy and an open-party system seemed to grow with the inscription of each new political group, many of which had ties with traditional parties, were strongly committed to Western representative democracy, or had already experienced the participatory democracy of the popular Christian movement.[7] Indeed, it could be argued that the particular forms that democracy took in Nicaragua were related to the specific (and very diverse) nature of the class coalition that overthrew the Somoza dictatorship and to the way in which the FSLN's political leadership conceived and interpreted those classes and their role in the continuing revolutionary process. Likewise, external pressures from the United States and other actors also conditioned the ways in which democracy developed during *Sandinista* rule and under the Chamorro administration.

In that the triumphant coalition of forces (and classes) became very broad indeed, the invocation of democracy by the new government at the time of the revolutionary triumph was less of a commitment to a specific program to institutionalize democratic participation than a general commitment to democratic ideals similar to that first invoked by Simon Bolívar at the end of the struggle for Latin American independence.

If the new leadership acknowledged a diversity of political groupings ranging from traditional parties to ultra-left movements, it also tacitly acknowledged several different conceptions about exactly what democracy was, or more specifically, which structures maximized its realization. Thus, members of the two traditional parties, the Liberals and the Conservatives, wanted Western-style elections, a traditional party system and representative government as did most of the bourgeoisie and quite a few in the middle class. Members of the popular classes, who had mobilized for the revolution or who had participated in local community or Church organizations, wanted to make sure that their direct participation would continue and would be given effect. Rural and urban workers and peasants wanted more power over where they labored, as well as in national affairs. *Sandinistas* wanted to ensure the predominant position of the *Sandinista* movement and make sure that the lower classes would be enfranchised for participation that would guarantee ongoing, effective involvement in decision-making *and* economic justice for the toiling masses. And many *Sandinista* militants wanted to ensure the hegemonic position of a vanguard party in which democratic centralism would be practiced.

Much of the *Sandinista* leadership was skeptical of a narrow, bourgeois definition of democracy that reinstated the traditional party system, minimized direct popular participation, and did not include a social and economic dimension. They also wanted to make sure that the democracy that was implemented did not block necessary social and economic restructuring and did not facilitate foreign manipulation. "Democracy neither begins or ends with elections. . . ."[8] "Effective democracy, like we intend to practice in Nicaragua, consists of ample popular participation; a permanent dynamic of the people's participation in a variety of political and social tasks. . . ."[9]

What leading *Sandinistas* did envision was a popular democracy that would not just allow participation by the few (or domination by the upper classes), but would build democracy from below through the construction of neighborhood, gender or functional grass-roots, mass organizations. In that traditional parties had been dominated by political élites, this conception mitigated against the creation of a competitive party system. Rather, the idea of meaningful democratic participation (though sometimes defined differently) became a strong symbolic value that was readily adopted by wide sectors of the population. Newly-formed mass organizations—and not traditional political party structures—became an important mechanism for popular empowerment. These organizations were also the direct communication link between the masses and the political leadership. They informed the people of new political directions and channeled popular demands through the party to the National Directorate.[10]

To hold the victorious coalition together and transform society, some form of political representation that would allow the participation of anti-Somoza elements from the upper and middle classes but would facilitate direct representatives from the lower classes and the *Sandinistas* was needed. Initially, different organizations were able to send the representatives they chose to an appointed council of state, which served as the national legislature, albeit with limited powers. The council of state was eventually expanded to 50 members. Virtually all groups, including AMNLAE (the national women's organization), peasant and small farmer groupings, workers, the Catholic Church, and COSEP (Superior Council of Private Enterprise), were included. Here parties were but one group among many. This was one of the most radical experiments in direct participation and functional representation in the history of the Americas. However, rather than incorporate this institution in the reconfigured post-1984 structure of government, it was dropped entirely. After the 1984 election this institution was replaced by an elected National Assembly. Representatives were now chosen by a system of proportional representation and there were no longer representatives sent directly by different organization. Forms of representative democracy began to supplant the attempt at direct democracy represented by the mass organizations and the council of state. Opposition parties were represented in the new legislature and were given a forum.

Elections had been on the agenda ever since the *Sandinista* victory in 1979. As enunciated by Humberto Ortega in 1980, the FSLN position had been that elections should be held within five years, but that some waiting period was necessary in order to develop election laws and to give the populace time to become accustomed to the new society and the pluralist possibilities it presented. Thus, the council of state (which included representatives of opposition groups including COSEP) passed the Political Parties Law in August of 1983. In fall 1983 the Socialist International joined opposition groups like the Social Christian Party (PSC) in calling on the government to move up elections to 1984. Washington was also able to point to the absence of elections as a verification of its claims that the *Sandinistas* were totalitarian Marxist-Leninists who, like Fidel Castro, would not hold elections as promised. These events prompted considerable discussion within the FSLN, which once again opted for a pragmatic course.

In February 1984 it was announced that elections would be held on November 4th of that year (two days before the U.S. elections). An electoral law was introduced in the Council of state during February and, after considerable debate, passed in mid March. Ironically, the debate in the Council of state was periodically boycotted by some opposition members who in the end reversed their previous calls for an earlier election by claiming that the accelerated timetable did not allow them adequate preparation time. The PSC, the Social Democratic Party, COSEP, and other parties that followed this path eventually joined the *Coordinadora* and abstained from the election. This led many critics to claim that their actual intent was never to participate in elections, but, like the Reagan administration in Washington, to use every possible pretext to embarrass the *Sandinistas* and discredit the electoral process.[11] Further credence was lent to this view when, under opposition criticism, the *Sandinistas* lifted the declared state of emergency in July 1984, only to be confronted with yet other reasons why such opposition parties would not participate in the election. Thus, even returning to more traditional Western democratic structures was not sufficient to convince the Reagan administration and many of its Nicaraguan allies that the *Sandinistas* really were good democrats. The move did, however, succeed in taking power from the common people and their mass organizations. As the full consequences of this restructuring settled in, many in the popular organizations began to question whether the elections may have diminished their power and limited their access to decision-making.

Though some press censorship persisted, it was mostly limited to military matters. Adequate media access was guaranteed to each of the seven participating parties. The government allocated each party 30 minutes of state television time and 45 minutes of state radio time each week. Further, each party received 9 million Córdobas (U.S. $ 900,000 at the official exchange rate) in order to buy additional T.V. and radio time and to purchase other campaign materials.

II. The 1984 Election

And so it was that on 4 November 1984 Nicaragua experienced a unique experiment in democracy. Guided by a nationalist ideology that was Marxist in orientation and a political movement that had incorporated some Leninist elements, the revolutionary government nonetheless held Western-style elections that invited the opposition parties to compete for power through the electoral process and encouraged the world to watch as they did. The result was a rare event in Nicaraguan history—an honest election. Further, it engendered real electoral competition among seven different parties and gave the Nicaraguan people one of their few experiences with democratic competition in this century. It also helped to embed representative democracy in the new governmental structure and diminish the construction of direct, participatory democracy.

The ground rules had been set before the election began. Elections would be held for representative institutions. Suggestions that direct democracy be retained in the form of a second house composed of legislators who were chosen directly by the members of their mass organizations (Yugoslavia had developed such a second house) were not persuasive. Rather traditional Western representation would be employed through elections for a National Assembly wherein parties would compete for seats. Despite some initial governmental resistance, the opposition parties had been able to achieve an electoral party law that defined political parties as "groups of Nicaraguan citizens who have similar ideologies and who have come together, among other reasons, *to vie for power with the purpose of carrying out a program responding to the needs of national development.*"[12] This statute and the pluralist philosophy that engendered it were a far cry from the special status reserved for the vanguard party in Marxist-Leninist states.

The inclusion of the phrase "*to vie for power*" defined the elections as instruments that would determine who would rule, not—as had been the case in traditional Marxist-Leninist states—how the official party would generate obligatory ratification of its policies. It was an example of how Nicaragua had broken out of the traditional East-West mold to forge its own policies and institutions. However, although this allowed for real political competition among parties it was not consistent with direct popular empowerment of the masses. Nor is it clear that this process served as a model for how participatory democracy might be developed.

There was, however, vigorous campaigning throughout the country. Even days after the election one could see numerous posters and slogans on walls, trees, and utility poles. The populace was very much involved in the electoral process. Participating parties included the FSLN; the PLI-Independent Liberal Party; the PDC-Democratic Conservative Party; the PSN-Nicaraguan Socialist Party; the PPSC-Popular Social Christian Party; the PCdeN-Communist Party of Nicaragua; and the MAP-ML-Marxist-Leninist Popular Action Movement.

For the purpose of electing candidates to the National Assembly, the country was divided into nine territorial districts and proportional representation was used to award seats from party lists in each of these. In addition a seat was awarded to each of the six presidential candidates who did not win. All of the 96 new members were to serve six-year terms. The Assembly's first task was to act as a constituent assembly to determine the exact organizational structure for the new government.

Seven widely different parties and 1.17 million voters (out of a total population of 3 million) participated in what was reported to be Nicaragua's most honest election to date. A wide variety of observer groups attested to the honesty of the process. Other than the CIA-trained and backed

Counter-revolutionaries (*Contras*), the only group not to participate in the electoral process was the Nicaraguan Democratic Coordinating Committee. Headed by Arturo Cruz and supported by the United States, it consisted of three small parties, the Social Christians (PSC), the Social Democrats (PSD), and the Constitutionalist Liberals (PLC). The *Coordinadora,* as it was known in Nicaragua, ignored several extended deadlines to register for the elections, claiming that freedom of the press and other necessary conditions for fair elections did not exist.

A general calm prevailed on election day. Despite Rightist efforts, *Contras* threats, and U.S. pressure not to vote, participation was extremely high. Almost 40 percent of the total population voted in the election. All citizens 16 years or older were able to vote and 93.7 percent of those eligible registered. Of these, 75 percent cast ballots on election day. The big winners were the *Sandinistas,* who garnered 62.9 percent of the votes for president and vice president and 62.3 percent of the National Assembly votes. The six opposition parties divided 33 percent of the vote, while blank or invalid ballots accounted for a little more than 6 percent of the votes cast.

Judged against Nicaragua's historic authoritarian tradition, the 1984 elections were an immense success. Although political conditions prior to the election were not perfect, the voting itself did not see the type of corruption and vote fraud that had been so common in countries like Nicaragua, Guatemala, and El Salvador. The opposition was allowed to run and to win a third of the seats in the National Assembly. The government and its policies were openly criticized during the campaign. This was a major accomplishment for a country like Nicaragua and was done despite the best efforts of the Reagan administration which, according to a National Security Council document leaked to the *Washington Post,* had actively campaigned to convince the north American public that the elections were a farce.[13] Subsequent developments suggest that Reagan had pressured the *Coordinadora* not to participate in the elections and tried to do the same with elements of the Independent Liberal Party. Like virtually all the other outside observers, the electoral observation team from the Latin American Studies Association found the 1984 electoral process to be a far cry from elections held in the past.[14]

It was the first time in which a Marxist movement that had come to power by revolution was willing to allow opposition groups to challenge it in an open balloting process and actually share power with these groups in an elected assembly. In retrospect, this process proved to be a precursor of many similar elections in Eastern Europe. As also was the case in Eastern Europe, this type of election and the representative institutions that resulted were a major concession to Western-style representative democracy. This process seemed to contradict earlier *Sandinista* pledges to enact a democratic system that more fully empowered the masses.

As the structure of the new legislative assembly was debated in the Council of state prior to the 1984 elections, the opposition parties were able to successfully remove any structures that would give the mass organizations a role in the new assembly. As the newly elected National Assembly first convened, the mass organizations no longer had their own direct representatives. This ended the strong, direct participation of these popular organizations in the legislature and thus in the governmental structure as a whole.[15] George Vickers argues that the actual 1984 election and "more importantly, the decision to replace the Council of state with a National Assembly constituted by political party representatives, drastically undermined the role of mass organizations in shaping the course of the revolution."[16] He further suggests that this represents the beginning of a movement away from the initial *Sandinista* conception of revolutionary (direct) participatory democracy to "the more traditional notion of democracy based on political parties and representative elections."[17]

In his seminal article on representative and participatory democracy in Nicaragua under the new (1987) Constitution, Jules Lobel noted that "the attempt to develop representative institutions in the context of a dominant role for participatory democracy [presented] several important contradictions."[18] He further argues that such representative government acted as a brake on the political demands that flowed from the mass-movement.[19] The new political institutions facilitated and became increasingly responsive to middle-class and bourgeois mobilization as manifest in the opposition parties who had gained seats in the National Assembly and became increasingly less responsive to the lower class constituency of the mass organizations, which no longer had seats in the new legislative body.

The new régime was setting the ground rules for the evolution to a more vigorous and competitive party system. The verticalist authoritarian structure of the FSLN had not permitted the strong exercise of internal party democracy that champions of one-party rule, like then President of Tanzania Julius Nyerere had envisioned for Third World countries.[20] Indeed, the government had often curtailed the operation of the main opposition newspaper, *La Prensa,* and had sometimes harassed opposition groupings. Even worse, it frequently subordinated the autonomy of the mass organizations it had initially encouraged (as decided by the FSLN), thus robbing many of these organizations of the independence and autonomy that was essential for their growth and development.[21] In most cases, the opposition parties that reemerged were creatures of narrow political groupings that did not incorporate mass participation (the Social Christian Party as headed by Maurecio Díaz was one exception). With the abolition of the Council of State, the only organizations in which the rank and file actually exercised some degree of power on a regular basis lost their only direct access to governmental decision-making. Nor did the multi-party—but *Sandinista*-dominated—representation in the National Assembly provide alternate avenues of access to power. Ironically, then, the return to representative democracy and the first steps towards invigorating a multi-party system, served to diminish, rather than enhance, the democratic empowerment of the great majority of Nicaraguans. Further, it could well be argued that the masses were much better represented and exercised much more power under the appointed Council of state than under the elected National Assembly.[22]

There was, however, one last attempt to directly involve the masses. As a means of continuing popular participation in the governmental process, a series of open forums were scheduled after the National Assembly, acting as a constituent assembly, fashioned a draft for a new constitution. The Assembly (primarily functioning through its Constitutional Commission, which included representatives of *all parties* in the Assembly) had considered 24 constitutional proposals submitted by different political parties and other groups. The first draft was completed in February of 1986. In an effort to harmonize representative and participatory democracy, the draft obligated the state to remove obstacles that effectively impeded the equality of Nicaraguans and their participation in the political, social, and economic life of the country. Consistent with that intent, 150,000 copies of the draft were distributed and 12 televised debates were held between representatives of opposing parties. Thereafter, a series of 73 open forums, or *cabildos abiertos*, were held across the country. Two thousand five hundred Nicaraguan citizens made presentations and 100,000 attended.[23] Several of the more conservative, middle-class parties like the Democratic Conservative Party and the Independent Liberal Party refused to participate in the *cabildos* on the grounds that since the population had already elected its representatives to draft a constitution, there was no need for further popular participation.[24] Quite a few provisions were challenged in these meetings and many were changed. Of particular note were the spirited attacks that the National Women's Association (AMNLAE) led on the concept of *patria potestas* (Article 102), which referred back to Roman law and the dominant position of the *pater familias* in the household.[25]

Another demand that came out of several *cabildos* was a proposal for a permanent legislative chamber for popular organizations. Such an institution would give direct representation to the mass organizations and again incorporate them in the mechanism of the state. However, when this measure was debated in the National Assembly, it was strongly resisted by the traditional parties. Although other aspects of the constitution such as the *patria potestas* were deleted and others were added, the proposal for direct representation for the mass organizations was not included. As time went on and Nicaragua moved towards new elections in 1990, the FSLN tried to encourage all opposition parties to participate in the political process. Meanwhile the mass organizations became less powerful as these traditional political groupings played an ever growing role in decision-making.

Jules Lobel concluded that participatory and representative mechanism of democracy could be combined.[26] The 1984 Nicaraguan election and the resultant constitutional structure suggest, however, that in such combinations great care must be taken to nourish direct participation lest it be subordinated to traditional representative institutions and party structures. The failure to do so may greatly diminish popular democracy and the direct participation of the masses in governance. It may even be argued that direct participatory democracy offers "greater potential for building democratic political culture than do sporadic voting, campaigning and party activism."[27]

Nor did the Nicaraguan people recover any greater democratic power in the presidential term of Violeta Chamorro (1990–96). And five years after the successful 1990 election, the subsequent reversion to factionalism and infighting prompted a well-respected observer of national politics to conclude that democracy had still not matured in Nicaragua.[28] The *Sandinista* leadership seemed to have assumed that representative structures for the national and local governments would indeed constitute democracy. Thus, even before the vote in the elections in 1990, it could be argued traditional, representative forms of democracy had already triumphed at the expense of direct, more participatory democratic forms.

III. The 1990 Election and the End of One-Party-Dominant Rule

The 1990 election was held after more than a decade of *Sandinista* rule and after the general outlines of a transformed Nicaraguan society were already in place. During these years, many traditional values had been challenged, if not replaced, by modern values in some sectors of the population. There were also many external factors that were brought to bear on the electoral process and the ensuing Chamorro administration. The vote occurred as the United States was poised to again extend its power through the region and— as became apparent—further project it in much of the rest of the world. As it turned out, the election occurred in an international and regional context over which the Nicaraguan government had only limited control despite its often brilliant use of diplomacy and the international legal system. From 1982 on, the United States had used military, diplomatic, and economic means to impose its will on the *Sandinista* government and the Nicaraguan people. Although the Reagan and Bush Republican administrations were not able to realize their primary objective of overthrowing the *Sandinistas*, they could make sure that the new government would have very difficult going, would have very limited options, and would be hard put to claim it could be a model for other Central or Latin American countries.

Although the FSLN had been able to maintain unity while it was in power, most of the other parties had not been able to overcome the traditional Nicaraguan proclivity for factionalism and internecine struggle. Although only six opposition parties had opposed the FSLN in the 1984 election (encouraged by the United States, the *Coordinadora Democratica* boycotted the elections), by the beginning of 1988 there were 14 opposition parties plus a few opposition political groupings.[29] The Reagan administration had pushed the military side of low-intensity conflict and discouraged parties from participating in 1984. As Bush took office, U.S. policy began to emphasize an electoral challenge to the *Sandinistas*.

If traditional factionalism had held sway, there would have been some 20 opposition parties on the ballot. This would have splintered the opposition vote and allowed the FSLN an easy victory. Realizing this, the Bush administration pushed for a unified opposition coalition and strongly encouraged the selection of a fresh opposition candidate who could serve as a symbol around which the opposition could rally. Although lacking political experience, Violeta Chamorro filled this role very well. With U.S. support, she was able to edge out Enrique Bolaños, a traditional political leader and head of COSEP, and become the National Opposition Union (UNO) candidate. By the time of the election, the U.S.-supported unity of the National Opposition Union had held. Included in the new coalition were parties that traced their origins to the old Conservative and Liberal Parties as well as Social-Democratic Parties, Social-Christian parties, a party tied to *Contra* leaders, and even two Communist Parties—the Nicaraguan Socialist Party (PSN) and the Communist Party of Nicaragua (PC de N).

The 1990 campaign proved to be quite lively, and the besieged *Sandinista* leadership was thrown into a different kind of battle. In order to be able to successfully compete against the U.S.-supported UNO coalition, the *Sandinista* leadership had to devote its organizational and human resources to an expensive electoral contest that ate up better than $7 million in very scarce funds. The cost of preparing and administering the election was itself enormous (this would also be the case for the 1996 election). The Supreme Electoral Council, the independent governmental body responsible for overseeing and running the election, spent in excess of $15 million.[30] Given the miserable economic conditions in which most workers and peasants found themselves by 1989, they might well have preferred to forgo the election in favor of a direct dispersal of funds, which would have guaranteed jobs, increased real wages, and thus gained relief from hyper-inflation.

The *Sandinista* leadership knew that conditions were bad, but thought their political base could endure a little longer while they employed the human and material resources at their disposal to win the election. They mobilized their followers well and spent $7 million on a very fancy campaign that featured not only door-to-door organizing and mass rallies, but giveaway FSLN baseball caps, straw hats, t-shirts, back packs, and cigarette lighters.[31] The FSLN used outside media and public relations consultants to develop a very slick, rock star-like presentation of Daniel Ortega. The *Sandinistas* reasoned that such extravagant spending was necessary to win the election so as to secure their position and legitimize their political system in the eyes of the West. They also realized that they were playing a high stakes game and that the United States had designated huge sums of money for the UNO campaign. This was epitomized by the 1989 U.S. Congressional authorization of $9 million in overt funding for the opposition. It was to be dispensed through the National Endowment for Democracy. The result was, however, that the *Sandinista* campaign was in stark contrast to the austere, impoverished conditions in which most Nicaraguans found themselves. This was clearly a contributing factor to the *Sandinista* defeat.

Up to the time of the February election it seemed that the Nicaraguan revolution might be able to build on the experiment with Socialist democracy that developed in Chile in the early 1970s. The *Sandinistas* reasoned that they would give an expanded electorate the opportunity to decide if they wanted to continue in the process of Socialist construction, or opt for another type of régime. Down to the eve of the election most opinion polls suggested that the Nicaraguan people would ratify the Socialist, mixed economy experiment and continue with *Sandinista* democracy. However, the *Sandinistas'* stunning defeat at the hands of the U.S.-sponsored National Opposition Union (UNO) suggested that the *demos* (the people) were not entirely satisfied with *Sandinista* rule, or the type of socialist democracy that was developing in Nicaragua. The real battle for Nicaragua had become economic and would continue to be economic through 1995. Careful analysis of the facts suggests the low-intensity conflict that the Bush administration waged against Nicaragua had disastrous effects on the economy.[32] Nor was the Nicaraguan government well prepared to manage the deteriorating economic conditions.

By 1988 inflation had reached some 36,000 percent, real wages had fallen to 29 percent of their 1980 value, milk consumption had fallen by 50 percent, and production reached levels that were abysmally low.[33] In that same year, the deteriorating economy began to heavily impact daily life and increasingly became a subject of intense public concern. The government clearly assigned blame to the U.S. actions. However, like the neo-liberal policies the Chamorro administration followed, the governmental response was an austerity program that was modeled on the "heterodox shock" treatments that Brazil and Argentina employed in 1985 and 1986 and as such fell disproportionately on the poor.[34] This marked a shift in *Sandinista* policy, because it was the first time since the *Sandinista* insurrection that "the Nicaraguan government ha[d] begun a program of economic reforms that d[id] not include steps to protect the poor, the social base of the *Sandinistas,* from its harshest effects."[35] By mid 1988 prices for basic commodities had risen 600 percent, while the government lifted price controls on most goods and services, with devastating results for wage-earners.

By the late 1980s, the harm had been done and there was a growing perception that the *Sandinistas* were not in control or were selling out their poor supporters to gain the economic cooperation of middle and upper class commercial interests.[36] It seemed that the only response to the economic crisis that the *Sandinista* leadership could agree to implement was one that sought to activate traditional commercial groups in the hope that they would lead the recovery. But by the end of 1989 it seemed to many that the economic dimension of the *Contras'* War, coupled with internal deficiencies in management and allocation, had caused the *Sandinista* government to ignore the economic plight of the masses.

In order to diminish any remaining *Sandinista* support, the Bush administration cranked up the *Contras* again in summer 1989. As they rampaged though the countryside, they spread political messages for the election: "Only UNO can end the economic crisis"; "There will be no peace under a *Sandinista* government"; "A *Sandinista* government means war and a continuation of the military draft. Only UNO can bring peace."[37] The *Contras* became an active part of the anti-*Sandinista* campaign that was organized by the United States. The sophisticated low-intensity conflict campaign was clearly having a dual effect. By January 1990, 52 percent of those registered voters surveyed believed that the economy was the most important issue for them in deciding how to vote in the coming election. By comparison 37 percent thought the *Contras* War was the most important issue.[38]

As the economic conditions deteriorated, and the political support for the direct, participatory democracy of the mass organizations was diminished by their exclusion from the legislative body after 1984 and their frequent subordination to FSLN control, there were fewer channels through which the masses could effectively communicate the gravity of their plight. Thomas Cronin suggests one reaction to such a situation is that when "there is growing suspicion that privileged interests exert far greater influences on the typical politician than does the common voter," there is a demand for more democracy.[39] But neither the official party nor the mass organizations seemed willing or able to provide greater democratic participation. And by lauding the election and the connected Western-style representative demo cracy, the *Sandinistas* themselves seemed to be telling the people that this (and not participatory democracy) was the only democratic instrument through which they could express themselves. Meanwhile, the UNO coalition was arguing that its fundamental objective was to "construct democracy" and that it planned to "profoundly democratize the nation and the society." (UNO 1990). UNO was the only party on the ballot that had any chance of challenging *Sandinista* political hegemony. Since Sandinista dominance appeared to many to be ever less responsive to popular democracy, there were very limited choices for most voters.

Many felt that the *Sandinista* leaders were isolated from the hardships of the masses and that their political position facilitated access to goods that the poor could no longer afford. Many were also angered by what they perceived as increasing bureaucratization in government offices. They saw the formation of a bureaucratic class that was not particularly sympathetic to popular needs and was the beneficiary of a disproportionate share of scarce resources. This created a considerable amount of resentment. Thus it seemed to many that the Vanguard Party had lost contact with the very people it was suppose to represent and consequently was not responding to their needs and feelings. Rather—they felt—it had become an institution that was ruled from the top down ("National Directorate commands") and had established a set of interests that was not always the same as those of the people.

As the election results trickled in it soon became apparent that—believing they had been abandoned by the *Sandinistas*—the residents of many working-class neighborhoods in the capital (Julio Bultrago, Las Brisas and San Judas among them) had given UNO the majority. And so it went in other urban areas and in much of the countryside as well. UNO got 54.7 percent of the vote while the *Sandinistas* received only 40.8 percent (most polls had predicted a substantial *Sandinista* victory; the ABC/*Washington Post* poll predicted 48 to 32 percent). To the FSLN's credit, Daniel Ortega announced early the day after the election that the government would abide by the election results and would cooperate in transferring power to the new government. Later statements specified conditions for doing so. Nor could the *Sandinistas* expect to control the National Assembly (they would control only 39 of the 92 seats, while the UNO coalition would have 51), or very many municipalities across the country (UNO won 102 of the 131 municipal councils).

Careful analysis suggests that it was the U.S.-induced economic crisis and the ineffective way it was handled by the government that most hurt the *Sandinistas* in their traditional bastions of working-class support. By ignoring those aspects of direct, participatory democracy that were part of the initial *Sandinista* program, and by failing to economically support its mass base (and natural constituency), the FSLN unwittingly left the door wide open for popular discontent to be channeled towards the rival Western-style institutional democratic system. In this way, the *Sandinista* leadership undermined the dominance of their party in the Nicaraguan political system and set the stage for the creation of a multi-party system where no party dominated.

The newly refined electoral framework was imperfect, but still provided a mechanism by which a growing desperation with conditions could be registered. The 1990 election proved to be a very effective means of registering a massive protest vote. Indeed, many later said they believe the *Sandinistas* would win anyway, so they voted for Violeta Chamorro's UNO just to let the *Sandinista* leadership know that their needs were not being met and that they felt they were being ignored. Given the conditions that existed, it is remarkable that the FSLN could still garner even 40.8 percent of the vote. The fact that they did, suggests the ambivalence the popular masses felt about their rule.

Many political observers celebrated the 1990 election as a return of true (Western, representative) democracy and the end of the *Sandinista* one-party dominance. One could equally argue that it was an imposed régime, which resulted from economic and military pressure from the United States and its allies and from pro-U.S. conservative groups inside Nicaragua. During the election these forces employed a variety of tactics to induce a majority of the population to vote against the *Sandinista* government. In all, the U.S. had invested heavily in supporting opposition forces in Nicaragua—some $26 million in overt and covert aid since the 1984 election.[40] *Newsweek* suggested that $5 million in covert funds had been used for the 1990 election alone.[41] Overt funding for the election was estimated at $12.5 million.[42] Many Nicaraguan voters came to believe that the only way things were going to improve was if they removed the *Sandinistas* from office. The authoritarian decision-making style of the government and the arrogance of many government and FSLN party leaders also convinced many other voters to sanction the party in office the only way they could: by voting for the only viable opposition—UNO.

In an action that further reduced the possibility of a return to a one-party-dominant régime under *Sandinista* control, the *Sandinista* government engaged in what came to be a very controversial action. Soon after the 1990 election they rushed legislation through the National Assembly that granted title to confiscated property to those who had occupied it during the *Sandinista* years. While this did give title to some peasants and cooperatives and other small property owners, it also gave quite a few *Sandinista* leaders title to expensive properties they had used or been awarded as compensation for their years of service and sacrifice. Known as the *Piñata* (because of all the "treats" disbursed to those at the *Sandinistas'* "going-away party") it came to be regarded as a way for the *Sandinista* leadership to enrich themselves before leaving office. As time progressed and poverty among the masses increased, the *Piñata* bred increasing resentment, helped to erode support for the *Sandinistas,* and seemed to confirm the growing popular perception that government, while paid for by the many, was by and for the few.[43]

In retrospect, it would seem that the 1990 election marked the beginning of a return to political decision-making by political *and economic* élites that was conducted far from institutions in which the masses could exercise any real power. Indeed, the next six years saw the development of a political system that was increasingly characterized by intense competition among political élites about issues that were often irrelevant to the daily lives of the Nicaraguan masses. As unemployment and poverty became more generalized, and income and wealth more concentrated, it became increasingly clear those aspects of economic democracy that had grown during the earlier years of *Sandinista* rule were severely eroded by successive waves of neo-Liberal policies.

The popular expectation was, however, quite different. It was expected that the new government would heed the democratic mandate, utilize the bountiful aid and support that (UNO voters believed) would surely be offered by the U.S. government, and begin to listen to popular political demands and respond to the masses' often desperate needs. In reality, it seems that the real electors were not the majority who voted for UNO, but the external and internal economic élites who had engineered the *Sandinista* electoral demise. It was their demands—and not those of the common people—that would get the greatest attention.

What the majority that voted for UNO did not realize was that Violeta Chamorro had been chosen as an electoral tool to unseat the *Sandinistas.* Thus, there would be strong pressure to dismantle the type of state apparatus that had developed under *Sandinista* rule, implement a conservative, neo-Liberal economic program, strengthen traditional parties, and further reduce the power and size of the mass organizations and the *Sandinista* Party. Nor would these changed give the masses any more power in the new system.

As the new president began her term, she initially relied on the now famous *Mayor* Plan,[44] which was designed to revise the structure of the Nicaraguan state and fully reintegrate Nicaragua into the capitalist world economy on terms that would be favorable to foreign investors and the dependent Nicaraguan bourgeoisie. This process continued over the next six years and was buttressed with the election of Alemán in 1996. Initially, however, it was tempered and at times blocked by the political power that the FSLN had developed. The FSLN was able to allude to its institutionalized power in state structures like the *Sandinista* army and supported sporadic popular mobilizations. The mass mobilizations at the time of the revolution and during the first years of *Sandinista* rule also set the stage for an often tenacious popular resistance against many of the unpopular economic policies that the Chamorro government tried to implement. As resistance was worn down, elements of the new policies were, however, gradually put in place. Meanwhile other political parties occupied more and more political space.

Nor did the FSLN prove to be an adequate channel for popular resistance. The initial *Sandinista* commitment to participatory democracy was never reinstitutionalized in the party or in its ties to mass organizations.[45] By 1991 it was becoming increasingly apparent that the Chamorro government was unable to solve basic economic problems for the common people. The fact that conditions actually deteriorated after the 1990 election did little to convince the masses of the ultimate utility of Western-style representative democracy. Nor were conflicts and centripetal forces limited to the *Sandinista* Party.

An uneasy alliance between Violeta Chamorro and her vice presidential candidate Virgilio Godoy barely endured through the electoral victory. Godoy was rapidly eclipsed by Chamorro's son-in-law, Antonio Lacayo. Upon her inauguration, he assumed the office of minister of the presidency. Thereafter Lacayo operated as de facto head of government, performing most of the executive functions for the president (who was more head of state than head of government). This left Vice President Godoy not only outside the decision-making process, but literally outside the presidential palace. Eventually, the UNO members in the National Assembly divided into two often hostile camps: one group, led by Conservative leader Miriam Arguello, was aligned with Godoy and the other, led by Alfredo César, was allied with the president.

The National Assembly became a focal point for political competition and deal making. While the economy continued to deteriorate, political conflict increased. A dispute between the president and many Assembly members of her own UNO coalition in 1992 worsened the situation. This angered the other UNO delegates who questioned the legitimacy of the institution and began to boycott Assembly sessions. They believed that the understanding on which their coalition was based had been betrayed and further accused Chamorro and Lacayo of collaborating with the *Sandinistas* in a co-government. On the Left, worker and peasant organizations, and the increasingly militant ex-*Sandinista* fighters (*Recompas*), who had still not received land, accused the *Sandinista* leadership of collaborating with the government at their expense. Former-*Contras* (*Recontras*) who had not received their promised land either, also became increasingly militant.

As the generalized political infighting continued, more and more Nicaraguans became disillusioned with the political process. The evolution beyond a one-party-dominant régime did not seem to have solved Nicaragua's political problems. In many ways, they seemed even worse. By early 1993, 85 percent of Nicaraguans indicated that they were not interested in the fights between the various political groupings. Indeed, 61 percent said they had no faith in any political party. Many took matters into their own hands. Land take-overs continued and the armed *Recompas* and *Recontras* clashed with government forces. Hostages were taken and one group of rearmed ex-*Sandinista* fighters even occupied the city of Estelí until they were dislodged by a bloody army attack that left scores dead.[46]

These events seemed to confirm earlier observations. "By moving into the realm of secret, bartered pacts, the government surrendered the power of its overwhelming public mandate and unquestioned international legitimacy. . . ."[47] Another well-respected Nicaraguan political observer noted that the government seemed "to be continuing the long practice of exercising leadership by cutting deals in back rooms with ranking representatives of powerful political actors." He went on to note that such deals eroded faith in the government and opposition alike.[48]

IV. The Developing Crisis

Many factors converged in 1994 to precipitate a crisis that shook the Nicaraguan state to its very foundations. Unemployment and underemployment were at horrendous levels (well over 50 percent) and economic conditions generally were approaching those of Haiti. But the political deterioration was equally bad. Coalitions and alliances that had been forged previously continued to unravel as the political setting became ever more contentious. The common vision and collective dedication that had characterized the uprising against Somoza and the first years of *Sandinista* rule were gone. Also forgotten by the leadership of the FSLN was how much of the revolutionary victory was owed to the masses' involvement in the insurrection and how important unity had been to their victory. Co-government had tied the FSLN to many government policies, and the continuation of autocratic decision-making policies by the *Sandinista* party leadership had angered many party loyalists. The perception that elements of the leadership—and not the movement generally—had most benefited from the *Piñata* added to dissatisfaction.

Matters came to a head at the May 1994 party congress. Tensions had continued to mount between Daniel Ortega, Thomas Borge, and the more orthodox party leadership on one hand, and ex-*Sandinista* vice president and acclaimed author Sergio Ramírez and a group of *Sandinista* representatives from the National Assembly, led by Dora María Téllez, on the other. The latter group sought to reform the party, but got short shrift at the party congress.

Ramírez was even removed from his seat on the newly constituted FSLN National Directorate. Others associated with him were also removed from their party posts. The way the recent party congress was conducted and a subsequent nasty personal attack involving Ramírez's daughter (who was also a member of the National Assembly) and Dora María Téllez only exacerbated tensions and began an exodus from the party in the months that followed. The famed priest-poet and ex-Minister of Culture, Ernesto Cardinal, finally resigned his party membership, saying "The truth is that since the last congress, a small group led by Daniel Ortega has taken over the FSLN . . . they've kidnapped it. They've imposed an authoritarian, hierarchical structure on it and exalted party bosses. . . ."[49] Sergio Ramírez, Dora María Téllez and quite a few prominent intellectuals left the party and eventually formed the *Sandinista* Renovation Movement (MRS). They held their first party congress in May of 1995 and vowed to run their own slate of candidates in the 1996 election. All but 7 of the 39 *Sandinista* deputies in the National Assembly opted to form part of the MRS bench. Led by Dora María Téllez, this became one of the stronger blocks in the Assembly.

But the dissension within the *Sandinista* ranks was only part of a growing political crisis. Backed by the UNO Centrist group, that part of the FSLN bench that eventually declared itself MRS, and Assembly speaker Luís Guzmán's Christian Democratic Union (UDC), there was a movement to reform the 1987 constitution. Pushed by a coalition made up of parties and individuals who currently did not have easy access to power, it envisioned increasing the power of the National Assembly at the expense of the executive. The constitutional reforms would transfer some fiscal power from the executive to the legislature, prohibit nepotism, expand constitutional liberties, abolish the draft, clarify the right to private and other forms of property, reduce the presidential term from six to five years, and stipulate that a second round of voting would need to be held in those elections where the leading candidate did not get at least 45 percent of the vote. The net effect would have been to considerably strengthen the legislature at the expense of the presidency and (through the prohibition against nepotism) eliminate Lacayo from future governmental positions, including that of the presidency. Begun in 1993, this process gained momentum during 1994. It led to much heated discussion between the two branches of government, but no consensus or compromise.

When the package of constitutional reforms was finally sent to the executive in January 1995, President Chamorro did not promulgate them (by publishing them in the official newspaper) in the required 15-day period, and then announced in February that her government did not recognize them. The next day several national newspapers published the texts of the reforms as signed by President of the National Assembly Luís Humberto

Guzmán, thus—it could be argued—promulgating them. This led to months of wrangling and mutual recrimination. For a while there were two constitutions, with each of the two branches declaring that theirs was the legal one. The situation worsened when the legislature would not accept Chamorro's recommendations for supreme court justices, and instead sent their own list back to the executive, who in turn refused to appoint them. This left the nation's highest court without a quorum.

The severity of the crisis was such that it took the combined effort of the major donor nations to convince the governmental institutions that cooperation was necessary to move beyond the breach. The impending June 1994 Paris meeting of donor nations acted as a catalyst. But the political immaturity of the political actors was so great that the U.S. Embassy had to pressure both sides, and recourse to the good offices of Cardinal Obando y Bravo was necessary to force both parties to resolve their differences. Many saw this as a serious erosion of fledgling democratic political institutions, since it was necessary to go to foreign brokers and extra governmental actors and employ extra-legal political deals to resolve the crisis. This further increased the general population's negative perception of the political class and their confidence in Nicaraguan democracy.[50]

V. The 1996 Elections and the Evolving Party System

The return of a multi-party system did not resolve fundamental problems of political legitimacy nor did it vest additional power in the hands of the masses. Indeed, by the end of this process, "The majority of the population . . . fed up with these duels by politicians brandishing cardboard swords, [was] gazing upon the outcome with consummate indifference."[51]

The participatory democracy that was developing in the mass organizations in the early 1980s did not triumph. Indeed, the authoritarian, verticalist tendencies in the FSLN had won out over democratic reformist possibilities and the party had factionalized. The U.S. type of representative democracy that had been imposed on Nicaragua proved to be a totally inadequate means of governing. The people, it seemed, had been abandoned by the political élites who ever more consistently turned to traditional struggles for power and influence and turned a deaf ear to popular needs. Indeed, by July 1995 some 40 percent of the electorate were so disillusioned with the existing political parties and their leaders and with the political system in general that they were considering not even voting in the 1996 election. As one researcher observed after a July 1995 poll, "with adults there is despair, deceit, and frustration . . . people say 'I have been deceived, I feel frustrated, I don't see what good voting is going to do.'" As one Managua resident put it, "the way we are going, no government does anything."[52] These feelings were a far cry from the generalized optimism that characterized the vast majority of Nicaraguans in the first years of *Sandinista* rule.

As the 1996 elections approached, the orthodox *Sandinista* faction (FSLN) began to ally itself with Minister of the Presidency Antonio Lacayo's newly formed National Project. The *Sandinista* Renovation Movement (MRS) was making common cause with the Christian Democratic Union, Virgilio Godoy's Independent Liberal Party, Miriam Arguello's Popular Conservative Alliance, the Nicaraguan Democratic Union (MDN), and the National Conservative Party (PNC). The strongest contender for the 1996 presidential election was Managua's conservative mayor, Arnoldo Alemán. Alemán was using his Constitutionalist Liberal Party (PLC) to gain control of the now factionalized old Liberal Party (including Liberal groups who were allied with Somoza). In the end, this strategy, and his successful public works campaign in Managua, combined to give him victory in the first round of the election. Amid fears that Alemán would bring back the *Somocistas* and allow them to retake their confiscated land and properties and reconstitute Liberal Party dominance there was a surge in support for Daniel Ortega and the FSLN in the final months of the campaign. Some polls even mistakenly gave the FSLN an edge on the eve of the election. The final results proved otherwise. Alemán won the October 20 contest. There were, however, charges of tampering with the transmittal of the returns from the polling places to the central tallying point in the Supreme Electoral Council (a part of the process not overseen by the electoral observers). Some seven parties requested that the electoral results for Managua be annulled. Fourteen parties petitioned that the same occur in the Department of Matagalpa. Nonetheless, the Supreme Electoral Council finally tallied the votes and declared that Alemán received 51 percent of the votes to Daniel Ortega's 37 percent. Alemán's Liberal Alliance was also a big winner elsewhere, winning many municipalities including Managua and 42 of 93 seats in the National Assembly. The FSLN won 36 seats in the Assembly and the smaller parties 15.

In 1996 it was the vestiges of the old Liberal Party, reorganized as the Liberal Alliance, that had once again united to claim victory. The FSLN's 11 years of party dominance had been refuted in the 1990 and again in the 1996 elections. Although still a power contender, it was far from being the dominant party in Nicaragua. The *Sandinista* Renovation Movement ran as a separate party, but got only a small percentage of the vote. Other political grouping were fractionalized as well. There were 24 parties on the ballot, but Alemán's Liberal Alliance and the FSLN secured 89.8 percent of votes.

It still, however, may be said that Nicaragua maintained some aspects of a one-party-dominant system. Not only was the FSLN a major contender for power, but it had been defeated by none other that a recast coalition of Liberal Party groupings, which included strong participation from the Somoza faction of the Liberal Party. The political hegemony of the FSLN had been broken, the Liberal Alliance had gained power. There was a possibility that a one-party-dominant system under Liberal hegemony would develop under Alemán's rule. Yet, the Nicaraguan proclivity for factionalism and FSLN strength continued to threaten this project.

It remains to be seen if the old Somoza dominated Liberal Party can claim party hegemony once again. Alemán campaigned on the platform of returning property taken during *Sandinista* rule to its previous owners, most of whom benefited from, or were strongly tied to, the Somozas. In the first months of Alemán's rule there was a strong upsurge in returning *Somocistas,* and shortly after the election Somoza's nephews returned to Nicaragua to reclaim much of Somoza's property.

At least for now Nicaragua is no longer a one-party-dominant system. Yet, the survival of the newly restructured competitive party system will depend on many factors. Apart from the issue of whether the Liberal coalition holds, there is the question of economic conditions (at the time of the election, the per capita income was $470 per year and unemployment was above 50 percent). As this and other questions come to the fore, the evolving system will be challenged to provide effective democratic representation and participation for the masses. If it becomes a mechanism for competition among the political élites to the exclusion of popular participation and popular concerns, the probability of system break-down and eventual return to some form of hegemonic rule increases dramatically.

Notes

1. T. J. Pempel, ed., *Uncommon Democracies: The One-Party Dominant Regimes* (Ithaca NY: Cornell University Press, 1990), p. 4.
2. George Vickers, "A Spider's Web," in *NACLA Report on the Americas,* vol. 30, no. 1 (June 1990): p. 18–27.
3. Humberto Ortega, *50 años* (Managua, 1980), p. 83.
4. This section relies on my earlier writing on Sandinista ideology and the development of Sandinismo. Fred Murphy was instrumental in developing some of this material. See Harry E. Vanden, "The Ideology of the Sandinista Revolution," in *Monthly Review,* no. 34 (June 1982); Harry E. Vanden & Gary Prevost, *Democracy and Socialism in Sandinista Nicaragua* (Boulder, CO: Lynne Rienner, 1993), Chapter 2.
5. Victor Tirado López, *El pensamiento político de Carlos Fonseca Amador* (Managua: Secretaría Nacional de Propagnada y Educación Política del FSLN (1979–1980): p. 7.
6. Interview: Emilio Alvarez Montalván, Managua, 21 July 1995.
7. John Booth, *The End and the Beginning* (Boulder, CO: Westview, 1985).

8. Humberto Ortega as quoted in Gary Ruchwarger, *People in Power: Forging a Grassroots Democracy in Nicaragua* (Boston: Bergin & Garvey, 1987), p. 34.
9. Sergio Ramírez, as quoted in Ruchwarger, *People, p. 4.*
10. Dennis Gilbert, *Sandinistas, The Party and the Revolution* (London: Basil Blackwell, 1988), particularly Chapter 3, "The Party in the state and Mass Organizations."
11. *Coordinadora* head, Arturo Cruz also came to the same conclusions see: Kinzer, "Ex-Contra Looks Back, Finding Much to Regret," in *New York Times* (15 October 1984).
12. See the "Political Parties Law" passed by the Nicaraguan Council of state in February 1984 after considerable debate by the opposition parties and some re-drafting. See also the Nicaraguan "Electoral Law," passed by the Council of state on 15 March 1984.
13. *Washington Post* (6 November 1984).
14. Ibid.
15. Jules Lobel, "The Meaning of Democracy and Participatory Democracy in the New Nicaraguan Constitution," in *University of Pittsburgh Law Review,* vol. 49 (1988): p. 868. It should be noted, however, that the FSLN did include mass organization members on its slate of candidates, even though some of these were not themselves FSLN members. Several of these candidates were so elected, but became part of the FSLN bloc, rather than direct delegates of the mass organizations.
16. George Vickers, "A Spiders Web," in *Report on the Americas,* vol. 15, no. 1 (June 1990): p. 23.
17. Ibid.
18. Lobel, "The Meaning of Democracy," p. 867. See also Chapter 8 of Kenneth J. Mijeski, ed., *The Nicaraguan Constitution of 1987, English Translation and Commentary* (Athens: Ohio University Monographs in International Studies, Latin American Series, no. 17, 1991).
19. Lobel, *The Meaning of Democracy,* p. 867–868.
20. Julius Nyerere, *Ujamaa: Essays on Socialism* (New York: Oxford, 1968).
21. See Vanden & Prevost, *Democracy and Socialism,* especially Chapter 4.
22. See the concluding chapter of Vanden & Prevost, *Democracy and Socialism;* plus Pierre LaRamée & Erica Polakoff, "The Evolution of the Popular Organizations in Nicaragua," and Harry Vanden, "Democracy Derailed," both in Gary Prevost & Harry E. Vanden, eds., *The Undermining of the Sandinista Revolution* (London: Macmillan-St. Martin's Press, 1997).
23. Andrew Reding, "By the People: Constitution Making in Nicaragua," in *Christianity and Crisis,* vol. 46, no. 18 (8 December 1986): p. 435.
24. Lobel, "The Meaning of Democracy," p. 868–869.
25. See Martha I. Morgan's excellent "Founding Mothers: Women's Voices and Stories in the 1987 Nicaraguan Constitution," in *Boston University Law Review,* vol. 70, no. 1 (January 1990): p. 1–107.
26. Lobel, "The Meaning of Democracy," p. 877.

27. John Booth, "A Framework for Analysis," in John Booth & Paul Seligson, eds., *Elections and Democracy in Central America* (Chapel Hill: University of north Carolina Press, 1989), p. 21.

28. Interview: Emilio Alvarez Montalván. Managua, 21 July 1995.

29. Interview: Dr. Mariano Fiallos, President, Supreme Electoral Council, Managua, 15 December 1987.

30. Interview: Dr. Roberto Estevez, Managua, 24 February 1990; Interview with Dr. Mariano Fiallos, President of the Supreme Electoral Council, Managua, 20 February 1990. Dr. Fiallos stressed the difficulty to estimate the total cost of running the election, but said that his organization had a budget of $18 million.

31. Daniel Ortega Press Conference, Managua, 22 February 1990.

32. Harry E. Vanden & Thomas Walker, "The Reimposition of U.S. Hegemony Over Nicaragua," in Kenneth M. Coleman & George C. Herring, *Understanding the Central American Crisis* (Wilmington: Scholarly Resources, 1991), p. 12.

33. Carlos Vilas, "What Went Wrong," in *NACLA: Report on the Americas,* vol. 30, no. 1 (June 1990).

34. Michael Conroy, "The Political Economy of the 1990 Elections," paper presented at the Coloquio sobre las Crises Económicas del Siglo XX" (Madrid: Universidad Compultense de Madrid, April 1990), p. 21.

35. IHCA (Central American Historical Institute), "The New Economic Package," in *Envío* (September 1988), cited in Conroy, "Political Economy," p. 21.

36. These opinions were frequently being voiced to the author when he visited Nicaragua in 1987. They were widely discussed on a second visit in early 1990.

37. David McMichael, "U.S. Plays Contra Card," in *The Nation* (5 February 1990): p. 166.

38. Conroy, "Political Economy," p. 30.

39. Thomas Cronin, *Direct Democracy: The Politics of Initiative, Referendum and Recall* (Cambridge, MA: Harvard University Press, 1998), p. 10.

40. Mark Cook, "Unfit to Print about Nicaragua's Election," in *Extra* (October-November 1989): p. 2–4.

41. "Washington Wants to Buy Nicaraguan Election," in *Newsweek* (5 September and 9 October 1989).

42. Holly Sklar, "Washington Wants to Buy Nicaragua's Election Again," in *Z Magazine* (December 1989): p. 50.

43. Reinaldo Antonio Téfel, "La mancha más fea: la Piñata," in *La Prensa* (19 July 1995).

44. Richard Stahler-Sholk,"Structural Adjustment and Resistance: The Political Economy of Nicaragua under Chamorro," in Prevost & Vanden, *The Undermining of the Sandinista Revolution.*

45. Pierre Laramee & Erica Polakoff, "The Evolution of the Popular Organizations in Nicaragua," in Prevost & Vanden, *The Undermining of the Sandinista Revolution.*

46. Richard Millett, "Central America's Enduring Conflicts," *Current History,* vol. 89 (February 1994): p. 124–128.

47. Mark Uhlig, "Nicaragua's Permanent Crisis: Ruling from Above and from Below," in *Survival*, vol. 33, n.5, p. 408 as cited in Forrest Colburn, "The Fading of the Revolutionary Era in Central America," in *Current History*, vol. 91 (February 1992): p. 70–73.
48. Colburn, "The Fading of the Revolutionary Era in Central America," p. 73.
49. Scarlet Cuadra & Leonardo Coca, "Gaines and Losses," in *Barricada Internacional* (October-November 1994): p. 7.
50. IHCA-Central American Historical Institute, "The Foes are Infighting; But the Hens Aren't Laughing," in *Envío* (April 1995).
51. IHCA, "Not Yet to the Root of the Crisis," in *Envío* (August 1995): p. 3.
52. Edgar S. Barberena, "Abstencionismo a la vista!" in *El Nuev Diario* (24 June 1995): p. 8. This article cites a survey by the M & R and the Fundación Centroamericana 2000 of 825 people in Managua and the other departmental capitals. In the survey 21.9 percent said they would not vote and 17.9 percent said they were not sure if they would vote or not. The article also cited another survey of people in the streets of Managua conducted by *Esta Semana*, which found even greater disillusionment. The quote is from this latter survey.

PART III

Democratization Among Third World Single-Party-Systems

TEN

Mexico:
Revolution in the Revolution?

Waltraud Q. Morales & Corinne B. Young

Recent political and economic events have left Mexico-watchers wondering which of the different faces of this nation of over 94 million people reveals the reality and probable future of Mexico. On the one hand, there is the Mexico that has prided itself for decades on being the most stable country in Latin America and the Third World, even claiming First World status. And on the other, there is the recent Mexico of political assassinations, Indian and guerrilla insurgencies, drug mafias, and economic chaos. Is Mexico on the verge of a revolution in the revolution, with the democratic transformation of the oldest remaining one-party-dominant system in the world? More immediately, will the mid 1997 elections see the ruling Party of the Institutionalized Revolution, or PRI, lose control of the National Congress and the Mexico City government for the first time in 68 years?[1] Is one of the most successful cases of one-party dominance since the disintegration of the former Soviet Union coming to an end? After all, we are reminded that "one-party dominance is an art far more than it is an inevitability."[2]

The irony of Mexican democratization is that its progress has occurred both because of and in spite of electoral reforms, passed after the suspect 1988 national elections which brought Carlos Salinas de Gortari to the six-year (non-renewable) presidency. If the political opening moderating one-party rule succeeds, will Mexico become a more traditional two-party or multi-party system; or will Mexico inherently remain a more authoritarian version of an "uncommon democracy," T. J. Pempel's term for one-party-dominant régimes? And how will the process of democratic change impact and respond to the regional and global forces of privatization, capitalist development, and modernization? Have the very forces of "neo-Liberal" privatization, as some charge, "accentuated the nation's deep social inequalities, particularly among the *campesinos?*"[3] Will political reforms within continued one-party dominance be sufficient to address the crisis of legitimacy for Mexican citizens and the crisis of confidence in economic circles? Finally, has democratization become essential to restart and maintain international investment and growth, and to provide a better economic future for all Mexicans?

I. The PRI's One-Party Dominance

Since 1929 the *Partido Revolucionario Institucional* (PRI) has won every presidential election, governed alone, and singularly dominated the political and economic landscape.[4] Indeed the persistence and extent of PRI's control places the Mexican system closer to a one-party state than a one-party dominant one. T. J. Pempel characterizes one-party-dominant régimes in industrialized nations as ones where "despite free electoral competition, relatively open information systems, respect for civil liberties, and the right of free political association," a single party has governed for substantial periods of time alone or in coalition.[5] In the Mexican case, key conditions of this model remain absent, notably, free electoral competition, relatively open information systems, and extensive industrialization and economic modernization. The PRI has never permitted real competition or coalition government, and has consistently dominated the media. Mexican industrialization and economic modernization has been highly uneven, concentrated in the northern states, but so absent in the backward agrarian south that Chiapas (the southernmost state bordering Guatemala) is often dismissed as Central America. Only if democratic reforms correct such critical deficiencies can Mexico approximate the authentically democratic single-party-dominant system that Pempel's theory describes.

To date, Mexico's electoral history, although stable and relatively non-violent, has been plagued by fraud and corruption. In 1940 and 1952 challenges to PRI from ex-party dissidents were met with fraud and violence, and despite recent electoral reforms in 1986, 1990, 1993, and 1994, "nearly every election at the municipal, state, or federal levels continues to yield a disputed result."[6] Even with the playing field for inter-party competition a bit more level, the two most recent presidential elections encountered problems. In 1988 the PRI's victory was clouded by charges of massive fraud. Cuauhtémoc Cárdenas, son of the legendary 1930s revolutionary, President Lázaro Cárdenas and candidate of the Left-of-Center opposition party, the PRD, Party of the Democratic Revolution (*Partido de la Revolución Democrática*), claimed that he had won. Although the 1994 presidential elections, despite irregularities, were cleaner and more competitive, they were not necessarily fair.[7] Virtual PRI-government control of the media, extravagant (and illegal) PRI campaign spending, and what one writer characterized as the "distinct symbiosis of government administration and partisan political structures," ensured the dominant party's victory, although a more narrow one.[8]

Since 1976, PRI's share of the vote has steadily fallen from 99 to 74 percent in 1982, and 51 percent and 50 percent in the 1988 and 1994 elections.[9] Conversely, the vote for PAN (*Partido de Acción Nacional*), the conservative opposition party based in the industrialized, north Americanized northern states, has been steadily increasing. Founded in 1939, the *Partido de Acción Nacional*, or National Action Party, has struggled to become Mexico's second major party, and since 1989 (when PAN won the gubernatorial elections in Baja) has controlled major state governorships, mayoral offices, and for the first time, a cabinet position in the PRI government of President Ernesto Zedillo Ponce de León. In the 1994 elections PAN officially received 27 percent of the vote, and President Zedillo appointed Antonio Lozano Gracia, PAN's opposition leader in Congress, his attorney general.

Analysts have hailed the PRI's decreasing electoral margins as proof of democratization and the party's weakening; most elected presidents never received less than 70 percent of the vote.[10] Clearly, today's opposition has more of a voice than in the 1920s when General Alvaro Obregón claimed 1.7 million supporters against zero-negative votes.[11] Nevertheless, PRI's slipping electoral control is all the more amazing considering the media empire and oligarchic wealth at its behest. Despite a new party-financing law, which limited individual contributions to $650,000 (compared to $20,000 in the United States) and contributions of interest groups to $3.25 million, the PRI secretly violates these limits. Press exposure of the infamous fundraising dinner in February 1993, which requested Mexico's wealthiest men (most billionaires known as the "Mexico Twelve") to contribute $25 million each to party coffers, only encouraged more creative and subversive measures.[12]

Another reform ostensibly capped spending for presidential campaigns at $103 million (about what both Bush and Clinton together spent on their presidential races in 1992).[13] The richest billionaire in the group and Mexico's *Televisa* telecommunications tycoon, Emilio Azcarraga, was estimated to be worth $5.1 billion and reportedly promised $50 million for the party's electoral bid. *Miami Herald* correspondent Andrés Oppenheimer writes that "the billionaires' pledges were a startling symptom of the massive corruption in Mexico's official circles—a world where publicly disclosed funds amounted to a small fraction of the fabulous sums that were moved under the table."[14] Even with officially reported campaign expenditures of $105 million, PRI far outspent all opposition contenders combined.[15] Amazingly, PRI has even bankrolled smaller opposition parties, which traditionally receive no more than three percent of the vote, in order to divide the opposition and reinforce the perception of free democratic contestation.

Oppenheimer also criticizes the PRI-government's manipulation of information. A staunch PRI loyalist, Don Emilio Azcarraga's pro-government *Televisa* has a virtual monopoly of Mexico's airwaves, owning four of the five television channels in Mexico City and controlling 95 percent of the national audience. Most print media, particularly the larger dailies of the 23 newspapers in Mexico City, are heavily subsidized by the government and often disseminate paid political advertising and campaign propaganda as news.[16] The media's campaign strategy in 1994, according to Oppenheimer, was to convince the voter that in the aftermath of the Chiapas peasant revolt, political assassinations, and drug violence, Mexico still needed the stability of a PRI victory more than ever.[17]

II. PRI's Corruption: Guerrillas and Mafias

The explosion of the Chiapas rebellion on New Year's Day 1994 set into motion a chain of events that would graphically expose the political corruption of the Mexican political system and of the entrenched old-guard clans in PRI's revolutionary family. Despite intelligence reports within Mexico and in Washington as early as 1990, Mexico's interior minister, the wealthy former governor of Chiapas, strongly denied the existence of guerrillas in Chiapas. With strong opposition to the North American Free Trade Agreement (NAFTA) in 1993, both the Salinas and Clinton administrations feared bad publicity. Desperate Mayan Indians and Leftist revolutionaries overrunning towns in Chiapas, Mexico's most underdeveloped region which had much in common with neighboring Guatemala (with its own 38-year history of violent internal war), would certainly have derailed passage of NAFTA and slowed down integration initiatives.

Quickly, ski-masked Subcommandante Marcos emerged as spokesman of the *Zapatista* National Liberation Army (EZLN, *Ejército Zapatista de Liberacíon Nacional*) of 2,500 rebels, and as an international Robin Hood. By the time President Zedillo purportedly unmasked Marcos on national television as Rafael Sebastián Guillén, a former UNAM (National Autonomous University of Mexico) student and architecture professor, and a member of the Marxist National Liberation Forces, the issue of the guerrilla leader's identity was basically moot. To many Mexicans, Subcommandante Marcos had come to embody the myth of Emiliano Zapata's agrarian revolution. And despite official attempts to discredit the local and indigenous nature of the *Zapatista* insurrection, the appallingly feudal economic conditions, corrupt oligarchic power structure, and routine violation of human rights by police and military forces in Chiapas, proved more convincing.[18]

Chiapas' civil society had responded to local backwardness and repression with intense organizing, forming thousands of functional popular organizations, solidarity committees, and non-electoral associations.[19] These included an active local human rights center, hundreds of Christian Base Communities (CBCs), and thousands of indigenous lay catechists. Within the Roman Catholic Church was the voice of the outspoken liberationist Bishop Samuel Ruiz Garcia, spiritual leader of the Mayan diocese of San Cristóbal de las Casas for over 30 years and long-time opponent of ex-Governor Patrocinio González Garrido, who was Salinas's secretary of interior in 1994. Bishop Ruiz became a fierce defender of Indian rights, condemning the PRI-government for its continued betrayal of Mayan peasants and abandonment of the agrarian program of the Mexican Revolution.[20] Officially promised land, the majority of Chiapas' six million indigenous people remained landless, unemployed, abandoned by Mexico's modernization, oppressed by the local cattle-ranching élite, and disenfranchised by the corrupt and entrenched PRI machine that ran the state.[21]

Whatever the origin or ideological complexion of the *Zapatista* insurgency, local conditions were at the root of social unrest. In the end the *Zapatistas'* "Declaration of the *Lacandon* Jungle" generated popular sympathy with its basic demands for jobs, land, justice, democracy, and freedom. Under NAFTA, the peasants of Chiapas feared an even greater agricultural depression in prices for coffee, corn, and fruits and vegetables. To defuse the crisis, Salinas and Zedillo promised more (largely inappropriate social works which sometimes generated more kick-backs for PRI cronies than actual economic development) and relied upon various peace initiatives and ineffective army operations to capture Marcos. Although the Chiapas stalemate has faded from the limelight, it has further tarnished the image of the ruling party, encouraged guerrilla uprisings in Guerrero, Oaxaca, and other regions of the country, and fueled dissent within PRI's ruling family, particularly the military sector, which had favored repression over negotiation.[22]

In the face of rising social conflicts since 1990, the Mexican Army, some 170,000 strong, has operated like the rural police of old, sweeping into the countryside to quell peasant unrest. One great success of the Mexican Revolution was to remove military men from power politics and to stabilize civil-military relations. The result was an end to the chronic military coups and dictatorships that have plagued Mexico's other Latin American neighbors. The *Zapatistas* uprising in Chiapas, plus the militarization of Mexico's drug war, may have seriously upset that balance. Expenditures for the armed forces are up by nearly 50 percent, and for the first time for many Mexicans, "soldiers in the streets have become a part of everyday life."[23] Also, more conflicts, such as the June 1995 massacre of 17 peasants in Guerrero, even if on a smaller scale than the Chiapas rebellion in which over a hundred died and several hundreds were wounded, will further worsen the military's already abysmal human rights record. Not since the 1968 Tlatelolco Square Massacre of students has the Mexican military found itself under such negative scrutiny; and neither the PRI of Salinas or Zedillo came to its rescue.[24] The military's direct involvement in the drug war has fared little better and has raised fears that the military's new powers may permit it to rival both local and national civilian authority, or more likely serve as a tool of internal control by a beleaguered PRI-government.[25]

PRI's corruption and debility has been further exposed by a year of political and drug-related assassinations and cover-ups, the most notorious being the killings of PRI presidential candidate Luis Donaldo Colosio on 23 March 1994, and of José Francisco Ruiz Massieu, former brother-in-law to President Salinas and General-Secretary of the PRI, on 28 September, 1994. Arrested by Zedillo's new opposition Attorney-General for Ruiz Massieu's murder, Raúl Salinas, former President Salinas's brother, has also been implicated in widespread drug corruption. The United States' Drug Enforcement Agency (DEA) has estimated that 75 percent of Colombian cocaine enters the United States through Mexico. After over $120 million was discovered in Raúl Salinas' foreign bank accounts, drug corruption seemed to taint the presidency and electoral politics.[26] This high-level drug corruption involved extensive complicity by federal and state police and military forces.[27] Among many conspiracy theories circulating, the so-called "Colombianization" of Mexico attributed the rash of assassinations, including the 1993 killing of Guadalajara's Cardinal Juan Jesús Posadas Ocampo, to vicious turf wars between rival Pacific and Gulf Coast drug cartels.[28]

Narco-funding of electoral campaigns poses a particular danger to future Mexican democracy. As one expert explained, elections are extremely expensive and "money buys votes and influences policy."[29] In Mexico these problems may become more acute with dwindling resources and increasing demands on them, and the sheer wealth of Mexican drug traffickers. One Mexican attorney general stated that Mexico's drug barons earned $27 billion annually.[30] Despite President Zedillo's goal to stamp out government corruption, without campaign financing reform and effective control of money laundering, the power of such illegal wealth and NAFTA's opening of the border has the potential to turn Mexico into an uncommon democracy indeed—a narco-democracy![31]

III. Revolving Dictatorship or Uncommon Democracy?

Although Pempel's theory of one-party-dominant régimes assumes a group of advanced industrialized democracies with significant political openness and without "authoritarian controls," quite unlike the present Mexican system, one can argue that Mexico represents a one-party-dominant regime according to the more general criteria of political theorists like Duverger, Sartori, Blondel, McDonald, and Pempel himself. Application of Pempel's scheme to Mexico confirms that, as a party, the PRI has been dominant in numbers and bargaining position, both chronologically and governmentally. However, the current post-revolutionary Mexican system, with its remaining uneven industrialization and authoritarian controls, falls short of Pempel's classic one-party-dominant model. Pempel argues that long-term one-party rule is not "difficult to comprehend in countries where social stagnation and rule by a limited oligarchy prevail," as in Franco's Spain, or in "authoritarian régimes where the sole legal party serves as a key element in a broad arsenal of rigid state controls," such as the former Soviet Union or Communist China.[32] Clearly the Mexican model does not represent either extreme, but future democratization is essential in order to realize the uncommon democracy that Pempel describes. Both the Indian unrest and guerrilla insurgency in Chiapas, and the growing power of narco-trafficking in Mexico's society and economy, underline the critical absence of social dynamism and political openness integral to single-party dominance in industrialized democracies. If, as Pempel asserts, the hallmark of democracy is a people's ability to change their government and throw the rascals out, then what is the prognosis for democracy in any régime dominated by PRI, which has never conceded a presidential election in 68 years? Is there a special relationship in Mexico between elections, democracy, and alterations in power?

The PRI's vital role has been its ability, as is the case with one-party-dominant régimes, "to dominate the nation's policy agenda, and to use that agenda to recreate and reconstitute the dominant party's own following."[33] Beyond electoral politics, the PRI, as its very name implies, successfully institutionalized the policy-making roles of interest associations in Mexico (labor, business, Church, military, and peasants) and served as the glue in the political system. However, in the process the interests of the Mexican state and the PRI (especially powerful cliques in the party) increasingly diverged. PRI party politics are now increasingly influenced by the impact of new domestic and international forces, market globalization, Mexico's national debt restructuring, and the NAFTA free-trade association with the United States and Canada. Equally important is the impact of the domestic diffusion of democracy through the intervention of international non-governmental organizations concerned with human rights and sustainable development. As a result, PRI's greater vulnerability has necessitated a closer reliance on Mexican civil society, especially grass-roots organizations, industry and business, and economic privatization and selective liberalization. The sell-off of hundreds of state enterprises has forced PRI and the Mexican state to rely more heavily on private wealth and competitive campaign fund-raising. In short, economic privatization may be forcing a dramatic realignment between Mexico's ruling class and its relationship with future PRI governments and the state. Reductions in state enterprises continue to shrink the government's economic pie and challenge PRI, which has historically relied upon pork and co-optation to forge consensus and loyalty among the party's competitive *camarillas*. The PRI has lost its former hegemony, making it more difficult for Mexican presidents, especially weak ones like Zedillo, to delay the democratic transition and still maintain investor confidence and critical economic stability.

IV. Political Economy of One-Party Dominance

Mexico has, for the past 15 years, appeared to be on the verge of breaking through the Third World barrier, but its "old" political order, financial crises in 1982, 1987, and 1994, and recent social unrest have made the transition into the global economy a very difficult one. If the pressure for major political reform has not been greater since the Mexican Revolution, the pressure for major economic reform had already reached an all-time high when the bottom fell out of the oil market and world interest rates soared in the early 1980s. Mexico was unable to pay its international debt and IMF austerity measures had to be implemented. Political stability was vital to the PRI and the ruling party leaders saw the inevitability of the globalization of markets and chose to address the immediate economic problems and give lip service to the needed political reforms. Possibly, the liberalization of the economy would cause sufficient "political realignment" for the PRI to maintain its power base and still capitalize on globalization.

The late 1980s and early 1990s were economic boom years for Mexico, and economists were predicting that the Mexican economy would take off and be able to sustain impressive growth rates. But disaster struck once more in 1994 when peasants and the *Zapatistas* rebelled in Chiapas, then Donaldo Colosio was assassinated, and finally the new Zedillo government had to significantly devalue the peso, throwing Mexico into its worst recession ever. What had gone wrong with the well-laid plans of President Carlos Salinas and the PRI Party? Had political instability triggered economic crisis once again? Simple explanations such as that the peso needed to be devalued faster than the current devaluation rate, or that interest rates needed to be increased even higher, or that information on the critically low level of foreign reserves was too slow in being reported and therefore took the market by surprise, were insufficient to explain Mexico's latest crisis. The explanation runs much deeper and leads economists and political scientists to revisit an age-old policy debate as to whether it is better for a country to enact economic reforms before political reforms, in order to stimulate growth and thus improve the standard of living for its people, or whether it is necessary to also address civic issues of representation and equity.

Most mainstream political economy theorists would agree that more economic freedom is obtainable in a democracy and that greater economic freedom is essential to economic growth. According to the 1997 *Index of Economic Freedom Rankings*, Mexico is "mostly unfree."[34] Mexico's low ranking on economic freedom might explain why growth has not been consistent or sustainable. In fact, low economic freedom has threatened the political stability of Mexico because the living standards of the majority of the population have not improved since the 1982 crisis. In addition, a mostly unfree economy is often burdened with an overabundance of regulations which give rise to more opportunity for corruption, and which in themselves are inefficient and undemocratic.[35] When one looks at South Korea, Japan, and Chile democratization was not a part of the initial liberalization policies to increase economic freedom. And although the improvement in GDP per capita in each of these countries has been noteworthy, and their governments today are generally stable, and in the case of Chile more democratic, social pressures for political reform, especially in South Korea, have been increasing steadily.

Despite major economic liberalization efforts in the last decade, Mexico continues to have a mixed economy, meaning that the state plays a much more significant role than it would otherwise play in a purer capitalist economy.[36] The private sector has always played an important role in the Mexican economy, providing at least 50 percent of the total capital in Mexico.[37] Recently, the political leaders have turned to the private sector to be the engine of economic growth, and a major privatization program has been undertaken. The Mexican economy is in the hands of a relatively small number of very large corporations concentrated in a few industrial cities, namely Mexico City, Monterrey, and Guadalajara. It is believed that the country's top industrial groups and banks (approximately 40 companies) control 27 percent of the Mexican economy and therefore can exert enormous influence on government policy-making. While many large corporations have faired better under more liberal market policies, the medium and smaller-sized companies, for the most part, have not. This means that the majority of Mexican workers have not shared in the economic growth over the past decade.[38]

The business sector is not incorporated into the official PRI Party in Mexico and some business leaders have changed their party allegiance to the

PAN but continue to vote PRI in the presidential elections to maintain political stability.[39] The private sector has historically had its collective political power grounded in government-mandated business chambers and in economic power. Business chambers, by law, are consulting agents of the government and they tend to be well-organized and well-financed with significant influence in legislation and policy-making.[40] According to Robert Jones Shafer, "since the early 1940s the history of the *empresarial* organizations of Mexico has been one of almost unbroken growth in membership and other resources, of multiplication and strengthening of programs, of simultaneous proliferation of forms and flexibility of organization and aggregation of those components into peak institutions for consolidated action on selected issues."[41] Basically, these numerous chambers provide the private sector with a direct inroad into the process of political decision-making without the obligations of official party membership.[42] It should also be noted here that individual chambers as well as individual corporations can and do have direct access to the president of Mexico and/or his advisors.[43]

The relationship between the state and the private sector has been ever-changing and was described by Roderic Camp as a "love-hate" relationship.[44] There is an underlying alliance for profit but there have been, and will continue to be, periods of conflict between the two sectors.[45] The relationship between the two sectors is further complicated by the fact that government officials sometimes have personal investments in the private sector.[46] These close economic ties provide opportunities for conflict of interest and corruption. From World War II until the early 1970s there were no major fundamental philosophical differences between government and business because the state had defined its role as one which would control labor, stimulate foreign investment in specific, prescribed industries, protect domestic industry from foreign competition, and provide fiscal and other types of incentives for business.[47] The recent pressures of globalization and the implementation of NAFTA have begun to redefine this relationship. Both the state and the private sector have historically had very potent weapons to use against each other. The state can increase taxes, tighten credit, increase minimum wages, control prices, withhold licenses, and easily add red tape with its "plethora of regulations."[48] The private sector can reduce its domestic investment and take its capital out of the country, a strategy that generally served to pressure administrations that were insufficiently pro-business. Since the late 1970s the government has been trying to win the confidence of the private sector because its support is crucial to the success of the economic policies of the country.

When President López Portillo began his *sexenio* in 1976, he immediately sent his economic advisors to meet with private sector leaders in order to try to regain their confidence and their capital, which had been lost under the previous administration.[49] An agreement known as the "Alliance for Production" was made between the state and the private sector, and soon the economy began to improve.[50] This and other positive economic signs, along with the discovery of new oil wealth, all helped Portillo gain some of the private sector's confidence back as their profits soared.[51] Unfortunately this honeymoon between the private sector and the state was short-lived and what confidence Portillo had regained was lost, and then some. Whether the reasons for the economic crisis were external and/or internal or mainly bad policy decisions did not matter, the fact was that Mexico was in the most severe economic crisis of this century, and the private sector was caught in the middle. Inflation, unrest due to dramatic loss of purchasing power, price controls, and an overvalued peso, were attributed to excessive government spending by the Portillo administration.[52] When the government failed to act on private sector recommendations, rampant capital flight resumed. Due to enormous capital outflow and, in turn, doubt concerning Mexico's creditworthiness, the finance minister, in August of 1982, announced a three-month moratorium on external debt principal payments. In subsequent weeks he also announced a major devaluation of the Peso, the forcible conversion of all Mexdollar accounts into Pesos, stringent foreign exchange controls and the nationalization of the banking system.[53] The fact that the private sector was making significantly greater profits for the first half of the Portillo *sexenio* did not keep the private sector from bailing out when the tables were turned. Private transfers of large amounts of capital out of the country proved how tenuous the relationship between the state and the most powerful industrialists remains.[54]

Obviously, when President de la Madrid began his term in office he had numerous crises to confront. He began a severe austerity program, causing investment and real wages to decrease significantly during the first two years of his administration.[55] De la Madrid, under pressure, removed the austerity measures too quickly, causing inflation and the public sector deficit to grow. When the catastrophic earthquake hit Mexico City in 1985, all confidence in the country's economic future was forfeited, and once again the private sector defected, taking its dollars with it. Naturally, this legacy of distrust, which faced President Carlos Salinas de Gortari when he took office in 1988, seemed almost insurmountable.[56]

Because the state must appease so many constituents of which the private sector is only one, oftentimes the political costs outweigh the economic costs. As Dale Story writes, "the state has employed many more inducements than constraints on the private sector in trying to enlist their support."[57] Naturally, those constituents which have "lost out" to the private sector are very resentful when they see no increase in total welfare as a result of these inducements. Levy and Székely also feel that "the government has gone a long way to facilitate capital accumulation in the private sector through such policies as the provision of goods and services at subsidized prices and low levels of taxation."[58] Whether the private sector was deserving of these subsidies is immaterial; the fact of the matter is that the private sector had, and continues to have, considerable influence over the state. Roderic Ai Camp argues that the relationship between the state and the private sector is one which "exposes a significant weakness in a semi-authoritarian, state-led political model" because the state nurtures the private sector, but when this subsidized group reaches a certain level of power and success it no longer wishes to follow the lead of its mentor because it no longer results in maximization of wealth for the private sector.[59] This certainly has been the experience of economic liberalization in Mexico's one-party system. Only time will tell if an anticipated transition to democracy will reenergize both economic and political development.

The years of the Carlos Salinas administration were very profitable years for Mexico and its leading industrialists. Salinas sold off hundreds of the state-owned enterprises, initiated and signed the North American Free Trade Agreement, brought down inflation, increased foreign direct investment, regained private sector confidence, defended the value of the Peso, and initiated and sustained a comprehensive strategy of economic reform. Wall Street and the world were touting Mexico as a newly industrializing country worthy of investment. When Salinas, like all PRI presidents before him, "handpicked" his successor, Donaldo Colosio, who vowed to continue Salinas's economic reforms, all seemed well with Mexico. But Colosio, head of the National Solidarity Program initiated by Salinas to co-opt opposition popular movements and regenerate grass-roots support for PRI through generous public works and local development funding, also promised political reforms in his campaign speeches. Fear of a political opening may have panicked PRI's old guard. Moreover, a sharp widening in the distribution of wealth and escalating charges of corruption in the PRI, ultimately led to an uprising in Chiapas and the assassination of Colosio (allegedly as part of a PRI sectoral conspiracy to stop reforms). All was not well with Mexico.

President Ernesto Zedillo began his *sexenio* in 1994, with little party support, an impending economic crisis, social unrest, and public allegations of political corruption in the PRI. Zedillo rose through the party ranks on his abilities, rather than his "connections" in the party, and might therefore be considered an "outsider."[60] He began his term in office by ordering investigations of corruption in PRI and by having to make the inevitable decision to sharply devalue the Peso. The result was a severe economic recession in Mexico, loss of investor confidence, and massive capital flight. While the crisis of 1994–95 was deep, it was not as long lasting as the 1982 crisis. Many believe this is because Mexico is more structurally sound than it was 15 years ago. The institutional changes made have given Mexico a stronger base on which to expand economic reforms and initiate political ones. Pedro Aspe argues that under the Mexican constitution it is the government's duty to ensure that all Mexican families live at a level capable to meet all basic needs. Aspe sees leadership, rather than paternalism, moving Mexico forward.[61] But this vision of Mexico requires greater efforts in democratic political reform and an unwavering commitment to economic reforms.

In the future, the private sector in Mexico will continue to demand both economic and political stability, because most industry leaders are convinced that the key to long-term national stability is economic growth and prosperity for all citizens. Over the past 30 years, the PRI lost support on both the Left and Right, due to its many failed economic policies and, most recently, rampant corruption and fraud.[62] The private sector would prefer to invest its capital in Mexico and see the country join the ranks of the world's industrialized nations, but cannot risk such investment until the government proves its wholehearted commitment to free market and political reform.

V. Conclusion

Whether the Mexican political system, and most particularly PRI, its dominant party, will risk full democratization in the years ahead is dependent on both political and economic factors, and the complex relationship between the two. To date, the relatively rapid, but limited and fragile post-1994 economic recovery has served to reinforce declining electoral support for PRI and has allowed President Zedillo to successfully control the pace of liberalization. Not only has economic growth been a function of political continuity and stability, but the reverse has also been true, especially in the 1990s when economic transformation "inevitably brought pressure for political change," and forced economic restructuring since 1982 opened up not only "Mexico's creaking, protected economy" but its creaking, one-party-dominant rule.[63] Mexico and Mexicans have changed, but can PRI change along with the country? Although President Zedillo has staked his presidency on a more open political system, the chance of electoral defeat that openness would bring has drawn him closer to PRI's traditional partisan interests. For the first time since the revolution the possibility exists that national power will be shared by opposing parties.[64]

Two experts remind us that "in Mexico the legacy of 'the Revolution' remained a key issue of contestation."[65] Precisely because the direction and content of future change will become more difficult to predict with democratization, contemporary Mexican political and economic reforms have the great potential to unleash a revolution within the Mexican Revolution, exposing old divisions and betrayals. In this sense, the uprising in Chiapas would represent a cry for revolutionary reform and not "revolution as a relic come to life."[66] Will a Mexican-style *glasnost* stimulate the resurgence of populist forces and Leftist political parties, and in the process polarize political life? Or will limited PRI-led reforms continue to freeze out Leftist party alternatives, while co-opting and incorporating moderate popular sectors, a strategy that has worked in the past? And will the delicate recovery of the Mexican economy (now dominated by a powerful and increasingly autonomous private sector) persist and provide the necessary political incentives and space for liberalization?[67]

Not unlike Octavio Paz's description of the Mexican Revolution as an incredible compromise of opposing forces, Mexico's revolution in the revolution, if that is what it will become, entails a struggle to officially recast that historic compromise in favor of free market over statist economic forces and towards democratic, rather than single-party, hegemony.[68] Traditionally, that compromise has occurred exclusively within PRI itself. By the end of the century, the technocratic wing of Mexico's dominant one-party, and PAN, its most powerful opposition, which conveniently shares the technocratic PRI's ideological and policy vision and is fast outdistancing PRI in voter popularity, may make common cause in a coalition government in order to forge that post-revolutionary compromise together. In the twentieth century, Mexican political stability has been achieved at the price of democracy. As Mexico approaches the twenty-first century, however, the very "factors that had previously contributed to political stability could have the opposite effect."[69] In the end, constraining change and democracy may contribute to further régime instability.

Notes

1. Julia Preston, "Retaliating, Mexico Increases 8 Tariffs on U.S.," in *New York Times* (13 December 1996): p. C1; Julia Preston, "Mexico Leader Shifts to Political Gear," in *New York Times* (19 January 1997): p. 7.
2. T. J. Pempel, ed., *Uncommon Democracies: The One-Party-Dominant Regimes* (New York: Cornell University Press, 1990), p. 32.
3. "Latin America forming new political profile," in *Latin America Press*, vol. 25, no. 48 (30 December 1993): p. 2; David Barkin, "The Specter of Rural Development," in *NACLA Report on the Americas*, vol. 28, no. 1 (July-August 1994): p. 29–34.
4. For a comprehensive history of the party, see: Dale Story, *The Mexican Ruling Party: Stability and Authority* (New York: Praeger, 1986).
5. Pempel, *Uncommon Democracies*, p. 1; Stephan Haggard & Robert R. Kaufman, *The Political Economy of Democratic Transitions* (Princeton, NJ: Princeton University Press, 1995).

6. Wayne A. Cornelius, "Mexico's Delayed Democratization," in *Foreign Policy*, no. 95 (summer 1994): p. 61, 53–55. Philip L. Russell quotes a noted Mexicanologist who noted that "the reform of election laws has been a regular feature of Mexican politics, responding to a periodic need to defuse and direct political opposition into manageable channels." A similar comment was made by PAN's Diego Fernández de Cevallos, who complained that "we cannot continue the vicious cycle of legal reforms and fraudulent elections, followed by more legal reforms and more fraudulent elections," see Diego Fernández de Cevallos, *Mexico Under Salinas* (Austin, TX: Mexico Resource Center, 1994), p. 67.

7. Dan A. Cothran, *Political Stability and Democracy in Mexico: The "Perfect Dictatorship"?* (Westport, CT: Praeger, 1994), p. 210–211.

8. *Latin America Press,* vol. 25, no. 48 (30 December 1993): p. 2.

9. Isidro Sepúlveda, "Mexico's Political Transition: The Emergence of Civil Society," in Donald E. Schulz & Edward J. Williams, *Mexico Faces the 21st Century* (Westport, CT: Greenwood Press, 1995), p. 47. Also, for slightly different percentages, see: Andrés Oppenheimer, *Bordering on Chaos: Guerrillas, Stockbrokers, Politicians and Mexico's Road to Prosperity* (New York: Little, Brown, 1996), p. 169. For the PRI presidential vote since 1934 see: Daniel Levy & Gabriel Székely, *Mexico: Paradoxes of Stability and Change* (Boulder, CO: Westview Press, 1987), p. 72.

10. James L. Busey, *Latin American Political Guide* (Boulder, CO: Juniper Editions, 1995), p. 8; Levy & Székely, *Mexico: Paradoxes of Stability and Change,* p. 72.

11. Oppenheimer, *Bordering on Chaos,* p. 169.

12. Joseph L. Klesner, "Broadening toward Democracy?" in Laura Randall, ed., *Changing Structure of Mexico: Political, Social and Economic Prospects* (Armonk, NY: M.E. Sharpe, 1996), p. 282–83; Oppenheimer, *Bordering on Chaos,* p. 83–90.

13. "Mexico awaits naming of new PRI candidate," in *Latin America Press,* vol. 25, no. 40 (4 November 1993): p. 5; Klesner sets the spending limits for the 1994 presidential elections at the "very high levels" of $42 million, in "Broadening toward Democracy?" p. 282.

14. Oppenheimer, *Bordering on Chaos,* p. 89.

15. Oppenheimer, *Bordering on Chaos,* p. 110, 144. The PRI had $700 million in campaign funds at its disposal; versus PAN or the National Action Party's reported expenditures of $5 million, and the PRD's campaign budget of $3 million.

16. Klesner, "Broadening toward Democracy?" p. 282–283.

17. Oppenheimer, *Bordering on Chaos,* p. 128–135.

18. Alma Guillermoprieto, "The Shadow War," in *The New York Review of Books,* vol. 42, no. 4 (2 March 1995): p. 34–43; Oppenheimer, *Bordering on Chaos,* p. 244, 256. Oppenheimer quotes Zedillo's memorable assertion that the Zapatistas were "neither popular, nor Indian, nor from Chiapas."

19. Klesner, "Broadening toward Democracy?" p. 283–287.

20. Julio C. Tresierra, "Mexico: Indigenous Peoples and the Nation-state," in Donna Lee Van Cott, ed., *Indigenous Peoples and Democracy in Latin America*

(New York: St. Martin's Press, 1995), p. 188–189, drawn from an ethnographic demography series by Mexico's *Instituto Nacional de Antropología e Historia* (1987). This is a conservative estimate which would make the Indian population about 6 percent of a total national population of 94 million. Another source estimates the Indian population at 16 million; "This Land Is Our Land," in *Latin America Press,* vol. 27, no. 36 (5 October 1995): p. 3.

21. On the rural crisis in Chiapas see: Nora Lustig, "The 1982 Debt Crisis, Chiapas, NAFTA and Mexico's Poor," in Randall, *Changing Structure of Mexico,* p. 157–165; also entire issue entitled "Chiapas: Challenging History," in *Akwe:kon* (summer 1994); David Barkin, "The Specter of Rural Development," and Julio Moguel, "Salinas' Failed War on Poverty," both in *NACLA Report on the Americas,* vol. 28, no. 1 (July-August 1994): p. 29–41.

22. Sam Dillon, "Mexicans Trace Rebels' History," in *New York Times* (5 September 1996): p. A1, A3; Oppenheimer, *Bordering on Chaos,* p. 242–244.

23. Thomas Catan, "Giant Stirs," in *Mexico Business* (October 1996): p. 45.

24. Stephen J. Wager & Donald E. Schulz, "The Zapatista Revolt and Its Implications for Civil-Military Relations and the Future of Mexico," in Schulz & Williams, *Mexico Faces the 21st Century,* p. 165–186.

25. Catan, "Giant Stirs," p. 47–52; Kate Doyle, "The Militarization of the Drug War in Mexico," in *Current History,* vol. 92, no. 571 (February 1993): p. 88. Doyle here cites Roderic Ai Camp, *Generals in the Palacio: The Military in Modern Mexico* (New York: Oxford University Press, 1992).

26. Joachim Bamrud, "Corruption, the Other Face of Business in Latin America," in *Latin Trade* (September 1996): p. 38; Sam Dillon, "A Fugitive Lawman Speaks: How Mexico Mixes Narcotics and Politics," in *New York Times* (23 December 1996): p. A6; Julia Preston, "Salinas Denies Being Told His Brother Might Have Drug Ties," in *New York Times* (25 December 1996): p. A4.

27. Julia Preston, "Another Top Drug Official Is Gunned Down in Mexico," in *New York Times* (16 September 1996): p. A6.

28. Oppenheimer, *Bordering on Chaos,* p. 305–307.

29. Eduardo A. Gamarra, "The Art of Narcofunding," in *Hemisphere,* vol. 7, no. 2 (1996): p. 26.

30. Samuel Blixen, "Money laundering taints much of the region," in *Latin America Press,* vol. 25, no. 18 (20 May 1993): p. 1.

31. Silvana Paternostro, "Mexico as a Narco-democracy," in *World Policy Journal,* vol. 12, no. 1 (spring 1995): p. 41–47.

32. Pempel, *Uncommon Democracies,* p. 5.

33. Pempel, *Uncommon Democracy,* p. 7.

34. Kim R. Holmes & Melanie Kirkpatrick, "Freedom and Growth," in *The Wall Street Journal* (16 December 1996): p. A16.

35. Carlos A. DeJuana, "Uphill Struggle," in *Mexico Business* (October 1996): p. 40; "Emerging Mexico," in *National Geographic,* vol. 190, no. 2 (August 1995).

36. Dale Story, *Industry, the state and Public Policy in Mexico* (Austin: University of Texas Press, 1986), p. 33.

37. Story, *Industry, the state and Public Policy in Mexico*, p. 66, 73.
38. Lucy Conger, "Power to the Plutocrats," *International Investor* (February 1995), in Alex López-Ortiz, ed., *Documents on Mexican Politics*, World Wide Web (January 1997).
39. Interviews conducted pre- and post-election 1994 by Corinne B. Young, Monterrey, Mexico.
40. Menno Vellinga, *Economic Development and the Dynamics of Class* (Netherlands: Van Gorcum Assen, 1977), p. 45.
41. For an in-depth look at Business Chambers in Mexico see: Robert Jones Shafer, *Mexican Business Organizations* (New York: Syracuse University Press, 1973), p. 49–50.
42. Vellinga, *Economic Development and the Dynamics of Class*, p. 45.
43. Keith Bradsher, "Back from the Brink, Mexico's Giant Alfa Slims Down for Hard Times," in *International Management* (September 1986): p. 66.
44. Roderic Ai Camp, *Entrepreneurs and Politics in Twentieth Century Mexico* (New York: Oxford University Press, 1989), p. 245.
45. Judith A. Teichman, *Policy-Making in Mexico: From Boom to Crisis* (Boston: Allen & Unwin, 1988), p. 114.
46. Camp, *Entrepreneurs and Politics in Twentieth Century Mexico*, p. 245.
47. Alan Riding, *Distant Neighbors: A Portrait of the Mexicans* (New York: Knopf, 1985), p. 124.
48. Miguel Basañez, *La lucha por la hegemonía en México, 1968–1980* (Mexico City: Siglo XXI, 1981), p. 193; quote from Camp, *Entrepreneurs and Politics in Twentieth Century Mexico*, p. 28.
49. Teichman, *Policy-Making in Mexico*, p. 114.
50. Paul Luke, "Debt- and Oil-led Development: The Economy Under López Portillo, 1977–1982," in George Philip, ed, *The Mexican Economy* (London: Routledge, 1988), p. 51.
51. Luke, "Debt- and Oil-led Development, 1977–1982," p. 51.
52. Teichman, *Policy-Making in Mexico*, p. 117.
53. Luke, "Debt- and Oil-led Development, 1977–82," p. 70.
54. Teichman, *Policy-Making in Mexico*, p. 125.
55. Levy & Székely, *Mexico: Paradoxes of Stability and Change*, p. 163.
56. Ibid., p. 163–164.
57. Story, *Industry, the state and Public Policy in Mexico*, p. 95.
58. Levy & Székely, *Mexico: Paradoxes of Stability and Change*, p. 136.
59. Camp, *Entrepreneurs and Politics in Twentieth Century Mexico*, p. 251.
60. Douglas P. Handler, "The Mexican Economy in Perspective," in *A.C. Neilson Company* (1996).
61. Pedro Aspe, *Economic Transformation the Mexican Way* (Cambridge, MA: MIT Press, 1993), p. 248–249.
62. Haggard & Kaufman, *The Political Economy of Democratic Transition*, p. 181.
63. Anthony DePalma, "Losing Control, for Mexicans, Democracy Exacts a Scary Price," in *New York Times* (27 March 1994): Sec. 4, p. 1.
64. Preston, "Mexico Leader Shifts to Political Gear," p. 7.

65. Haggard & Kaufman, *The Political Economy of Democratic Transitions,* p. 291.
66. Clifford Krauss, "Revolution as a Relic Come to Life," in *New York Times* (29 December 1996): Sec. 4, p. 1.
67. Julia Preston, "In Mexico, an Uneven Recovery," in *New York Times* (2 January 1997): p. C13.
68. Oppenheimer, *Bordering on Chaos,* p. 97. In an interview with Paz, Mexico's great literary figure, he argued that the revolution was a "compromise between opposing forces: nationalism and imperialism, workers' rights and industrial development, state-managed economy and free market, democracy and state tutorship."
69. Cothran, *Political Stability and Democracy in Mexico,* p. 209.

ELEVEN

Peaceful Democratic Change in Brazil and Argentina

Franco Mazzella

I. Comparative Transition of Régimes: Blending Old and New

The wave of democratization in the 1980s has produced a vast literature on transition from authoritarian rule, especially the military type. The transition literature has attempted to explain rather convincingly the variety of paths towards democratic politics.[1] Argentina and Brazil moved away from military authoritarianism with different means and at different times. Argentina ended its military rule in 1982 abruptly and with some help from exogenous conditions in the form of a military-induced, disastrous war with Great Britain over the Falkland/Malvinas Islands. Brazil, on the other hand, moved towards democratization in the late 1970s under the tutelage of the military, which tried to control the increasing uneasiness of élites and masses over the slow progress towards civilian-led democratic politics.[2] The Brazilian military sought to manage the transition to civilian-led democracy by establishing manipulative alliances with key élite sectors of civil society, while the Argentine armed forces were unable to link up with the political world. The mode, strategies, and timing of régime transition are not uniform, even in a regional context such as Latin America where countries share several similarities. One of the key experiences Argentina and Brazil have shared is a cycle of democratic and military "bureaucratic authoritarianism" from which they are trying to escape. They also share the burden of finding a new way towards economic and social modernization. The two countries in the early 1990s are at relatively similar levels of development according to key indicators of the World Bank (see Appendices 11.1 and 11.2). Although Argentina had started at a higher level than Brazil, it suffered a "reversal development."[3]

Régime transitions are characterized by significant differences. Military interventions in the politics of the two countries were responses to a different set of factors with little regional demonstration effect. The governing practice and the modus operandi of the military in power have exhibited important differences as well. The Argentine military was actually threatened, or perceived a threat to the internal security of the country, in the face of highly politicized social segments mobilized by the radical and Peronist movements, which aggressively pursued power at the expense of conservative groups.[4] The Brazilian military, on the other hand, sought to continue a "moderating power" among the diverse clientelistic élites, which seldom threatened the integrity of the state. The guerrilla movements of the 1960s–70s, and the "Cuban threat," were more quantitatively and qualitatively significant in Argentina than Brazil.

The Argentine military sought to restore order out of civil war in their overthrow of Isabela Peron, while the Brazilian military in 1964 sought to impose peacefully their brand of "revolution" over President Goulart's Marxist temptations. The Argentine armed forces established a brutal dictatorship and unleashed a "dirty war," which terrorized the nation from 1976 to 1982. The Brazilian officers decided to manage a fluid authoritarianism characterized by low-level state terrorism. The number of disappeared is estimated in the thousands in Argentina, while in Brazil the number is over 300 persons.[5] The nastiness of military authoritarianism in Argentina is demonstrated by the controversy over President Menem's pardon of top generals, revelations about people being dropped into the ocean by the air force, and continuing debate over human rights violations during the years of the "dirty war." In Brazil the armed forces were spared the humiliation of trials, and President Cardoso has sought to compensate the families of persons disappeared in the 1960s.

The transition from a régime of authoritarianism is affected by the legacy of previous democratic experiences, political expectations, political tolerance among political leaders, and the management of economic systems. Argentina's democratic governance was led by agrarian conservative élites who guided the democratic institutions with little consent and accountability to the growing masses. The rise of Radicalism and Peronism discredited the representative model of democratic decision-making and replaced it with a mass-based, plebiscitarian system. Ideological intolerance drove a wedge among social classes and key élites in civil society. Political parties in Argentina performed poorly the function of democratic aggregation, but did well in raising popular expectations. The two main parties used the power of the state to maneuver the economy towards autarkic practices and distributive outcomes.[6] The Peronists were perhaps more ideologically driven than the radicals in this type of governance, but both had the responsibility to create a political culture of collectivism, intransigence, and absolutism.[7]

Both countries have suffered a democratic lag and democratic deficiency because in times of crisis no political movement emerged to guarantee stable constitutional life for all groups in society, especially those threatened by the traditional power holders. The Radical Party in Argentina lost the opportunity to become a dominant party in the 1930s–40s because of its strategy, disunity, and identity. The Peronist Movement of the 1950s, as well as the *Estado Novo* of Getulio Vargas, were of short duration and do not fit T.J. Pempel's concept of "uncommon democracy."[8] In both countries these two populist movements were viewed with suspicion and were not "true believers" in liberal constitutional democracy. The traditional, somewhat expected, and self-imposed role of the military as "constitutional guarantor" has made it impossible for a political party to establish the conditions for a "one-party dominant régime."

The presidential system, antiquated federalist structures, and the lack of sub-cultures on which to anchor the electoral dominance of a political party did not facilitate the rise of that type of democracy. The rise of Peronism in Argentina created feeble conditions for a two-party, alternating system of governance, while the régime of Getulio Vargas in Brazil failed to transform the localistic, personalistic, fragmented, and clientelistic party politics into a coherent strategy for the growth of a national, mass-based, political party. Political alliances, through patronage and distributive policies were not a common strategy for the enhancement of democracy in the 1950s. In fact, the Alfonsin (1983–89) administration in Argentina attempted a strategy to create democratic space by distributing significant resources to state governments led by Peronist administrations, including the poor state of La Rioja where Governor Carlos Menem launched his presidential bid. President Alfonsin's policies failed to make the UCR a dominant party, but it formed the nucleus for future negotiations aimed at the legitimation of constitutional democracy.

The international environment was not conducive to the growth of a dominant party in charge of the democratic future. In both countries the populist and somewhat popular movements of the 1950s–70s were nationalistic with strong anti-American and anti-capitalist prescriptions. The United States provided neither a democratic anchor nor a reliable interlocutor for mass-based parties that could be used as democratic walls against extremist movements. The United States, during the Cold War period, was the beneficiary of anti-populist, anti-Marxist policies of military authoritarianism. The outcome did not help to build a case for a one-party-dominant régime.

Brazilian democratic politics were prone to soften the sharp edges of political conflicts; regional, economic, military, and sectoral élites were driven less by ideologies than pragmatic ideals. Brazilian political parties continue to be influenced by *personalismo,* factionalism, and localism to a greater degree than their Argentine counterparts.[9] The Brazilian state historically played a lesser role in management of the economy than the Argentine state. The political economy of President Juan Peron was more nationalistic and statist-oriented than that of President Getulio Vargas because Argentina's level of industrialization and urbanization was higher than that of Brazil during the time of the two régimes. Foreign control over important sectors of the Argentine economy gave more credence to Peron's nationalization policies than was the case with Brazil under the government of *Estado Novo* of Vargas.[10]

The rule of the bureaucratic-military governments in both countries did not change the legacy of the past in these areas. The Argentine military tried to govern by exclusion and depoliticization. while the Brazilian military authoritarianism tended to be more inclusive and operated an accordion-type politics whereby some semblance of electioneering, political participation, and rule of law could be restricted or enlarged depending on the relative threat of the power holders. A minor difference between the two cases existed in their economic policies. The Brazilian military increased the scope of the state, while the Argentine armed forces tried to somewhat reverse the statist trend. The Argentine government's share of the GNP was 40 percent in 1976 and 18.4 percent in 1980, while the Brazilian government used 20.9 percent (1980) and 25.6 percent (1992) of its GNP. The military authoritarian régime in Brazil privatized some public companies and sold 30 percent of its holdings in 140 companies.[11]

II. Economic Dilemmas of the New Governance: From Statism to Free Market

The literature on democratic governance has discovered a direct relationship between economic growth and the political fortunes of democracy.[12] Economic transitions, like political transitions, are often dictated by the weight of the past. The new rulers of Argentina and Brazil have inherited heavy burdens in the transition. They have to manage a peaceful redemocratization, redirect the public responsibilities of governments, rebuild public confidence in civilian-run institutions, and correct the inequities of a poor society. The success of the new democratic governance depends on the ability to deliver.[13] Students of "transitology" have become more cautious after the initial euphoria over the demise of military authoritarianism and the rise of democratic governance.[14]

The Latin American case is particularly instructive because the economies of the area have been constrained by high levels of poverty (60 million people of which 89 percent live in urban areas), tremendous inequalities, and sharp philosophical disagreements over the relation between the public and private sectors.[15] Argentina and Brazil have not been spared the costs of economic transformations: Brazil has 26.8 percent of its population classified as poor (39 percent of them live in urban areas), while Argentina has experienced for the first time in its history unusually high levels of poverty (25 percent to 37 percent). Both countries have unequal distribution of household incomes. In the 1970s, Argentina's highest ten percent of households shared 35 percent of household income, while their Brazilian counterparts shared 51 percent (1980); the lowest 20 percent of households in Argentina took 4.4 percent of household income, while in Brazil the same income group took 2 percent of income. The middle class ("third and fourth quintiles") took 35.6 percent of household income in Argentina, and in Brazil the same income bracket shared 26.4 percent of household income.[16] Argentineans have always enjoyed a higher standard of living than other Latin Americans. In general, however, Argentina can claim a higher level of economic and social development than Brazil, although both countries are classified as "upper-middle income" by the World Bank Report (see Appendices 11.1 and 11.2).[17]

The two countries compete in a global economy composed of giants (economies of over $500 billion) and pygmies (economies of less than $100 billion). Both countries have accumulated large amounts of foreign debt (Brazil's $146 billion and Argentina's $85 billion) which continue to absorb over one-third of their export earnings. Brazil out-exported Argentina in 1993 ($32.2 billion vs. $13.3 billion), while both countries depend heavily on imports (Brazil imported $21.1 billion against $14.4 billion for Argentina). The globalization of the economy has forced a change in the political economy of both countries. The state, since the 1930s, has played a dominant role in the economy. The free-market model did not operate without government-induced investments in the form of nationalization, redistributive policies, and a large bureaucracy. According to one school of thought, the unchecked expansion of state function has brought neither a liberal democracy nor the desired economic development, especially in Argentina where Peronism took charge of the state, helped by a militant labor movement.[18]

Both governments invested in petrochemicals, steel, electricity, television, oil, gas, telecommunications, nuclear plants, armament industry, transportation, and general infrastructures. The private sector was either included as a partner or excluded from investing in those areas. Statism was often the result of nationalism and protectionism that played to a fear of foreign control over public economic policies. The public role in the economy was reaffirmed in the

1988 Brazilian constitution which can be changed only through 60 percent of the vote by the Brazilian bicameral legislature. Foreign investments were discouraged by placing restrictions on their activities, and foreign borrowing was often a way to subsidize inefficient industries or to substitute for investments that the domestic private sector was unwilling or unable to provide.

The breakdown of military authoritarianism has revived the debate over the role of the state and democratic governability. The discrediting of military handling of public decisions and the demonstration effect from successful free-market models has renewed enthusiasm for the private market unfettered by government controls. The post-authoritarian governments sought privatization of publicly owned enterprises, protection of domestic and foreign investments, elimination of protective policies, and fiscally austere public policies. A turn-around in public opinion and changes among political groups previously hostile to free-market economies, such as the Peronists, helped the new governments. Argentina and Brazil have privatized public firms worth $24 billion and $6.7 billion respectively. Certain types of public enterprises have so far escaped because they have been competitive or are backed by powerful political forces. For example, state-owned oil companies such as Argentina's Y.P.F. (*Yacimentos Petroliferos Fiscales*) or Brazil's Petrobras, and the armament industry in both countries, have not been totally privatized, while Argentina has privatized 80 percent of Y.P.F.

Private foreign investments have come more slowly than expected for several reasons. They are volatile and can move around the globe very rapidly as political events influence investment climates and private decisions. Argentina has attracted less foreign money than Brazil—about $13 billion (1994), which declined to $7.5 billion (1995) against Brazil's $12 billion (1995) with a projected increase to $17 billion.[19] The majority of investments go into stock ownership, government bonds, and ownership of privatized firms.[20]

Foreign investments and borrowing from international monetary institutions such as the International Monetary Fund (I.M.F.) continue to pressure for privatization, lower taxes and decreased government expenditures. These policies have reduced the ability of both governments to deal with declining wages, unemployment, public service, and poverty. Labor costs in Argentina have declined from 125 to 85 (1993–95) and unemployment hovers around 16 percent to 17 percent (1996). President Menem and his Economic Minister continue to struggle with a government deficit produced by decreased taxes, tax evasions (estimated at $24 billion, almost 50 percent of the federal budget) and costs of public service. The number of government-owned or partially owned firms in Argentina has been cut to about 20 to 30 percent of the total, and since 1989 the number of government workers has been reduced from 800,000 to 308,000; further privatization is likely to generate less revenues and more political conflicts with the congress, civil society, and provincial politicians. President Menem successfully extracted from parliament public emergency powers to deal with changes in tax structures, privatization, and administrative reforms at the national (federal) and provincial level. The Peronist majority in Congress reluctantly agreed to delegate, with severe restrictions, some of its legislative prerogatives to the executive branch. President Menem's objective is to reduce the number of government units and eliminate several thousand jobs. The task is extremely difficult at the provincial government level, where 9 percent of the economically active population was employed in 1991. President Cardoso of Brazil has been less successful with the Brazilian congress than President Menem. The Brazilian congress is not controlled by the president's political party, and state politicians are more independent and driven by personal political calculus. Constitutional reforms to change government pensions, welfare, and to redefine federal-state relations have met with strong opposition.

The revitalization of a global, competitive, aggressive capitalism has spurred the establishment of regional economic cooperation in the form of customs unions with the objective of lowering tariffs and expanding commercial relations. Argentina, Brazil, Paraguay, and Uruguay formed MERCOSUR in 1995. This potential market has a population of about 195 million and a GNP of about $795 billion. Trade between Argentina and Brazil has already doubled, but so far Argentina has registered a trade deficit of $619 million (1995), most of it caused by imports from Brazil. Onefourth of Argentina's exports go to Brazil, which imports foodstuff and has invested about $300 million in Argentina.[21]

The redirection of the economy has brought about a rethinking of the functions of the state in both countries.[22] The decline of statism in the political economy of the new governance tends to add to the dilemma because it shrinks the activities of the public sector at a time of major need for economic and social infrastructures, and it enhances the economy with the international system of free-marketing with its regulative web that places constraints on public choices. The loan policies practiced by the International Monetary Fund (IMF) have forced austere budgets that make government responses to crises very difficult.

Argentina is more vulnerable than Brazil in its relation between state and society, and the role of the central government and its provincial federal units. The shrinking of government responsibilities in Argentina has so far resulted in significant riots in three provinces from Cordoba to San Juan, where public employees were not paid for months or their salaries were cut by 30 percent (from 400 Pesos to about 280 Pesos a month).[23] President Menem backed the decision of his Economic Minister, Domingo Cavallo, not to help the provincial governments unless they privatized some of their public services. Thereafter, the reduction of the burden of the central government since 1991 has been met by the growth of local responsibilities. In Argentina local government spending increased by 75 percent at the time of declining aid from the central government (from 11 to 9 percent of the national budget) and increased tax evasion at $20 billion depriving local governments of revenue.[24]

The Brazilian government of the *Nova Republica,* which is slowly taking shape after the authoritarian years, is having difficulty implementing the promise of a new federalism approved by the 1988 constitution, where the states would have more autonomy, funds, and cooperative responsibilities with the federal government.[25] The reasons are two-fold: (1) The responsibility of the federal government is decreasing; in 1980–83 the federal "social expenditures" represented over 10 percent of Brazil's GDP, while in the 1990s they are down to 9 percent.[26] The states and local governments have also abused the new delegation of responsibility by consuming more than their revenues and by contributing to the total public debt by borrowing over $50 billion.[27] The loss of local revenues due to inefficiency and government tax evasion added to fiscal problems. In 1993 over 2,600 Brazilian local governments reported a tax load of $10, while 900 did not collect any tax, and 638 collected a combined total revenue of $600.[28] (2) The new governability of democracy is often valued in the abstract, while public decisions contribute to the erosion of whatever legitimacy the new governance built up on the way towards the consolidation of democracy.

III. The Dilemma of Consolidating Democratic Governance

The governance of post-military authoritarianism follows different patterns in the consolidation of democracy because of the transition circumstances, historical experiences, and commitments to that "distinct political order and a particular form of human existence" called democratic governance.[29] The literature on "transitology" is being replaced by the science of "consolidology," i.e., "a preoccupation among students of politics with the conditions underlying régime stability."[30] The organization of transition is a process of acting on circumstances, timing, exploitation of dictator's mistakes, and is often led by "advocates" who work to shape winning coalitions, strategies and objectives.[31] In the period of consolidation, however, the governor's job is to choose carefully both partners and the least damaging public choices. The consolidation is "a process of transforming the accidental arrangements, prudential norms and contingent solutions that have merged during the transition into relations of cooperation and competition that are reliably known, regularly practiced, and voluntarily accepted by those persons or collectivities, (i.e., politicians and citizens who participate in democratic governance).[32]

The timing and conditions of consolidation of democratic stability are almost unpredictable because complex factors influence the process such as past history, levels of trust, behavior of political activists, tolerance of dissent, and acceptance of the rules of the game, often expressed in the political culture of the citizenry. Argentina and Brazil are building new institutions and forms of political relationships, while retaining significant components of political practices that existed prior to their authoritarian experience.

The political culture that is emerging in both countries tends to reflect changing values. Support for democracy seems to be higher in Argentina than Brazil as 74 percent of the people agreed in 1988 with the statement: "Democracy is always preferable to any other system," while only 43 percent of Brazilians did so (see Table 11.1). The élites and the masses hold different views of democracy and of people's ability to make wise decisions. The extension of voting rights in Brazil to illiterates and sixteen-year-old youths was not viewed favorably by a significant number of élites. Brazilian élites also disagree with the masses on the representative institutions: 69 percent favored a parliamentary system, while only 10 percent of the masses supported it. In 1993 Brazilian voters rejected a parliamentary system and kept the presidential system that was established in the 1988 constitution. The general mistrust of Brazilian politicians is reflected in the low esteem of congress: 55 percent felt that the legislative body is "bad," 31 percent "fair," 8 percent "good," and 43 percent believed that the country would fare as well without congress.[33] Surveys also show that 65 percent believed that democracy would be consolidated in the 1990s; 63 percent, however, also felt that Brazil would face "a chronic state of social convulsions" if the country failed to improve social conditions. The democratic political culture is also helped by changes in information levels and the relative low level of class or ethnic cleavages, but the legacy of clientelism, party fragmentation, and populist styles of politics is still significant.[34]

Argentina, on the other hand, has been more divided along social classes and issue orientations. People support democracy in general, but democratic dimensions such as political pluralism and tolerance generate disagreements: 52 percent are identified as "democratic" and 48 percent as élitists and populists. Support for procedural democracy is strong: 79 percent favor elections as a way to settle political disputes and denial of voting rights on the basis of education is rejected by 77 percent.[35] Although the "fundamental core of the political culture is both individualistic and collectivist," the number of people who favor "gradual reforms" increased from 67 percent (1984) to 74 percent (1991).[36] Changes in political culture are especially important in voters' views on the privatization of important state-owned enterprises and on controversial economic decisions by the democratic rulers. In the midst of austerity programs that are causing hardship in Argentina, 54 percent of the people supported President C. Menem's decision not to remove his unpopular Economic Minister Cavallo, whose presidential aspirations are opposed by

86 percent.[37] Brazilian President H. Cardoso's decision to stand up against a long strike by workers of the state-owned oil giant (*Petrobras*) increased support for its privatization among members of the Brazilian Congress. President Cardoso's administration approval rate at a time of crisis governance was substantial (39 percent "very good," 40 percent "fair," and 16 percent "very bad"), and 52 percent of those polled felt that the government could solve the economic crisis, while 22 percent believed that no government can solve Brazil's problems.[38]

IV. Rebuilding Procedures and Structures of Democratic Government

The consolidation of democracy is heavily dependent on the rebuilding of representative democratic institutions after years of neglect. Brazil's military authoritarianism allowed the Brazilian congress to function on and off under severe constraints, while the armed forces of Argentina shut off any means of participant politics and representative democracy. The civil-military relations in Brazil were less exclusionary than those in Argentina where the process of transition to the return of democracy under civilian governance was more divisive. The legislative institutions performed poorly on all expected representative functions in both countries. A strong presidentialism has been the preferred form of popular representation, and almost always the intervention of the armed forces against a president encountered no opposition by any legislative body in Latin America.[39]

The separation of powers between the civilian presidents and the armed forces were poorly drawn in the process of the transition. The Brazilian military negotiated an amnesty for violations of human rights, while the work of human rights activists in Argentina forced the Alfonsin administration to prosecute a handful of generals and low-level officers. Several officers were jailed but were pardoned by President C. Menem who has extracted military loyalty towards civilian rulers. The Argentinean military launched three insurgencies against President Alfonsin and two against President Menem. In both cases, President Menem has punished the military insurgents. The Brazilian military, however, has not threatened the civilian governors, even in the face of the impeachment crisis of President F. Collor de Mello in December 1992. In both countries the civilian president was forced to grant the military an increasing role in areas that constitutionally belong to civilian-operated institutions.

The governing structures sometimes found it difficult to operate without some unexpected interruptions. People in Argentina and Brazil voted for president almost at the same time. President R. Alfonsin was reelected in 1983 and handed over the office peacefully to President C. Menem (1989), who was elected in 1995. Brazilians elected President T. Neves in

1985, who died in office after a few months and was replaced by J. Sarney, who was not elected but served longer. Brazilian voters voted again in 1989 and elected F. Collor de Mello, who was impeached after three years on charges of corruption. Itamar Franco replaced him until the 1994 election of H. Cardoso. Brazilians ended up with only two elected presidents, but five different administrations that muddled through the consolidation of democracy, while Argentina has had three elected administrations for the first time in its history. Voters in Argentina have influenced political choices, as well as drastic economic and social changes, much more significantly than their counterparts in Brazil.

The success of the governing structures depends on the load factor, which is a composite of programmatic choices available to governors. In both countries the load factor is controlled by the executive. In Argentina the political parties are less personalistic, factionalized, and more issue-oriented and disciplined than in Brazil. The executive normally can expect a higher level of party support in Argentina than in Brazil, where the government initiatives quite often lose the backing of 50 to 60 percent of the pro-government parties.[40] The program of the Alfonsin administration in Argentina was limited in scope in economic and social issues and dictated more by the need to recreate a sense of national reconciliation and legitimacy for civilian representative institutions under a regime of law. However, in Brazil the presidencies of Neves, Sarney, and Franco were driven by the same concerns but with less pressure on the dimensions cited: one of the chief reasons for the difference in the two cases is that key political players in Brazil came predominantly from groups that were connected with the past and ensured more continuity than sharp detours in governing.

The first Presidencies of C. Menem in Argentina and F. Collor de Mello in Brazil were driven to changes in economic and social policy. Both administrations pushed forward initiatives to reduce the burden of government and the statist political economy. Menem, however, surprised the Argentinean economic and political establishment and shocked the Peronist Party's traditionalists (industrial workers in Buenos Aires and suburbs, the middle and lower classes in the interior provinces) anchored to the safety net of the state and small industry protected by the government.

Menem's program was more ambitious and challenging to old ways of governing than Collor's, whose government had a brief term. Menem's style was aggressive, personalistic, on the edge of legalism, unconcerned with political party loyalty, and prone to make deals with both political "friends" and enemies. His most ambitious programs were to move Argentina's economy towards a free market, promote changes in the Constitution, and reduce tension between the armed forces and the new civilian governors. His key constitutional targets were the elimination of the electoral college and the one-term, six-year, presidential office. Menem was seeking reelection and plebiscitarian confirmation. Constitutional amendments needed a two-thirds approval in both houses of congress. President Menem's party did not have the required votes, because in the 1993 legislative elections his party improved only slightly (126 seats in the house with 42 percent of the national vote). President Menem, in an unprecedented strategic move, pursued an agreement with the least anti-Peronist faction of the Radical Party (UCR) led by ex-President Raul Alfonsin. The Pact of Olives (December 1993) was somewhat uncharacteristic of Argentina's political culture. The pact was achieved through political bargaining between the dominant political rivals by downplaying confrontation and intransigence that had weakened democracy for the last 50 years. The pact passed in both houses of congress with Radical and Peronist votes, and the 1994 constitutional assembly ratified its provisions by 177–to–27.

The Constitutional reform amended 40 articles, added 19, contained a chapter on the rights of citizens, and legalized democratic procedures as a system of government. The incumbent President is allowed to run for reelection once, and after a period of four years he/she is eligible to run again. The President's term of office was reduced from six to four years. The electoral college was abolished, and the President is now elected by a direct vote of the people in a two-round process, which is triggered if the top candidate receives less than 45 percent of the popular vote or his margin of victory over the second-place candidate is less than 10 percent. The Constitution abolished the requirements that Presidential candidates be Roman Catholic. The President's constitutional powers include a "decree authority" in time of "urgent necessity," which is not subject to congressional approval except on matters of election, freedom of assembly, operation of the judicial system, and activities of political parties. The Constitution created a new government structure in the form of a chief-of-cabinet in charge of policy implementation, chosen and responsible to the President but subject to removal by a two-thirds vote of congress. The document introduces the direct election of senators, increases their number from two to three from each province (one senator must come from the minority party), and it reduces their term of office from nine to six years. The constitution strengthens the independence of the judicial branch.[41]

The 1993 Argentine and the 1988 Brazilian constitutions tried to structure a government in the direction of democratic consolidation, which includes a provision to strengthen the legislature, protect civil liberties, and ensure judicial independence and the rule of law. Both documents grant the executive decree powers in case of "emergency" or "necessity." These provisions could bring unintended weakening of representative bodies and lead to abuses of power. Brazilian presidents have issued 1004 decrees in the

1988–95 period, of which 274 were approved by congress, 18 rejected, and 640 reissued.[42] Some scholars have cast doubt or pessimism on the way the consolidation game is being played out in both countries. The experiments in Argentina have been criticized as being manipulated for personal gain in a political environment that does not have "mutually acceptable rules of the game to regulate competition between the political forces"[43]

V. Democratic Consolidation through Disassembling Electioneering

The stability and endurance of democracy depend on the institutionalization of regular, free, competitive, unrestricted, public civilian contests, whose results are accepted by the players involved as the only means to achieve political power, respect people's sovereignty, and preserve democracy. Argentina and Brazil have held public contests much longer than post-Communist systems in Eastern Europe. The authoritarianism of Latin America has been quite often the result of an unpredictable electioneering process. In the last 50 years the problem has been not whether elections were held but whether the results would stick! The process of electioneering in Argentina and Brazil in the 1990s, at a time of severe economic crisis, shows that so far electoral outcomes have not caused a reversal of democracy, but they have presented risks for incumbent governors and produced voting volatility exacerbated by volatile political leaders and redefined party structures.[44]

The cultural and historical legacy has influenced the evolution of key institutions such as political parties. In both countries the military structures have taken advantage of the weak presence of mediating organizations in civil society that demand accountable democratic governing. In Argentina the culture of class antagonism, with fragile ties to political parties and mistrust of opposition, has led to political movements identified in a strong, i.e., authoritarian, leader whose job in office is to hegemonize political power on behalf of winners. Both Radicals and Peronists have exhibited such a trend. President Menem's control over the *Justicialista* Party in the 1990s has virtually marginalized that organization as a vehicle for the recruitment of candidates for public office, the selection of a cabinet, and the political program of the party. President Menem's neo-Liberal economic team, led by Economic Minister Cavallo, has clashed with the "social justice" wing of the party represented by some Peronist governors of states like Santa Cruz and La Pampa, who believe that "Menemismo" is just a cast of characters without convictions, desperately loyal to the president who can ensure their political survival. Cabinet infighting is occurring more often in the second administration over economic policies and the "withering of the state" under the slash and burn privatization program. In March of 1996

President Menem supported the creation of an economic advisory board composed of representatives of government, labor, and industry. The economic minister opposed the board as a corporatist attempt to derail his economic program. President Menem's decision to redefine Argentina's statecraft by remaking the Peronist Party into a model of free-market, anti-government, anti-collectivist, virtuous democratic organization carries more risk than Cardoso's attempts to make Brazil a "more just society." President Menem's program is being subjected to more national debate. The opposition from the Radical Party (UCR), the Center-Left Coalition (FREPASO), the Catholic Church, and the major labor unions (CGT) forced President Menem to dismiss Cavallo, the architect of Argentina's economic austerity program. Argentina's defense minister and minister of justice were also dismissed under a cloud of corruption. President Menem's political future was jolted by the results of the local election in Buenos Aires where the Radical candidate (UCR) won the mayor's office and 60 percent of the council, the candidate of the Center-Left (FREPASO) received 27 percent of the votes, and the Peronist candidate, strongly backed by President Menem, came a distant third with only 18 percent of the votes.

President Menem is not yet a beleaguered executive. He reassured the financial markets that he "runs the government and leads the way." He replaced Harvard-educated Cavallo with the chief of the Central Bank, Roque Fernandez, a graduate of the University of Chicago and a follower of the free-market, low-tax policies advocated by U.S. economist and Nobel winner, Milton Friedman. Cavallo's destitution however, did not end the long feud between President Menem and the labor movement. The two largest labor groups—the General Confederation of Labor (CGT) and Congress of Argentine Workers (CTA)—called two general strikes against additional austerity policies, reforms and cuts in the pension system, and restructuring of labor-management relations. Menem also threatened to privatize the health system run by the labor unions. The Argentine president faced also a mini-rebellion from his own party in the legislature. Several Peronists joined the radicals and FREPASO lawmakers in a boycott of the lower house to prevent a quorum. The autumn of popular discontent plunged the approval rate of Mr. Menem's administration to 15 percent of the people 16 months after he was reelected with 50 percent of the votes.

President Cardoso of Brazil faces a different connection between democracy and political parties. The Brazilian political parties are the reflection of political élitism and corporatism anchored in state politics and kept alive by repressive social relationships. Patronage and privileges extensively used for political purposes are the cornerstone of a patrimonial political style and politics still present in Brazil. The building of enduring political structures with national purposes are a recent phenomenon. The danger for Brazil's democracy lies in the lack of national civil structures such as political parties providing democratic opposition and channeling demands to the governing institutions. The results are often disastrous as private interests limit or prevent the enactment of public interest.

The management of agrarian problems in Brazil is an example of the difficulties of democratic reforms in the absence of stable institutions. The rapid urbanization of the country (only 25 percent of the population now lives in a rural setting) has not ended the inequity of land distribution (1 percent of farmers own 44 percent of the total land which is mainly uncultivated). Since the 1960s the federal government has been unable and unwilling to deliver promised land distribution. President Cardoso promised land to 280,000 families, but only 42,900 have received land (1995). The movement of Workers without Land (MST) in the last few years has led a militant campaign against exploitation and land concentration through land invasions and land occupation. The conflicts have often ended in death (200 in the last 15 years). The last serious confrontation (in April 1996) took place in the southern state of Pará, where a peaceful peasant demonstration was broken up by military police: 19 people were killed and, according to a congressional investigation, some of the deaths were execution style. The search for a new minister of agriculture in charge of the National Institute for Agrarian reform (INCRA) was delayed for several days because of bargaining among rural-based congressmen of several parties. President Cardoso was able to get an agreement from the third largest component of the Brazilian congress, the P.P.B., whose commitment to President Cardoso's program is doubtful since one of its leaders is thinking about the 1998 Presidential election.

The management of the economic crisis and the reinvention of the state's role in post-military authoritarianism are taking place in an environment of disassembling electioneering. This type of process is evident in repeated reshuffling of existing political parties and their factions. It takes place in a political marketplace characterized by the widespread use of television, weak party identification, weak internal party discipline, and the rise of a new type of political leader. Disassembling electioneering tends to occur more in multiparty systems than in stable, two-party systems, and in a political culture of personalistic nature that fosters élite accommodations. The two elections of President C. Menem and the elections of F. Collor de Mello and H. Cardoso of Brazil, analyzed below, are examples of this type of electioneering.

A. Argentina

President Menem's nomination (1989) in the Peronist primary was made possible by the reshuffling of the Peronist Party in the late 1980s. The "renovators" faction took charge of the neo-Peronist movement in the northwest provinces, which spread throughout the country including Buenos Aires and Cordoba, the strongholds of orthodox Peronism. The renovators are less labor-centered, less statist, more prone to make deals, less anti-military, and potentially lean towards a plebiscitarian relation with the masses. As the governor of a relatively small, poor, province—La Rioja—Carlos Menem gave some indication of his abrasive style, aggressive deal-making ability, and a manipulator of factionalism in the Peronist Party.[45] He won the nomination by 53 to 47 percent over a more popular candidate—A. Cafiero of Buenos Aires—because he moved to make deals with several factions of the labor movement. He won the 1989 Presidential election with 47 percent of the popular vote (310 electoral college votes) over the Radical Party candidate, C. Angeloz, who received 32.4 percent of the popular vote (211 electoral college votes). President Menem's new coalition is centered on economic conservatism, big domestic and foreign capital, free-market groups that favored government deregulation, and privatization of government-owned firms. Menemismo was turning traditional Peronism upside down. The surplus labor helped "Menemismo" as the president was able to split the working class between displaced workers and those afraid of being displaced.

The increasing provincialization of the Peronists, i.e., shift of party influence from Buenos Aires to the provinces, contributed to the disassembling and allowed Mr. Menem to reassemble the party leaders. He established a direct dialogue with Peronist voters, and in many ways he marginalized the party as an instrument of governing. The changes in Peronism were evident also in the occupation of Peronist deputies elected in 1989: lawyers and liberal professions declined from 48 percent (1963) to 28 percent, and 23 to 15 percent respectively; employers and entrepreneurs increased 16 and 6 percent, while workers virtually disappeared from Peronist deputies (2 percent).[46] The declining approval rate of President Menem's policies (Table 11.2) did not help to stop the declining vote of the two major parties. The combined vote of Peronists and Radicals went from 86.6 percent (1983) to 79 percent (1989), and 66 percent (1995). The decline of the major parties is accompanied by the rise of new political forces such as the *Frente Grande* (FG), a break-away group of dissident Peronists, and MODIN (Movement for National Dignity) led by Colonel A. Rico. The *Frente Grande* polled 10 percent of the national vote (13 percent in Buenos Aires).

The reelection of President Menem (1995) was an unprecedented event in Argentina. For the first time in 70 years, three consecutive civilian presidents took office peacefully; it was only the second time since the second election of Juan Peron (1952) that an incumbent president had won a second term. In the absence of the electoral college, the election was based on the popular vote, which favored disassembling of existing parties and forced the reassembling of three large blocks: the radical bloc whose candidate was Horacio Massaccesi, Menem's Peronist Movement, and a new political actor, FREPASO, led by Peronist Senator José O. Bordon, who assembled dissident Peronists, Christian Democrats, Social-Democrats, dissident Radicals and Marxist independents.

The Radical candidate was doomed because of his association with Mr. Alfonsin who negotiated the unpopular *Pacto de Olives*. Senator Bordon's campaign was centered on the premise that President Menem's economic program was too extreme and destroyed the main ideals of Christian and Peronist social values. Senator Bordon's FREPASO was not well-organized outside the metropolitan area of Buenos Aires and a few other cities. He established himself as the only candidate who could deny President Menem the required 10 percent margin of victory and force a run-off election. One week before the election Menem was ahead by only 9 percent (43 to 34 percent), and he urged Radical voters to cast their ballot for the Radical Party candidate in order to preserve Argentina's traditional two-party system.[47]

Senator Bordon was not able to overcome the widespread belief of many voters that continuity and incumbency were the acceptable, safe course for political stability. The business community, the upper middle class, and Conservative groups shared that same belief. Senator Bordon carried Buenos Aires (44 to 41 percent), but secured in the upper–30 percent only in the provinces of Santa Fé, Mendoza, Corrientes, and San Juan.[48] President Menem's slight plurality was a bit larger than his victory in 1989, as he lost only Buenos Aires but secured 50 percent of the vote in 17 of 23 provinces. He never trailed in the polls and his message was "stay the course" on economic policies, but he paid more attention to social concerns in the second administration. He convinced the middle class and workers that the end of statism and national reconciliation would be the best safeguards against the two traditional enemies of economic growth and democracy—excessive reliance on government and attempts to delegitimize and demobilize the Peronist Movement—that would trigger military interventions. Moreover, he presented himself as the guarantor of a stable transition for both, while promising job creation and some further investigations in the "dirty war."

Revelations of the macabre killing of political opponents during the military dictatorship by an ex–navy captain, A. Scilingo, embarrassed the Menem administration and reopened unwelcome wounds. Mr. Scilingo admitted that a number of people were thrown alive into the ocean from helicopters.[49] The military, which had enforced a total silence ban over the "dirty war," now began to break ranks, with even the chief of staff, General

M. Bolza, criticizing the methods used during the "dirty war." These revelations and the ensuing debate however, did not greatly affect President Menem's reelection campaign, which enjoyed a huge advantage in organization and public resources. Menem announced several public works projects a few weeks before the election and showed more sympathy for the hardships caused by his economic policies. Many undecided voters (28 percent a week before the elections) voted for Mr. Menem, while the widespread split-ticket voting indicated that Mr. Menem was more popular than his own party because the president out-polled the Peronist candidate in the lower house and gubernatorial candidates (Table 11.4). The president's popularity in fact, captured 9 of 14 governorships and a comfortable majority in the house.

B. Brazil

The 1989 election of F. Collor de Mello in Brazil bears some resemblance to the first election of Menem of Argentina. Both started as governors of small, relatively poor states. Collor de Mello was from Alagoas in northeast Brazil where his family wealth and political connections helped him create a new party, the PRN (National Renewal Party), composed of groups that favored the free market, government efficiency, privatization of state-owned firms, and an end to corruption.[50] Collor de Mello also took advantage of a weak national party system, more prone to disassembling than that of Argentina because oligarchic factions are often run by family clans entrenched in regional political strongholds (*filhotismo*), with weak party discipline, ideological inconsistency, and frequent party switching. The two-round presidential election favors the reassembling process: Collor de Mello received only 28.5 percent of the popular vote in the first round, against 16 percent for Iñacio "Lula" de Silva, the founder of the Workers Party (PT), by 53 to 46.9 percent. The President's party elected only 24 deputies, against 200 for the PDS, and 234 for the PMDB. When soon afterwards, Collor de Mello was indicted for financial scandals, his administration went into decline until his impeachment in 1992. Thereafter, his successor, Itamor Franco, began to make deals that kept statism alive and left the country in a state of "hyperactive paralysis."[51]

The presidential and congressional elections in 1994 tended to confirm the disassembling-reassembling nature of Brazilian electoral politics. The Workers Party (PT) candidate was again Lula, who tried to assemble the Left-Progressive political groups from the many existing parties. Lula's opponent was Henrique Cardoso, one of the founders of the recently created PSDB. He is a distinguished sociologist and was the Minister of Treasury in Franco's administration and author of the *Real-Plan* (the eighth economic plan in eight years), designed to fight triple-digit inflation and to tie the currency to the U.S. dollar (R$1 = 0.850 US$). Cardoso was the representative of moderate political forces and the business community. The slow decline of inflation and the backing of many factions within the three major parties (PMDB, PDS, and PFL) propelled him to the lead in pre-election polls (38 percent to 42 percent versus 22 to 26 percent for Lula).[52] He won in the first round with 54.5 percent (he needed only 43 percent in a field of six candidates) against a very disappointing 27 percent for Lula. The candidate of the Workers Party won only in Brasilia and six state capital cities, while Cardoso carried the industrial south and southeast by large margins.

Cardoso won with a message of moderate change. He advocated constitutional reforms in order to change the role of the state in the divisive issues of privatization, state pensions, taxation, and responsibilities of government at all levels. He has often written that Brazil is an "unjust nation." Cardoso draws a difference between an authoritarian state and a strong state that is competent to protect the public interest.

The results of the congressional election will provide a challenge, if not an obstacle, to Cardoso's governance. His political party won only 62 deputies and 8 senators (Table 11.5). According to a study of the new congress, Cardoso can count on 334 deputies (66 percent of the house) and 54 senators (63 percent of the Senate) "depending on the issue."[53] The ideological composition of the Congress tends to be Center-Left (53 to 47 percent), while a majority of people in one poll (59 percent) perceived him to be "Center-Right/Right."[54] Since Brazilian political parties are a motley crew of factions tied by personal loyalty and characterized by the ritual of *"Troca-Troca"* (switching parties), the president will have advantages and disadvantages. He needs a three-fifths majority in both houses (about 306 in the House and 48 in the Senate) to get major reforms to change some provisions of the 1988 constitution that protect many special categories of people.

The new Brazilian congress is also a mixture of old and new politicians. Some of the incumbents come from the ranks of "traditional" career-politicians (271 deputies and 46 senators) and are former governors, senators, and local office-holders. There are 53 percent freshmen deputies and 60 percent freshmen senators, many of whom are supportive of change. Women constitute 6 percent of the House (34 deputies) and 6 percent of the Senate (5 members).

The Congress elected two experienced politicians tied to the authoritarian past—J. Sarney (PMDB) as president of the Senate and L. E. Magalhaes (PFL) as president of the house. Cardoso also lost when the President's party (PSDB) was excluded from the major congressional committees which will consider constitutional reforms. Senate President Sarney is not fond of many of the constitutional reforms, and he has complained that the repeated use of presidential decrees (1000 so far) weakens the prerogatives of Congress.[55]

President Cardoso has scored well on a few important issues. He broke a month-long strike by the powerful labor unions of *Petrobras*—the government-owned petrochemical company—which caused a $750 million loss and public hardship. The opposition of workers and other groups to a constitutional amendment to end government monopoly over refinery, exploration, marketing, and private investment in the oil industry failed, and congress approved the amendment (357 to 136 in the house). The president also won on a less controversial constitutional amendment to end the government monopoly over the vast industry of telecommunications (348 to 140 in the house). The congressional votes so far indicate that President Cardoso is forging a coalition majority in the Brazilian Congress and is building a "presidential party" among public opinion makers. A recent poll revealed that 51 percent support a constitutional change to allow Cardoso to run for reelection in 1998, a "Menem-type" solution in Argentina.[56] The House chairman, Luise Magalhaes (PFL), has not opposed the amendment approved by a house committee.[57]

The two presidents face similar issues, but also differences. Administrative reforms to reduce the number of public employees and control the deficit of the government at all levels are key issues in both countries. The state governments have a deficit of over $1 billion, while that of the municipalities is over $11 billion. Constitutional barriers and political parties are big hurdles for the two presidents. In both countries, but especially in Brazil, parties are led by strong local notables who are protective of patronage and public jobs. The reforming of public pensions is also a common problem, and the two presidents are asking their respective legislative branches to give them "extraordinary" powers to deal with the reforms. President Menem has been more decisive and has issued "emergency decrees" for 18 months to restructure the public administration, privatize additional public enterprises, and restructure the budgetary procedures.[58]

Brazil also faces a severe crime problem in big cities, especially in Rio de Janeiro, and 70 percent of the people blame the government, while Argentina has to be concerned with political violence. Brazil also has an agrarian problem in the form of land seizures in Ceará, Paraná, and Rio Grande do Sul, with violent confrontations between rural families and the police. President Cardoso has asked the Brazilian congress for compensation of 100,000 acres of land to be distributed in 11 states. Argentina, on the other hand, has experienced more unemployment and lower economic growth than Brazil, where inflation tends to be more problematic than in Argentina (51 percent of people expected inflation to increase in 1996).[59] Both societies have severe social dislocations and social conflicts, but neither country tends to have ethnic, religious, or separatist cleavages that could make the consolidation of democracy more difficult.

The political system that is emerging, however, may not fit the liberal, representative, democratic model, but rather a new type called "delegative democracy."[60] In both countries, democracy is not consolidated or "institutionalized" in a set of popular, civic institutions that allow participatory mechanisms in government decisions after the electoral procedure. Presidents like Menem and Cardoso are elected "for a chance to rule virtually free of all constraints . . . [and] voters/delegates are expected to become a passive but cheering audience of what the president does." The factors that make possible this type of democracy are the propensity of Presidents to ask and receive from legislative branches "extraordinary powers" and the support of "electorally weighty segments of population," which regard as successful the government policies.[61] The failure to organize countervailing power and the passage of policies without serious debates carries a real danger in post-authoritarian politics, especially in countries where a strong presidentialism and a weak democratic tradition have contributed very often to the rise of authoritarian solutions. Consolidation is a learning process that requires time and an environment of negotiated stability, both in short supply in Argentina and Brazil where the peoples' problems are not merely political.

The reelection of Fernando H. Cardoso in 1998 was not unexpected after his presidential party anchored on a Center-Right coalition composed of the PFL, PMDB and PSDB amended the Brazilian Constitution to allow him to run a second term. President Cardoso barely escaped a second round of elections by receiving 51 percent of the votes, while the Left-oriented voters split between Luiz Iñacio "Lula" da Silva of the PT with 31 percent and a Social Democratic candidate Ciro Gomes, who polled 11 percent. Cardoso's campaign, centered on the promise of "four more years of economic development for all," did not energize Brazilian voters who were more interested in effective crisis-management than moved by deep-seated ideological values. The president's coalition has a majority in both houses of Congress and the election of Governor Mario Covas in São Paulo will help Cardoso to forge a governing coalition necessary for crucial reforms of local government finances, constitutional reforms on retirement, entitlements, the strengthening of human rights, and the construction of a fair society. But the president faces severe obstacles in his effort to build a cohesive, enduring, and dominant political movement capable of supporting austerity measures that will hurt the lower middle classes and lower classes. The victory of opposition candidates in the important states of Rio de Janeiro, Minas Gerais, and Rio

Grande do Sul, where governors tend to become rivals of the president will test the ability of Cardoso to convince people that his national vision is more viable than that of a faction-ridden, disassembled party system. The reelection of the presidents in Argentina and Brazil does not seem to open the way to a dominant political party as envisioned by T.J. Pempel's *Uncommon Democracy*. The two historic events tend to fit the typology of G. O'Donnell's *Delegative Democracy*, and the personalization of decision-making.

VI. Conclusion

The process of learning how to do politics in a democratic way requires political leaders to overcome the fear of impending Caesaristic solutions and to resist the temptation to use all government institutions for denying power to political opponents. Democracy in both countries faces the challenge of recruiting leaders with three key characteristics: the virtue to separate the public from private affairs, the fortitude to accept defeat, and the wisdom to oppose for the sake of finding better solutions to the problems of governing. Political leaders in both countries have not scored well on these components. Presidents Menem and Cardoso are being presented as the "new leaders" in the age of democracy. They bring a set of experiences to public life that makes them open to the inherent values of a truly republican democracy. Both presidents have had the opportunity to learn the differences between democracy and authoritarianism. Both opposed authoritarianism in different ways, and both approach the management of democracy differently. President Menem operates in a political environment where politics is often played as a histrionic game with tragic outcomes, while in Brazil political leaders learn how to make deals behind the scene in smoke-filled rooms. President Menem is flamboyant, arrogant, and at ease with the 'rich and famous' as well as the forgotten poor. President Cardoso is reserved, intellectually detached, and an acute diagnostician of the Brazilian road to democracy. President Menem demands personal loyalty and loves to exercise power, as he demonstrated in 1991 when he became president of the party. Menem comes from the world of business, and politics are natural to him, while Brazil's president comes from the world of academia and he likes to delegate power and to move adroitly in the complex world of Brazilian factional politics. He does not have a loyal cadre of followers and does not demand absolute loyalty.

The political leaders in charge of reinventing democracy in Argentina and Brazil have been spared so far the trauma of post-Communism experienced in Eastern Europe and Russia. The two countries do not exhibit elements of national disintegration. There are no ethnic, religious, and territorial cleavages that either threaten the viability and integrity of the nation-state or present political leaders with unmanageable, unpleasant alternatives. Social unrest and class tensions reflect the reordering of public priorities and the conflict between state and régime, where the civil society is trying to find new space for democratic action. guerrilla movements do not constitute a threat nor do they provide viable answers to the problems of social justice, poverty, and human rights in either country. Democracy in both countries faces the challenge of redefining citizenship on the premise of free, civic participation. In the past, Argentina and Brazil tolerated government-protected terrorism, lack of public accountability, and defiance of the rule of law. The new constitutions of both countries have taken up the challenge by instituting a system of civil rights guarantees unprecedented in the history of both countries. Civic organizations are freely monitoring the activities of public authority, and the judicial system is enforcing more accountability in both countries. New political actors are emerging in a variety of ways. Lay Catholic groups, feminist organizations, investigative commissions for human rights' violations and neighboring communities are creating new channels of political demands instrumental in the rise of the Brazilian Workers Party and the FREPASO movement in Argentina.

Both presidents are interpreting democracy in different ways. Menem is recasting Peronism as a neo-Liberal movement where respect for the market must be accompanied by opening channels of democracy. The temptation of Peronist populism is evident at times, not so much in the reluctance to compromise, but in the desire to carve a dominant position for the "president's party" and by treating political opponents as enemies. President Cardoso of Brazil operates in a gradualist setting of oligarchic party structures and solutions managed by élitist groups, which includes the military. Argentina is moving more rapidly towards a free-market model than Brazil where some statist policies are not unpopular among many segments of the public opinion. Cardoso's style is less personalistic, and he has less political experience than Menem. Menem's reelection was historic, but his party leadership has been severely tested at the most recent polls. Cardoso's weakness is the lack of public support and of a strong "presidential" party to carry his policies through the Brazilian congress. He can turn his weakness into strength by reassembling the various factions of the Brazilian parties in a bloc to sustain democracy and policies for a more just society. Menem turned his popular strength into weakness for democracy, overestimating the wisdom and popularity of his changes, and misjudged the degree of tolerance for economic hardship in the society, which has had a history of economic success and egalitarianism. Thus, in the October 1999 elections, Argentina repudiated Menem by voting in Fernando de la Ruá, the Radical candidate.

Table 11.1 Political Attitudes in Four Countries (1988) in Percentages

Question	Brazil	Argentina	Chile	Uruguay
People cannot vote wisely (Agree)	68.0	48.0	29.0	59.0
Communist Party should be outlawed (Agree)	36.0	19.0	49.0	17.0
It would be better if the military came back to govern (Agree)	40.0	15.0	—	6.0
The best politcal system is based on elections (Agree)	80.0	86.0	82.0	81.0

Source: Bolivar Lamounier & Amaury De Souza, "Changing Attitudes toward Democracy and Institusional Reform in Brazil," in Larry Diamond, *Political Culture and Democracy in Developing Countries* (Boulder, CO: L. Rienner, 1993), p. 304.

Table 11.2 Public Reactions to President Menem's Policies (September 1994) in Percentages.

Policy	Good	O.K.	Bad	D.K.
Economic Plan	36.0	32.5	28.3	3.2
Privatization	29.3	24.9	40.5	5.3
Economic Growth	23.2	34.3	37.9	4.6
Foriegn Policy	26.0	22.7	27.5	23.8
Improving Haelth	14.8	29.4	53.6	9.0
Fighting Corruption	10.1	17.4	68.3	4.2
Improving Education	9.8	24.3	64.1	1.8
Improving Justice	6.9	15.9	76.5	0.7

Source: The Economist (26 November 1994): p. 14.

Table 11.3 1995 Presidential Election in Argentina

Political Party Canidate	National Percentage
Carlos Menem (*Partido Justicialista*)	49.0
José O. Bordon (*FREPASO*—Front of Argentine Solidarity)	29.0
Horacio Massaccesi (UCR—*Union Civica Radical*)	17.0
Colonel A. Rico (Movement of National Dignity)	1.8
Other	2.2
	100.0

Source: La Nacion (Buenos Aires, 15 May 1995).

Table 11.4 1995 Argentine Election for the Lower House

Political Party	Vote in Percentages	Number of Seats 1995	1993 House
Peronist	23	137	125
U.C.R.	20	69	83
Frepaso	35	26	13
Other	22	25	25
Total		257	257

Source: La Nacion (Buenos Aires, 15 May 1995); *Keesing's Record of World Events*, vol. 41, no. 5 (27 June 1995).

Table 11.5 The Federal Congress of Brazil Elected in 1994.

Party	Number of Seats in the Senate (81)	Number of Seats in the House (513)
PMBD	23	107
PFL	17	90
PSDB	9	62
PPR	8	52
PDT	6	33
PTB	5	30
PP	5	35
PT	5	50
PSB	1	16
PPS	1	2
PCB	—	10
PMN	—	4
PSC	—	2
PL	1	—

Source: Journal do Brazil (16 October 1994). In 1994, 17 political parties gained representation in the Federal Congress (nine less than in 1980). Five poltical parties are dominant PMDB (The ex-Brazilian Democratic movement which eventually became the key opposition to the continuation of authoritarianism; the PFL recently formed out of splits in the PSD and conservatives that supported the previous régime; PSDB, the Social Democratic Party of Brazil, began to fragmentize as authoritarianism paved the way to redemocratization. It was the main pro-auhtoritarian party now in search of a new role; th PT (Worker's Party) formed circa 1979 in order to create a non-Communist, European-type labor movement; the PPR formed in the late-1980's to help the candidacy of impeached President F. Collor De Mello. The Left is fragmented into five parties, including the Communist Party of Brazil; the Center also claims five political parties, and the middle at least three parties; also the conservative Right can rely on three parties.

Table 11.6 Congressmen's Attitudes towards Constitutional Amendent Issues

Government should end state monoploy over:	Congressmen's Agreement
Oil	58%
Telecommunication	78%
Energy	84%
Easing Restrictions on Foriegn Companies	70%
Revise Constitution to Allow Independence of Central Bank	69%
Reduce Federal Taxes	86%
Abolish Life-time Job Provisions for Public Employees	51%

Source: *O Estado de São Paulo* (6 March 1995).

Notes

1. Guillermo O'Donnell & Philippe Schmitter, *Transitions From Authoritarian Rule* (Baltimore, MD: Johns Hopkins Press, 1986); Samuel Huntington, "How Countries Democratize," in *Political Science Quarterly,* vol.106, no.4 (1991–92).
2. Huntington, "How Countries Democratize," p. 580.
3. D. Ethier, ed., *Democratic Transition and Consolidation in Southern Europe, Latin America and South-East Asia* (London: McMillan, 1990); Carlos H. Waisman, *Reversal of Development in Argentina* (Princeton: Princeton University Press, 1987).
4. Waisman, *Reversal of Development in Argentina,* Ch. 6.
5. Frances Hagopian, "Brazil," in G. Almond & G. Bingham Powell, eds., *Comparative Politics Today* (New York: Harper Collins, 1996), p. 566.
6. Carlos H. Waisman, "Argentina: Autarkic Industrialization and Illegitimacy," in Larry Diamond, Juan Linz & S.M. Lipset, eds., *Democracy in Developing Countries: Latin America* (Boulder, CO: L. Rienner, 1989), p.59–104.
7. Peter G. Snow & Luigi Manzetti, *Political Forces in Argentina* (New York: Praeger, 1993); Frederick C. Turner, "Reassessing Political Culture," in Peter H. Smith, ed., *Latin America in Comparative Perspectives* (Boulder, CO: Westview Press, 1995), p. 210–213; Edgardo Catterberg, "Attitudes towards Democracy in Argentina during the Transition Period," in *International Journal of Public Opinion Research,* vol. 2, no. 2 (1990): p.155–167.
8. T. J. Pempel, ed., *Uncommon Democracies: The One-Party Dominant Regimes* (Ithaca, NY: Cornell University Press, 1990), especially the Introduction.
9. Ruth Berins Collier & David Collier, *Shaping the Political Arena* (Princeton: Princeton University Press, 1991); Torcuato Di Tella, "The Popular Parties: Brazil and Argentina in Latin American Perspective," in Jorge I. Dominguez, ed., *Essays on Mexico, Central America,* vol. 2 (New York: Garland, 1994); Scott Mainwaring, "Political Parties and Democratization in Brazil and the South-

ern Cone," in Jorge I. Dominguez, ed., *Parties, Elections and Political Participation in Latin America,* vol. 5 (New York: Garland, 1994).

10. Lawrence S. Graham, *The State and Policy Outcomes in Latin America* (New York: Praeger, 1990).

11. *The Economist* (26 January 1980).

12. Kenneth A. Bollen, "Comparative Measurements of Political Democracy," in *American Sociological Review,* vol.45, no.3 (June 1980); David Beetham, ed., *Defining and Measuring Democracy* (London: Sage, 1994), p.370–390; Gary Marks & Larry Diamond, eds., *Reexamining Democracy* (London: Sage, 1992).

13. James G. March & Johan P. Olsen, *Democratic Governance* (New York: Free Press, 1995).

14. Peter Hakim & Abraham Lowenthal, "Democracy on Trial: Politics in Latin America," in *Current History* (February 1992): p. 28–35; Guillermo O'Donnell, "Delegative Democracy," p. 55–67, and Bolivar Lamounier, "Brazil at an Impasse," p. 72–87, both in *Journal of Democracy,* vol.5, no.1 (January 1994).

15. Atilio Boron, *State, Capitalism and Democracy in Latin America* (Boulder, CO: L. Rienner, 1995).

16. Diamond, Linz & Lipset, eds., *Democracy in Developing Countries: Latin America,* p. 40.

17. *World Development Report for 1994* (World Bank: Oxford University Press, 1994).

18. Theda Skocpol, "Bringing the State Back In," in *Items,* vol.36, no.1–2 (June 1982): p.1–8; Waisman, *Reversal of Development in Argentina;* Lawrence Graham & H. Robert Wilson, eds., *The Political Economies of Brazil* (Austin: University of Texas Press, 1990).

19. *Excelsior* (Mexico City, 23 May 1995).

20. *Excelsior* (15 July 1995).

21. *The Economist* (26 November 1994).

22. Lawrence Graham, *The State and Policy Outcomes in Latin America* (New York: Praeger 1990).

23. *Excelsior* (5 August 1995).

24. *Excelsior* (24 October 1994).

25. Graham & Wilson, eds., *Political Economies of Brazil,* p. 33.

26. V. Faria & Castro H. Guimaraes, "Social Policy and Democratic Consolidation in Brazil," in Graham & Wilson, eds., *Political Economies of Brazil,* p.125–128.

27. Hagopian, "Brazil," p. 601.

28. *Excelsior* (28 October 1994).

29. March & Olsen, *Democratic Governance,* p. 2.

30. Philippe Schmitter, "Transitology: the Science of Democratization," in Joseph Tulchin, ed., *The Consolidation of Democracy in Latin America* (Boulder, CO: L. Rienner, 1995), p. 13.

31. March & Olsen, *Democratic Governance,* p. 13.

32. Philippe Schmitter, "Interest Systems and the Consolidation of Democracies," in Marks & Diamond, eds., *Reexamining Democracy,* p. 158.

33. Hagopian, "Brazil," p. 571.
34. Lamounier, "Brazil at an impasse," p. 82.
35. Catterberg, "Attitudes towards Democracy in Argentina during the Transition Period," p.164.
36. Frederick Turner, "Reassessing Political Culture," in Peter Smith, ed., *Latin America in Comparative Perspective* (Boulder, CO: Westview Press, 1995), p. 214.
37. *Excelsior* (29 August 1995).
38. *Datafolha,* poll as published in *Excelsior* (2 April 1995).
39. Juan Linz & Arturo Valenzuela, eds., *The Failure of Presidential Democracy, Comparative Perspectives* (Baltimore, MD: Johns Hopkins Press, 1994).
40. Snow & Manzetti, *Political Forces in Argentina,* p. 83; David Fleischer, "The Constituent Assembly and the Transformation Strategy: Attempts to Shift Political Power in Brazil from the Presidency to Congress," in Graham & Wilson, eds., *The Political Economies of Brazil,* p. 224–230.
41. *Keesing's Record of World Events,* vol. 39, no.11 (11 November 1993): p. 39734.
42. Hagopian, "Brazil," p. 588.
43. Schmitter, "Transitology," p. 12.
44. James W. McGuire, "Political Parties and Democracy in Argentina," in Scott Mainwaring & Timothy R. Scully, eds. *Building Democratic Institutions: Party Systems in Latin America* (Stanford: Stanford University Press, 1995); "Brazil: Weak Parties and Feckless Democracy," Ch.11; Frances Hagopian, "The Compromised Consolidation: the Political Class in the Brazilian Transition," in Scott Mainwaring, Guillermo O'Donnell & J. Samuel Valenzuela, eds., *Issues in Democratic Consolidation: the New South America Democracies in Comparative Perspective* (Notre Dame: University of Notre Dame, 1992); O'Donnell, "Transitions, Continuities and Paradoxes."
45. Karen Remmer, "The Political Impact of Economic Crisis in Latin America in the 1990s," *The American Political Science Review,* no. 85 (September 1991): p. 777–799.
46. Snow & Manzetti, *Political Forces in Argentina,* p. 62–68.
47. Ibid., p. 74–75.
48. *Excelsior* (9 May 1995).
49. *La Nacion* (Buenos Aires, 15 May 1995).
50. *Le Monde* (Paris, 8 March 1995).
51. Hagopian, "The Compromised Consolidation in the Brazilian Transition," p. 265–270.
52. Lamounier, "Brazil at an impasse," p. 75.
53. The polling data are from *Excelsior* (May-October 1994).
54. *Jornal do Brasil* (11 October 1994).
55. *Excelsior* (28August 1995).
56. *O Globo* (5 March 1995).
57. *Excelsior* (28 August 1995).
58. *Folha de São Paulo* (23 October 1995).
59. *Excelsior* (19 November 1995).

60. Guillermo O'Donnell, "Delegative Democracy," in *Journal of Democracy*, vol.5, no.1 (January 1994): p.55–69.
61. *Excelsior* (25 November 1995).

Appendix 11.1 The Economy of Argentina and Brazil

		Argentina	Brazil
Selective Indicators			
Population (1992: millions)		33	154
GDP (Million $)	1970	30,660	35,546
	1992	228,779	360,405
Distribution of GDP (%)			
Agriculture	1970	10	12
	1992	6	11
Industry	1970	44	38
	1992	31	37
Manufacturing	1970	32	29
	1992	22	25
Services	1970	47	49
	1992	63	52

Source: World Development Report 1994 (World Bank: Oxford University Press, 1994), p. 167.

Appendix 11.2 Levels of Social Development

	Argentina	Brazil
Selective Indicators		
GNP Per Capita (1992: Dollars)	6,050	2,770
Adult Illiteracy	5%	9%
Infant Mortality Rate	29%	57%
Urban Population (1992: Percentages)	87%	77%
Households with Electricity (% of Total: 1984)	87%	79%

Source: World Development Report 1994, p. 163, 215–225.

TWELVE

The Political Party System of India: From One-Party Dominance to No-Party Dominance

Renu Khator

I. Democracy and Party Dominance in India

The Indian party system is one of the most paradoxical systems in the world. As a system, it is rigid enough to withstand continuous defections and yet fluid enough to absorb new alliances; inclusive enough to accommodate the immense diversity and yet exclusive enough to be controlled by one family; mature enough to allow peaceful turnovers and yet inapt enough to arouse spontaneous violence; and, finally, old enough to become "one of the world's oldest" and yet youthful enough to produce new parties overnight. Its ever-evolving character, with strong qualities of adaptation and resilience, defies the conventional wisdom on political parties.

Needless to say, the paradoxical party system is the result of several underlying tendencies. First, the unique texture of the Indian political fiber itself necessitates the existence of a complex party system. India is a federal state with a powerful parliament at the national level and a strong *panchayati raj* at the local level. Social identities based on caste, class, religion, region, ethnicity, language, and gender constantly overlap and undercut each other in the political arena, giving rise to new political alliances and fresh socio-political conflicts. There are 25 linguistically distinct states that generally harbor an anti-center sentiment; 82 percent of the population practices Hinduism, although Muslims, who comprise only 11 percent, still constitute the world's third largest Muslim population. Women occupy only 7 percent of the national and state government seats, although they are now legally entitled to occupy 33 percent of all local government seats. Even though only 50 percent of the adult population is literate, approximately two-thirds of them turn out to vote. In this context, political parties have become the primary medium through which social and political interactions get expressed and managed. The impressive scope of political participation guarantees a central place for political parties. It is important to note that social diversity has not led to political instability, for India has held only 11 parliamentary elections in its 50 years of history, giving an average of 4.5 years to a parliamentary life span (the perfect term would be 5 years).

The Indian party system consists of one historically dominant party (Indian National Congress), less than half a dozen national opposition parties[1] (Communist Party of India and Communist Party of Marxists, *Bhartiya Janata* Party or *Jana Sangh*), several national alternatives (National Front, *Janata* Party),[2] and over two dozen regional and state parties. Ranging from the extreme Right (*Bhartiya Janata* Party) to the extreme Left (Communist Party of India), they offer a real ideological choice to the nation's 400 million plus voters. Their platforms also vary from religious issues to linguistic agendas to economic platforms.

Born in 1885 with the creation of the Indian National Congress, the Indian party system has evolved through a multitude of stages. From 1885 to 1947, it existed in the form of a movement, with the Indian National Congress forming the core and the Indian Muslim League and two Communist parties constituting the periphery. Prior to 1947,[3] the party system did not have the need to connect to the people and create a popular agenda because electoral prizes, even though in existence since the first popularly held elections in 1935, were insignificant. However, the Congress Party underwent a massive transformation from being an élitist movement to a true grass-roots political party during the first 20 years (1947–67) following national independence. Under Jawaharlal Nehru's premiership, the Indian National Congress expanded its sphere of influence and introduced the concept of formal membership and group representation. No other viable parties were on the horizon, as most were either starved to death or reduced to a dismal existence by the Congress. Rajni Kothari described the early years of the Indian party system as the "Congress System."[4]

A significant change in the party system came in 1967 when the Indian National Congress faced its first serious electoral challenge from a coalition called *Samyukta Vidhayak Dal* who succeeded in winning half of the states in state assembly elections. This public humiliation for the Indian National Congress was followed by another wave of local electoral defeats in 1968.

Unable to cope with public opposition and internal squabbling following Nehru's death, the Indian National Congress finally split in 1969, thus ending the aura of immortality.

The period of 80 years beginning in 1969 was a transitional period for the Indian party system. In 1971, the Indian National Congress (functioning under the leadership of Indira Gandhi) regained its claim over the "Congress" name, however the party's image as "the party above politics" was already lost. Indira Gandhi tried to connect to the voters by offering populist programs, but in 1974 she herself was charged for engaging in illegal electoral practices. Gandhi responded by tightening her grip on the party and declaring a national emergency.[5] A second wave of internal squabbling and mass defections followed the emergency. For the first time after the 1977 elections, the Indian National Congress (I)[6] failed to form a national government. Thus began the era of coalition politics, which lasted for the next two decade.

The Indian party system turned over a new leaf in 1996 when 590 million voters went to the polls to select 535 parliamentarians from a field of 14,000 candidates offering more than 30 party platforms. In some districts, the number of candidates vying for one single seat was as high as 90. The candidate to seat ratio of 26:1 was one of the highest in the world. The results of the elections were as astonishing as the exercise itself: the Indian National Congress (I) secured only one-fourth of the parliamentary seats, the lowest level of seats ever. Not only did it fail to become the winner, but it also failed to become the runner-up, if electoral alliances are taken into consideration. Furthermore, for the first time the Congress Party was defeated by a single political party (BJP), not a political alliance (as observed in 1977, 1989, and 1991).[7]

As India celebrates the 50th anniversary of its independence, it can boast of a functionally sound and adaptable party system. The form and shape of the party system—multi-party or single-party or single-party dominance—are not of as much interest to comparativists as the party-system's evolution and adaptability. According to T. J. Pempel, one-party dominance or lack thereof in a system is reflective of its social, political, economic, and historical development.[8] While Pempel does not arrive at this conclusion directly, he offers four conditions that make single-party dominance likely or unlikely in a political system. Pempel stresses that his "virtuous cycle of dominance theory," or single-party dominance, is unlikely in societies that are: (a) socially dynamic; (b) economically industrialized; (c) politically democratic; (d) historically free of colonial experiences.[9] Pempel's analysis suggests that development can be measured on a new continuum, ranging from single-party dominance to multi-party dominance where single-party dominance would indicate the presence of social stagnation, political oligarchy, economic non-industrialization, and historical oppression, whereas the absence of single-party dominance would suggest the presence of social dynamism, political democratization, economic industrialization, and freedom from a colonial past.

Admittedly, Pempel identifies several outliers, including Japan, Sweden, Israel, and Italy, where single parties have existed, or continue to exist in socially dynamic, politically democratic, or economically industrialized societies. However, these cases, argues Pempel, involve "a serendipitous congruence of effort and luck [and] interplay of highly idiosyncratic factors different from those in others."[10] The only factor common in these cases is that for one reason or another, the parties there were able to establish a virtuous cycle of dominance. The cycle of dominance refers to the situation where causes and consequences reinforce each other and where each successive victory provides increased chances of dominance and each increased chance of dominance provides a new opportunity to put in place policies that further facilitate dominance.

This study of the Indian party system relies on the above thesis, but takes a reverse approach to testing it. The central question being raised here is not "why do some industrialized countries have a single-party-dominant political system?" But "why do some non-industrialized countries do not have a single-party-dominant system?" A more specific question in the context of the Indian political system is "under what conditions does a party system change from single-party dominance to no-party dominance?" A closer look at the Indian party system proves that simplistic models, such as developed by Pempel, fail to capture the complexity of inter-group and intra-group interactions in a culturally rich society like India. It further proves that a single-party system can be as dynamic and democratic as a multi-party system and that party systems change not because of, but in spite of, other ongoing social, economic, and political changes.

Following Pempel's line of reasoning, I offer four hypotheses, which must prove to be true in order for us to accept Pempel's proposed linkage between party system and its larger social, political, economic, and historical context:

Hypothesis 1: *India harbored a single-party-dominant system in the past.*
Hypothesis 2: *India no longer has a single-party-dominant system.*
Hypothesis 3: *Given that Hypotheses 1 and 2 hold true, the transition from the single-party- dominant system to the no-party-dominant system is the result of: (a) social dynamism, (b) economic "industrialization," (c) political competition and the weakening of historical experiences.*
Hypothesis 4: *The transition in Hypothesis 3 provides a greater degree of democratization.*

II. A Numeric Profile of the Party System

Capturing the evolution of parties in India is like constructing a family tree. Each part has its own defining characteristics—just enough to make it a distinguishable entity and yet not enough to separate it from the rest. Parties in India form, merge, and split with amazing regularity. Most sound similar in name and platforms. There are several Congress, Socialist, and *janata* parties. Among the best known-national names in the party system are:

Bhartiya Jan Sangh	*Jan Morcha*
Bhartiya Janata Party (BJP)	*Janata* Party
Bhartiya Lok Dal (BLD)	*Janata* Party (Secular)
Communist Party of India (CPI)	*Kisan Mazdoor Praja* Party (KMPP)
Communist Party of Marxists (CPM)	*Lok Dal* (B)
Dalit Mazdoor Kisan Party	National Front
Indian National Congress	*Praja* Socialist Party
Indian National Congress (Organization)	*Samajwadi Janata* Party
Indian National Congress (Indira)	*Samyukta* Socialist Party
Indian National Congress (*Urs*)	Socialist Party
Indian National Congress (*Jagjivan Ram*)	*Swatantra* Party
Indian National Congress (Socialist)	United Front

In addition to the national parties, a large number of strong, electorally winnable, and governmentally viable regional and state parties also exist. These parties command a substantial support base, albeit their appeal is concentrated in small areas consisting of one of more states. Among the most successful regional parties are: DMK, *AIADMK, Akali Dal,* National Conference, *Telugu Desam, Asom Gana Parishad* and *Shiva Sena.* The regional parties not only play a dominating role at the state level, but also exert significant influence at the national level, especially when no single party is able to win a parliamentary majority. Table 12.1 summarizes party positions in 11 parliamentary elections.

Table 12.1 illustrates that the Indian National Congress enjoyed a position of uncontested supremacy in the first three parliamentary elections: 1952, 1957, and 1962. Even though it did not win a majority of the popular votes, it had a decisive majority of over 70 percent in terms of parliamentary seats. However, even in its heyday it was never able to win 50 percent of the popular votes.

Figure 12.1 analyzes the position of the Indian National Congress (I) and its nearest rival. The analysis suggests that in the past 50 years the Congress dominance has all but eroded. The Indian National Congress has now failed

Table 12.1 Percetage of Votes (and Seats) Won by Selected Political Parties

Election Year	Indian National Congress	Other versions of Congress	Bhartiya Janata Party (later BJP)	Communist Party of India	Communist Party-Marxist	Janta Dal
1952	45.0 (74.4)		3.1 (0.6)	3.3 (3.3)		
1957	47.8 (75.1)		5.9 (0.8)	8.9 (5.5)		
1962	44.7 (73.0)		6.4 (2.8)	9.9 (5.9)		
1967	40.8 (54.4)		9.4 (6.7)	5.0 (4.4)	4.4 (3.7)	
1971	43.7 (68.0)	10.4 (3.0)	7.4 (4.2)	4.7 (4.4)	5.1 (4.8)	
1977	34.5 (28.4)	1.7 (0.6)		2.8 (1.3)	4.3 (4.1)	
1980	42.7 (66.7)	5.3 (2.5)		2.6 (2.1)	6.1 (6.8)	
1984	48.1 (76.6)	1.6 (0.9)	7.4 (0.4)	2.7 (1.1)	5.7 (4.1)	
1989	39.5 (37.2)	0.3 (0.2)	11.4 (16.1)	2.6 (2.3)	6.5 (6.2)	17.8 (27.0)
1991	36.4 (44.5)	0.4 (0.2)	20.2 (23.3)	2.5 (2.7)	6.3 (6.9)	11.6 (11.0)
1996	28.1 (25.3)		23.5 (30.0)	(2.2)	(6.1)	(8.0)

to secure a majority in four of the most recent six elections. In the 1996 elections, it placed second as a single party and third as an electoral alliance. The Indian National Congress and its allies received only 139 of the 537 seats, while the *Bhartiya Janata* Party and its allies secured 194 seats and the Third Front (a conglomeration of 14 national and regional parties) received 179 seats. The 1996 elections were a landmark in the transformational journey of the Indian party-system, for they ended even the illusion of the Congress's dominance.[11] They marked the end of the Congress supremacy, both as an organization and as a political party.

The following are some observations from the 1996 elections: (1) For the first time, the Indian National Congress received less than 30 percent of the popular votes, a level considered critical for a party to claim dominant status. (2) For the first time, the Indian National Congress was defeated by another party, not an alliance, in getting the largest number of parliamentary seats. (3) The Bhartiya Janata Party, the nearest rival, gained an additional 44 seats without receiving any significant increase in popular votes. The Indian National Congress converted its 28 percent popular votes into 25 percent of seats, while BJP converted its 23 percent votes into 30 percent of seats. (4) The Indian National Congress (I) had double-digit losses in popular votes in all major states. (5) With the exception of the states of Andhra Pradesh, Himachal Pradesh, and Orissa, the Congress (I) did not finish at the top in any state having more than one parliamentary seat. (6) The Congress (I) lost its traditional "rainbow" votes: support waned among the young, the educated, Muslims, Hindus, and Dalits. Only the Christian minority remained compact behind the Congress (I). (7) Voters were polarized on caste, religion and education, as parties courted distinct groups. (8) The post-election politics suggests that the Congress (I) still plays a critical role at the bargaining table, nonetheless it is no longer the only game in town. Immediately following the elections, the BJP formed the shortest surviving government in the history of India.[12] At that point, the Congress (I) offered its support to the National Front-Left Front Alliance. Without the Congress's support, the new government could not have been formed.

Based on the above analysis, it is clear that no single party enjoys the status of a dominant party today. The numeric profile of the Indian party system supports Hypothesis 1, that the Indian National Congress Party held a dominant position in its early years. This dominance was visible both in absolute numbers and relative party strength. The 1977 elections, which gave the Indian National Congress (I) its first experience on the opposition bench, proved to be an exception rather than a rule, as the Congress (I) gained back its position in the 1980 elections.

Throughout the 1970s–80s, the challenge to the Congress (I) came from coalition parties, such as *Janata Dal* and *Janata* Party. However, since these

Figure 12.1 The Congress(I) and Its Rival

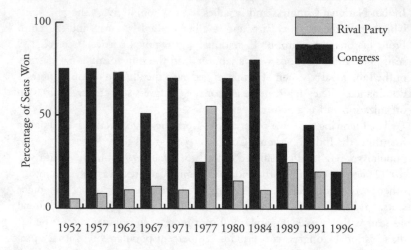

coalitions were electoral coalitions loosely put together to win elections, they did not form a formidable challenge to the Congress (I). In fact, history proves that even when in power, the coalitions were unable to make their niche in the political system. The Congress (I) continued to hold a strong bargaining position in the national political arena. It was only in the 1990s and with the emergence of the BJP—an ideologically based party—that the sharing of power among parties really began. The numerical profile of the Indian party system suggests that the system has gone through four distinct stages of development:

1947–1967: Single-Party-Dominant System, where the Congress dominated the political scene and other parties existed only on the periphery. The level of competition was low and no real internal or external challenge to the Congress Party was evident. The Congress was the party of consensus while opposition parties were the parties of pressure.

1967–1977: Sub-Party-Dominant System, where factions within the Congress Party dominated the political scene and served the functions typically performed by political parties in a multi-party system. The Congress Party split in 1969 leaving Congress (I) led by Indira Gandhi as its real successor in terms of public appeal and political clout. The level of competition was limited to the boundaries defined by the Congress Party. The Congress (I) Party was the only sustainable party and did not face any serious external threat at the polls.

1977–1996: Confederation Party System, where the Congress (I) faced real opposition and even lost control of the government. The opposition came from electoral alliances of several parties rather than any single party. Consequently, the Congress (I) succeeded in retaining its dominant position. While these alliances undermined the Congress supremacy, they themselves did not offer a viable electoral alternative to voters.

1996-beyond: No-Party-Dominant System, where no single party, including the Congress (I), can claim dominance based on either the number of votes or seats.

Thus, the numeric profile suggests that Hypotheses 2 and 3 are true and that the Indian party system has transformed from a single-party-dominant to a no-party-dominant system.[13] A closer look at the political, social, and economic undercurrents is necessary at this point to test the validity of Hypotheses 3 and 4. Pempel himself argues that numbers, even though an important indicator of party dominance, do not conclusively determine a party's true strength. Below is an analysis of Congress (I) numerical strength in the larger historical, political, economic and social context.

III. A Political and Historical Profile of the Party System

India's first political party, the Indian National Congress, was established by the British in 1885 to provide a forum for political debate for the "India-born, but Western-educated" élite. However, following the reawakening in the early 1900s, the party transformed itself into a nationalist movement. Congress's nationalist stance lasted for another three decades when Mahatma Gandhi's leadership turned it into a mass party by extending its support base to the rural population.[14] When the nation received its freedom in 1947, the Indian National Congress was the only organization, besides the bureaucracy, capable of penetrating the multiple layers of social identity and reaching out to the people. In fact, it was the only political organization familiar to the people. In the minds of many, the party system was the political system. While several other parties on both sides of the ideological spectrum—Left and Right—existed and won seats in the early elections of 1952, 1957, 1962, 1967, and 1971, the Indian National Congress Party emerged as the only electorally viable and politically sustainable party. It received at least 40 percent of the popular votes and 55 percent of seats in each of the first five parliamentary elections.[15] It won the elections defeating its next rival by a 4:1 ratio.

The Congress's domineering position in the political system was of critical importance to the long-term survival of the Indian democracy itself. In

1947, the nation lacked experience in modern governance. The 1947–71 period was dominated by infrastructure-building where two of the most critical needs were to establish state legitimacy and national identity.[16] State-building was of great significance because having been under foreign domination for more than a thousand years, the country did not have an established place for an autonomous state in its scheme of things. Similarly, nation-building was also important because the country had just been divided in two and the scars of the break-up were still fresh in people's minds. During this critical phase of political development, the Indian Congress served as "India's central integrating institution."[17] It served as a political laboratory allowing political ideas such as interest articulation, distribution of power, federalism, functional alliances, vertical and horizontal competition, resource allocation, etc., to be tested and perfected before being introduced to the larger political system.[18]

The Congress Party, in its early years, developed a functional form of federalism within its own structure. It was parallel to a governmental system in the sense that its local organizational units corresponded with administrative districts rather than electoral districts. The local units were brought together under several state-level Pradesh Congress Committees, forming a system similar to state governments. The Pradesh Congress Committees were further tied into a national level organization, called the All-India Congress Committee, mirroring the structural arrangements of a national government. The All-India Congress Committee selected from within its own members a Working Committee comprising approximately 20 members (similar to the cabinet in a parliamentary system). At the top of this organization was the Congress president elected by the members of the All-India Congress. It is noteworthy that the Congress provincial units during the nationalist struggle were drawn on the basis of linguistic identities, the same basis used later on to draw state boundaries by the Nehru administration.[19]

Table 12.2 offers a sample list of political ideas introduced in the Congress Party and then applied to the larger political system.

During the country's first 20 years of life, much of national politics took place within the Congress system. Initially, there was a power tussle between the party and the government. However, the system resolved this tension by merging the two top leaderships—prime minister and congress president—into one person. Jawaharlal Nehru served as both and ensured that the party stayed subservient to the government rather than vice-versa.[20]

The Nehru administration consciously designed a two-pronged strategy for the party-government partnership. Under this strategy, the government provided the nexus for forging national unity, while the Congress offered the place for groups (ethnic or otherwise) to express their diversity. In the 1950s–60s, when national leaders asked the people to identify themselves as

Table 12.2 Experiments in the Congress System and the Politcal System

Principles as experimented in the Congress Party System	Principles corresponding to the Indian Political System
Federalism within the party structure.	Drawing of state boundaries based on language and evolution of the center-state realtionship.
Political competion practiced by different factions within the party.	Political competition later on adopted by political parites and their alliances.
Plurality and absorption of new interest through patron-client networks.	Absorption of new interest groups in the politcal system.
Identity-building within the party by creating an over-arching loyality to the party and creating a rainbow coalition of different ethnic groups.	Nation-building: developing a common identity over and beyond ethnic identities.
Cooptation of other parties, aggrandization of issues, and forging alliences based on issues.	State-building: coopting of secessionist tendencies, forging policy alliances, preserving and enhancing state autonomy.

"*Bhartiyas*" (Indians), party leaders encouraged them to assert themselves as *Tamils,* or *Bengali,* or *Maharashtriyans.* The Congress not only sustained, but promoted, regionalism among groups by letting them scuffle for power as regionalists within the party. Social complexities made the Congress a necessary feature of the political system, just as they ensured that the Congress would remain a broad coalition of interests. According to Balveer Rora:

> As late as 1963, Nehru made a major concession to regionalist sentiment on the language issue; with his profoundly intuitive understanding of India's historical and social complexities, he realized, perhaps more than any other centralist leader in the party at that time, the developing contradictions which threatened his party and the country.[21]

Evidence shows that the state-level party committees were often controlled by locals.[22] The localities found appeasement in the Congress patronage, since it offered them the source of power and influence. Thus, in a diverse society like India, the party-government partnership succeeded in creating a two-tier political agenda—a national agenda with issues of stability and unity, and a state/local agenda with issues of self-assertion and diversity. This duality was apparent in all pre-1985 elections where voters often voted for the Congress at the national level but chose regional parties at the state level. Needless to say, this system was in the best interest of the Congress Party, for it practically assured its dominance at the national level.

The statistics on election results belie the level of pluralism and competition that existed within the "Congress System." Indeed, Congress was the most, and in some areas the only, recognizable party name, and voters often voted for the name. In reality, the party was an umbrella organization assimilating many different views and ideals. It was home to some of the most visionary philosophers and leaders, many of whom differed in their political views, but found the Congress to be the only forum available for meaningful expression. Consequently, as early as the 1950s, Congress had already emerged as a "catch-all" party accommodating every ideology, but prescribing none. Describing the Indian National Congress, the ruling party for all but a handful of India's 50-year history, Rasheeduddin Khan offers a good portrayal of the party system itself:

> The Congress is the counterpart of Hinduism in political culture. Like Hinduism it is amorphous, resilient, hospitable to diverse strands of dogma and interpretation, non-rejectionist, tolerant and accommodating, capable of internalizing dissent, and seeking to reconcile the irreconcilable. And like Hinduism it is multi-level and multi-structured, including the sublime and the ridiculous. India is a classic de-polarised polity. . . . This given dominant ethos of India has been utilised by the Congress, both by accident and design.[23]

The Congress Party also assisted the government in absorbing new political groups into the system.[24] As the level of industrialization and urbanization increased in the 1960s, the level of mass mobilization also increased, creating several new groups, such as women, backward classes, scheduled castes, industrial workers, and new property owners.[25] Until 1971, the Congress absorbed these groups by appeasing their needs on one hand and diversifying its own organization on the other. However, after 1971 the number and size of the new groups became too large to be contained within the party boundaries.[26]

Consequently, the nature of the party organization changed following Indira Gandhi's victory in the 1971 general elections. The party became less open, more rigid, and less reliant on its grass-roots organization. Indira Gandhi's style also proved to be different from that of her father, Jawaharlal Nehru. She preferred to appeal directly to the voters rather than work through intermediaries and party brokers. This exercise in direct democracy, scholars argue, crippled the party organization and left the government to fend for itself.[27] Personification of power, centralization, alienation, organizational instability, and the weakening of state and local organizations were some of the side-effects of Indira Gandhi's management style.[28]

During the 1970s, as the Congress (I) turned its energies inwards and became exclusive, the newly entering groups searched for other alternatives to exert their influence on the political system. Consequently, several new parties found their way into the system and many existing ones experienced increased levels of popular acceptance. Many of the Congressional factions that were fighting for their cause from within the party also found it in their self-interest to separate from the Congress and press for issues from the outside. By 1980, the party system that Morris-Jones had once described as the system of "dominance co-existing with competition but without a trace of alternation"[29] had changed into a system of "competition resulting in continuous alternation."

The Indira Gandhi era ended suddenly in 1984 with her assassination, but her son Rajiv Gandhi, a novice in politics, accepted the reign of the Congress (I). Rajiv won the 1984 elections riding on the sympathy wave created by his mother's death, but failed to convert this electoral victory into political charisma. The Rajiv era was marked by failed policies and scandalous practices. Rajiv himself was accused of taking several million dollars as kick-back on a major defense contract from a Swedish company. By 1991, the political scene had changed remarkably and the Congress (I) party had lost most of its historical advantage. Even though the Congress (I) formed governments in the 1980s and early 1990s, its base was never secure enough for it to transform its platform into policies. The *Bhariya Janata* Party (BJP) had emerged as a significant challenge to the Congress (I) party's catch-all policies. The BJP was a party of ideology, offering a distinctly different agenda based on "*Hindutsava*" (Hindu identity) in a nation that housed 82 percent Hindus. The BJP, however, was a geographically constrained party in the sense that its support came only from the northern-belt states. Consequently, it, too, failed to offer a viable alternative to the voters.

After Rajiv's assassination in 1991, the voters again supported the Congress (I). Scholars called this another wave of sympathy votes. Narsimha Rao, a seasoned politician from the south, took the leadership of the party and formed a coalition government. The BJP and its allies formed a unified opposition and offered a two-party system challenge at least for the first few years. In 1991–96, the Rao government ruled amidst political confusion and electoral insecurity. Rao started several promising programs in economic liberalization, industrialization, technologization and social harmony. He also made an attempt to reform the party by decentralizing power and initiating elections to all party posts.

However, the party continued to face the crisis as several scandals involving Rao and his top ministers were being exposed. By the end of the Rao era, the Congress (I) party could no longer function as a cohesive party let alone a political laboratory for the political system. Its weaknesses are portrayed by Hardgrave and Kochanek as follows:

> Organizational elections had not been held since 1972. The All-India Congress Committee and the Working Committee, once the crucial decision-making center of the party, were moribund. State party units had no autonomy, and provincial, district, and local Congress committees, insofar as they functioned at all, were creatures of the central party high command—a euphemism for Mrs. Gandhi. The grass roots had been cut, and the Congress, as it approached its centenary year, was an organization with no base.[30]

Thus, the Congress Party served as a parallel government performing the functions of a political system until 1971. The transfer of function from the party to the government seems to have coincided with Indira Gandhi's arrival on the scene; however, it is possible that the political system had also matured by this time and was ready to assume the responsibility. The Congress Party's unwillingness to adapt and expand to the changing circumstances also facilitated this shift. By 1991, this transfer was complete and the Congress (I) was ready to begin its role as one of many political parties vying for office. Today, it still retains a historical appeal and plays a key role. However, it no longer has a free hand in converting its agenda into national policies.

At the present time, the *Bhartiya Janata* Party (BJP) offers the single most viable alternative to the Congress (I). A party of upper cast, educated, urban, and professional voters, the BJP now holds the single largest number of seats in the parliament. It is increasingly more successful in designing campaign strategies. In recent years, the BJP has also shown the signs of adaptability by promoting a Hindu nationalist agenda with a moderate theme. Nonetheless, voters still find the BJP exclusionary and discriminatory in its policies. Other parties also find the BJP programs hard to swallow. It is evident from the fact that even after holding the largest number of seats in the 1996 parliament, the BJP could not succeed in withstanding its first confidence challenge on the floor. Its government, lead by Atal Bihari Bajpeyi, lasted for only 12 days.

IV. A Social and Economic Profile of the Party System

The Congress Party grew out of India's social diversity, economic necessity, and political confusion.[31] The social fabric of India included threads of various textures, colors, and sizes, as dimensions of social diversity cut across many lines. While India was declared to be a secular state, the declaration was more a result of historical experiences and Nehru's personal philosophy than the demographic reality. As carved out in 1947, the nation was predominantly Hindu with more than 80 percent of its population classifying itself as practicing Hindus. While the Muslim minority was only 11 percent, their sensitivity score, due to the creation of the nation of Pakistan on religious lines in 1947, was relatively high. However, Muslims were unable to use any historical leverage due to the dispersion of their population throughout India. In contrast, other religious minorities, such as the Sikhs and the Christians, were geographically concentrated, but they too lacked the numerical strength to exert power in the political arena. The Congress could have become a Hindu party had it not been for the inherent diversity of Hinduism imposed by the caste system. The caste system nullifies the Hindu identity as a people by dividing them into several hundred mutually exclusive, rigid categories and sub-categories, further complicated by linguistic diversity.[32]

From early on, the Congress applied the strategy of appealing to all groups over and beyond their social, religious, and linguistic identities. Its birth as an intellectual forum and existence as a nationalist movement afforded it the opportunity to extend its boundaries beyond social lines. At the time of independence, when the role of the Congress changed from that of a nationalist movement to a political party, it became incumbent upon the Congress to accommodate these groups to the extent that they would not gravitate towards other parties. The Congress Party met this challenge by creating a "federal system" within itself, at a time when the political system was unclear about its own federalist nature. The Congress not only used the patronage system[33] to undermine the social identities, but it also succeeded in co-opting regional parties into its federal structure. Many regional parties joined hands with the Congress in forging state-level electoral alliances, while many others sought Congress's assistance in forming local governments. In reality, the Congress succeeded in creating a parallel or shadow political system within its own structure. This shadow system served the political needs of the society when its political system was not capable of managing it.

A number of major and minor factions based on caste, religion, region and language emerged as shadow parties within the system and offered opportunities for all groups to express and champion their interests. Most shadow politics were intense, due to the multi-party system. Factions constantly formed and reformed; resources were allocated and reallocated; issues were debated and decided upon; voices were heard through the shadow parties; and constituencies were responded to through patron-client networks. Kothari called this a system of "consensus and pressure," where Congress was the party of consensus and the opposition parties were parties of pressure.[34]

During the coalition party system (1977–96), the party-voter link went through a major transformation. Prior to 1977, voting behavior in India was predictable. The Congress secured at least 40 percent of the votes and these votes came from a unified India irrespective of cast, religion, region, class, or language. According to scholars, voters formed vote banks and voted in blocks honoring the social hierarchical order. Women voted according to the advice of their husbands; peasants of the landlords; and the youth of the elderly. The vote bank system served its purpose of linking people to the political system, especially in the rural areas, where village leaders were able to trade village vote banks in return for favors of electricity, roads, hospitals, or schools. However, as parties entered the coalition game following the emergency in 1977, they spent more energy in appeasing their fellow parties than their own voters. More often than not, coalitions were formed irrespective of ideological or political preferences, leaving voters confused and alienated. The most recent elections reveal that the voter-party link is still on shaky ground, and the vote bank system is fast disappearing, if not already extinct. A 1996 news poll by the Center for the Studies of Developing Societies revealed that the Indian electorate, similar to the Indian party system, defies the conventional models of political behavior.[35] They feel less aligned with parties, yet have more faith in the power of their vote. While they vote less on ethnic lines, they feel that certain parties look after their ethnic interests better than others. Similarly, voters believe that while their vote has a greater value today, they feel that the people they elect do not care for them (Table 12.3).

Table 12.3 Voter's Opinions on Issues of Party-Voter Realtionship in 1996 & 1971[36]

Statements	Agree in 1996 (%)	Agree in 1971 (%)	Change in 25 years (%)
Governance is better without parties and elections.	11	14	-3
Does your vote make a diiference?	59	48	+11
Do representatives care for the people?	22	27	-5
Do you feel close to any party?	31	37	-6
Are you a member of any political party?	6	4	+2
Does your caste/community generally vote for one party?	27	35	-8
Is it important to you to vote the way your catse/community votes?	30	51	-21
Does your party look after the interests of your caste/community?	17	14	+3

The results further show that voters display a very low level of trust towards political parties. On a scale of 0 to 100, voters designate a score of 39 for political parties, 57 for central government, and 59 for state governments. A report in *India Today*[37] summarizes the voter-party relationship as:

> The effect of the decline in voters' identification with parties can be seen in the timing of their voting decision. The proportion of voters who make up their mind during the days of the election campaign has nearly doubled since 1971. In addition to this, about one-quarter of them make up their minds on the day of polling itself, as in 1971. Very few democracies have recorded such a high level of potentially unattached and politically fluid voters.

The 1996 elections also marked clear boundaries between parties based on voters' age, religion, caste, gender, and class identities. Table 12.4 depicts the support base for the Congress (I), the BJP, and the National Front-Left Front Alliance. Thus, in 50 years the Indian party system seems to have come full circle. Whereas earlier, all voters could be represented by a single party, today all of the parties combined fail to satisfy the voters' need for representation. In the words of Sunil Khilnani, "India's new government is suffering from fragmentation and none of the three major ruling parties represent the people. Instead, political issues are being addressed at the state and local level, rather than in a centralized manner."[38] Similarly, whereas social complexity was viewed as a positive factor in the development of a representative democracy, it is now viewed as the biggest source of political instability.[39] Some recent studies on voting behavior claim that Western models of party politics (social cleavage and consociational theories) now explain Indian politics, but held no explanatory power in 1960s–70s.[40]

According to Pempel, India should have also gone through the experience of industrialization during its shift from the a single-party-dominant system to a no-party-dominant state. India adopted a policy of five-year economic plans under the Nehru administration and has followed the same model since then. This kind of planning, argues the government, gives it more flexibility over a long period of time.[42] While the Indian economy has done exceedingly well in many areas of traditional growth indicators,[43] its performance stands undermined by its exponentially growing population which has already crossed the 900 million mark. During the past 50 years, the Indian economy grew by an average of 3–3.5 percent annually. Its industrial growth rate ranged from 6.7 percent annually during the first five-year plan (1953–57) to 9.3 percent during the second five-year plan (1957–65). It stayed 5.5 and 7 percent during the 1970s and rose to about 8 percent in the 1980s. The liberalization policies adopted

Table 12.4 Voter Support Base for the Top Three Parties in the 1996 Election[41]

Factor	Congress (I) %	BJP %	NF-LF %
Age			
18–25	27	25	20
26–35	28	25	20
36–45	29	22	23
46–55	32	21	20
56+	33	22	20
Religion			
Hindu	29	27	18
Muslim	28	3	48
Christian	46	3	12
Sikh	29	10	7
Education			
Illiterate	32	17	24
Middle	29	22	21
High School	27	30	18
Graduate	25	36	16
Gender			
Male	29	25	20
Female	30	21	21
Caste			
Forward	29	33	17
Backwards	25	23	25
Scheduled	31	11	21
Sch. Tribes	47	17	15

by the Rao government facilitated India's entry into the global market, sustaining the high growth rate in the first five years of the 1990s. Today, the Indian industry contributes 29 percent towards the nation's income, while it contributed only 5 percent in 1947. Nonetheless, India is not an industrialized economy. Over 67 percent of its population depends on agriculture for livelihood; per capita income is only $310; nearly 37 percent of the population lives below the poverty line; and 40 percent are still illiterate.

V. The Myth of Causations

Hypotheses 3 and 4 rely on causational links—linking, first, the larger system (political, social, and economic) to the party system, and subsequently the party system to the process of democratization. Based on the historic, political, social and economic profile of the party system, it is evident that

India always had a high level of social dynamism and political competition. Even during the first 25 years when the Congress Party held numerical supremacy, social and political groups existed and asserted themselves on the political scene. This competition, however, took place within the confines of the Congress rather than the system at large. The Congress carefully channeled the group energy through its own patronage system. The Congress supremacy helped the political system by providing it a safety valve and allowing it the time to build a national and state identity. In this context, the Congress, serving as the dominant party in a single-party-dominant system, perpetuated the cycle of dominance. It promoted the policies (regionalism, internal competition, federalism, co-opting) that allowed it to sustain its numeric supremacy, while at the same time converting its positional strength into more policy-related dominance.

Thus, Hypothesis 3 cannot be fully accepted. There is no evidence to prove that over the years the levels of social dynamism and political competition have increased, although it is true that the ways in which the dynamism and competition are expressed and managed have been evolving over the years. The Congress Party, which managed competition during the first two decades, failed to do so in the later years. What caused it to fail is a puzzling question whose answer lies only partially in Pempel's historical argument. During 1947–71 India fought four major wars, keeping the historical images of suppression and dominance alive. However, it has not faced any significant external threat since then. Furthermore, the Congress Party, no matter how internally divided, offered a cohesive front to the voters during the first two decades. Its split in 1967, followed by massive defections in 1969, and loss of majority in 1977, eroded the unifying image of the party from the voters' minds. The role of scandals and the level of corruption also played a key role in undermining the Congress's credibility. First, Indira Gandhi was charged with election fraud, then Sanjay's[44] name was linked with emergency excesses, then Rajiv's name was attached to the *Bofors* scandal, and, finally, Rao's image was tarnished with the allegations made in 1993–94. Admittedly, other political parties, including the Congress rival, the BJP, have also fallen from their clean image, but the Congress, being the dominant party, had the most to lose.

It must be acknowledged that social dynamism was already present in India in 1947. The Congress chose to manage this dynamism by ethnicizing the party system which eventually led to the ethnicization of the political system. What we see today is not the emergence of, but the expression of, social identities at the national level. The presence of the so-called social dynamism at the national level should not lead scholars to conclude that the level of social interaction has increased, instead the evidence suggests that the mechanism used to contain this interaction within local boundaries has now weakened, leading to the decline of the single-party-dominant system. In brief, the absence of a single-dominant party does not signal the presence of social dynamism or industrialization in India; it merely signals the changing nature of institutional arrangements. Thus, we must accept that Hypothesis 3 holds only partially true in India's case: the historical link has weakened but the nation has not industrialized; new groups have emerged but they are not based on the industrial identity; and the social groups are more assertive in politics but they were always a part of the political scene, albeit in a different form.

It is the last hypothesis, Hypothesis 4, claiming a natural link between the decline of the single-party dominance and the level of democratization that I find most exceptional in the case of India. The evidence of democratic governance—political competition, fair and frequent elections, freedom of press, professional civil service, apolitical military and effective means of mass participation—can be traced as early as 1950. On many accounts, such as the level of corruption and political violence, one would find a greater degree of disorder now than during the days of the Congress dominance. It is misleading to assume that India of the 1950s was any less democratic than India of the 1990s. Even within a single party, there was sufficient room for free expression of political ideas, electoral competition, interest articulation, and political communication. The methods of delivering these were indeed different. In earlier days, the Congress Party provided the sole forum and managed political competition within that forum. The systems of patronage, patron-client network, vote bank, and functional federalism filled the need of the time. As the political system gained experience, the same political processes found different modes of expression. The decline of the Congress Party today only mirrors the transfer of functions from one system to another; it does not prove the absence of these functions in the past.

Since 1996, the Indian electorate has gone through two government fallouts, owning to coalition party politics. In March 1998, the BJP won 33 percent of the total seats, while Indian National Congress occupied 26 percent. BJP with its 11 allies succeeded in getting 252 seats (46 percent), up significantly from 187 in 1996 and thus forming a coalition government with the help of additional support. Congress and its allies were able to increase their seat share only by 1 percent from 143 seats in 1996 to 148 in 1998. The support for the BJP was strongest among the upper-caste Hindus (40 percent). While OBCs (other backward castes) featured significantly (24 percent) in the BJP's support-base, the Muslims almost completely boycotted the party. The 1998 elections reaffirmed that urbanity, ritual hierarchy, education, respectable occupations, and wealth were all associated with a greater propensity to vote for the BJP. Under Prime Minister Atal Bihari Vajpeyi, the BJP formed the government and made some bold moves, including the testing of India's nuclear warhead capability. Realizing the limitations of its narrow base, the Vajpeyi government also tried to dilute the Hindustava platform and speak the language of conciliation and compromise. In early 1999, the coalition again fell apart, forcing the Indian people to face yet another round of elections in September, although early polls from *India Today* suggest that the result will again usher in a hung parliament and another fragile, coalition government.

Notes

1. Labeled as opposition parties because their minor strength never allowed them to become viable ruling options.
2. These are loose party alliances that come together at election time to offer a real electoral alternative.
3. India received its independence from the British on 15 August 1947.
4. Rajni Kothari, "The Congress 'System' in India," *Party System and Election Studies,* occasional papers of the Centre for Developing Societies, No. 1 (Bombay: Allied Publishers, 1967), p. 1–11.
5. According to the Indian Constitution, the president can declare a state of emergency, on the advice of the prime minister, for one year. During the emergency all functions of State and local governments cease to exist and the governments are controlled through presidential ordinances. The emergency is renewable for another year.
6. After the split, the Indian National Congress under Indira Gandhi became the Indian National Congress (I).
7. http://india.bgsu.edu/arch/india-l/May96/0049.html
8. T. J. Pempel, "Introduction," in T. J. Pempel, ed., *Uncommon Democracies: The One-Party Dominant Regimes* (Ithaca, N.Y.: Cornell University Press, 1990), p.1–32.
9. Ibid., p.5.
10. Ibid., p.334.
11. *India Today* (31 May 1996).
12. Prime Minister Atal Bihari Vajpeyi's BJP government lasted only 12 days due to a "no confidence" vote.
13. Paul R. Brass, *The Politics of India since Independence* (Cambridge: Cambridge University Press, 1994).
14. Paul R. Brass, "Democracy and Political Participation in India," in Myron L. Cohen, ed., *Asia: Case Studies in the Social Sciences: A Guide for Teaching* (New York: M.E. Sharpe, 1992).
15. In the first three elections, its share of parliamentary seats was at least 73 percent.
16. The processes of state-building and nation-building are the most critical for newly independent nations.
17. James Manor, "Party Decay and Political Crisis in India," *The Washington Quarterly* (1981): p. 25–40.

18. This opinion is shared by Rajni Kothari, who stresses that: "The Congress got converted into not just a ruling party, but a dominant framework of institutionalizing the whole process of power. The "party system" that emerged from such a framework was distinctive and served the Indian democracy well during its period of consolidation and consensus-making," in *Politics and the People* (New York: New Horizon Press, 1989), p.4.

19. Myron Weiner, *Party-Building in a New Nation: Indian National Congress* (Chicago: University of Chicago Press, 1967).

20. Stanley A. Kochanek, *The Congress Party of India* (Princeton, NJ: Princeton University Press, 1968).

21. "Centralist and Regionalist Parties in India's Federal Polity," in Zoya Hasan, S. N. Jha & Rasheeduddin Khan, eds., *The State, Political Processes and Identity* (New Delhi: Sage Publications, 1989), p.191–204.

22. A term used to refer to the local élite who claim their power on the basis of their regional/local identity.

23. "The Total State: the Concept and its Manifestation in the Indian Political System," in Hasan, Jha & Khan, eds., *The State, Political Processes and Identity*, p.64.

24. Membership of the Congress grew from 500,000 in 1947 to 11 million before the split in 1967. Since then its membership has stood around nine million, making it the largest party in the non-Communist world.

25. Rajni Kothari, *Politics and the People* (New York: Horizon, 1989).

26. Kothari, Morris-Jones, and James Manor agree that by the 1970s, the new groups constituted a market polity.

27. Paul R. Brass agues that due to these practices, the Congress (I) Party turned into a cadre party in the 1970s–80s. See, Paul R. Brass, *Caste, Faction and Party in Indian Politics* (Delhi: Chanakya, 1983).

28. There is a near consensus on the after-effects of Mrs. Gandhi's governance style. See, Henry C. Hart, ed., *Indira Gandhi's India: A Political System Reappraided* (Boulder, CO: Westview Press, 1976).

29. Wyndraeth H. Morris-Jones, "Dominance and Dissent," in Morris-Jones, *Politics Mainly Indian* (Madras: Orient Longman, 1978), p.217.

30. Robert L. Hardgrave & Stanley A. Kochanek, *India: Government and Politics in a Developing Nation* (Fort Worth: Harcourt Brace Jovanovich, 1993), p.258.

31. Interesting views on the topic are held by James Monor, Morris-Jones, Kothari, and Lloyd Rudolph.

32. India has 15 official languages and over 2,000 dialects. Since the major languages have their own script, it is not possible for people from different language groups to communicate without proper training or experience.

33. The patronage system refers to a large number of positions—including cabinet ministers, governors, non-political appointees, presidential candidate support—that are under the control of the ruling party.

34. Kothari, "The Congress System in India."

35. For the brief report on the survey results, consult *India Today* (31 August 1996): p. 28–43.

36. The data are taken from the report published in *India Today* (31 August 1996).
37. Ibid., p.39–40.
38. Sunil Khilnani, "Beyond the fragments," in *New Statesman and Society* (17 May 1996): p.26.
39. James Manor's studies discuss notions of state-society link and the prevailing trends of decay and awakening.
40. Pradeep K. Chhibber, "The puzzle of Indian Politics: Social Cleavages and the Indian Party System," in *British Journal of Political Science*, vol. 19 (1989): p.191–212.
41. The data are taken from the report published in *India Today* (31 May 1996).
42. C. Rangarajan, et alia, *Strategies for Industrial Development in 1980s* (New Delhi: Oxford University, 1981).
43. On the physical quality of life index, India ranks at the same level as many countries showing a steep increase in per capita income, life expectancy (32 years in 1947 compared to 60 today) and literacy (55 percent today versus 16 percent in 1947).
44. Sanjay was Indira Gandhi's younger son and her natural successor until his 1980 death in a car accident.

THIRTEEN

Local and Provincial Elections in Taiwan: Appraising Steps in Democratization

James A. Robinson[*]

This chapter analyzes Taiwan's 1994 elections for provincial governor, provincial assembly, Taipei City, and Kaohsiung City mayors and councils, as well as legislative recalls as trends towards greater democratization in Taiwan. It appraises electoral administration, voter participation, inter-party competition, and election campaigns according to criteria of normative theories of democracy. The appraisal identifies biased electronic media, high costs of campaigns, and allegations of corruption as problems for attention if Taiwan is to sustain democratic institutions that distinguish it from its former Leninist-like policies and practices.

I. Standpoint of the Observer[1]

As a "world democrat," I follow Taiwan as an example of a polity in gradual pursuit of a policy of power-sharing. This is the political equivalent of the so-called "economic miracle," the root of the much acclaimed "Taiwan experience."[2] In 1994 Taiwan voters took further steps towards democratization. One significant step was the election of Taipei's mayor from the élite of the main opposition. Chen Shui-bian's plurality victory over both the ruling party's incumbent, Huang Ta-chou, and the New Party's champion campaigner, Jaw Shau-kong, made him the opposition's most successful candidate to date in competition for high political offices throughout Taiwan. The Democratic Progressive Party (DPP) previously had established itself as a formidable and promising opposition, but until 1994 its highest office was that of county magistrate, including the larger county, Taipei, which surrounds Taipei City, but is a sub-provincial jurisdiction. With success in Taipei City, DPP wrested an office of status and power from control by the ruling *Kuomintang* (KMT). This surrender of office from one party to another, voluntarily and at the hands of votes not of violence, marked an advanced state of democratization. It is one thing to have frequent elections, as Taiwan does, but another when those elections become competitive. Until 1994, Taiwan resembled Japan so far as concerns inter-party competition; it was a predominant one-party state, in the jargon of political scientists.[3] Taipei mayoral results showed that the major opposition party actually can win one of the major elective offices.

A second significant effect of the voting was the apparent diminution of ethnic or national origin issues. Despite the efforts of the New Party to make a controversy of independence versus reunification, voters elected two island-born candidates and one mainland-born candidate. President Lee Teng-hui was said to have insisted on naming James Soong, a Mainlander, to the governorship of Taiwan Province in 1993 and thus to break the practice of reserving that post for a Taiwanese. Soong's success in being elected in his own right seemed to vindicate the president's efforts to reduce a divisiveness that some élites have promoted. While the DPP and the KMT leaders differ over policies domestically, they have been closer to one another about cross-Strait relations, as well as democratization, than either has been to the New Party strategists' usual positions. Thus, a national consensus appeared in the making and the risks of polarization of the electorate reduced.

A third effect, likely to flow from the second, was the way in which the election was expected to be interpreted by élites in Taiwan's greatest source of worry, the People's Republic of China (or Mainland China). While it is difficult for foreigners to divine the thought processes of political figures in the PRC, one of the latter's chief interests is assumed to be "stability." Electoral results in Taiwan rather closely followed results that had been expected for months. Thus, they could be read as stabilizing on both sides of the Taiwan Strait. Stability not only promotes peace across this 100-mile passageway, but it helps to secure the processes of democratization within Taiwan. For several years, the greatest threat to continuing democratic progress had not been internal but external. External dangers remained, but the election helped to calm, rather than excite, such threats.

With this added security, Taiwan resumed its pursuit of a democratic agenda. Much remained to be done, as the 1994 campaign revealed, but Taiwan, for the time being, could continue its own course. That democratic course need not imitate any other democracy in particular, but blend American, European and Asian experiences.

II. Provincial Governors, Assembly, Metropolitan Mayors, and Councils: Appraising Criteria

On 3 December 1994, Taiwan held its fourth round of elections in one year and a week. At stake were the governorship of Taiwan Province and the mayoralties of the two largest metropolitan areas, Taipei and Kaohsiung. During the previous year, voters in local elections chose 23 county-level and large city executives, their county or city councils, and the chiefs and councils of the smallest units of local government. Voting in late 1993 and twice in early 1994 followed annual trips to polling stations every year since 1989. Taken together, the frequency of elections and the number of offices filled by popular vote give Taiwan the distinction of relying more heavily on ballot boxes than any other polity, perhaps with the exceptions of the United States and Switzerland.

Local elections are not new to Taiwan.[4] They have occurred regularly in most areas since 1950. What gave special significance to the late 1994 voting was that this was the first time ever for voters in Taiwan Province to elect their governor. Heretofore, the official had been appointed by the central government. Similarly, Taipei voters would elect their mayor for the first time in 30 years. The last mayor to be elected, in 1964, was an independent, Kao Yu-shu. Since Taipei became a special municipality in 1967, the central government had appointed the city's chief executive, once including Kao himself, until the 1994 occupant, Huang Ta-chou. Kaohsiung also had lost an elected mayor when its population size qualified it as a special municipality in 1979. The last elected mayor was also the first appointed incumbent. Wang Yu-yun of the prominent Wang family of southern Taiwan was retained as mayor and had been succeeded by four incumbents, including the 1994 mayor, Wu Den-yih.

Taiwan Province, Taipei City, and Kaohsiung City are separate administrative jurisdictions and therefore separate constituencies for electoral purposes. No one votes in more than one of these elections, as determined by place of residence. Every voter, however, is also eligible to cast a ballot for the legislative body that corresponds with the provincial or city executive. The Taiwan Provincial Assembly had been increased in size from 77 to 79, and all seats were up for election. In the Taipei City Council, 52 seats would be filled, and in Kaohsiung City Council 44 seats.

The assembly and council elections are notable for their use of "Multi-Member, Single Vote" constituencies. As is also the practice in electing members of the National Assembly and the Legislative Yuan, each voter casts one vote among a number of candidates of all parties running for several seats from the same geographic sub-area. This method, dubbed MM-SV, is used now almost exclusively by Taiwan voters. In 1995 Japan changed to a combination of single-member districts and proportional representation for elections to the Lower House of the Diet. Only a few multi-member districts survive in some local elections in the United States and in Thailand's Lower House of parliament, but this method is virtually untried elsewhere. This procedure is widely thought to favor large, well-established parties and to disadvantage small parties. At the same time, it sometimes seems to encourage splinter parties, which by selectively nominating only one candidate in a few districts and concentrating their scarce votes can successfully elect a handful of members.[5]

Electoral processes and procedures for these offices may be appraised according to standard criteria applicable almost everywhere. These criteria apply both to the administration of the election and to the outcomes (who wins) and effects (what wins, or what parties and policies win). A common basis of comparison is percentage of eligible voters who actually cast ballots, or "turn-out." Voter turn-out in Taiwan has been consistently high. In elections for thousands of offices filled since 1950, 70 percent of voters typically have visited their polling station on election day. A number of factors account for high voter participation. One is that election commissions in Taiwan rely on up-to-date household registration lists to notify voters of time and place of voting and to inform them, through an election bulletin mailed to every residence, of the candidates for each office being filled. Elections have been scheduled on Saturdays, treated as work-holidays, and extra trains and buses run to carry urban workers to their provincial places of registration. Another element encouraging high voter participation is competition between parties. As Taiwan has become a more competitive party-system—that is as the ruling party, the *Kuomintang,* faced increasing electoral opposition from first the Democratic Progressive Party and later the New Party—interest and motivation among voters was expected to rise, and apparently did.

This election, or rather these elections, had something special to attract voters. They were, as noted earlier, the first time in a generation that Taipei and Kaohsiung voters had the opportunity to vote for mayor, and the first time in history that voters in the Province had chosen their own governor. This alone was expected to maintain the 70 percent level of turn-out, perhaps even increase it. Moreover, mayoral and gubernatorial campaigns featured several novelties that also may have stimulated voter attention. Debates and joint appearances among candidates in Taipei and Kaohsiung attracted much media notice. Other new techniques for promoting candidates among voters included endorsements from prominent actors and entertainers. And not to be overlooked were contentious controversies that divided candidates, particularly debate of the status and defense of Quemoy and Matsu, Taiwan-controlled islands within sight of Mainland China.

Hence, observers expected a relatively high rate of voter participation. Anything under 70 percent would have been cause for comment; anything above, no surprise.

How shall we know who won? By who got the most votes in each contest, of course. Analyzing elections, however, is more complicated than that. Whenever a polity matures, as Taiwan's democratic processes have been becoming more routine, *expectations* of victory are almost as important as actual victories. The ruling party, the KMT, had held office for so long that any defeats for its candidates defied expectations of its inevitable governing. In fact, a sign of Taiwan's political maturation is success among opposition candidates. Power-sharing through elections testifies to the KMT's success in devolving power and promoting democratization.

So, any success among the DPP and the New Party candidates became special evidence of victory. Likewise, unanticipated outcomes drew notice. For example, at the time candidates for the three main offices were nominated in August, it was widely expected that the KMT would win the governorship and the Kaohsiung mayoralty, while DPP would win the race for Taipei mayor. Any divergence from this expectation would surprise many observers, although one could find election-watchers with counter predictions.

Still another effect of the voting was its impact on future competition between the political parties. If the KMT should win all three executive offices—an unlikely prospect—opposition parties would be handicapped severely. If the KMT should win two of the three, and the DPP one, the existing balance of power would be maintained. On the other hand, if the KMT should lose all three or even two major elections, either to the DPP or a combination of the DPP and the New Party winners, one would identify the 1994 elections with increasing competition between parties. Taiwan would be less a one-party and more a competitive or multi-party system.

Not to be overlooked in defining "winners" were the post-election distribution of seats in the provincial assembly and metropolitan councils. Historically, each of them had been dominated by the KMT. Indeed, in previous elections in the province and in Taipei and Kaohsiung, opposition parties had fielded few candidates, with the effect that the KMT had enjoyed large working majorities in legislatures (the same had been true in county councils and city councils throughout the island). This time, however, the DPP had nominated enough candidates that if they all won, the party could have a small majority in the assembly and in the Taipei council. This was not considered likely, but a possibility was that a high DPP success rate, combined with selective victories by the New Party candidates, could threaten KMT's working majorities in one or more legislative bodies.

Such an effect would be important in its own right, but like all other consequences of these interrelated elections set the stage for the *next round* of elections. If any Taiwanese voter felt fatigued from going to the polls so frequently, he could look at the calendar. Within another year, the campaign to elect the president for the first time would be underway, and the terms of members of the Legislative Yuan and the National Assembly would have expired, leaving those bodies open for reelection. So, the results of voting on December 3 promised much—to voters, of course; to winning candidates, to be sure; to the fortunes of parties, also; and to prospects for candidates and parties in the next year's elections. Most of all they would mean much to the stability and continuity of democratic reform, long devolving, now rapidly accelerating, in Taiwan. And beyond Taiwan, the example would be of interest to much of the rest of the world for which democratization remains a goal, not a reality.

More than ten and a half million Taiwanese voters, in elections for provincial governor and assembly and metropolitan mayors and councils, delivered significant rewards and punishments to candidates, political parties, and proponents of major issues on 3 December 1994. With a near-record 76 percent of eligible voters casting ballots for the three highest offices, Taiwan's citizens once again affirmed their attachment to electoral democracy and to continuing, gradual devolution of power.

If one considers the vote from several points of view, each of the political parties had a new balance sheet of assets and liabilities. The ruling *Kuomintang* won two of the highest level offices ever elected in Taiwan. In Kaohsiung it reelected Wu Den-yih, who had served as appointed mayor since 1989, with 55 percent of the votes among more than 80 percent of the eligible electorate who went to the polling stations. As the newly elected mayor of Taiwan's second city, Wu continued the KMT's electoral dominance from the days before 1979 when the city's population surpassed one million and qualified it for status as a special municipality.

The KMT leaders enjoyed even greater satisfaction from the election of James Soong as governor of Taiwan Province with 56 percent of the total vote. This was the first time in the province's 400 years that its governor derived office from the suffrage of constituents rather than from the sufferance of a superior central government. As a Mainland-born citizen of the Republic of China on Taiwan, Soong won office among a population, 85 percent of whom were born in Taiwan from families that date their island ancestry as far back as 300 years.

The Democratic Progressive Party, the largest opposition party, staked a claim for further power-sharing by its victory for Chen Shui-bian as Mayor of Taipei. As noted earlier, this was the first time for this office to be elected popularly since 1964, when after losing it to independent Kao, the KMT altered rules for urban elections and made cities larger than one million special municipalities with appointive rather than elective executives. In the

Table 13.1 Gubernatorial and Mayoral Election Outcomes

Candidate	Party	Vote	Percent
Taiwan Governor			
James Soong	KMT	4,726,012	56
Chen Ding-nan	DPP	3,254,887	39
Ju Gau-jeng	NP	362,377	4
Tsai Cheng-chih	Ind.	37,256	—
Wu Tzu	Ind.	25,398	—
Taipei Mayor			
Chen Shui-bian	DPP	615,090	44
Jaw Shau-kong	NP	424,905	30
Huang Ta-chou	KMT	364,618	26
Jih Rong-ze	Ind.	3,941	—
Kaohsiung Mayor			
Wu Den-yih	KMT	400,766	54
Chang Chun-hsiung	DPP	289,110	39
Tang A-ken	NP	25,113	3
Shih Chung-hsiang	Ind.	13,084	2
Cheng Te-yiao	Ind.	7,513	1

Source: Chung-yang hsüan-chu wei-yuan-hui, *Sheng shih I hui I yuan chi sheng shih hsuang chu* (Hsuan-chu kai-kuang, 3 December 1994).

wake of consensus formulated at the 1990 National Affairs Conference, called by President Lee Teng-hui to promote continuing democratization, local governmental autonomy from central government was enlarged and election of Taipei and Kaohsiung Mayors devolved to voters.[6]

DPP Taipei candidate, Chen-Shui-bian, widely respected as an effective opposition leader in the Legislative Yuan, won nomination in a close primary election over fellow legislator, Hsieh Chang-ting. With a united party supporting him against adversaries divided between the KMT and former KMT members in the year-old New Party, Chen became an early favorite among election observers. In the week before voting, *Time* included him among 100 promising leaders in all fields throughout the world.[7] Despite the mid campaign suggestion by DPP Chairman Shih Ming-the that the future of Quemoy and Matsu be negotiated with Mainland China, Chen held onto his apparent early advantages. He hastened to Quemoy to explain his own position, somewhat different from Shih's, and returned to Taipei to refocus his campaign on the capital city's special problems, among them transportation, pollution, alleged corruption, and more amenable conditions for living. In winning a 43.6 percent plurality of votes, Chen overcame efforts of the New Party's legendary election campaigner, Jaw

Shau-kong, to divide voters between mainlanders and islanders. Taipei's population consists of just more than one-third of people with Mainland origins, the largest such concentration on Taiwan.

Jaw, who had never lost an election in Taipei and held records for most votes ever won in a city council or a Legislative Yuan election, could not repeat his campaign magic. He was left to be content with having denied the KMT-appointed incumbent Huang Ta-chou reelection with 20 percent of the total vote. Thus, the New Party, despite Jaw's 30 percent showing, reconfirmed its role as a spoiler party, which it had established in county magistrate elections just a year beforehand. Moreover, the poor showing of the New Party candidates for races outside Taipei—for Kaohsiung mayor and council and for provincial governor and assembly—revealed the limited constituency available to it, as well as the shortness of its list of articulate and attractive candidates for high offices. That the New Party performed successfully in contests for Taipei City Council, winning 11 of 54 seats, further testified to its limited geographic appeal, however enthusiastic. Taiwan's unusual "Multi-Members-Single Vote" legislative constituencies worked to the New Party's advantage, which strategists exploited effectively.

Also in the Taipei City Council, the DPP improved its representation from 14 to 18 members. The biggest change in power distribution, however, was the KMT's decline from 37 seats to 20, fewer than a majority. Both the DPP and the New Party apparently targeted their resources on fewer candidates more successfully than did the KMT, which heretofore had enjoyed a reputation for effective mobilization of voters behind selected candidates. The peculiar electoral system and party strategies for implementing it probably did not account for all of the KMT's declining fortunes in the council. Council members were subject to criticisms over policies and issues similar to those lodged against Mayor Huang, especially by the New Party.

City council politics now likely would be coalition politics. Recent experience among the three parties in the Legislative Yuan only partially guided expectations of things to come in Taipei's council. In the legislature, the DPP alternately had coalesced with the KMT and the New Party. In the city council, however, which must work with the new DPP mayor, a more stable coalition was expected to be required than in the Legislative Yuan whose executive counterpart, the premier, is a leader from the KMT. This suggested a possible alliance between the two major parties, the KMT and the DPP, with the effect of freezing out the New Party, at least in selecting the speaker and organizing the council.

Beyond Taipei, the New Party made negligible progress. Gubernatorial candidate Ju Gau-jeng won only 4.3 percent, not enough to have his preelection deposit refunded by the Election Commission. In the provincial assembly, the New Party won only two seats of 79, in Kaohsiung City Council three of 44. In both bodies, the New Party's showing was less successful than that of independents who claimed eight seats each in the assembly and the Kaohsiung Council. These results also deserved interpretation that left the New Party largely a Taipei regional or sub-regional phenomenon, yet an element in position to broker and bargain between the two major parties. The New Party's fortunes did not appear promising enough to lure away remaining dissidents within the KMT, as might have been the case had Jaw been a victorious candidate. On the other hand, loyalty and cohesion among the New Party adherents permitted its leaders to occupy a position on one side of the KMT with the DPP on the other.

If this was the shape of things to come, at least in Taipei City, the KMT was a reluctant beneficiary of its defeats in that city's mayoral and council races. Certainly KMT national leaders campaigned with a view to getting along with and accepting gracefully the consequences of an opposition victory. This seemed evident in the different role President Lee Teng-hui played in this campaign. In the previous year, he participated unprecedently and visibly in county magistrate and city mayor elections. In 1994, he appeared to give more attention to selecting nominees for the three high elective offices than to campaigning for them after nomination. The president spoke for and endorsed Governor Soong and Mayors Huang and Wu, but not with the frequency or intensity of the previous year. This different strategy may have stemmed from either or both of two factors. One was an early anticipation that Mayor Huang could not win, hence the president should invest little in a losing cause. The other was to signal that any fair outcome was acceptable to the leadership of Taiwan's democratization movement. Premier Lien Chan and most members of the executive cabinet also were reticent about participating in campaign activities.

These elections augured a period of inter-party cooperation, especially in the assembly and councils, as well as cabinet in which the mayor of Taipei (now an opposition figure), like the Mayor of Kaohsiung, takes a seat. Such cooperation would promote the oft-acclaimed goal of "stability," which business as well as political leaders, and perhaps a considerable proportion of the citizenry, demand and expect. Stability in internal political affairs also provides for continuity in the conduct of cross-Strait relations. Mainland China, a hundred or so nautical miles away, remained a primary source of latent, often manifest, concern. Whatever intentions officials in Beijing had about Taiwan, they too, as we have said, were presumed to favor stability over instability. That these elections adhered to and extended a devolutionary trend begun nearly a decade earlier on Taiwan may not have pleased those in the PRC who regard Taiwan as a "renegade province." Yet the orderliness and predictability of the trend also may have served both Mainland's interests and those of Taiwan.

The sharing of victory between the major parties (the governorship and one mayoralty to the KMT and the other mayoralty to the DPP) induced stability in the gradual devolution of power. A devolutionary equilibrium also drew support from the "anti-provincial" outcomes of the provincial governorship and Taipei mayor contests. DPP legislator and former city councilor Chen Shui-bian would be Taipei's mayor and his election achieved another first. His would be the highest office yet yielded by the ruling KMT to the opposition as a result of an election. Taiwan had crossed another threshold in its long march to democratization. After establishing well-rooted traditions of holding regular elections for many offices through high voter turnout and efficient administration, Taiwan's voters now attained the final democratic practice of voting out one party and voting in another.

Taipei City was especially symbolic for the opposition as it is the capital city. It also is the residence of the largest concentration of Mainland-born citizens in Taiwan. Its last election of mayor was in 1964, after which the ruling party altered the rules and made mayors appointive in cities of one million population and larger. And Taipei's incumbent mayor was Huang Ta-chou, considered a protégé of President Lee Teng-hui. The competition between the DPP and the KMT was infused with challenge from the energetic and enthusiastic New Party. The New Party had been founded only 15 months earlier by KMT dissidents. Led by legislators and the ex-cabinet Ministers Jaw Shau-kong and Wang Chien-shien, the New Party had won few votes and fewer offices in late 1993 and early 1994 regional and local elections. Now with the dynamic and experienced Jaw as its candidate in Taipei, the New Party threatened to win a vital contest in its own right.

Jaw's rallies were something never seen before in Taiwan. Friendly, happy, chanting crowds interacted with speakers and singers. Enormous gatherings and congregations of cheering supporters were preceded by miles of caravans of taxis, private cars, trucks, and buses bearing New Party flags and RCC emblems, which filled streets leading to rally sites. If crowd size and collective noise determined winning platforms and victorious candidates, the New Party principles and Jaw Shau-kong would have been installed in Taipei's cavernous new City Hall. According to procedures associated with modern democracy, voices of the people ordinarily are counted neither by decibel levels or stomping feet but by a show of hands or secret ballots. When ballots not boots were counted, results gave the DPP control of the Taipei executive branch.

DPP rejoicing in Taipei was matched by KMT gratitude in Taichung and Kaohsiung. At campaign headquarters (Chung Hsing Village, Nantou County, site of the provincial government), James Soong greeted cheers from faithful supporters. His landslide victory was distinctive for several reasons. Although a life-time member of KMT and a party functionary all his adult career, Soong had never run for public office. He climbed to prominence on rungs of party and bureaucratic ladders. He had been secretary and translator for President Chiang Ching-kuo; director of party propaganda and government information; KMT deputy Secretary-General, and finally Secretary-General after Lee Teng-hui succeeded the late President Chiang Ching-kuo as party chairman.

Soong's period as party leader and confidant of the new president coincided with numerous reforms in the KMT's and the ROC's democratization. When DPP scored impressive gains in the 1992 Legislative Yuan vote, Soong took responsibility by offering his resignation. Worn by years of party controversy, his future seemed unclear. President Lee and Premier Lien Chan appointed him governor of Taiwan Province, making him the first Mainland-born governor in a generation. This office had been reserved for a Taiwanese as part of KMT's "Taiwanization program" initiated in the 1960s by Chiang Ching-kuo. President Lee had served in this post before becoming vice president.

Soong used the appointment as a stepping stone to election, against odds set by many observers who did not imagine that a Mainland-born KMT candidate would win the allegiance of the island's largest electoral unit made up of 85 percent provincial-born. In a year and a half, Soong reportedly visited every one of 309 towns and townships. He became a household name through cultivation of mass media, especially by vigorous and thorough exposure of his ceremonial visits by local newspapers, including provincial papers, weekly paid advertisements in Taipei papers, and island-wide broadcast of provincial-owned Taiwan Television. He soon reversed the odds and became the hands-down favorite to be the KMT's candidate. He elbowed aside the popular and ambitious Minister of Interior Wu Poh-hsiung, a Hakka (a Chinese ethnic minority among the Fukienese majority of Taiwanese people).[8] Minister Wu withdrew rather than contest Soong, who then was nominated easily by KMT leaders and cadres.

Soong campaigned intensively from August to December. Despite concern in his entourage about DPP opponent Chen Ding-nan, Soong left no stone unturned in relentless pursuit of victory. Chen, former independent magistrate of Ilan County, member of the Legislative Yuan, and recent convert to the DPP had narrowly won nomination in July. Soong ran as if Chen might be snapping at his heels and in the end left more than a million votes between them. With ineffective support and reportedly sometimes inactive participation from DPP county magistrates and city mayors, Chen won only Ilan County among the 21 cities and counties of the province.

Soong's victory opened reinterpretations of "provincialism." Though the population of the province is overwhelmingly Taiwanese, a Mainland-born KMT stalwart was accepted readily. Some attribute this to the KMT's experience and advantaged organizational resources. These cannot explain all

Soong's success because they were available also to the KMT's candidate in Taipei City, who suffered a humiliating defeat. Nor can the outcome be put down to vote-buying, which by now universally acknowledged, at last, was also more vigorously prosecuted and better understood. Soong's enormous outlay of NT dollars must have gone to more substantial purchases than traditional vote-bribery—travel, advertisement, staff, printing, communications. In the end, many Taiwanese did not take easily to the DPP's slogan, "Taiwanese vote only for Taiwanese."

III. Recall Elections

In the midst of the provincial and metropolitan elections, more than two million eligible voters in the largest county constituency on Taiwan had an opportunity on Sunday, 27 November, 1994, to add another chapter to the book on democratization (Taipei County's Mayor You Ching, was a member of the DPP, and as chair of the County Election Commission he managed to schedule this vote on Sunday, in hopes of increasing turnout; the DPP has held its party primaries on Sunday for the same purpose). Only 21 percent, the smallest vote ever in an important Taiwan election, cast ballots for or against retaining four Kuomintang legislators in an unprecedented "recall election." The four defied an unofficial referendum in May by voters in Kungliao Township, Taipei County, who overwhelmingly opposed the construction of a nuclear power plant. As members of the Legislative Yuan, they were forced to choose between demands of constituents that elected them and the policies of the KMT leaders, and President Lee Teng-hui, a native of Sanchih in the county.

Although more than 80 percent voted to terminate terms of offices of the four legislators, the 21 percent participation rate fell below that required in the Public Officials Election and Recall Law. The Legislative Yuan had only recently raised this requirement from one-third to one-half of eligible voters, at the behest of the KMT leadership, to increase the probability that recalls would be defeated. Some supporters of the controversial legislators urged voters to boycott the recall balloting. For whatever reason, an insufficient number of participants doomed the outcome, whether the voting rate requirement was 33 or 50 percent. The legislators, accordingly, retained their offices for the balance of terms to expire in January 1996.

On the same day, at sites adjacent to the 883 polling stations in Taipei County, residents could express their approval or disapproval of the proposed nuclear power plant, the fourth such facility in Taiwan. In all 29 county administrative districts, results ranged from 80 to 96 percent against construction. This vote, organized by the county government rather than the county election commission, was unofficial because Taiwan as yet has no provision for referenda. If recall voting settled the fate of four legislators, the unofficial referendum left unsettled whether and where nuclear power was to be expanded. Recall elections, in which voters decide whether to continue or terminate terms of officials previously elected, are rare except in the United States. The U.S. constitution provides no opportunity to recall a president or a member of Congress. Only some of the 50 states of the United States, especially in the south and west, allow recall elections. They are not nearly so popular as other methods associated with "progressive" or "direct" democracy, including initiative and referenda (sometimes called plebiscites).

In Dr. Sun Yat-sen's philosophy of democracy, borrowed partly from practices in the United States and Western Europe, four methods of popular representation held prominence—elections, recall elections, initiative, and referenda. For 40 years, Taiwan has held regular, periodic elections of local officials, and in the last decade of reform, similar voting opportunities have devolved to the electorate for mayors in the two largest metropolitan areas, for provincial governor, and in 1996 for president of the republic. Although the Public Officials' Election and Recall Law includes a section on recall voting, this event in Taipei County was its first serious test. Recall elections are a form of initiative that results from citizen petitions to call an election on retaining (recalling) an incumbent official or adopting (initiating) a law or policy. Referenda differ from initiatives in that they are devolved (referred) to voters by the government, usually a legislative body.

The history of these forms of direct democracy is recent, roughly the last 100 years in the United States, Switzerland, and some Scandinavian countries. Taken together, they represent a series of checks and balances between elected or appointed representatives and the people they are chosen to represent. Recalls, initiatives, and referenda came late in the development of representative government, after direct election of legislatures. When elected legislators behaved in ways some thought contrary to popular will, they could be countered with a variety of means. One method was to organize political parties to mediate between voters and representatives. Another was to defeat offending politicians when they stood for reelection at the end of short and fixed terms (two to four years, typically). Still another was to limit the number of terms or years that a person could hold any particular office without a period of inactivity between terms. Recall elections are a kind of last resort of voters when other checks and balances seem ineffective. One reason for the absence of such elections in Taiwan is the relatively short experience there with democratic practices and institutions. Voters first experience representative government, then perfect it with more direct forms of popular government, as Dr. Sun observed in the growth of democratic institutions in the West.

Thus one would expect the recent recall election eventually to be emulated by other occasional but not frequent attempts to terminate legislative service between regular elections. This vote in Taipei County was as much about the merits of nuclear power as about the merits of recall elections. Likewise, future introduction of official initiatives or referenda would depend on demands over controversial matters, as well as expectations about the effectiveness of democratic procedures.[9]

IV. Appraising the Electoral Process

In a culture in which public opinion polls apparently are not trusted by respondents, it is difficult to infer voters' motivations. It is less difficult to draw implications from their votes. Post-election interpretations often confuse motives with effects. Whatever the intentions of provincial voters, the consequences of their 1994 electoral choices promoted the status quo and preserved stability in the democratic transformation of Taiwan and the mid course of pragmatic diplomacy between independence and reunification. If this was the mandate of voters, it coincided with the major trend lines of Taiwan politics, since before Chiang Ching-kuo formally launched what became known as the Democratization Period.[10] Taiwan now enjoyed standing, for however long, as the most democratic polity in Asia. It is not a perfect democracy. It never will be. No democracy is complete. None ever has been or will be.[11] But Taiwan's record of frequent, free and fair elections entitles it to some kind of comparative prize for establishing electoral democracy.

The next agenda of democratic reform emerged rather clearly. Major challenges included perfecting electronic media coverage of parties and candidates to increase the flow of reporting and analysis and to decrease the streams of bias and propaganda. Another challenge flowed from the continually rising expense of election campaigns. Taiwan has earned world respect for its rising wealth, yet Japan and the United States have per capita incomes 2.5 times greater. Taiwan elections are more expensive than those in Japan or the United States, while campaign costs will escalate further when parties and candidates are allowed to buy time on television.[12]

With all its residual imperfection, Taiwan democratization earned distinction for having been realized with minimum violence and threats of violence. Sun Yat-sen was an apostle of Asian, or more exactly Chinese, democracy. He was also an advocate of gradualism, and his heirs have made a metaphor of his idea of tutelage. Political élites gradually have devolved political power from a narrow band of participants to virtually all adult citizens who desire to participate (three-fourths of whom do). Gradual non-violent transformation has been the ruling party's objective. More rapid, but also non-violent, transition has been the opposition's goal. In tandem they have cooperated to make the "Taiwan Experience" more than an example of economic growth. They have given the world, still mostly undemocratic, an unusual lesson in devolution rather than revolution.

For these reasons, the significance of the 1994 elections was larger than which candidates from which parties won which offices on a small island of 21 million people. It testified to the fact that within a generation-and-a-half, leaders and followers could relate together to transform a non-democratic polity into an increasingly democratic one. Moreover, this was done in a region of the world said to be inhospitable to an idea thought to be exclusively relevant to another region of the world. The suggestion that Taiwan imported an ill-fitted suit of electoral clothes is a variant of assertions that Asian values and institutions conflict with Western values and institutions. So far as the appropriateness of democracy to Taiwan is concerned, Dr. Sun infused Chinese nationalism with some Western ideas, but he also modified them to fit the contexts established by Chinese history and culture. Moreover, particular electoral procedures have been borrowed, not exclusively from U.S. or European practice, but from elsewhere in Asia. Taiwan's unusual "multi-member, single vote" legislative constituencies apparently derived from Japan, which introduced this method in 1925 and retained it until 1994. Taiwan thus, is an instance of gradual non-violent democratic devolution, and a blend of practices and institutions that is at once universal and provincial. Taken together, they provide a clear formula for preserving stability for the people of Taiwan.

The relatively optimistic projection of the penultimate paragraph more or less coincided with subsequent developments in Taiwan politics and in cross-Strait relations. It did not anticipate, however, the belligerent response of the People's Republic of China to President Lee's June 1995 visit to Cornell University. Following that event, officials of the PRC initiated both propaganda campaigns and campaigns of military threats prior to the December 1995 Legislative Yuan elections and the March 1996 National Assembly and presidential elections. Notwithstanding these influences on Taiwan's elections, voters, candidates and parties successfully conducted their competitive contests. Thus, participants did reconfirm that democratic electoral practices and institutions do indeed offer "one formula for continuing peace and well-being of the people of Taiwan."[13]

Notes

* This is one of a series of essays identifying trends in increased power-sharing in Taiwan since 1986. See James A. Robinson, "Local Elections in Taiwan,

1993–94: Appraising Steps in Democratization," in *Political Chronicle,* vol. 6, no. 2 (1994): p. 1–9. For citations of companion articles, see: Deborah A. Brown, Eric P. Moon & James A. Robinson, "Taiwan's 1998 Legislative and Metropolitan Elections: Appraising Steps in Democratization," in *China Perspectives,* no. 21 (1999): p. 29–37, footnote 1. All papers derive from fieldwork concurrent with the elections.

1. See Robinson, "Local Elections in Taiwan, 1993–94," p. 1–9.

2. Jason C. Hu, ed., *Quiet Revolutions on Taiwan, Republic of China* (Taipei: Kwang Hwa, 1994); Peter Ferdinand, ed., *Taiwan Takeoff* (London: Royal Institute of International Affairs, 1996).

3. Hung-chao Tai, "The Kuomintang and Modernization in Taiwan," in Samuel P. Huntington & Clement H. Moore, eds., *Authoritarian Politics in Modern Society* (New York: Basic Books, 1970), p. 406–436.

4. John F. Copper & George P. Chen, *Taiwan's Elections: Political Development and Democratization in the Republic of China* (Baltimore: University of Maryland Law School, 1984), p. 40–58; Lai Tse-han, Ramon H. Myers & Wei Wou, *Tragic Beginning: Taiwan's Uprising of 1947* (Stanford University Press, 1991), p. 67–70.

5. Andrew J. Nathan, "The Legislative Yuan Elections in Taiwan: Consequences of the Electoral System," in *Asian Survey,* vol. XXXIII, no. 4 (April 1993): p. 424–438.

6. James A.Robinson,"ROC's 1990 National Affairs Conference," in *Issues and Studies,* vol. 26, no. 12 (1990): p. 23–35.

7. *Time,* vol. 144, no. 23 (5 December 1994): p. 30.

8. Clyde Kiang, *The Hakka Search for a Homeland* and *The Hakka Odyssey and their Taiwan Homeland,* both (Eglin, PA: Allegheny Press, 1991 & 1992).

9. John T. Rourke, Richard P. Hiskes & Cyrus Ernesto Zirakzadih, *Direct Democracy and International Politics: Deciding International Issues Through Referendums* (Boulder CO: Lynne Reinner, 1992); David Butler & Austin Ranney, eds., *Referendums around the World* (Washington, DC: AEI Press, 1994).

10. References are innumerable. A comprehensive review is Tun-jen Cheng and Stephan Haggard, eds., *Political Change in Taiwan* (Boulder, CO: L. Rienner, 1992).

11. Robert A. Dahl, *Polyarchy: Participation and Opposition* (New Haven: Yale University Press, 1971), p. 8.

12. James A. Robinson, "Shuan-chu ping fan zhen-ma fu tan teh chi," in *Chung-kuo shih-pao* (29 November 1993): p. 8; "Te hsing hou hsuan jen hui hi mei jih hua chien to," in *Lien-he pao* (29 January 1994): p. 11.

13. This essay, like others in the series, derives from observations made in the field during the election campaigns described and published contemporaneously in *Asian Wall Street Journal, Chung-kuo shih-pao, Lien-he pao, Free China Review,* and especially *Free China Journal* (19 August 1994): p. 7; (25 November 1994): p. 7; (2 December 1994): p. 6; (9 December 1994): p. 7. Many observations are retained, others corrected in light of subsequently obtained information, but the observational standpoint remains that of the on-site field-worker.

FOURTEEN

South Africa

Charles W. Arnade & Keith Tankard

I s there a relationship between autocratic, single individual governments and single or dominant party rule? A valid question. Often strong and dictatorial leaders, such as Juan Peron in Argentina, created a party (such as the Peronist Party) with a democratic façade and trappings to legalize their government. Often the party, as in the case of Argentina, continues after the death of the autocrat. In the case of democratic France a strong and charismatic leader originated a strong party still identified as Gaullist. On the other hand, Mexico, a country with a long period of ruthless dictators (*caudillos*), which finally was able to establish a dominant party, made sure that the party was the ultimate power and that no single individual would be supreme over it. Therefore there are various models that have emerged mainly because of different historical developments—different histories of nations.

What about South Africa? Only a few years have passed since 1990 when the apartheid government under the leadership of F. W. de Klerk opened the political process to the banned parties (ANC, PAC, and SACP). De Klerk's party, the NP, was the dominant party of the enfranchised white minority. It took until 1994 to have a nonracial election giving the vast number of previously disfranchised inhabitants of South Africa the right to vote. The result was the emergence of the ANC as the dominant party of the nation and also the dominant voice of the non-white voters, just as the NP had previously been the dominant voice of the white voters. Have the radical changes since 1990 really not changed the political habits and nature of South Africa? Is it based on strong rule by strong person, rooted in its unique history?

South Africa's history in the last 150 years is one of strong personalities with autocratic tendencies. The long rule of the NP is characterized by leadership of strong men, including De Klerk, who terminated apartheid. Only a forceful leader could have done this, bending the institutionalized party to his will. The phenomenal success of the ANC was mainly due to a strong leader, Nelson Mandela, who opted for peaceful means. They were able to accomplish this, a unique event in history. Mandela is certainly dominant in the dominant party. Will the ANC continue in that position after Mandela relinquishes power to Thabo Mbeki?

The ANC's greatest challenge is probably not the weakened NP, which has opened its ranks to non-whites, but the Zulu-dominated IFP, directed by a powerful personality of an authoritarian nature, Chief Mangosuthu Gatsha Buthelezi. The IFP is more regional than national as it is ethnically oriented, dominant in the KwaZulu area. One can say with good reason, and most studies will confirm this, that the ANC is mainly Xhosa in composition. Mandela is a Xhosa and so are most of its leadership. Also the NP white party has been largely Afrikaners, descendants of the Boers (Dutch settlers). Certainly the history of South Africa has shaped the present. While this is true with all nations, in South Africa it is particularly significant and important. South Africa in the last one or even two centuries is an example of the emergence of dominant parties. But when looked at from a global point of view South Africa's political realities are unique and its past is unique. What is today's South Africa is the result of a complex and fascinating history. Without some knowledge of this past it is difficult to understand the events during the last 60 or more years. Leonard Thompson in his *History of South Africa* laments that those who write and discuss South Africa make little reference to what occurred before 1652 when the first white settlers arrived.[1]

The area of the modern south and Namibia (the old South-West Africa)[2] were rather isolated from the mainstream of human world history. Neither the ancestors of the present-day black majority population, nor the whites, were present. Today's blacks (Bantu-speaking)[3] began arriving in A.D. 300 and whites in 1652. Before A.D. 300 and into the very far past the land was inhabited by indigenous persons of whom today's Bushmen and Hottentots[4] are direct descendants. We call these early people the Khoisan and San. The overwhelming majority of the population of the south of today cannot trace their origins to what we now call the pre-Christian era. While 1652 is the date of the first white settlement, the Portuguese sailors of the Bartholomeau Dias expedition made contact in 1487 at Mossel Bay. Not until 1652 did the Dutch establish a station at the Cape of Good Hope. And, by 1652, the Europeans had already established themselves in the Americas. In Africa, north of southern Africa, great civilizations existed and had existed.

Only in Australia was the isolation of its original population more severe. Not until the late eighteenth century did Europeans start to settle in Australia. There was a simple clash between a technologically far more advanced people and a gathering and hunting people with millennia of isolation from the development of human history. The clash pushed the Australian aborigines into unoccupied lands or killed them. It was similar to what happened in North America when the Europeans arrived in the sixteenth century. Today Australia and the United States have vibrant democracies. The development of democracy in each country was based on a cruel past of the genocide of a people. The development of democracy in South Africa was more complicated.

Geographically, southern Africa is also isolated. The coast is inhospitable and access was limited and difficult, with few good harbors. Large areas are arid and desert. Rainfall is limited, but occasionally heavy. The original population, the Khoisan and San, were reasonably well adjusted to the harsh land, which had sufficient game. They were undisturbed for millennia, and around 3000 years ago people in the northern part of today's Botswana acquired cattle and "took to herding."[5]

These herders later expanded south. Therefore there existed basically a hunting-gathering people and those who herded cattle in the more northern regions. All this changed in what we now call the Christian Era. After A.D. 300, Bantu-speaking people began to drift South Africa of the Limpopo River. They began farming and herding and also extracting and processing metals, including copper and iron. They probably migrated in an earlier period from east and central Africa.

South Africa gives 1652 as the beginning of its history, when the Dutch East Indian Company founded a fort at Table Bay where today's Cape Town is located. Often a rationale for white supremacy was the assertion that the European colonists came and expanded into "empty land." A more moderate version asserts that European colonization was contemporary with African colonization. This is not accurate. Until recently South African official history was used to justify European minority rule.[6]

Another crucial year was 1795, the year the British occupied the Cape Colony. It marked the end of a century and a half of rule by the Dutch East India Company. It started the history of the Anglo-whites different from the Boers, the Dutch-Huguenot white settlers. By now there were about 20,000 Boers, the greatest number in Cape Town and the Western Cape, where some kind of local government had come into existence. A small number had gone to the east and taken to cattle farming. The Boers, especially those in the east, were ferociously independent and narrow-minded. As Gailey wrote, "They disliked any authority, believed in their God-given superiority over all Black men, were normally uneducated and fiercely Calvinistic and wandered freely over the countryside to stake their claims to huge cattle ranges."[7]

Those in the east towards the Fish River had, about 20 years earlier, encountered and clashed with the Bantu-speaking Xhosa. It was the first real opposition by non-whites. The Khoisan and San of the first contact days, over 100 years ago, had been reduced "to a servile state of landless men."[8] With the Xhosa encounter South Africa's history begins a long and ruthless struggle, which basically lasted until the present and shaped the demand for absolute white supremacy—the roots of the National Party. It should be recalled that the ANC is heavily Xhosa in composition and that Mandela is Xhosa. The NP and the ANC are certainly dominant parties, and historical roots are deep.

English attempts to be more conciliatory and less racially ardent had only slight effect. Conflict continued, and is now known as the Frontier Wars (previously the derogatory term "*Kaffir*" wars was used).[9] By 1803 the Dutch, representing the Batavian Republic, regained control of the colony. But the British returned in 1806 (all this because of the Napoleonic Wars) and the British possession was legalized in 1814 in the final peace settlement. The nineteenth century is one of immense complexity because of the convergence of many peoples—whites of varying roots, behaviors and cultures; Africans of different roots, behaviors and cultures; Asians with dissimilar cultures and religions. There were also new economic forces, especially the discovery of diamonds and gold. Then the new authority of Britain, the now prime global power with more humane ideologies inspired by the Enlightenment, created tensions. A more benevolent religious outlook clashed with the entrenched prejudices of white and Christian superiority. One cannot forget climatological and environmental changes in Southern Africa along with an expanding population. All these came together and produced a century of confusion, violence, cruelty, and some heroic, charismatic leaders. Eventually, nations were born in our century: Botswana, Namibia, Swaziland, Lesotho, and the regional power that is South Africa. Can we say that by now (nearly 200 years later) South Africa has reached democracy without a Western-style democratic tradition (except for the British component)?

The early eighteenth century attests to these new forces, especially a population explosion and drought. Three pivotal events, resulting in clashes with much violence, set the stage for the coming decades and all of the twentieth century. First is what is known as *Mfecane*. It means, in English, "crushing" or "time of crushing" and has been modified as a "time of troubles."[10] This time of trouble was a massive movement of Africans, mostly South Africa and westward. Second was the celebrated Boer trek north and east, which encountered the African migration coming in the opposite direction. Third, there was the growing presence of the English in the eastern coastal areas and its hinterland in what is now Natal and central and northern parts of the Eastern Cape.

In the 1810s the Zulus, a clan of the Nguni-speaking Africans, under their great leader Shaka, had become a dominant force. They established a powerful and well-organized kingdom between the coast and the mountain escarpment and north of the far earlier arrivals, the Xhosas. The Zulu genesis was a part of the vast movements, which earlier had only been a trickle of Africans across the Limpopo River to the fertile and rather disease-free land between the coast and the mountains (Drakensberg), partly caused by a population explosion. The Zulu "outburst" intensified the *Mfecane*.[11] There were movements in all directions, fleeing, migrations, integrations. It was an ever-increasing circle of disarray. One could compare it to what happened in the first centuries A.D. in Europe with the migrations from the east and north towards and into the Roman Empire, which a standard text calls the "forces of disruption."[12] That could be termed a European *Mfecane*.

While the *Mfecane* was underway, the Boers of Dutch, German, and some Huguenot stock began their trek. It mostly took place between 1836 to 1854, crossing the Orange River towards the Vaal River and west of the mountains into the high veld. Some then crossed the Drakensberg mountains towards the more productive region between the mountains and the coast, where, among others, the Zulus had settled. These Boers, originally over 12,000, also were land-hungry, but wanted to escape as well the more enlightened policies of the new English administration. They believed that there were unreasonable restrictions to their individual rights and their beliefs.

Thirdly, the British began to enforce their authority north of the Orange River. By 1824 some English merchants were present in what is today Durban. Settlers continued to come, and it is estimated that around 5,000 had arrived before 1852. Most were English, but some were Germans and a few were from the not-too-distant Indian Ocean island of Mauritius. The increasing presence of the English coincided with the Boer trekkers who had crossed the Drakensberg into the rich land that stretched to the Indian Ocean. The trans-Drakensberg trekkers had among its leaders Andreas Pretorius, after whom the South African capital, Pretoria, was named.

The stage was set for confrontation. The Zulus, among others, had established a viable and strong kingdom. The English, now permanently in their Cape Colony, undertook as the leading European power of the Enlightenment, some political, cultural, social, and economic reforms and set out to extend their authority over a far wider area. Reform-minded missionaries and their societies became influential. The Boers felt threatened and migrated. With it a distinct people emerged who eventually, in the twentieth century, developed "the ideology of apartheid."[13]

On 16 December 1838 (later a national holiday in South Africa) the trekkers defeated the Zulus, they claimed by "Divine Sanction," in the Battle of Blood River.[14] Soon afterward these Boers established the Republic of Natal. In 1842 the British annexed Natal and the Boers trekked back across the mountains to the high veld. Thus ended the Zulu nation and the Boer Republic of Natal, while the Zulu nation resigned to British rule. They became aware of the more benevolent attitudes of the British as compared to the Boers. And the British never lost their respect for the Zulus.

Eventually the Boer trekkers were successful in the high veld, and two Boer nations were established. Their lasting heritage was the creation of the Orange Free State and Transvaal, which became two of the four provinces of the Union of South Africa. The Afrikaner Republic of Orange Free State came into existence in 1854 and that of Transvaal in 1852—both claiming independence from the British. Relations with the British were complex and strained. In 1862 diamonds were found along the Orange and Vaal Rivers, and in the next decades gold was discovered in Transvaal. The economy was profoundly changed. These new riches were not an "unmixed blessing for the farmers and burghers."[15] Outsiders in the thousands arrived. These "*Uitlanders*" constituted a threat.[16] Britain was ready to claim its presence by various means and proposals. Again the Boers felt victimized. Eventually their two republics succumbed after two wars, the first one in 1880–81 and the far more significant Anglo-Boer War of 1899–1902, which was a major event in British history. Two years after the war the white population of South Africa climbed to over one million, having more than tripled in three decades. In the meanwhile, since 1860 thousands of Indians had arrived in the province of Natal, most in indentured service, and the great majority remained when their contracts ended, becoming laborers, artisans, and some small land-holders. In number they would soon equal the whites in Natal. In 1910 the Cape Colony, the Orange Free State, the Transvaal, and Natal were joined by Britain to form the Union of South Africa. Racial harmony was elusive.

What about the Western concept of democracy and within it the role of political parties? Today the new South Africa, whose laudable goal is ethnic integration, has adopted the Westminster/U.S. model. The British part of the South African–roots equation represents the standard evolution of English political, cultural, and economic attitudes and emerging structures in its numerous colonies, be it in north America, the Caribbean, Asia, Oceania, or Africa. Most of the colonies on becoming independent adopted representative democracy that emphasizes individual rights and a multi-party system. In South Africa there was another important factor in the equation: another white people, the Boers, whose established ideology was very different. Its ideology became the ideology of apartheid.

The Boers, who proudly called themselves Afrikaners, separated from the British by declaring their grievances. It reminds us of those Americans, who in 1776, also declared their independence from the English. The philosophy of the Boers (Afrikaners) when they trekked to independence was quite different. The Piet Relief Manifesto of January 1837 (Piet Relief was a trek leader who was killed by the Zulus) was a clear presentation of the Afrikaner grievances, reminiscent of the grievances enumerated in the American Declaration of Independence.[17] To be sure, in the U.S. Declaration the true native Americans (Indians) are identified as "merciless Indian savages" supposedly supported by the English. However, the document is still an expression of the enlightenment of the age to which Jefferson, its author, and the other leaders of the revolution, such as Madison, John Adams, and Hamilton, were devoted.[18] The Afrikaner expressions are basically a negation of the Enlightenment. While it stated that "wherever we go, we will uphold the just principle of liberty . . . that no one shall be held in a state of slavery, it is our determination to maintain . . . and preserve proper relations between master and servant" (Relief Manifesto).[19]

In June 1837, the first meeting of the *Volksvergadering* (Peoples' Assembly) of the trekkers took place, and they wrote what "were the foundation of the future Boer republics." Nine articles were adopted. They declared that the law would be that as was in use in the colony in 1795, the Roman-Dutch law, that there would be a court of magistrates, a parliament, and the executive power was the commandant general. Finally, no one was permitted to have "any connection and never correspond with the London Missionary Society."[20] It meant their fundamental brand of Christian dogma was the sole and divinely inspired religion. This union of Church and state, which later became the union of the party (NP) and religion (Dutch Reformed Church), was a cornerstone of apartheid. What emerged was what author Norval identifies as "Christian Afrikaans national socialism."[21] She says "it recognized only one (and therefore no) political party; government and the state were elevated above the *Volk;* and it disregarded the autonomy of spheres of human life. . . ."[22] Professor J. A. Wiid states that the "native policy of the *Trekkers* was later copied, not only in the Boer Republics, but also in the Union of South Africa."[23] The British, who militarily won the Anglo-Boer War and then created a unified British colony in 1910, eventually lost out to the ideology of the Boers. We can say what Andre Du Toit and Hermann Giliomee write in their first sentences of their book, *Afrikaner Political Thought,* that "the political hegemony on Afrikaner nationalism is a central product of South African history."[24] The Afrikaners ferociously believed that they had been mistreated. The principal manifesto of the Transvaal Republic, adopted in 1899 when the Anglo-Boer War started and entitled, "A Century of Wrong," lucidly expresses their anger.

They were determined to be vindicated and to rule in the next century. From 1910 their ideology was in ascendancy, reaching their goal in 1948 with the general election resoundingly won by the Afrikaner National Party.[25]

But what about the great injuries to the majority population—the non-whites? From early times the population has always been unofficially or officially classified by color or race. Just before World War II the African population was 69 percent, the so-called coloreds 8 percent, and the Asian-Indians (nearly all in Natal) 2 percent. By that time, the population was close to ten million. Urbanization had accelerated: 65 percent of whites lived in urban areas, 44 percent of colored, 66 percent of Asians and only 17 percent of the Africans. The government had schemes, including pass laws, to limit the African population in the cities.[26] Just before 1986 the population had grown to 27.6 million of, which 19 million were classified as black; 2.8 million as colored; 861,000 as Asian; and 4.8 million as white. Of the latter, there were now 70,000 Portuguese, who mostly had migrated from the ex-Portuguese African colonies.[27]

"Colored" was one of the defined racial categories. It needs an explanation because of its uniqueness. Coloreds are mostly located in the Cape Province and sometimes referred to as Cape Colored. The original Cape inhabitants eventually came to be known as Khoikhoi (Hottentots) and the San (Bushmen). Later, slaves were brought from Asia and some other African regions. Abolition of slavery took effect in 1837. Emancipation resulted in equal status for the ex-slaves and Khoikhoi and San. "Officials soon began to refer to them comprehensively as the Cape Colored people. The term has stuck."[28] In the next century the strict classification of white, black, colored and Asian emerged during the ages of segregation (1910–48) and apartheid (1948–92). In the age of segregation, when the Afrikaners still had not gained complete power through limited democratic elections, racial laws, decrees, statutes, and provisos came into existence, some legalizing white-imposed customs. The thriving gold mines, which had become the vital element of the nation's economy, employed a vast number of workers. Over 80 percent were Africans and the rest whites. As early as 1911 rigid racial laws were introduced through the Mines and Work Act. Two years later the monumental Native Land Act was promulgated creating "reserves" and prohibiting Africans from purchasing land outside these reservations. Thus, the vast majority of the population, the Africans, lost their land. The small white minority now claimed the vast majority of the land. This law is the forerunner of the homelands of the apartheid period, which stripped the blacks of their citizenship and made them all foreigners within the country, but citizens in their respective homelands. No country in the world recognized their existence of these homelands (Bantustans).[29]

In 1936 various acts were passed strengthening the racial laws. They fully or partially disenfranchised non-whites, placing them on separate voter rolls. While in World War I, black South Africans fought in the war against Germany, in World War II, the Africans and colored could serve only as laborers and drivers. The slow, but ever increasing, humiliation of non-whites was glaringly evident. Democracy and all its trappings were only for whites. It was the rule of a single race with a democratic façade. Soon after 1910 Africans began to react, but interestingly within the parameters of democratic behavior. There had been lukewarm initiatives before 1910. But not until the Union of South Africa was established did more organized efforts take place. The ANC, now led by President Nelson Mandela, came into existence in 1912. It was originally called the South African Native National Congress, and was set up to oppose the Native Land Act of 1913. Eventually other resistance organizations, some non-African, began to participate. This included multiracial unions, addressing the exploitation of laborers and rural workers. In the face of government repression and internal squabbling these proved ineffective. It has to be recognized that the vanguard were the black organizations.

The black leaders who emerged at the time of the 1910 union and in the post-union era were a new type. The power of the old tribal chiefs, rooted in the communal African culture, had been eroded and many had become subservient to the dominant white establishment. The new Western educated blacks and coloreds had received their education mainly in the various liberal churches, which had become centers for African gatherings and education, semi-protected from white reprisals. The influence of these churches cannot be underestimated. While the ideology of the Afrikaner is according to Norval, "Christian Afrikaans National Socialism,"[30] the emerging non-white opposition is embodied in what we call today liberation theology. We cannot forget the influence of passive resistance of Mahatma Gandhi, who as a young man lived in Natal.[31]

Western ideologies, too, profoundly influenced the resistance leaders. These ranged from traditional democracy to various brands of socialism to Marxism and Leninism and also various shades of U.S. civil rights and anti-Vietnam ideologies.[32] Basically five leading organizations emerged during the segregation and apartheid periods: the ANC; the SACP, organized in 1921; the PAC, founded in 1959 as a more radical splinter of the ANC; the Black Consciousness Movement of the late 1960s; and, finally, the IFP, founded in 1928 and later revitalized by Chief Buthelezi as a Zulu identity organization. By the end of apartheid period and the collapse of white supremacy rule, only the ANC, the NP of the apartheid white exclusivistic rule, and to a somewhat lesser extent, the IFP were the main political players. But the SACP, closely allied to the ANC, was and still is a party to consider. One of the reasons why the ANC and the SACP assumed more significance is that their programs were multiracial. The crucial ANC Freedom Charter, issued in 1955, emphasized this. The charter "recognized that cultural, linguistic and religious pluralism are not only permissible, but desirable."[33] Kathryn Manzo clearly tells us the term black (as in the Black Consciousness Movement) "refers to Africans only."[34] The PAC, which came into existence a few years after the Charter proclamation, was disturbed by its all-embracing nature.[35] The SACP believed that racism was a product of class struggle, which also marginalized many exploited whites. There is no doubt that after 1948 the whites imposed total control over the other races.

In her recent study, Marina Ottaway writes that the NP "did not depend on votes alone. It was more than just a political party; it had become a state as well, a *party-state*." This was, Ottaway tells us, a term used by President Sekou Touré of Guinea.[36] We are reminded that a number of African leaders (as well as others in Latin America and Asia) had established single and totally dominant parties to govern. Was the totally white NP of South Africa just another manifestation of the political realities of the post–World War II era? But here it was based completely on a minority race that used a "party-state" to dominate, disenfranchise, segregate the great majority and marginalize those whites who opposed strongly, moderately, or even mildly their policies. There is no doubt that the NP membership and voters support was mainly those of the Afrikaners. Therefore, this dominant, single-rule party or "party-state" was not only white, but a brand of whites—the Afrikaners speaking *patois* Dutch.

Another crucial date in South Africa's history is 1948. It is the year that the period of apartheid started, escalating racial discrimination of the era of segregation to the separation and total disenfranchisement of non-whites. That year the NP won a greater than expected victory in the general election. While their vote was under 50 percent, they won a majority of the seats in parliament—70 seats mainly from the rural regions. The United Party, which was expected to win, received 65 seats, mainly from urban voters. From that date until 1994 the NP ruled South Africa, marginalizing all other white opposition and the non-white voters, even taking away their citizenship. Within the white electorate a façade of democracy was presented. Whites in 1948 were 12 percent of the total population; NP received 48 percent of their vote in the election, meaning that they became the dominant party with a vote of less than 6 percent of what in a true democracy constitutes the eligible electorate.[37]

The NP-dominant government rapidly developed into apartheid rule. One author writes that apartheid was to "further the aim and interests of either an atavistic group of white Afrikaner racists, or of the Afrikaner petty bourgeois."[38] Historian Thompson believes that the apartheid system dealt with four ideas. These were strict racial groupings (whites, coloreds, Asians, and blacks); white superiority with whites "entitled to have absolute control over the state"; white interests must prevail; no "equal facilities for the subordinate races." Only the whites "formed a single nation." Indeed, this was accomplished.[39]

The collapse of apartheid and the reasons for it remain to be studied when time gives us a better perspective, and more data emerges. Professor Thomashaversusen states that apartheid only stood "for a vast range of policies adopted over decades in an unsystematic fashion. . . ." Thomashaversusen insists that it did not collapse but was "dismantled."[40] In the opinion of this author (Arnade), it was a system imposed by a people of West European roots. It was imposed in the mid twentieth century. It was an absurdity and an aberration of democracy and even of single-party dominance. But the post-1990 events must be addressed with a 1999 perspective.

By 1990 the phenomenon of apartheid was rapidly losing its grip in the face of social and economic pressure. Such was the nature of change during the 1980s that it was becoming virtually impossible to continue to enforce the system except at massive cost in both blood and money. At the heart of the change was rapid urbanization. For the first time in its history, the majority of South Africans lived in the towns and cities, with the urban Africans outnumbering their white counterparts. Already by the mid 1970s, white education had reached its ceiling, which meant that future expansion of the South African economy rested with the black people. Financial pressure alone was therefore causing many local institutions to defy government regulations by applying voluntary desegregation.[41] Pressures of an expanding population also saw urban segregation erode ever more rapidly during the 1980s. Housing surpluses in white neighborhoods, combined with critical shortages in the black townships, encouraged the African middle class to migrate in defiance of the law. Once there, they found that South Africa's law courts were reluctant to send them back.

Social structures were therefore integrating and that, in turn, put pressure on the very foundations of the apartheid legal system. Furthermore, limited reform under the P.W. Botha régime tended also to undermine the structure. Once the Immorality Act was scrapped in 1985, thereby allowing sexual relationships across the color line, it became almost impossible to apply the other apartheid laws. If white and black people were allowed to cohabit, where were they to live? Where would their children go to school?[42] By 1990, therefore, the apartheid system was on the brink of expiring. It needed, however, the political will-power to perform the act of euthanasia to consign it legally to the grave. President P.W. Botha promised such in his much vaunted Rubicon speech from Durban in August 1985, but perceived pressure for change from the international community made him stubborn and he balked from reform at the very last moment.

There were nevertheless serious problems for the many players in this complicated political game. In the first place, the radical Left would not give cognizance to the changes that were evolving quite naturally, believing that the only form of revolution was the bloody sort. The NP, on the other hand, although long admitting that continued segregation was enforceable only at unacceptable cost, was nevertheless witnessing a hemorrhage of membership to the neo-Nazi ultra-Right.

Even in 1990, however, the government was still very much in control of the country and had the confidence of the powerful South African army, which had scarcely flexed its muscles as far as internal politics was concerned. Furthermore, by then Communism had collapsed in the Soviet Union and the Cold War was over. Because the liberation struggle was far from bringing about a violent overthrow of the régime, the government could then negotiate from a position of strength.[43]

On the other hand, the continual violence after the Soweto massacre of 1976 had been accelerating through the 1980s. When combined with the economic and cultural strangulation that sanctions was producing, it was bringing home to the government quite forcibly that the black majority had to be given a voice. The alternative was decades of violence, which would destroy not only the South African economy but the very fabric of its society. Far better, therefore, to negotiate a change while still dominating the political arena.

The principal tactic employed by the liberation forces, on the other hand, was to make the South African townships ungovernable. This, however, saw the opposition forces themselves lose control. With so many of its real leaders in detention, the townships were falling increasingly into the hands of an immature, self-styled despotism that had no use for democracy. Indeed, the favorite punishment for suspected informers was "necklacing," an inhuman system whereby a tire was placed around the victim's shoulders, after which he or she was doused in fuel and set alight.

Such a state of chaos afforded criminal elements ample room for fostering their own ends. It also gave rise to vigilante groups, which reacted against the excesses of the kangaroo courts, often with the tacit support of the state security system. This meant that the brutality was giving rise to a neo-feudalism as warlords in the squatter camps afforded protection, sometimes together with such essential services as water and electricity, in return for loyalty and a payment of dues.

While the government appeared to be losing control of the townships, however, two other factors were coloring the political arena. The first was the success that the military forces were having at destabilizing the economies of

South Africa's neighbors, which largely prevented these states from participating in the sanctions campaign. At the same time, a carrot was offered: that such destabilization would cease if support for the liberation forces was withdrawn. In this way, ANC and PAC bases had to be moved farther and farther from the scene of action. While this was happening, Natal and KwaZulu were degenerating into a civil war. Unlike the other homelands, where support for the ANC was strong, it was probably weakest in Natal as an IFP autocracy was able to muscle opposition out of the vast rural areas, leaving the ANC mainly with an urban power-base.

The government was nevertheless beset with a sinking economy as sanctions bit ever deeper. The value of the South African currency tumbled and there was a negative growth rate for the first time since the NP had taken control in 1948. Moreover, opposition in the workplace had taken a new form with the organization of COSATU in 1985, producing a new record of 793 strikes in 1986 alone.[44] The NP was also aware of the hemorrhage of white voters to the militant ultra-Right. The general election of May 1987 saw the Liberal PFP ousted as the official opposition, and its place taken by the CP. It was quite clear, moreover, that the NP was holding onto power because of a swing from the Liberal, English-speaking community. It was therefore a matter of time before the ultra-Right would topple the government.

The turning point arrived suddenly and dramatically. Just when the "imperial presidency" appeared unable to make the necessary steps towards reform, Botha suffered a stroke. Although he valiantly clung on, he was forced to let go leadership of the NP to F. W. de Klerk. Immediately there followed a power struggle, for it was unheard of that the leader of the NP was not also head of government. Ultimately, on 10 August, 1989, Botha's hand was forced and he grudgingly stepped down as president. Although de Klerk had never been known as a reformist, he quickly showed that his presidency would be more flexible. After weathering a grueling snap general election called by his predecessor for September, he immediately reshuffled his cabinet to bring more enlightened men to the fore. The following month he announced the release of some of the most prominent political prisoners. It was in February 1990, however, that de Klerk stunned the world with two dramatic announcements. First was the unbanning of the major liberation parties, namely the ANC, the PAC and the SACP. Just over a week later he revealed that Mandela himself would be released the following day. As the "prisoner of the century" walked to freedom on 11 February, the NP revealed the greatest policy shift in its entire history, and the road was open for a negotiated settlement rather than a bloody revolution.

Events thereafter moved rapidly. In May the first "talks about talks" were held between the government and the ANC, to be repeated in July and again in August. By December 1991 the two parties had moved sufficiently forwards to begin the first round of negotiations towards setting up a new constitution. This was CODESA, a forum comprising most of the major political parties in the country with the notable exceptions of the ultra-Left PAC and the ultra-Right CP.[45]

Behind the scenes, however, a jockeying for power had already begun in earnest, taking on many forms. The liberation forces were, up until 1990, united in a common cause but once it became clear that South Africa was moving inexorably towards a new democracy, fracturing occurred as each of the parties began to seek its own constituency. The ultra-Right parties, on the other hand, believed that the NP was fast losing its support and was no longer a legitimate authority. They therefore concentrated their actions on destabilizing the peace process while at the same time demanding the general election, which they believed would sweep them into power.

While moderates hoped that de Klerk's initiatives would restore peace to the ravaged country, the opposite happened. South Africa was catapulted into new crises of unrest and violence. In the townships, left-wing "comrades" sensed an imminent overthrow of the government and their excesses caused the vigilante groups to retaliate, creating a spiral of violence, which was driven to greater heights through the savagery of the criminal elements that milked the situation.

At the same time, trouble erupted in various homelands. Bloody conflict exploded in KwaZulu as the IFP and the ANC clashed for the hearts and minds of the Zulu people, a struggle which spilt over into the mine hostels on the Witwatersrand gold-fields where Zulu migrant workers lived. Coups d'états saw the Transkei and Ciskei governments topple, while unrest caused the South African government to take action in Bophuthatswana, Venda, and Gazankulu. In all of this there was suspicion, later corroborated, of the existence of a so-called "third force," being the South African security network operating undercover to bolster opposition to the ANC.[46]

Meanwhile, the ANC and its SACP ally made a last-ditch attempt to smuggle arms into the country to test the state for a possible weak underbelly. "Operation Vula" in July 1990 revealed, however, that the government was indeed still a viable force, and the failed mission caused such tension to the negotiators that the ANC at last announced the official end to its armed struggle.

Right-wing opposition was of a different nature. The government's legitimacy amongst the white populace hinged upon a democratic process, and the general elections of September 1989 had seen the NP majority shrink to a mere 20 seats. The CP, together with its neo-Nazi allies, wished therefore to force the government into calling yet another general election, which it believed would oust the de Klerk administration.

At the same time, the president was himself in an awkward position because he had promised in 1990 that the new constitution would eventually be submitted to the white electorate for its approval. The ANC, on the other hand, refused to enter long-term dialogue with the prospect that the negotiated settlement would ultimately hinge on a white minority referendum.

Early in 1992 a bye-election had to be held in the western Transvaal constituency of Potchefstroom. The NP, renowned for its well-oiled political machine, fought a particularly inept campaign, which stunned many of its supporters. It is possible, however, that this was a deliberate ploy, a calculated risk that would see the CP win the seat, but give de Klerk an excuse for calling a snap referendum to test his mandate for a negotiated settlement.

If so, then his gamble paid off handsomely, with 69 percent of the white electorate supporting his position and thereby strengthening his hand in several directions. First, it indicated that the vast majority of whites did indeed want a negotiated settlement to the conflict. On the other hand, it also gave de Klerk the excuse he needed to avoid another bruising general election. At the same time he could claim that this was the referendum he had promised, thereby tempering ANC fears.

Despite the overwhelming mandate for negotiation, however, the second round of CODESA collapsed in May 1992 when it became clear that none of the parties were yet prepared to go the whole distance in terms of essential compromises. The failure led almost immediately to renewed crises which took two forms. In the first place, the ANC, SACP, and COSATU alliance called upon its members to embark on a "rolling mass action" that would bring the government to its knees, but the day before the campaign was due to begin a massacre took place in a squatter camp at Boipatong in the southern Transvaal. Although the killers were all Zulus and members of the IFP, allegations of "third force" involvement further tarnished the image of the NP.

Yet the events also had unexpected consequences for the liberation parties. The massacre, together with the "rolling mass action," was crippling the fragile South African economy, which the ANC would eventually inherit. Moreover, a mass-meeting at a sports stadium in Bisho led to the Ciskei police opening fire on the crowds, killing many and injuring hundreds. It was clear that any further action would cost the nation dearly in money and blood.

Both the ANC and the NP were therefore ready to resume negotiations, but it had become apparent that the multi-party CODESA discussions were clumsy and inflexible. Instead, the two primary role-players appointed a negotiator each to break the deadlock, and behind the scenes dialogue was launched between the ANC's Cyril Ramaphosa and the NP's Roelf Meyer. In this way the two parties were able to move forward and reach what they termed a "Record of Understanding."

The agreements, however, threw the smaller parties into disarray. They objected to the fact that they were no longer being consulted, and that decisions made by the ANC and NP were simply being thrust upon them as a *fait accompli*. Because of this, several organizations representing the IFP, the Zulu monarchy, the various homeland governments, and the ultra-Right wing left the negotiations in protest and formed themselves into an alliance called the Concerned South Africans Group (COSAG). Nevertheless, the Record of Understanding did enable the remaining parties to begin negotiations once again, but this time it was at the World Trade Center, and the new forum would be called the Multi-Party Negotiating Process and no longer CODESA. Its first decision was a surprising one for, instead of thrashing out an interim constitution and then deciding on a date for South Africa's first democratic election, the council opted rather to declare the election date and then sort out the constitution.

The ANC was concerned with establishing a sense of urgency that would prevent the NP from dragging its heels. That, in turn, would ensure that major stumbling blocks would be overcome rapidly. It was also decided that a Transitional Executive Council (TEC) would be established, a kind of super-cabinet consisting of members of the Negotiating Process who would keep a watch over government policy during the run-up to the elections. All agreements were now reached by a tactic known as "sufficient consensus." No one knew exactly what this meant but it was interpreted to mean that if the ANC and NP reached agreement, then sufficient consensus had occurred. Frustrated by this apparent dictatorship, the delegates from the Ciskei and Bophuthatswana thereupon walked out to join COSAG, and a new opposition was formed known as the Freedom Alliance. However, because its foundation was the IFP and the ultra-Right, the Freedom Alliance transmitted ominous signals of an imminent civil war in South Africa.[47]

Two events subsequently substantiated this apprehension: an invasion of the World Trade Center by a heavily armed ultra-Right para-military force, and a march through the streets of Johannesburg by traditionally armed IFP supporters. Although the former was costly in terms of structural damage to the building, the latter caused mayhem when sharp-shooters on the roof of the ANC headquarters at Shell House opened fire, leaving 18 dead and hundreds injured.

Another serious clash occurred in Bophuthatswana on the eve of the election. Civil servants panicked, believing that if Bophuthatswana failed to join the new South Africa their jobs and pensions would be in jeopardy. Violence thereupon erupted and the homeland president called in support from the ultra-Right. The event turned into a fiasco. Neo-Nazis drove through the streets of the capital, Mmabatho, randomly shooting at passers-by and killing many. One of their vehicles was stopped, however, and two of its injured occupants were summarily executed by the Bophuthatswana police in full view of a press contingent.[48]

The incident sent waves of nausea through the white community but, at the same time, the débâcle of the ultra-Right's ridiculous invasion essentially destroyed the credibility of that movement. Indeed, the more level-headed General Constand Viljoen immediately abandoned his former allies and announced the formation of the new Freedom Front Party to represent the Afrikaners in the negotiation process. Then, with only days to go to the election itself, the IFP announced its participation. Immediately the country breathed a sigh of relief as the very real threat of civil war dissipated. The week leading up to the elections was marred by sporadic outbursts of violence, particularly in the form of random bombings by the ultra-Right in a last-ditch attempt to destabilize the process. The targets were various polling stations, as well as Johannesburg's international airport. Yet, when 27 April dawned, an uncanny peace broke out, which was to last for the duration of the election.

The polling produced some unexpected results. First, the ANC failed to win its expected two-thirds majority, which would have enabled the party to rewrite unilaterally the Constitution. Yet, more surprising was the weak support for the PAC, which won a mere 5 seats in the 400-seat National Assembly. The Liberal DP was another victim, with moderate whites giving their vote either to the ANC or the NP. The latter, in turn, found unexpected support from the colored community of the western cape and so was enabled to win 20 percent of the votes, entitling de Klerk to become the second deputy president. The IFP, too, defied predictions and scored third place in the overall ratings, while taking control of the new KwaZulu-Natal province.[49]

On 10 May 1994 Nelson Rolihlahla Mandela was sworn in as South Africa's first black president. The initial phase of the struggle was now over, but in many ways a more important one was beginning because the new government had urgent duties to attend. Not only did it have to begin putting the economy back on track but it also had a mere two years to reach agreement on a final constitution. The new administration was to be a government of national unity, with one ministerial post to be apportioned for each 5 percent of the votes, based on a system of proportional representation. Although the ANC was therefore dominant, the NP and the IFP were brought into the ministerial fold. Given the divided nature of their constituencies, however, this was by no means an easy task, since the ANC was, in 1994, still a full-blooded Socialist party with a strong Communist base, while the NP and IFP were both essentially ultra-conservative. Unlike most governments, in which the majority of ministerial appointees have had years of political experience through parliamentary debate, the Mandela administration had no such experience. Indeed, until 1990 many of the new parliamentarians and ministers had either been languishing on the infamous Robben Island or living abroad in exile. Furthermore, there is a major difference between being a freedom fighter and managing a government of a modern industrial state.

A pressing problem confronting the new administration was how to deliver on its many promises made during the liberation struggle. Indeed, so many unattainable commitments had been made that it was a common joke amongst the white electorate on election day that anybody venturing outdoors during the next week would be crushed to death when all the houses, cars, and utilities showered down from the sky. At the same time, the new government had no concept of the amount of money that would be needed for the development of South Africa, nor how limited were the funds at its disposal. Very quickly, therefore, the expectations of such things as free education, free medicine, and houses for all, had to be radically adjusted.[50]

There was also the knowledge that the aging Mandela could not go on forever. Initially it was believed that he would step down in 1999, which meant that almost immediately a low-key power struggle was commenced between Deputy President Thabo Mbeki and ANC leader Cyril Ramaphosa. Such a struggle necessarily diverted attention away from the important task of restructuring as well as the "Reconstruction and Development Programme" (RDP).

By mid 1996 it was clear that Mbeki had won, whereupon two things happened. First, Mandela declared that he would step down as early as 1997 to give his deputy a clear two years at the helm before the next general election. Second, Ramaphosa announced his retirement from politics and his dramatic entrance into the world of big business. Some, mainly those who lack confidence in Mbeki's abilities, believe that Ramaphosa's move might be calculated to give the president-elect time to reveal his ineptitude, at which stage he would make his dramatic re-entry from a successful business career to become the future savior of the nation.

Although the post-election years have seen a marked decline in political violence—even the 1996 local elections in war-torn KwaZulu-Natal were conducted in relative peace—there has been an alarming rise in all other forms of violence. South is now the most dangerous country in the world in which to live. There are many reasons for this. First, during the years of the liberation struggle, much criminal activity was happening under the banner of political struggle. This affected both sides in the conflict because, while supporters of the struggle were sometimes causing mayhem in the name of liberation, the police tended to focus their attention almost solely on eradicating the anti-apartheid forces rather than combating crime. At the same time, the police was open to corruption and officers often worked with known criminals in order to eliminate political opposition.

Since the 1994 elections, moreover, those criminal elements have used their new-found freedom to inflict their horrors on an ever-increasing mass of the people, while the loyalty of the police force is still under deep suspicion. At the same time, drug lords, finding themselves under increasing pressure in other parts of the world, have moved into South Africa to utilize the weak state of civil control to establish their springboard into Africa.

Mandela himself is possibly a major problem. He is a folk-hero and everywhere he goes he is swamped with adulation, having become almost a demi-god to his people. The international community likewise bestows honors on him far in excess of those showered on other world leaders, as was seen in July 1996 when eight British universities simultaneously awarded him honorary doctorates at a grand banquet at Buckingham Palace. Mandela's adulation, together with his advanced years and lack of basic economic expertise, effectively left the state almost leaderless in the pragmatic political sphere. More and more responsibilities devolved to his deputy president, but Mbeki in turn did not have the political clout to carry through the necessary programs until he finally replaced Mandela in power in 1999. Essential development, therefore, languishes and the economy is failing to make the breakthrough that was anticipated.

At the same time, the much-vaunted reconstruction languishes because of lack of local infrastructure to carry it through. Many of the provincial governments have yet to be granted sufficient powers, while local elections took place only in November 1995. In many cases, therefore, the Transitional Regional Councils, as they are called, are still in the process of finding their feet. A serious problem in this regard is the tradition of non-payment for essential services started in the 1980s as an economic tool to make South Africa ungovernable.

Now that democratic councils are in place, an effort has been made to get the people to start paying, but the "*Masikane* Campaign" to end the rent and services boycott is still largely a dead-letter. The government learned the hard way that it is easier to start a culture of non-payment than to end it. Indeed, today that same culture is beginning to spread to the still predominantly white neighborhoods, which increasingly perceive the state to be like Robin Hood, robbing them to give to the non-paying black communities.

The government must also give serious attention to macro-economic policy to reduce South Africa's estimated 40 percent unemployment rate. Although economic policy was initially the strong point in South Africa's favor, the appointment early in 1996 of ANC stalwart Trevor Manuel has caused jitters in the finance market because of his former Communist inclinations.[51] This, together with ever-present question marks over Mandela's future, saw the southern currency devalue by almost 30 percent in relation to the U.S. dollar between January and November 1996.

At the same time, sharp rifts and tensions are beginning to fracture the ANC itself. In 1994 the party was perceived to be the leader in the liberation struggle and much was expected of it. By the end of 1996, however, inefficiency and corruption were beginning to make their mark. New leaders are starting to show their mettle, like the enigmatic Bantu Holomisa whose accusations of ANC corruption have led to his dismissal from the party and who could possibly head a powerful new challenge in the 1999 elections.

South Africa's unacceptable crime rate, high taxation, devaluing currency, and falling educational standards are pushing up the emigration rate of white professionals, causing what is known locally as the "brain-drain." Although Mandela repeatedly calls on these people to rethink their stance and invest in South Africa, they are nevertheless lured by greener and more tranquil pastures, particularly in Australia, New Zealand, and Canada.

On the other hand, South Africa, in turn, presents greener pastures to the rest of the African community, and many black people desire to migrate southwards. This is a two-fold problem: there is a brain-drain of African professionals to South Africa and there is growing illegal immigration as the poor people migrate across the borders to seek a haven in an already over-supplied job market. Already changing attitudes are being evinced. While before 1994 the black electorate was united in the concept of a pan-African brotherhood and sisterhood that aimed to liberate South Africa, now the illegal immigrants are being seen as a public enemy who take away jobs and vital income from South Africans themselves. Although the government hesitates to take action, the thousands of jobless people are beginning to take the law into their own hands in their attempt to evict the unwanted foreigners.

At the same time, South Africa constitutes a power house on the African continent. Even in the days of sanctions, most states in southern Africa were unable to break free from the stranglehold that the South African economy placed on them. With sanctions gone, there is a distinct danger that South Africa could completely outstrip her neighbors. Instead of contributing to the greater benefit of the sub-continent, the country could in fact monopolize the economy to the detriment of her neighbors. By the end of 1996, several things are still in South Africa's favor. Despite fears to the contrary, the country does have a depth of leadership far greater than that of any other state in Africa. The scenario that South Africa will go the way of other tin-pot republics, through rampant nationalization, has also not happened. Indeed, the ANC has moved in the opposite direction. Despite its early policy of nationalization, the government has, in fact, shifted towards a market economy and the privatization of existing state assets. More importantly, it has also convinced the powerful COSATU to accept this decision. A few years is still too short a time to judge the new multi-party democracy. The government needs time to find its feet, to convert from the liberation struggle to being a public administrator. Nevertheless, the rank-and-file want to see some improvement to their lot. They need to feel liberated or else they will be tempted to offer allegiance elsewhere. For its part, the government desperately needs to get the economy on the move, boosting revenue without increasing the tax load on the already overburdened individual, while at the same time providing work for the ever-increasing numbers of school-leavers.

For the moment, the threat from the neo-Nazis appears to have dissipated and the ultra-Right is seen mostly as a lunatic fringe that waves the old flag at rugby matches. The more moderate Afrikaner politicians, in the meantime, go about their task of trying to demarcate boundaries for a future national state in the hopes that they will then be able to convince the government to make that further concession. The real threat to stability now lies to the Left as the poor, the homeless, and the unemployed watch with growing anger while parliamentarians and civil servants board the "gravy train," enriching themselves through bigger salaries, and move into the sumptuous neighborhoods once reserved for the affluent whites. Unless something is done quickly, the government may quickly lose the groundswell of support. But the 1999 elections, while reconfirming that the multi-party democracy is alive and well in South Africa, did surprisingly revamp the popular and political support for the ANC, now under Mbeki's leadership, giving it an almost crushing majority (but just short of the numbers needed to amend the Constitution).

South Africa is a paramount nation in Africa. Adebayo Adedeji, a previous under-secretary of the United Nations, states that South Africa will "become a self-confident force reinvigorating Africa's drive and resourcefulness and playing a leadership role."[52] A vigorous democracy grounded on strong political parties and an active global role, as well as a pivotal status in Africa, is a definite possibility for this diverse and multicultural nation.[53]

ACRONYMS:
ANC - African National Congress
PAC - Pan-Africanist Congress
SACP - South African Communist Party
NP - National Party
CP - Conservative Party
PFP - Progressive Federal Party
DP - Democratic Party (successor to the PFP)
IFP - *Inkatha* Freedom Party
COSATU -Congress of South African Trade Unions

Notes

1. Unfortunately authoritative histories of South Africa such as the *Oxford History of South Africa* were published during the apartheid period. While of quality and scholarship they do reflect prevalent attitudes. Leonard Thompson, *A History of South Africa* (Yale University Press, 1995), is a more recommended book which adds new dimensions (Professor Thompson is co-author of the *Oxford History*). See Nigel Worden, *The Making of Modern South Africa* (Oxford: Blackwell, 1994), p. 1–4.

2. To have a clear knowledge of South African history, especially its evolution as a nation, one needs to know the topography of southern Africa. The names of rivers, their courses, the mountain ranges, dry and wetlands, and prairies especially need to be known.

3. The term "Bantu" is problematic. It is derived from the Nguni language and means "people." Anthropologists have used the term to denote those African peoples who migrated into southern Africa after about 200 A.D. and to differentiate between the original Khoisan (Hottentot) and San (Bushmen). Anthropologists also find the term "Bantu-speaking" useful because the languages spoken by this group have a fundamental similarity. The actual languages of the various sub-divisions (Zulu, Tswana, Venda) are however, as different as French, Italian and Greek. A further complication is that the National Party used the term Bantu as a fundamental concept to explain its apartheid policy and it has now become an abusive word for the African people.

4. Hottentots and Bushmen are often considered derogatory terms. They were given to the natives by the early white arrivals and continue to be used. The British during the Nineteenth Century often called the Bantu-speaking blacks *Kaffirs* (or Caffres), which means unbelievers, and eventually it became a "term of racial abuse." Also the term Boer (which means farmer) is often used interchangeably with Afrikaaner (also Afrikaander) but the modern spelling is Afrikaner. They are the descendants of the Dutch settlers and slowly adopted a dialect which eventually became a patois known as Afrikaans, which is widely used and rivals English. It is an official language of South Africa and its status is gradually being challenged and reduced in post-apartheid South Africa. See G.H.L. Le May, *The Afrikaners: An Historical Interpretation* (Oxford: Blackwell Publishers, 1995), p. 1–2.

5. Worden, *Making of Modern South Africa,* p. 6.

6. Ibid., p. 5.

7. Harry A. Gailey, *A History of Africa from Earliest Times to 1800* (New York: Holt, Rinehart & Winston, 1970).

8. Ibid.

9. Roland Oliver & J.D. Fage, *A Short History of Africa* (Baltimore: Penguin Books, 1962), p. 162.

10. Thompson, *History of South Africa,* p. 81. See Robert W. July, *A History of the African People* (New York: Scribner's, 1970), p. 235. The *Mfecane* has become a controversial and disputed event. Some revisionists even deny what happened

or some of what has been presented. Yet standard texts and studies by renowned experts continue to accept and mention the *Mfecane*. See a clear and short summary in Worden, *Making of Modern South Africa,* p. 14–15. Detailed presentations of *Mfecane* revisionism is in Carolyn Hamilton, ed., *The Mfecane Aftermath: Reconstruction in Southern African History* (Johannesburg: Witwatersrand University Press, 1995).

11. Oliver & Fage, *Short History of Africa,* p. 164.
12. Ibid.
13. Shepherd P. Clough, *A History of the Western World* (Boston: D.C. Heath, 1964), p. 111.
14. Hermann Giliomee & Lawrence Schlemmer, *From Apartheid to Nation-Building* (Cape Town: Oxford University Press, 1989), p. 401.
15. Vernon February, *The Afrikaners of South Africa* (London: Kegan Paul International, 1991) p. 50.
16. Harry A. Gailey, *History of Africa from 1800 to Present* (New York: Holt, Rinehart & Winston, 1996), p. 167.
17. Ibid.
18. February, *The Afrikaners of South Africa,* p. 48.
19. Adrienne Koch, ed., *The American Enlightenment* (New York: George Brazillier, 1965), p. 19–48.
20. February, *The Afrikaners of South Africa,* p. 48.
21. Ibid., p. 50.
22. Norval, *Deconstructing Apartheid Discourse* (London: Verso, 1996), p. 71.
23. Ibid.
24. André Du Toit & Hermann Gilliomee, *Afrikaner Political Thought,* vol. I (Analysis & Documents: 1780–1850), (Berkeley: University of California Press, 1983) p. Xlll.
25. Le May, *The Afrikaners,* p. 4, 112, 126, 137.
26. Thompson, *History of South Africa,* Chp. 5.
27. *Yearbook of the Republic of South Africa, 1988–1989,* p. 66–70. The population estimated is far higher than the official numbers: by 1996 the South African population was about 40 million.
28. Thompson, *History of South Africa,* p. 65.
29. Mary Benson, *South Africa: The Struggle for a Birthright* (New York: Funk & Wagnall, 1969), p. 23–26.
30. Norval, *Deconstructing Apartheid,* p. 71.
31. See the *"Passive Resister"* of December 1947 in Benson, *South Africa,* p. 118.
32. Heidi Holland, *The Struggle: History of the African National Congress* (New York: Brazillier, 1989), Chp. 12.
33. E. S. Sachs in Norval, *Deconstructing Apartheid,* p. 355, note 87.
34. Kathryn Manzo, *Domination, Resistance and Social Change in South Africa* (London: Praeger, 1992), p. 209.
35. Ibid., p. 186.
36. Marina Ottaway, *South Africa. Struggle for a New Order* (Washington DC: Brookings, 1993), p. 24.

37. Gailey, *History of Africa from 1800*, p. 373.
38. Norval, *Deconstructing Apartheid*, p. 3.
39. Thompson, *History of South Africa*, p. 190.
40. André E. A. M. Thomashaversusen, *The Dismantling of Apartheid* (Cape Town: Printpak Books, 1987), p. 1.
41. John Kane-Burman, *South Africa's Silent Revolution* (Johannesburg: S. A. Institute of Race, 1991), p. 7–29.
42. On the erosion of apartheid: M. Lipton, *Capitalism and Apartheid* (Cape Town: David Philip, 1989), p. 49–83.
43. See J.E. Spence, ed., *Change in South Africa* (London: Pinter, 1994), p. 22–23
44. See D. Oakes, ed., *Illustrated History of South Africa: Real Story* (Cape Town: Reader's Digest, 1994), p. 489.
45. CODESA: Convention for a Democratic South Africa.
46. See J. Crush & W. James, eds., *Crossing Boundaries: Mine Migrancy in a Democratic South Africa* (Cape Town: Idasa, 1995), p. 43–50.
47. Spence, *Change in South Africa*, p. 24–29.
48. *Time* (21 March 1994).
49. Oakes, *Illustrated History of South Africa*, p. 528–529. For an evaluation of the Interim Constitution, see Spence, *Change in South Africa*, p. 29–33, and chart below:

SOUTH AFRICAN ELECTIONS' FINAL RESULTS:

African National Congress:	62.7 percent (252 seats)
National Party:	20.4 percent (82 seats)
Inkatha Freedom Party:	10.5 percent (43 seats)
Freedom Front:	2.2 percent (9 seats)
Democratic Party:	1.7 percent (7 seats)
Pan-Africanist Congress:	1.3 percent (5 seats)
African Christian Democratic Party:	0.5 percent (2 seats)

50. Conversation with Deputy President Thabo Mbeki in *Time* (London, 16 September 1996).
51. Initially Mandela appointed two people with good international reputations to key economic portfolios: Chris Stals as governor of the Reserve Bank and Derek Keyes as finance minister. The latter soon stepped down in favour of Christo Liebenberg, who also enjoyed international confidence.
52. Adebayo Adedeji, ed., *South Africa and Africa* (London: Zed Books, 1996), p. 13; Gavin Maasdorp & Alan Whiteside, eds., *South Africa* (New York: St. Martin's Press, 1992), p. 211–215.
53. A renewed presence in various parts of South Africa in December 1996 through January 1997, Charles Arnade revealed two interesting matters related to this chapter. Several times an opinion was expressed, coming from all races and sections of the population, that the modus operandi of the dominant ANC party was not at all different from that of the dominant NP of the apartheid era. This shows that South Africa was, and, in the foreseeable future,

will be governed by a dominant party within the framework of a democracy guaranteed by a brand new constitution (1996) containing all modern features for individual rights.

Secondly, when the respected General-Secretary of the ANC, Mr. Cyril Ramaphosa (rumored to be the successor to President Mandela), resigned to enter the private sector, the Vice Secretary Ms. Cheryl Carulus (who is colored), became the acting general-secretary. Her chances of becoming secretary are nil. She is competent and she would like the position. The general opinion (which included press opinions) is that she is not Xhosa, not black, and she is a woman. In the past, the NP represented a small minority of the population (Afrikaner white). Now the ANC represents a majority, but is still black and Xhosa-dominated. And the NP and the ANC still favor men for top positions. It is true that both parties are trying now to recruit persons of all races and genders but so far have failed to give them equal access to leadership positions.

FIFTEEN

The Dilemmas of
Democracy in Nigeria

Festus Ugboaja Ohaegbulam

I. The Elusive Quest for Democracy in Nigeria

The quest for democracy was the driving force and political objective of intensified anti-colonial nationalism in Africa after the end of World War II. African nationalists sought to overthrow Western European imperial control of Africa because they believed that no section of the human family had an inherent right to rule, dominate, and exploit another section of that family; that all men and women have natural rights, as equal members of the human family, to participate in reaching decisions that affect their lives either directly or indirectly; that freedom from alien control would help to promote and sustain the civic virtues and ideals of obligation to freedom, justice, equality, accountability, and truth in Africa. These democratic values and ideals still elude Africa more than three decades after the formal termination of Western European imperial control from most of the continent. Why? What went wrong?

Africa had made a false start. Thus, instead of the promises of independence, the social reality in many an independent African state has been one of massive poverty, despotism and abuse of fundamental human rights, violent intra-communal conflicts, corruption, military coups and misuse of political power. Such a situation has promoted neither economic growth, nor democracy. Neither of these, together with requisite political stability, can take root until the government becomes accountable and relevant to the people, and has the capacity to sustain the minimum functions of a modern state.

The social reality described above has been most in evidence in Nigeria, Africa's most populous nation. Nigeria, to date, has been under two civilian administrations and *seven military régimes* since its political independence from Britain in October 1960. Traditionally, the military is under civilian control and performs a variety of functions designed, above all, to protect the national security interests of the state—its political independence, domestic and external sovereignty, territorial integrity, and its citizens' well-being. The Nigerian military establishment departed from this traditional civilian-military relationship to become preoccupied with a role of political administration for which it is neither suited nor designed. Capitalizing on the complexity and hard realities of the Nigerian polity, and the admittedly palpable errors of inexperienced civilian administrators, the military seized political power from civilians. It has ruled Nigeria for most of the period of its independence. It found political administration materially lucrative and thus became preoccupied with that role rather than with its development for the performance of its traditional functions.[1] The efforts, since 1993, of its leaders to retain power, contrary to their assertions, do not arise from a strong sense of public service but from their naked desire for wealth accumulation and grandiose living. Their interest in financial rewards and tight control over imports and exports impede foreign investment and development. As a consequence, the military establishment has victimized Nigeria's national unity and damaged its own unity as well. The late military head of state himself, Sani Abacha, admitted that the Nigerian military is "perpetuating an illegality."[2]

Military intervention in Nigerian politics, which has severely damaged the promises of Nigeria's independence and the prospects of democratic governance in the republic, began in mid January 1966. On that date Prime Minister Abubakar Tafawa Balewa, and a few of his associates were killed in a poorly executed military coup to rid Nigeria of a corrupt and discredited despotism, as the coup leaders explained. It was a popular coup for many reasons. Sir Abubakar's government had been riddled with political crises, increasing ethnic and regional polarization, political violence, repression and corruption. At a critical stage in its development, Nigeria was cursed with a subaltern executive head of state who lacked the power and a free hand to deal with the reality of Nigeria's problems. Sir Abubakar was the lieutenant of Sir Ahmadu Bello, one of the founders and the leader of the northern People's Congress. Sir Ahmadu was widely believed to be the most powerful Nigerian politician of his time. But, more loyal to Nigeria's northern region than to the Federal Republic of Nigeria, Sir Ahmadu opted to remain premier of the region. To complicate Nigeria's difficulties he allowed his lieutenant at the federal capital in Lagos no flexibility at all to deal with Nigeria's problems at a very crucial period. This led to drift, political brinkmanship and ineffectiveness of the Abubakar government. A succession of political crises, violence and repression, which Sir Abubakar could not stop, provoked junior military officers to stage the poorly executed coup which overthrew his government on 15 January 1966. The leader of the coup, Major Kaduna Nzeogwu, identified its targets as the main enemies of Nigeria:

> the political profiteers, the swindlers, the men in high and low places . . . who seek to keep the country divided permanently so that they can remain in office as ministers or VIPs at least; the tribalists, the nepotists. . . . who make [Nigeria] look big for nothing before international circles, those who have corrupted our society and put the Nigerian political calendar back by their words and deeds.[3]

That coup established Nigeria's first military government under General John T. U. Aguiyi-Ironsi. Aguiyi-Ironsi had been the general officer commanding the Nigerian Army and had been one of the intended victims of the coup plotters. Like most of the leaders of the 15 January 1966, coup that overthrew Abubakar's government, Aguiyi-Ironsi was an Igbo from eastern Nigeria. He and the January coup that catapulted him to power were immediately seen by the Muslim leaders of northern Nigeria as a plot to impose Igbo-domination on Nigeria. In particular, the north and the military officers from that region were incensed that none of the leading politicians and only one of the senior military officers who were killed in the course of the military coup that put Aguiyi-Ironsi in power was Igbo. For this reason, resentment in northern Nigeria against Aguiyi-Ironsi's government grew fast. Its corrective policy of centralization of power led to a counter-coup which swept away the six-month-old régime on 29 July 1966.

The Aguiyi-Ironsi régime was replaced by another military government led by Lieutenant Colonel Yakubu Gowon, a member of a northern Nigeria minority ethnic group. Gowon's ascendancy to power was a compromise and the result of a tragic breakdown of command and internal conflict within the army hierarchy, which was exacerbated by external political dissension, largely in northern Nigeria. Initially his régime was uncertain and unstable. It witnessed an orgy of ethnic bloodletting which finally led to the 30-month Nigeria-Biafra War (July 1967–January 1970).

Thousands of Igbo residents in the north had been brutally massacred before and after the overthrow of Aguiyi-Ironsi. Other hundreds of thousands of them, in the Western and northern regions of Nigeria, began a mass flight to their homeland seeking safety. Faced with a situation in which Igbo and other easterners were no longer safe in other parts of Nigeria it seemed to Col. C. Odumegwu Ojukwu—the military governor of eastern Nigeria—and other leaders of the region, to look for a drastic solution. First, they looked into a constitutional revision that would assure the people complete regional autonomy while preserving the unity of Nigeria. When various attempts to do so, inside and outside Nigeria (the last at Aburi in Ghana), failed, Colonel Ojukwu prepared his people for the assertion of their right of self-determination. Before that step was taken, Gowon assumed emergency powers on 28 May 1967. He proceeded thereafter to reorganize Nigeria's four regions into 12 states. He did this for three reasons: (1) to keep Nigeria one through winning and galvanizing the sympathy, loyalty and support of Nigeria's ethnic minority groups; (2) to attempt an equalization of the treatment of various areas and ethnic groups in Nigeria; (3) above all, to deprive Ojukwu and the Igbo majority of the loyalty and support of the non-Igbo inhabitants of the eastern region for a drive towards a separate and independent nation. Ojukwu and the leaders of the eastern region responded by declaring the region a sovereign and independent state on 30 May 1967. This precipitated the tragic, bloody Nigeria-Biafra War, from which Nigeria emerged with her territorial integrity intact.

Achievement of post-war reconciliation and reconstruction goals was remarkably smooth. Magnanimous in victory, Gowon worked to reintegrate the Igbo into Nigerian national life. The oil boom of the early 1970s facilitated the process. But Gowon suspended the country's normal political life beyond his promises and the expectations of eager politicians. He was also unable to curb widespread government corruption as well as a scandalous clogging of Lagos port facilities with excessive cement imports. His régime had indeed reneged on its promise of a six-year program of transition to civilian rule. It had mismanaged the economy, and had at the same time become increasingly corrupt. Gowon was consequently overthrown in a bloodless military coup on 29 July 1975 by General Murtala Muhammad.

In February 1976 Muhammad, who had already initiated a plan for return to civilian rule over a period of four years, was himself assassinated in an attempted coup. He was succeeded by his second-in-command, General Olusegun Obasanjo. After a transition period of three years Obasanjo transferred political power in 1979 to a civilian administration led by President Shehu Shagari. Shagari's administration marked the beginning of Nigeria's Second Republic. After a four-year rule, senior military officers intervened again and overthrew the Shagari government on 31 December 1983. From that time to the present, Nigeria experienced socio-economic and political subjugation under three military dictators—Muhammadu Buhari (1983–85), Ibrahim Badamasi Babangida (1985- 93), and Sani Abacha (1993–98). The dictators not only withered the Nigerian economy but also smothered opposing voices and made Nigeria Africa's new pariah state. Unprincipled, unproductive, corrupt, and weak political élites, unable to resist the military, joined them to obliterate the rule of law and asphyxiate all democratic liberties and opportunities in the country. It is no wonder that Nigeria, 36 years after independence, is now teetering ominously on the brink of political dissolution and economic ruin.[4]

This process began on 31 December 1983 when Buhari and other senior military officers overthrew the Shehu Shagari civilian administration. In a radio broadcast to the nation, one of the coup plotters, Brigadier Sani Abacha, told Nigerians:

> "You are all living witnesses to the grave economic predicament . . . which an inept and corrupt leadership has imposed on our beloved nation. . . . Our economy has been hopelessly mismanaged. We have become a debtor and beggar nation. There is an inadequacy of food at reasonable prices. . . . Health services are in a shambles as our hospitals are reduced to mere consulting clinics without drugs, water, and equipment. Our education system is deteriorating at an alarming rate. Unemployment figures, including the graduates, have reached embarrassing and unacceptable proportions."[5]

For two years after seizing power, Buhari and his military co-plotters politically and economically mismanaged Nigeria. In fact, they surpassed, in every respect, the failings of the Shagari administration, which they had so loudly decried and condemned. On 27 August the Buhari régime was overthrown in a bloodless coup by General Ibrahim Badamasi Babangida and other members of its ruling council. Upon seizing power, Babangida pledged to end the cycle of political and economic instability and the corruption that plagued Nigeria for most of the 36 years of its independence and to transfer power to civilian administrators in 1990.

Babangida remained in office for eight years, having postponed his promised departure three times during the period. To do so, he skillfully exploited regional rivalries and alleged electoral fraud, while at the same time using other forms of intrigue, deceit and manipulation.[6] In the final stages of a scheduled presidential race in 1992, he disqualified all the candidates for the office over alleged vote-rigging. In June 1993 a presidential election, which he had orchestrated, was conducted. The office was contested on 12 June by two political parties—the Social Democratic Party and the National Republican Party—which he had created by decree. He nullified the election on 23 June 1993 when he did not like the result—the victory of a Yoruba businessman from southwestern Nigeria, Moshood Abiola. He had concluded that, once in office, Abiola could not be relied upon to do the bidding of the military. By most accounts, the annulled election had been fair and free for the first time since independence appeared to have transcended Nigeria's practice of voting along ethnic, religious, and regional lines. The annulment of the election cost more than 200 lives. General Sani Abacha, Chief of Defense Staff at the time, had ordered the murders. Yet, Babangida ignored these facts as it was, among other reasons, his intention to remain in office for at least four more years. In this he was supported by an organization—the Association for a Better Nigeria—that his régime had backed and funded. He had fooled the people on three previous occasions. This time he had miscalculated the intensity of the people's bitterness against military rule and had totally lost his credibility. As this reality dawned on him and as pressure was exerted by his military cohorts anxious to succeed him, Babangida promised on 17 August to hand over power to an elected government on 27 August 1993.

The ever-manipulating Babangida had other plans for continued military control of Nigeria. On 26 August he stepped down. In his place he installed a military-backed interim government headed by a southwestern Nigerian businessman, Ernest Shonekan. Shoneken was perceived as another strategic tool of the military, dictating the tune from behind the scenes, and so received little popular support. Two weeks later, on 16 September 1993, his government scheduled presidential elections for February 1994. Those were not to take place. On 17 November 1993 the defense minister under the Babangida régime and a notorious coup plotter, Sani Abacha, removed Shonekan and assumed full political authority. The following day he dissolved political parties, state and local governments, and the federal legislature. Abacha proceeded to rule by decree, arrest opponents, muzzle the labor unions, ban leading opposition publications, and trample upon civil liberties.

Abacha tried to quiet the call for turning over power to Abiola or to provide a transition to civilian rule by summoning instead a ruse constitutional conference as if the problem of Nigeria was just one of constitution writing. He nominated a third of the conference's members and pledged that it would deliberate, unhampered, with full authority. He never kept the pledge. For no sooner had the delegates to the conference, boycotted by the supporters of Abiola in Southwest Nigeria, adopted a resolution urging him to hand over power by January 1996, than he dismissed them from further deliberation for an extended period. The exit date was removed from the final report of the reconvened conference.

The Abacha régime's secret military tribunal arrested, tried, and sentenced an ex-Nigerian head of state, Obasanjo Olusegun, his second-in-command, Shehu Musa Y'Ardua, and 40 others to death or life imprisonment for allegedly plotting to overthrow the military régime. A barrage of international protests persuaded Abacha to commute the death and reduce the life sentences. Finally, in a speech on 1 October 1995, Abacha outlined his plan for a three-year transition to civilian rule by October 1998:

1. His régime—the Provisional Ruling Council—had approved a "new constitution in which bold attempts to redress the factors and forces that have impaired [Nigeria's] political stability and national integration will certainly provide the necessary base."[7]

2. His régime had also accepted a proposal for rotational power-sharing at all levels of the national government. It had endorsed a modified presidential system in which six key executive and legislative offices will be zoned and rotated among six identifiable geographical groupings. For that purpose, the country was divided into six zones: North-East, Northwest, Middle belt, Southwest, East Central and Southern minority.

3. The concept of power-sharing would be entrenched in the constitution and applied for an experimental period of 30 years. Six national political offices—the president, vice president, prime minister, deputy prime minister, senate president, speaker of the house of representatives—are to be filled by candidates on a rotational basis.

4. Regarding revenue allocation, his government approved a recommendation by the constitutional conference to set aside 13 percent of all revenues accruing to the federal account directly from natural resources as derivation. This fixed percentage of the revenue would compensate communities which suffer severe ecological degradation as a result of the exploitation in their areas.

5. His administration would commute the sentences on alleged coup plotters—two former military rulers, army officers, journalists and human rights activists. It would review the situation at the appropriate time. Some saw this as a ploy to assuage local and foreign critics of his human rights record and to use the victims of the secret military tribunal as pawns in future negotiations.

6. His administration would not release Chief Moshood Abiola, but would allow the ongoing judicial process to continue its course. Abacha later offered to release Abiola from prison if he agreed to leave Nigeria upon his release. Abiola declined the offer.

7. To implement the three-year transitional plan, his régime would encourage the establishment of new political parties; establish an electoral commission; seek political reconciliation; create new local government areas and new states. Subsequently, Abacha established a commission to supervise the new transition to civilian rule, oversee elections from local to the national level, and to review the number and composition of states and local governments. In October 1996, the commission announced that five political parties (none opposed to Abacha's régime), out of 15 that had applied for recognition, would participate in the transition. Also, Abacha created six additional

states, surely to increase the military's patronage network. His political reconstruction initiatives were designed to justify the continuation of his régime's tenure. His rider that the duration of the transition schedule would be determined by the time required to complete each phase of the plan was considered ominous, given the experience with his predecessor, Babangida, who postponed the terminal date of his transfer of power at least three times. The complexity of implementing the concept of power-sharing on rotational basis raises an additional question regarding the observance of the terminal date of the transition program. What appears likely is that the transition he is dictating (already behind schedule) is ensuring the tenure of his régime until the inevitable day it will be forced out.

II. Unfulfilled Expectations and Promises of Independence

Many a Nigerian is disappointed, frustrated, and bitter about these developments, which have undermined Nigeria's potential to emerge as a major democracy. On the eve of its formal political independence, its political élites and its overseas admirers had cherished the hope, which hardly anyone in the continent now entertains, that Nigeria would emerge as a major democracy that would spearhead the regeneration of Africa.[8] Such hope was based on identifiable potential assets. Nigerians are not only vigorous, industrious, and economically responsive, they also have "a superabundance of . . . entrepreneurial attributes: willingness to work hard for economic gain; to take risks; to persevere and persist; to undertake new occupations and new ways of doing things."[9]

Also, Nigeria's geographical location on the western shores of the Atlantic Ocean and in tropical Africa, as well as its geographical size, gives it geopolitical advantage. Its relatively diverse rich natural resources—oil, natural gas, coal, tin ore, and timber—enhance its stature. Potentially, they provide it enormous economic and political leverage in Africa and in international politics. Moreover, Nigeria's relatively rapid national reconciliation, after a 30-month civil war, strengthened the hope that the Nigerian federation would emerge as a major democracy in Africa. This expectation was further enhanced by the fact that its civil-war trauma in the era of the Cold War did not leave the nation beholden, that is overly indebted, to any of the world's major powers. Indeed, Nigeria, by doing so, had been able to deny the major powers a special position in the post-war management of Nigerian affairs.

As promising as its potential has been, Nigeria, however, has historically been afflicted with enormous contradictions and a colonial legacy, which have collectively militated against its emergence as a stable democracy. Political turmoil has thwarted its economic potential. Bedeviled by a national question, social injustice and inequality, and the domination by one component unit of the federation over the other units, the Nigerian federation has been under severe strain since attaining independence in 1960. Its leaders have lacked the political will and vision to address its national question. They adopted merely diversionary tactics and palliatives in their attempts to deal with that question. To date, therefore, Nigeria's social reality and overall impact on African and world affairs have remained marginal and unrepresentative of its potential 36 years after its political independence from Britain. In spite of this reality, Nigeria's military dictators and their civilian cronies cling to the belief that Nigeria will soon secure a permanent seat in the United Nations Security Council.

In the late 1980s, especially after the collapse of Euro-Communism in 1989, several African states embarked upon the process of making democracy an integral part of their societies' development. Consequently, over the first half of the 1990s, remarkable political restructuring occurred in several countries, including Malawi, Zambia and Benin. Authoritarian one-party states and military régimes were exchanged for relatively democratic, multiparty systems of government. The Republic of South Africa reversed course from years of denial of political rights to the majority of its population under the apartheid system to a multiracial democracy led by the black majority. After years of political struggle with south, Namibia experienced a successful transition to majority rule in 1990. Growth in private ownership of newspapers and radio stations occurred in states like Ghana, Cameroon, Côte d'Ivoire, and Malawi, all once dominated by state-owned newspapers and broadcasting. This is a remarkable transformation, although much work remains to be done to entrench democracy and improve on governance throughout the continent.

The trend in Nigeria, by contrast, is completely different. It has been marked by the entrenchment of a military dictatorship that has obstructed every attempt at democratic governance. The military rulers have turned Nigeria upside down politically and economically. They have created more economic, social, and political problems than solutions, undermined Nigeria's fragile civil society, and made the Nigerian state irrelevant to the masses of its people. Under their rule, therefore, whatever reputation Nigeria had has been tarnished by a legacy of public corruption, international business scams, and Nigeria's perceived role as a conduit on the international narcotics circuit. The World Bank ranked Nigeria among the 20 poorest countries of the world in 1993. Further, all efforts since 1979 at developing truly Nigerian national institutions were suppressed. The nation has been fortunate that it has had no external military threats: its defense, given the current low morale of the masses, would be very precarious indeed. Babangida himself admitted that the involvement of the military in Nigerian politics has eroded its professional standing and prestige.[10]

This state of affairs in Nigeria is a product of Nigeria's political, historical, and cultural realities. It reflects the dilemmas and contradictions within the Nigerian federation. Part of the contradiction is that Nigeria, with its virile population, including the political class, democracy advocates, journalists, trade unionists, university students, religious leaders, hundreds of thousands of unemployed able-bodied men and women, has endured military dictatorship for so long. It is this anomaly that has fostered military rule and kept opposition to that rule weak. The opposition is not only weak, it is also fragmented by its lack of a common ideology and clearly defined objectives and its division along ethnic, religious, and regional lines. The opportunism of its leaders and the divide and rule tactics of the military weaken it further. It is not even united on such issues as whether Moshood Abiola should be installed as president to actualize his election on 12 June 1993. Some of his own supporters, including his running mate in the nullified 12 June 1993 election, abandoned him to join Abacha's military rule. Nor is there any agreement within the military as to whether to establish a government of national unity or create and support a Nigerian government-in-exile.

So far, the opposition has failed to mobilize the masses to promote some kind of violent tension and armed resistance, or develop other effective strategies against the military. Exile, arrests, restrictions, incarceration of members of its leadership, frequent closure of universities—the seedbed of nationalism—contributed to reduce the effectiveness of the opposition. Because of its weakness and lack of capacity for armed resistance the opposition is not credible, and has no potential national influence. Neither the military régime, whose continued tenure in office is supported by organizations such as the Fourth Force and the National Youth Movement,[11] nor the great powers have taken it seriously. This brief documentation and analysis of the dilemmas of democracy in Nigeria shows that Nigeria cannot realize its promise until its people realistically tackle their national question. It highlights the need for sacrifices for national consolidation, to make all the ethnic groups of Nigeria an organic whole owing allegiance to one indivisible nation—Nigeria. It also points to the need for Nigerians to eschew the current voracious appetite for the materialistic comforts and luxuries of the industrialized Western democracies, which breed rampant corruption and destructive struggle for power in the land.

It is the failure of Nigeria's political élites to live within their means and to address decisively these issues that obstructs Nigeria's capacity to provide for all its people. This same failure has been the bedrock of the military's excuse to intervene and entrench itself in Nigerian politics and thus to compound Nigeria's dilemmas. Having convincingly demonstrated that it is incapable of creating a democratic and stable Nigeria, the military, therefore, must be expunged from Nigerian politics. Nothing else will do more damage to the prospect of democratic governance in Nigeria, not to mention its survival as a nation, than allowing the military to remain in control of the federation.

Masses of Nigerian citizens—the working-classes, peasants, students and unemployed—who have refused to share part of the responsibility for Nigeria's dilemmas and failures. They must reexamine not only their uncritical identification with the military/political élites but also their characteristic patience and tolerance of greedy, corrupt and despotic rulers. Often revolutionary change does not come from above, but from below. Indeed, seldom does it come from above without the sacrifice, blood, sweat, and tears of those below.

III. Major Elements of the Dilemmas of Democracy in Nigeria

At least five major elements of the dilemmas of democracy in Nigeria can easily be identified. First is the national question, which is fundamentally a legacy of British colonial rule. The most salient aspect of the national question is the existence of deep ethnic and regional divisions, which have been a continuous source of ethnic and regional conflicts in Nigeria's history as a nation. Nigeria's federal structure, up to seven years after independence, in which one region was larger and more populous than the others combined, heightened the regional cleavage and ethnic insecurity in general. So far Nigeria's historical experience is that ethnic and regional conflicts have been deliberately provoked as a strategy to retain or obtain power.

A second element of the dilemmas of democracy in Nigeria derives from the first one. It is the very shallow sense of nationhood among the Nigerian populace. Nigerians have yet to develop a deep sense of loyalty to a multinational Nigerian state, which transcends their loyalty to their traditional states based on ethnicity. Their loyalty to Nigeria as a nation is proportional to the range of benefits and security Nigeria confers upon them and the degree to which the Nigerian nation makes itself relevant to them and to their needs. The dilemma arising from this situation is manifest in the rivalry among Nigeria's major ethnic groups for group and regional advancement and security, and the feeling of domination among all minorities within their midst.

Thinly established political institutions in Nigeria with little depth of experience make up the third element. Nigeria's political parties are largely non-ideological, ethnically based, corrupt, and prone to violence. Nigeria's judiciary tends to be prone to political manipulation. It has frequently failed to demonstrate any independence or to mediate political conflict and fraud in Nigeria. The fourth major element of democracy's dilemma in Nigeria is the crisis of political leadership. The fifth derives from that crisis; it is the role of the military in intervening in civilian politics.

IV. The National Question

The problems of democracy in Nigeria are deeply rooted in the political history of the nation, a British creation out of many diverse ethnicities.[12] The estimated population in 1996 of the British-created federation was 101.2 million. This population comprises 250 ethnic groups, including the four largest and most dominant—Hausa (21 percent), Yoruba (20 percent), Igbo (19 percent) and Fulani (9 percent). The Hausa and the Fulani (or Hausa-Fulani) live largely in the north which comprises more than half the size of the entire federation. The Yoruba and Igbo are concentrated in the west and southeast respectively. Between 1861 and 1900 Great Britain acquired three colonial entities—the colony of Lagos, and the protectorates of southern and northern Nigeria—which it amalgamated in 1914 as the Colony and Protectorate of Nigeria. Thus, Nigeria began as a colonial territory of many ethnicities with differing political cultures, religions, and traditions. While there were adherents to traditional African religion in all regions of the territory, Islam and Christianity had their adherents mainly in the north and the south respectively. Also, Islamic theocracy prevailed in most of the north, while the traditional political systems in the south included definite measures for limiting arbitrary use of power by the rulers. In the traditional political systems in the south, rulers performed their functions within the framework of existing custom, which imposed considerable restrictions on their behavior. A ruler who ignored such restrictions or traditional customs was deposed. The people, not the king or ruler, were sovereign. The ruler spoke and acted in their name.[13] The amalgamation, crafted by Frederick Lugard, Britain's first governor general of Nigeria, took no cognizance of these differences. Rather, it was carried out to suit British administrative goals and convenience, rather than to produce an organic union and democratic rule of all ethnic groups.

In particular, British colonial policy required colonial territories to be self-supporting and not be a burden on British taxpayers. Thus, financing the administration of the newly acquired colonies in Africa was a major problem for which a variety of measures was adopted. In Nigeria's case a commercial company was granted royal charter as the Royal Niger Company to administer the territory from its profits. Accordingly, the Royal Niger Company did so in 1886–1900 when its charter was revoked because other British companies had accused it of running a monopoly of trade in the territory. From 1900, the colony and the two protectorates were strictly required, according to British colonial policy, to provide sufficient revenues for their administration. The colony of Lagos and the Protectorate of southern Nigeria, which were merged in 1906, more than met the requirement. The Protectorate of northern Nigeria could not meet the revenue requirement, thereby creating the economic necessity to amalgamate the Colony of Lagos and the Protectorates of southern and northern Nigeria in 1914 as a single political territory.

Neither of the amalgamated Protectorates was ethnically, politically, and culturally homogeneous. Nor did any of the dominant ethnic groups regard themselves as belonging to a single sovereign state or political territory prior to the British occupation and amalgamation. Rather, without exception, each saw itself as comprising separate and autonomous states. Each ethnic group decided the ways and for what purpose it interacted with others within it. The British occupation and amalgamation transformed and fused the groups into political ethnic groups within the political territory named Nigeria. After this fusion, historical circumstances forced each ethnicity to act politically to defend its perceived interests against those of other competing groups. Also, they began to identify themselves thereafter as Hausa-Fulani, Igbo, and Yoruba, first within the context of a British colony and later in the context of a multi-national Nigerian state. Loyalty to the ethnic group, thus fostered by perceived group interest and historical circumstances, undermined loyalty to the colonial territory and subsequently to sovereign multi-national Nigeria.

British colonial administrators who had not gone to Africa to build nations used this political fact to their advantage when Frederick Lugard adopted a dual policy for the administration of Nigeria. At the national level, Nigeria was ruled by British administrators in an essentially authoritarian fashion, and was maintained by a free use of violence and repression.[14] Its governors who ruled by decree—"Orders in Council"—"enjoyed very wide powers without brakes from below,"[15] in addition to "the symbolic trappings of supreme and exalted status."[16] Immediate post-colonial rulers of Nigeria employed authoritarianism, violence and repression similar to what they had witnessed during colonial rule. Outside the political center Lugard employed the policy of Indirect Rule both as a basis for local government, and the implementation of central government laws affecting the entire Nigerian territory. Accordingly, in the Islamic theocracies of the north he co-opted the emirs into subordinate positions as local administrators in his colonial hierarchy, and as labor recruiters and revenue collectors. In the south he used the traditional rulers of the centralized Yoruba, Bini, and other ethnic groups in a similar manner. For the Igbo of the southeast and other acephalous states in the territory, he created "warrant chiefs" for the same purpose. By 1948 the policy of Indirect Rule was abandoned in eastern Nigeria where it had fared poorly and had been a source of great irritation and conflict against the colonial order. However, by then, the application of the policy had already left its impact and legacy for contemporary and future Nigeria.

Indeed, under Indirect Rule the local rulers carried out British imperial policies, while educated Nigerians were excluded from practical politics in their localities as well as in the center. The policy undermined traditional political systems of the Igbo, Yoruba, and other ethnicities as well. It swept away constitutional limitations of monarchical authority in western Nigeria and undermined the individualistic and participatory democratic tradition, known as gerontocracy, of the Igbo of southeast Nigeria. Hence, it undermined the accountability of rulers to the ruled in most of the societies of southern Nigeria. The policy, on the other hand, preserved the authoritarian Muslim theocracies of the Hausa-Fulani emirates in northern Nigeria. This culture of lack of accountability of the governors to the governed became a major character of political administration in post-colonial Nigeria under both civilian and military rulers. In addition, Indirect Rule solidified local and regional particularisms in colonial Nigeria. It did so at the expense of nation-building. Consequently, the Nigerian nationalities merely mixed but did not combine. Hence participatory or electoral democracy, which was introduced into the country less than ten years before the British departure, was difficult to sustain after independence was achieved. Ethnic interests and regional divisions fostered by the policy of Indirect Rule culminated in the democratic breakdown in Nigeria in 1962–70 and the military rule that lasted from 1966 to 1979 and from 1983 to the present.

The 1914 amalgamation, which brought about the adoption and application of the policy of Indirect Rule in colonial Nigeria, contributed in other ways to sow the seeds of future problems for independent Nigeria. British administrators, for their own imperial interests, failed to use the colonial amalgamation to create in Nigeria political regions comparatively equal in size to each other. Instead, in 1939, they divided Nigeria into four administrative units—the Colony of Lagos, the Western, Eastern and Northern Provinces. In 1951 the provinces were designated as regions, each with a dominant nationality group—the Yoruba in Western Nigeria, the Igbo in Eastern Nigeria and the Hausa-Fulani in Northern Nigeria. By this action the northern region, almost the size of all the southern regions combined, became the largest and most favored political unit within colonial Nigeria. Until 1947 the north was kept legislatively separate from the southern regions, while each region developed each along its own path. When the north and the south began to interact legislatively in 1951, under the James

Macpherson constitution, the north enjoyed a preponderant position in the central legislature by having as many seats as the East and West combined, and by enjoying distinct preferences and advantages over the southern regions.[17] That was the aim of the British administrators who regarded the political leaders of the Northern region as less radical and more predisposed to protect British interests in post-colonial Nigeria. Furthermore, during the period of nine years (1951–60), when the regions interacted legislatively before independence, only a small élite of their populations was allowed very limited popular participation in government. This nine years' preparation for independence was, certainly, insufficient either to instill in the small élite modern democratic values or to equip them adequately for assuming the functions of the executive, legislative and bureaucratic organs of an independent Nigerian government. It was under these circumstances that the three regions and the Lagos colony became the component political units of the Federation of Nigeria. This flawed federal structure, tracing back to the amalgamation of 1914, contributed much to the polarization of politics around ethnicity and regionalism in the federation since independence. Sir Ahmadu Bello, in his day the most powerful leader in northern Nigeria, asserted that the amalgamation of 1914 was a mistake.

Separate regional emphasis and development made the regions the primary centers of power and wealth in Nigeria. This tilted the political balance in favor of conservative forces and protected the position of the aristocratic rulers of the northern region, especially, from interference from the federal government.[18] It ensured the organization of political parties, for example the four leading ones—the Action Group (AG), the National Council of Nigerian Citizens (NCNC), the Northern Peoples Congress (NPC) and the northern Elements Progressive Union (NEPU)—along regional lines. Separate regional emphasis and development also brought about the regionalization of the civil service. These features of separate regional development in Nigeria culminated in struggles for socio-economic resources and political conflicts over such issues as the timing of independence and revenue allocation (the two southern regions became independent in 1957, the north in 1959, and the federation in 1960, the date the northern region preferred). The struggles were clearly manifested in the fierce electoral competition for power at the center, anti-democratic currents, and bitterness in the pre-independence elections of 1959. This was the climate under which Nigeria became independent, on 1 October 1960, to operate a parliamentary democracy under a constitution guaranteeing civil liberties and other fundamental freedoms to citizens.

In the meantime, the regional governments, which had achieved independence earlier than the federation, had systematically become one-party states, harassing and repressing political opponents. The national government, instead of restraining, aided and abetted them. At the national level, loopholes in the constitution, crafted under British tutelage, facilitated abuse. For example, it allowed the declaration of a state of emergency by a simple majority vote of each house of the parliament, and the takeover of the administration of a regional government by the federal government (by two-thirds vote of each house of the parliament). The declaration of a state of emergency in 1962, and the subsequent take-over of the government of Western Nigeria by these means, became a major cause of the breakdown of law and order in Western Nigeria in 1962–65. In addition, the actions weakened the legitimacy of the ruling party at the national level and brought about the eventual demise of the First Republic on 15 January 1966 after a series of crises.

Another crucial component of the national question and colonial legacy in Nigeria is the Hausa-Fulani domination of Nigerian life since the end of British imperial rule. They apparently want to maintain and perpetuate that domination at all costs. This seemed to be the best way to ensure their regional and ethnic interests and to preserve their class dominance against the mobilization of radical elements in the north and the winds of change blowing up from the south. It does not matter that their region is landlocked and that most of the critical resources that make the federation politically and economically viable lie in the south, outside their region. This perpetuation of northern domination of the Nigerian federal government was in large measure responsible for the polarization and bitterness of Nigerian politics during the First Republic.

The perpetual northern political control of Nigeria is reinforced by the influence of Islam, the major religion in the region. This religion makes no distinction between Church and state. Prior to the British colonial occupation, the emirates in Northern Nigeria had been ruled as Islamic theocracies. Adherents would like to impose such rule on Nigeria despite a constitutional provision that Nigeria is a secular state. Further, Islam enjoins its adherents to remain combative and exclusive, an injunction which reinforces among its faithful a desire to hold on to power.

Confronted with this question of place and role of the Hausa-Fulani in Nigerian politics, the two largest nationality groups in the south—the Igbo and Yoruba—appear unable to find common ground to convince the Hausa-Fulani to share power and distribute social and economic amenities equitably among all Nigerian nationalities. Lacking the political cohesion of the Hausa-Fulani dominated North, and engaged in their own politics of ethnic security, the Igbo and Yoruba of the south become easily manipulated by the North and the northern-dominated military. At one time or another, each teamed up with the North as a junior partner to control and mismanage national power and economy. Many of their intelligentsia and political élites are guilty of intellectual dishonesty. They are advocates of democratic rule but have no scruples in accepting ministerial and other appointments from Nigerian autocratic military régimes. All these elements of the national question helped the military to play a disproportionate political role in Nigeria.

Another aspect of Nigeria's national question is the role of minority groups in political and economic life. This aspect of the national question is also a legacy of British colonial rule. It derived in part from the administrative division of Nigeria into political units, each with a major and dominant ethnic group, administered by the policy of Indirect Rule. It derived also from the oppressive nature of colonial domination, which fostered the natural desire of the ethnic groups to search for their own security and advancement, which the colonial order could not provide.

Under the colonial policy of Indirect Rule, traditional rulers served as colonial agents in both majority and minority ethnic group areas within each region. Colonial oppression was therefore inclusive of majority and minority groups. But as the policy of Indirect Rule was modified and regional governments were set up, members of the majority ethnic groups began to exercise whatever powers colonial authorities devolved to the regions. Also, at the national level, as progress was being made towards independence, it was largely the majority groups who constantly struggled for political power at the center. This colonial reification of the political importance of the three majority ethnic groups effectively denied the numerous minority ethnic groups significant political power. Naturally, therefore, the realities of the political situation at both the national and regional levels, as they experienced them, caused the minorities real concern. Therefore, for over a decade, during the twilight of British imperial tutelage, all minority groups agitated for an effective administrative mechanism to allay their fears of domination by the majority groups. The question of allaying such fears featured prominently in Nigeria's constitutional development and in the appointment of a commission to inquire into and recommend remedies for them. The major opposition to the idea of breaking up the existing regions and creating new states as a means of allaying the fears of minorities came from the British government and the leaders of Northern Nigeria. The two major southern political parties at the 1957 London Constitutional Conference were already committed to supporting the creation of additional states so as to allay the fears of minorities. The northern leaders instead "repeatedly and emphatically rejected any suggestion either to alter the present northern boundaries in order to assuage aggrieved minorities, or to create new states."[19] The British government based its strong opposition on the economic and administrative viability of additional states. Tinkering with the regions in order to allay those fears would have upset the political status quo, and so British interests, in both the north and the two southern regions. Thus, British colonial authorities adroitly avoided the issue altogether.

After independence a fourth region—the Midwest—was created out of the western region by the ruling NPC/NCNC (Northern Peoples Congress/National Council of Nigerian Citizens) coalition government. The NPC/NCNC coalition did so more to clip the political wings of the most prominent Yoruba leader at the time, Obafemi Awolowo, than to allay the fears of minorities in Nigeria's Midwest. Eight more states were created in 1967 by the military régime of Yakubu Gowon, partly to cripple the rebellious state of Biafra and also to win the loyalty and support of the minorities in the struggle to keep Nigeria one. By 1986 Nigeria had been carved up into 30 states by the military, as various groups agitated for more states as a means of obtaining their "fair share" of national power and "cake." The military dictators also used the process of creating states as a ploy to stay in power. The military's execution in November 1995 of the Ogoni leader and human rights advocate, Ken Saro-Wiwa, and his eight associates, for agitating for the rights of the Ogoni people shows that the fears of minorities were not totally allayed by these measures. Hence, in 1996 Abacha employed the same ruse to create six more states. The majority ethnic groups still jockeyed with the military for power and revenue allocation at the national level, using the minorities as pawns or allies, while the military consolidated its own hold on power and national resources.

These issues are the fundamental causes of the national question in Nigeria—the question of relations between Nigeria's ethnic groups, problem of power-sharing among them, the allocation of national resources, and social and economic amenities. Proposals, made at Abacha's 1994 decreed constitutional conference, regarding power-sharing through a rotational presidency and revenue allocation that designates 13 percent of mineral revenue to the areas of derivation were vehemently opposed by northern delegates. Outside the conference, the northern Elders Forum completely rejected the revenue allocation proposal. It said it was not completely against rotational presidency so long as it was not permanent, began with the north, and rotated only for a period of ten years.[20]

V. Inter-ethnic Rivalry

Another major dilemma of democracy in Nigeria is the practice whereby ethnic group interests have been accorded paramountcy over the collective interests of the majority of Nigerian citizens. This practice is a function of the natural evolution of nations from groups that desire and seek the preservation and promotion of their natural rights and self-interests. Historically, this phenomenon, according to Thomas Hobbes, created the need for the establishment of a centralized government (a "Leviathan," a monarchy), to avoid the chaos and ultimate destruction of all that would result from "the war of every man against every other man." In a multi-national state, such as Nigeria, a primary function of the national or central government is to mediate the rivalries and conflicts that result from such desire of specific groups in a way that ensures the basic rights, interests, and needs of all groups, and their collective survival as a political entity. This requires the existence of a social contract created by the people and stipulating the principles and terms of their union as a nation. Above all, it demands, first, a selfless leadership with vision to apply judiciously the principles and provisions of the constitution. Secondly, it demands an independent judiciary to ensure the respect for and the nurturing of the rule of law and a fair administration of justice. A stable democracy develops when these values and a specific liberal philosophy are instilled in the society and the functions are faithfully executed. In Nigeria no particular liberal philosophy has developed. Neither have these values been deeply instilled, nor is there a genuine commitment to the principles and terms of the organic union. Also, the central function is not being faithfully executed—hence, the failure of democracy to take a deep root in Africa's largest federal republic.

A factor contributing to this failure is the fact that Nigeria is an embryonic, multi-national state of extraordinary complexity. Its diversity in ethnic groups, cultures, political traditions and languages, while one of the sources of its strength, has also been an impediment to its national cohesion and development as a democracy. The depth and complexity of the federation's ethnicity have made its management by either democratic or authoritarian means extremely difficult. The clash among the centralized politico-ethnic majorities of the north, southwest, and southeast, and the dispersed ethnic minorities of the federation have been dysfunctional to inter-ethnic cooperation. The centralized politico-ethnic majorities have tended to impede inter-ethnic cooperation, whereas the dispersed ethnic minorities, which could have abetted such cooperation, have consistently been drawn into the morass of the power struggle among the ethnic majorities. Thus, it has been the practice that in electoral campaigns majority ethnic groups vigorously mobilized the ethnic minorities against other ethnic majorities. This situation has persisted in the federal republic despite "the quiet but steady growth of the social infrastructure of democracy—a (relatively) free press," an educational system (which although currently being stymied, had been rapidly expanding since independence), and "a diverse array of autonomous social, cultural, and economic organizations."[21] This is certainly one of the major dilemmas of democracy in Nigeria.

Rivalries among the major ethnic groups—first between the Igbo and Yoruba, and later between these two ethnic groups and the Hausa-Fulani—over the distribution of power and national resources were a major cause of political instability and breakdown of the civilian administration of the First

Federal Republic of Nigeria in January 1966. Because of this rivalry, every election and political contest became a struggle for supremacy, in which everything was at stake and no one ethnic group or region could afford to lose. Accordingly, this unhealthy rivalry over the distribution of power and wealth frustrated several efforts at census enumeration in Nigeria between 1962 to 1991. It has affected the voting patterns and results of national elections since 1959, notwithstanding the division of the federation into 36 states, a step that was expected to counter such behavior.

Between 1961 and 1966 a series of crises escalated ethnic rivalry and regional polarization. The first such crisis began in Western Nigeria between the Yoruba leaders of the AG—Obafemi Awolowo, who had become leader of the opposition in the federal legislature after the 1959 general elections, and Samuel L. Akintola who had succeeded Awolowo as premier of the western region. The crisis soon split both the party and the region into two factions and ultimately drew the federal, the eastern, and the northern regional governments into a heightened conflict. Following the removal of Akintola as premier by the Awolowo faction, the NPC/NCNC federal government coalition used the internal disorder in the western house of assembly to intervene. The federal legislature declared a state of emergency in the region, set up a six-month emergency administration there, and effectively prevented the Awolowo faction from selecting a new premier. Thereafter, Akintola was reinstated as premier. He had formed a new party—the Nigerian National Democratic Party (NNDP)—and had also succeeded in aligning himself with the leaders of the NPC who perceived Awolowo as a threat to their power and political role in Nigeria. Furthermore, the NPC/NCNC coalition charged, convicted, and imprisoned Awolowo and his associates for treason. At the same time, it exploited these developments to carve the midwest region out of the western region, but left the eastern and the largest northern region intact. In the process, Awolowo's Yoruba-based party, the AG, was devastated as a political force, leaving the Yoruba, as they saw themselves, emasculated in Nigerian national politics by the Hausa-Fulani/Igbo federal government coalition. But it did not take long for the Igbo-based NCNC, which had supported the destruction of the AG and Yoruba political power, to realize the folly of its role. New crises, beginning with the census enumeration of 1962, emphasized the folly and the consequent concentration of power into the hands of the conservative northern leaders of the NPC.

Nigeria's attempt at census enumeration in 1962 provoked another major crisis which aggravated inter-ethnic rivalry. For Nigeria's majority ethnic groups, census enumeration was, and has remained, politically significant. Under civilian rule, political representation, on the basis of population, determined the control of power at the federal legislature and so the control of the allocation of the federation's resources and wealth. The NPC had always demonstrated dexterity in playing the politics of controlling the center through sheer numbers. It did so in 1961, when, as the senior partner in the federal coalition government, it flatly refused to campaign vigorously in a UN-supervised plebiscite in the trust territory of Southern Cameroon to make the territory part of Eastern, and thus Southern, Nigeria. A positive vote by Southern Cameroon in that plebiscite to unite with Nigeria would have increased southern representation in the federal legislature and reduced the power of the north in that body. Instead, the NPC campaigned more vigorously and sue Northern Cameroon, which eventually became part of Nigeria's northern region as Sardauna province. This further ensured the strength of the region's representation at Nigeria's federal legislature.

The initial results of the 1962 census showed larger population increases in the south, a development that would have reduced the north's hegemonic control of the federal legislature. The north sought to prevent such a situation by claiming that it had discovered eight million more people in the region. A crisis ensued. The census was canceled and a new one was ordered. The resulting figures from the new census gave the north continued population majority and were rejected by the NCNC government of the Eastern region. However, the NPC, with its parliamentary majority and the acquiescence of its ally, Akintola of the Western region was able to win acceptance of the figures. This development contributed to weaken the marriage of convenience between the NPC and the NCNC and hastened political realignments in the federation: the Igbo-dominated NCNC-AG-NEPU United Progressive Grand Alliance [UPGA] against the Hausa-Fulani-dominated NPC-NNDP Nigerian National Alliance [NNA]. These alliances contested the 1964 federal elections. The elections became a bi-polar struggle, punctuated with acrimony, violence, official obstruction, and repression of opposition campaigns. The UPGA unwisely boycotted the balloting. The NPC and its allies triumphed, but only after President Nnamdi Azikiwe, a founder of the NCNC, desiring to avoid civil war and bloodshed, asked them to form a broad-based coalition government with the NCNC and its allies.

The brinkmanship of 1964, however, was undermined by another crisis among the Yoruba of the Western region in October 1965, which soon revived the north/south dichotomy in Nigerian politics. In the meantime, in "Essentials for Nigerian Survival," published in *Foreign Affairs* (April 1965), President Azikiwe articulated what he believed were contradictions in the Nigerian polity. He referred to how provisos in the 1960 constitution encouraged discrimination against Nigerians in their own country. He cited how certain nationality groups had made allegations of neglect by the federal and regional governments to provide them with essential infrastructure of roads, telecommunications networks, general and specialist hospitals, secondary industries, and postal facilities. Such discrimination, he said, was a fundamental cause of bad faith and suspicion in the Nigerian democracy. He lamented the "logic in depriving a Nigerian . . . of liberty to lease or purchase land, to seek employment, and to enjoy all the rights, and fulfill all the obligations of Nigerian citizenship anywhere in Nigeria, simply because he comes from a different region."[22]

To remedy these anomalies, Azikiwe called for a revision of the constitution. No immediate steps were taken in that direction but developments in western Nigeria in October 1965 were to starkly emphasize other realities and the anomalies Azikiwe had denounced. At that time, the AG and Akintola's party, the NNDP, contested the regional election. Most Yoruba people hated Akintola, whose régime, supported by the NPC-controlled federal government, was widely known to be corrupt, oppressive, and a sell-out to the north. The people were shocked to disbelief when his party was declared the victor in the political contest. They rose up in rebellion. The federal government refused to protect the oppressed. This, among other reasons, led to Nigeria's first military coup of 15 January 1966.

The head of the federal military government, Aguiyi-Ironsi, lasted six months. He was assassinated in July, more because he was an Igbo of southeast Nigeria than because of the charge that his administration was turning Nigeria into a unitary state at the expense of the north. The massacre of about 30,000 Igbo residents in Northern Nigeria and scores of military officers in both Northern and Western Nigeria between July 1966 and May 1967 forced most Igbo people to retreat to the Igbo heartland and to declare a separate and independent state of Biafra. The ensuing civil war lasted until January 1970 when Biafra was defeated.

In 1976, after the traumas of the civil war, two military coups, and assassinations, a step was taken in the direction advocated 11 years earlier by Azikiwe to revise the Nigerian constitution and to remedy the anomalies in the federation. The civil war traumas had generated renewed interest in carving up the nation's four regions into smaller states to allay the fears of minorities and to minimize the rivalries among the dominant nationality groups. Thus, on the eve of the civil war in 1967, Nigeria was divided into 12 states in the hope that such division would strengthen democracy in the federation. After the civil war, the creation of additional states remained so volatile an issue and so much the focus of intense ethnic and sub-ethnic political mobilization that seven more states were created in 1976, and 11 more in 1991. It was expected that this exercise would weaken ethnic and regional solidarities that had bedeviled the First Republic and at the same time generate a more fluid and shifting pattern of alignment in the federation. It did not. Rather, it activated sub-ethnic cleavages, which produced a much more decentralized pattern of ethnic rivalry. Notwithstanding this, General Abacha created six additional states in 1996 as part of his transition program.

Salvation from ethnic and regional rivalry was also sought in constitution-making. In 1976, Nigerians drafted a new constitution, similar in several respects to the U.S. constitution. By several of its provisions, the draft constitution, ratified by the military in 1979, sought to tackle Nigeria's problem of ethnic and regional cleavages and to provide the nation a more durable foundation for democratic governance and respect for the rule of law. It instituted an executive presidential system, a bicameral legislature, and an independent judiciary. It explicitly prohibited sectional parties and required broad ethnic representation in each party as a condition for registration and participation in electoral politics. It created a Federal Electoral Commission to certify political parties, regulate campaigning, and ensure fair and free elections. It forbade crossing the carpet by parliamentarians, a practice that had been abused during the First Republic. It required that federal institutions and establishments should reflect the heterogeneous character (multi-ethnicity) of its population, of Nigeria. It established an elaborate Code of Conduct for Public Officials and a bureau and tribunal for monitoring and enforcing compliance with its provisions.

These major steps have not resolved the problem of inter-ethnic and regional rivalry in Nigeria. The political parties that emerged to contest power in the Second Republic "bore strong resemblance to the parties of the First Republic, in part because of significant continuities in their leadership and [their] regional basis."[23] Thus, they tended to retreat "into convenient and familiar ethnic alignments," and to produce "a sad level of regional and [ethnic] correlation in voting behavior."[24] Electoral malpractices in the 1979 elections and thereafter eroded the legitimacy of the Federal Electoral Commission as a regulatory agency. The result of all this was that the Second Republic, heralded by the new constitution, which lasted barely four years under Alhaji Shehu Shagari. Although he was admired for his restraint and fine human qualities, Shagari failed to demonstrate the ability to take hard-nosed political decisions in the interest of democratic governance and a stable and economically vibrant Nigerian nation. He was unable to control the undemocratic and venal tendencies of his closest advisers, and of his party machinery. Under his administration, competition for wealth and power and for the award of government contracts among the ethnicities of Nigeria remained a clear source of tension. To this situation was added an unending succession of scandals and glaring corruption at all levels of government. To cap it all, the federal and state elections, held in August and September 1983, were marred by violence and fraud. These brought about the overthrow of the

Shagari administration and the Second Republic on 31 December 1983 by the military, which eliminated democracy and imposed authoritarian rule on Nigeria.[25]

VI. Political and Judicial Institutions

Nigeria's multi-party system emerged in the 1940s during the waning years of British colonial rule. The emergent political parties were generally ethnic and regionally based, fragile, shallow, and weak. Throughout the period, heated and bitter political polarization in Nigeria consistently resulted not from class or ideology but from the coincidence of party cleavage with region and ethnicity. This major characteristic of the emergent party system remained so throughout the years of the First Republic (1960–66). During that period, politicians deliberately provoked ethnic and regional conflicts as a strategy to obtain or retain power as a means of amassing private wealth and dispensing favors. They turned political competition into mortal warfare, which increased ethnic and regional insecurity, suspicion and hostility. Intolerant of political opposition, the political parties were also generally afflicted with defections and expulsions, while their members lacked experience.

The earliest party to emerge, the Nigerian Youth Movement, was ineffective in dealing with British colonial administrators because of internal dissensions. It broke up in 1941. The next to emerge, in 1944, the NCNC, although a national movement, was in essence a "confederation of trade unions, smaller parties, [ethnic] unions and literary groups."[26] Its major goal was to ensure Nigeria internal self-government and the exercise of executive, legislative, and judicial powers. Two other competing parties emerged from cultural organizations among the Yoruba of the west and the Hausa-Fulani of the north respectively. The AG emerged from Egbe Omo Oduduwa (Society of the Descendants of Oduduwa) in 1947, and the NPC from the Bauchi Improvement Association in 1951. NEPU, led by Mallam Aminu Kano, a founding member of the NPC, was a break-away party from the NPC, just as the United Independent Party (UNIP) broke away from the NCNC. The three major parties—NCNC, AG, NPC—contested Nigeria's first general elections in 1951/52. The NCNC won the Eastern region with a large majority; the NPC won the North. Victorious NCNC candidates in the West crossed the carpet to give the AG 49 out of 80 seats in the region. Each party was thus in control in its ethnic and regional stronghold.

While the NCNC wanted a more powerful central government, the other parties wanted as much power in the regions as possible and a less powerful central government. Also, while the NCNC and the AG demanded independence for Nigeria by 1956, the NPC rejected the idea as its leaders felt the Northern region would not be ready for self-government by that date. Its leaders asked instead for self-government as soon as it was practicable. The resulting ethnic and regional tensions from this disagreement over a date for self-government culminated in riots in Kano in 1956. By official account, 36 people were killed and 277 others were wounded during the riots.

The three major parties were able to bury their differences over the timing of independence, revenue allocation, and the issue of creating more states to assuage the fears of minorities in all regions of the country, as they worked with British colonial authorities to produce Nigeria's 1954 constitution. After minor revisions of the 1954 constitution, general elections to lead Nigeria to independence were held in 1959. No single party won a large enough majority to form the government. What emerged after negotiations was an NPC-NCNC coalition, despite the considerable differences in their political views. The NPC, as the senior partner, appointed its deputy leader, Abubakar Tafawa Balewa, as the prime minister. Obafemi Awolowo, leader of the AG, became leader of the opposition at the federal legislature.

Each of the parties remained in power in its regional stronghold, which was already self-governing: the east and the west in 1957, and the north in 1959. Each espoused parliamentary democracy while negating the basic principles of the system. The NPC never lost an election either in its region or at the federal level. Instead, it consolidated its power and dominance at both the national and regional levels after each subsequent election. The NCNC prospered in its stronghold in the eastern region, just as the AG did in the west. Without shame, without honor, each of the parties freely used political violence and electoral fraud to retain power.

The cause of political violence and fraud during the First Republic, and indeed during the Second Republic, was the nature and role of the state as the primary means for the accumulation of personal wealth, the source of wage employment, and the primary source of money expenditures, contracts, licenses, scholarships, development projects, public loans, and investment funds. This role of the state put too much at stake in the competition for state power, for the authoritative allocation of resources and national wealth. Nigerian politicians vested so much emotional stake in electoral competition that no one dared to contemplate, or accept defeat. Thus, the enormous premium Nigerian political parties vested in winning elections and political power produced political thuggery, rioting, arson, and massive electoral fraud, which ultimately drained the First Republic, and later the Second Republic, of their legitimacy.[27]

It was through the process of electoral competition that during the First Republic the AG fell victim to internal dissension and to its ultimate destruction, as the NPC-NCNC coalition brought its dominant political position to bear on the party's internal squabbles. That development precipitated the series of crises which, among other causes (including NPC-NCNC rift after the crushing of the AG, rampant corruption and indiscipline among the politicians, and the erosion of their legitimacy), led to the collapse of the First Republic in January 1966. Consequently, partisan politics was suspended by military dictators until 1978.

In 1978, three years after it began the preparation for the Second Republic, the military lifted the ban on political parties. Various electoral provisions were adopted, requiring that political parties should have broad ethnic representation as a condition for registration. Of the 19 out of about 50 emergent political parties that applied by mid December 1978 for certification, only five were certified by the Federal Electoral Commission. However, the certified parties—National Party of Nigeria (NPN), Unity Party of Nigeria (UPN), Nigerian Peoples' Party (NPP), Great Nigerian Peoples' Party (GNPP), a breakaway from the NPP, and Peoples' Redemption Party (PRP)—fell victim to time constraints. With the advance of the full onset of electoral competition, they were unable "to develop fresh leadership, new and coherent identities and broad constituencies."[28]

The results were predictable. They became the reincarnation of the parties and politics of the First Republic in their leadership, regional bases, weakness and extraordinary volatility. The characteristic politics of ethnic and regional security reemerged. Alhaji Shehu Shagari, a former NPC federal minister, led the NPN. Chief Obafemi Awolowo, the jailed former leader of the Yoruba-based AG, and of the opposition in the First Republic's federal legislature, became the leader of the UPN. The NPP was led by Nnamdi Azikiwe, an Igbo, and formerly leader of the NCNC and president of the First Republic. The former leader of NEPU, Mallam Aminu Kano, led the PRP while Waziri Ibrahim led the GNPP, based in northern Nigeria. Thus, in the north, where there had been only two parties during the First Republic, a third party had emerged. The NPN, with its core leadership in the north, managed to penetrate the south, winning followers among minority as well as majority ethnic groups throughout southern Nigeria.

The campaigns and the subsequent state and federal balloting were relatively fair and free although there were charges of corruption and electoral malpractices. The NPN won the presidency. A constitutional provision that the presidential candidate should win 25 percent of the votes in two-thirds of Nigeria's 19 states (at the time) became the basis of a challenge to the legitimacy of the NPN victory. Awolowo, leader of the UPN, argued that the NPN candidate, Shehu Shagari, had not won the required 25 percent of the votes in two-thirds of the 19 states but only 25 percent of the votes cast in 12 states. The Federal Electoral Commission and the Supreme Court upheld the NPN victory, a ruling that engendered lasting political hostility between the NPN and the UPN, similar to that during the First Republic between the NPC and the AG.

Coupled with charges of corruption and abuse of political authority by the NPN government of the Second Republic, the political hostility produced new political alignments by the UPN, GNPP, and the PRP, on the one hand, and political cooperation and sharing of executive and legislative offices between the NPN and the NPP, on the other. Intra and inter-party alignment, polarization, and bickering dominated Nigerian politics thereafter.

The UPN-NPP alliance had collapsed by July 1981. Shortchanged on bilateral political consultations and patronage-sharing from the NPN, the NPP withdrew from the alliance and some of its governors moved closer to UPN. Internal dissension split the PRP into radical and traditional establishment factions, which played into the hands of the NPN and facilitated the impeachment of the PRP Governor of Kaduna State. While the NPN and UPN remained mostly intact, the two other parties—the NPP and the GNPP—like the PRP suffered internal bickering, expulsions, and defections, which, as in the First Republic, produced political intolerance, violence, and public disillusionment. Public disillusionment was aggravated not only by the behavior of the politicians in their quest for personal power and wealth, but also by evidence of massive corruption and mismanagement within the Shagari-led NPN government, and by the inability of the state governments to pay their employees and maintain public works, hospitals, and schools. This general situation set the stage for speculation that a military intervention would pre-empt 1983 scheduled elections. Although there had been allegations of plots to overthrow the Shagari government, the military establishment bided its time and allowed the elections to take place.

From the start the Federal Electoral Commission mismanaged the electoral process—from registration through certification of political parties, campaigns, to the casting of ballots. The general impression was that during both the First and the Second Republics the National Electoral Commission, the judiciary, and the police were partisan instruments of the ruling party and were frequently manipulated by corrupt and partisan pressures. Because of the role of the state as the primary source of wealth and personal advancement, these political institutions lacked the independence, resources, and effective power to mediate political fraud and to safeguard respect for the rule of law and impartial administration of justice. The high court demonstrated its lack of independence vividly in 1993 when it was asked by the Association for a Better Nigeria, a clique of Babangida's sycophants, to issue an injunction against a presidential election planned for June 1993. The election was to have been held in 1992, but Babangida, wanting to remain indefinitely in power, had found one excuse after another to postpone it. The high court obliged his agents. However, the judicial ban was ignored by the National Electoral Commission. The balloting process run its course relatively smoothly and satisfactorily.

When early returns showed that Abiola, the SDP candidate, had a commanding lead over the NRC candidate, whose victory Babangida and his military colleagues preferred, pressure was again brought upon the high court to issue an injunction suspending the counting and official verification. Again, the high court succumbed to their pressure. The National Electoral Commission was similarly pressured to suspend its official verification of the results. Thereafter, Babangida proceeded to annul the election, throwing the nation into a political crisis that ultimately forced him from power by 26 August 1993. For their part, despite the relative degree of their autonomy and repeated warnings about the dangers of political violence and fraud, the print media were also implicated by their lack of independence. As organs of the government or political parties, they reflected or accommodate the polarization of partisan loyalties. The electronic media, too, are a state monopoly and articulate mainly the views of the government or party in power.

The 1983 electoral campaigns, which culminated in the establishment of the Second Republic, were accompanied by violence and thuggery in various states of the federation. While the UPN and NPP, whose leaders had failed to yield one to the other the presidential candidacy, campaigned against the corruption and mismanagement of the NPN government, the NPN itself branded them advocates of ethnic, regional, and religious interests. In the end, widespread electoral malpractices produced a landslide victory for the NPN and the second inauguration of Alhaji Shehu Shagari's administration on 1 October 1983. The Shagari administration, however, was overthrown by the military on 31 December 1983, thus burying Nigeria's second attempt at democracy. The corruption and mismanagement of Shagari's first administration and the economic malaise of the country had gone too far to be redeemed by the belated austerity and remedial measures he had taken after his second inauguration.

VII. The Crisis of Leadership

The crisis of leadership is, perhaps, the root cause of the failure of democratic governance in Nigeria.[29] The Nigerian constitution, whether that of 1979 or its predecessor, the independence constitution, was basically sound especially because constitutions work by interpretation. An imaginative leadership can interpret the constitution and mobilize competing groups of people, as those of Nigeria, to achieve what is in the overall interest of all the groups. Nigerian leaders have not genuinely demonstrated that very critical quality. Rather, they have allowed themselves to be bound by their economic need and personal ambition, and the dictates of the structure of Nigeria, in their operation of the Constitution and in their role as leaders. Ethnicity, the most politically significant aspect of that structure, has been the ultimate factor in the recruitment of leaders for the top political positions in Nigeria. This truly limited the choice of individuals to serve in executive positions in the state during the First and the Second Republics. Hence, simply because of their ethnic origins, potentially capable individuals were unable to win power to serve as head of state or in similar leadership positions.

Once such individuals lost at the polls, political ambition, combined with the politics of ethnic and regional security, crippled their ability to play a more constructive role in the democratic governance of Nigeria. They failed "to rise to the responsibility, to the challenge of personal example which are the hallmarks of true leadership."[30] For example, the judges who tried Chief Obafemi Awolowo on charges of treason during the First Republic stated in their judgment that when his ambition of becoming the first prime minister of Nigeria did not materialize, his hopes were shattered and he lost faith in the ballot box. As a consequence, he developed a sense of frustration, which culminated in plots to seize the government.[31]

On the other hand, the two men who, after their electoral victory, served in Nigeria's highest political office, Sir Abubakar and Alhaji Shehu Shagari, while good and honest men, were weak and overcautious. They were encumbered by domineering forces—Sir Ahmadu Bello over Sir Abubakar, and the aristocrats of the National Party of Nigeria over Alhaji Shagari—whose chief concerns were not democracy, not national but parochial. In addition, the political élites in Nigeria have not been a cohesive group. They have been, and still remain, divided along ethnic, regional and religious identifications. They employ such divisions as tools to mobilize masses of Nigerians to facilitate their access to state power and thereby to accumulate personal wealth. But after acquiring such wealth they pay little or no attention to the economic and social concerns of the masses they manipulated to achieve their goals.

In Nigeria's political history up to 1983, Alhaji Shehu Shagari was the only leader who rejected, and reduced by half, the salary recommended for him by members of the National Assembly, who approved for themselves salaries completely out of line with the economic realities of Nigeria.[32] For the most part, political leaders of Nigeria's First and Second Republics lacked integrity and commitment to the democratic system. They had no vision for the nation, but were motivated by the ambition to exercise power, and in the process, to appropriate for themselves and their supporters the perquisites of office. They consistently mismanaged Nigeria's human and natural resources. They wasted Nigeria's oil wealth, which had held out a great promise in national economic and social development. Intolerant of political criticism and debate, they frequently resorted to violence in dealing with critics and opponents. Such leaders as Sir Abubakar, Shehu Shagari and General Yakubu Gowon, who generally were not known to be corrupt, displayed remarkable weakness to discipline corrupt officials in their own administrations. Collectively, therefore, the political leadership undermined not only the legitimacy of the democratic process, but its own legitimacy through weakness, fraud, indiscipline, rampant corruption, and authoritarianism.

Military rule exacerbated the crisis of political leadership in Nigeria. It became infected by the same ethnic, regional, and religious divisiveness that crippled civilian rule. It was unable to resolve the contradictions and crises that caused it to overthrow the civilian governments. It has inaugurated a unique transition to civilian rule that never ends, thereby engendering new contradictions within Nigerian society. Its stay in power has not altered the fact of the Nigerian state as the primary source of wealth and personal advancement. For the military rulers, the state has served that function very well. Under military authoritarianism, corruption has not diminished either within the military régime itself or within the civilian society. Rather, the military leaders, like their deposed civilian counterparts, used state power to accumulate wealth and to advance their own interests and those of the bureaucrats with whom they forged an alliance of silence to defraud the nation. Because the military has been accountable to nobody, its abuses have surpassed even those of the civilian rulers, and aroused counter-coups by other members of the military who had not been party to the loot.

Military rule has caused the most severe setback for the growth and development of democracy in Nigeria. It has inflicted increasing political, material, and psychological damage on Nigeria. It has nullified the rule of law, killed and scorched the spirit and the seeds of democracy that had been sprouting in the country. It stifled press freedom, repressed; and trampled upon basic human rights; and exploited ethnic, regional, and religious cleavages to justify continued authoritarian rule. It depressed the economy, and caused stark inequities through structural adjustment programs it imposed on the nation. Historical experience of military dictatorships and their prolonged rule eliminates any hope that the military, which has indeed become part of Nigeria's political problem, is capable of resolving the dilemmas of democracy in the federation.

VIII. Conclusion

Since the end of World War II, enormous efforts and resources have been devoted to addressing the deep cleavages of ethnicity, regionalism, religion and economic inequalities in Nigeria so as to facilitate the entrenchment of democracy in the country. Before independence in 1960, a series of constitutional conferences in which Nigerian leaders participated fully, under the auspices of the British Colonial Office, were devoted to devising a political system that would ensure the rule of law and the protection and promotion of fundamental human rights throughout the land. No less than four constitutional conferences were held between 1966 and 1995 to devise a political system that could effectively accommodate the political, economic, and religious fissures that continued to confound Nigeria. In the process, constitutional provisions, administrative and electoral institutions, designed to guarantee Nigeria's cultural diversity within a legitimate democratic framework, were crafted. Systems of revenue allocation aimed at fairness and minimizing economic inequities and inequalities were adopted. A grueling civil war was fought in 1967–70. Reconciliation was rapidly achieved. No less than six "corrective" military régimes have been imposed on the country to save it from "mismanagement, corruption, and indiscipline" by civilian, even military, administrators. The nation has been divided into 36 states of relatively comparable population to strengthen the federal system and reduce the real or imagined fear of political domination by majority groups or by one group or region over all others. Indeed, the creation of more states produced a multi-state federal system and a corresponding break-up of the hegemony of the three largest nationality groups. This has strengthened the federal system, dispersed development activity, and taken such activity closer to people in the more remote and rural areas of the country.

In spite of these efforts and measures, democratic governance still eludes Nigeria. Ethnic group interests continue to be accorded paramountcy over the collective good of Nigerian nationals. The military establishment continues to hold sway over the entire nation. Despite some of its more positive effects, the creation of more states has not helped to promote democratic governance. Rather, it has exposed intra-ethnic tensions in all regions of Nigeria. What accounts for this failure of democracy to establish deep roots in Nigeria?

The cause is not a lack of effort to seek modalities for solutions. Nigeria's road to democratization is rough. The foundations for democracy in the federation are weakened by internal contradictions and, especially, by the fundamental handicap of Nigeria's pluralism—ethnic, religious, and regional diversity, and civil/military dichotomy. The glaring condition of poverty, economic deprivation, and skewed distribution of national wealth further handicaps the process. These handicaps are aggravated by a lack of will to make the necessary sacrifices for the critical solutions, and to implement strategies already devised for resolving the problems. This lack of a will to make necessary sacrifices is a function of misplaced priorities, a lack of vision and a crisis of leadership in Nigeria. Despite their achievements in peacefully negotiating independence from British colonial rulers, the first generation of Nigerian political leaders were myopic in that they placed the interests of their regions and ethnic groups above those of an organic Nigerian nation, worthy of the sacrifices of its citizens and their leaders. Their misconduct and the interference of a politicized military progressively stymied democracy in Nigeria.

The priority of those leaders was not Nigeria for its sake, but Nigeria as it served their own parochial interests and those of their region and ethnic group. This may be a reflection of the colonial origins of Nigeria in which the state controlled most avenues of amassing and transferring wealth from the colony to the imperial metropole. Although Nigerian nationalists opposed colonialism for many reasons (including democratic governance, to terminate all forms of exploitation), upon their victory they put more focus on exploiting post-colonial Nigeria for themselves and their ethnic and regional supporters than upon its democratic administration. At one time Sir Ahmadu Bello said that, "the East was for the easterners, the West for the Westerners, the North for the Northerners, and the federal government for all of us." Therefore, to Nigeria's political leadership, civilian and military, acquiring state power became the primary means of acquisition and allocation of national wealth and resources. Hence, politics was no longer the art of compromise but a zero-sum game, a total war, to be won at any cost.

The materialistic spirit that produced these behavioral patterns accounts also for the indiscipline, misplaced priorities, and lack of vision among Nigeria's leaders and their followers. To it also should be attributed the failure of the leaders to effectively enforce the provisions of the constitution, to implement legal rules and regulations, and to uphold the rule of law and the principles of fairness and justice. In spite of these, prospects for democracy in Nigeria remain alive. Nigerians are resilient. Their indigenous political cultures and autonomous interest groups and associations, which survived British imperial rule, have tended to prevent absolute rule and to limit, although not prevent, authoritarian rule. Institutionalized authoritarian rule would require more widespread violence, which Nigeria has not experienced yet. Nigeria's volatile ethnic and religious diversity militates against such a rule, which would threaten groups, ethnic or religious, not party to it, and would increase not only political and economic instability, but also the urge for separatism.

These realities in themselves will not restore democracy in Nigeria. The most immediate strategy to adopt in the efforts to revive the spirit and bones of democratic governance in Nigeria is to alter the relationship between the Nigerian state, as the source of all wealth, and the society, composed of competing consumers of wealth. All the ingredients essential to bringing about such a revolution are already present in Nigeria: egregiously corrupt rulers and bureaucrats who have lost the confidence of the people, rampant inflation, abject poverty of the masses, intolerable unemployment rate among high school leavers and college graduates, vast numbers of economic and political refugees overseas, wasted resources, a potentially rich country hovering on the brink of economic and political collapse, and recently, a series of unprecedented bomb blasts targeted at the military.[33] But yet there is no leadership to capitalize on these conditions to mobilize the people for such a change. Nigerian leaders need a national conference that could produce a transitional government of shared powers, accountable to the people, over a minimum period of seven years. Such a transition could lead to the emergence of mutual trust and a truly national leader, "the fashioning of a common political program, together with a commitment to overcome the country's regional, ethnic and religious divisions, and make possible the national concord that could sustain an extended period of civilian rule." That may be the only remaining hope for the survival of Nigeria as one organic political entity.[34]

IX. The Dilemmas of Democracy in Nigeria: Postscript

Since the completion of this chapter, Nigeria has experienced a number of significant developments which can only be briefly summarized here. First, Sani Abacha, who had inaugurated a period of transition to civilian rule in 1997, and had promoted the emergence of five political parties, decided instead on a program of self-succession. He created and financed a youth movement and other paid political sycophants, civilian as well as military, to advocate his self-succession. He adroitly manipulated the five political parties to adopt him as their candidate for the presidency. In this manner, the national election that had been planned for August 1998 was to become a referendum on Abacha's self-succession. Every measure of opposition against this plan was thwarted, while lavish national resources were spent to promote it.

In the meantime, about 21 military officers, including Abacha's second-in-command, Lieutenant General Oladipo Diya, were arrested and charged with treason for an alleged plot (covertly videotaped) to overthrow the Abacha régime. The accused coup-plotters were tried by the military, which found most of them guilty.

In the scheme of things by the great ruler of all things, as many Nigerians believed, the referendum on Abacha's self-succession did not take place. On Sunday night, 7 June 1998, Abacha died suddenly from natural causes and was buried shortly afterward according to established Muslim tradition. The nation was thus spared incalculable dangers into which his self-succession plan would have plunged it. Upon Abacha's death, General Abdulsalami Abubakar was selected by the military leadership to succeed him.

Abubakar worked to calm the tempers of an agitated nation and promised to end military dictatorship through a genuine transition by the end of May 1999. He proceeded to release most of Abacha's political prisoners, including journalists and human rights activists. He reached understanding to release Moshood Abiola—the presumed winner of the June 1993 presidential election annulled by Abacha—from detention, but Abiola died of a heart attack in August, while talking to visiting U.S. government officials, before he could be released.

In a further move, Abubakar dissolved the five Abacha-régime political parties. In their place emerged 15 others, only three of which—Peoples Democratic Party, All Peoples Party, and Alliance for Democracy—were certified to contest elections of local, state, and national governments, including the presidency. The elections would be completed by 20–27 February 1999, when the National Assembly and the president respectively would be elected, thus returning Nigeria, by the end of May, to civilian rule. However, deep concerns about the future of Nigeria and democratic rule in the republic remain. One of the leading candidates for the presidency, Olusegun Obasanjo, Nigeria's former military head of state, is widely believed to be sponsored by powerful political forces in Northern Nigeria and by past and present military rulers as the one who can best protect their respective interests. Furthermore, the nation is experiencing severe problems from falling revenues from crude oil, rebellion in the Delta, a major oil-producing region, and from dilapidated economic infrastructure.

Notes

1. General Sani Abacha, the late military head of state (1995–98) and his immediate predecessor, Ibrahim Babangida, are believed to be billionaires. Many retired and active senior military officers are multimillionaires due to their control of the oil sector, which provides more than 80 percent of Nigeria's foreign exchange earnings.

2. *West Africa* (25 September–8 October 1995): p. 1515; Adonis Hoffman, "Nigeria: the Policy Conundrum," in *Foreign Policy*, no. 101 (winter 1995–96): p. 146–158.

3. Richard Joseph, "Nigeria: Inside the Dismal Tunnel," in *Current History*, vol. 95, no. 601 (May 1996): p. 194.

4. Wole Soyinka, *The Open Sore of a Continent: A Personal Narrative of the Nigerian Crisis* (New York: Oxford University Press, 1996); Richard Joseph, "Nigeria's Long, Steep, Bloody Slide," *The New York Times OP-ED* (22 August 1994); "Let Down Again: A Survey of Nigeria," in *Economist* (21–27 August 1993): p. 36.

5. Quoted in "Let Down Again: Survey of Nigeria," p. 36.

6. Joseph, "Nigeria: Inside the Dismal Tunnel," p. 193–200; Peter M. Lewis, "Endgame in Nigeria: the Politics of a Failed Transition," in *African Affairs*, vol. 93, no. 372 (July 1994): p. 323–340; Obasanjo Olusegun's Keynote Address, "state of the Nation: Which Way Forward?" delivered at the Arewa House Conference, Kaduna, Nigeria (2 February 1994).

7. *West Africa* (9–15 October 1995): p. 1556.

8. Nnamdi Azikiwe, "Nigeria in World Politics," in *West African Pilot* (6–7 August 1959); Olajide Aluko, "Nigeria's Role in Inter-African Relations with Reference to the Organization of African Unity," in *African Affairs*, vol. 72, no. 287 (April 1973): p. 163; A.A. Haastrup, "Nigeria's Role in World Affairs," in *Africa Quarterly*, no. 4 (January-March 1965): p. 240–248; Abubakar T. Balewa, "Nigeria Looks Ahead," in *Foreign Affairs*, no. 41 (October 1962): p. 131–140; Jean Herskovits, "Dateline Nigeria: A Black Power," in *Foreign Policy*, no. 29 (winter 1977–78): p. 167–188; Jean Herskovits, "Democracy in Nigeria," in *Foreign Affairs*, vol. 58, no. 2 (winter 1979–80): p. 314–333.

9. Sayre P. Schartz, *Nigerian Capitalism* (Berkeley: University of California Press, 1977), p. 1–2; Timothy M. Shaw & Orobole Fasehun, "Nigeria in the World System: Alternative Approaches, Explanation and Projections," in *The Journal of Modern African Studies* (vol. 18) n.4 (1980): p. 560.

10. *West Africa* (25 September–8 October 1995), p. 1515.

11. *Africa Confidential*, vol. 37, no. 17 (25 August 1995): p. 3.

12. On Nigeria's nationality groups see: Onigu Otite, *Ethnic Pluralism and Ethnicity in Nigeria* (Ibadan, Nigeria: Shaneson C.I. Ltd., 1990).

13. Festus Ugboaja Ohaegbulam, *Towards an Understanding of the African Experience from Historical and Contemporary Perspectives* (Lanham, MD: University Press of America, 1990), p. 101–103; Nnamdi Azikiwe, "Essentials for Nigerian Survival," in *Foreign Affairs*, vol. 43, no. 3 (April 1965): p. 447–448.

14. Michael Crowder, "Whose Dream Was It Anyway? Twenty-Five Years of African Independence," in *African Affairs*, vol. 86, no. 342 (January 1987): p. 7–24, especially p. 11–13.

15. Crowder, "Whose Dream Was it Anyway?" p. 16.

16. Larry Diamond et al., eds., *Democracy in Developing Countries: Africa* (Boulder, CO: Rienner,1988), p. 7.

17. Obaro Ikime, "Nigeria: the National Question," in *Africa Events*, vol. 3, no. 6 (June 1987): p. 21.

18. Diamond et al., eds., *Democracy in Developing Countries*, p. 37.

19. James S. Coleman, *Nigeria: Background to Nationalism* (Berkeley: University of California Press, 1958), p. 390–396, quote from p. 393; Diamond et al., eds., *Democracy in Developing Countries: Africa, p. 9*.

20. *West Africa* (25 September–8 October 1995): p. 1515; Paul Adams, "Nigeria: Next Pariah?" in *Africa Today* (May-June 1995): p. 43–45.

21. Diamond et al., eds., *Democracy in Developing Countries: Africa*, p. 33.

22. Nnamdi Azikiwe, "Essentials For Nigerian Survival," in *Foreign Affairs*, vol. 43, no. 3 (April 1965): p. 447–461.

23. Diamond et al., eds., *Democracy in Developing Countries: Africa*, p. 48.

24. Ibid., p. 49.
25. Larry Diamond, "Nigeria in Search of Democracy," in *Foreign Affairs*, vol. 62, no. 4 (spring 1984): p. 905–927.
26. Michael Crowder, *The Story of Nigeria* (London: Faber and Faber, 1978), p. 223.
27. Chinua Achebe, *A Man of the People* (London: Heinemann, 1982).
28. Diamond et al., eds., *Democracy in Developing Countries: Africa*, p. 19–20.
29. Chinua Achebe, *The Problem with Nigeria* (London: Heinemann, 1983).
30. Achebe, *The Problem with Nigeria*, p. 1.
31. Jean Herskovits, *Nigeria: Power and Democracy in Africa* (New York: Foreign Policy Association, 1982), p. 20.
32. *West Africa* (26 November 1998), Colin Legum ed., *Africa Contemporary Record, 1979–1980*, p. B590.
33. Anthony Gouldman, "Nigeria's Leaders Keep Mum as Bombs Target the Military," in *The Christian Science Monitor* (10 January 1997): p. 7.
34. Richard Joseph, "Nigeria: Inside the Dismal Tunnel," in *Current History*, vol. 95, no. 601 (May 1996): p. 199.

Notes on Contributors

The Editor

DR. MARCO RIMANELLI is Director of the Center on Inter-American and World Studies of Saint Leo University, Tampa, Florida, and tenured Associate Professor in European Affairs, U.S. Foreign Policy and International Security. Currently on leave, he is a NATO expert for the U.S. government and Research Associate at the Elliott School of International Affairs–George Washington University, Washington, DC. From 1993–96 he was Editor of *Political Chronicle*, The Journal of Florida's Political Science Association. He has worked in 1991–92 on U.S.-Soviet/Russian nuclear arms reductions at the U.S. Arms Control and Disarmament Agency/state Department, Washington, DC. He has authored, edited, and co-edited works on U.S.-European security: *Strategic Challenges to U.S. Foreign Policy in the Post–Cold War* (Tampa, FL: Saint Leo Press–Center on Inter-American and World Studies, 1998); *Italy between Europe and the Mediterranean: Diplomacy and Naval Strategy from 1800s to NATO* (New York: Peter Lang Publishing, 1997); *The 1891 New Orleans Lynching and U.S.-Italian Relations: Immigration, Mafia and Diplomacy* (New York: Peter Lang Publ., 1992). He is currently completing a manuscript on NATO.

The Contributors

DR. CHARLES W. ARNADE is Professor of International Affairs at the University of South Florida–Tampa (USF). He is an expert on Third World politics, on which he has published several works.

DR. ROBERT V. BARYLSKI is Associate Professor of Government and International Relations at the University of South Florida–New School, Sarasota, Florida. He is an expert on post-Soviet politics, civil-military relations, problems of new state construction, and Russian policy towards Islamic people. He has published several works on these issues.

DR. ANTHONY N. CELSO is Assistant Professor of Government at Valley Forge Military College, Wayne, Pennsylvania. He is an expert on Spanish politics, on which he has published several works.

DR. ALFRED G. CUZÁN is Professor of International Affairs and Chairman of the Department of Government at the University of West Florida–Pensacola. He is an expert on Latin America, Portugal, and the Ibero-Latin region, on which he has published several works.

Mr. JACK P. HORGAN is the former President of Tampa Overseas Associates, a consulting company working with Japanese and U.S. companies. He is retired from the CIA, the U.S. Foreign Service, and the U.S. Army. Previously he studied Japanese Affairs at Harvard under Dr. Edwin O. Reishauer, worked in Japan with General Douglas MacArthur after World War II, and has lived in Japan over 16 years. He is currently working on a manuscript on Japanese affairs and society.

DR. RENU KHATOR is Associate Professor of Government at the University of South Florida–Tampa (USF), and is a close collaborator of USF President Betty Kastor. He is an expert on Public Administration, and on Indian politics, on which he has published several works.

DR. BEAT KERNEN is Associate Professor in Eastern European Affairs at Southwest Missouri State University–Springfield. He is an expert on post-Soviet politics, governments and politics of Eastern Europe, and the European Union, on which he has published several works.

DR. FRANCO MAZZELLA is Professor of Political Science at Southwest Missouri State University–Springfield. He is an expert on Latin America, and on Italy, on which he has published several works.

DR. JACK J. McTAGUE is Professor of History and International Affairs at Saint Leo University, Tampa, Florida. He is an expert on Israel, Middle-East, and Third World issues.

DR. WALTRAUD QUEISER MORALES is Professor of Comparative and International Studies and is the former Director of the Office of International Studies at the University of Central Florida–Orlando. She is also the new Editor of *Political Chronicle*, the Journal of Florida's Political Science Association. She is an expert on Latin American and Third World politics, on which she has published several works.

DR. FESTUS UGBOAJA OHAEGBULAM is Professor of International Affairs at the University of South Florida–Tampa (USF) and former Chairman of African and African American Studies. He is an expert on African issues and Nigerian politics, on which he has published several works.

DR. PLATON N. RIGOS is Professor of Government and Director of Public Administration at the University of South Florida–Tampa (USF). He is an expert on U.S. and comparative public administration, as well as on Greek/Mediterranean issues, on which he has published several works.

DR. JAMES A. ROBINSON is Professor of International Affairs at the University of West Florida–Pensacola. He is an expert on Asia, China, and Taiwan, on which he has published several works.

DR. KEITH TANKARD is Lecturer of Government and African Issues in Cape Town, South Africa.

DR. HARRY VANDEN is Professor of International Studies at the University of South Florida–Tampa (USF), and previously Director of the USF Center for Latin American Studies. He is an expert on political issues in Latin America and Nicaragua, on which he has published several works.

DR. CORINNE B. YOUNG is Director of International Programs and is Associate Professor of Management, International Business, and Latin American Studies at the University of Tampa, Florida. She works with companies doing business in Latin America, and has published several works.

Index